Java 2
In Plain English

Java 2
In Plain English

Brian Overland and Michael Morrison

M&T Books
An imprint of IDG Books Worldwide, Inc.

Foster City, CA • Chicago, IL • Indianapolis, IN • New York, NY

Java 2 In Plain English

Published by
M&T Books
An imprint of IDG Books Worldwide, Inc.
919 E. Hillsdale Blvd., Suite 400
Foster City, CA 94404
www.idgbooks.com (IDG Books Worldwide Web site)

ISBN: 0-7645-3539-0

Printed in the United States of America

10 9 8 7 6 5 4 3 2 1

1O/QV/QS/QR/FC

Distributed in the United States by IDG Books Worldwide, Inc.

Distributed by CDG Books Canada Inc. for Canada; by Transworld Publishers Limited in the United Kingdom; by IDG Norge Books for Norway; by IDG Sweden Books for Sweden; by IDG Books Australia Publishing Corporation Pty. Ltd. for Australia and New Zealand; by TransQuest Publishers Pte Ltd. for Singapore, Malaysia, Thailand, Indonesia, and Hong Kong; by Gotop Information Inc. for Taiwan; by ICG Muse, Inc. for Japan; by Intersoft for South Africa; by Eyrolles for France; by International Thomson Publishing for Germany, Austria, and Switzerland; by Distribuidora Cuspide for Argentina; by LR International for Brazil; by Galileo Libros for Chile; by Ediciones ZETA S.C.R. Ltda. for Peru; by WS Computer Publishing Corporation, Inc., for the Philippines; by Contemporanea de Ediciones for Venezuela; by Express Computer Distributors for the Caribbean and West Indies; by Micronesia Media Distributor, Inc. for Micronesia; by Chips Computadoras S.A. de C.V. for Mexico; by Editorial Norma de Panama S.A. for Panama; by American Bookshops for Finland.

For general information on IDG Books Worldwide's books in the U.S., please call our Consumer Customer Service department at 800-762-2974. For reseller information, including discounts and premium sales, please call our Reseller Customer Service department at 800-434-3422.

For information on where to purchase IDG Books Worldwide's books outside the U.S., please contact our International Sales department at 317-572-3993 or fax 317-572-4002.

For consumer information on foreign language translations, please contact our Customer Service department at 800-434-3422, fax 317-572-4002, or e-mail rights@idgbooks.com.

For information on licensing foreign or domestic rights, please phone + 1-650-653-7098.

For sales inquiries and special prices for bulk quantities, please contact our Order Services department at 800-434-3422 or write to the address above.

For information on using IDG Books Worldwide's books in the classroom or for ordering examination copies, please contact our Educational Sales department at 800-434-2086 or fax 317-572-4005.

For press review copies, author interviews, or other publicity information, please contact our Public Relations department at 650-653-7000 or fax 650-653-7500.

For authorization to photocopy items for corporate, personal, or educational use, please contact Copyright Clearance Center, 222 Rosewood Drive, Danvers, MA 01923, or fax 978-750-4470.

Library of Congress Cataloging-in-Publication Data

Overland, Brian R.
    Java in plain English / Brian Overland.--3rd ed.
        p. cm.
    ISBN 0-7645-3539-0 (alk. paper)
    1. Java (Computer program language)
I. Morrison, Michael (Michael Wayne), 1970-
QA76.73.J38 O83 2001
005.13'3--dc21   00-053869

 is a registered trademark or trademark under exclusive license to IDG Books Worldwide, Inc., from International Data Group, Inc. in the United States and/or other countries

 is a trademark of IDG Books Worldwide, Inc.

ABOUT IDG BOOKS WORLDWIDE

Welcome to the world of IDG Books Worldwide.

IDG Books Worldwide, Inc., is a subsidiary of International Data Group, the world's largest publisher of computer-related information and the leading global provider of information services on information technology. IDG was founded more than 30 years ago by Patrick J. McGovern and now employs more than 9,000 people worldwide. IDG publishes more than 290 computer publications in over 75 countries. More than 90 million people read one or more IDG publications each month.

Launched in 1990, IDG Books Worldwide is today the #1 publisher of best-selling computer books in the United States. We are proud to have received eight awards from the Computer Press Association in recognition of editorial excellence and three from Computer Currents' First Annual Readers' Choice Awards. Our best-selling ...For Dummies® series has more than 50 million copies in print with translations in 31 languages. IDG Books Worldwide, through a joint venture with IDG's Hi-Tech Beijing, became the first U.S. publisher to publish a computer book in the People's Republic of China. In record time, IDG Books Worldwide has become the first choice for millions of readers around the world who want to learn how to better manage their businesses.

Our mission is simple: Every one of our books is designed to bring extra value and skill-building instructions to the reader. Our books are written by experts who understand and care about our readers. The knowledge base of our editorial staff comes from years of experience in publishing, education, and journalism — experience we use to produce books to carry us into the new millennium. In short, we care about books, so we attract the best people. We devote special attention to details such as audience, interior design, use of icons, and illustrations. And because we use an efficient process of authoring, editing, and desktop publishing our books electronically, we can spend more time ensuring superior content and less time on the technicalities of making books.

You can count on our commitment to deliver high-quality books at competitive prices on topics you want to read about. At IDG Books Worldwide, we continue in the IDG tradition of delivering quality for more than 30 years. You'll find no better book on a subject than one from IDG Books Worldwide.

John Kilcullen
Chairman and CEO
IDG Books Worldwide, Inc.

Eighth Annual
Computer Press
Awards ≥1992

Ninth Annual
Computer Press
Awards ≥1993

Tenth Annual
Computer Press
Awards ≥1994

Eleventh Annual
Computer Press
Awards ≥1995

IDG is the world's leading IT media, research and exposition company. Founded in 1964, IDG had 1997 revenues of $2.05 billion and has more than 9,000 employees worldwide. IDG offers the widest range of media options that reach IT buyers in 75 countries representing 95% of worldwide IT spending. IDG's diverse product and services portfolio spans six key areas including print publishing, online publishing, expositions and conferences, market research, education and training, and global marketing services. More than 90 million people read one or more of IDG's 290 magazines and newspapers, including IDG's leading global brands — Computerworld, PC World, Network World, Macworld and the Channel World family of publications. IDG Books Worldwide is one of the fastest-growing computer book publishers in the world, with more than 700 titles in 36 languages. The "...For Dummies®" series alone has more than 50 million copies in print. IDG offers online users the largest network of technology-specific Web sites around the world through IDG.net (http://www.idg.net), which comprises more than 225 targeted Web sites in 55 countries worldwide. International Data Corporation (IDC) is the world's largest provider of information technology data, analysis and consulting, with research centers in over 41 countries and more than 400 research analysts worldwide. IDG World Expo is a leading producer of more than 168 globally branded conferences and expositions in 35 countries including E3 (Electronic Entertainment Expo), Macworld Expo, ComNet, Windows World Expo, ICE (Internet Commerce Expo), Agenda, DEMO, and Spotlight. IDG's training subsidiary, ExecuTrain, is the world's largest computer training company, with more than 230 locations worldwide and 785 training courses. IDG Marketing Services helps industry-leading IT companies build international brand recognition by developing global integrated marketing programs via IDG's print, online and exposition products worldwide. Further information about the company can be found at www.idg.com.   1/26/00

Credits

Acquisitions Editor
Debra Williams Cauley

Project Editor
Sharon Nash

Technical Editor
David Williams

Development Editor
Gus A. Miklos

Copy Editor
Richard H. Adin

Proof Editor
Cordelia Heaney

Project Coordinators
Louigene A. Santos
Danette Nurse

Graphics and Production Specialists
Robert Bihlmayer
Rolly Delrosario
Jude Levinson
Michael Lewis
Victor Peréz-Varela
Ramses Ramirez

Quality Control Technician
Dina F Quan

Book Designers
London Road Design
Kurt Krames

Illustrator
© Noma/Images.com

Proofreading and Indexing
York Production Services

Cover Image
© Noma/Images.com

About the Authors

Brian Overland worked for Microsoft for 10 years, where he was a software tester, senior technical writer, and manager. Before working for Microsoft, he was an applications programmer using both C and Basic. While at Microsoft, he was on the development teams of both Visual C++ 1.0 and Visual Basic 1.0, the latter as project lead of documentation. He also worked on Assembler and interactive television. His books have been translated into several languages, including French, German, Polish, and Croatian. He is currently at work on his second novel.

Michael Morrison is a writer, developer, and generally creative guy who has written books such as *The Unauthorized Guide to Pocket PC, XML Unleashed, Complete Idiot's Guide to Java 2,* and *Teach Yourself Internet Game Programming with Java in 21 Days.* Michael is also the instructor of several Web-based courses including DigitalThink's Introduction to Java 2 series, JavaBeans for Programmers series, and Win32 Programming series. These courses are available at Digital-Think's Web site, which is located at http://www.digitalthink.com. Michael is also the creative lead at Gas Hound Games, a game company he co-founded with his wife and two close friends. Gas Hound's first commercial debut is Inc. The Game of Business, a fast-paced financial board game based upon starting and growing businesses (http://www.incthegame.com). When not glued to his computer, playing hockey, skateboarding, mountain bike racing, or watching movies with his wife, Masheed, Michael enjoys hanging out by his koi pond.

*To Matthew, Aaron, and Katelyn, who are
the light of the world and the promise of the
future, and to Mom, who was right about
the stock market — Brian*

*To my wife, Masheed, who makes my life a
joy to live — Michael*

Preface

There's a warm, familiar scent as you enter the kitchen in the morning. The coffee is brewing, you go to your computer, and . . . it's Java! There are good reasons for learning Java in today's competitive world.

The Increasing Acceptance of Java

Since its release, Java has become more than just another language; it has become a fundamental new architecture. Moreover, it's becoming an industry. By the hundreds of thousands (or even more), people are looking for ways to learn it and master it, or at least to have a basic understanding of what it's about.

It is not hard to understand why. Beyond its networking capabilities, Java has a multi-platform design. This means that for the most part, a Java program doesn't care whether it's running on Windows, Macintosh, or UNIX. As we move further into an era of more communication between computers, this flexibility is vital.

Strengths and Weaknesses of Java

You can use Java to create applications, as well as applets for the Web. To this extent, it's fair to compare Java to other programming languages. A couple of points emerge from this comparison.

On the one hand, some things are easy to do in Java. Its application programming interface (API) makes handling graphics, threads, and network operations easier than with many other APIs. Additionally, Java 2 introduces the Swing toolkit, which makes it possible to build powerful and compelling graphical user interfaces (GUIs) with relative ease. If you are interested in object-oriented programming, you'll find that Java lives up to your best hopes.

On the other hand, some things that are easy to do in other languages are not at all obvious in Java. *Java 2 In Plain English* emphasizes how to do these simple tasks. (See, for example, Part II, Chapter 8, "Common Programming Tasks.")

How This Book Is Organized

I mentioned that Java training is almost an industry. Wandering through any bookstore, you can get the impression that there are almost as many people writing about Java as there are trying to learn it!

So, a book must justify its right to exist. The goal of *Java 2 In Plain English* has always been to summarize the language and its API so that you can use it to get a simple, straightforward answer to almost all day-to-day programming questions — all without having to look to another source (in most cases). I understand that this aim is ambitious; one could easily devote a couple of thousand pages (larger pages!) to explaining the arcane use of each method and field in the API. What you hold in your hands is a good compromise.

It's hard to cover everything, but this book features:

- The "Java 2 API Reference" (Part I, Section 7), which includes more examples on everything, including difficult areas such as networking and Swing GUI construction.

- Part II, "A Java Programming Tutorial," which includes extensive coverage of the Swing toolkit, JavaBeans, and the Java delegation event model. This part of the book is packed with practical examples and sample code.

- An expanded Glossary to address some of the new concepts and emerging technologies.

Here is a blow-by-blow summary of what you can expect to find:

Part I: Java 2 Reference

This part includes an extensive reference that is broken down into several sections focusing on the Java 2 language and API:

- Section 1, "Java 2 Language in Plain English," provides a listing of common tasks performed with the Java language and cross-references each task with the Java 2 Language Reference.

- Section 2, "Java 2 Language A to Z," serves as a topical and keyword cross-reference to the Java 2 Language Reference.

- Section 3, "Java 2 Language Reference," contains syntax and discussion of each Java keyword, as well as other basic parts of the language such as arrays, methods, classes, and objects.

- Section 4, "Java 2 API in Plain English," provides a listing of common tasks performed with the Java API and cross-references each task with the Java 2 API Reference.

- Section 5, "Java 2 API by Category," breaks down the main packages in the Java 2 API and provides a description of each of the classes and interfaces within. This section is useful in that it presents a quick overview of the majority of the Java 2 API.

- Section 6, "Java 2 API A to Z," provides a class and interface cross-reference to the Java 2 API Reference.

- Section 7, "Java 2 API Reference," contains syntax and discussion of the most important classes, interfaces, and methods that make up the Java 2 API. This is probably the most important part of the book; it says something about almost every class and interface in the API, along with many methods and fields.

Part II: A Java Programming Tutorial

This concise tutorial is aimed mainly at people who already understand C or C++. We don't spend 100 pages, as do many books, rehashing the while and do loops that you already know from C/C++. The material includes updated coverage of the Java delegation event mode, along with chapters on the Swing GUI toolkit and JavaBeans.

The following enhanced reference material is included at the back of the book:

- Appendix A, "Java Exceptions and Errors" — The tables in Appendix A summarize the different errors and exceptions that are capable of being generated by Java 2 code. The package for each exception is listed, along with its superclass.
- Appendix B, "Useful Tables" — The tables in Appendix B summarize fonts, colors, key codes, and other information.
- "Glossary — The Glossary presents an explanation of the terminology used throughout Java 2 programming. The focus is to simplify each concept and give it a broader context rather than explain syntax.

Java: The Versions March On . . .

Java 1.0 was the original version, of course.

Java 1.01 primarily fixes bugs in Java 1.0.

Java 1.1 added new areas to the core API, including JavaBeans and more techniques for customized event handling. Java Beans — much like custom controls in Visual Basic — enable you to create graphical objects that work with integrated development systems. (Whew! That's a mouthful.) This means that you create objects with "design-time" behavior.

Also note that beginning with Version 1.1, Java strongly encourages you to adopt the new event-handling model. Code that does things the 1.0 way is "deprecated," meaning that you are discouraged from using it. The new event-handling model requires slightly more work at first, but provides a good deal more flexibility.

Java 2 added significantly to the core API with the introduction of the Swing toolkit, which is a rich suite of classes and interfaces for building high-powered graphical user interfaces.

There is some discussion of these features in the Glossary, but size considerations make it harder to cover them in detail; coverage awaits a future book. . . .

Conventions

Java sometimes employs complicated syntax, reflecting the power and flexibility of the language. To summarize the possibilities, this book makes use of some typographical conventions. Although overuse of such conventions can make life complicated, we've employed them wherever we thought we could use them to simplify things.

The main convention is that anything in **bold** is meant to be typed in exactly as shown. Anything in both *italics* and monospace is a placeholder, which means that you replace it with an item of your own choosing.

Anything in brackets is an optional item — you can choose whether to include it. Exceptions: when the material gives syntax for arrays, and where the brackets are intended literally, in which case they are in bold (**[ ]**).

Ellipses (. . .) indicate a repeated series or, in some cases, part of an example that has been omitted for brevity's sake.

Other Icons

This book employs several types of icons to draw attention to different kinds of notes.

NOTE

This icon signifies a technical note that digresses from the main discussion. There are many ands, ifs, and buts in C++. To be technically correct without being too distracting, the text relegates additional information to Notes.

TIP

A Tip recommends an alternative way to do something that might be faster or more convenient. These tips are always in the form of a suggestion.

How to Reach the Authors

Comments on the book — including how to improve it — are more than welcome. You can send feedback to Briano2u@aol.com.

Acknowledgments

*J*ava 2 In Plain English involved modifying, refining, and then further modifying. It took a concerted effort by a couple of busy authors and a patient staff at IDG Books to make it happen. We are very grateful to the folks at IDG Books for helping to make this third edition a reality. Debra Williams Cauley, Sharon Nash, and Gus Miklos were unfailingly patient, responsive, and capable, and made significant contributions toward improving the usability of the book.

And thanks go to Sun Microsystems, for providing a language that is fun to learn and well supported on the Web.

Contents at a Glance

Preface ix
Acknowledgments xv

Part I: Java 2 Reference 2

Java 2 Language in Plain English 5
Java 2 Language A to Z 13
Java 2 Language Reference 19
Java 2 API in Plain English 105
Java 2 API By Category 131
Java 2 API A to Z 153
Java 2 API Reference 163

Part II: A Java Programming Tutorial 502

Chapter 1: Applets and Oranges 505
Chapter 2: Java Building Blocks 519
Chapter 3: Fun with Graphics 539
Chapter 4: Components and Events 561
Chapter 5: Moving to Swing 587
Chapter 6: Animation and Threads 617
Chapter 7: Working with JavaBeans 633
Chapter 8: Common Programming Tasks 663

Appendix A: Java Exceptions and Errors 673
Appendix B: Useful Tables 679
Glossary 687
Index 728

Contents

Preface. ix

Acknowledgments xv

Part I: Java 2 Reference 2

Java 2 Language in Plain English 5

Java 2 Language A to Z 13

Java 2 Language Reference 19

Java 2 API in Plain English 105

Java 2 API By Category 131

Java 2 API A to Z 153

Java 2 API Reference 163

Part II: A Java Programming Tutorial 502

Chapter 1: Applets and Oranges 505

Preparing to Run Java 506

Applications: Remember the main 507

Compiling and running the application 507

Understanding the code 508

Summary: Application syntax 509

What are Classes and Methods? 511

Applets: Getting into a Web Page 511

Compiling and running the applet 512

Understanding the code 514

Summary: Applet syntax 516

How Java Works on Multiple Platforms 516

Chapter 2: Java Building Blocks 519

Doing More with Classes 520

A Class that Creates Objects 522

Creating data types 523

Allocating objects 524

Background: Object Orientation 525
   Manipulating objects with methods 526
   Using constructors 528
Program Organization and Packages 529
   How packages work 530
   Packages and directory structure 532
   How Java searches for classes and packages 534
   The import statement 535

Chapter 3: Fun with Graphics 539

   Applets, Applications, and Graphics 540
   The Graphics Object 540
   Displaying Text 542
      Setting background and foreground colors 542
      Setting the font 544
      Using font metrics 545
      Using other font metrics: A summary 547
   Drawing Figures 548
   Blasting Pictures to the Screen 552
   Grabbing a Graphics Context (Scribble) 556

Chapter 4: Components and Events 561

   The Java AWT Hierarchy 561
   Background: Inheritance 563
   Overview of Java UIs 565
   An Applet with Components 566
   Responding to Events 570
      Low-level events 571
      Semantic events 575
      Event delivery 577
      Event adapters 580
   An Application with Components 583

Chapter 5: Moving to Swing 587

   Swing and the AWT 588
   Inside Swing 589
      Getting started with Swing frames 589
      Understanding panes 590
      Mixing Swing with the AWT 591
   Laying Out GUIs with Swing 592
      Getting to know layout managers 592
      Using layout managers 593
   Using Swing Components 600
      Icons 600

Labels 601
Buttons 604
Borders 604
Lists and combo boxes 605
More Swing components 607
Using Menus and Toolbars 608
Dialog Boxes, Option Panes, and Choosers 611
Using option panes 612
Using choosers 613
Pluggable Look and Feel 614

Chapter 6: Animation and Threads **617**

The Java Thread/Animation Model 618
Creating a thread 618
Implementing the runnable interface 619
Background: Threads 619
What is a thread? 620
Why are threads needed for animation? 620
The Basic Animation Applet 621
Creating a Simple Animation 623
Smoothing Out the Animation 624
Technique 1: Clipping 625
Technique 2: Double buffering 626
The revised animation code 627
Final Touches: Follow the Bouncing Ball 628

Chapter 7: Working with JavaBeans **633**

What are JavaBeans? 634
The JavaBeans component model 634
JavaBeans versus ordinary Java objects 635
Inside a Bean 636
Bean properties 636
Accessor methods 638
Advanced Bean properties 638
Understanding Bean Introspection 642
Property design patterns 643
Event design patterns 644
Explicit Bean information 645
Bean Persistence 646
Serialization 647
Versioning 648
Customizing Beans 649
Property editors 649
Property sheets 650

Customizers 651
Creating a Simple Bean 652
Packaging Beans in JAR Files 654
Testing Beans in the BeanBox 656
Advanced JavaBeans 660
EJB: JavaBeans and the Enterprise 660

Chapter 8: Common Programming Tasks 663

Converting between Numbers and Strings 663
String to integer 664
String to floating point 664
Numeric to string 665
Console Input and Output 665
Basic File Operations 667
Reading the directory 668
Reading file contents 669
Other file-handling techniques 671

Appendix A: Java Exceptions and Errors 673

Appendix B: Useful Tables 679

Glossary 687

Index 728

Java 2
In Plain English

Java 2 Reference

english in plain english in pl
lain english in plain english in
plain english in plain english
english in plain english in pl
plain english in plain english
english in plain english in pl
lain english in plain english in
plain english in plain english
english in plain english in pl
lain english in plain english in
plain english in plain english
english in plain english in pl

Part I provides a detailed reference to the core Java language and the standard Java Application Programming Interface (API). Use Section 1, "Java 2 Language in Plain English," to look up a Java language topic by task. This section is organized alphabetically by key phrase. Similarly, Section 4, "Java 2 API in Plain English," presents Java API programming topics by task. Use Section 2, "Java 2 Language A to Z," to conveniently find the location of any Java language construct instantly. Section 6, "Java 2 API A to Z," presents a similarly organized index of important Java API classes and interfaces. Also, Section 5, "Java 2 API By Category," provides a categorical breakdown of the Java 2 API. Finally, Sections 3 and 7 serve as detailed references for the most important areas of the Java language and API, respectively. For a general introduction and exploration of Java programming, see Part II, "A Java Programming Tutorial."

IN THIS PART

- Java 2 Language in Plain English

- Java 2 Language A to Z

- Java 2 Language Reference

- Java 2 API in Plain English

- Java 2 API By Category

- Java 2 API A to Z

- Java 2 API Reference

Java 2 Language in Plain English

The following table lists the topics discussed in Part I, Java 2 Language Reference. The table is an alphabetically arranged master list of Java 2 programming topics and language constructs, along with the page number on which each topic begins.

If you want to...	Use this language construct	Located on page
create an *abstract method*	abstract keyword	20
create an *abstract class*	abstract keyword	20
advance a loop to the next iteration	continue statement	40
use *aggregates* to create an array	aggregates	21
allocate space for an object	new operator	74
create an *application entry point*	main() method	67
create an *array*	arrays	23
obtain the length of an *array*	arrays	23
assign a value to a variable	assignments	25
use *bitwise operators*	bitwise operators	26
create a *Boolean* expression	Boolean expressions	27
create a *Boolean* variable	Boolean expressions	27
test *Boolean* conditions	Boolean expressions	27
break out of a loop	break statement	28
create a *byte* variable	byte data type	29
determine the size of a *byte* variable	byte data type	29
call a constructor from within another constructor	this keyword	96
cast between data types	casts	30
catch an exception	catch keyword	32
create a *character* variable	char data type	33
determine the size of a *character* variable	char data type	33
declare a *class*	class keyword	34
create *class fields*	static keyword	87
create *class members*	static keyword	87
understand *class methods*	functions (C++)	55
use *class modifiers*	class keyword	34
handle *command-line arguments*	main() method	67
comment your code	comments	36
create a *compound statement*	compound statements	37
create a *conditional expression*	conditional operator (?:)	38

If you want to...	Use this language construct	Located on page
use the *conditional operator*	conditional operator (?:)	38
conditionally execute a statement	if statement	57
declare a symbolic *constant*	final keyword	51
create a *constant value*	final keyword	51
constructing an object	constructors	39
creating *constructors*	constructors	39
convert between data types	casts	30
create *critical sections* of code	synchronized keyword	94
label a *default switch branch*	default keyword	42
create a *default switch branch*	default keyword	42
derive a class from another class	extends keyword	49
create a *do loop*	do keyword	44
create a *do-nothing statement*	empty statements	45
create javadoc *documentation*	comments	36
use a *documentation comment*	comments	36
create a *double* variable	double data type	44
determine the size of a *double* variable	double data type	44
create an *else clause*	else keyword	45
create an *empty statement*	empty statements	45
declare an *exception*	exception handling	46
respond to an *exception*	catch keyword	32
pass an *exception* to another context	throw keyword	97
enclose code that may throw an *exception*	try keyword	98
understand *exception handling*	exception handling	46
extend a class from another class	extends keyword	49
use the *false Boolean constant*	false keyword	51
check for a *false condition*	false keyword	51
create a *float* variable	float data type	52
determine the size of a *float* variable	float data type	52

Continued

If you want to...	Use this language construct	Located on page
create a *for* loop	`for` statement	53
utilize Java *garbage collection*	`delete` operator (C++)	43
use *hexadecimal notation*	hexadecimal notation	56
create an *identifier*	identifiers	56
understand the rules of *identifier names*	identifiers	56
create an *if statement*	`if` statement	57
provide an alternate path to an *if statement*	`else` keyword	45
implement an interface	`implements` keyword	58
import a class	`import` statement	59
import a package of classes	`import` statement	59
understand *inheritance*	inheritance	61
create an *inner class*	inner classes	61
use the *instanceof* operator	`instanceof` operator	63
create an *integer* variable	`int` data type	63
determine the size of an *integer* variable	`int` data type	63
branch on an *integer test expression*	`switch` statement	93
create an *interface*	`interface` keyword	64
understand the *Java variable naming convention*	identifiers	56
assess Java *keywords*	keywords	65
label a statement	labels	66
use a *line comment*	comments	36
create a *long* variable	`long` data type	67
determine the size of a *long* variable	`long` data type	67
loop as long as a condition is true	`do` keyword	44
mask bits of a value	bitwise operators	26
create a *main() method*	`main()` method	67
define a *method*	methods	69

If you want to...	Use this language construct	Located on page
create multiple versions of a *method*	method overloading	72
understand a *method argument list*	methods	69
utilize *method modifiers*	methods	69
understand *methods*	methods	69
use the *modulus operator*	modulus operator (%)	73
use a *multiline comment*	comments	36
utilize *native code* for a method	native keyword	74
declare a *native method*	native keyword	74
use the *new operator*	new operator	74
assign *null* to an object variable	assignments	25
test for an object being *null*	null constant	75
use the *null constant*	null constant	75
create an *object instance*	new operator	74
understand *object references*	references	84
reference the *object with scope*	this keyword	96
understand *objects*	objects	76
use *octal notation*	octal notation	76
determine *operator precedence*	operators	77
assess Java *operators*	operators	77
overload a method	method overloading	72
specify that a method cannot be *overridden*	final keyword	51
organize classes into a *package*	package statement	79
understand *package directory structure*	package statement	79
use the *package statement*	package statement	79
understand why Java doesn't have *pointers*	pointers (C++)	80
use *primitive data types*	data Types	41
use the *private keyword*	private keyword	81
declare a *private method*	private keyword	81
declare a *private variable*	private keyword	81

Continued

If you want to...	Use this language construct	Located on page
use the *protected keyword*	protected keyword	82
declare a *protected method*	protected keyword	82
declare a *protected variable*	protected keyword	82
use the *public keyword*	public keyword	83
declare a *public class*	public keyword	83
declare a *public method*	public keyword	83
declare a *public variable*	public keyword	83
obtain the *remainder* of an integer division	modulus operator (%)	73
repeatedly execute statements	for statement	53
return from a method	return keyword	85
return a value from a method	return keyword	85
return nothing from a method	void keyword	101
declare a method that *returns nothing*	void keyword	101
obtain *run-time object information*	instanceof operator	63
shift data a number of bits	shift operators	86
use *shift operators*	shift operators	86
create a *short* variable	short data type (C++)	87
determine the size of a *short* variable	short data type (C++)	87
create a *static initializer*	static keyword	87
create a *string*	strings	89
obtain the length of a *string*	strings	89
understand *string escape sequences*	strings	89
use a *string literal*	strings	89
compare *strings*	strings	89
specify that a class cannot be *subclassed*	final keyword	51
reference a *superclass*	super keyword	92
call a *superclass constructor*	super keyword	92
create *switch* branches	case keyword	30
label a *switch* branch	case keyword	30

If you want to...	Use this language construct	Located on page
create a *switch statement*	switch statement	93
create a *synchronized method*	synchronized keyword	94
terminate a switch branch	break statement	28
throw an exception	throw keyword	97
specify that a method may *throw* an exception	throws keyword	97
use the *true Boolean constant*	true keyword	97
check for a *true condition*	true keyword	97
create *uninitialized variables*	default argument values (C++)	42
declare a *variable*	variables	99
specify that a *variable* may be changed externally	volatile keyword	102
utilize *variable modifiers*	variables	99
create a *while loop*	while statement	103
use the *+ operator* with strings	operator overloading (C++)	79

Java 2 Language A to Z

The following table lists the topics discussed in Part I, Java 2 Language Reference. The table is an alphabetically arranged master list of Java 2 programming topics and language constructs, along with the page number on which each topic begins.

Topic	Located on this page in Part I
abstract keyword	20
Aggregates	21
Arrays	23
Assignments	25
auto (C++)	26
Bit fields (C++)	26
Bitwise operators	26
Boolean expressions	27
break statement	28
byte data type	29
case keyword	30
Casts	30
catch keyword	32
char data type	33
class keyword	34
Comments	36
Compound statements	37
Conditional operator (?:)	38
const keyword (C++)	38
Constructors	39
Context operator (C++)	39
continue statement	40
Data members	41
Data types	41
Default argument values (C++)	42
default keyword	42
#define directive (C++)	43
delete operator (C++)	43
Destructors (C++)	43
do keyword	44
double data type	44
else keyword	45
Empty statements	45
Exception handling	46

Topic	Located on this page in Part I
extends keyword	49
extern declarations (C++)	50
false keyword	51
final keyword	51
float data type	52
for statement	53
friend keyword (C++)	55
Functions (C++)	55
goto statement(C++)	56
Hexadecimal notation	56
Identifiers	56
if statement	57
#if Directive (C++)	58
implements keyword	58
import statement	59
#include directive (C++)	60
Inheritance	61
Inner classes	61
instanceof operator	63
int data type	63
interface keyword	64
Keywords	65
Labels	66
long data type	67
main() method	67
Methods	69
Method overloading	72
Modulus operator (%)	73
Namespaces (C++)	73
native keyword	74
new operator	74
null constant	75
Octal notation	76

Java 2 Language A to Z

Continued

Java 2 Language A to Z

Topic	Located on this page in Part I
Objects	76
Operators	77
Operator overloading (C++)	79
package statement	79
Pointers (C++)	80
private keyword	81
protected keyword	82
public keyword	83
References	84
return keyword	85
Shift operators	86
short data type (C++)	87
static keyword	87
Strings	89
struct declarations (C++)	92
super keyword	92
switch statement	93
synchronized keyword	94
Templates (C++)	96
this keyword	96
throw keyword	97
throws keyword	97
true keyword	97
try keyword	98
typedef declarations (C++)	98
Unsigned types (C++)	98
Variables	99
virtual keyword (C++)	101
void keyword	101
volatile keyword	102
while statement	103

Java 2 Language Reference

This section presents a series of alphabetically arranged topics related to Java 2 keywords and programming constructs. Each topic includes a detailed description, along with an analysis of its syntax and in many cases example code. Most of the topics also include a "Java vs. C++" section that clarifies the relationship between the topic in Java and its equivalent feature in C++.

The section "Conventions" (p. xii) at the beginning of the book explains the notational conventions used in syntax displays in this chapter. These conventions include the use of brackets to indicate optional items (except where the brackets are bold), and the use of bold font to indicate a keyword or punctuation to be entered precisely as shown. Placeholders are in italic font.

abstract Keyword

Java vs. C++

The abstract keyword can be used to create abstract methods in Java; abstract methods are the equivalent of pure virtual functions in C++.

Syntax

To create an abstract method, place the abstract keyword at the beginning of a method declaration and terminate the declaration immediately with a semicolon. Optionally, the method can have other modifiers, such as public.

```
abstract [other_modifiers] type method_name(args);
```

An abstract method has no definition — that is, no executable code.

Any class that has at least one abstract method is an abstract class and must be declared with abstract. (See "Example.") An abstract class cannot be used to create objects, but it can be used as a base class for other classes. A derived class can provide definitions for an inherited method so that the method is no longer abstract.

Abstract methods and classes have an important connection to interfaces. See the topic "interface Keyword," page 64, for more information.

Example

The following code declares a generic Shape class with two abstract methods:

```
import java.awt.Graphics;
abstract public class Shape {
    abstract public void moveTo(int newx, int newy);
    abstract public void reDraw(Graphics g);
}
```

The next class, MyRectClass, is an example of a class that can be derived from Shape. Although Shape cannot be used to create objects, MyRectClass can. Note that the methods are not declared with abstract in the MyRectClass class.

```
import java.awt.Graphics;
public class MyRectClass extends Shape {
    public void moveTo(int newx, int newy) {
        x = newx;
        y = newy;
    }

    public void reDraw(Graphics g) {
        g.drawRect(x, y, 20, 20);
    }
}
```

Aggregates

Java vs. C++
Aggregate syntax is roughly the same in Java as in C and C++, but Java treats strings differently. In Java, strings are not arrays of bytes but are simple objects.

Syntax
An aggregate is a literal constant for a string or an array. An aggregate has one of the following forms:

```
"string_of_characters"
{item, item, ...}
```

Here, the ellipses (...) are not intended literally but are used to indicate that there may be any number of items. Each *item* is a constant, variable, or other object. In any case, an item must be either an object or an instance of a primitive data type.

Java allocates memory for a string or array object whenever it encounters an aggregate. In the case of string literals, Java allocates an object of the `String` class. Such an object is not equivalent to an array of `char` as it would be in C or C++. See the topic "Strings," page 89, for more information.

When the set aggregate form is used, Java creates an array object of the appropriate size. (The set form uses the `{item, item, ...}` syntax.) This is the only way to create arrays other than using the new operator. For example, the following array declaration creates an array variable, `manyInts`, but it allocates no integers in memory:

```
int manyInts[];
```

However, the following declaration allocates an array of five integers, in which the variable `manyInts` refers to the array:

```
int manyInts[] = {1, 2, 3, 4, 5} ;
```

Usage 1: Character Strings
As in C and C++, string literals can be used to initialize string variables or can be passed as arguments. However, string literals are used to initialize variables of the `String` class, and not arrays of `char`, as in C and C++. For example:

```
String s = "Here is a string";
String Name = "John Doe";
System.out.println("My name is " + Name);
```

The last example uses the concatenation operator (+), which creates a `String` result from two `String` operands.

Characters in a string can include any Unicode character, including a number of characters specified by an escape sequence (such as to indicate a newline). For a table of escape sequences and other details of string behavior, see the topic "Strings," page 89.

Usage 2: Set Aggregates (Arrays)

In Java, set aggregates are only used to initialize arrays. In the simple case of initializing an array of numbers, Java accepts the same code as C and C++. For example:

```
int countdown[] = {10, 9, 8, 7, 6, 5, 4, 3, 2, 1} ;
```

You can initialize other kinds of arrays, but each item inside the brackets must be one of the following:

- An object
- An instance of primitive data type, such as a number
- A nested aggregate — which itself is actually an object, either of String type or an array

The third category is not really a separate category. A set aggregate is itself an array object. In Java, multidimensional arrays are arrays of arrays, so you can initialize them as follows:

```
int matrix[][] = {{1, 2} , {4, 5} , {9, 10} } ;
```

This declaration creates matrix as a 3×2 array. In Java, there is no requirement that nested arrays have the same size. You can therefore create arrays like this:

```
int matrix[][] = {{1, 2, 3, 4} , {4} , {9, 10} } ;
```

This declaration creates matrix as an array of three array objects. The first object is an array of four integers, the second is an array of one integer, and the third is an array of two integers.

Except for strings, initializing an object (an instance of a user-defined class) always requires the use of the new operator. You can initialize arrays of objects, but each instance of a class must involve new and a constructor. For example:

```
class Pnt {
    int x, y;
    Pnt(int x, int y) {
        this.x = x;
        this.y = y;
    }
}
//...
Pnt pts[] = {new Pnt(10, 20), new Pnt(3, 4)} ;
```

As long as each object has been allocated somewhere, you can use any combination of variables and other objects. Each object, of course, must have the appropriate type. For example:

```
Pnt p1 = new Pnt(3, 4);
Pnt pts[] = {p1, new Pnt(10, 20), new Pnt(3, 4)} ;
```

Strings, of course, are the one kind of object that can be created without using new. The following example creates a valid array of strings:

```
String words[] = {"Welcome", "to", "Java"} ;
```

Arrays

Java vs. C++

Java treats arrays as objects and not as compound types. This means that an array cannot hold elements until you use new or aggregate initialization to allocate space for the array. In other respects, Java arrays behave like arrays in C and C++, with indexes running from 0 to size-1.

In Java, arrays do not equate to pointers or addresses. You must use the index notation to access array elements.

Syntax

Typically, arrays are allocated with the new operator and are associated with an array variable in the same declaration:

```
type array_name[] = new type[size];
type array_name[][]... = new type[size1][size2]... ;
```

Note that throughout this syntax, the brackets are intended literally.

Arrays can also be declared and initialized through the use of aggregates:

```
int iarray[] = {1, 2, 3, 4, 5} ;
```

After an array is declared and allocated, its legal indexes (or each dimension, if it's multidimensional) run from 0 to size-1. Thus, an array of size 100 runs from array[0] to array[99]. At runtime, the Java interpreter catches illegal indexes and raises them as exceptions of the class ArrayIndexOutOf BoundsException.

Array variables can be declared without immediately allocating an array in memory. An array can be allocated later using new. In multidimensional arrays, each element can be individually associated with a row of different length. (See "Examples.") When the new operator is applied to multidimensional arrays, any number of dimensions can be left blank as long as all the blank sizes are to the right of the fixed sizes. Such expressions create arrays of arrays, in which not all dimensions are yet allocated.

```
new type[size1][size2]...[ ][ ]...
```

Syntax: Variation

In declaring an array variable, you can choose to place brackets (instead of the variable name) after the type. For example:

```
int[] iarray = {1, 2, 3, 4, 5};
```

The choice of syntax is a matter of personal style.

Examples

This example declares a simple array of 100 integers and initializes each element to 5:

```
int iarray[] = new int[100];
for (int i = 0; i < 100; i++)
  iarray[i] = 5;
```

The next example declares a two-dimensional array and initializes each element to 0:

```
int matrix[][] = new int[ROWS][COLS];
for (int i = 0; i < ROWS; i++)
  for (int j = 0; j < COLS; j++)
    matrix[i][j] = 0;
```

The third example creates an uneven two-dimensional array; that is, a matrix with rows of different length. This is uncommon but legal.

```
// Create weirdMatrix as array of two elements, each
//   element being a one-dimensional array of int not
//   yet allocated.
int weirdMatrix[][] = new int[2][];
weirdMatrix[0] = new int[3];       // First row: size 3
weirdMatrix[1] = new int[7];       // Second row: size 7
```

Array Arguments and Array Length

Although you should generally know the length of your own arrays, it is sometimes useful to determine their length dynamically. This is especially true of methods that take arrays as arguments. In Java, arrays are objects and have a built-in length field.

```
array_name.length
```

The preceding expression produces the length of the first-order dimension. In a two-dimensional array, the size of the second dimension could be produced by an expression such as this:

```
array_name[0].length
```

A simple example uses a method that takes an array of long, of any size, as an argument:

```
void zeroLongArray(long array[]) {
```

```
   for(int i = 0; i < array.length; i++)
      array[i] = 0;
}
```

Array parameter declarations never include sizes. The size of an array is an attribute (available in the length field) and not a determinant of type.

Assignments

Java vs. C++
Java's assignment syntax is similar to that of C and C++. However, assignment to an object changes the reference instead of performing a copy operation.

Syntax
The Java assignment operator creates an expression from two operands:

```
variable = value
```

The variable can be a variable, a data member, or an element of an array. The notion of "lvalue" is less important in Java than in C and C++, because Java does not support pointers. In general, expressions are legal on the left side as long as they are neither constants nor complex expressions.

As in C and C++, assignment expressions are expressions just like any other, so they can be reused in larger expressions. After assigning the value to variable, the expression evaluates to the value of variable after assignment. (See "Examples.")

Because object variables are references in Java, assignment to one of these variables does not result in copying of data between objects, as it would in C++. Instead, assignment to an object variable associates that variable with a new object in memory. You can also assign the special value null to an object variable, which causes the variable to have no current association with any actual object.

Examples
As in C and C++, you can take advantage of assignment being an expression and not a statement. The following statement uses nested assignment expressions. The effect is to assign the value 0 to all four variables. Associativity of assignment is right-to-left, so after 0 is assigned to d, it is assigned to c, and so on:

```
a = b = c = d = 0;
```

The next example demonstrates assignment to an object variable. The effect of this code is to make obj2 an alias for the same object that obj1 refers to. In other words, only one object is allocated, but it has two names.

```
MyClass obj1, obj2;
obj1 = new MyClass(); // Allocate an object.
```

Java 2 Language Reference

```
obj2 = obj1;    // Make obj2 an alias for this same object.
```

If you want to get an actual copy of an object, use the clone() method. This method is defined in the Object class, which all other classes inherit from directly or indirectly. Note that all API classes that have a usable clone() method also implement the Cloneable interface.

```
MyClass obj1, obj2;
obj1 = new MyClass(); // Allocate an object.
obj2 = obj1.clone();  // Create a copy and assign to obj2.
```

Auto (C++)

Java vs. C++
Not supported in Java.

The auto keyword has an obscure use in C and C++; it is a way to declare that a variable is local and that the variable has an automatic storage class. It is generally unnecessary even in these languages. Java does not support auto because all variables are class variables, instance variables, or local to a method (a member function). This arrangement tends to make scope and storage class simpler and better defined in Java.

Bit Fields (C++)

Java vs. C++
Not supported in Java.

See "BitSet Class" in Section 7, "Java 2 API Reference" (p. 182) for a capability similar to bit fields.

Bitwise Operators

Java vs. C++
Java supports the same bitwise operators that C and C++ support. However, these operators work differently with Boolean expressions and integer expressions.

Syntax
Java supports the bitwise operators: AND (&), OR (|), and exclusive OR (^). When both the operands are integers, the operation compares bits in the two operands to determine the corresponding bit in the result.

```
integer & integer
integer | integer
integer ^ integer
~ integer
```

However, when the two operands have type boolean, the operations are actually logical operations. These operators always evaluate both sides of the expression fully. This is different from the operators && and ||, which use "short-circuit" logic to evaluate just one side when appropriate. (For example, if the first operand connected by && is false, then the second operand is not evaluated.)

```
boolean & boolean
boolean | boolean
boolean ^ boolean
! boolean
```

The symbols ˜ and ! perform bitwise and logical negation, respectively. In the other expressions, both expressions must be integer, or both must be Boolean.

See also "Shift Operators," page 86.

Examples

The following example masks out all bits except the two least-significant bits:

```
int test_value, result;
//...
result = test_value & 0x03;
```

The following figure illustrates bitwise AND, OR, and exclusive OR between two sample integer operands.

|0|0|0|0|1|0|0|1| First operand (1001 binary = 9)

|0|0|0|0|0|1|1|1| Second operand (0111 binary = 7)

AND (&) |0|0|0|0|0|0|0|1| Both bits in operands set?

OR (|) |0|0|0|0|1|1|1|1| Either bit in operands set?

XOR (^) |0|0|0|0|1|1|1|0| Either bit in operands set, but not both?

Bitwise operators

Boolean Expressions

Java vs. C++

In Java, boolean is a distinct type rather than just another way of using integers. What's more, Java does not accept an integer expression when the syntax calls for a Boolean expression. Thus, Sum > 0 is accepted as a conditional expression for an if, for, or while statement, but Sum is not. (See "Example.")

Java 2 Language Reference

Syntax

A Boolean expression consists of one of the following:

- The result of a comparison, such as `Sum == 0` or `N > 5`
- A Boolean variable
- The constant `true` or `false`
- Boolean expressions combined with one or more of the Boolean operators: And (`&&`), Or (`||`), Not (`!`)

Java supports the `boolean` keyword for the declaration of Boolean variables. Such variables might be useful in storing part of the result of a complex logical expression.

```
boolean variable [= Boolean_expression];
```

Example

Assume that n is declared as an integer. The following `while` statement is legal, because it uses a Boolean expression (n > 0) for the conditional:

```
while (n > 0)
    amount = amount * n--;
```

but this `while` statement is illegal:

```
while (n)                    // ERROR! while(n) not valid
    amount = amount * n--;
```

break Statement

Java vs. C++

The break statement does the same thing in Java as in C and C++; it terminates a branch of a `switch` statement or breaks out of a loop. Java extends break syntax by adding an optional label target.

Syntax

The break statement has two forms:

```
break;
break label;
```

The statement transfers execution to the first statement past the end of the innermost loop or `switch` statement. If `label` is specified, execution is transferred to the first statement past the end of the statement block (loop or `switch` statement) identified by the label.

Examples

This example uses break to terminate two branches of a `switch` statement. Without break, execution would fall through from one case to the next.

```
int n;
String NumberString;
// ...
switch(n) {
case 1:
  NumberString = "One";
  break;
case 2:
  NumberString = "Two";
  break;
```

This next example breaks directly out of two loops as soon as a zero element is found.

```
major_loop: for(int i = 0; i < 20; i++) {
  for(int j = 0; j < 20; j++) {
    if (matrix[i][j] == 0) {
      zero_found = true;
      break major_loop;
    }
  }
}
```

byte Data Type

Java vs. C++
The byte data type is a primitive data type in Java that is equivalent to signed char in most C/C++ implementations. byte is an 8-bit signed number, whereas the Java char type is actually 16 bits, not 8 bits.

Syntax
The byte keyword can be used to create 8-bit (1-byte) integer variables:

```
byte declarations;
```

The range is −128 to 127.

Example
The byte data type is most frequently used to create compact arrays of small numbers.

```
byte lottery_numbers[] = {2, 9, 13, 27, 55, 57};
```

case Keyword

Java vs. C++

The case keyword does the same thing in Java as in C and C++; it labels a branch inside a switch statement.

Syntax

This keyword turns a statement into a labeled statement:

```
case constant_integer_expression:
   statement
```

Within a switch statement, if the test value matches constant_integer_expression, execution transfers to statement (unless another branch was taken first).

Example

The case keyword is only a label and not a control structure. This is why execution falls through unless you use break. In the following example, break prevents falling through to the default case.

```
switch(c) {
case 'a':
case 'e':
case 'i':
case 'o':
case 'u':
      is_a_vowel = true;
      break;
default:
      is_a_vowel = false;
}
```

Casts

Java vs. C++

Casting is critical with certain parts of the Java API. A number of methods return type Object, which usually must be cast. Rules for casting in Java are similar to those for C and C++ except that you can only cast up and down through the class hierarchy.

Casting converts the type of an expression. Some casting is automatic, but Java will not automatically convert a data type if there is the possibility of loss of information; this situation requires an explicit cast. It's Java's way of making sure that you know what you're doing.

Syntax: Explicit Cast

You can recast an expression to a different type by using the following syntax. The resulting expression, assuming it is valid, has the specified type.

```
(type) expression
```

You need a cast in two common situations:

- Assigning primitive data when it would result in loss of precision or range. The most common example is assigning a floating-point literal (which by default has type double) to a float variable:

  ```
  float f = (float) 3.97;   // Convert from double.
  double d = 3.97;          // No cast needed.
  ```

- Assigning an object to a subclass type. A number of API methods return an expression of type Object that needs to be cast to a subclass:

  ```
  Long theLong = (Long) theStack.pop();
  ```

Java requires the cast because Stack.pop() always returns a result of type Object. We can assume from the example that theStack is being used to hold Long objects, but there is no way for Java to know this. It would be too risky for Java to automatically cast an Object to Long, because an Object does not necessarily support all the fields that a Long supports.

You can assign to a superclass for free. For example, Stack.push() takes an Object argument — Object being the ultimate superclass — and no cast is required:

```
theStack.push(theLong);   // Automatic cast to Object
```

A Long object supports all the fields of the Object class, so there is no danger in passing a Long (or an instance of any class) when type Object is expected. It is only assigning to a subclass that requires a cast.

The principle behind all casting is consistent: it is the potential loss of information that requires a cast. You can easily get yourself into trouble by using casts that don't make sense, but the assumption is that you're an adult and have good reasons for whatever you do.

You also need a cast when you assign a long to an int:

```
long theLong = 100;       // 100 cast to long.
int i = (int) theLong;    // Cast required to go back to int!
```

Restrictions on Casting

You cannot cast outside the class hierarchy when dealing with objects. For example, the following code is illegal if neither A nor B is a subclass of the other. (In this context, "subclass" means a direct or indirect subclass, so that, for example, all classes are subclasses of Object.)

```
A a;
B b = (A) a; // Legal only if A is superclass or subclass.
```

With a little thought, you can see how to cast between any two classes if you do it in two steps (because all classes are related through Object). However, there is never a reason to do something like that. If you want to create different classes that support the same methods, you should relate them through inheritance. If classes do not support the same methods, casting between them is dangerous.

Another restriction that should be clear by now is that you can't cast between primitive data types and classes. However, the wrapper classes (such as Long, used in previous examples) are valid parts of the class hierarchy.

Implicit Casting and Promotion

Usually, numeric data can be combined into expressions without having to use explicit casts. Numeric expressions are cast according to a well-defined hierarchy. In the following list of types, whenever two types of expression are combined, the type lower in the list is cast to the type higher on the list:

double

float

long

int

short

char

byte

Casts between boolean and other types are never permitted. The easiest way to effect a conversion between boolean and an integer is to use the conditional operator (?:):

```
boolean b;
//...
int i = b? 1 : 0;
```

catch Keyword

The catch keyword is used to define an exception handler. See the topic "Exception Handling" (p. 46) for description, syntax, and an example.

The catch keyword has the following syntax. A try block must precede any catch block.

```
catch (exceptionClass e) {statements}
```

Here, e is an argument name of your choice. You can use it within *statement* to refer to the exception that was caught.

char Data Type

Java vs. C++

In Java, the char data type is a 16-bit-wide integer that stores a single Unicode character value. Strings are not arrays of char as they are in C/C++, although you can convert string data to the char format.

Syntax

The char keyword can be used to declare variables that hold individual characters:

```
char declarations;
```

The range is the entire set of Unicode characters. Although these are 16-bit values, the lowest 128 values are equal to their counterparts in standard ASCII. Note that individual character constants use single quotation marks. (See "Examples.")

In Java, strings are instances of the String class and are not arrays of char. However, you can convert String objects to arrays of char by using the toCharArray() method of the String class. The String class also has a number of class (static) methods for dealing with arrays of char. See the topic "String Class" in Section 7, "Java 2 API Reference," page 457, for more information.

For a list of escape codes that can be used for special character constants, see the topic "Strings," page 89.

Examples

This example declares a variable holding a single character initialized to a newline:

```
char end = '\n';
```

This next example declares an array of char and initializes it by calling the toCharArray() method:

```
String str = "data";
char charray[] = str.toCharArray();
```

This code does not copy over a null-terminated string. In the example just shown, the variable charray is associated with a char array in memory containing exactly four characters: d, a, t, and a. There is no fifth byte for a null.

Another way to fill a character array is to use the StringBuffer class. This approach is most likely to appeal to die-hard C fans:

```
char carr[] = new char[MAXSIZE];
StringBuffer buffer = new StringBuffer("data");
buffer.getChars(0, 3, carr, 0);
```

Java 2 Language Reference

For more information, see the topic "StringBuffer Class" in Section 7, "Java 2 API Reference," page 460.

class Keyword

Java vs. C++
In Java, classes are the most basic part of program organization, even more so than in C++. Java classes can be defined only with the class keyword; struct and union are not supported.

NOTE
Unlike C and C++, Java has no problem with forward references to classes and methods. Consequently, you can declare classes in any order.

Syntax
A class declaration has the following syntax. Unlike C++, Java does not terminate class declarations with a semicolon.

```
[public] [final] [abstract] class class_name [extends
super_class] [implements interfaces] {
   declarations
}
```

Here, brackets indicate optional items. The declarations consist of any number of method and variable definitions. Unlike C++, the default access level is not private; in this respect, Java classes are more similar to C structures. See the topics "Methods" (p. 69) and "Variables" (p. 99) for more information.

Syntax: Modifiers
The modifiers include any of the following, in any order: abstract, final, and public. Table 1 summarizes the meaning of each modifier.

Table 1 *Modifiers of the class keyword*

Modifier	Description
abstract	The class contains one or more abstract methods (methods without definitions). If any method is declared abstract, then its class must also be declared abstract.
final	The class may not be subclassed.
public	The class is accessible both inside and outside the package. Methods and variables of the class are accessible outside the package if they are also declared public.

For more information, see individual topics for the keywords.

In each source file, there can be at most one class declared public. This class must also have a name that precisely matches the base name of the source file. Public classes and methods are significant because they are accessible outside the package and because they serve as entry points into the application or applet.

Syntax: extends Clause

The optional extends clause specifies a single superclass (also called a *base class*). You can only specify one superclass because Java does not support multiple inheritance.

```
extends super_class
```

All the fields (members) of the superclass are automatically fields of the current class. See the topics "Inheritance" (p. 61) and "extends Keyword" (p. 49) for more information.

Syntax: implements Clause

The optional implements keyword is followed by one or more interfaces. If there is more than one interface, they are separated by commas.

```
implements interface1 [,interface2]...
```

An interface is similar to an abstract class, but interfaces are declared with a different keyword and have special restrictions placed on them. When a class implements an interface, it must provide a definition for each method declared in the interface. See "interface Keyword" (p. 64) for more information.

Examples

The following example declares a Pnt class with two members and a constructor, which is a method with the same name as the class. (See the topic "Constructors," page 39, for more information.)

```
class Pnt {
   int x, y;

   Pnt(int x, int y) {  // Constructor
      this.x = x;
      this.y = y;
   }
}
```

The next class declaration creates a subclass of Pnt by using the extends keyword. The class inherits x and y and adds a variable and some methods, one of which is a constructor.

```
class PointTemp extends Pnt {
   private double degreesC;
```

```
PointTemp(int x, int y, double d) {  // Constructor
    super(x, y);
    degreesC = d;
}

void Set_Fahrenheit(double degreesF) {
    degreesC = (degreesF - 32) / 1.8;
}
}
```

The previous two examples use the keywords this and super. See the topics "this Keyword" (p. 96) and "super Keyword" (p. 92) for more information.

The final example shows the declaration of a class creating an applet. The class must be declared public and must be placed in a source file with the same name (Life). It implements Runnable because the applet involves more than one thread.

```
public class Life extends java.applet.Applet
    implements Runnable {
    boolean Grid[][] = new boolean[20][20];
    int Totals[][] = new int[20][20];
    int cellx, celly;
    Thread runner;

    // Method declarations follow
    //...
}
```

Comments

Java vs. C++

Java supports the same comment symbols that C and C++ support.

Syntax

Both the line comment (C++) and the multiline comment (traditional C) are supported:

```
// comment_to_end_of_line
/* comment_text
...
  more_comment_text */
```

All text that appears inside a comment is simply ignored by the Java compiler. Comments may contain any information, preferably in human-readable form, that you find helpful when reviewing the source code.

Java also supports comments beginning with /**. This syntax creates a documentation comment, which is the same as a standard comment, except that the javadoc compiler can be used to extract the comment text into a documentation file:

```
/** doc_comment_text
...
more_comment_text */
```

Documentation comments enable you to add special markup tags that help describe the code being commented. For example, you can use special tags to identify method parameters and return values.

Example

This example uses comments to describe the purpose of each of its variables:

```
/* Declare a 2D array and two indexes. */
double matrix[][];    // 2D array; allocate space later
int r;                // Index to rows
int c;                // Index to columns
```

Example: Viewing Comments

You can view documentation comments by using the javadoc compiler provided in the Java SDK. (As explained earlier, a documentation comment begins with /**.) Simply specify the name of one or more source files as the argument to javadoc:

```
javadoc myclass.java
```

The javadoc compiler produces a file with an HTML extension; in this example, it produces a file called myclass.html. This HTML file displays information summarizing classes and fields in a .class file. It also includes documentation comments that were placed in the source code.

Compound Statements

Java vs. C++

Java uses the same compound-statement syntax that C and C++ use.

Syntax

A compound statement consists of one or more statements enclosed in braces:

```
{ statements }
```

A compound statement can appear anywhere a single statement can appear. Variables and objects declared inside the compound statement are local to the statement block. Unlike C, Java has no requirement that all variables and object declarations precede all executable statements.

Example

The following example executes two statements if the variable x is out of range. The two statements are grouped in a compound statement and therefore are both executed if the condition is true.

```
if (x < 0 || x > 100) {
    x_in_range = false;
    return -1;
}
```

Conditional Operator (?:)

Java vs. C++

Java provides the same support for the conditional operator (?:) that C and C++ provide. However, note that the conditional expression must be a genuine Boolean expression, such as the result of a comparison.

Syntax

The conditional operator forms an expression from three subexpressions:

```
conditional_expr ? expr1 : expr2
```

The conditional expression, which must be Boolean, is evaluated first. If the result is true, *expr1* is evaluated; if it is false, *expr2* is evaluated. The result of the entire expression is *expr1* or *expr2*, whichever was evaluated.

Example

The following statement sets MaxNum to a if it is greater than b; otherwise, MaxNum is set to b:

```
MaxNum = (a > b ? a : b);
```

const Keyword (C++)

Java vs. C++

Not supported in Java. However, const is a reserved word and may be supported in future versions of Java.

You can use the final keyword to create variables with constant values in Java. When a variable is declared static final and is initialized with a constant, it creates a compile-time constant rather than an actual variable.

See the topic "final Keyword," page 51.

Constructors

Java vs. C++

In Java, as in C++, a constructor is a method that is automatically called when an object is created. Constructors are useful for initialization.

Because all Java objects are references, Java does not make the extensive use of copy constructors that C++ does. See "Example" for the Java equivalent of a copy constructor.

Syntax

A constructor has the same name as its class:

```
class(args)
```

For any given class, you can provide any number of different constructors, each with a different argument list. Note that constructors have no return type, not even void.

Example

This example declares a class with three constructors. Each constructor, like the class, is named `Point`.

```
class Point {
    int x, y;

    Point() {        // default constructor
        x = 0; y = 0;
    }

    Point(int newx, int newy) {
        x = newx; y = newy;
    }

    Point(Point p) { // copy constructor
        x = p.x; y = p.y;
    }

// ...
```

Context Operator (C++)

Java vs. C++

Not supported in Java.

Although Java supports classes and objects, elimination of the context operator (:) is one way that Java is smaller than C++. The context operator performs several important roles in C++ programming that are handled differently in Java:

- Clarification of scope: Java uses the dot (.) notation rather than the context operator. For example, `Color.red` is a valid expression, even though `Color` is a class and not an object.
- Referring to a member defined in a base class: In Java, you can use the `this` and `super` keywords to clarify scope. For example: `this.x` or `super.x`. The expression `super.x` refers to a member of the base class. This usage is unambiguous, because Java does not support multiple inheritance. See the topic "super Keyword," page 92.
- Defining a member function (method) outside the class declaration: In Java, all methods must be defined within the class declaration, so this is not an issue.
- Referring to symbols in namespaces: Java does not support namespaces, although packages can be used in a way similar to the way namespaces are used.

continue Statement

Java vs. C++

The `continue` statement does the same thing in Java as it does in C and C++: it advances to the next iteration of a loop. Java also permits specification of a label to identify the loop. This arrangement helps make up for the lack of a `goto` statement, although you should really never write code that requires a `goto` statement.

Syntax

The `continue` statement has two forms:

```
continue;
continue label;
```

If `label` is specified, execution transfers to the top of the loop identified; the label must be attached to the first line of the loop. Otherwise, execution transfers to the top of the innermost loop. In either case, if the affected loop is a `for` loop, the increment portion of that loop is executed before the next iteration.

Example

In this example, if `end_of_row` returns the value `true`, the `continue` statement advances execution to the next iteration of the outer `for` loop. Note that continue does not cause skipping of the increment (in this case, i++).

```
major_loop: for(int i = 0; i < 20; i++) {
    for(int j = 0; j < 20; j++) {
```

```
        amount += matrix[i][j];
        if (end_of_row())
            continue major_loop;
    }
}
```

Data Members

Java vs. C++
Java classes have data members just as C++ classes do; in Java, however, they are usually called class variables and instance variables. In Java, all variables are class, instance, or local, a policy that simplifies scope issues.

See the topic "Variables," page 99.

Data Types

Java vs. C++
Java does not support unsigned integers, and it introduces the byte and boolean types. The sizes of some integers are different from those in typical C and C++ implementations.

Primitive Types
In Table 2, all integer values (byte, short, int, and long) are signed, and all of them use two's complement format to represent negative numbers. In contrast to C and C++, the use of two's complement and data types of the size shown is not implementation dependent.

Table 2   *Primitive data types*

Type	Description	Range and precision
boolean	Boolean value (stored in 1 bit)	Two possible values: true or false
char	Unicode character (2 bytes)	\u0000 to \uFFFF
byte	1-byte integer	−128 to 127
short	2-byte integer	−32,768 to 32,767
int	4-byte integer	Approximately −2.147 billion to 2.147 billion
long	8-byte integer	Approximately $\pm 9 \times 10^{18}$

Continued

Table 2 *Continued*

Type	Description	Range and precision
float	4-byte floating point	Approximately $\pm 3.4 \times 10^{38}$; 7 digits of precision
double	8-byte floating point	Approximately $\pm 1.7 \times 10^{308}$; 15 digits of precision

Note that although the char type holds a single character, the String type is not equivalent to an array of char. See the topic "Strings" (p. 89) for more information.

Default Argument Values (C++)

Java vs. C++
Not supported in Java.

Although the capability to declare argument lists with default values is sometimes a useful feature of C++, Java drops support for this feature in the name of simplifying the language. The same functionality, it should be noted, can be achieved by using method overloading.

Java has a related feature found in neither C nor C++: guaranteed variable values for primitive data variables. In Java, uninitialized variables have the value 0, 0.0, or false, as appropriate for the data type. This arrangement works for all kinds of variables that have a primitive data type. It does not work for objects, which must be explicitly initialized.

default Keyword

Java vs. C++
The default keyword does the same thing in Java as it does in C and C++: it labels a default branch inside a switch statement.

Syntax
This keyword turns a statement into a labeled statement:

```
default:
    statement
```

Within a switch statement, if none of the case labels matches the test expression, execution transfers to the statement. Only one use of default can occur inside each switch statement.

Example
See the topic "switch Statement," page 93, for an example.

#define Directive (C++)

Java vs. C++
Not supported in Java.

One purpose of the #define directive in C and C++ is to create symbolic constants. You can do this in Java by modifying a variable declaration with the final keyword. Moreover, if you declare a variable as static final, you create a constant that can be used in calculations at compile time. The effect is to achieve the same optimization benefits that a #define constant has in C.

The other purpose of #define is to create macro functions. The Java alternative is to rely on writing methods, which can be overloaded to accommodate different types as needed. A sufficiently powerful Java compiler can inline functions in an optimal fashion, producing the same benefit as macro functions.

See the topic "final Keyword," page 51.

delete Operator (C++)

Java vs. C++
Not supported in Java.

Java eliminates the need for this operator. C++ expects you to use the new operator to release any allocated memory. Java, in contrast, keeps track of memory associated with each object, automatically releasing the memory after determining that no object is still using the memory. This process, called *garbage collection*, runs in the background as a low-priority thread.

When an object variable goes out of scope, Java recognizes this and notes that the variable no longer refers to memory or other objects. When there are no references left to an area of memory, it can be freed by the garbage collector. There is, in effect, an internal "reference count" for objects and memory.

The longer the existence of an object variable, the longer it will hold onto memory. You can therefore influence memory management by making objects local wherever appropriate. Aside from this fact, however, you can program in Java without worrying about deleting objects or memory.

Destructors (C++)

Java vs. C++
Not supported in Java. Java does support a similar concept in the form of the finalize() method.

The Java garbage collector takes care of all the details of releasing objects and memory. See the topic "delete Operator (C++)" for more information. Because most destructors in C++ are concerned with releasing memory and because this is automated in Java, destructors are seldom necessary in Java.

When a class owns resources other than memory, you may need to write a finalize() method to perform cleanup.

do Keyword

Java vs. C++

The do statement does the same thing in Java as it does in C and C++: it executes one or more statements as long as a condition is true. However, the condition must be a genuine Boolean expression, such as a comparison.

Syntax

The do statement is one of the Java loop structures.

```
do
   statement
while (condition);
```

The statement is executed at least once. After each execution of statement, if condition is true, the statement is executed again. The do statement differs from the while statement in that at least one execution of statement is guaranteed. See "while Statement" (p. 103) for the alternative syntax.

The condition must be a Boolean expression, such as Sum > 1.

Example

This example multiples amount by n as long as n is greater than zero.

```
do {
   amount = amount * n;
   n--;
}  while (n > 0);
```

double Data Type

Java vs. C++

The double data type has essentially the same characteristics as it has in C and C++, but its size is fixed for all time at 64 bits (8 bytes).

Syntax

The double keyword can be used to create 64-bit (8-byte) floating-point variables:

```
double declarations;
```

The range is approximately $\pm 1.8 \times 10^{308}$, with 14 places of precision after the decimal point. Tiny, nonzero values can get as close to zero as approximately $\pm \text{pm} 4.9 \times 10^{-324}$. The type can also hold the value zero precisely.

The java.lang.Double class includes a number of class constants of type double, including NEGATIVE_INFINITY, POSITIVE_INFINITY, and NaN ("Not a Number"). Floating-point arithmetic never raises exceptions, but it may result in one of these values.

Example
The first example creates temperature as an 8-byte floating-point variable with an initial value of 98.6. The second example declares two floating-point variables.

```
double temperature = 98.6;
double x, y = 2.0;
```

else Keyword

Java vs. C++
The else keyword does the same thing in Java as it does in C and C++: it provides an alternative execution path to an if statement.

Syntax
The else keyword appears in the following syntax:

```
if condition
    statement1
[ else
    statement2 ]
```

Here, the brackets indicate that the else clause is optional. If included, both else and *statement2* must appear. See the topic "if Keyword" (p. 57) for more details and for an example.

Empty Statements

Java vs. C++
Empty statements are legal in Java as they are in C and C++.

Syntax
An empty statement consists of a lone semicolon:

```
;
```

Java has relatively little use for empty statements. However, they are legal anywhere a complete Java statement would be legal. This means that Java is relatively forgiving (as are C and C++) if you type extra semicolons at the end of a statement. On the other hand, a semicolon is not legal anywhere a complete statement would not be legal.

Example

The example shows how to use an empty statement to create a do-nothing if statement, which might be useful as a placeholder if you plan to add code later in response to the if test:

```
if (temp < 32)
    ;
```

Exception Handling

Java vs. C++

Java's exception-handling syntax is close to that of C++. The main differences are that all exception classes are derived from the Throwable class, and any method that you write that might generate an exception without handling it must declare the exception with a throws clause.

Syntax

An exception is an unusual runtime event that must be handled immediately. Errors are the most typical cases of exceptions but are not the only ones. See the Glossary for a fuller description.

Java uses the following exception-handling syntax. Brackets indicate optional items.

```
try {
    statements
}
[ catch(ExceptionClass1 e1){
    statements
}]
[ catch(ExceptionClass2 e2){
    statements
}]
...
[finally {
    statements
}]
```

The statements inside the try block are executed unconditionally as part of the normal flow of execution. During execution of try block statements, an exception might be raised by one of these statements or during a method call. If a more tightly nested block or method does not handle the exception, the Java interpreter checks to see if one of the catch blocks can handle the exception.

Each exception is thrown in the form of an object, enabling exceptions to contain status information or error strings. Every exception class must be derived from the `Throwable` class. When the Java interpreter responds to an exception, it checks `ExceptionClass1`, `ExceptionClass2`, and so on until it finds a class that matches the type of the exception: There is a match if the exception's type is `ExceptionClass` or is derived from `ExceptionClass`. The statements inside the `catch` block are then executed. A `catch` block is not part of the normal flow of execution.

●—NOTE

Some early versions of Java supported the use of simple statements; that is, omission of the braces (`{}`) if `try` and `catch` blocks had only one statement each. However, not all versions of Java support this syntax, and many people discourage it as bad style anyway. To be safe, always use braces with `try`, `catch`, and `finally` keywords.

Inside the `catch` block, the code may decline to handle the exception by executing a `throw` statement:

```
throw;
```

In this case, the exception is passed along and the Java interpreter must search for another handler. Exceptions not handled by any code eventually reach the Java default exception handler, which prints a message and terminates execution.

Code in the `finally` block is executed unconditionally after execution leaves the `try` block. The `finally` block is guaranteed to be executed, whether the try block terminated normally or exited early due to an exception or break statement. The `finally` block is a logical place to put code that cleans up resources such as open file handle.

Example

This example shows a skeletal outline of exception-handling code.

```
try {
    // Open data file.
    // Attempt to read.
}
catch(EOFException e1) {
    // EOF reached; stop reading file.
}
catch(FileNotFoundException e2) {
    // File not found; print error msg.
}
catch(IOException e3) {
    // Misc. IO exception; print error msg.
```

```
   }
   finally {
      // If file still open, close it.
   }
```

Declaring Exceptions (throws)

As Appendix A, "Java Exceptions and Errors," illustrates, there are two kinds of exceptions: those that you must handle and those whose handling is optional. The optional exceptions are those derived from the Error and RuntimeException classes: each of these exceptions involves a common runtime error occurring in programs generally. Such exceptions are difficult to foresee when programming.

An exception such as FileNotFoundException happens only in response to certain method calls. Not surprisingly, Java requires you to handle these exceptions, because you have a good idea when they may or may not occur. For example, you watch for I/O exceptions (of which FileNotFoundException is a subclass) when you are doing file I/O work.

When you call a method that throws one of these mandatory exceptions, you have two choices. You can handle it in the code using a try-catch block, as explained in the previous section. Or you can declare your method with a throws clause: this tells the compiler, "I may throw this exception without handling it. Whoever calls me must handle it." For example:

```
   void readFile(String s) throws IOException {
      // ...
   }
```

Every caller of this method must include a try-catch block for type IOException, or else include throws IOException in its own declaration. This is the Java equivalent of passing the buck.

Simplified Exception Handling

The paradox of exception handling is that it's bothersome in simple programs but necessary in professional-quality software. For your first programs, you probably should include a few lines that handle exceptions in a concise way.

You must place a statement after a catch clause, but it is legal to use an empty statement (;):

```
   try {
      Thread.sleep(250);
   }
   catch (InterruptedException e) {
      ;
   }
```

I don't recommend this technique unless you never expect to see the exception. In this case, `InterruptedException` is unlikely to be thrown in a simple thread program, so it's fairly safe to ignore this exception.

However, it's usually a good idea to at least print a simple diagnostic. You can print an exception by passing it to the `println()` method. This method can take any object as argument. It responds by calling the object's `toString()` method, which, in this case, identifies the particular type of exception.

```
try {
    Thread.sleep(250);
}
catch (InterruptedException e) {
    System.out.println(e);
}
```

For more diagnostic information, you can use a *stack trace*, which prints a list of all Java methods currently executing at the time of the exception. The exact place where the exception was thrown is listed first. All exception classes inherit the stack-trace capability from `Throwable`.

```
try {
    Thread.sleep(250);
}
catch (InterruptedException e) {
    e.printStackTrace();
}
```

Another strategy is to place a `throws` clause in the current method's declaration, removing the need for a `try-catch` block. This means that the `caller` of the method must deal with the possibility of the exception. You can, if you choose, propagate the exception all the way up the line, even placing a `throws` clause in `main()`, thereby kicking back all responsibility to Java. Then you never need deal with the exception; but doing this tends to defeat the purpose of having exception handling in the first place.

extends Keyword

Java vs. C++

In Java, extends designates a superclass; C++ uses a colon (`:`) for this purpose.

Syntax

When you declare a class, place `extends` and a superclass name immediately after the class name. (The superclass is sometimes called `base class` or `parent class`.)

```
[public] [abstract] [final] class class_name [extends
super_class_name] {
```

```
declarations
}
```

Use of extends *super_class_name* is optional. If omitted, the superclass
is Object by default. Only single inheritance is supported for classes. The
effect of inheritance is to implicitly include all the declarations of the superclass (except for constructors) in the current class declaration. See the
topic "Inheritance" (p. 61) for more information. Also, see the topic
"class Keyword" (p. 34) for additional class syntax.

The extends keyword can also be used in interface declarations. An interface
can inherit only from other interfaces.

```
[public] [abstract] interface interface_name [extends interface1
[,interface2]...] {
    declarations
}
```

Any number of interfaces can follow extends. If more than one interface
follows extends, separate them by commas.

Examples

This class declaration indicates that Pubs is the superclass for Newspaper.
The effect is to create Newspaper as identical to Pubs except for the addition
of two new members.

```
class Newspaper extends Pubs {
    public String   editor;
    public long     circulation;
}
```

In an interface declaration, the interface may inherit from any number of
other interfaces:

```
interface Lang_Translator extends English, French, German {
    // declarations...
}
```

extern Declarations (C++)

Java vs. C++

Not supported in Java.

Java does not have global variables in the sense that C and C++ have them,
so there is no external storage. However, within the definition of a method,
you have access to members of the same class. You also have access to
members of another class as long as the following things are true:

- The compiled class information (.class file) is available in the appropriate directory. By default, this is the current directory. For information on how Java searches directories, see Part II, Chapter 2, "Java Building Blocks."
- The class is in the same package, or the class is declared public — in which case, the class can be in any package. If the class is in another package, both the class and individual members to be accessed must be declared public.

If you refer to a class in another package, you need to qualify the name of the class by using the syntax package.class, unless you use the import statement to abbreviate the name as Class.

See the topics "class Keyword" (p. 34), "package Keyword" (p. 79), and "import Statement" (p. 59) for more information. See also Part II, Chapter 2, "Java Building Blocks."

false Keyword

Java vs. C++
Because Boolean expressions are not the same as integers, Java provides the Boolean constants true and false. In C and C++, the values 1 and 0 suffice.

Syntax
The false keyword is a predefined constant in the Java language. It represents one of two possible values for expressions of type boolean:

```
false
```

Example
Comparing a condition to false reverses its logical meaning:

```
boolean outa_range = false;
outa_range = (X < 0 || X > 100);
if (outa_range == false)
    // X is in range...
```

Note that using the logical negation operator (!) has the same effect:

```
if (!outa_range)
    // X is in range...
```

final Keyword

Java vs. C++
In addition to providing some other uses, the final keyword provides the only way to declare symbolic constants in Java.

Syntax

When applied to a variable definition, final specifies that the value cannot change. The variable must be initialized in the definition. If the variable is also declared static and is initialized to a constant value, the variable becomes a compile-time constant (equivalent to a #define constant in C/C++), meaning that it can be folded into calculations at compile time.

```
final [other_modifiers] type variable = value;
```

When applied to a class declaration, final specifies that the class can never be subclassed (made a superclass for any other class).

```
final [other_modifiers] class class_name [extend, implement
clauses] {
   declarations
}
```

When applied to a method definition, final specifies that the method can never be overridden by a subclass. If the method is also declared static, the compiler might be able to inline the method to optimize the program.

```
final [other_modifiers] return_type method_name(args) {
   statements
}
```

Example

This class declaration shows examples of each use of final:

```
final class MyClass {
   final float pi = 3.141592;
   final int freeze = 0, boil = 100;

   final float pi_quot(float x) {
      return pi/x;
   }
}
```

float Data Type

Java vs. C++

The float data type has essentially the same characteristics as it does in C and C++, but its size is fixed for all time at 32 bits (4 bytes).

Syntax

The float keyword can be used to create 32-bit (4-byte) floating-point variables:

```
float declarations;
```

The range is approximately $\pm 3.4 \times 10^{38}$, with six places of precision after the decimal point. Tiny, nonzero values can get as close to zero as approximately $\pm 1.4 \times 10^{-45}$. The type can also hold the value zero precisely.

The java.lang.Float class includes a number of class constants of type float, including NEGATIVE_INFINITY, POSITIVE_INFINITY, and NaN ("Not a Number"). Floating-point arithmetic never raises exceptions, but may result in one of these values.

Examples

The first example creates temperature as a 4-byte floating-point variable with an initial value of 98.6. The second example declares two floating-point variables.

```
float temperature = (float) 98.6;
float x, y = (float) 2.0;
```

Note that floating-point constants must be cast to type float before being assigned.

for Statement

Java vs. C++

The for statement does essentially the same thing in Java as it does in C and C++: it executes statements repeatedly. However, in Java, the for statement enables special use of the comma (,) as an expression separator, and it also enables declaration of variables local to the for statement itself.

Syntax

The basic syntax of the for statement is the same as the syntax in C and C++:

```
for (initializer; condition; increment)
   statement
```

As in C and C++, the for statement syntax is equivalent to the following while loop (except for effects on the behavior of the continue statement, as described on page 40):

```
initializer;
while(condition) {
   statement
   increment;
}
```

See the topic "while Statement" (p. 103) for more information.

Each expression has special features that are not present in the C/C++ for statement, so you should examine the next few sections if you are new to its use in Java.

The initializer Expression

The initializer expression is executed just once, before the rest of the loop begins. Typically, it initializes a loop variable:

```
i = 0
```

You can use the comma to insert multiple expressions. This (along with the increment portion of the for statement) is the only place that Java enables this use of the comma:

```
i = 0, j = 0
```

A feature unique to Java lets you declare variables "on the fly" in the initialization expression. When you do this, the comma can be used only to separate variables in the list. You cannot combine this technique with the multiple-expression technique just shown.

```
int i = 0, j = 0
```

Variables have the same scope as the for loop when they are declared this way.

The condition Expression

The for loop executes as long as the condition is true. As elsewhere in Java, condition must be a genuine Boolean expression. Booleans include comparisons but not simple integer expressions. The condition in a for loop is typically a test to see whether a loop variable has reached a limit of some kind. For example:

```
i < array.length
```

The increment Expression

The increment expression is executed at the end of each iteration of the loop. Typically, this involves updating a loop variable:

```
i++
```

As with the initializer expression, Java permits the use of multiple expressions here, separated by commas:

```
i++, j++, k++
```

Examples

This simple example initializes all the members of an array:

```
int(i = 0; i < array.length; i++)
    array[i] = 0;
```

The second example uses a for statement to copy all the elements of arrayA to arrayB but in reverse order. The initializer declares the variables i and j and initializes them. These variables are local to the for statement. The increment expression uses the comma to separate two independent expressions, i++ and j--.

```
int arrayA[] = new int[50];
int arrayB[] = new int[50];
// ...
for (int i = 0, j = 49; i < 50; i++, j--)
  arrayA[i] = arrayB[j];
```

friend Keyword (C++)

Java vs. C++

Not supported in Java.

Elimination of the C++ friend keyword is another way in which Java reduces the size of the language. In C++, the friend keyword is used principally as an aid for writing binary operator functions (operator overloading). The only other use for friend is to break encapsulation, which runs counter to the goals of object-oriented programming and design. Because Java does not support operator overloading, there is little reason to support friend.

Functions (C++)

Java vs. C++

Technically, Java does not have functions; it only has methods (member functions). In practical terms, this means that you must place all function code inside class declarations.

To use C++ terminology, we should say that Java has no global functions. However, Java supports and encourages the use of class methods, as opposed to instance methods. Class methods are declared with the static keyword and correspond closely to static member functions in C++.

A class method works very much like a global function. Class methods are not tied to individual objects (instances) and can be used without regard to whether you have instantiated a particular object. If you call a class method from within its own class, you can use the method directly as though it were a global function. You can also call class methods from other classes as long as the names are properly qualified. Using the import statement enables you to use the method name without worrying about the package name.

See the topics "Methods" (p. 69), "static Keyword" (p. 87), and "import Statement" (p. 59).

goto Statement (C++)

Java vs. C++
Not supported in Java, although it is a reserved word.

Structured programming generally discourages the use of the direct-jump statements such as goto. In C and C++, goto is still useful for breaking out of several loops directly and for responding to error conditions. Java provides labeled **break** and **continue** statements to break out of nested loops, eliminating the major use for goto. In addition, exception handling provides a way to respond to errors from anywhere in the program.

See the topics "break Statement" (p. 28), "continue Statement" (p. 40), and "Exception Handling" (p. 46).

Hexadecimal Notation

Java uses the same notation for hexadecimal notation that C and C++ use. The syntax is 0x*num*; for example, 0x1A. See the topic "int Data Type" (p. 63). You can also use hexadecimal to specify a character code, as shown in Table 8, "Java escape sequences in strings" (p. 681).

Identifiers

Java vs. C++
Java uses the same rules for forming identifiers that C and C++ use.

Syntax
An identifier is a name that you create, as opposed to a keyword or operator. Identifiers serve as names for variables, classes, packages, and methods. As in C and C++, identifiers in Java observe these rules:

- An identifier must not be a reserved word (this includes all keywords).
- Identifiers consist of any of the following: the letters A to Z (uppercase and lowercase), the digits 0 to 9, and the underscore (_).
- The first character cannot be a digit.

Example
The following are all valid identifiers:

```
a
x04
count
this_is_Java
cuppaCoffee
MyClass
```

The Java API uses a naming convention that I have adopted in this book. The names of classes have the first letter capitalized. The names of all other symbols — including variables, methods, and packages — have the first letter in lowercase. Although the language itself does not require this approach, it is a useful convention for making programs easier to read.

if Statement

Java vs. C++
The if statement does the same thing in Java as in C and C++; it executes one or more statements if a condition is true. However, the condition must be a true Boolean expression, such as a comparison.

Syntax
The if statement constitutes a single complex statement.

```
if (condition)
   statement1
[ else
   statement2 ]
```

The brackets indicate that the else clause is optional. You can, in effect, create else if clauses by making statement2 an if statement. (See "Examples.")

The condition must be a Boolean expression, such as Sum > 0. An integer expression, such as Sum, is not a valid condition. In other words, the expression must always evaluate to a value of true or false.

Examples
The first example prints a message if n is not equal to zero. Note that using n itself as a condition would not be valid.

```
if (n != 0) {
   System.out.println("n not equal to zero.");
   return true;
}
```

The next example performs a series of comparisons.

```
if (a > b)
   System.out.println("a is greater than b");
else if (a == b)
   System.out.println("a is equal to b");
else
   System.out.println("a is less than b");
```

#if Directive (C++)

Java vs. C++
Not supported in Java.

The #if directive is supported in C and C++ primarily to support conditional compilation. This technique enables you to maintain one set of source code files from which different versions of the software are generated. Conditional compilation is far less necessary or useful in Java, because a Java binary file executes equally well on all platforms that support a Java interpreter. Contrast this with C and C++, where you might well need to maintain different source files for 16-bit Intel systems, 32-bit Intel systems, Macintosh, and so on. Because #if is not necessary in Java, eliminating it is another way of reducing the size of the language.

Java does not support any of the C/C++ preprocessor commands, including #ifdef, #else, #endif, for the same reasons that it does not support #if. Eliminating the preprocessor step also helps make the Java interpreter much more efficient. It also eliminates the chance of programmers creating complex nested macros, which often make poorly designed C and C++ programs virtually impossible to maintain.

implements Keyword

Java vs. C++
In Java, implements is used to indicate a special kind of inheritance, in which a class inherits declarations from an interface and provides implementations (definitions) for all its methods. In C++, this can be done by simply inheriting from abstract classes. Java uses the implements keyword because it treats interfaces in a privileged way. Only with interfaces can you get around Java's restriction against multiple inheritance.

Syntax
The implements keyword can be used within a class declaration. (This syntax does not include the use of throws. See the topic "class Keyword," p. 34, for more information.)

```
[modifiers] class class_name [extends super_class_name]
[implements interface1 [,interface2...] ]
{
    declarations
}
```

Here, the brackets indicate optional items. After implements appears, one or more *interfaces* appear. If there is more than one, they must be separated by commas.

For each interface that the class implements, it must provide method-definition code for all the methods declared in that interface. See the topic "interface Keyword" for more information on interfaces.

Example

The following code declares an interface called Shape, which declares two methods. Because Shape is an interface, the methods are implicitly declared abstract and are not given definitions.

```
import java.awt.Graphics;
interface Shape {
   public void moveTo(int newx, int newy);
   public void reDraw(Graphics g);
}
```

The class MyRectClass inherits declarations from the Shape interface. MyRectClass inherits from Shape and implements Shape by providing definitions for each of the two Shape methods (moveTo() and redraw()).

```
import java.awt.Graphics;
class MyRectClass implements Shape {
   int x, y;
   public void moveTo(int newx, int newy) {
      x = newx;
      y = newy;
   }

   public void reDraw(Graphics g) {
      g.drawRect(x, y, 20, 20);
   }
}
```

import Statement

Java vs. C++

At first glance, the Java import statement seems to work much like the C/C++ #include directive: it makes classes declared in other files available. However, any compiled, public class in the current directory (or a CLASSPATH directory, if CLASSPATH is used) is available without special declarations. The purpose of import is to let you refer to classes and interfaces without spelling out their package names.

Syntax

The import statement has two forms. In each case, package must be a complete package name such as java.awt or java.applet. You may include any number of import statements, but they must appear after the package statement, if any, and before the first class or interface declaration.

The first version of import lets you subsequently refer to the specified class without qualifying the name with the package. (See "Example" for clarification.)

```
import package.class;
```

The other version of import is similar except that it lets you refer to *all* the classes and interfaces in the package without qualifying the names with the package.

```
import package.*;
```

Example

Without an import statement, references to the Graphics class must be qualified by its package, java.awt:

```
paint(java.awt.Graphics g) {
}
```

However, after using the import statement shown, you can refer directly to the Graphics class:

```
import java.awt.Graphics;
//...
paint(Graphics g) {
}
```

● **NOTE**

The package java.lang is implicitly imported into all Java code, so you do not need to import it yourself. In other words, all classes in java.lang are directly available without the need to use the package name.

#include Directive (C++)

Java vs. C++

Not supported in Java.

The purpose of the #include directive in C and C++ is to support the inclusion of header files, which (among other things) include external declarations of variables and functions. In Java, however, all public classes and interfaces are available as long as they have been compiled and the appropriate class information is present in the current directory (or a directory listed in the CLASSPATH environment variable, if CLASSPATH is used). In short, class information previously compiled is automatically available to your Java applications and applets.

Java's import statement is an aid to the use of other classes, because it enables you to refer to classes and methods more directly. The effect is vaguely similar to that of the #include directive in C and C++, although it does not actually do the same thing. None of the C/C++ preprocessor directives is supported in Java.

See the topic "import Statement" (p. 59) for more information.

Inheritance

Java vs. C++

Java and C++ support a similar inheritance mechanism. Inheritance is based on classes, which are object types (although interfaces can also inherit from one another). In Java, the extends keyword specifies a superclass. See "extends Keyword" (p. 49) for more information.

There are two key differences between the inheritance mechanism in Java and that in C++:

- By design Java classes cannot directly inherit from multiple classes. Eliminating multiple inheritance keeps the language simpler. It also enables the Java super keyword to be used unambiguously. At the same time, Java helps get around the limitations of single inheritance by letting a class implement any number of interfaces; in Java, an interface is a special kind of abstract class. See the topic "interface Keyword" (p. 64) for more information.
- All classes, with the exception of one, have a superclass. If you do not explicitly declare a superclass, the special class Object is the superclass by default. This class is part of the Java API and is defined in java.lang. All classes inherit, either directly or indirectly, from Object, which means that the Object class sits atop the Java hierarchy of classes. A number of universal methods are defined in this class, including equals(), wait(), finalize(), toString(), and clone(). Some of these methods can be overridden. See the topic "Object Class" in Part I's "Java 2 API Reference," page 407, for more information.

Limitations

In Java, a derived class automatically inherits all the members of the base class except for constructors. However, superclass constructors may be called from the derived class through the use of the super keyword. Private members of the superclass are inherited but are invisible, so they may appear not to have been inherited.

Inner Classes

Most Java classes are defined at the package level, meaning that each class is a member of a particular package. Even if you don't explicitly specify a package association for a class, the default package will be assumed. Classes defined at the package level are known as top-level classes. Prior to Java 1.1, top-level classes were the only types of classes supported. However, Java 1.1 has ushered in a more open approach to class definition. I'm referring to *inner classes*, which are classes that can be defined in any scope. This means that a class can be defined as a member of another class, within a block of statements, or anonymously within an expression.

Inner classes, although seemingly a minor enhancement to the Java language, actually represent a significant modification to the language. In fact, the Java delegation event model utilized by the AWT specifically requires a mechanism like inner classes to function properly.

Rules governing the scope of an inner class closely match those governing variables. An inner class's name is not visible outside its scope, except in a fully qualified name, which helps in structuring classes within a package. The code for an inner class can use simple names from enclosing scopes, including class and member variables of enclosing classes, as well as local variables of enclosing blocks.

In addition, you can define a top-level class as a static member of another top-level class. Unlike an inner class, a top-level class cannot directly use the instance variables of any other class. The capability to nest classes in this way allows any top-level class to provide a package style organization for a logically related group of secondary top-level classes.

Example

Following is a simple example of an inner class:

```
public class Outer {
  public outerMethod() {
    // Outer class method
  }

  class Inner {
    public innerMethod() {
      // Inner class method
    }
  }
}
```

In this example, the Inner class is an inner class defined within the Outer class, which makes Inner only usable within the Outer class. This might seem like a serious limitation of inner classes, but they can serve a vital role as helper classes. More specifically, inner classes are very valuable at simplifying the manner in which events are handled in Java. To learn more, check out Chapter 4, "Components and Events," page 561, in Part II.

instanceof Operator

Java vs. C++

The Java instanceof operator has the same general purpose of the runtime type information (RTTI) operators in ANSI C++.

Syntax

The instanceof operator is a Boolean operator that returns information on an arbitrary object at runtime. It is particularly useful for determining whether a random object supports a particular method.

When used with a class, the instanceof operator returns true if the object is an instance of class or a subclass derived, directly or indirectly, from class.

```
object instanceof class
```

When used with an interface, the instanceof operator returns true if the object's class implements interface or is derived from a class that implements interface.

```
object instanceof interface
```

Example

In this example, the Test() method is passed a random object, obj, which may be of type Object or a class derived from Object (in other words, any class). The example tests whether obj is an instance of the String class. If it is, then it is safe to call the toLowerCase() method, which is a method of this class.

```
void Test(Object obj) {
   if (obj instanceof String)
      System.out.println(obj.toLowerCase());
   //...
```

int Data Type

Java vs. C++

The Java int data type is similar to int in C and C++ except that its size is fixed at 32 bits (4 bytes) for all implementations.

Syntax

The int keyword can be used to create 32-bit (4-byte) integer variables:

```
int declarations;
```

The range is approximately plus or minus 2 billion: –2,147,483,648 to 2,147,483,647.

You can use hexadecimal and octal notation in Java just as you can in C (using 0x*num* and 0*num*). For example, 255 can also be written as 0xFF or 0377.

Examples

This example creates a variable named score as a 4-byte integer with an initial value of 100. The second example declares two integer variables.

```
int score = 100;
int i, j;
```

Unlike C and C++, Java automatically sets uninitialized variables of primitive type to 0, although explicitly initializing them is good programming practice:

```
int i = 0, j = 0;
```

interface Keyword

Java vs. C++

In Java, an interface is like an abstract class — a class with methods that are not implemented. However, Java recognizes interfaces as distinct from classes and imposes a different syntax. The distinction is important in Java, because although interfaces have some limitations, they offer the only way around the restriction against multiple inheritance. In C++, an interface is coded as just another class.

Classes inherit methods from an interface by the use of the implements keyword. See the topic "implements Keyword" for more information.

Syntax

An interface is declared with the following syntax:

```
[public] [abstract] interface interface_name [extends interfaces]
{
    declarations
}
```

Here, brackets indicate optional items. Interfaces are automatically abstract, so the abstract keyword is unnecessary, although legal. The optional extends clause may specify any number of other *interfaces* to inherit from. If there are more than one, they must be separated by commas (,).

The declarations can contain variables. The variables are automatically static and final, whether or not you use these keywords, and must be initialized to a constant expression. Interface variables are automatically public if the interface is public.

```
[static] [final] [public] type variable = value;
```

The declarations can also contain methods (usually the most important part of an interface). The methods are automatically abstract and do not contain a method definition; you must terminate such a declaration with a semicolon. Interface methods are automatically public if the interface is public. The methods cannot include constructors, and the only legal modifiers are those shown:

```
[public] [abstract] return_type method_name(args);
```

Example
An interface declares a list of services that each class implements in its own way. The class implements the interface by using the implements keyword and providing a definition (implementation) for each method declared in the interface. A class can have only one superclass, but it can implement any number of interfaces.

The following interface declares services for reporting status. Any class that implements this interface must provide a definition for each of the four methods listed.

```
public interface Status {
    boolean is_multithreaded();
    boolean is_active();
    int number_of_threads();
    void set_priority(int priority_num);
}
```

Keywords

Java vs. C++
The Java, C, and C++ keywords include many of the same words. All but a few C++ keywords are also Java keywords. Java has some additional keywords, such as package, that support Java's unique features.

Summary
Table 3 summarizes Java reserved words; most of these are keywords. However, there are some, marked by an asterisk (*), that have no current use but are reserved for use in future versions of Java.

Java 2 Language Reference

Table 3 *Java reserved words and keywords*

abstract	boolean	break	byte	byValue*
case	cast*	catch	char	class
const*	continue	default	do	double
else	extends	false	final	finally
float	for	future*	generic*	goto*
if	implements	import	inner*	instanceof
int	interface	long	native	new
null	operator*	outer*	package	private
protected	public	rest*	return	short
static	super	switch	synchronized	this
throw	throws	transient	true	try
var*	void	volatile	while	

Labels

Java vs. C++

In Java, statement labels are used in switch statements (as in C and C++)
and as targets for break and continue statements. Java does not support
a goto statement. The label syntax is the same as the syntax for C/C++.

Syntax

A labeled statement has one of three forms:

```
identifier: statement
case constant_expression: statement
default: statement
```

The first form is used to create a target of a break or continue statement.
The other two forms are used only inside a switch statement block.

Example

This example labels the top of a for statement, giving it the name top_of_loop:

```
top_of_loop:
  for(int i = 0; i < 100; i++)
  //...
```

For more information, see the topics "break Statement" (p. 28), "continue
Statement" (p. 40), and "switch Statement" (p. 93).

long Data Type

Java vs. C++

The long data type has a size fixed at 64 bits for all implementations.

Syntax

The long keyword can be used to create 64-bit (8-byte) integer variables:

```
long declarations;
```

The range is −9,223,372,036,854,775,808 to 9,223,372,036,854,775,807 (approximately $\pm 9 \times 10^{18}$).

You can use hexadecimal and octal notation in Java just as you can in C (using 0xnum and 0num). For example, 255 can also be written as 0xFF or 0377. You can also use the L suffix, as in 10L, to force a small constant to be stored as a long.

Examples

The first example creates score as a 64-bit integer variable with an initial value of 100. The second example declares two integer variables.

```
long score = 100;
long i, j;
```

Unlike C and C++, Java automatically sets uninitialized variables of primitive type to 0, although explicitly initializing them is good programming practice:

```
long i = 0, j = 0;
```

main() Method

Java vs. C++

The main() method in Java has roughly the same purpose as the main() function in C and C++; however, it is an entry point only for applications and not for applets. Furthermore, in Java, main() is a method like any other, and it must be declared inside a public class.

Syntax

The main() method is the entry point for an application and must be declared inside a public class. It should be given the attributes shown:

```
public static void main(String args[]) {
    statements
}
```

The main( ) method can instead be given an integer return type, in which case it must return a value. This value is received by the operating system.

```
public static int main(String args[]) {
    statements
}
```

Here, *statements* must include at least one return statement.

In either case, args is an array of strings, each string containing a command-line argument. The first string in the array is the first argument on the command line after the class name itself. You can determine the number of command-line strings by referring to the length field of args.

Getting the Command Line

When using args, you may find it useful to review the unique features of Java arrays since args contains an array of strings. (See the topic "Arrays," p. 23.) args[0] and args[1] refer to the first and second command-line arguments, respectively, and args.length is equal to the total number of arguments. The following figure shows how Java would parse the sample command line java Printarg aa bb cc.

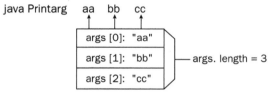

Getting arguments from a command line

Example

The following example prints command-line arguments to the display, printing one to a line:

```
public class Printarg {
    public static void main(String args[]) {
        for (int n=0; n < args.length; n++)
            System.out.println(args[n]);
    }
}
```

This application must be contained in a source file named Printarg.java. When compiled and run, the application will be named Printarg. Consider the following command line:

```
java Printarg this is a test
```

This command line will result in the following output:

```
this
is
a
test
```

Methods

Java vs. C++

Methods in Java are similar to function members in C++, but there are many differences. In particular, Java has no global functions and requires methods to be defined entirely within class declarations.

Unlike C and C++, Java has no problem with forward references to classes and methods. Consequently, you can declare methods in any order without the need for prototypes.

Syntax

Every method definition must occur inside a class declaration:

```
[modifiers] class class_name [extends, implements clauses] {
   ...
   method_declaration {
     statements
   }
   ...
}
```

This book assumes that all method definitions are inside a class declaration. The full syntax for a method declaration is:

```
[modifiers] return_type method_name(args) [throws exceptions] {
   statements
}
```

Here, brackets indicate optional items. Return type is not optional, although it may be void. (Exception: Constructors have no return type.) This syntax is complete except for the case of abstract and native methods, which are terminated by a semicolon (;) in place of {statements}. See "abstract Keyword" (p. 20) and "native Keyword" (p. 74) for more information.

Syntax: Modifiers

The modifiers include any of the following, in any order: abstract, final, native, static, synchronized, public, private, and protected. The modifiers private protected can be used together, but neither one can be used with public. Table 4 summarizes the meaning of each modifier.

Table 4 *Modifiers for Java methods*

Modifier	Description
abstract	No definition is provided for the method. Definitions must be provided in subclasses.
final	Method may not be overridden in subclasses.
native	No definition is provided for the method. Definition is provided by another language such as C.
private	Method can be accessed only within the class. This is not the default behavior; see discussion following this table.
private protected	Method can be accessed only within the class and subclasses.
protected	Method can be accessed anywhere in the package and also by subclasses in other packages (if the class is public).
public	Method has same access level as the class.
static	Method is a class method; may refer only to static (class) variables.
synchronized	Two threads cannot execute this method simultaneously.

For more information, see individual topics for the keywords. If none of the access-level keywords is used (public, private, and protected), then the method is visible to all other methods in the package but not outside the package. In contrast to C++ rules, in Java, a method must be specifically declared private to be hidden to code outside the class.

Syntax: args

The Java argument-list syntax is almost identical to the C++ syntax but may not include default arguments. Also, if there are no arguments, leave the argument list blank; do not use void. In Java, unlike C, an empty argument list is unambiguous and means that the method takes no arguments.

```
type arg_name [, type arg_name]...
```

This syntax indicates that there may be any number of arguments. If there is more than one, separate them with commas.

Syntax: throws Clause

A method declaration may include an optional throws clause, which lists exceptions that a method may throw:

```
throws exception1 [,exception2]...
```

This syntax indicates that the throws keyword is followed by one or more exceptions and that if there is more than one exception, commas are used to separate them.

The throws clause informs the compiler of exceptions that the method may throw without handling. Code that calls the method, therefore, should expect the possibility of being thrown these exceptions. Each such exception thrown must be declared in the throws clause, except for the classes Error and RuntimeException and their subclasses.

Examples

This example shows a simple method, Set_Pnt(). This method is an instance method (it is not declared static) and is accessible throughout the package in which it appears.

```
class Pnt {
  int x, y;

  void Set_Pnt(int newx, int newy) {
    x = newx;
    y = newy;
  }

//...
```

This next example shows the method resetVars(), which is private to the class and is a class method (because it is declared static).

```
class Myclass {
  private static int x, y;
  private static double ratio;
  private static displayString;

  private static int resetVars() {
    x = 0;
    y = 0;
    ratio = 0.0;
    displayString = "";
    return 0;
  }

//...
```

This last example shows a method that uses a throws clause. Because the method is public, it is accessible to code in other packages if the class is also public.

```
public long scanFile(File theFile)
```

```
        throws FileNotFoundException {
        long size;
        //...

        throw new FileNotFoundException();
        //...

        return size;
    }
```

Method Overloading

Java vs. C++

Method overloading is supported in Java just as in C++. (In C++, it is usually called *function overloading*.)

Example

Method overloading is a technique for creating different versions of the same method within the same class; each version has the same name but a different argument list. The different versions are actually separate methods, and each version has its own definition. During a method call, the Java compiler determines which version to call by examining the argument list.

As in C++, the argument lists must differ in the number of arguments, the types, or both. You cannot have two different methods with the same name and argument list, but with different return values. However, as long as the argument lists differ, the return types do not necessarily have to be the same.

This example overloads the method named SetPnts():

```
    class Pnt {
        private float x, y;

        void setPnts(Pnt pt) {
            x = pt.x;
            y = pt.y;
        }

        void setPnts(float newx; float newy) {
            x = newx;
            y = newy;
        }

        // ...
```

Modulus Operator (%)

Java vs. C++

The modulus operator (`%`) does exactly the same thing in Java as it does in C and C++: it returns the remainder of the division of two integers. (It is also called the remainder operator.)

Syntax

The modulus operator (`%`) forms an expression from two integer subexpressions:

   quantity `%` *divisor*

The syntax is the same as division (`/`), but the remainder is the result. For example, 7 divided by 2 is 3 with a remainder of 1, so the expression 7 `%` 2 evaluates to 1.

Example

A common use is to determine when an integer is exactly divisible by another integer. For example, the following function determines whether a number is odd or even. It returns `true` if the number is even; otherwise, it returns `false`.

```
boolean is_even(int n) {
    return (n % 2 == 0);
}
```

In general, if a number n is exactly divisible by a divisor d, then n `%` d evaluates to 0.

Namespaces (C++)

Java vs. C++

Not supported in Java.

You can use classes and packages in a way that's similar to using namespaces. Declaring class methods and class variables (as opposed to instance methods and classes) has an effect similar to that of declaring global functions and variables, as you would in C and C++. References to class methods and variables must be qualified, although you can use Java's `import` statement to abbreviate the reference to the class. You can therefore manage access to symbols defined in another class or package just as you can manage access to symbols in a C++ namespace.

See the topics "package Statement" (p. 79) and "import Statement" (p. 59) for more information.

Java 2 Language Reference

native Keyword

Java vs. C++

The native keyword is an extended feature of Java not supported by C or C++.

Syntax

The native keyword can be applied to method declarations to indicate that the method is implemented with native code. The declaration must be terminated by a semicolon (;).

```
native [other_modifiers] return_type method_name(args);
```

Native code consists of code that runs directly on a particular platform. A native-code method would therefore consist of machine instructions instead of Java byte codes. A method declared as native is generated by another language (such as assembler or a C compiler) and linked to a Java program at run time.

Example

This example declares a single native method.

```
native void set_protection_level(int level);
```

new Operator

Java vs. C++

The new operator returns a reference, not a pointer. This means that you assign the result to an object variable and not to an address expression. (See "Examples.")

In Java, it is usually necessary to use new to allocate actual space for an object. This makes new more important than it is in C++, which provides other ways to create an object. When you define an object variable in Java, it is merely a *reference* to an object. The variable must be associated with an actual object in memory (allocated with new) before it can be used.

In contrast to C++, there is no matching delete operator and no need to explicitly release memory in the source code. The Java interpreter handles object destruction and memory management for you through its garbage collection process.

Syntax

The new operator can be used to create one or more objects:

```
new type()           // Calls default constructor
new type(args)       // Calls constructor that takes args
```

```
new type[size]          // Creates array object
new type[size1][size2]... // Creates multidimensional array
                        //  object
```

In each case, the new operator returns a reference to the appropriate type of object. In the last two cases, the operator returns a reference to an array. (Arrays are also types of objects in Java.)

Note that throughout this syntax, the brackets are intended literally.

Some of the sizes in the multidimensional case can be left blank. See the topic "Arrays" (p. 23) for more information.

Examples

The first declaration shows the new operator used to allocate a single object. The second example shows the new operator used to allocate an array of objects.

```
MyClass obj = new MyClass();
MyClass arrayObj[] = new MyClass[10];
```

Note that you do not need to use new when defining primitive type variables (int, short, long, float, double, boolean, char) or String type variables. Primitive data allocates actual space in data storage, and String objects can be initialized with quoted strings.

```
int  a, b, c = 200;
String  Name = "John Q. Public";
```

null Constant

Java vs. C++

Although Java does not support pointers, the Java predefined null constant is similar to the null pointer value in C and C++, usually defined as ((void *) 0).

Syntax

In Java, null is a literal constant:

```
null
```

This value can be assigned to, or compared to, object variables. (An object is an instance of a class and not a primitive data type.) An object variable with the value null is not associated with any actual object in memory; instead, it is only an empty reference. In other words, an object with the value null currently holds the value "no object."

Assigning the value null to a thread causes the thread to stop running.

Example
One use of null is to test an object variable to see whether it really holds an object. Only if the variable holds an object is it safe to refer to instance variables or methods:

```
if (myObject != null)
    System.out.println(myObject.toString());
```

Octal Notation

Java uses the same notation for octal notation that C and C++ use. The syntax is 0*num*; for example, 057. See the topic "int Data Type" (p. 63). You can also use octal to specify a character code, as shown later in Table B-4, "Java escape sequences," page 681.

Objects

Java vs. C++
The concept of objects is roughly the same in Java and C++: an object is a packet of data with associated functions. Objects are distinct from classes in that an object is an instance of a class and therefore has a specific value; a class is an object's type.

There are some significant differences between the Java class-object model and the C++ model:

- Unlike C++, Java considers objects and primitive data to be two different categories, and different rules apply. Most important, variables of a primitive data type contain actual data, but object variables are only *references* to objects — you must allocate objects in memory and then associate them with the object variables. Usually, this means that the use of the new operator (or calling a method that uses new) is required to allocate a new object in memory:

  ```
  class object_name = new class();
  ```

- String is a special type. It is the only class that supports an extended operator (+, for concatenation). In contrast to objects of other classes, you can allocate a String object simply by using a quoted literal string. See the topics "Aggregates" (p. 21) and "Strings" (p. 89).
- Because object variables are references, assignment has the effect of simply associating one variable with the same location in memory as another variable; testing for equality (==) tests references to see whether they are associated with the same memory. To get around this behavior, which is counterintuitive for most people, Java provides the equals() and clone() methods, which are inherited from the Object class. See the topic "References" (p. 84) for additional discussion.

- All Java classes inherit, directly or indirectly, from the Object class. Therefore, all objects have the built-in functionality defined in Object. This is not true of primitive types, although primitive types have corresponding "wrapper" classes. These classes include Boolean, Character, Integer, Long, Float, and Double. For more information on the Object class, see the topic "Object Class" in the Part I's "Java 2 API Reference," page 407.

For information on classes, see the topic "Classes" (p. 34). For examples of object allocation, see the topic "new Operator."

Operators

Java vs. C++
Nearly all Java operators are also found in C and C++, but the Java operator set is somewhat smaller because it does not support pointers.

Summary of Precedence
Table 5 shows precedence and associativity of Java operators.

Table 5 *Precedence of Java operators*

Operator(s)	Type of operation (if not binary)	Association
++, —, +, -, ~, ! (type)	Unary	Right-to-left
*, /, %		Left-to-right
+, -, + (string concatenation)		Left-to-right
<<, >>, >>>		Left-to-right
<, >, <=, >=, instanceof		Left-to-right
==, !=		Left-to-right
&		Left-to-right
^		Left-to-right
|		Left-to-right
&&		Left-to-right
||		Left-to-right
?:	Ternary	Right-to-left

Continued

Table 5 *Continued*

Operator(s)	Type of operation (if not binary)	Association
=, +=, -=, *=, /=, %=, +=, -=, <<=, >>=, >>>=, &=, ^=, |=		Right-to-left

Description of Operators (by Group)

The use of some operators is obvious (at least if you've programmed in another high-level language). Table 6 provides an overview of some of the less-obvious operators and suggests where to go for further information.

Table 6 *Groups of operators*

Operators	Description
==, !=	Test for equality and nonequality, respectively, as in C/C++.
~, !	Bitwise and logical negation. See the topic "Bitwise Operators" (p. 26).
%	Remainder (modulus) division. See the topic "Modulus Operator" (p. 73).
<<, >>, >>>	Left shift, right shift, and unsigned right shift. Valid only on integer operands. See the topic "Shift Operators" (p. 86).
&, ^, |	AND, exclusive OR, and OR, respectively; can be used on two integer or two Boolean operands. See the topic "Bitwise Operators" (p. 26).
&&, ||	Logical AND and OR.
? :	See the topic "Conditional Operator" (p. 38).
++, --	Incremented and decremented operators.

As in C and C++, Java supports a set of assignment operators that have the following form:

    operand1 op = operand2

Such expressions are equivalent to the following expression:

    operand1 = operand1 op operand2

For example, a + = b is equivalent to:

```
a = a + b
```

The target, *operand1*, must be an expression that can legally appear on the left of a regular assignment (=). Such an expression could be a simple variable or array element. In any case, *operand1* is evaluated only once.

●—NOTE

> The Java language set also supports characters for field access (.) and for array indexing ([ ]). Technically, these are not considered operators; they have the effect of qualifying a name, as in Basic and FORTRAN. This arrangement is appropriate in Java, because it does not translate field and element access into pointer arithmetic. Use of these symbols is resolved before operators are applied.

Operator Overloading (C++)

Java vs. C++

Not supported in Java.

Although operator overloading is a useful technique in C++, Java did not adopt it. This omission serves the purpose of keeping Java a smaller, leaner language. All the operator functions you might write in C++ can be realized in Java by simply writing ordinary methods.

Java supports operator overloading in a very limited sense. For example, the addition operator (+) is reused by the String class to indicate string concatenation. However, Java does not extend the ability to define operators to user-defined classes, so, in that sense, there is no operator overloading.

package Statement

Java vs. C++

Packages have no close parallel in C or C++, although there are similarities to the concepts of module and namespace. However, a single Java package can extend over multiple source files. All the classes in the same package have access to one another.

Syntax

The package statement, if it occurs, must be the first statement in a Java source file.

```
package package_name;
```

The *package_name* can contain embedded dots (.) to separate different parts of the package name. The name must represent a subtree in the directory structure. For example, if the package name is briano.util.tools, then all the classes in this package must reside in the directory briano\util\tools, in which briano is a subdirectory of a directory that Java normally searches. For more information on the intricacies of package naming and locations, see Part II, Chapter 2, "Java Building Blocks," p. 519.

The statement places all the classes defined in the source file into the specified package. Other source files may contribute to this same package. Classes declared in the same package, even if declared in different source files, have access to one another. From outside the package, only public classes are accessible.

If a source file specifies no package, it is placed in the default package. Consequently, until you start placing code in packages, all the classes you write have access to one another, and name conflicts are possible.

Example

This example specifies that the classes defined in the source file are to be placed in the package briano.util.tools, which must reflect the directory structure.

```
package briano.util.tools;
```

Pointers (C++)

Java vs. C++

Java does not support pointers. This is the most dramatic difference between Java and C/C++. Java provides alternative mechanisms for things that involve pointers in C and C++:

- Arrays. In Java, you must use array indexing, just as you would in most languages, including Basic or FORTRAN. This is a small concession, because array indexing is only slightly less efficient than pointer access. Java has better security and error checking, because it enforces array bounds instead of translating indexes into pointer expressions.
- Memory allocation. Java supports dynamic use of the new operator, just as in C++ (and in C with the malloc( ) function). However, in Java, the new operator returns a reference; this means that it associates the appropriate address with a target object variable but avoids pointer syntax.
- Pointers to callback functions. Because Java methods are polymorphic — meaning late bound — they work like virtual functions in C++. Consequently, it is easy to create a callback by building an interface or abstract class around it. Such an interface or class declares at least one method, which, in effect, is a callback function. Again, Java avoids the pointer syntax that C would require.

- Passing by reference. Java is least flexible in this area, although workarounds are possible. In Java, object variables are references, so they can be associated with different addresses just as pointers are. All objects, therefore, are automatically passed by reference. If you want to simulate passing by value (perhaps to make sure you preserve the value of the original argument), you can use a copy constructor or clone() function, if available. For example:

```
// Copy the value, then modify ONLY the copy,
// not the original.
public void doCalc(MyClass object) {
    MyClass objectCopy = new MyClass(object);
    // ...
```

Passing a primitive data type (such as int) by reference is more problematic. Primitive data is always passed by value. However, you can pass numeric data by reference by declaring an argument of class Boolean, Character, Integer, Long, Float, or Double. These types correspond to the primitive data types, but because these types are classes, the data is passed by reference. For example:

```
Float x = new Float(0.0);
Float y = new Float(1.5);
Translate_Points(x, y);  // Changes values of x and y.
```

This example assumes that Translate_Points takes two objects of type Float (rather than float).

private Keyword

Java vs. C++

The private keyword has a general meaning in Java similar to that in C++. However, the keyword must be applied to methods and variables individually. In Java, a method or variable can be declared public, protected, private, or private protected (using both keywords).

Syntax: private

Unlike C++, Java requires that private be declared for each individual member to which it applies. The declaration for a data member (variable) is as follows:

```
private [other_modifiers] type items;
```

The declaration for a method is as follows:

```
private [other_modifiers] return_type method_name(args)
[throws_clause] {
```

```
    statements
}
```

In each case, brackets indicate optional items.

A member that is declared `private` but not `protected` has no visibility outside the class. Even derived classes cannot access the member. A member that is declared `private` and `protected` is similar, but it can be accessed in classes derived from the current class.

Example

In this example, the instance variables x and y have private access. They cannot be accessed except within code for the `Point` class:

```
class Point {
    private float x, y;
    //...
}
```

protected Keyword

Java vs. C++

The protected keyword has a general meaning in Java similar to that in C++. However, the keyword must be applied to a method or variable individually. In Java, a method or variable can be declared `public`, `protected`, `private`, or `private protected` (using both keywords).

Syntax: protected

Unlike C++, Java requires that `protected` be declared for each individual member to which it applies. The declaration for a data member (variable) is as follows:

```
protected [other_modifiers] type items;
```

The declaration for a method is:

```
protected [other_modifiers] return_type method_name(args)
[throws_clause] {
    statements
}
```

In each case, brackets indicate optional items.

A member that is declared `protected` but not `private` has general visibility within the package. The member can also be accessed within the method definitions of subclasses declared in other packages. This assumes that the class itself is declared `public`; otherwise, `protected` declarations have no effect.

A member that is declared protected and private does not have visibility outside the class except within subclasses. This state is closest to the C++ meaning of protected.

Example

In this example, the instance variables x and y have private protected access: they cannot be accessed except within code for the Point class and classes derived from Point:

```
class Point {
    private protected float x, y;
    //...
}
```

public Keyword

Java vs. C++

Although the public keyword has a general meaning in Java similar to that in C++, there are many differences. Java has public classes that can be accessed from anywhere, including other packages. Within public classes, the public keyword can be used to extend this access to individual methods and variables.

Syntax: Class Declarations

The public keyword is one of the modifiers of a class declaration. (But note that private and protected cannot be used this way.)

```
[public] [abstract] [final] class class_name [extends
super_class_name] {
    declarations
}
```

Here, brackets indicate optional items. When public is applied to the class declaration, it makes the class available to all other classes, if the class is placed in the appropriate directory. The default behavior is for a class to be available only to classes in the same package. (See "package Keyword," page 79.) Even though a class is available outside its package, members are not available outside the package unless they are individually declared public as well.

In each source file, there can be at most one class declared public. This class must have the same name as the file. In addition, a class must be public to serve as the entry point of an applet or application.

Syntax: Members

Unlike C++, Java requires that public be declared for each individual field to which it applies. Here is the declaration for a public variable:

```
public [other_modifiers] type variable_declarations;
```

The declaration for a public method is as follows:

```
public [other_modifiers] return_type method_name(args)
[throws_clause] {
  statements
}
```

In each case, brackets indicate optional items. A member that is declared public cannot be declared private or protected.

If the member declaration occurs in a public class, then the effect of public is to let the member be accessed by classes outside the package as well as inside the package. Otherwise, public has no effect. The default behavior is for a member to be accessible by classes in the same package. To prevent this access, a member must be specifically declared private.

Example

In the following example, both the class Hello and the method main() must be declared public.

```
public class Hello {
  public static void main(String[] args) {
    System.out.println("Hello, Java!");
  }
}
```

References

Java vs. C++

In Java, all object variables, arguments, and return types are references. There is no need for a reference operator as there is in C++.

If you have programmed in C, you can think of references as pointer variables without the pointer syntax. If you have not programmed in C or C++, you can think of references as variables that first must be *associated* with actual objects in memory before being used.

In Java, assigning one object to another does not invoke a copy or assignment operator function. (You can copy between objects by using the clone() function, inherited from the Object class, but only if the class implements the Cloneable interface.) Instead, assigning to an object has the effect of associating the variable with another location in memory, much like pointer assignment.

Example

In the following example, the variables one_obj and arr_obj are associated with actual objects in memory; some_obj is not.

```
MyClass one_obj = new MyClass();
MyClass arr_obj[] = new MyClass[100];
MyClass some_obj;
some_obj = one_obj;        // some_obj is an alias for one_obj.
some_obj.update();         // Updates one_obj.
some_obj = arr_obj[10];    // some_obj an alias for arr_obj[10].
some_obj.update();         // Updates arr_obj[10].
some_obj = new MyClass();  // Create a new object.
```

The object variable some_obj is at first not associated with any object. However, it is used as an alias, first for one_obj and then for arr_obj[10]. The call to the update() function applies to a different object in each case. Finally, in the last line, a new object is allocated in memory and then associated with some_obj.

register Keyword

Java vs. C++

Not supported in Java.

In C and C++, register is used to indicate that a variable is to be stored directly in a microprocessor register, which is an optimization for frequently used variables. Since Java attempts to remain very hardware independent, the register keyword isn't supported.

return Keyword

Java vs. C++

Java supports the same syntax for return that C and C++ support.

Syntax

There are two versions of the return statement:

```
return expression;
return;
```

The first version returns a value to the caller of a method. It should be used in any function that does not have a void return type. The second version does not return a value. Both versions have the effect of immediately exiting the current method.

Example

This example uses return to report the results of a calculation:

```
long factorial(int n) {
    long result = 1;
    while (n > 1) {
```

```
      result = result * n—;
   }
   return result;
}
```

Shift Operators

Java vs. C++

Java supports left and right shift operators, as in C and C++. Java also supports an additional right-shift operator (>>>) that treats integer data as unsigned.

Syntax

Java supports three shift operators, as explained in Table 7.

Table 7 *Shift operators in Java*

Operator and Syntax	Description
data << *num_bits*	*data* shifted left by *num_bits*.
data >> *num_bits*	*data* shifted right by *num_bits*. Data is considered signed, so result is sign-extended into the leftmost bit.
data >>> *num_bits*	*data* shifted right by *num_bits*. Data is considered unsigned, so 0 is always placed into the leftmost bit.

In each case, *data* is the data to be operated on. The operand *num_bits* is also an integer, but it should be a relatively small positive number. Shifts greater than 31, in the case of int, or 63, in the case of long, have the effect of losing all the original data.

None of these operations changes the original data operated on, integer; they simply evaluate to the indicated result. The assignment-operator versions (<<=, >>=, and >>>=) perform the same operations but change the original data.

Example

The following statements return different results. In the first case, the digit 1 is shifted into the leftmost position, preserving the negative sign of the number. In the second example, a 0 is shifted into this position.

```
int test = 0xFFFE;
int result1, result2;
result1 = test >> 1;     // Result is 0xFFFF;
result2 = test >>> 1;    // Result is 0x7FFF;
```

short Data Type (C++)

Java vs. C++

The short data type has the same characteristics in Java as it does in C and C++, but its size is fixed at exactly 16 bits (2 bytes) for all time and is not in any way implementation-dependent.

Syntax

The short keyword can be used to create 16-bit (2-byte) integer variables:

```
short declarations;
```

The range is –32,768 to 32,767.

Examples

The first example creates a variable named score as a 2-byte integer with an initial value of 100. The second example declares two integer variables.

```
short score = (short) 100;
short i, j;
```

Unlike C and C++, Java automatically sets uninitialized variables of primitive type to 0, although explicitly initializing them is good programming practice:

```
short i = 0, j = 0;
```

static Keyword

Java vs. C++

Java supports the use of static with class fields, just as in C++. However, Java does not support the use of static with local variables. You refer to a static field as *class.field* and not *class::field*.

Java introduces a new syntax for static. Called the *static initializer*, it is occasionally useful for initializing class variables.

Syntax: Declarations

In Java, the static keyword is valid in three contexts: variable declarations, method declarations, and special blocks of code preceded by static (static initializers). In all three cases, these structures must appear at the class level and not inside method definition code.

When applied to variable declarations, static creates class variables. A class variable is created only once, and it is shared by all instances of a class:

```
static [other_modifiers] type variable_declarations;
```

When applied to a method declaration, static creates a class method. A class method cannot refer to other fields of the class unless they are also declared static. (This limitation applies to variables and to other methods.)

```
static [other_modifiers] return_type
method_name(args)[throws_clause] { statements }
```

You can also place static in front of a block of code to create a static initializer. Such a block is executed just once, when Java loads the class:

```
static { statements }
```

Syntax: Access to Static Fields

A distinctive feature of static fields, which are also called *class fields*, is that they can be referred to by their class name:

```
class.staticfield
```

Nonstatic fields, also called *instance fields*, can be referred to only by means of an instance. This means that you must create an object before you can refer to an instance field. Note that objects can be used to refer to *both* kinds of fields:

```
object.nonstaticfield
object.staticfield
```

For example, NaN is a variable in the Float class declared static and is therefore a class field. You can use the class name Float to refer to this field, or you can use a Float object:

```
Float.NaN
myfloat.NaN
```

Within a class's own methods, you can refer to other fields of the class without qualification (that is, without a class or object name as a prefix). However, the use of static modifies this access:

- Within a static method, statements can refer only to other static fields of the class.
- Within a nonstatic method, statements can refer to any field whether or not it is static.

Example: Static Fields

In the following example, the static method ZeroStatic() can refer to other fields of the same class only if they are static:

```
class MyClass {
    static int i, j;
    static double x;
    double y;
```

```
static void ZeroStatic () {
   i = j = 0;    // Legal: i and j are static.
   x = 0.0;      // Legal: x is static.
}

// ...
}
```

A reference to y, a nonstatic field, would be illegal inside ZeroStatic():

```
y = 0.0;      // ERROR! y is not static.
```

Example: Static Initializer

You can use a static initializer to assign initial values to static fields. Usually, this assignment isn't necessary, but it might be useful if you need to set initial values before a constructor is ever called (or if the class is never instantiated). In this example, the block of code performs only simple assignments:

```
class MyClass {
   static int i, j;
   static double x;
   double y;
   static {
      i = j = 0;   // Legal: i and j are static.
      x = 0.0;      // Legal: x is static.
   }

   // ...
}
```

Unlike the function ZeroStatic(), it is impossible for the static initializer to be executed more than once. As with static methods, the statements can refer only to static fields of the class.

Strings

Java vs. C++

Java does not treat strings as arrays of char; instead, it treats strings as objects of the class String. Strings are not null-terminated; size is determined by using the length() method of the String class.

Syntax: String Variables

Character strings, including all string literals, are objects of the class String. As part of the java.lang package, the String class is directly available without an import statement.

Although string objects are not primitive data types, you can create string variables by using the type name String. You can use string literals rather than the new operator to allocate string objects.

String declarations;

Java strings are similar to Basic strings in some respects. You can declare Java strings without worrying about how much space is needed to hold individual characters. At the same time, Java string variables are object references and follow the general rules for Java objects. For example:

```
// Create three string variables, associate s3 with an actual
// string.
String s1, s2, s3 = "the end";
s1 = "the ";              // Allocate string and associate with s1.
s2 = "the " + "end ";     // Create string thru concatenation,
                          // and associate with s2.

// If s2 and s3 refer to the same object, return true.
if (s2 == s3)
    String displayString = "s2 equal to s3";
```

In the preceding example, the conditional does not test the contents of s2 and s3 for equality but instead tests s2 and s3 themselves to see whether they refer to the same object in memory. In this case, the test would result in false, because s2 and s3 refer to two different objects, each of which happens to contain "the end." To test object contents for equality, use the equals() method inherited from the Object class:

```
if (s2.equals(s3))
    String displayString = "s2 equal to s3";
```

This approach to string comparisons, which may seem counterintuitive at first, follows from the way Java handles all objects (as opposed to primitive data).

●—NOTE

Although string variables can be associated freely with different string data, the actual contents of a String object cannot be changed. To do complex and efficient string manipulation, you should transfer string data to a StringBuffer object, which can be manipulated. You can also transfer string data to an actual array of char by using the String class toCharArray() method.

For more information on the capabilities of the String class, see the topic "String Class" in Part I's "Java 2 API Reference," page 457.

Syntax: String Literals

As described in the topic "Aggregates" (p. 21), Java allocates an actual string object in memory whenever it encounters a quoted string. The object becomes an instance of the String class.

```
"string_of_characters"
```

Java represents string data as a series of Unicode character codes. Unicode characters are 16 bits wide and can represent a much larger character set than ASCII can. Because of the potential need to represent international character sets and because of the need for Java programs to work consistently on all platforms, Java uses Unicode as a universal standard.

In addition to alphanumeric characters (see the previous section, "Syntax: String Variables"), Java accepts escape sequences to represent special characters, as shown in Table 8.

Table 8 *Java escape sequences in strings*

Escape sequence	Description of character
\b	Backspace
\f	Form feed
\n	New line
\r	Carriage return
\t	Tab
\"	Double quotation mark
\'	Single quotation mark
\\	Backslash
\xxx	Character corresponding to Unicode octal value; range is 000 to 0377
\uxxxx	Character corresponding to Unicode hexadecimal value; sequence may include one to four hexadecimal digits

Individual characters that are primitive data of type char can also be represented with escape sequences. The representation of an individual character, as in C and C++, is as follows:

```
'c'
```

String Operations

The String type is unique among all classes in that it is the only class to support an operator:

```
string1 + string2
```

This expression forms a new string from two existing string objects. By assigning to a string variable (as shown earlier in this topic), you associate that variable with the new string.

As with all classes, the String class inherits methods from the Object class. Among the most useful of them is the equals() method introduced earlier in this topic. The String class does not support a usable clone() method, but you can create an independent copy of a string by using the String copy constructor:

```
String s1 = "A string."
String s2 = new String(s1);       // Make a copy from s1
if (s1 == s2)
  System.out.println("s1 == s2"); // This won't be printed.
if (s1.equals(s2))
  System.out.println("s1 eq. s2"); // This will.
```

The String class defines a number of useful methods of its own, including charAt(), compareTo(), length(), substring(), toLower(), toUpper(), and toCharArray().

struct Declarations (C++)

Java vs. C++
Not supported in Java.

All the uses for struct can easily be realized with the use of the class keyword, which in Java (unlike C++) is the only keyword that is used to declare classes. Classes do not necessarily need to define new methods; classes can be used strictly as data types. The main reason struct is supported in C++ is for backward compatibility with C. In Java, compatibility with C takes a backseat to the goal of creating a smaller, simpler, leaner language. Thus, the struct keyword was not included.

See "Classes" (p. 34) for information about declaring user-defined types.

super Keyword

Java vs. C++
Java's super keyword is equivalent to a superclass (base class) reference in C++. It is also used to call a superclass constructor.

Syntax
Within a method, the super keyword refers to a member of the superclass. This arrangement is useful when you want to use the superclass version of a method, for example, rather than the overridden version.

```
super.member
```

You can also use super from within a class constructor to call a base-class constructor. In some cases, this may be the only way to initialize data declared private in the superclass. If used, the call to super must be the first statement in the constructor.

```
super(args);
```

Example

In this example, assume that members x and y are inherited from the superclass Point, and that they are declared private there. The use of super in this example invokes the Point constructor, Point(int, int).

```
class PointTemp extends Point {
    float temp;

    PointTemp(int x, int y, float temp) {
      super(x, y);
      this.temp = temp;
    }

    // ...
}
```

switch Statement

Java vs. C++

The switch statement does the same thing in Java as it does in C and C++: it jumps to a different branch depending on the value of a test expression, which must be an integer.

Syntax

A switch statement contains a statement block, which contains statements labeled with case, and no more than one statement labeled as default.

```
switch (expression) {
case constant_expression_1:
   [statements]
case constant_expression_2:
   [statements]
...
case constant_expression_n:
   [statements]
[ default:
   statements ]
}
```

Here, brackets indicate optional items. The action of the switch statement is to evaluate the expression and then jump to the case label with the value that matches the result (or default, if none of the case labels has a matching value).

In each block of statements, the last statement executed should usually be a break statement; otherwise, execution falls through to the next case. The reason break is needed is that the case keyword is just a label and not a statement, and it does not alter the flow of control. The switch statement jumps to one of the labeled statements, but from there, execution continues normally unless interrupted with break.

Example

A switch statement is generally a more compact, more efficient version of a series of if-else statements. Consider this series:

```
if (n == 1)
   System.out.print("one\n");
else if (n == 2)
   System.out.print("two\n");
else if (n == 3)
   System.out.print("three\n");
else
   System.out.print("greater than three\n");
```

You can get the same functionality from a switch statement:

```
switch (n) {
case 1:
   System.out.print("one\n"); break;
case 2:
   System.out.print("two\n"); break;
case 3:
   System.out.print("three\n"); break;
default:
   System.out.print("greater than three\n");
}
```

synchronized Keyword

Java vs. C++

The synchronized keyword is an extended feature of Java that is not supported by C or C++. The synchronized keyword has only two uses, both of which create critical sections of code.

Syntax

The synchronized keyword can be applied to method declarations to specify that only one thread can execute the method at any given time. This requires all threads to obtain a lock before executing the method. If a thread attempts to gain the lock but another thread owns it, then the first thread must wait. When you use this approach to synchronization, the entire method is considered a critical section of code.

```
synchronized [other_modifiers] return_type method_name(args){
    statements
}
```

The synchronized keyword can also be used to create a critical section of code within a method, causing a thread to wait for ownership of a particular resource:

```
synchronized (object)
    statement
```

When a thread reaches this code, it attempts to gain ownership of the lock for the specified *object*. If another thread owns the lock for this same *object*, the first thread must wait until the lock becomes available. After executing *statement* (which is usually a compound statement), the lock is relinquished.

●—**NOTE**───────────────────────────────

Java's handling of locks is deliberately kept at a high level of abstraction. Individual operating systems may include many specific kinds of threads and locks (semaphores, read-write locks, and so on), but Java's thread model is sufficiently general that correctly written code should behave reliably and predictably on all platforms. With rare exceptions, Java programmers need not concern themselves with how locks are obtained or what form they take: the Java interpreter handles it.

Example

In the following example, no two threads are allowed to sort the same array at the same time. However, because of the way the code is written, two different threads can enter the critical section of code simultaneously as long as they are sorting different arrays.

```
// Synchronize on array of double (darr), which can
//  be passed different values each time. Thread is
//  locked out only if another thread calls the method
//  with the same argument for darr.
void sortMe(double[] darr) {
    synchronized (darr) {
        // Insert code to sort the array.
    }
}
```

Templates (C++)

Java vs. C++
Not supported in Java.

Templates are a feature of ANSI-compliant C++ (supported by most recent C++ compilers). Templates enable you to specify types as parameters. The most practical application of templates is the ability to write generalized collection classes. However, because all Java objects inherit from the root class Object, it is not difficult to write generalized collection classes building upon the Object class as the base type. Any type of object may be passed as a parameter where Object is the type expected.

this Keyword

Java vs. C++
The this keyword has roughly the same purpose in Java as it does in C++, but with two important differences. First, in Java, this is a reference and not a pointer. Second, in Java, this can be used within one constructor to call another constructor.

Syntax
Within a method, the this keyword refers to the current object being operated on: the object to which the method is attached. There are several ways to use this.

When combined with dot notation (.), this helps specify a member of the current object. This use is usually unnecessary unless there is a conflict in scope. (See "Example.")

```
this.member
```

You can also use this to specify the current object as an argument to a method. This usage assumes that the class itself is the argument type expected:

```
method(this);    // Note: there may be other arguments.
```

Finally, Java enables use of this to call a constructor from within another constructor. When used this way, this must be the first statement in the constructor. This use is a coding convenience.

```
this(args);
```

Example
This example illustrates two ways of using the this keyword:

```
class Size {
    public double width, height;
```

```
public Size(width, height) {
  this.width = width; this.height = height;
}

public Size() {
  this(0.0, 0.0);      // Call Size(width, height)
}                      // and set to 0,0.
}
```

throw Keyword

This keyword raises or passes an exception and should not be confused with the throws keyword. (See the topic "Exception Handling," page 46, for information on exceptions.) The throw keyword supports two versions of syntax:

```
throw exceptionObject;
throw;
```

The first version raises a new exception of type *exceptionObject*, which must be a class derived from Throwable. The second version is valid only inside a catch block; it passes the buck to another exception handler.

The following example shows how you can use the throw keyword to throw an exception of type IOException. Remember that it is an instance class that is thrown, and that new is required to create it.

```
if (! file_readable)
  throw new IOException("Goofy i/o error.");
```

throws Keyword

The throws keyword is an optional part of a method declaration, which indicates that the method may generate a specified exception. See the topic "Methods" (p. 69) for description, syntax, and an example. See also "Exception Handling" (p. 46).

true Keyword

Java vs. C++

Because Boolean expressions are not the same as integers, Java provides the Boolean constants true and false. In C and C++, the values 1 and 0 suffice.

Java 2 Language Reference

Syntax

The true keyword is a predefined constant in the Java language, representing one of two possible values for expressions of type boolean.

```
true
```

Example

One possible use of true is to create an endless loop. Such a loop needs an alternative mechanism to exit:

```
while (true) {
  // Do something.
  if (exit_condition)
    break;
  // Do some more.
}
```

try Keyword

The try keyword is used to create a block of code that is protected by an exception handler. See the topic "Exception Handling" (p. 46) for description, syntax, and an example.

The try keyword has the following syntax:

```
try {statements}
// Exception handlers ("catch" blocks) should follow.
```

typedef Declarations (C++)

Java vs. C++

Not supported in Java.

The typedef keyword is not needed as much in Java as in C++, because Java eliminates pointer syntax and therefore tends to have simpler type declarations. The typedef keyword is also provided in C to create type names from structure declarations. In Java, the use of typedef is unnecessary because class declarations create type names directly.

Unsigned Types (C++)

Java vs. C++

Not supported in Java.

A C/C++ unsigned type has the same storage size as its counterpart (for example, unsigned int is the counterpart to int), but it does not represent any negative numbers. Instead, the negative half of the range is interpreted as representing large positive numbers. Thus, the range of unsigned short is 0 to 65,535 instead of –32,768 to 32,767. Unsigned types are useful when you need a variable that will never need to hold a negative value but can benefit from having the higher range available.

But eliminating unsigned types from Java makes the language smaller (one of the key design goals) and is unlikely to seriously hinder programming. If you need to represent larger positive numbers, simply switch to a larger type. Integer data types in the following series have progressively larger ranges: byte, short, int, long.

See the topic "Data Types" (p. 41) for more information.

Variables

Java vs. C++

Java does not support global variables. In addition to local variables, Java supports class variables and instance variables, which are the same as C++ static and nonstatic data members, respectively.

Syntax

All Java variables that are not local must be declared within a class. Variables may be either class variables (declared with static) or instance variables (not declared with static). Class variables are created once for the class and have the same lifetime as the program. Instance variables are associated with objects.

Java supports the following general form of variable declaration:

```
[modifiers] type items;
```

A variable declaration has one or more items. If there are more than one, they are separated by commas. Each item has the following form:

```
name [= initial_value]
```

In these syntax displays, the brackets indicate optional pieces of syntax. The initial_value may be any valid expression. If type is a class, then it is common for the initial_value to be an expression using the new operator.

In any case, type creates actual data if the type is a primitive data type (such as int or long). Otherwise, the variable declaration creates only a variable that serves as a reference to a potential object.

Unlike C and C++, Java provides reasonable default values for all variables of primitive type, regardless of scope. These values are 0 for integers, 0.0 for floating point, false for Booleans, and null for object variables. However, it is always a good idea to explicitly initialize variables yourself.

Syntax: Modifiers

The modifiers include any of the following, in any order: final, static, volatile, public, private, and protected.

The three access-level modifiers (public, private, protected) apply only to class and instance variables and not to local variables. The modifiers private and protected may be used together, but neither may be used with public. Table 9 summarizes the meaning of each modifier.

Table 9   *Modifiers for Java variables*

Modifier	Description
final	Value cannot change. The variable must be initialized. If declared static and initialized to a constant, the variable is a compile-time constant rather than a true variable.
private	Variable can be accessed only within the class. This is not the default behavior; see discussion following this table.
private protected	Variable can be accessed only within the class and subclasses.
protected	Variable can be accessed anywhere in the package, and by subclasses in other packages (if the class is public).
public	Variable has same access level as the class.
static	Variable is a class variable. This means the variable is shared by all instances of the class and can be referred to through the class name rather than an instance.
volatile	Value of variable is subject to external change; compiler will not optimize by placing in temporary locations.

For more information, see the individual topics for the keywords. Note that if none of the access-level keywords areused (public, private, and protected), the variable is visible to all other methods in the package but is not visible outside the package. In contrast to C++ rules, in Java, a variable must be specifically declared private to be hidden to code outside the class.

Examples

The following declarations show examples of class and instance variables. The variable secret may be accessed only by the class's own methods. The other variables may be accessed from anywhere, if the code has access to an instance of the class. The variable number_of_uses requires access to the class but not necessarily to an instance.

```
class Point {
  static int number_of_uses;   // class variable
  double x, y;                 // instance variables
  private long secret;         // instance variable, private
  //...
}
```

virtual Keyword (C++)

Java vs. C++

Java does not use the virtual keyword from C++, but Java methods (except for those declared final) are similar to virtual functions. To facilitate Java's dynamic loading of classes, Java methods are late bound. This means that each object maintains its own pointer to the method table for its class. A method's address is not finally determined until runtime.

The practical significance is that you can safely override methods that are inherited from a base class. The appropriate method is called at runtime. For example, suppose that RoundedRect inherits from the class Rect, and that both define the method DrawMe():

```
// Declare object of a base type (Rect),
// then allocate an object of the derived type (RoundedRect).
Rect theRect;
theRect = new RoundedRect(10, 10, 50, 50);
theRect.DrawMe(); // Which version of DrawMe is called?
```

Which implementation of the method does this code call? Does it call Rect.DrawMe() (from the base class) or RoundedRect.DrawMe() (from the object's actual class)? Because of late binding, the correct implementation, RoundedRect.DrawMe(), will be called. This is exactly how virtual functions work in C++.

Java does not support virtual base classes. They are unnecessary, because Java does not support multiple inheritance.

void Keyword

Java vs. C++

As in C and C++, Java uses void as a return type for methods that do not return any value. However, Java does not use void as a pointer type (because there are no pointers in Java) or for empty argument lists.

Syntax

A method that does not return a value is declared with void return type:

```
[modifiers] void method_name(args) {
    statements
}
```

As in C++, you must use void in declaring methods that do not return
a value.

Example

This example features a void method, draw_me(). Note that void is not used
in the argument list, which is empty.

```
class Box {
    int top, left, height, width;

    public void draw_me() {
        //...
    }
}
```

volatile Keyword

Java vs. C++

The volatile keyword does the same thing in Java as it does in C and C++:
it identifies a variable whose value is subject to change from a source external
to the program.

Syntax

The volatile keyword is a modifier that may be applied to a variable
definition:

```
volatile [other_modifiers] type variable_list;
```

Declaring a variable as volatile informs the compiler that the variable's
value is subject to change without warning; therefore placing it in a temporary location or a register cannot optimize it. Every time the value is read,
the compiler must access the variable's own memory address.

Example

This example declares system_clock as volatile:

```
volatile long system_clock;
```

while Statement

Java vs. C++

The while statement does the same thing in Java as it does in C and C++: it executes one or more statements repeatedly as long as a condition is true. However, note that the condition must be a genuine Boolean expression, such as a comparison.

Syntax

The while statement is one of the Java loop structures.

```
while (condition)
    statement
```

The condition is first evaluated; if it is true, statement is executed, control returns to the top of the loop, and the cycle is repeated. If condition is false, the loop exits. The condition must be a Boolean expression, such as Sum > 1.

Example

This example multiplies amount by n as long as n is greater than zero.

```
while (n > 0) {
    amount = amount * n;
    n—;
}
```

Java 2 Language Reference

Java 2 API in Plain English

This section will help you find the information that you need to complete Java programming tasks. The alphabetical list of keywords and phrases in the left-hand column describes the topic or task you want to accomplish. The associated Java 2 API class, interface, or method on the right will send you to the appropriate place in the API.

Task or subject	API reference
3-D drawing methods	`Graphics.draw3DRect()` (p. 263), `Graphics.fill3DRect()` (p. 265)
Absolute value, getting	`Math.abs()` (p. 391)
Abstract border, creating	`AbstractBorder` (p. 164)
Action events, responding to	`ActionListener` (p. 169), `ActionEvent` (p. 168), `Action` (p. 166)
Adding a component	`Container.add()` (p. 221)
Adding a menu	`MenuBar.add()` (p. 399), `JMenuBar.add()` (p. 324)
Adding a menu bar	`Frame.setMenuBar()` (p. 262), `JFrame.setJMenuBar()` (p. 314)
Adding a menu item	`Menu.add()` (p. 398), `JMenu.add()` (p. 322)
Adding a menu separator	`Menu.addSeparator()` (p. 398), `JMenu.addSeparator()` (p. 322)
Adding items to a list	`List.add()` (p. 378)
Adding points to a polygon	`Polygon.addPoint()` (p. 418)
Address on the net, specifying	`InetAddress` (p. 285), `URL` (p. 486)
Adjustment events, responding to	`AdjustmentListener` (p. 172), `AdjustmentEvent` (p. 170)
Appending string text	`String.concat()` (p. 458), `StringBuffer.append()` (p. 461)
Applet parameters	`Applet.getParameter()` (p. 174)
Applet, starting another	`AppletContext.showDocument()` (p. 176)
Application, loading images for	`Toolkit.getImage()` (p. 483)
Arc, drawing	`Graphics.drawArc()` (p. 263)
Arrays, using flexible	`Vector` (p. 492)
Arrow keys, codes for	`Event` (p. 241)
Attributes, file	`File` (p. 244)
Audio clip, loading	`Applet.getAudioClip()` (p. 173)
Audio clip, playing	`AudioClip.play()` (p. 178)
Background color, setting	`Component.setBackground()` (p. 216)
Bell-curve distribution	`Random.nextGaussian()` (p. 427)
Bevel border, creating	`BevelBorder` (p. 181)
Bevel border, creating soft	`SoftBevelBorder` (p. 452)

Task or subject	API reference
Black	Color.black (p. 208)
Blue	Color.blue (p. 208)
Bold, getting and setting	Font (p. 258)
Boolean, reading from a file	DataInputStream.readBoolean() (p. 228)
Boolean, writing to a file	DataOutputStream.writeBoolean() (p. 230), PrintStream.print() (p. 421)
Box layout, creating	BoxLayout (p. 187)
Brightening a color	Color.brighter() (p. 209)
Browsing the file structure	File, JFileChooser (p. 309)
Buffering data input	BufferedInputStream (p. 188)
Buffering data output	BufferedOutputStream (p. 189)
Button, creating	Button (p. 190), JButton (p. 293)
Bytes, reading from a file	DataInputStream.readBytes() (p. 228)
Bytes, writing to a file	DataOutputStream.writeBytes() (p. 230)
Card stack layout	CardLayout (p. 199)
Case-insensitive string test	String.equalsIgnoreCase() (p. 458)
Case, testing and converting	Character (p. 201)
Character dimensions, getting	FontMetrics (p. 259)
Character processing	String (p. 457), StringBuffer (p. 460)
Character, testing type of	Character (p. 201)
Characters, reading from a file	DataInputStream.readChars() (p. 228)
Characters, writing to a file	DataOutputStream.writeChars() (p. 230), PrintStream.print() (p. 421)
Checking a menu item	CheckboxMenuItem (p. 204), JCheckBoxMenuItem (p. 296)
Checking image status	MediaTracker.checkID() (p. 395)
Circle, drawing a	Graphics.drawOval() (p. 264)
Class, getting information on	Class (p. 206)
Client, acting as a	Socket (p. 450)

Java 2 API in Plain English

Continued

Task or subject	API reference
Client, creating	Socket (p. 450)
Clipping a rectangle	Graphics.clipRect() (p. 263)
Cloning an object	Cloneable (p. 207), Object.clone() (p. 408)
Closing a file	InputStream.close() (p. 286), OutputStream.close() (p. 410)
Closing a port	Socket.close() (p. 451)
Color filtering	RGBImageFilter (p. 433)
Color model, getting	Component.getColorModel() (p. 212)
Color model, getting	Toolkit.getColorModel() (p. 483)
Color Model, setting	ColorModel (p. 209)
Color number, translating from	IndexColorModel (p. 284), Color.getHSBColor() (p. 209)
Command button	Button (p. 190), JButton (p. 293)
Communicating across a network	Socket (p. 450), ServerSocket (p. 444)
Component, adding	Container.add() (p. 221)
Component, removing	Container.remove() (p. 222)
Compound border, creating	CompoundBorder (p. 220)
Concatenating text	String (p. 457), StringBuffer.append() (p. 461)
Connecting an image filter	FilteredImageSource (p. 251)
Connecting to a Web page	URL (p. 486), URLConnection (p. 488), AppletContext.showDocument() (p. 176)
Console metrics	Toolkit (p. 482)
Console, reading from	DataInputStream (p. 227)
Console, writing to	PrintStream (p. 420), System.in (p. 466), System.out (p. 466)
Constants, color	Color (p. 207)
Constants, event	Event (p. 241)
Constants, scroll pane	ScrollPaneConstants (p. 440)
Constants, Swing	SwingConstants (p. 463)
Constants, window	WindowConstants (p. 498)
Constraints, setting layout	GridBagLayout (p. 270)
Container, getting reference to	Component.getParent() (p. 213)

Task or subject	API reference
Controlling document printing	PrinterJob (p. 419)
Controlling image loading	MediaTracker (p. 394)
Controls	Component (p. 210), JComponent (p. 300)
Converting a character case	Character.toUpperCase() (p. 202), Character.toLowerCase() (p. 202)
Converting a string to bytes	String.getBytes() (p. 458)
Converting to a double	Double (p. 236)
Converting to a float	Float (p. 254)
Converting to a long	Long (p. 387)
Converting to an integer	Integer (p. 288)
Coordinates, translating	Event.translate() (p. 244)
Copying an object	Cloneable (p. 207), Object.clone() (p. 408)
Counting menu items	Menu.countItems() (p. 398)
Creating a checkbox	Checkbox (p. 202), JCheckBox (p. 294)
Creating a color	Color (p. 207)
Creating a command button	Button (p. 109), JButton (p. 293)
Creating a custom component	Canvas (p. 199), JComponent (p. 300)
Creating a custom layout	BoxLayout (p. 187), GridBagLayout (p. 270)
Creating a dialog box	Dialog (p. 234), FileDialog (p. 247), JFileChooser (p. 309)
Creating a frame	Frame (p. 261), JFrame (p. 313)
Creating a label	Label (p. 371), JLabel (p. 314)
Creating a list box	List (p. 379), JList (p. 318)
Creating a menu	Menu (p. 397), JMenu (p. 321)
Creating a menu bar	MenuBar (p. 398), JMenuBar (p. 324)
Creating a menu item	MenuItem (p. 401), JMenuItem (p. 325)
Creating a network client	Socket (p. 450)
Creating a network server	ServerSocket (p. 444)
Creating a new directory	File.mkdir() (p. 246)
Creating a new thread	Thread (p. 472), Runnable (p. 435)

Continued

Task or subject	API reference
Creating a panel	Panel (p. 412), JPanel (p. 331)
Creating a polygon	Polygon (p. 417)
Creating a push button	Button (p. 190), JButton (p. 293)
Creating a radio button	Checkbox (p. 202), CheckboxGroup (p. 203)
Creating a rectangle	Rectangle (p. 431)
Creating a scroll bar	Scrollbar (p. 437), JScrollBar (p.342)
Creating a separate process	Runtime.exec() (p. 435)
Creating a window	Frame (p. 261)
Creating an image from a source	Component.createImage() (p. 212)
Creating an image object	Component.createImage() (p. 212)
Creating an option button	Checkbox (p. 202), JCheckBox (p. 294)
Cropping an image	CropImageFilter (p. 222)
Current date, getting	Date (p. 231)
Current time, getting	Date (p. 231)
Cursor type, setting	Frame.setCursor() (p. 262)
Custom components	Canvas (p. 199), JComponent (p. 300)
Customizing a layout	BoxLayout (p. 187), GridBagLayout (p. 270)
Cyan	Color.cyan (p. 208)
Cycling through an enumeration	Enumeration (p. 239)
Darkening a color	Color.darker() (p. 209)
Dark Gray	Color.darkGray (p. 208)
Data types, and stream I/O	DataInputStream (p. 227), DataOutputStream (p. 230)
Date of last file modification	File.lastModified() (p. 245)
Date, getting today's	Date (p. 231)
Day of the week, getting	Date.getDay() (p. 232)
Defining thread behavior	Runnable (p. 435)
Descriptor, getting a file	FileDescriptor (p. 246)
Dialog box, creating	Dialog (p. 234), FileDialog (p. 247), JFileChooser (p. 309)
Digits, converting radix of	Character.forDigit() (p. 201)
Dimensions, getting component	Component.size() (p. 217)

Task or subject	API reference
Dimensions, getting image	Image (p. 277), ImageIcon (p. 281)
Directory, access to a	File (p. 244), JFileChooser (p. 309)
Directory, creating a new	File.mkdir() (p. 246)
Directory, looking at contents of	File.list() (p. 246)
Disabling a menu item	MenuItem.disable() (p. 402)
Display device metrics	Toolkit (p. 482)
Display, writing output to the	PrintStream (p. 420)
Displaying a window	Frame (p. 261), Component.show() (p. 217)
Displaying a window or component	Component.show() (p. 217)
Displaying an image quickly	Part II, Chapter 3, "Fun with Graphics" (p. 539)
Displaying a text message	JOptionPane (p. 327)
Displaying an option menu	Choice (p. 205), JComboBox (p. 297)
Displaying status-bar message	Applet.showStatus() (p. 175)
Double type, converting	Double (p. 236)
Double type, reading from a file	DataInputStream.readDouble() (p. 228)
Double type, writing to a file	DataOutputStream.writeDouble() (p. 231), PrintStream.print() (p. 421)
Downloading from a Web page	URL (p. 486)
Drawing a pie-shaped wedge	Graphics.fillArc() (p. 265)
Drawing an arc	Graphics.drawArc() (p. 263)
Drawing lines	Graphics.drawLine() (p. 264)
Drawing methods	Graphics (p. 262)
Drawing shapes	Graphics (p. 262)
Drawing to in-memory image	Image.getGraphics() (p. 278)
e, getting value of	Math.E (p. 391)
Editing text (components)	TextArea (p. 468), TextField (p. 470), JTextArea (p. 351), JTextField (p. 355)
Editing text (string manipulation)	String (p. 457), StringBuffer (p. 460)

Continued

Task or subject	API reference
Empty border, creating	EmptyBorder (p. 238)
Enabling a menu item	MenuItem.enable() (p. 402)
Enumeration, using	Enumeration (p. 239)
Equality, testing objects for	Object.equals() (p. 407)
Error, getting standard	System.err (p. 466)
Etched border, creating	EtchedBorder (p. 240)
Event constants	Event (p. 241)
Events, basic concepts	Part II, Chapter 4, "Components and Events" (p. 561)
Events, action	ActionListener (p. 169), ActionEvent (p. 170), Action (p. 166)
Events, adjustment	AdjustmentListener (p. 172), AdjustmentEvent (p. 170)
Events, component	ComponentListener (p. 219), ComponentAdapter (p. 218), ComponentEvent (p. 218)
Events, focus	FocusListener (p. 258), FocusAdapter (p. 256), FocusEvent (p. 257)
Events, item	ItemListener (p. 291), ItemEvent (p. 290)
Events, keystroke	KeyListener (p. 370), KeyAdapter (p. 365), KeyEvent (p. 365), KeyStroke (p. 370)
Events, mouse	MouseListener (p. 405), MouseMotionListener (p. 406), MouseAdapter (p. 402), MouseMotionAdapter (p. 405), MouseEvent (p. 403)

Task or subject	API reference
Events, window	WindowListener (p. 500), WindowAdapter (p. 497), WindowEvent (p. 499)
Exceptions, basic methods of	Throwable (p. 477)
Executing a separate process	Runtime.exec() (p. 435)
Exponential functions	Math (p. 391)
File attributes, getting	File (p. 244)
File dialog box	FileDialog (p. 247), JFileChooser (p. 309)
File, getting separator character	File.separator (p. 245)
File, random access to	RandomAccessFile (p. 427)
File, reading from a	FileInputStream (p. 248), often converted to DataInputStream (p. 227)
File, writing to	FileOutputStream (p. 250), often converted to DataOutputStream or PrintStream (p. 420)
File name, specifying	File (p. 244)
Filtering an image	FilteredImageSource (p. 251), ImageFilter (p. 280)
Filtering color settings	RGBImageFilter (p. 433)
Filtering image by cropping	CropImageFilter (p. 222)
Finding a substring	String.substring() (p. 460)
Finding length of an array	"Arrays" (p. 23)
Finding string length	String.length() (p. 459)
Float type, converting	Float (p. 254)
Floating-point, reading from a file	DataInputStream.readFloat() (p. 228)
Floating-point, writing to a file	DataOutputStream.writeFloat() (p. 231), PrintStream.print() (p. 421)
Focus, moving	Component.requestFocus() (p. 216)
Focus, responding to change in	Component.gotFocus() (p. 213), Component.lostFocus() (p. 215)

Continued

Java 2 API in Plain English

Task or subject	API reference
Font metrics, getting	`Component.getFontMetrics()` (p. 212)
Font properties, getting	`FontMetrics` (p. 259)
Font, setting	`Graphics.setFont()` (p. 265), `Component.setFont()` (p. 265)
Forcing a repaint	`Component.repaint()` (p. 216)
Foreground color, setting	`Component.setForeground` (p. 217), `Graphics.setColor()` (p. 265)
Formatting a printed page	`PageFormat` (p. 411)
Formatting text output	`PrintStream` (p. 420)
Gaussian distribution, creating	`Random.nextGaussian()` (p. 427)
Getting a class from its name	`Class.forName()` (p. 206)
Getting a component's container	`Component.getParent()` (p. 213)
Getting a file descriptor	`FileDescriptor` (p. 246)
Getting a property setting	`Properties.getProperty` (p. 425)
Getting a reference to an applet	`AppletContext.getApplet()` (p. 175)
Getting a toolkit	`Component.getToolkit()` (p. 213)
Getting an image object	`Component.createImage()` (p. 212)
Getting an image source	`Image.getSource()` (p. 278), `ImageProducer` (p. 283)
Getting class information	`Class` (p. 206)
Getting component size	`Component.size()` (p. 217)
Getting current date and time	`Date` (p. 231)
Getting current font	`Component.getFont()` (p. 212), `Graphics.getFont()` (p. 265)
Getting dimensions of an image	`Image` (p. 277), `ImageIcon` (p. 281)
Getting file attributes	`File` (p. 244)
Getting file input	`FileInputStream` (p. 248), often converted to `DataInputStream` (p. 227)
Getting file length	`File.length()` (p. 246)
Getting file output	`FileOutputStream` (p. 250), often converted to `DataOutputStream` (p. 230) or `PrintStream` (p. 420)
Getting file position	`RandomAccessFile.getFilePointer()` (p. 428)

Task or subject	API reference
Getting file separator character	`File.separator` (p. 245)
Getting font metrics	`Component.getFontMetrics()` (p. 212)
Getting font properties	`Font` (p. 258), `FontMetrics` (p. 259)
Getting image property	`Image.getProperty()` (p. 278)
Getting list-box selection	`List.getSelectedItem()` (p. 381), `JList.getSelectedValue()` (p. 320)
Getting list of a container's components	`Container.getComponents()` (p. 221)
Getting local URL	`Applet.getCodeBase()` (p. 174), `Applet.getDocumentBase()` (p. 174)
Getting RGB values	`Color` (p. 207)
Getting scroll-bar position	`Scrollbar.getValue()` (p. 438)
Getting screen metrics	`Toolkit` (p. 482)
Getting text	`TextComponent` (p. 469)
Grabbing the graphics context	`Applet.Component.getGraphics()` (p. 213)
Graphics context, grabbing	`Applet.Component.getGraphics()` (p. 213)
Graphics operations	`Graphics` (p. 262)
Graphics, synchronizing	`Toolkit.sync()` (p. 483)
Gray	`Color.gray` (p. 208)
Green	`Color.green` (p. 208)
Grouping components	`CheckboxGroup` (p. 203), `Panel` (p. 412), `ButtonGroup` (p. 191), `JPanel` (p. 331)
Growing arrays	`Vector` (p. 492)
Handling actions	`ActionListener` (p. 169), `ActionEvent` (p. 168), `Action` (p. 166)
Handling adjustments	`AdjustmentListener` (p. 172), `AdjustmentEvent` (p. 170)

Continued

Java 2 API in Plain English

Task or subject	API reference
Handling items	ItemListener (p. 291), ItemEvent (p. 290)
Handling keystrokes	KeyListener (p. 370), KeyAdapter (p. 365), KeyEvent (p. 365), KeyStroke (p. 370)
Handling mouse events	MouseListener (p. 405), MouseMotionListener (p. 406), MouseAdapter (p. 402), MouseMotionAdapter (p. 405), MouseEvent (p. 403)
Handling window changes	WindowListener (p. 500), WindowAdapter (p. 497), WindowEvent (p. 498)
Height of font, getting	FontMetrics.getHeight() (p. 260)
Height of screen	Toolkit.getScreenSize() (p. 483)
Height, getting component	Component.size() (p. 217)
Height, getting image	Image.getHeight() (p. 278)
Hierarchical tree, creating	JTree (p. 361)
Hiding a component	Component.hide() (p. 214)
Hue, getting from color	Color.RGBtoHSB (p. 208)
Hue, setting	Color.HSBtoRGB (p. 208)
Hypercard-like interface	CardLayout (p. 199)
Icon, setting	Frame.setIconImage() (p. 262)
Ignore-case string test	String.equalsIgnoreCase() (p. 458)
Image filter, connecting an	FilteredImageSource (p. 251)
Image loading, tracking	MediaTracker (p. 394)
Image source, getting	Image.getSource() (p. 278), ImageProducer (p. 283)
Image, cropping an	CropImageFilter (p. 222)
Image, getting instance of	Component.createImage() (p. 212)
Image, getting raw data from	PixelGrabber (p. 415)

Task or subject	API reference
Image, loading an	Applet.getImage() (p. 174), Toolkit.getImage() (p. 483), Graphics.drawImage() (p. 264)
Image, providing raw data for	MemoryImageSource (p. 396)
Implementing thread behavior	Runnable (p. 435)
In-memory files	ByteArrayInputStream (p. 193), ByteArrayOutputStream (p. 194)
In-memory image data, using	MemoryImageSource (p. 396)
In-memory image, drawing to	Image.getGraphics() (p. 278)
Indexing a string	String.charAt() (p. 458)
Infinity, testing for	Double.isInfinite() (p. 237), Float.isInfinite() (p. 254)
Initializing an applet	Applet.init() (p. 174)
Input from a file	FileInputStream (p. 248), often converted to DataInputStream (p. 227)
Input, getting standard	System.in (p. 466)
Input, keyboard	DataInputStream (p. 227), System.in (p. 466)
Inserting string text	StringBuffer.insert() (p. 461)
int type, converting	Integer (p. 288)
Integers, reading from a file	DataInputStream.readInt() (p. 288)
Integers, writing to a file	DataOutputStream.writeInt() (p. 231), PrintStream.print() (p. 421)
Internet address, specifying	InetAddress (p. 285), URL (p. 486)
Interpreting special key codes	Event (p. 241)
Intersection of rectangles	Rectangle.intersection() (p. 432)
IP address, using	InetAddress (p. 285)
Italic, getting and setting	Font (p. 258)
Iterating through a list	Enumeration (p. 239)
Keyboard input, reading	DataInputStream (p. 227), System.in (p. 466)
Keystroke codes	Event (p. 241)
Keystrokes, responding to	KeyListener (p. 370), KeyAdapter (p. 365), KeyEvent (p. 365), KeyStroke (p. 370)

Java 2 API in Plain English

Continued

Task or subject	API reference
Label, creating	Label (p. 371), JLabel (p. 314)
Laying out a UI	Part II, Chapter 4, "Components and Events" (p. 561)
Layout manager, setting	Container.setLayoutManager() (p. 222)
Layout, creating a custom	GridBagLayout (p. 270)
Layouts, introduction to	Part II, Chapter 4, "Components and Events" (p. 561)
Length of an array	array.length (p. 23); see Part II, "Arrays" (p. 23)
Length of file, getting	File.length() (p. 246)
Light Gray	Color.lightGray (p. 208)
Line border, creating	LineBorder (p. 373)
Line, drawing a	Graphics.drawLine() (p. 264)
List box, creating	List (p. 379), JList (p. 318)
Listing options, component for	Choice (p. 205), List (p. 379), JComboBox (p. 297), JList (p. 318)
Loading an image	Applet.getImage() (p. 174), Toolkit.getImage() (p. 174), Graphics.drawImage() (p. 264)
Loading an image, tracking	MediaTracker (p. 394)
Loading image in an application	Toolkit.getImage() (p. 483)
Loading pixel data for image	MemoryImageSource (p. 396)
Logarithmic functions	Math (p. 391)
Long integer, reading from a file	DataInputStream.readLong() (p. 228)
Long integer, writing to a file	DataOutputStream.writeLong() (p. 231), PrintStream.print() (p. 421)
Long type, converting	Long (p. 387)
Look and feel, setting	LookAndFeel (p. 389)
Low-level network I/O	DatagramPacket (p. 224)
Lowercase, converting to	Character.toLowerCase() (p. 202)
Magenta	Color.magenta (p. 208)
Making a new directory	File.mkdir() (p. 246)

Task or subject	API reference
Masking password entry	JPasswordField (p. 332)
Mathematical functions	Math (p. 391)
Matte border, creating	MatteBorder (p. 393)
Memory, used as a stream	ByteArrayInputStream (p. 193), ByteArrayOutputStream (p. 194)
Menu bar, adding to frame	Frame.setMenuBar() (p. 262)
Menu bar, creating a	MenuBar (p. 398)
Menu command, responding to	MenuItem (p. 401)
Menu item, creating a	MenuItem (p. 401)
Menu items, with check mark	CheckboxMenuItem (p. 204)
Menu, adding to menu bar	MenuBar.add() (p. 399)
Menu, creating a	Menu (p. 397)
Menu, removing from bar	MenuBar.remove() (p. 399)
Message, status-bar	Applet.showStatus() (p. 175)
Metrics for a font	FontMetrics (p. 259)
Modal, setting condition	Dialog (p. 234), JDialog (p. 305), JOptionPane (p. 327)
Modification date, for a file	File.lastModified() (p. 245)
Monitoring image loading	MediaTracker (p. 394)
Monitoring an input stream	ProgressMonitorInputStream (p. 423)
Mouse events, responding to	MouseListener (p. 405), MouseMotionListener (p. 406), MouseAdapter (p. 402), MouseMotionAdapter (p. 405), MouseEvent (p. 403)
Moving scroll-bar indicator	Scrollbar.setValue() (p. 438)
Moving the file pointer	RandomAccessFile.seek() (p. 430)
Moving the focus	Component.requestFocus() (p. 216)
Multiline text editing	TextArea (p. 468), JTextArea (p. 351)
Multiple list-box selection	List.setMultipleSelections() (p. 382)
Music, playing	AudioClip (p. 178), Applet.play() (p. 174)
Network operations, performing	Socket (p. 450), ServerSocket (p. 444)

Java 2 API in Plain English

Continued

Task or subject	API reference
Normal distribution, creating	`Random.nextGaussian()` (p. 427)
Not a Number, testing for	`Double.isNaN()` (p. 237), `Float.isNaN()` (p. 254)
Notifying other objects	`Observable` (p. 408), `Observer` (p. 409)
Numbered line input	`LineNumberInputStream` (p. 374)
Observing another object	`Observable` (p. 408), `Observer` (p. 409)
On/off conditions	`Checkbox` (p. 202), `JCheckBox` (p. 294)
Opening a file	`FileDialog` (p. 247), `JFileChooser` (p. 309), `FileInputStream` (p. 248), `FileOutputStream` (p. 250)
Opening a server socket (to listen for connections)	`ServerSocket` (p. 444)
Opening a client socket (to transmit and receive data)	`Socket` (p. 450)
Option	`Checkbox` (p. 202), `JCheckBox` (p. 294)
Option menu	`Choice` (p. 205), `JComboBox` (p. 297)
Orange	`Color.orange` (p. 208)
Output to a file	`FileOutputStream` (p. 250), often converted to `DataOutputStream` (p. 230) or `PrintStream` (p. 420)
Output, getting standard	`System.out` (p. 466)
Paginating printable information	`Pageable` (p. 411), `Book` (p. 183)
Paint mode, setting	`Graphics.setXORMode()` (p. 265)
Painting a component	`Component.paint()` (p. 215), `Component.repaint()` (p. 266)
Painting a pie-shaped wedge	`Graphics.fillArc()` (p. 265)
Painting an image	`Graphics.drawImage()` (p. 264)
Painting child components	`Component.paintAll()` (p. 215)
Painting methods	`Graphics` (p. 262)
Painting shapes	`Graphics` (p. 262)
Pane, using an editor	`JEditorPane` (p. 307)
Pane, using a layered	`JLayeredPane` (p. 316)
Pane, using an option	`JOptionPane` (p. 327)
Pane, using a scroll	`JScrollPane` (p. 344)
Pane, using a split	`JSplitPane` (p. 350)

Task or subject	API reference
Pane, using a tabbed	JTabbedPane (p. 350)
Pane, using a text	JTextPane (p. 357)
Parameters, getting applet	Applet.getParameter() (p. 174)
Parent, getting reference to	Component.getParent() (p. 213)
Pathname, getting	File.getPath() (p. 245)
Pausing for a specified time	Thread.sleep() (p. 473), Object.wait() (p. 408)
Performing security checks	SecurityManager (p. 441)
pi, getting value of	Math.PI (p. 391)
Pie-shaped wedge, painting a	Graphics.fillArc() (p. 265)
Pink	Color.pink (p. 208)
Pipe, data	PipedInputStream (p. 414), java.io.PipedOutputStream (p. 415)
Pixel data, getting	PixelGrabber (p. 415)
Pixel data, producing image from	MemoryImageSource (p. 396)
Pixel data, saving	PixelGrabber (p. 415)
Placing a border around a component	Border (p. 185)
Placing a check mark on a menu	CheckboxMenuItem (p. 204)
Playing an audio clip	AudioClip (p. 178), Applet.play() (p. 174)
Point, finding inside a shape	Polygon.inside() (p. 418)
Polygon methods	Graphics (p. 262)
Port, using for net I/O	Socket (p. 450)
Position on scroll bar, getting	Scrollbar.getValue() (p. 438)
Positioning a component	GridBagLayout (p. 270)
Primitive data, and stream I/O	DataInputStream (p. 227, DataOutputStream (p. 230)
Printing a document	Printable (p. 418)
Printing child components	Component.printAll() (p. 216)
Printing component contents	Component.print() (p. 215)
Priority, setting thread	Thread.setPriority() (p. 474)
Process, starting a	Runtime.exec() (p. 435)
Producing image from pixel data	MemoryImageSource (p. 396)

Java 2 API in Plain English

Continued

Task or subject	API reference
Progress monitor, creating	ProgressMonitor (p. 422), ProgressMonitorInputStream (p. 423)
Properties, system	System.getProperties() (p. 467)
Properties, getting image	Image.getProperty() (p. 278)
Property, getting and setting	Properties (p. 424)
Push button	Button (p. 190), JButton (p. 293)
Radio button	Checkbox (p. 202), JRadioButton (p. 338)
Random access, using	RandomAccessFile (p. 427)
Random number, getting	Math.random() (p. 392), Random (p. 427)
Range, double	Double (p. 236)
Range, float	Float (p. 254)
Range, int	Integer (p. 288)
Range, long	Long (p. 387)
Raw image data, getting	PixelGrabber (p. 415)
Raw image data, using	MemoryImageSource (p. 396)
Reading a sequence of files	SequenceInputStream (p. 443)
Reading across the net	Socket.getInputStream() (p. 451)
Reading data across a network	Socket.getInputStream() (p. 451)
Reading double type from a string	Double (p. 236)
Reading file attributes	File (p. 244)
Reading float type from a string	Float (p. 254)
Reading from a file	FileInputStream (p. 248), often converted to DataInputStream (p. 227)
Reading from the keyboard	DataInputStream (p. 227), System.in (p. 466)
Reading integers from a string	Integer.parseInt() (p. 289)
Reading keyboard input	DataInputStream (p. 227), System.in (p. 466)
Reading long integers from a string	Long.parseLong() (p. 388)
Reading random-access records	RandomAccessFile (p. 427)

Task or subject	API reference
Receiving low-level net data	DatagramPacket (p. 224)
Rectangle, drawing a	Graphics.drawRect() (p. 264)
Red	Color.red (p. 208)
Refreshing the display	Component.repaint() (p. 216)
Region, painting a	Graphics.fillRect() (p. 265)
Remainder, taking the	Math.IEEEremainder() (p. 392)
Removing a component	Container.remove() (p. 222)
Removing a menu item	Menu.remove() (p. 398)
Renaming a file	File.renameTo() (p. 246)
Repaint, forcing	Component.repaint() (p. 216)
Repainting the display	Component.repaint() (p. 216)
Replacing string text	String.replace() (p. 459)
Requesting the focus	Component.requestFocus() (p. 216)
Resizing a frame or window	Frame.setResizable (p. 262), Component.resize() (p. 216)
Resolution, getting screen	Toolkit.getScreenResolution() (p. 483)
Responding to a menu command	MenuItem (p. 401), JMenuItem (p. 325)
Responding to an action	ActionListener (p. 169), ActionEvent (p. 168), Action (p. 166)
Responding to an adjustment	AdjustmentListener (p. 172), AdjustmentEvent (p. 170)
Responding to a component event	ComponentListener (p. 219), ComponentAdapter (p. 218), ComponentEvent (p. 218)
Responding to focus changing	Component.gotFocus() (p. 213), Component.lostFocus() (p. 215), FocusListener (p. 258), FocusAdapter (p. 256), FocusEvent (p. 257)

Continued

Java 2 API in Plain English

Task or subject	API reference
Responding to an item event	ItemListener (p. 291), ItemEvent (p. 290)
Responding to keystrokes	Component.keyDown() (p. 214)
Responding to mouse events	MouseListener (p. 405), MouseMotionListener (p. 406), MouseAdapter (p. 402), MouseMotionAdapter (p. 405), MouseEvent (p. 403)
Responding to window events	WindowListener (p. 500), WindowAdapter (p. 497), WindowEvent (p. 499)
RGB, creating color with	Color (p. 207)
Rounded rectangle, painting	Graphics.drawRoundRect() (p. 264), Graphics.fillRoundRect() (p. 265)
Rounding a floating-point	Math.round() (p. 393)
Running another program	Runtime.exec() (p. 435)
Saving pixel data from image	PixelGrabber (p. 415)
Screen metrics, getting	Toolkit (p. 482)
Screen resolution, getting	Toolkit.getScreenResolution() (p. 483)
Screen, writing output to	PrintStream (p. 420)
Searching a directory	File (p. 244)
Searching a string	String.substring() (p. 460)
Searching vectors (arrays)	Vector.firstElement() (p. 493)
Security checks, controlling	SecurityManager (p. 441)
Seeking to new file position	RandomAccessFile.seek() (p. 430)
Selecting a file	FileDialog (p. 247), JFileChooser (p. 309)
Selecting and replacing text	TextArea (p. 468), TextField (p. 470)
Selecting list box items	List.select() (p. 382)

Task or subject	API reference
Sending data across a network	`Socket.getOutputStream()` (p. 451)
Sending low-level data on the net	`DatagramPacket` (p. 224)
Separating menu items	`Menu.addSeparator()` (p. 398), `JSeparator` (p. 346)
Separator, file	`File.separator` (p. 245)
Separator, menu	`Menu.addSeparator()` (p. 398), `JSeparator` (p. 346)
Sequence of files, reading from	`SequenceInputStream` (p. 443)
Series of files, reading from	`SequenceInputStream` (p. 443)
Server, acting as a	`ServerSocket` (p. 444)
Server, creating	`ServerSocket` (p. 444)
Setting a clipping rectangle	`Graphics.clipRect()` (p. 263)
Setting a dialog box title	`Dialog.setTitle()` (p. 234)
Setting a frame title	`Frame.setTitle()` (p. 262)
Setting a frame's icon	`Frame.setIconImage()` (p. 262)
Setting a menu bar	`Frame.setMenuBar()` (p. 262)
Setting a property	`Properties` (p. 424)
Setting a timer	`Timer` (p. 477)
Setting background color	`Component.setBackground()` (p. 216)
Setting bold and italic	`Font` (p. 258)
Setting font in a menu item	`MenuComponent.setFont()` (p. 400)
Setting font style	`Font` (p. 258)
Setting foreground color	`Component.setForeground()` (p. 217)
Setting list box selection	`List.select()` (p. 382), `JList.setSelectedIndex()` (p. 321)
Setting scroll bar coordinates	`Scrollbar` (p. 437), `JScrollBar` (p. 342)
Setting text	`TextComponent` (p. 469)
Setting the font	`Component.setFont()` (p. 217), `Graphics.setFont()` (p. 265)
Setting the paint mode	`Graphics.setXORMode()` (p. 265)
Setting thread priority	`Thread.setPriority()` (p. 474)

Java 2 API in Plain English

Continued

Task or subject	API reference
Shapes, displaying	`Graphics` (p. 262)
Shift (modifier) keys, codes for	`Event` (p. 241)
Showing a window or component	`Component.show()` (p. 217)
Size, getting component	`Component.size()` (p. 217)
Size, getting image	`Image` (p. 277), `ImageIcon` (p. 281)
Size of an array	`array.length` (p. 23); see "Arrays" (p. 23)
Size of file, getting	`File.length()` (p. 246)
Sleeping	`Thread.sleep()` (p. 473)
Soft bevel border, creating	`SoftBevelBorder` (p. 425)
Sound, producing	`AudioClip` (p. 178), `Applet.play()` (p. 174)
Special keys, codes for	`Event` (p. 241)
Specifying an Internet address	`InetAddress` (p. 285), `URL` (p. 486)
Splitter window, creating	`JSplitPane` (p. 350)
Splitting a pane	`JSplitPane` (p. 350)
Spreadsheet, creating	`JTable` (p. 350)
Square, drawing a	`Graphics.drawRect()` (p. 264)
Stack collection class	`Stack` (p. 453)
Standard input, output, error	`System.in` (p. 466), `System.out` (p. 466), `System.err` (p. 466)
Starting a new thread	`Thread.start()` (p. 474)
Starting another applet	`AppletContext.showDocument()` (p. 176)
Static text	`Label` (p. 371), `JLabel` (p. 314)
Status bar, displaying in	`Applet.showStatus()` (p. 175)
Stream input	`DataInputStream` (p. 227)
Stream output	`DataOutputStream` (p. 230), `PrintStream` (p. 420)
String methods	`String` (p. 457)
String representation, getting a	`Object.toString()` (p. 408), `String.valueOf()` (p. 458)
Strings, reading from a file	`DataInputStream.readLine()` (p. 228), `DataInputStream.readUTF()` (p. 228)

Task or subject	API reference
Strings, reading from the keyboard	DataInputStream (p. 227), System.in (p. 466)
Strings, writing to a file	DataOutputStream.writeUTF() (p. 231), PrintStream (p. 420)
Style, setting font	Font (p. 258)
Superclass, finding object's	Class.getSuperclass() (p. 207)
Swing, creating an applet	JApplet (p. 292)
Swing, creating a button	JButton (p. 293)
Swing, creating a checkbox	JCheckBox (p. 294)
Swing, creating a checkbox menu item	JCheckBoxMenuItem (p. 296)
Swing, creating a color chooser	JColorChooser (p. 296)
Swing, creating a combo box	JComboBox (p. 297)
Swing, creating a component	JComponent (p. 300)
Swing, creating a dialog box	JDialog (p. 305)
Swing, creating a file chooser	JFileChooser (p. 309)
Swing, creating a frame window	JFrame (p. 313)
Swing, creating a label	JLabel (p. 314)
Swing, creating a list	JList (p. 318)
Swing, creating a menu	JMenu (p. 321)
Swing, creating a menu bar	JMenuBar (p. 324)
Swing, creating a menu item	JMenuItem (p. 325)
Swing, creating an option pane	JOptionPane (p. 327)
Swing, creating a password field	JPasswordField (p. 332)
Swing, creating a popup menu	JPopupMenu (p. 333)
Swing, creating a progress bar	JProgressBar (p. 336)
Swing, creating a radio button	JRadioButton (p. 338)
Swing, creating a radio button menu item	JRadioButtonMenuItem (p. 339)
Swing, creating a scroll bar	JScrollBar (p. 342)
Swing, creating a separator	JSeparator (p. 346)
Swing, creating a slider	JSlider (p. 347)
Swing, creating a table	JTable (p. 350)

Continued

Java 2 API in Plain English

Task or subject	API reference
Swing, creating a text area	JTextArea (p. 351)
Swing, creating a text field	JTextField (p. 355)
Swing, creating a toggle button	JToggleButton (p. 357)
Swing, creating a tool bar	JToolBar (p. 358)
Swing, creating a tool tip	JToolTip (p. 360)
Swing, creating a tree	JTree (p. 361)
Swing, creating a window	JWindow (p. 363)
Swing, using utilities	SwingUtilities (p. 464)
Sync, ensuring graphics are in	Toolkit.sync() (p. 483)
System properties, getting	System.getProperties() (p. 467)
Table, creating	JTable (p. 350)
Testing character type	Character (p. 201)
Testing object for equality	Object.equals() (p. 407)
Text components	TextArea (p. 468), TextField (p. 470)
Text processing	String (p. 457), StringBuffer (p. 460)
Text string methods	String (p. 457)
Threads, introduction to	Part II, Chapter 6, "Animation and Threads" (p. 617)
Time of last file modification	File.lastModified() (p. 245)
Time, getting current	Date (p. 231)
Timer, creating	Timer (p. 477)
Title, setting a frame (window)	Frame.setTitle() (p. 262)
Title, setting dialog box	Dialog.setTitle() (p. _234)
Titled border, creating	TitledBorder (p. 480)
Tokenizing file contents	StreamTokenizer (p. 454)
Tokenizing string contents	StringTokenizer (p. 462)
Toolkit, getting	Component.getToolkit() (p. 213)
Tracking image loading	MediaTracker (p. 394)
Translating coordinates	Event.translate() (p. 244)
Tree, creating hierarchical	JTree (p. 361)
Trig functions, using	Math (p. 391)
Union of rectangles	Rectangle.union() (p. 432)
Uppercase, converting to	Character.toUpperCase() (p. 202)

Task or subject	API reference
URL, getting local	`Applet.getCodeBase()` (p. 174), `Applet.getDocumentBase()` (p. 174)
Using a properties table	`Properties` (p. 424)
Using I/O streams	`InputStream` (p. 286), `OutputStream` (p. _410)
Validating text	`InputVerifier` (p. 287)
Virtual files	`ByteArrayInputStream` (p. 193), `ByteArrayOutputStream` (p. 194)
Waiting for a specified time	`Thread.sleep()` (p. 473)
Waiting for a thread	`Thread.join()` (p. 474)
Waiting for client request	`ServerSocket.accept()` (p. 445)
Waiting for image completion	`MediaTracker.waitForID()` (p. 395)
Web page, downloading from	`URL` (p. 486)
White	`Color.white` (p. 208)
Width, getting component	`Component.size()` (p. 217)
Width, getting image	`Image.getWidth()` (p. 278)
Width of characters	`FontMetrics.stringWidth()` (p. 260)
Width of screen	`Toolkit.getScreenSize()` (p. 483)
Window, displaying a	`Frame` (p. 261), `JFrame` (p. _313)
Window, showing	`Component.show()` (p. 217)
Window, splitting	`JSplitPane` (p. 350)
Writing across the net	`Socket.getOutputStream()` (p. 451), often converted to `PrintStream` (p. 420)
Writing random-access records	`RandomAccessFile` (p. 427)
Writing thread code	`Runnable` (p. 435)
Writing to a file	`FileOutputStream` (p. 250), often converted to `PrintStream` (p. 420) or `DataOutputStream` (p. 430)
XOR painting mode	`Graphics.setXORMode()` (p. 265)
Yellow	`Color yellow` (p.208)

Java 2 API in Plain English

Java 2 API By Category

This section presents the most important standard Java AWT packages, along with a paragraph description of the package and a table containing an alphabetic listing of the interfaces and classes in the package. A brief description of each interface and class in the package tables is also provided.

The java.applet Package

The java.applet package contains one class (Applet) and three interfaces that support the creation of applets. Applet code typically makes frequent use of the Applet class. Two related interfaces — AppletContext and AppletStub — are lower level and used less often; they must be implemented by applications (such as browsers) that load and run applets.

java.applet.AudioClip interface	Defines audio play methods.
java.applet.AppletContext interface	Provides an interface to the browser; interface provides applet support methods, including inter-applet communication.
java.applet.Applet class	Defines applet methods. Extends java.awt.Panel.

The java.awt Package

The java.awt package implements the Java Abstract Window Toolkit (AWT). It contains all the classes and interfaces for creating a basic user interface. Although classes in other packages can affect the display, java.awt is the package most directly concerned with UI issues. This package includes all component and windows classes along with the important Event, Graphics, and Image classes.

java.awt.Adjustable interface	Describes a bounded range of numeric values.
java.awt.ItemSelectable interface	Describes a set of items for which zero or more can be selected.
java.awt.LayoutManager interface	Declares methods required for all layout managers.
java.awt.AWTEvent class	Serves as the base class for all AWT events.
java.awt.BorderLayout class	Layout manager that places components along edges.
java.awt.Button class	Push-button component.
java.awt.Canvas class	Blank component: subclass to create custom components.
java.awt.CardLayout class	Layout manager that simulates a card stack.
java.awt.Checkbox class	Check-box component — can be used as a radio button.

`java.awt.CheckboxGroup` class	Groups check boxes to create radio button groups.
`java.awt.CheckboxMenuItem` class	Menu item that has checked state.
`java.awt.Choice` class	Option-menu component.
`java.awt.Color` class	RGB color value. This class also defines color constants.
`java.awt.Component` class	Superclass for all component classes. This class defines many methods for showing, moving, and handling events.
`java.awt.Container` class	Superclass for all components that can contain other components. Extends `Component`.
`java.awt.Cursor` class	Represents the bitmap associated with the mouse cursor.
`java.awt.Dialog` class	Dialog-box class. Extends `Window`.
`java.awt.Dimension` class	Class that contains height and width.
`java.awt.Event` class	Objects of this class contain information on one event. This class defines many useful constants such as key codes and event IDs.
`java.awt.FlowLayout` class	Layout manager that uses straight left-to-right placement.
`java.awt.Font` class	Each `Font` object describes a font.
`java.awt.FontMetrics` class	Provides detailed measurements for characters in a font.
`java.awt.Frame` class	Window with borders, system bar, and optional menu bar. Extends `Window`.
`java.awt.Graphics` class	Provides all drawing and painting methods.
`java.awt.GridBagConstraints` class	Defines set of constraints for one component; used with `GridBagLayout`.
`java.awt.GridBagLayout` class	Layout manager that accepts constraints for each component; provides maximum flexibility in layout.
`java.awt.GridLayout` class	Layout manager that uses tabular arrangement.

java.awt.Image class	Encapsulates an image loaded from disk or created as an offscreen buffer.
java.awt.Insets class	Margins around a component.
java.awt.Label class	Static-text component.
java.awt.List class	List-box component.
java.awt.MediaTracker class	Monitors loading of an image.
java.awt.Menu class	Pull-down menu component. Extends MenuItem.
java.awt.MenuBar class	Menu bar attached to a frame. Extends MenuComponent.
java.awt.MenuComponent class	Abstract class that declares common methods for menus.
java.awt.MenuContainer class	Declares methods used in Menu, interface MenuBar, Frame.
java.awt.MenuItem class	An item on a menu. Extends MenuComponent.
java.awt.Panel class	Container without definite borders. Extends Container.
java.awt.Point class	Class that contains x and y coordinates.
java.awt.Polygon class	Set of points that define a polygon.
java.awt.Rectangle class	Measurements defining a rectangular region.
java.awt.Scrollbar class	Scroll-bar component.
java.awt.ScrollPane class	Implements a container that supports horizontal and vertical scrolling.
java.awt.TextArea class	Multi-line edit-text component. Extends TextComponent.
java.awt.TextComponent class	Defines common text-handling methods.
java.awt.TextField class	Single-line edit-text component. Extends TextComponent.
java.awt.Toolkit class	Provides access to image-file loading (for applications) and to screen display measurements.
java.awt.Window class	Generic window class; usually, you should use Frame instead. Extends Container.

The java.awt.event Package

The java.awt.event package contains:

java.awt.event.ActionListener interface	Describes an interface for handling action events.
java.awt.event.AdjustmentListener interface	Describes an interface for handling adjustment events.
java.awt.event.ComponentListener interface	Describes an interface for handling component events.
java.awt.event.ContainerListener interface	Describes an interface for handling container events.
java.awt.event.FocusListener interface	Describes an interface for handling focus events.
java.awt.event.HierarchyBounds Listener interface	Describes an interface for handling hierarchy bounds events.
java.awt.event.HierarchyListener interface	Describes an interface for handling hierarchy events.
java.awt.event.InputMethodListener interface	Describes an interface for handling input method events.
java.awt.event.ItemListener interface	Describes an interface for handling item events.
java.awt.event.KeyListener interface	Describes an interface for handling key events.
java.awt.event.MouseListener interface	Describes an interface for handling mouse events.
java.awt.event.MouseMotionListener interface	Describes an interface for handling mouse movement events.
java.awt.event.TextListener interface	Describes an interface for handling text events.
java.awt.event.WindowListener interface	Describes an interface for handling window events.
java.awt.event.ActionEvent class	Encapsulates the information associated with an action event.
java.awt.event.AdjustmentEvent class	Encapsulates the information associated with an adjustment event.
java.awt.event.ComponentAdapter class	A helper class that provides empty handler methods for a component listener. Implements ComponentListener.

`java.awt.event.ComponentEvent` class	Encapsulates the information associated with a component event.
`java.awt.event.ContainerAdapter` class	A helper class that provides empty handler methods for a container listener. Implements `ContainerListener`.
`java.awt.event.ContainerEvent` class	Encapsulates the information associated with a container event.
`java.awt.event.FocusAdapter` class	A class that provides empty handler methods for a focus listener. Implements `FocusListener`.
`java.awt.event.FocusEvent` class	Encapsulates the information associated with a focus event.
`java.awt.event.HierarchyBounds Adapter` class	A helper class that provides empty handler methods for a hierarchy bounds listener. Implements `HierarchyBoundsListener`.
`java.awt.event.HierarchyEvent` class	Encapsulates the information associated with a hierarchy event.
`java.awt.event.InputMethodEvent` class	Encapsulates the information associated with an input method event.
`java.awt.event.InvocationEvent` class	Encapsulates the information associated with an invocation event.
`java.awt.event.ItemEvent` class	Encapsulates the information associated with an item event.
`java.awt.event.KeyAdapter` class	A helper class that provides empty handler methods for a key listener. Implements `KeyListener`.
`java.awt.event.KeyEvent` class	Encapsulates the information associated with a key event.
`java.awt.event.MouseAdapter` class	A helper class that provides empty handler methods for a mouse listener. Implements `MouseListener`.
`java.awt.event.MouseEvent` class	Encapsulates the information associated with a mouse event.
`java.awt.event.MouseMotionAdapter` class	A helper class that provides empty handler methods for a mouse motion listener. Implements `MouseMotionListener`.
`java.awt.event.TextEvent` class	Encapsulates the information associated with a text event.

`java.awt.event.WindowAdapter` class	A helper class that provides empty handler methods for a window listener. Implements `WindowListener`.
`java.awt.event.WindowEvent` class	Encapsulates the information associated with a window event.

The java.awt.image Package

The `java.awt.image` package should not be confused with the `Image` class, which is a part of the `java.awt` package and not `java.awt.image`. The classes and interfaces in this package are concerned with low-level manipulation of images. Typical application programmers will probably not use this package often. You can ignore the existence of image producers and image sources (which are defined in this package) unless you are using an image filter or extracting pixel data from an image.

`java.awt.image.ImageConsumer` interface	Declares methods implemented interface by image consumers, which are objects that have requested pixel data.
`java.awt.image.ImageObserver` interface	Declares `imageUpdate()` method, interface which is called during loading of data for an Image object.
`java.awt.image.ImageProducer` interface	Declares methods implemented interface by image producers (or image sources), which are objects that produce pixel data.
`java.awt.image.ColorModel` class	Converts to RGB from another color scheme.
`java.awt.image.CropImageFilter` class	Filters an image by cropping a region. Extends `ImageFilter`.
`java.awt.image.DirectColorModel` class	Uses different bit patterns from standard RGB scheme. Extends `ColorModel`.
`java.awt.image.FilteredImageSource` class	Converts an image filter to a class and image producer, which you can use to create new `Image` objects.
`java.awt.image.ImageFilter` class	Superclass of image filters.
`java.awt.image.IndexColorModel` class	Color model that uses simple class integers to represent colors. Extends `ColorModel`.

java.awt.image.MemoryImageSource class	Image producer that class provides pixel data from a memory location.
java.awt.image.PixelGrabber class	Image consumer that copies pixel data from an image to memory.
java.awt.image.RGBImageFilter class	Filter that changes color values for each pixel. Extends ImageFilter.

The java.awt.print Package

The java.awt.print package contains:

java.awt.print.Pageable interface	Describes an interface for paginating printable information.
java.awt.print.Printable interface	Describes an interface used to print a page.
java.awt.print.PrinterGraphics interface	Describes an interface that an application uses to determine the print job controlling the printing.
java.awt.print.Book class	Breaks a document into pages that are capable of having different formatting. Implements Pageable.
java.awt.print.PageFormat class	Encapsulates the information associated with the format of a printed page.
java.awt.print.Paper class	Represents the physical attributes of a piece of paper.
java.awt.print.PrinterJob class	Controls the printing of a document.

The java.io Package

The java.io package is mainly concerned with file and console input/output. (The java.awt package handles GUI I/O by itself, and java.net is involved with network I/O.) The File class encapsulates file path, name, and attributes for files and directories. To read and write to files, use FileInputStream and FileOutputStream and then convert the object to a more flexible type such as DataInputStream. The DataInputStream class can also be used for reading the keyboard (see the example in the topic). The java.io package is relatively large, because it supports a number of variations on basic file input/output.

java.io.DataInput interface	Declares methods for reading Java primitive data types.

java.io.DataOutput interface	Declares methods for writing Java primitive data types.
java.io.FilenameFilter interface	Declares method for accepting or rejecting a file name. Typically used to filter out file names in a dialog box.
java.io.BufferedInputStream class	Input stream that uses a buffer. Extends FilterInputStream.
java.io.BufferedOutputStream class	Output stream that uses a buffer. Extends FilterInputStream.
java.io.ByteArrayInputStream class	In-memory input stream. Extends InputStream.
java.io.ByteArrayOutputStream class	In-memory output stream. Extends OutputStream.
java.io.DataInputStream class	Input stream that handles all Java primitive data types. Extends FilterInputStream.
java.io.DataOutputStream class	Output stream that handles all Java primitive data types. Extends FilterOutputStream.
java.io.File class	Encapsulates file and directory attributes (but not contents).
java.io.FileDescriptor class	Encapsulates low-level file descriptor.
java.io.FileInputStream class	Opens an input stream from a file. Extends InputStream.
java.io.FileOutputStream class	Opens an output stream to a file. Extends OutputStream.
java.io.FilterInputStream class	Superclass for filtered input classes. Extends InputStream.
java.io.FilterOutputStream class	Superclass for filtered output classes. Extends OutputStream.
java.io.InputStream class	Superclass for all input streams.
java.io.LineNumberInputStream class	Keeps track of line count. Extends FilterInputStream.
java.io.OutputStream class	Superclass for all output streams.
java.io.PipedInputStream class	Reads (sinks) a data pipe. Extends InputStream.
java.io.PipedOutputStream class	Writes to (sources) a data pipe. Extends OutputStream.

`java.io.PrintStream` class	Writes text representations of data. Extends `FilterOuputStream`.
`java.io.PushbackInputStream` class	Stream that enables unreading of last character read. Extends `FilterInputStream`.
`java.io.RandomAccessFile` class	Provides read/write data methods, along with a `seek()` method, for a random-access file.
`java.io.SequenceInputStream` class	Reads two or more streams as if they were one unbroken stream. Extends `InputStream`.
`java.io.StreamTokenizer` class	Reads an input stream as a series of tokens.
`java.io.StringBufferInputStream` class	Reads stream input from an in-memory string. Extends `InputStream`.

The java.lang Package

The `java.lang` package provides strings, threads, and wrapper classes for Java primitive types as well as access to system functions. Note that you can always use the classes and interfaces in this package without having to qualify their names or use an import statement.

`java.lang.Cloneable` interface	Implementing this class indicates that a class provides a usable definition of the `Object.clone()` method.
`java.lang.Comparable` interface	Describes a means of comparing objects with one another.
`java.lang.Runnable` interface	Declares `run()` method, which you implement to define behavior for a thread.
`java.lang.Boolean` class	Wrapper class for `boolean` type.
`java.lang.Byte` class	Wrapper class for `byte` type.
`java.lang.Character` class	Wrapper class for `char` type.
`java.lang.Class` class	Provides information about the class that a given object belongs to.
`java.lang.Double` class	Wrapper class for `double` type.
`java.lang.Float` class	Wrapper class for `float` type.
`java.lang.Integer` class	Wrapper class for `int` type.

java.lang.Long class	Wrapper class for long (integer) type.
java.lang.Math class	A collection of useful math routines and constants.
java.lang.Object class	Ancestor class of all Java classes.
java.lang.Process class	Provides control over a process returned by Runtime.exec().
java.lang.Runtime class	Provides access to system and Java interpreter routines.
java.lang.SecurityManager class	Sets permissions for various Java operations.
java.lang.Short class	Wrapper class for short type.
java.lang.String class	Standard text-string class.
java.lang.StringBuffer class	Special text-string class for more efficient in-memory manipulation of a string.
java.lang.System class	Provides access to system routines and standard i/o streams; overlaps with Runtime.
java.lang.Thread class	Encapsulates a thread.
java.lang.ThreadGroup class	Enables operations on a set of threads.
java.lang.ThreadLocal class	Supports thread-local variables.
java.lang.Throwable class	Ancestor class for Java exceptions and runtime errors.
java.lang.Void class	Wrapper class for void type.

The java.net Package

The java.net package provides access to network communications through several different levels: connectionless I/O (UDP), which sends data without requiring acknowledgments of a connection; connection-based socket I/O; and URLs, which can be used to download information from a Web page. Several of the classes in this package (ContentHandler, SocketImpl, URLStreamHandler) provide alternative or extended implementations of network I/O; you can generally ignore these classes unless you're dealing with low-level platform issues.

java.net.Authenticator class	Used as a means of authenticating a network connection by prompting the user for information.

java.net.DatagramPacket class	Data packet using a simple protocol (UDP).
java.net.DatagramSocket class	Encapsulates a socket; can send and receive packets.
java.net.InetAddress class	Encapsulates a network address.
java.net.PasswordAuthentication class	Stores the user name and password associated with a network authentication.
java.net.ServerSocket class	Encapsulates connection-based port I/O; can listen and respond to clients.
java.net.Socket class	Encapsulates connection-based port I/O.
java.net.URL class	Encapsulates a Web page as a URL specification.
java.net.URLConnection class	Similar to URL, but provides more methods.
java.net.URLDecoder class	Provides a method for converting strings in a standard form to URL strings.
java.net.URLEncoder class	Provides a method for converting URL strings to a standard form.

The java.util Package

The java.util package includes a number of support classes that are frequently useful in programming. The Enumeration and Properties classes, in particular, are used by a number of other Java packages. Other collection classes in this package include Hashtable, Stack, and Vector.

java.util.Enumeration interface	Declares methods for traversing an enumerated list.
java.util.List interface	Describes an ordered collection, also known as a sequence.
java.util.Map interface	Describes a map collection that is used to map keys to values.
java.util.Set interface	Describes a collection of elements where no two elements are alike.
java.util.SortedMap interface	Describes a map collection that is sorted in ascending order according to the keys contained within.

java.util.ArrayList class	Implements a list that functions as a resizable array.
java.util.BitSet class	Provides capabilities similar to C bit fields.
java.util.Calendar class	Base class for calendar classes that support the conversion of a Date object to a set of individual date integers.
java.util.Date class	Represents a date and time. Constructor gets value of "now."
java.util.Dictionary class	Superclass to Hashtable class.
java.util.GregorianCalendar class	Implements a standard Gregorian calendar as a subclass of the Calendar class.
java.util.HashMap class	Implements a hash table based upon the Map interface.
java.util.Hashtable class	Provides storage for a set of elements, each identified by a key.
java.util.LinkedList class	Implements a linked list based upon the List interface.
java.util.ListResourceBundle class	Used to package resources in a list for internationalization.
java.util.Locale class	Represents a specific geographical, political, or cultural region for purposes of localizing program content.
java.util.Observable class	Provides ability to maintain and notify a list of observers.
java.util.Observer interface	Declares methods that enable an object to act as an observer.
java.util.Properties class	A specialized form of Hashtable in which both keys and values are strings. Can include default property values.
java.util.PropertyResourceBundle class	Used to package a set of properties for a specific locale.
java.util.Random class	Generates random numbers using a variety of schemes. Note that Math.random( ) is often simpler.
java.util.ResourceBundle class	Represents a bundle of information that is specific to a given locale.

java.util.SimpleTimeZone class	A time zone that is compatible with a Gregorian calendar.
java.util.Stack class	Collection class providing push( ) and pop( ) methods. Extends Vector.
java.util.StringTokenizer class	Tokenizes strings. See also java.io.StreamTokenizer.
java.util.TimeZone class	Represents a time zone that supports daylight savings time.
java.util.TreeMap class	Implements a tree map based upon the SortedMap interface.
java.util.TreeSet class	Implements a tree set based upon the Set interface.
java.util.Vector class	Collection class that encapsulates an expandable array.
java.util.WeakHashMap class	Implements a weak hash map, which is a hash map whose entries are automatically removed when their keys are no longer in use.

The javax.swing Package

The javax.swing package contains:

javax.swing.Action interface	Describes a generic action that can apply to multiple user interface elements.
javax.swing.Icon interface	Describes a small rectangular image that is used to accentuate other components.
javax.swing.MenuElement interface	Describes an interface for interacting with menu items.
javax.swing.Scrollable interface	Describes an interface for scrolling within a container.
javax.swing.ScrollPaneConstants interface	Defines the constants associated with a scroll pane.
javax.swing.SwingConstants interface	Defines constants used throughout the Swing toolkit.
javax.swing.WindowConstants interface	Defines constants associated with windows.

`java.swing.AbstractButton` class	Contains generic methods used by buttons.
`javax.swing.AbstractionAction` class	Provides a base class for implementations of the `Action` interface.
`javax.swing.Box` class	A container that uses a box layout as its layout manager.
`javax.swing.Box.Filler` class	An inner class that supports invisible fillers for use in controlling the space between components in a box.
`javax.swing.BoxLayout` class	A layout manager in which components are arranged either vertically or horizontally. This layout manager is particularly useful when nested within other box layouts.
`javax.swing.ButtonGroup` class	Establishes multiple-exclusion for a group of buttons. Only one button in a button group can be selected at any given time.
`javax.swing.ImageIcon` class	Uses an image as the basis for an icon. Implements Icon.
`javax.swing.InputVerifier` class	Validates text entered by the user according to some predetermined validation criteria.
`javax.swing.JApplet` class	An extended applet class that utilizes the Swing architecture.
`javax.swing.JButton` class	An extended button class that utilizes the Swing architecture.
`javax.swing.JCheckBox` class	An extended check box class that utilizes the Swing architecture.
`javax.swing.JCheckBoxMenuItem` class	An extended check box menu item class that utilizes the Swing architecture.
`javax.swing.JColorChooser` class	A special pane of controls that is used to provide a standard user interface for selecting a color.
`javax.swing.JComboBox` class	A component consisting of a text field or button combined with a drop-down list.
`javax.swing.JComponent` class	An extended component class that utilizes the Swing architecture.

javax.swing.JDialog class	An extended dialog class that utilizes the Swing architecture.
javax.swing.JEditorPane class	A component that supports the editing of various types of text content.
javax.swing.JFileChooser class	A special pane of controls that is used to provide a standard user interface for selecting a file.
javax.swing.JFrame class	An extended frame class that utilizes the Swing architecture.
javax.swing.JLabel class	An extended label class that utilizes the Swing architecture.
javax.swing.JLayeredPane class	A special container that supports multiple layers for overlapping components.
javax.swing.JList class	An extended list class that utilizes the Swing architecture.
javax.swing.JMenu class	An extended menu class that utilizes the Swing architecture.
javax.swing.JMenuBar class	An extended menu bar class that utilizes the Swing architecture.
javax.swing.JMenuItem class	An extended menu item class that utilizes the Swing architecture.
javax.swing.JOptionPane class	A standard dialog box used to display messages to the user.
javax.swing.JPanel class	An extended panel class that utilizes the Swing architecture.
javax.swing.JPasswordField class	A special text field that hides what is typed to protect sensitive data entry such as password entry.
javax.swing.JPopupMenu class	An extended popup menu class that utilizes the Swing architecture.
javax.swing.JProgressBar class	A component that provides a visual indicator of the progress of a certain task, displayed as a percentage of completion.
javax.swing.JRadioButton class	A component that can be selected or deselected, and can be combined with other radio buttons in a button group to present a mutually exclusive list of options.

`javax.swing.JRadioButtonMenuItem` class	A menu item containing a radio but ton that can be selected or dese-lected, or used in a group of radio button menu items to form a mutu-ally exclusive list of options.
`javax.swing.JRootPane` class	A container that is used behind the scenes to manage the different panes in a top-level Swing container such as `JApplet` or `JFrame`.
`javax.swing.JScrollBar` class	An extended scroll bar class that uti-lizes the Swing architecture.
`javax.swing.JScrollPane` class	An extended scroll pane class that utilizes the Swing architecture.
`javax.swing.JSeparator` class	A visual divider used to separate items on a menu.
`javax.swing.JSlider` class	A component that provides a sliding knob that can be dragged back and forth within a bounded region to select a specific numeric value.
`javax.swing.JSplitPane` class	A component used to divide a pane into two separate panes that can be resized by the user.
`javax.swing.JTabbedPane` class	A component that establishes a tabbed user interface where the user can select different tabs to reveal different groups of compo-nents.
`javax.swing.JTable` class	A two-dimensional table component that presents information in rows and columns, much like a spread-sheet.
`javax.swing.JTextArea` class	An extended text area class that uti-lizes the Swing architecture.
`javax.swing.JTextField` class	An extended text field class that uti-lizes the Swing architecture.
`javax.swing.JTextPane` class	A component that supports the edit-ing of various types of styled text content. Unlike `JEditorPane`, `JTextPane` displays styled content such as HTML and RTF graphically as opposed to showing it as simple text.

`javax.swing.JToggleButton class`	A two-state button that can be turned on and off.
`javax.swing.JToolBar class`	A component that serves as a container for commonly used components within the context of an application.
`javax.swing.JToolTip class`	A visual tip that appears over a component and provides helpful but brief information to the user.
`javax.swing.JTree class`	A hierarchical tree component that consists of nodes and leaves.
`javax.swing.JViewport class`	A logical view through which you can see underlying data. Viewports are useful for implementing scrolling.
`javax.swing.JWindow class`	An extended window class that utilizes the Swing architecture.
`javax.swing.KeyStroke class`	A keystroke typed on the keyboard.
`javax.swing.LookAndFeel class`	Describes the look and feel of a program's graphical user interface.
`javax.swing.OverlayLayout class`	A layout manager that supports the arrangement of components over each other in layers.
`javax.swing.ProgressMonitor class`	A special class that monitors the progress of an operation. If the operation takes longer than a certain amount of time, a progress bar is automatically displayed.
`javax.swing.ProgressMonitorInput Stream class`	A progress monitor that is specially designed to monitor the progress of reading from an input stream.
`javax.swing.ScrollPaneLayout class`	A layout manager designed specifically for use with scroll panes.
`javax.swing.SizeRequirements class`	A special class used by layout managers to calculate the size and position of components.
`javax.swing.SwingUtilities class`	A suite of helper methods used throughout the Swing toolkit.
`javax.swing.Timer class`	A class that provides a timing function that triggers an action event at a specified rate.
`javax.swing.ViewportLayout class`	A layout manager designed specifically for use with viewports.

The javax.swing.border Package

The javax.swing.border package contains:

javax.swing.border.Border interface	Describes a generic border that appears around the edge of a component.
javax.swing.border.AbstractBorder class	An empty border with no size. Serves only as a base class for other types of borders.
javax.swing.border.BevelBorder class	A border containing a 3D bevel that is two pixels thick.
javax.swing.border.CompoundBorder class	A special border used to combine two other borders to form a compound border.

The javax.swing.event Package

The javax.swing.event package contains:

javax.swing.event.ChangeListener interface	Describes a change event listener that is used to handle change events.
javax.swing.event.HyperlinkListener interface	Describes a hyperlink event listener that is used to handle hyperlink events.
javax.swing.event.ListSelectionListener interface	Describes a list selection event listener that is used to handle list selection events.
javax.swing.event.ChangeEvent class	Represents a change event that is delivered in response to a change occurring in an event source.
javax.swing.event.HyperlinkEvent class	Represents a hyperlink event that is delivered in response to a hyperlink being updated.
javax.swing.event.ListSelectionEvent class	Represents a list selection event that is delivered in response to an item or items in a list being selected or deselected.

The javax.swing.text Package

The javax.swing.text package contains:

java.swing.text.JTextComponent class	Defines generic text-component methods used by both **JTextArea** and **JTextField**.

Java 2 API A to Z

This section presents a table of the API classes and interfaces covered comprehensively in "Part I, Java 2 Reference." Here, you'll find an alphabetically arranged master list of Java 2 API classes and interfaces, along with the page number on which each corresponding topic starts.

Java 2 API A to Z

Topic	Located on page
AbstractBorder class	164
Action interface	166
ActionEvent class	168
ActionListener interface	169
AdjustmentEvent class	170
AdjustmentListener interface	172
Applet class	173
AppletContext interface	175
AudioClip interface	178
BevelBorder class	181
BitSet class	182
Book class	183
Boolean class	184
Border interface	185
BorderLayout class	186
Box class	187
BoxLayout class	187
BufferedInputStream class	188
BufferedOutputStream class	189
Button class	190
ButtonGroup class	191
ByteArrayInputStream class	193
ByteArrayOutputStream class	194
Canvas class	199
CardLayout class	199
ChangeEvent class	200
ChangeListener interface	200
Character class	201
Checkbox class	202
CheckboxGroup class	203
CheckboxMenuItem class	204
Choice class	205
Class class	206
Cloneable interface	207

Topic	Located on page
Color class	207
ColorModel class	209
Component class	210
ComponentAdapter class	218
ComponentEvent class	218
ComponentListener interface	219
CompoundBorder class	220
Container class	221
CropImageFilter class	222
Cursor class	223
DatagramPacket class	224
DatagramSocket class	225
DataInput interface	226
DataInputStream class	227
DataOutput interface	229
DataOutputStream class	230
Date class	231
Dialog class	234
Dictionary class	234
Dimension class	235
DirectColorModel class	236
Double class	236
EmptyBorder class	238
Enumeration interface	239
EtchedBorder class	240
Event class	241
File class	244
FileDescriptor class	246
FileDialog class	247
FileInputStream class	248
FilenameFilter interface	249
FileOutputStream class	250
FilteredImageSource class	251

Java 2 API A to Z

Continued

Topic	Located on page
FilterInputStream class	252
FilterOutputStream class	253
Float class	254
FlowLayout class	255
FocusAdapter class	256
FocusEvent class	257
FocusListener interface	258
Font class	258
FontMetrics class	259
Frame class	261
Graphics class	262
GregorianCalendar class	266
GridBagConstraints class	267
GridBagLayout class	270
GridLayout class	271
Hashmap class	272
Hashtable class	274
HyperlinkEvent class	275
HyperlinkListener interface	276
Icon interface	276
Image class	277
ImageConsumer interface	278
ImageFilter class	280
ImageIcon class	281
ImageObserver interface	282
ImageProducer interface	283
IndexColorModel class	284
InetAddress class	285
InputStream class	286
InputVerifier class	287
Insets class	288
Integer class	288
ItemEvent class	290
ItemListener interface	291
ItemSelectable interface	291

Topic	Located on page
JApplet class	292
JButton class	293
JCheckBox class	294
JCheckBoxMenuItem class	296
JColorChooser class	296
JComboBox class	297
JComponent class	300
JDialog class	305
JEditorPane class	307
JFileChooser class	309
JFrame class	313
JLabel class	314
JLayeredPane class	316
JList class	318
JMenu class	321
JMenuBar class	324
JMenuItem class	325
JOptionPane class	327
JPanel class	331
JPasswordField class	332
JPopupMenu class	333
JProgressBar class	336
JRadioButton class	338
JRadioButtonMenuItem class	339
JRootPane class	341
JScrollBar class	342
JScrollPane class	344
JSeparator class	346
JSlider class	347
JSplitPane class	350
JTabbedPane class	350
JTable class	350
JTextArea class	351

Java 2 API A to Z

Continued

Topic	Located on page
JTextComponent class	353
JTextField class	355
JTextPane class	357
JToggleButton class	357
JToolBar class	358
JToolTip class	360
JTree class	361
JViewport class	361
JWindow class	363
KeyAdapter class	365
KeyEvent class	365
KeyListener interface	370
KeyStroke class	370
Label class	371
LayoutManager interface	372
LineBorder class	373
LineNumberInputStream class	374
LinkedList class	375
List class	379
Long class	387
LookAndFeel class	389
Map interface	390
Math class	391
MatteBorder class	393
MediaTracker class	394
MemoryImageSource class	396
Menu class	397
MenuBar class	398
MenuComponent class	399
MenuContainer interface	400
MenuElement interface	400
MenuItem class	401
MouseAdapter class	402
MouseEvent class	403

Java 2 API A to Z

Topic	Located on page
MouseListener interface	405
MouseMotionAdapter class	405
MouseMotionListener interface	406
Object class	407
Observable class	408
Observer interface	409
OutputStream class	410
Pageable interface	411
PageFormat class	411
Panel class	412
Paper class	412
PipedInputStream class	414
PipedOutputStream class	415
PixelGrabber class	415
Point class	417
Polygon class	417
Printable interface	418
PrinterGraphics interface	419
PrinterJob class	419
PrintStream class	420
Process class	422
ProgressMonitor class	422
ProgressMonitorInputStream class	423
Properties class	424
PushbackInputStream class	426
Random class	427
RandomAccessFile class	427
Rectangle class	431
ResourceBundle class	432
RGBImageFilter class	433
Runnable interface	435
Runtime class	435
Scrollable interface	437

Java 2 API A to Z

Continued

Topic	Located on page
Scrollbar class	437
ScrollPaneConstants interface	440
SecurityManager class	441
SequenceInputStream class	443
ServerSocket class	444
Set interface	445
SizeRequirements class	449
Socket class	450
SoftBevelBorder class	452
SortedMap interface	453
Stack class	453
StreamTokenizer class	454
String class	459
StringBuffer class	460
StringTokenizer class	462
SwingConstants interface	463
SwingUtilities class	464
System class	466
TextArea class	468
TextComponent class	469
TextField class	470
Thread class	472
ThreadGroup class	474
Throwable class	477
Timer class	477
TitledBorder class	480
Toolkit class	482
URL class	486
URLConnection class	488
URLDecoder class	491
URLEncoder class	492

Topic	Located on page
Vector class	492
ViewportLayout class	495
Void class	495
WeakHashMap class	495
Window class	496
WindowAdapter class	497
WindowConstants interface	498
WindowEvent class	499
WindowListener interface	500

Java 2 API A to Z

Java 2 API Reference

This section provides a comprehensive reference that covers the most important classes and interfaces that compose the Java 2 API. The classes and interfaces are arranged alphabetically and include detailed information such as their full name and inheritance. The various members of each class and interface are examined, along with numerous examples that demonstrate how to use many of the classes and interfaces.

AbstractAction Class

Full Name	javax.swing.AbstractAction
Extends	Object
Implements	Action.
Description	Public abstract class. This class provides a minimal but not-quite-complete implementation of the Action interface (p. 166). To declare a class that creates Action objects, first subclass this class, Abstract Action. Then, make sure that you implement action Performed(), which is the method called to actually perform the command. You should preferably implement some constructors, as well.

For methods supported, as well as a complete example, see Action interface.

Constructors

```
public AbstractAction();
public AbstractAction(String name);
public AbstractAction(String name, icon);
```

AbstractBorder Class

Full Name	javax.swing.border.AbstractBorder
Extends	Object
Description	Public class. This class implements an empty border and serves primarily as a base class for more interesting border classes, such as LineBorder (p. 373) and MatteBorder (p. 393).

Constructors

```
public AbstractBorder();
```

Class Methods

```
public static Rectangle getInteriorRectangle(Component c, Border b,
    int x, int y, int width, int height);
```

This method calculates an interior rectangle based on the *x,y* coordinates and dimensions specified; the interior rectangle is the given rectangle minus the insets of the border.

Instance Methods

```
public Insets getBorderInsets(Component c);
public Insets getBorderInsets(Component c, Insets insets);
```

These methods retrieve the insets for the border; the second version acts on the Insets object that is passed as an argument.

```
public Rectangle getInteriorRectangle(Component c, int x, int y,
    int width, int height);
```

This is a convenience instance method that calls the getInteriorRectangle() class method.

```
public boolean isBorderOpaque();
```

This method checks whether a border is opaque or transparent; opaque borders paint their own backgrounds, whereas transparent borders do not.

```
public void paintBorder(Component c, Graphics g, int x, int y,
    int width, int height);
```

This method paints the border for a component using the specified border *x,y* position and size.

AbstractButton Class

Full Name   javax.swing.AbstractButton

Extends   JComponent->Container->Component->Object

DescriptionPublic abstract class. This class provides common functionality used by Swing button classes including JButton (p. 293), JCheckBox (p. 294), and JRadioButton (p. 338).

This topic describes the more commonly used methods.

Instance Methods

```
public void addActionListener(ActionListener l);
public void addChangeListener(ChangeListener l);
public void addItemListener(ItemListener l);
```

These methods add an event handler for an action, change, or item event. The conditions under which these events are generated (if at all) depends on the type of the button. An action event indicates an active choice on the part of the user, such as clicking a command button. An item event is invoked when a component such as a checkbox is selected or de-selected, and a change event is a change in value. See ActionEvent, and ItemEvent (pp. 168, and 290).

```
public void doClick();
public void doClick(int pressTime);
```

These methods click the button programmatically; pressTime is a waiting interval in milliseconds.

```
public String getActionCommand();
```

Returns the action-command string, if any.

```
public Icon getDisabledIcon();
public Icon getIcon();
public Insets getMargin();
public Icon getPressedIcon();
public Icon getSelectedIcon();
public String getText();
```

These methods get various properties of the button. The getText() method replaces the getLabel() method, which is deprecated. Also note that getIcon() gets the default icon for the button, although other icons may be used for different button states.

```
public void removeActionListener(ActionListener l);
public void removeChangeListener(ChangeListener l);
public void removeItemListener(ItemListener l);
```

These methods remove a previously installed event handler.

```
public void setDisabledIcon(Icon disabledIcon);
public void setEnabled(boolean b);
public void setIcon(Icon defaultIcon);
public void setMargin(Insets m);
public void setMnemonic(int mnemonic);
public void setMnemonic(char mnemonic);
public void setPressedIcon(Icon pressedIcon);
public void setSelected(boolean b);
public void setSelectedIcon(Icon selectedIcon);
public void setText(String text);
```

These margins set various properties of the button. The setEnabled() and setSelected() methods use a Boolean argument (true or false) to enable, disable, select, or de-select the button. You can specify a mnemonic key using either an integer constant or a char value. See KeyEvent class on page 365. Finally, note that the setText() method replaces the setLabel() method, which is deprecated.

Action Interface

Full Name javax.swing.Action

Description Public interface. This interface describes an action, which is a command that is capable of being invoked by multiple GUI elements. An object implementing this interface (i.e., an Action object) bundles an identifying string or icon (or both), along with code that executes a command. You can streamline your code by creating an action once and then efficiently adding it to any element (toolbar, menu, or button) that invokes it.

The easiest way to use this interface is to subclass the
`AbstractAction` class, which provides a minimal implementation,
and then override methods of interest—particularly
`actionPerformed()`, which must be implemented.

The following code declares a class `MyCmd` that creates an `Action` object. Note
that the class subclasses the `AbstractAction` class and passes along arguments to `AbstractAction` constructors.

```
class MyCmd extends AbstractAction {
    public MyCmd(String text) {
        super(text);
    }

    public MyCmd(String text, Icon icon) {
        super(text, icon);
    }

    public void actionPerformed(ActionEvent e) {
        String s = "Action :" + e.getActioncommand();
        System.out.println(s);
    }
}
```

Interface Constants

```
public static final String DEFAULT;
public static final String LONG_DESCRIPTION;
public static final String NAME;
public static final String SHORT_DESCRIPTION;
public static final String SMALL_ICON;
```

These constants contain keys used to identify properties of an `Action` object.
For example, to get or set the command name, use the key `Action.NAME`.

Interface Methods

```
public abstract void actionPerformed(EventAction e);
```

This method contains the code that actually performs the action. Because the
method is abstract, a child class *must* implement this method to create a concrete class.

```
public void addPropertyChangeListener(
    PropertyChangeListener listener);
```

Registers a property change listener for events generated by the object supporting this interface.

```
public Object getValue(String key);
```

Returns the value of a property (such as name or icon) identified by key. See also putValue( ).

```
public boolean isEnabled();
```

Returns true if the action is enabled.

```
public void putValue(String key, Object value);
```

Assigns a value to a property identified by key. Keys are named by the class constants listed earlier: Action.NAME is the key for the command string; Action.SMALL_ICON is the key for the command icon. The value argument contains the value to be assigned.

```
public void removePropertyChangeListener(
    PropertyChangeListener listener);
```

Removes a previously registered property change listener.

```
public void setEnabled(boolean b);
```

Enables an action, if b is set to true; disables the action if b is false.

ActionEvent Class

Full Name java.awt.event.ActionEvent

Extends   AWTEvent->EventObject->Object

DescriptionPublic class. This class encapsulates the information associated with an action event. Action events are generated by action event sources and handled by objects that implement the ActionListener interface. An instance of the ActionEvent class is delivered to the action listener event response method to aid in handling action events.

Here is an example of using the ActionEvent class to check the name of the component that generated the event:

```
class MyApp extends Frame implements ActionListener {
    public void actionPerformed(ActionEvent e) {
        if (e.getActionCommand() == "OK")
            System.out.println("The OK button was pressed!");
    }
}
```

Constructors

```
public ActionEvent(Object source, int id, String command);
public ActionEvent(Object source, int id, String command,
    int modifiers);
```

The source argument is the object with which the action event is associated; id is an identifier that identifies the event; command is a string containing the command associated with the action; and modifiers contains a combination of flags specifying the keys held down when the event occurred.

Class Variables

```
public static final int ACTION_FIRST;
public static final int ACTION_LAST;
public static final int ACTION_PERFORMED;
public static final int ALT_MASK;
public static final int CTRL_MASK;
public static final int META_MASK;
public static final int SHIFT_MASK;
```

Class constants. These constants are flags used to describe the keys held down when the event occurred.

Instance Methods

```
public String getActionCommand();
```

Returns the command-name string associated with the action.

```
public int getModifiers();
```

Returns the keystroke modifiers associated with the action event. For example, the value returned from this method can be AND'ed with ActionEvent. CTRL_MASK to test if the CTRL key was pressed.

```
public Object getSource();
```

Returns the object that generated the event. (This method is actually inherited from EventObject, an ancestor class.)

ActionListener Interface

Full Name java.awt.event.ActionListener

DescriptionPublic interface. This interface defines a single method that is used to respond to action events. An action event is a semantic event that is generated in response to the user initiating an action or command through the use of a component. A good example of an action event is clicking a button with the mouse. To handle an action event, you must implement the ActionListener interface, provide an implementation of the actionPerformed() method, and then register the listener class with an event source.

This interface is parallel to, but distinct from, the Action interface (p. 166). The ActionListener interface is used to respond to user-level choices (such as clicking a command button) if the component does *not* have an Action object attached. If an Action object is attached, that object contains its own code for responding to actions, so it isn't necessary to install an ActionListener.

Here is an example of implementing the ActionListener interface to handle action events:

```
class MyApp extends Frame implements ActionListener {
    Button button1 = new Button("Click this.");
    button1.addActionListener(this);
    //...
    public void actionPerformed(ActionEvent e) {
        System.out.println("An action event occurred!");
    }
}
```

Interface Methods

```
public void actionPerformed(ActionEvent e);
```

This method is called in response to a user-level action, such as clicking a command button or choosing a menu item. Text fields (see JTextField, p. 355) and timers are among the other components that generate action events.

AdjustmentEvent Class

Full Name	java.awt.event.AdjustmentEvent
Extends	AWTEvent->EventObject->Object
Description	Public class. This class encapsulates the information associated with an adjustment event. Adjustment events are generated by adjustment event sources and handled by objects that implement the AdjustmentListener interface. An instance of the AdjustmentEvent class is delivered to the adjustment listener event response method to aid in handling adjustment events. Adjustment events are generated by the JScrollBar class (p. 342).

Constructors

```
public AdjustmentEvent(Adjustable source, int id, int type,
    int value);
```

The source argument is the object with which the adjustment event is associated; id is an identifier that identifies the event; type is the type of the adjustment; and value contains the value of the adjustment.

Class Variables

```
public static final int ADJUSTMENT_FIRST;
public static final int ADJUSTMENT_LAST;
public static final int ADJUSTMENT_VALUE_CHANGED;
public static final int BLOCK_DECREMENT;
public static final int BLOCK_INCREMENT;
public static final int TRACK;
public static final int UNIT_DECREMENT;
public static final int UNIT_INCREMENT;
```

Class constants. These constants are flags used to describe the adjustment event.

Instance Methods

```
public Adjustable getAdjustable();
public int getAdjustmentType();
public Object getSource();
```

These methods provide information about the event; getAdjustable() and getSource() return the object that was the source of the event. getAdjustmentType() returns one of the constants listed earlier.

```
public int getValue();
```

Returns the current setting of the value property of the object that generated the event.

Adjustable Interface

Full Name java.awt.Adjustable

DescriptionPublic interface. This interface describes a bounded range of numeric values; other objects implement the Adjustable interface to support the selection of a value from within the range.

Interface Constants

```
public static final int HORIZONTAL;
public static final int VERTICAL;
```

These constants describe the orientation of an adjustable object, which is either horizontal or vertical.

Java 2 API Reference

Interface Methods

```
public void addAdjustmentListener(AdjustmentListener l);
```

This method registers an adjustment listener for receiving adjustment events generated by the object that implements the Adjustable interface.

```
public int getBlockIncrement();
public int getOrientation();
public int getMaximum();
public int getMinimum();
public int getValue();
public int getVisibleAmount();
public int getUnitIncrement();
```

These methods get information pertinent to an adjustable object, such as the orientation, minimum and maximum values, and current value, to name a few.

```
public void removeAdjustmentListener(AdjustmentListener l);
```

This method unregisters an adjustment listener that is registered to receive adjustment events generated by the object that implements the Adjustable interface.

```
public void setBlockIncrement(int b);
public void setMaximum(int max);
public void setMinimum(int min);
public void setUnitIncrement(int u);
public void setValue(int v);
public void setVisibleAmount(int v);
```

These methods set information pertinent to an adjustable object, such as the orientation, minimum and maximum values, and current value, to name a few.

AdjustmentListener Interface

Full Name   java.awt.event.AdjustmentListener

DescriptionPublic interface. This interface defines a single method that is used to respond to adjustment events. An adjustment event is a semantic event that is generated in response to the user "adjusting" a component. A good example of an adjustment event is moving a scrollbar with the mouse. To handle an adjustment event, you must implement the Adjustment
Listener interface, provide an implementation of the adjustmentValueChanged() method, and then register the listener class with an event source. Adjustment event listeners are installed by the addAdjustmentListener() method of the JScrollBar() class (p. 342).

Interface Methods

```
public void adjustmentValueChanged(AdjustmentEvent e);
```

This method is called on a registered adjustment listener in response to an adjustment event occurring.

Applet Class

Full Name `java.applet.Applet`

Extends `Panel->Container->Component->Object`

DescriptionPublic class. You nearly always use this class by subclassing it and then overriding methods such as `init()`, `start()`, `stop()`, and `paint()` — which is inherited from Component. No Java code creates an Applet object unless it is a browser or applet viewer program (which it is possible to write in Java). Some Applet methods are used only internally and should never be called or overridden. In your own code, you may find it useful to call `getImage()`, `getAudioClip()`, and `getDocumentBase()`. When you're looking up methods, remember that many useful methods are inherited from the `Container` and Component classes.

Constructors

```
public Applet();
```

Instance Methods

```
public void destroy();
```

This method is called just before the applet is terminated. Occasionally, it is useful to override this method to clean up system resources that are not automatically released by Java.

```
public AppletContext getAppletContext();
```

This method is usually used internally, although it is sometimes useful for interacting with other applets and Web pages. This method returns an object that represents the browser or applet viewer running the applet. See Applet Context interface, page 175.

```
public String getAppletInfo();
```

Returns a string that contains information about the applet, including author and version.

```
public AudioClip getAudioClip(URL url);
public AudioClip getAudioClip(URL url, String name);
```

Java 2 API Reference

Returns an object that supports the AudioClip interface for playing audio clips. The string argument, if specified, is a file name. See also play( ), below

```
public URL getCodeBase();
public URL getDocumentBase();
```

These methods return a URL object that represents a Web-page address. These addresses are the location of the applet and the location of the document (HTML file), respectively.

```
public Image getImage(URL url);
public Image getImage(URL url, String name);
```

Returns an Image object that contains instructions for loading the image. Actual loading is initiated by calling Graphics.drawImage( ). The string argument, if specified, is a filename.

```
public String getParameter(String name);
```

Returns the value of the specified parameter. HTML files can pass parameter names and values to the applet by using <PARAM> tags.

```
public String[][][][] getParameterInfo();
```

Returns a two-dimensional string array that describes all the parameters understood by the applet. Each row contains three strings: name, type, and description. For example, if the result of the method is assigned to the variable parms, then the strings parms[0][0], parms[0][1], and parms[0][2] provide information describing the first parameter.

```
public void init();
```

This method is called when the applet is loaded into memory. Applets frequently override this method, using it to initialize instance variables.

```
public boolean isActive();
```

Returns true if the current applet is active.

```
public void play(URL url);
public void play(URL url, String name);
```

Plays an audio clip if the specified location implements the AudioClip interface. The string argument, if specified, is a file name.

```
public final void setStub(AppletStub stub);
```

Used internally. This method is called by the browser or applet viewer application shortly after creating the applet. The applet responds by storing a reference to the stub. The applet can then call the stub to perform certain services. This is one of those methods that your own applet subclass would have no reason to call.

```
public void showStatus(String msg);
```

Displays a message in the browser or applet viewer's status bar.

```
public void start();
```

This method is called when the applet starts running and whenever it resumes operation after being suspended. In contrast to init(), the start() method may be called more than once. Applets typically override this method to start or resume running of additional threads.

```
public void stop();
```

This method is called when running of the applet is suspended temporarily or because of applet termination.

```
public void resize(Dimension d);
public void resize(int width, int height);
```

Overrides method definitions in the Component class. The applet viewer program responds to this method as you would expect, resizing the window immediately. Behavior of a browser may differ.

AppletContext Interface

Full Name java.applet.AppletContext

DescriptionPublic interface. Browsers and applet viewer programs implement this interface to enable communication between the applet and the browser. The process of applet creation is as follows: browser creates an applet stub; browser calls applet constructor; browser calls the applet's setAppletStub() method to tell the applet where the stub is; applet uses the stub to get a reference to the applet context.

In general, you don't have to worry about this interface unless you're creating a browser or applet viewer program, although it is occasionally useful for interapplet communication.

Interface Methods

```
public abstract Applet getApplet(String name);
```

Returns the applet with the given name, as defined in the document (HTML file). The <APPLET> tag for an applet can optionally specify a name by using the NAME attribute.

```
public abstract Enumeration getApplets();
```

Returns an Enumeration object that contains references to all other applets in the context (started by the same browser). See Enumeration class, page 239.

```
public abstract AudioClip getAudioClip(URL url);
public abstract Image getImage(URL url);
```

These methods are called in response to the corresponding `Applet` class methods.

```
public abstract void showDocument(URL url);
public abstract void showDocument(URL url, String target);
```

Requests the browser to start the specified document (HTML file). The second argument, if included, is a filename.

```
public abstract void showStatus(String status);
```

Called in response to `Applet.showStatus()`.

ArrayList Class

Full Name `java.util.ArrayList`

Extends `AbstractList->AbstractCollection->Object`

DescriptionPublic class. This class implements a list that functions as a resizable array. The primary difference between this class and the `List` class is that `ArrayList` allows you to alter the size of the underlying array.

Creating an array list is very simple:

```
ArrayList list = new ArrayList(10);
```

This array list has an initial capacity of ten elements, although it may grow if you add more than ten elements. To add elements to the array list, simply call the add() method and pass in the element objects:

```
list.add("A string element");
list.add("Another string element");
list.add("One more string element");
```

If you want to insert an element somewhere specifically within the array, you can do so with a different version of the add() method:

```
list.add(1, "A sneaky string element");
```

Since array lists are zero-based, this string is inserted between the first and second strings, thereby moving the second and third strings down in the array.

To determine how many elements are in an array list, you call the size() method:

```
int numElements = list.size();
```

Removing elements from an array list is accomplished by calling the remove() method and specifying the index of the element:

```
list.remove(2);
```

This removes the third string in the array list since the first element is at position 0. To remove all of the elements in an array list, simply call the clear() method:

```
list.clear();
```

Constructors

```
public ArrayList();
```

Default constructor.

```
public ArrayList(int initialCapacity);
```

Creates an empty array list using the specific initial array size.

```
public ArrayList(Collection c);
```

Creates an array list that is initialized with the specific collection.

Instance Methods

```
public void trimToSize();
```

Minimizes the storage capacity of the array list by trimming it to the current list size, which may be smaller than the array capacity.

Overridden Instance Methods

```
public boolean add(Object o);
public void add(int index, Object element);
```

Appends the specified object to the array list, or inserts the object at the specified array index.

```
public boolean addAll(Collection c);
public boolean addAll(int index, Collection c);
```

Appends the specified collection of objects to the array list, or inserts the collection of objects at the specified array index.

```
public void clear();
```

Empties the array list of all elements.

```
public boolean contains(Object elem);
```

Searches the array list for the specified element, returning true if it is found.

```
public Object get(int index);
```

Retrieves the object at the specified array index in the array list.

```
public int indexOf(Object elem);
```

Searches the array list for the specified element, returning its array index if it is found.

```
public boolean isEmpty();
```

Checks to see if the array list is empty.

```
public int lastIndexOf(Object elem);
```

Retrieves the element located at the end of the array list.

```
public Object remove(int index);
```

Removes the element at the specified index.

```
public Object set(int index, Object element);
```

Replaces the element at the specified index with the specified object.

```
public int size();
```

Retrieves the number of elements in the array list, which may be smaller than the array capacity.

```
public Object[] toArray();
public Object[] toArray(Object[] a);
```

Returns an array containing all of the elements in the array list. The a parameter allows you to specify an array that determines the runtime type of the array returned by toArray().

AudioClip Interface

Full Name java.applet.AudioClip

DescriptionPublic interface. This interface declares services for playing and stopping audio clips. You can get a reference to an object that implements these services — for a particular audio clip — by calling the Applet.getAudioClip() method.

Interface Methods

```
public abstract void loop();
```

Does the same thing as play() except that the audio clip plays in a continuous loop until stopped.

```
public abstract void play();
```

Plays the audio clip from beginning to end. Immediately restarts from beginning if audio clip is currently playing.

```
public abstract void stop();
```

Interrupts and stops audio clip if it is currently playing.

Authenticator Class

Full Name java.net.Authenticator

Extends Object

DescriptionPublic class. This class is used as a means of authenticating a network connection by prompting the user for information.

Constructors

```
public Authenticator();
```

Class Methods

```
public static PasswordAuthentication
  requestPasswordAuthentication(InetAddress addr, int port,
  String protocol, String prompt, String scheme);
```

Obtains authentication for a network connection using the specified parameters including the IP address, port, and protocol of the connection, as well as a string prompt to be displayed to the user and the authentication scheme.

```
public static void setDefault(Authenticator a);
```

Sets the default authenticator to be used for authentication.

Instance Methods

```
protected PasswordAuthentication getPasswordAuthentication();
```

Obtains authentication for a network connection; this method must be overridden in subclasses of Authenticator in order to provide real functionality.

```
protected final int getRequestingPort();
protected final String getRequestingPrompt();
protected final String getRequestingProtocol();
protected final String getRequestingScheme();
protected final InetAddress getRequestingSite();
```

These methods obtain information about the authenticator including the port and protocol of the connection, as well as the string prompt displayed to the user, the authentication scheme, and the IP address of the site requesting the authentication.

Java 2 API Reference

AWTEvent Class

Full Name `java.awt.AWTEvent`

Extends `EventObject->Object`

DescriptionPublic class. This class serves as the base class for all AWT events.

Constructors

    public AWTEvent(Object source, int id);

Creates an AWT event based upon the specified source object and event type identifier.

Class Constants

    public static final long ACTION_EVENT_MASK;
    public static final long ADJUSTMENT_EVENT_MASK;
    public static final long COMPONENT_EVENT_MASK;
    public static final long CONTAINER_EVENT_MASK;
    public static final long FOCUS_EVENT_MASK;
    public static final long HIERARCHY_BOUNDS_EVENT_MASK;
    public static final long HIERARCHY_EVENT_MASK;
    public static final long INPUT_METHOD_EVENT_MASK;
    public static final long INVOCATION_EVENT_MASK;
    public static final long ITEM_EVENT_MASK;
    public static final long KEY_EVENT_MASK;
    public static final long MOUSE_EVENT_MASK;
    public static final long MOUSE_MOTION_EVENT_MASK;
    public static final long PAINT_EVENT_MASK;
    public static final int RESERVED_ID_MAX;
    public static final long TEXT_EVENT_MASK;
    public static final long WINDOW_EVENT_MASK;

Class constants. These constants represent different event types supported by the AWTEvent class.

Instance Methods

    public int getID();

Obtains the event type identifier of the AWT event.

    public String paramString();

Retrieves a string containing the state of the AWT event. This method is used only for debugging purposes.

BevelBorder Class

Full Name   javax.swing.border.BevelBorder

Extends   AbstractBorder->Object

DescriptionPublic class. This class implements a bevel border that is two lines in thickness. Note that some useful methods are inherited from the AbstractBorder class (p. 164).

Constructors

```
public BevelBorder(int bevelType);
public BevelBorder(int bevelType, Color highlight,
  Color shadow);
public BevelBorder(int bevelType, Color highlightOuterColor,
  Color highlightInnerColor, Color shadowOuterColor,
  Color shadowInnerColor);
```

These constructors create bevel borders with varying degrees of detail in terms of the colors used to shade the borders.

Class Variables

```
public static final int LOWERED;
public static final int RAISED;
```

Class constants. These constants represent the two different styles of bevel border.

Instance Variables

```
protected int bevelType;
protected Color highlightInner;
protected Color highlightOuter;
protected Color shadowInner;
protected Color shadowOuter;
```

These variables store the various pieces of information associated with a bevel border, including the type of the border and the highlight and shadow colors. The bevelType may be assigned one of the constants listed earlier.

Instance Methods

```
public int getBevelType();
public Color getHighlightInnerColor(Component c);
public Color getHighlightInnerColor();
public Color getHighlightOuterColor();
public Color getHighlightOuterColor(Component c);
public Color getShadowInnerColor(Component c);
```

```
public Color getShadowInnerColor();
public Color getShadowOuterColor(Component c);
public Color getShadowOuterColor();
```

These methods retrieve various pieces of information that describe the bevel border. The bevelType may be assigned one of the constants listed earlier.

Overridden Instance Methods

```
public Insets getBorderInsets(Component c);
public Insets getBorderInsets(Component c, Insets insets);
```

These methods retrieve the insets for the border; the second version acts on the Insets object that is passed as an argument.

```
public boolean isBorderOpaque();
```

This method checks whether the border is opaque or transparent; opaque borders paint their own backgrounds, whereas transparent borders do not.

```
public void paintBorder(Component c, Graphics g,
    int x, int y, int width, int height);
```

This method paints the border for a component using the specified border *x,y* position and size.

BitSet Class

Full Name   java.util.BitSet

Extends   Object

Implements   Cloneable

DescriptionPublic class. Creates a compact set of bit flags, not unlike the bit-field mechanism in C and C++; each bit in the set stores one independent Boolean value. This is the most efficient storage mechanism for a set of Boolean values, but it takes slightly more time than the use of the primitive Boolean type, which is not compact.

The following example declares a BitSet object and sets the three least significant bits, which are bits 0, 1, and 2. (This can be done more efficiently by using and(7) in place of set() calls.)

```
BitSet flags = new BitSet(5);  // Five bits: 0 to 4
flags.set(0);
flags.set(1);
flags.set(2);
```

Constructors

```
public BitSet();
public BitSet(int nbits);
```

The nbits argument, if given, specifies the number of bit flags.

Instance Methods

```
public void and(BitSet set);
public void or(BitSet set);
public void xor(BitSet set);
```

These methods all perform bitwise logical operations combining the current object with the specified argument. For example, the and() method can be used to apply bit masks.

```
public void clear(int bit);
public boolean get(int bit);
public void set(int bit);
```

Each of these methods clears, sets, or gets the value of an individual bit. The argument specifies bit position, in which 0 is the least-significant bit.

```
public int size();
```

Returns the number of bits.

Overridden Instance Methods

```
public Object clone();
public boolean equals(Object obj);
public int hashCode();
```

These methods override method definitions in the Object class.

Book Class

Full Name java.awt.print.Book

Extends Object

DescriptionPublic class. This class represents a printable document containing multiple pages that are capable of being printed. Each page of a Book object can have different formatting information, and therefore can be rendered differently when printed.

Constructors

```
public Book();
```

Default constructor. This constructor creates an empty book; you add pages via the setPage() or append() methods.

Java 2 API Reference

Instance Methods

```
public void append(Printable painter, PageFormat page);
public void append(Printable painter, PageFormat page,
    int numPages);
```

These method append a page to the end of the book; notice that a page is defined by a Printable object and a PageFormat object. The second version of the method appends multiple pages, the number of which is determined by numPages.

```
public PageFormat getPageFormat(int pageIndex)
    throws IndexOutOfBoundsException;
public Printable getPrintable(int pageIndex)
    throws IndexOutOfBoundsException;
```

These methods return the format of the page specified by pageIndex, as well as the Printable object associated with the page.

```
public int getNumberOfPages();
```

This method returns the number of pages currently in the book.

```
public void setPage(int pageIndex, Printable painter, PageFormat
page)
    throws IndexOutOfBoundsException;
```

This method sets the page at the specified index in the book; notice that a page is defined by a Printable object and a PageFormat object.

Boolean Class

Full Name   java.lang.Boolean

Extends   Object

DescriptionPublic final class. Wrapper class for the Boolean primitive data type. Most common use is to pass Boolean values by reference. Several methods read a string containing true or false. In these cases, case does not have to match, and false is assumed when the string does not match true.

The following example shows two equivalent ways of initializing a wrapper object for Boolean values. In any given example, you could use either statement but not both together.

```
Boolean b = new Boolean(true);
Boolean b = Boolean.TRUE;
```

Constructors

```
public Boolean(boolean value);
public Boolean(String s);
```

See class description for interpretation of string argument.

Class Variables

```
public final static Boolean FALSE;
public final static Boolean TRUE;
```

Class constants. Remember that these constants are objects and not primitive data.

Class Methods

```
public static boolean getBoolean(String name);
public static Boolean valueOf(String s);
```

These class methods read a string and return primitive data and an object, respectively.

Instance Methods

```
public boolean booleanValue();
```

Returns the primitive data value (true or false) of the current object.

Overridden Instance Methods

```
public boolean equals(Object obj);
public int hashCode();
public String toString();
```

These methods override method definitions in the Object class.

Border Interface

Full Name javax.swing.border.Border

DescriptionPublic interface. This interface describes a generic border that frames a rectangular GUI component.

Interface Methods

```
public Insets getBorderInsets(Component c);
```

This method retrieves the insets for the border.

```
public boolean isBorderOpaque();
```

This method checks whether a border is opaque or transparent; opaque borders paint their own backgrounds, whereas transparent borders do not.

```
public void paintBorder(Component c, Graphics g,
    int x, int y,  int width, int height);
```

This method paints the border for a component using the specified border *x,y* position and size.

BorderLayout Class

Full Name	java.awt.BorderLayout
Extends	Object
Implements	LayoutManager
Description	Public class. Creates layout manager objects that use the BorderLayout scheme described at the end of Chapter 4, "Components and Events." When this layout manager is in use, objects may be added in several zones: EAST, WEST, NORTH, SOUTH, and CENTER, all of which are constants of the BorderLayout class. Use of these zones enables you to add objects such as toolbars and menus along an edge of a container. See the Container class (p. 221) for the add() method.

The following example sets the current container to use an instance of BorderLayout:

```
setLayout(new BorderLayout());
```

Constructors

```
public BorderLayout();
public BorderLayout(int hgap, int vgap);
```

You can optionally specify horizontal and vertical margins (gaps) around components.

Instance Methods

```
public void addLayoutComponent(String name, Component comp);
public void layoutContainer(Container target);
public Dimension minimumLayoutSize(Container target);
public Dimension preferredLayoutSize(Container target);
public void removeLayoutComponent(Component comp);
```

These five methods implement the LayoutManager interface; none of these methods is normally called by applications.

Overridden Instance Methods

```
public String toString();
```

This method overrides the method definition in the Object class.

Box Class

Full Name	`javax.swing.Box`
Extends	`Container->Component->Object`
Description	Public class. The Box class implements a lightwieght container that utilizes the box layout as its layout manager. This Swing class is very flexible because it supports various invisible positioning elements (glue, struts, and rigid areas) that make it possible to highly customize the positioning of components within the box. The main purpose of this class is to enable you to add components easily, in either left-to-right or top-to-bottom fashion, without having to work out precise constraints.

Constructors

```
public Box(int axis);
```

This constructor creates either a horizontal or vertical box, based on the value of the axis argument; BoxLayout.X_AXIS creates a horizontal box and BoxLayout.Y_AXIS creates a vertical box.

Class Methods

```
public static Component createGlue();
```

Returns a component that acts as "glue," between components added to a container. Between adding two components, call add(Box.createGlue()) to force even spacing between the components.

```
public static Box createHorizontalBox();
public static Component createHorizontalGlue();
public static Component createHorizontalStrut(int width);
public static Component createRigidArea(Dimension d);
public static Box createVerticalBox();
public static Component createVerticalGlue();
public static Component createVerticalStrut(int height);
```

These methods create boxes and box components. A horizontal or vertical box draws a box within a frame, in which components added to the box or displayed left-to-right or top-to-bottom. Struts contain a specific number of pixels and can be added between components to achieve exact spacing. Glue, described earlier, causes even spacing between components.

BoxLayout Class

Full Name `javax.swing.BoxLayout`

Extends `Object`

Description	Public class. This class implements a layout manager that supports the arrangement of components either horizontally or vertically. The real power of the `BoxLayout` class is when multiple box layouts are nested within one another.

Constructors

```
public BoxLayout(Container target, int axis);
```

This constructor creates a box layout manager and associates it with the target container; the axis argument specifies whether the box layout is horizontal (BoxLayout.X_AXIS) or vertical (BoxLayout.Y_AXIS).

Class Variables

```
public static final int X_AXIS;
public static final int Y_AXIS;
```

Class constants. These constants establish whether the box layout is horizontal or vertical.

Instance Methods

```
public float getLayoutAlignmentX(Container target);
public float getLayoutAlignmentY(Container target);
```

These methods get the *x* and *y* alignment for the layout, which is a floating point number between 0.0f and 1.0f.

```
public void invalidateLayout(Container target);
```

This method indicates that a component within the container specified in target has changed and results in the container being laid out.

```
public void layoutContainer(Container target);
```

This method lays out the container specified in target and is called automatically whenever the layout needs to be laid out.

```
public Dimension maximumLayoutSize(Container target);
public Dimension minimumLayoutSize(Container target);
public Dimension preferredLayoutSize(Container target);
```

These methods get the maximum, minimum, and preferred size for the layout.

BufferedInputStream Class

Full Name	`java.io.BufferedInputStream`
Extends	`FilterInputStream->InputStream->Object`

DescriptionPublic class. This class takes an existing input stream and creates buffered input stream around it. Data is read directly from the buffer; when the buffer is exhausted, more data is read from the stream. If the underlying input stream is from a file, the buffering mechanism speeds file I/O, because it reduces the amount of disk access.

Constructors

```
public BufferedInputStream(InputStream in);
public BufferedInputStream(InputStream in, int size);
```

InputStream is the underlying stream to be buffered, and size is the buffer size to use. The default buffer size is 512.

Overridden Instance Methods

```
public int available() throws IOException;
public void mark(int readlimit);
public boolean markSupported();
public int read() throws IOException;
public int read(byte b[], int off, int len)
   throws IOException;
public void reset() throws IOException;
public long skip(long n) throws IOException;
```

These methods override method definitions in the InputStream class. markSupported() returns true for all instances of this class, indicating that the mark() and reset() methods are supported.

BufferedOutputStream Class

Full Name java.io.BufferedOutputStream

Extends FilterOutputStream->OutputStream->Object

DescriptionPublic class. This class takes an existing output stream and creates buffered output stream around it. Data is written directly to the buffer; when the buffer is full, the entire buffer is written to the stream. If the underlying output stream is to a file, the buffering mechanism speeds file I/O, because it cuts down on the amount of disk access.

Constructors

```
public BufferedOutputStream(OutputStream out);
public BufferedOutputStream(OutputStream out, int size);
```

OutputStream is the underlying stream to be buffered, and size is the buffer size to use. The default buffer size is 512.

190   BufferedOutputStream Class

Overridden Instance Methods

```
public void flush() throws IOException;
public void write(byte b[], int off, int len)
  throws IOException;
public void write(int b) throws IOException;
```

These methods override method definitions in the `OutputStream` class. The `flush()` method forces the current contents of the buffer to be written now. Then buffer is then emptied.

Button Class

Full Name   `java.awt.Button`

Extends   `Component->Object`

Description   Public class. A `Button` object is a command button or push button. This component generates all standard keyboard and mouse events except for `mousePressed` and `mouseReleased`. These actions translate into an `ActionEvent`. To respond to the user clicking the button, use the `addActionListener()` event to install an event handler. (For an example, see `ActionListener` inteface, p. 169.)

The following example creates a button and adds it to the current frame or applet:

```
Button btn1 = new Button("Press Me.");
add(btn1);
```

Constructors

```
public Button();
public Button(String label);
```

You can optionally specify initial button label text.

Instance Methods

```
public void addActionListener(ActionListener al);
```

Registers an event handler for responding to the user clicking the button. This is an "action" in the sense that it involves the user choosing to execute a particular command. See `ActionListener` (p. 169).

```
public String getLabel();
```

Gets the current label text.

```
public void removeActionListener(ActionListener al);
```

Removes an event handler previously installed with `addActionListener()`.

Java 2 API Reference

```
public void setLabel(String label);
```

Sets the current label text.

Overridden Instance Methods

```
public void addNotify();
```

Overrides the method definition in Component. Used internally.

ButtonGroup Class

Full Name   javax.swing.ButtonGroup

Extends   Object

Description   Public class. This class implements a button group that is
                 used to create a set of buttons for navigational purposes. The
                 significance of button groups is that they allow you to establish
                 multiple exclusion for buttons, which allows only one button to
                 be selected at any given time. Button groups are typically used
                 with the JRadioButton and JRadioButtonMenuItem
                 classes (pp. 338 and 401).

For example code, see JRadioButton and JRadioMenuButton. This topic
describes the more commonly used methods.

Constructors

```
public ButtonGroup();
```

Creates an empty group. Individual buttons must be added, one at a time,
with the add() method.

Instance Variables

```
protected Vector buttons;
```

This variable stores references to all the buttons that have been added to the
group.

Instance Methods

```
public void add(AbstractButton b);
```

Adds an individual button b. (This may be any type of button supported by
Swing.)

```
public int getButtonCount();
```

Returns number of buttons in the group.

```
public Enumeration getElements();
```

Returns all the buttons in an enumeration.

Java 2 API Reference

```
public void remove(AbstractButton b);
```

Removes the specified button.

Byte Class

Full Name	`java.lang.Byte`
Extends	`Number->Object`
Description	Public class. This class serves as a standard wrapper for primitive byte values.

Constructors

```
public Byte(byte value);
public Byte(String s) throws NumberFormatException;
```

Creates a `Byte` object using either a primitive byte value or a string containing a base 10 number.

Class Constants

```
public static final byte MIN_VALUE;
public static final byte MAX_VALUE;
```

These constants represent the minimum and maximum values allowed for a byte.

```
public static final Class TYPE;
```

This constant is an object representing the primitive byte type.

Class Methods

```
public static Byte decode(String nm)
   throws NumberFormatException;
```

Decodes a `Byte` object out of a string containing a number; the number in the string can be in decimal, hexadecimal, or octal format.

```
public static byte parseByte(String s)
   throws NumberFormatException;
public static byte parseByte(String s, int radix)
   throws NumberFormatException;
```

Parses a byte out of a string containing a byte number.

```
public static Byte valueOf(String s)
   throws NumberFormatException;
public static Byte valueOf(String s, int radix)
   throws NumberFormatException;
```

Parses a `Byte` object out of a string containing a byte number.

Instance Methods

```
public int compareTo(Byte anotherByte);
public int compareTo(Object o);
```

Compares this byte to the specified `Byte` object or other object; the return value is 0 if the objects are numerically equal, less than 0 if this byte is less than the argument, and greater than 0 if this byte is greater than the argument.

Overridden Instance Methods

```
public byte byteValue();
public double doubleValue();
public float floatValue();
public int intValue();
public long longValue();
public short shortValue();
```

These methods return the value of this byte as a byte, double, float, int, long, or short.

ByteArrayInputStream Class

Full Name   java.io.ByteArrayInputStream

Extends   InputStream->Object

Description   Public class. Creates an input stream from an array of bytes. The effect is to treat an area of memory as a virtual sequential-access file.

The following example creates an input stream object around an existing array, `dataArray`. The resulting stream can then be used in the same way as any instance of `InputStream`.

```
ByteArrayInputStream bytes_in =
    new ByteArrayInputStream(dataArray);
DataInputStream dis = new DataInputStream(bytes_in);
```

Constructors

```
public ByteArrayInputStream(byte buf[][]);
public ByteArrayInputStream(byte buf[][], int offset,
    int length);
```

Optional offset and length give starting point in the array and size. If these are not specified, the entire array is used.

Overridden Instance Methods

```
public int available();
public int read();
```

```
public int read(byte b[], int off, int len);
public void reset();
public long skip(long n);
```

These methods override method definitions in the InputStream class.

ByteArrayOutputStream Class

Full Name	java.io.ByteArrayOutputStream
Extends	OutputStream->Object
Description	Public class. Creates an output stream from an array of bytes. The effect is to treat an area of memory as a virtual sequential-access file. An object of this class automatically grows as it is written to. For this reason, it does not correspond to a fixed location in memory, as a ByteArrayInputStream object does. Instead, if you want to access the data, you need to periodically write it to another object by using the toByteArray(), toString(), or writeTo() method. These methods give snapshots of the current state of the output stream.

The following example creates a stream that can be written to as if it were a file. The result is an array, dataArray, containing all the data written.

```
ByteArrayOutputStream bytes_out =
    new ByteArrayOutputStream();
// ... Write to the bytes_out stream.
byte dataArray[] = bytes_out.toByteArray();
```

Constructors

```
public ByteArrayOutputStream();
public ByteArrayOutputStream(int size);
```

You can optionally specify an initial buffer size, but in any case this will grow as needed.

Instance Methods

```
public byte[] toByteArray();
```

Writes data from the buffer to a byte array, which is allocated with exactly the size needed.

```
public String toString();
public String toString(int hibyte);
```

These methods fill a string with the contents of the buffer. Each byte is written to a string character. The high order bits of each character are set to 0x00, or to the eight low-order bits of hibyte, if specified.

Overridden Instance Methods
```
public void reset();
public int size();
public void write(byte b[], int off, int len);
public void write(int b);
```

These methods override method definitions in the OutputStream class. Note that in this implementation, they affect the buffer maintained by the object. size() gives the number of bytes that have been written to.

Calendar Class

Full Name	java.util.Calendar
Extends	Object
Description	Public class. This class serves as the base class for calendar classes that support the conversion of a Date object to a set of individual date integers such as YEAR, MONTH, DAY, etc. Calendar subclasses such as GregorianCalendar implement calendars for specific calendar systems.

Unlike most classes, you don't create a Calendar object using the new operator and a constructor. Instead, you call one of the getInstance() class methods defined in the Calendar class. To create a Calendar object initialized with the current date and time, just call the getInstance() method with no arguments:

```
Calendar now = Calendar.getInstance();
```

If it seems strange to you that a Calendar object would store a time, consider the fact that a traditional calendar is just a more general way of keeping track of time. In Java, the Calendar class happens to provide a more specific approach, down to the second. You can also provide a specific time zone and locale when calling the getInstance() method to create a Calendar object. Once you've created a Calendar object, you can easily obtain a portion of the date and time using the get() method and one of the constants defined in the Calendar class:

```
int day = now.get(DAY_OF_WEEK);
if (day == FRIDAY)
    System.out.println("It's Friday!!!");
```

The Calendar class fully supports globalization for internationalized programs. Using the default getInstance() method like the earlier code example, the Calendar class automatically localizes the time to the default locale. To localize the time to another locale, you use a different getInstance() method.

Following is an example of retrieving the current time localized to the Korea locale:

```
Calendar now = Calendar.getInstance(Locale.KOREA);
```

Notice that the Locale.KOREA locale constant is used instead of creating a Locale object explicitly. You can use this approach any time a Locale object is required for an operation. The Locale class is covered on page ___.

Class Constants

```
public static final int AM;
public static final int AM_PM;
public static final int APRIL;
public static final int AUGUST;
public static final int DATE;
public static final int DAY_OF_MONTH;
public static final int DAY_OF_YEAR;
public static final int DAY_OF_WEEK;
public static final int DAY_OF_WEEK_IN_MONTH;
public static final int DECEMBER;
public static final int DST_OFFSET;
public static final int ERA;
public static final int FEBRUARY;
public static final int FIELD_COUNT;
public static final int FRIDAY;
public static final int HOUR;
public static final int HOUR_OF_DAY;
public static final int JANUARY;
public static final int JULY;
public static final int JUNE;
public static final int MARCH;
public static final int MAY;
public static final int MILLISECOND;
public static final int MINUTE;
public static final int MONDAY;
public static final int MONTH;
public static final int NOVEMBER;
public static final int OCTOBER;
public static final int PM;
public static final int SATURDAY;
public static final int SECOND;
public static final int SEPTEMBER;
public static final int SUNDAY;
public static final int THURSDAY;
public static final int TUESDAY;
```

```
public static final int UNDECIMBER;
public static final int WEDNESDAY;
public static final int WEEK_OF_YEAR;
public static final int WEEK_OF_MONTH;
public static final int YEAR;
public static final int ZONE_OFFSET;
```

Class constants. These constants represent requisite parts of a calendar, along with specific calendar-related names such as month and day names.

Class Methods

```
public static Locale[] getAvailableLocales();
```

Obtains a list of locales for which calendars are installed.

```
public static Calendar getInstance();
public static Calendar getInstance(TimeZone zone);
public static Calendar getInstance(Locale aLocale);
public static Calendar getInstance(TimeZone zone,
   Locale aLocale);
```

Obtains a Calendar object based upon the specified time zone, locale, or combination of time zone and locale; these methods are used to create a Calendar object as opposed to using a constructor.

Instance Methods

```
public boolean after(Object when);
public boolean before(Object when);
```

Compares the time of the current calendar with the specified time argument to see if the current calendar time is before or after the argument.

```
public final void clear();
public final void clear(int field);
```

Clears all of the time fields for the calendar, or only the field specified by the field argument.

```
public final int get(int field);
```

Retrieves the specified time field of the calendar.

```
public int getActualMaximum(int field);
public int getActualMinimum(int field);
```

Retrieves the maximum and minimum values the specified field can have given the current date.

```
public int getFirstDayOfWeek();
```

Retrieves the first day of the week for the current locale.

```
public int getMinimalDaysInFirstWeek();
```

Retrieves the minimal number of days required for the first week in the year.

```
public final Date getTime();
```

Obtains the calendar's current time as a Date object.

```
public TimeZone getTimeZone();
```

Obtains the calendar's current time zone.

```
public boolean isLenient();
```

Checks to see if the date/time interpretation of the calendar is lenient.

```
public final boolean isSet(int field);
```

Checks to see if the specified time field is set.

```
public void roll(int field, int amount);
```

Rolls the specified time field by the specified amount.

```
public final void set(int field, int value);
public final void set(int year, int month, int date);
public final void set(int year, int month, int date, int hour,
    int minute);
public final void set(int year, int month, int date, int hour,
    int minute, int second);
```

Sets the calendar based upon a series of arguments including a field/value pair, or specific fields including the year, month, date, hour, minute, and second.

```
public void setFirstDayOfWeek(int value);
```

Sets the first day of the week for the current locale.

```
public void setLenient(boolean lenient);
```

Sets the leniency of the calendar, which determines how strict it interprets date/time conversion.

```
public void setMinimalDaysInFirstWeek(int value);
```

Sets the minimal number of days required for the first week in the year.

```
public final void setTime(Date date);
```

Sets the time of the calendar based upon the specified date argument.

```
public void setTimeZone(TimeZone value);
```

Sets the time zone of the calendar.

Canvas Class

Full Name	java.awt.Canvas
Extends	Component->Object
Description	Public class. Creates components with no built-in redrawing or response to events. You can create custom components by subclassing Canvas and adding your own code to paint the component or to handle events. Canvas generates all the standard keyboard and mouse events.

Although there are no explicit constructors for Canvas, it implicitly supports a default constructor, Canvas( ).

Overridden Instance Methods

```
public synchronized void addNotify();
public void paint(Graphics g);
```

These methods override method definitions in Component. addNotify() is used internally.

CardLayout Class

Full Name	java.awt.CardLayout
Extends	Object
Implements	LayoutManager
Description	Public class. Creates layout manager objects that use the CardLayout scheme described in Chapter 5 on page 592. This scheme displays components in a way similar to HyperCard or a cardfile program.

The following example sets the current container to use an instance of CardLayout:

```
setLayout(new CardLayout());
```

Constructors

```
public CardLayout();
public CardLayout(int hgap, int vgap);
```

You can optionally specify horizontal and vertical margins (gaps) around components.

Instance Methods

```
public void first(Container parent);
public void last(Container parent);
public void next(Container parent);
```

```
public void previous(Container parent);
public void show(Container parent, String name);
```

These five methods bring a component to the top of the "stack." The component made visible is the first, last, next, or previous component on the stack, depending on which method you call. The show( ) method uses a name to identify a component; this is the same string that was specified when the add(String, Component) method was used to add the component to the container.

Instance Methods (Supporting Interface)

```
public void addLayoutComponent(String name, Component comp);
public void layoutContainer(Container target);
public Dimension minimumLayoutSize(Container target);
public Dimension preferredLayoutSize(Container target);
public void removeLayoutComponent(Component comp);
```

These five methods implement the LayoutManager interface; none of these methods is normally called by applications.

Overridden Instance Methods

```
public String toString();
```

This method overrides the method definition in the Object class.

ChangeEvent Class

Full Name	javax.swing.event.ChangeEvent
Extends	EventObject->Object
Description	Public class. This class represents a change event that is delivered in response to a change of some sort occurring in an event source.

Constructors

```
public ChangeEvent(Object source);
```

Creates a change event based upon the specified event source.

Instance Methods

```
public Object getSource();
```

Retrieves the object upon which the event originally occurred. (This method is actually inherited from the EventObject ancestor class.)

ChangeListener Interface

Full Name	javax.swing.event.ChangeListener

Extends   `EventListener`

DescriptionPublic interface. This interface describes a change event listener that is used to handle change events.

Interface Methods

```
public void stateChanged(ChangeEvent e);
```

This method is an event response method that is called when a change of some sort occurs in an event source.

Character Class

Full Name	`java.lang.Character`
Extends	`Object`
Description	Public final class. Wrapper class for the `char` primitve data type. This class contains many useful operations for testing and converting individual characters. Remember that strings are not arrays of char. See `String` class, page 457, for string operations.

The following example calls a `Character` class method to test a character:

```
char c;
// Read a character, c.
// ...
if (Character.IsDigit(c)) //...
```

Constructors

```
public Character(char value);
```

The value is a Unicode character value.

Class Variables

```
public final static int MAX_RADIX;
public final static char MAX_VALUE;
public final static int MIN_RADIX;
public final static char MIN_VALUE;
```

These constants specify the minimum and maximum value in the char data range, and the minimum and maximum radix that can be used in the digit() method.

Class Methods

```
public static int digit(char ch, int radix);
public static char forDigit(int digit, int radix);
```

These class methods convert between a printable digit character and its face value.

```
public static boolean isDefined(char ch);
```

Returns true if the argument has a meaningful value in the Unicode character set.

```
public static boolean isDigit(char ch);
public static boolean isJavaLetter(char ch);
public static boolean isJavaLetterOrDigit(char ch);
public static boolean isLetter(char ch);
public static boolean isLetterOrDigit(char ch);
public static boolean isLowerCase(char ch);
public static boolean isSpace(char ch);
public static boolean isUpperCase(char ch);
```

Java 2 API Reference

These class methods, starting with isDigit(), report a particular condition. The isJavaLetter() and isJavaLetterOrDigit() methods return true if the character is accepted as an initial character and a non-initial character, respectively, in a Java identifier.

```
public static char toLowerCase(char ch);
public static char toUpperCase(char ch);
```

These class methods return a converted character.

Instance Methods

```
public char charValue();
```

Returns the char value stored in the current object.

Overridden Instance Methods

```
public boolean equals(Object obj);
public int hashCode();
public String toString();
```

These methods override method definitions in the Object class. The toString() method returns a string of length 1 that contains the character stored in the current object.

Checkbox Class

Full Name java.awt.Checkbox

Extends   Component->Object

Description   Public class. Creates checkboxes with a simple on/off state, as well as checkboxes that work as part of a group (in which selecting one automatically deselects the others). These are often called radio buttons or option buttons. To create a group, create a `CheckboxGroup` object and then specify this group when you create a checkbox. You can also call the `setCheckboxGroup()` method after a checkbox has been created. A checkbox generates an `ItemEvent` whenever its state changes. Call the `addItemListener()` method to install an event handler for changes to the checkbox state.

For an example, see `CheckGroup` class.

Constructors

```
public Checkbox();
public Checkbox(String label);
public Checkbox(String label, CheckboxGroup group,
    boolean state);
```

The third constructor sets initial conditions as well as specifying a group (which can be set to null).

Instance Methods

```
public void addItemListener(ItemListener l);
```

Installs an event handler that responds to changes in the checkbox state.

```
public CheckboxGroup getCheckboxGroup();
public String getLabel();
public boolean getState();
```

These methods get various properties of the checkbox.

```
public void removeItemListener(ItemListener l);
```

Removes an event handler previously installed with addItemListener().

```
public void setCheckboxGroup(CheckboxGroup g);
public void setLabel(String label);
public void setState(boolean state);
```

These methods set a property of the component. Some checkboxes work as stand-alone components rather than as part of a group; calling getCheckbox Group(), in those cases, returns null.

CheckboxGroup Class

Full Name   `java.awt.CheckboxGroup`

Extends   `Object`

Java 2 API Reference

Description   Public class. A `CheckboxGroup` object can be used to place one or more check boxes in a common group. Boxes in a group are often called radio buttons or option buttons. A checkbox can be associated with a group when it is created. It can also be associated by calling its `setCheckboxGroup()` method. The checkbox group object is not very interesting, although you can use it to get or set the current item.

The following example creates a group of two checkboxes:

```
CheckboxGroup fruit = new CheckboxGroup();
Checkbox chkAp = new Checkbox("Applets", fruit, true);
Checkbox chkOr = new Checkbox("Oranges", fruit, false);
add(chkAp);
add(chkOr);
```

Constructors

```
public CheckboxGroup();
```

Instance Methods

```
public Checkbox getCurrent();
```

Returns a reference to the current item, if any, in the group. Returns null if there is no current item.

```
public void setCurrent(Checkbox box);
```

Sets the current item — that is, the specified object is selected as a result of this method call.

```
protected String toString();
```

Overrides the method definition in the `Object` class.

CheckboxMenuItem Class

Full Name   `java.awt.CheckboxMenuItem`

Extends   `MenuItem->MenuComponent->Object`

Description   Public class. Similar to `MenuItem` class except that it creates a menu item that optionally appears with a check mark. The Boolean (true/false) state determines whether the menu item is currently checked. See `MenuItem` for most fields.

The following example adds two menu items to an existing menu, m, and checks the first one. See `Menu` (p. 397) and `MenuItem` (p. 401) classes for more examples.

```
CheckboxMenuItem miBold = new CheckboxMenuItem("Bold");
CheckboxMenuItem miItal = new CheckboxMenuItem("Italic");
```

```
m.add(miBold);
m.add(miItal);
miBold.setState(true);
```

Constructors

```
public CheckboxMenuItem(String label);
```

The label must be specified at the time the object is created.

Instance Methods

```
public boolean getState();
public void setState(boolean t);
```

These methods get and set the state: true means that the menu item is checked.

```
public void addNotify();
```

Overrides the method definition in MenuItem. Used internally.

Choice Class

Full Name	java.awt.Choice
Extends	Component->Object
Description	Public class. In Java, a Choice object is much like a drop-down list or option menu. A set of choices is displayed when the object gets focus. Use the addItem( ) method to initialize the list. Selection of an item results in generation of an ItemEvent (p. 290). Some Choice methods use an index: this index is zero-based, so the first item is 0.

The following example creates and initializes a Choice component:

```
Choice chooseCountry = new Choice();
chooseCountry.addItem("Oh Canada!");
chooseCountry.addItem("La Belle France");
chooseCountry.AddItem("USA");
add(chooseCountry);
```

Constructors

```
public Choice();
```

Default constructor. Note that list must be initialized with addItem( ).

Instance Methods

```
public synchronized void addItem(String item)
    throws NullPointerException;
```

Java 2 API Reference

Adds item in string form. This is the only way to add items.

```
public void addItemListener(ItemListener l)
```

Installs an event handler for changes in item selection.

```
public int countItems();
public String getItem(int index);
public int getSelectedIndex();
public String getSelectedItem();
```

These four methods return information about the list: number of items, contents of selected item, zero-based index of current item, and current item in string form, respectively.

```
public void removeItemListener(ItemListener l)
```

Removes an event handler previously installed with addItemListener().

```
public synchronized void select(int pos)
    throws IllegalArgumentException;
public void select(String str);
```

The select() method changes current selection as indicated, if possible. The pos argument is a zero-based index.

Class Class

Full Name	java.lang.Class
Extends	Object
Description	Public final class. A Class object provides information about a Java class. The practical uses of a Class object are limited, but you can use it to browse the Java class system. The newInstance() method is one of the few ways to create an object other than using new. This class has no constructors, but the Object.getClass() method returns a Class object, as does Class.forName().

The following example registers the class imaginary.sql.iMsqlDriver, the mSQL driver for JDBC:

```
Class.forName("imaginary.sql.iMsqlDriver");
```

Class Methods

```
public static Class forName(String className);
```

Registers a class by name and then returns the corresponding Class object.

Instance Methods

```
public ClassLoader getClassLoader();
public Class[] getInterfaces();
public String getName();
public Class getSuperclass();
public boolean isInterface();
```

Each of these methods returns some information about the class. getClassLoader() returns a class loader object that loads Java classes over the network; few applications ever use this.

```
public Object newInstance() throws InstantiationException,
    IllegalAccessException;
```

Returns a new instance of the class. This object needs to be cast to the appropriate type.

Overridden Class Methods

```
public String toString();
```

Returns a string representation of the class.

Cloneable Interface

Full Name	java.lang.Cloneable
Description	Public interface. An API class that implements this interface indicates that it supports a usable definition for the Object. clone() method. In other words, if a class implements this interface, an object of the class can be cloned. The Vector and Hashtable classes are examples of cloneable classes.

This interface declares no fields.

Color Class

Full Name	java.awt.Color
Extends	Object
Description	Public final class. A Color object represents a color value. In addition, this class provides a number of useful constants and class methods. (Class constants and methods can be used without being accessed through an object.) Because it is a final class, Color cannot be subclassed.

The following example shows three ways to create the same Color object. In actual code, you would only use one of these constructors.

Java 2 API Reference

```
Color yuckGreen = new Color(212, 255, 0);
Color yuckGreen = new Color(0Xd4ff00);
Color yuckGreen = new Color(0.83, 1.0. 0.0);
setBackground(yuckGreen);
```

Constructors

```
public Color(int r, int g, int b);
public Color(int rgb);
public Color(float r, float g, float b);
```

In all cases, the color is specified as an RGB (red/green/blue) value. Where integers are used, each color intensity is specified as a number between 0 and 255. Where floating-point numbers are used, each color intensity is specified as a number between 0.0 and 1.0. The second constructor uses a packed value, in which each of the three lowest bytes holds a color value.

Class Variables

```
public final static Color black;
public final static Color blue;
public final static Color cyan;
public final static Color darkGray;
public final static Color gray;
public final static Color lightGray;
public final static Color magenta;
public final static Color orange;
public final static Color pink;
public final static Color red;
public final static Color white;
public final static Color yellow;
```

Color constants. You can refer to these constants directly without having to first instantiate your own color object. Each has the correct RGB value for the stated color. Although it is a standard Java convention to use all-upper-case names for constants, that convention is broken here.

Class Methods

```
public static int HSBtoRGB(float hue, float saturation,
    float brightness);
public static float[] RGBtoHSB(int r, int g, int b,
    float[] hsbvals);
```

The HSB class methods create a color value from values for hue, saturation, and brightness, in which each is a floating-point number ranging from 0.0 to 1.0. If you specify null for the array argument in the RGBtoHSB() method, the method allocates an array in which to return the hue, saturation, and brightness values.

```
public static Color getColor(String nm);
public static Color getColor(String nm, Color v);
public static Color getColor(String nm, int v);
```

The getColor() class method takes a string as input, which it looks up as a system property. The second argument, if specified, gives a default value to use if the color name is not found. Returns a Color object with the color value found.

```
public static Color getHSBColor(float hue, float saturation,
    float brightness);
```

This class method takes values for hue, saturation, and brightness (each ranging from 0.0 to 1.0) and returns the equivalent Color object.

Instance Methods

```
public Color brighter();
public Color darker();
```

These methods return a Color object that is a shade brighter or darker than the current object. These methods are useful for creating a palette of colors differing in degree of brightness.

```
public int getBlue();
public int getGreen();
public int getRed();
public int getRGB();
```

These four methods get the current setting of one or more of the primary colors associated with the current object. The getRGB() method returns an integer containing red, green, and blue intensities, each packed into a byte.

Overridden Instance Methods

```
public equals(Object obj);
public int hashCode();
public String toString();
```

These three methods override method definitions in the Object class.

ColorModel Class

Full Name	java.awt.image.ColorModel
Extends	Object
Description	Abstract public class. The API supports two usable sub-classes: DirectColorModel and IndexColorModel. Most applications and applets never have any reason to interact with these classes. In general, there is never any need to use a ColorModel class unless you're processing image data that does not use the default RGB model.

Constructors

```
public ColorModel(int bits);
```

Specifies number of bits per pixel.

Class Methods

```
public static ColorModel getRGBdefault();
```

Returns a color model that uses the RGB default.

Instance Methods

```
public abstract int getAlpha(int pixel);
```

Translates a pixel from the color model into the default model (RGB plus alpha). The alpha, which is returned by this method, gives a transparency number from 0 to 255, 0 being completely transparent and 255 being solid, or opaque.

```
public abstract int getBlue(int pixel);
public abstract int getGreen(int pixel);
public abstract int getRed(int pixel);
```

These methods translate a pixel from the color model into the default model (RGB), returning the particular color intensity (a number from 0 to 255).

```
public int getPixelSize();
```

Returns the number of bits per pixel.

```
public int getRGB(int pixel);
```

Translates a pixel from the model into its RGB representation.

Comparable Interface

Full Name	java.lang.Comparable
Description	Public interface. This interface is used to compare objects with one another. In order for an object to support comparisons, it must implement the Comparable interface.

Interface Methods

```
public int compareTo(Object o);
```

This method compares the specified object to the object that implements the Comparable interface.

Component Class

Full Name	java.awt.Component

Extends	Object
Implements	ImageObserver
Description	Abstract, public class. Cannot be directly instantiated. However, many classes in the Abstract Windowing ToolKit (AWT) inherit directly or indirectly from this class, which declares the sizing, movement, focus, and event-handling methods for all Java components (other than menus) as well as paint( ), setVisible( ), and related methods. In Java, a component is any graphical object that can be displayed and receive events. This class cannot be directly subclassed; to create a custom component, use the Canvas class.
	Note that this class has a number of methods added or replaced since Java 1.0. Java 1.1 replaced the reshape( ), resize( ), and show( ) methods with "set" methods whose names conform to JavaBeans design patterns. For example, to display a component, you now use setVisible(true) rather than show( ). Java 1.1 also added event-handling installers for the new event model and deprecated the old event-handling methods.

Java 2 API Reference

Instance Methods

```
public boolean action(Event evt, Object what);
```

This method was deprecated beginning with Java 1.1 because it has been supplanted by the new event-handling model. See the addActionListener( ) method of classes such as the Button class (p. 190).

```
public void addComponentListener(ComponentListener cl);
```

Registers an event handler for responding to visible changes to the component — resizing, showing, moving, or hiding. See ComponentListener (p. 219).

```
public void addFocusListener(FocusListener cl);
```

Registers an event handler for responding to focus events — both focus gained and focus lost. See FocusListener (p. 258).

```
public void addKeyListener(KeyListener cl);
```

Registers an event handler for responding to keystroke events. See KeyListener (p. 370).

```
public void addMouseListener(MouseListener cl);
```

Registers an event handler for responding to mouse click, press, and release events. See MouseListener (p. 405).

```
public void addMouseMotionListener(MouseMotionListener cl);
```

Registers an event handler for responding to mouse movement and dragging events. See MouseMotionListener (p. 406).

```
public void addNotify();
```

Causes the component to create a peer — this is an object that determines the look of the component on the specific platform. Although it is possible to override this method to create components with a different look (but same functionality), it is generally for internal use only.

```
public int checkImage(Image image, ImageObserver observer);
public int checkImage(Image image, int width, int height,
    ImageObserver observer);
```

Reports progress of a loading image by returning flags described in the ImageObserver class. Does not cause loading. Generally, you should use a MediaTracker object to monitor loading.

```
public boolean contains(int x, int y);
```

Checks to see if the component contains the specified point.

```
public Image createImage(ImageProducer producer);
public Image createImage(int width, int height);
```

Creates an Image object. The first version uses an image producer such as a filter or in-memory pixel data. (See FilteredImageSource, page 251, and MemoryImageSource, page 396, classes.) The second version is used to create an offscreen buffer. To load an image from a file, see Applet (p. 173) and Toolkit (p. 482) classes.

```
public final void dispatchEvent(AWTEvent e);
```

Dispatches an event to this component or one of its sub-components.

```
public void doLayout();
```

By default, this method does nothing. If the component is a container, layout() causes the layout manager to reposition components. This method is called by validate(). Application code should generally not call this method directly.

```
public Color getBackground();
public Rectangle getBounds();
public Rectangle getBounds(Rectangle r);
public synchronized ColorModel getColorModel();
public Component getComponentAt(int x, int y);
public Font getFont();
public FontMetrics getFontMetrics(Font font);
public Color getForeground();
```

These methods return basic information about the component, including foreground and background color. The color model is used internally to translate RGB values, if necessary, to the particular color scheme in use on this platform. Also, the getBounds() method returns a rectangle containing the size and position of the component; if a rectangle r is passed, the method initializes this object with bounds data as well as returning a Rectangle object.

```
public Graphics getGraphics();
```

Gets a graphic object, which can be used to draw to the component's screen area directly rather than waiting for a repaint.

```
public Point getLocation();
```

Returns the current location.

```
public Dimension getMaximumSize();
```

Returns the component's maximum size. (Introduced in Java .2.0.)

```
public Dimension getMinimumSize();
```

Returns the minimum size that the component takes up on the screen. For example, if the component is a button, its minimum size is the space needed to display the label along with a sufficient margin on each side. Used by layout managers.

```
public Container getParent();
```

Returns the component's container.

```
public Dimension getPreferredSize();
```

Returns the preferred size of the component. This is its "natural" size. This information can be used by some layout managers. Beginning in Java 1.1, this method replaces preferredSize().

```
public Dimension getSize();
```

Returns the component's current size. (Introduced in Java 1.1.)

```
public Toolkit getToolkit();
```

Returns the component's toolkit, which (especially in applications) is useful for loading an image or getting information about the platform's screen display.

```
public int getX();
public int getY();
```

These two methods return the X and Y coordinate, respectively, of the component. (Introduced in Java 2.0.)

```
public boolean gotFocus(Event evt, Object what);
```

Event handler for the gotFocus event. This method was deprecated starting with Java 1.1, because it has been supplanted by the new event handling model. This model uses addFocusListener().

```
public boolean handleEvent(Event evt);
```

The general event-handling dispatcher. This method was deprecated starting with Java 1.1, because it has been supplanted by the new event handling model.

```
public boolean hasFocus();
```

Returns true if the component currently has the focus. (Introduced in Java 2.0.)

```
public synchronized void hide();
```

Makes the component invisible until show() is called. Beginning with Java 1.1, this method is deprecated. Use setVisible(false) instead.

```
public boolean imageUpdate(Image img, int flags,
    int x, int y, int w, int h);
```

This method implements the ImageObserver interface. This method is called internally as new image data is loaded into memory. Default response is to repaint the display with the new image data. See ImageObserver (p. 282) for more information.

```
public synchronized boolean inside(int x, int y);
```

Returns true if the specified point is located in the component's region. Beginning with Java 1.1, this method is deprecated. Use contains() instead.

```
public void invalidate();
```

Marks the component as having changed. The next call to validate() causes the component to be laid out again if it is a container. Note that this method, along with validate() and layout(), is most relevant to containers and does not affect repainting. See also repaint(), page 216.

```
public boolean isEnabled();
public boolean isShowing();
public boolean isValid();
```

These methods return basic information about the component. The isValid() method returns false if the component is a container that needs to be layed out. See validate(), page 218.

```
public boolean keyDown(Event evt, int key);
public boolean keyUp(Event evt, int key);
```

Event handlers for all keystroke events. Beginning in Java 1.1, these methods are deprecated, because they are supplanted by the new event handling model. See addKeyListener().

```
public void list();
public void list(PrintStream out);
public void list(PrintStream out, int indent);
```

Prints a string representation of this component. This can be useful for debugging. Output is sent to a print stream, if specified, and to standard output by default. The optional indent argument specifies number of spaces to indent.

```
public boolean lostFocus(Event evt, Object what);
```

Event handler called just before the component loses focus. This method was deprecated starting in Java 1.1, because they were supplanted by the new event handling model. See addFocusListener().

```
public boolean mouseDown(Event evt, int x, int y);
public boolean mouseDrag(Event evt, int x, int y);
public boolean mouseEnter(Event evt, int x, int y);
public boolean mouseExit(Event evt, int x, int y);
public boolean mouseMove(Event evt, int x, int y);
public boolean mouseUp(Event evt, int x, int y);
```

These six methods are all handlers for mouse events. Beginning in Java 1.1, these methods are deprecated, because they are supplanted by the new event-handling model. See addMouseListener() and addMouseMotionListener().

```
public void paint(Graphics g);
```

Called when the display needs to be updated either because the component is being displayed for the first time, or part of the component is newly visible. This is a commonly overridden method in application and applet code.

```
public void paintAll(Graphics g);
```

Paints the component and all subcomponents, if any.

```
public Dimension preferredSize();
```

Returns the preferred size of the component. This method is now deprecated. Use getPreferredSize() instead.

```
public boolean prepareImage(Image image,
    ImageObserver observer);
public boolean prepareImage(Image image,
    int width, int height, ImageObserver observer);
```

Used internally to start image loading. In application code, using Graphics. drawImage() is much easier. prepareImage() returns true if all image data is available now.

```
public void print(Graphics g);
```

Called by a net browser to print the page that shows the component. Default behavior is to call paint(). Application code can override this method to do special processing, if any, before calling paint().

```
public void printAll(Graphics g);
```

Calls print() for the component and all child components, if any.

```
public synchronized void removeNotify();
```

Used internally to request that the component destroy its peer. See addNotify().

```
public void removeComponentListener(ComponentListener cl);
public void removeFocusListener(FocusListener cl);
public void removeKeyListener(KeyListener cl);
public void removeMouseListener(MouseListener cl);
public void removeMouseMotionListener(
   MouseMotionListener cl);
```

These methods each remove an event handler. See the corresponding "add" methods for a description of these handlers.

```
public void repaint();
public void repaint(long tm);
```

Forces a repaint, resulting in calls to update() and paint(). The optional tm argument specifies the number of milliseconds before repainting.

```
public void requestFocus();
```

Requests that the focus move to this component. Focus enables the component to get keyboard events.

```
public synchronized void reshape(int x, int y,
   int width, int height);
public void resize(int width, int height);
public void resize(Dimension d);
```

These methods change the size or position (or both) of the component. Beginning with Java 1.1, these methods are deprecated. Use setBounds() and setSize() instead.

```
public synchronized void setBackground(Color c);
```

Sets background color for drawing.

```
public synchronized void setBounds(int x, int y, int width, int
   height);
public synchronized void setBounds(Rectangle r);
```

This is now the preferred method for setting the extent (size and position) of the component. This method replaces `reshape()`. You can specify individual coordinates or a rectangle.

```
public void setEnabled();
```

This method enables and disables the component: disabling a component causes it be grayed out and to stop responding to the user.

```
public synchronized void setFont(Font f);
public synchronized void setForeground(Color c);
```

These methods set foreground color and default font for drawing.

```
public void setLocation(int x, int y);
```

Moves the top-left corner of the component to the indicated location within its container.

```
public synchronized void setSize(Dimension d);
public synchronized void setSize(int width, int height);
```

This is now the preferred method for setting the size of the component. This method replaces `resize()`. You can specify individual coordinates or a `Dimension` object.

```
public synchronized void setVisible(boolean b);
```

This is now the preferred method for displaying or hiding the component. This method replaces show(). The method shows the component if b is true and hides it if b is false.

```
public synchronized void show();
public void show(boolean cond);
```

Displays the object, or hides the object if cond is specified and is false. Beginning with Java 1.1, these methods are deprecated. Use setVisible() instead.

```
public Dimension size();
```

Returns the height and width of the component's area as a `Dimension` object. Beginning with Java 1.1, this method is deprecated. Use getSize() instead.

```
public void transferFocus();
```

Moves focus to the next component, in which "next" is defined by the container. Typically, the container uses the order in which components were added. This is an appropriate response to the Tab key.

```
public void update(Graphics g);
```

Called to repaint the component's display. The default behavior is as follows: fill region with background color; set graphics object to component's foreground color; call `paint()`. This method is sometimes overridden to eliminate the background repainting. This is safe only if the program is written so that the background color is not used.

    public void **validate**();

Calls the `layout()` method to cause the component to be laid out (assuming it is a container). Then the method marks the component as valid (meaning correctly laid out). See also `invalidate()`, page 214.

Overridden Instance Methods

    public String **toString**();

Overrides the method definition in the `Object` class.

ComponentAdapter Class

Full Name   `java.awt.event.ComponentAdapter`

Extends   `Object`

Implements   `ComponentListener`

Description   Public class. A helper class that provides empty implementations of the methods defined in the `ComponentListener` interface. This class serves as a convenience by allowing you to extend it and to override only the listener response methods that you need, as opposed to implementing all of the methods defined in the interface. After deriving an event-handling class from this one, you need to register it as an event listener.

Constructors

    public **ComponentAdapter**();

Instance Methods

    public void **componentHidden**(ComponentEvent e);
    public void **componentMoved**(ComponentEvent e);
    public void **componentResized**(ComponentEvent e);
    public void **componentShown**(ComponentEvent e);

These methods are called in response to a component being hidden, moved, resized, or shown.

ComponentEvent Class

Full Name   `java.awt.event.ComponentEvent`

Extends   `AWTEvent->EventObject->Object`

Description   Public class. This class encapsulates the information associ-
               ated with a component event, which is whether a component
               has moved, resized, been shown, or been hidden. Component
               events are generated by component event sources (compo-
               nents) and handled by objects that implement the Component
               Listener interface. An instance of the ComponentEvent
               class is delivered to the component listener event response
               methods to aid in handling component events.

Constructors

```
public ComponentEvent(Component source, int id);
```

The source argument is the object with which the component event is associated, and id is an identifier that identifies the event.

Class Variables

```
public static final int COMPONENT_FIRST;
public static final int COMPONENT_HIDDEN;
public static final int COMPONENT_LAST;
public static final int COMPONENT_MOVED;
public static final int COMPONENT_RESIZED;
public static final int COMPONENT_SHOWN;
```

Class constants. These constants are flags used to indicate the type of component event.

Instance Methods

```
public Component getComponent();
```

This method is used to retrieve the component that generated the component
event.

Overridden Instance Methods

```
public String paramString()
```

This method generates a parameter string that identifies the component
event.

ComponentListener Interface

Full Name   java.awt.event.ComponentListener

Description   Public interface. This interface defines methods that respond
               to component events. Component events are generated when
               a component is resized, moved, shown, or hidden. To handle
               component events, you can implement the Component
               Listener interface, provide implementations of component
               event response methods, and then register the listener
               class with an event source.

Alternatively, you can extend the ComponentAdaptor class and override only the component event response methods in which you are interested. A ComponentListener event handler is attached to a com-ponent by calling the addComponentListener() method declared in the Component class (p. 210).

Interface Methods

```
public void componentHidden(ComponentEvent e);
public void componentMoved(ComponentEvent e);
public void componentResized(ComponentEvent e);
public void componentShown(ComponentEvent e);
```

These methods are called on a registered component listener in response to a component being resized, moved, shown, or hidden.

CompoundBorder Class

Full Name   javax.swing.border.CompoundBorder

Extends   AbstractBorder->Object

Description   Public class. This class implements a compound border that consists of two borders used in conjunction with each other; one of the borders is an inside border and the other is an outside border.

Constructors

```
public CompoundBorder();
public CompoundBorder(Border outsideBorder,
    Border insideBorder);
```

These constructors create compound borders; the second constructor accepts two borders that form the inside and outside of the compound border.

Instance Variables

```
protected Border insideBorder;
protected Border outsideBorder;
```

These variables store the two borders that comprise a compound border.

Instance Methods

```
public Border getInsideBorder()
public Border getOutsideBorder()
```

These methods retrieve the outside and inside borders of the compound border.

Overridden Instance Methods

```
public Insets getBorderInsets(Component c, Insets insets)
public Insets getBorderInsets(Component c)
```

These methods retrieve the insets for the border; the latter version acts upon the Insets object that is passed as an argument.

```
public boolean isBorderOpaque()
```

This method checks whether the border is opaque or transparent; opaque borders paint their own backgrounds, whereas transparent borders do not.

```
public void paintBorder(Component c, Graphics g,
    int x, int y, int width, int height)
```

This method paints the border for a component using the specified border x,y position and size.

Container Class

Full Name	java.awt.Container
Extends	Object
Description	Abstract, public class. Because this class is abstract, you cannot instantiate it directly, but you can use a number of its subclasses, including Frame, Dialog, and Applet. Objects created from a Container subclass have the capability to physically contain other components. Each such object, or container, has a layout manager assigned to it, which you can change by calling the setLayout() method. The importance of containers and layout managers is described in Chapter 5, starting on page 592.

Instance Methods

```
public Component add(Component comp);
public synchronized Component add(Component comp, int pos);
public synchronized Component add(String name,
    Component comp);
```

Adds a child component to the container. Default order of components is the order in which they're added, although you can specify a position. The BorderLayout class uses the position to identify a zone: EAST, WEST, NORTH, SOUTH, and CENTER (all of which are constants defined in the BorderLayout class). See Chapter 5, page 592, for the meaning of these zones.

```
public synchronized Component getComponent(int n) throws
    ArrayIndexOutOfBoundsException;
public synchronized Component[] getComponents();
```

These methods return one or more child components. The parameter *n* is a zero-based index into the container's list of components.

```
public LayoutManager getLayout();
```

Returns the layout manager object currently in use by this container.

```
public void paintComponents(Graphics g);
```

Paints all the components in the container. Internally, this is called automatically as needed.

```
public void printComponents(Graphics g);
```

Prints all the components in the container. Internally, this is called automatically when the container is printed.

```
public synchronized void remove(Component comp);
public synchronized void removeAll();
```

These methods remove one or more components.

```
public void setLayout(LayoutManager mgr);
```

Sets a new layout manager.

Overridden Instance Methods

```
public synchronized void addNotify();
public void deliverEvent(Event e);
public void list(PrintStream out, int indent);
public synchronized void removeNotify();
public synchronized void validate();
```

These methods override method definitions in Component. The locate() method, although defined in Component, is almost always used by containers. Given internal coordinates, it returns the component at that location. addNotify(), deliverEvent(), and removeNotify() are used internally.

CropImageFilter Class

Full Name	java.awt.image.CropImageFilter
Extends	ImageFilter
Description	Public class. Creates an image filter that can be used to produce a new image from an old one, in which the old image is cropped to a specified rectangle. The image filter is connected to an actual image with the help of the FilteredImage Source class.

The use of the image filter, producer, and consumer classes and interfaces is not obvious at first. See the description of the FilteredImageSource class

(p. 251) for an example that takes you through the process of creating a filtered image.

Constructors

```
public CropImageFilter(int x, int y, int w, int h);
```

Arguments determine the region to be cropped from the original image.

Overridden Instance Methods

```
public void setDimensions(int w, int h);
public void setPixels(int x, int y, int w, int h,
   ColorModel model,
   byte pixels[], int off, int scansize);
public void setPixels(int x, int y, int w, int h,
   ColorModel model, int pixels[], int off, int scansize);
public void setProperties(Hashtable props);
```

These methods override method definitions in the ImageFilter class.

Cursor Class

Java 2 API Reference

Full Name	java.awt.Cursor
Extends	Object
Description	Public class. This class represents the bitmap associated with the mouse cursor.

You can assign different cursors to different components within an applet or application. Following is an example of how to use the Cursor class to assign a hand cursor to a component named window:

```
window.setCursor(Cursor.getPredefinedCursor(Cursor.HAND_CURSOR));
```

The setCursor() method is defined in the Component class (page 210), and is therefore available in all components.

Constructors

```
public Cursor(int type);
protected Cursor(String name);
```

Creates a Cursor object based upon the specified cursor type or name.

Class Variables

```
public static final int CROSSHAIR_CURSOR;
public static final int CUSTOM_CURSOR;
public static final int DEFAULT_CURSOR;
public static final int E_RESIZE_CURSOR;
public static final int HAND_CURSOR;
```

```
public static final int MOVE_CURSOR;
public static final int N_RESIZE_CURSOR;
public static final int NE_RESIZE_CURSOR;
public static final int NW_RESIZE_CURSOR;
public static final int S_RESIZE_CURSOR;
public static final int SE_RESIZE_CURSOR;
public static final int SW_RESIZE_CURSOR;
public static final int TEXT_CURSOR;
public static final int W_RESIZE_CURSOR;
public static final int WAIT_CURSOR;
```

Class constants. These constants define different types of cursors.

Class Methods

```
public static Cursor getDefaultCursor();
```

Retrieves the default system cursor.

```
public static Cursor getPredefinedCursor(int type);
```

Retrieves a predefined cursor of the specified type.

```
public static Cursor getSystemCustomCursor(String name)
    throws AWTException;
```

Retrieves a custom system cursor by name.

Instance Methods

```
public String getName();
```

Retrieves the name of the current cursor.

```
public int getType();
```

Retrieves the type of the current cursor.

DatagramPacket Class

Full Name	java.net.DatagramPacket
Extends	Object
Description	Public final class. Creates a packet that can be sent or received over the network. A datagram consists of a simple series of bytes. This form of communication uses the User Datagram Protocol (UDP): there is no guarantee that packets will be received in the same order sent, and the protocol requires no acknowledgment of receipt.

This is the most unreliable form of network I/O, but it is also the fastest. After creating a packet, you send it by using a DataSocket object. See Socket (p. 450) and URL (p. 486) classes for more-reliable network I/O.

The following example sends a packet of data to network address *iaddr*:

```
try {
    DatagramSocket sock = new DatagramSocket();
    DatagramPacket pack = new DatagramPacket(
        buffer, n, iaddr, portnum);
    sock.send(pack);
} catch(Exception e) {System.out.println(e);}
```

Constructors

```
public DatagramPacket(byte ibuf[], int ilength);
```

Creates a data-packet structure to receive data. After creating the object, the DatagramSocket.receive() method is called to get the data.

```
public DatagramPacket(byte ibuf[], int ilength,
    InetAddress iaddr, int iport);
```

Creates a packet to be sent, along with its destination address and destination port. After creating the object, the DatagramSocket.send() method is called to send the data.

Instance Methods

```
public InetAddress getAddress();
public byte[] getData();
public int getLength();
public int getPort();
```

These methods return information that was specified in the constructor.

DatagramSocket Class

Full Name	java.net.DatagramSocket
Extends	Object
Description	Public class. Creates an interface around a communications port, enabling the sending and receiving of datagram packets. These packets are simple arrays of bytes; see Datagram Packet (p. 224) for more information. For higher-level, more reliable network I/O, see Socket (p. 450) and URL (p. 486) classes.

See DatagramPacket class (p. 224) for an example.

Constructors

```
public DatagramSocket() throws SocketException;
public DatagramSocket(int port) throws SocketException;
```

Creates a datagram socket around the specified local port. If a port is not specified, one is assigned.

Instance Methods

```
public void close();
```

Closes the socket and frees the port.

```
public int getLocalPort();
```

Returns the socket's port number.

```
public void receive(DatagramPacket p) throws IOException;
```

Receives a datagram packet. This method assumes that data has been sent.

```
public void send(DatagramPacket p) throws IOException;
```

Sends a datagram packet. The packet must specify an Internet address and a port number.

DataInput Interface

Full Name	`java.io.DataInput`
Description	Public interface. This interface declares methods implemented by `DataInputStream` and `RandomAccessFile`. For descriptions of the methods, see `DataInputStream`, page 227.

Interface Methods

```
public abstract boolean readBoolean() throws IOException,
    EOFException;
public abstract byte readByte() throws IOException,
    EOFException;
public abstract char readChar() throws IOException,
    EOFException;
public abstract double readDouble() throws IOException,
    EOFException;
public abstract float readFloat() throws IOException,
    EOFException;
public abstract void readFully(byte b[]) throws IOException,
    EOFException;
public abstract void readFully(byte b[], int off, int len)
    throws IOException, EOFException;
```

```
public abstract int readInt() throws IOException,
   EOFException;
public abstract String readLine() throws IOException;
public abstract long readLong() throws IOException,
   EOFException;
public abstract short readShort() throws IOException,
   EOFException;
public abstract int readUnsignedByte() throws IOException,
   EOFException;
public abstract int readUnsignedShort() throws IOException,
   EOFException;
public abstract String readUTF() throws IOException;
public abstract int skipBytes(int n) throws IOException,
   EOFException;
```

DataInputStream Class

Full Name   java.io.DataInputStream

Extends   FilterInputStream->InputStream->Object

Implements   DataInput

Description   Public class. This class, along with DataOutputStream, lets
                  you read and write Java data types and strings in a platform-
                  independent way. You can produce output from any Java pro-
                  gram using DataOutputStream, and any program using
                  DataInputStream is guaranteed to read the same data
                  (provided that they agree on which data types and strings
                  to look for). See FileInputStream (p. 248) for information
                  about how to hook the stream to a file.

DataInputStream can be used to read input from the keyboard in a console
application. After reading a line of input, you can parse it by using Integer.
parseInt(), Long.parseLong(), and other wrapper classes.

```
DataInputStream dis = new DataInputStream(System.in);
String s = "";
try {
    s = dis.readLine();
}catch(IOException e){;}
```

Constructors

```
public DataInputStream(InputStream in);
```

Creates a DataInputStream object from the specified input stream.

Class Methods

```
public final static String readUTF(DataInput in)
   throws IOException;
```

Reads a string in UTF-8 format from the specified stream. See readUTF( ) near the end of this topic.

Instance Methods

```
public final boolean readBoolean() throws IOException;
public final byte readByte() throws IOException;
public final char readChar() throws IOException;
public final double readDouble() throws IOException;
public final float readFloat() throws IOException;
```

Each of these methods reads an instance of a primitive data type.

```
public final void readFully(byte b[]) throws IOException,
   EOFException;
public final void readFully(byte b[], int off, int len)
   throws IOException, EOFException;
```

Reads enough bytes to fill the array, or reads len bytes if specified. In either case, this method causes the current thread to wait until all the requested data is read.

```
public final int readInt() throws IOException;
```

Reads an instance of an int.

```
public final String readLine() throws IOException;
```

Reads a character string up to the first newline, carriage return, newline/carriage-return pair, or end-of-input stream; this method returns null if all lines of text have been read. This behavior enables you to set up a loop that tests for null as the end-of-file indicator. The terminating characters, if any, are included in the string returned. This method can be used to read from the keyboard; see the example at beginning of this topic. However, for reading strings written by DataOutputStream, the use of readUTF() is recommended.

```
public final long readLong() throws IOException;
public final short readShort() throws IOException;
public final int readUnsignedByte() throws IOException;
public final int readUnsignedShort() throws IOException;
```

Each of these methods reads an instance of a primitive data type. Although unsigned byte and unsigned short are not Java data types, Java can read them correctly and return them in an int field, which has sufficient range to store the number read.

```
public final String readUTF() throws IOException;
```

Reads a string in the Unicode transformation format (UTF). This format reads the first two bytes as an unsigned short integer indicating the length of the string. The rest of the data consists of UTF-8 character encoding. The UTF-8 format, which is compatible with ASCII, is described in Table B-5 in Appendix B, "Useful Tables." See also `DataOutputStream.writeUTF()`, page 231

```
public final int skipBytes(int n) throws IOException;
```

Skip n bytes before the next read.

```
public final int read(byte b[]) throws IOException;
public final int read(byte b[], int off, int len) throws
IOException;
```

These methods override method definitions in the `InputStream` class.

DataOutput Interface

Full Name   `java.io.DataOutput`

Description   Public interface. This interface declares methods implemented by `DataOutputStream` and `RandomAccessFile`. For descriptions of the methods, see `DataOutputStream`, page 230.

Interface Methods

```
public abstract void write(byte b[]) throws IOException;
public abstract void write(byte b[], int off, int len)
   throws IOException;
public abstract void write(int b) throws IOException;
public abstract void writeBoolean(boolean v)
   throws IOException;
public abstract void writeByte(int v) throws IOException;
public abstract void writeBytes(String s)
   throws IOException;
public abstract void writeChar(int v) throws IOException;
public abstract void writeChars(String s)
   throws IOException;
public abstract void writeDouble(double v)
   throws IOException;
public abstract void writeFloat(float v) throws IOException;
public abstract void writeInt(int v) throws IOException;
public abstract void writeLong(long v) throws IOException;
public abstract void writeShort(int v) throws IOException;
public abstract void writeUTF(String str)
   throws IOException;
```

DataOutputStream Class

Full Name	`java.io.DataOutputStream`
Extends	`FilterOutputStream->OutputStream->Object`
Implements	`DataOutput`
Description	Public class. This class, along with `DataInputStream`, lets you read and write Java data types and strings in a platform-independent way. You can produce output from any Java program using `DataOutputStream`, and any program using `DataInputStream` is guaranteed to read the same data (provided that they agree on which data types and strings to look for). See `FileOutputStream` for information about how to hook the stream to a file.

The following example writes an integer to a file, STUFF.DAT. The try-catch block is required because the `FileOutputSteam()` constructor may throw an exception.

```
try {
   FileOutputStream out = new
         FileOutputStream("STUFF.DAT");
   DataOutputStream dataOut = new
         DataOutputStream(out);
   dataOut.writeInt(5);
} catch (IOException e) {System.out.println(e);}
```

Constructors

```
public DataOutputStream(OutputStream out);
```

Creates a `DataOutputStream` object from the specified output stream.

Instance Methods

```
public final void writeBoolean(boolean v)
   throws IOException;
public final void writeByte(int v) throws IOException;
```

These methods write an instance of a primitive data type.

```
public final void writeBytes(String s) throws IOException;
```

Writes a string to the output stream, converting each character to a byte by discarding the eight high bits. Note that `DataInput-Stream.readLine()` will not read such a string correctly unless you terminate it with a newline or carriage return. See also `writeUTF()`, page 231.

```
public final void writeChar(int v) throws IOException;
public final void writeChars(String s) throws IOException;
```

```
public final void writeDouble(double v) throws IOException;
public final void writeFloat(float v) throws IOException;
public final void writeInt(int v) throws IOException;
public final void writeLong(long v) throws IOException;
public final void writeShort(int v) throws IOException;
```

Each of these methods writes the appropriate primitive data type.

```
public final void writeUTF(String str) throws IOException;
```

Writes a string in the Unicode transformation format (UTF). This format writes the first two bytes as an unsigned short integer indicating the length of the string. The rest of the data consists of UTF-8 character encoding. The UTF-8 format, which is compatible with ASCII, is described in Table B-5 in Appendix B, "Useful Tables." See also `DataInput-Stream.readUTF()`, page 228.

Overridden Instance Methods

```
public void flush() throws IOException;
public final int size();
public void write(byte b[], int off, int len)
    throws IOException;
public void write(int b) throws IOException;
```

These methods override method definitions in the `OutputStream` class.

Date Class

Full Name	`java.util.Date`
Extends	`Object`
Description	Public class. A `Date` object combines complete year, day, and time of day information down to milliseconds. The class has many uses: you can use the `Date` default constructor as a seed value for the `Random` class, you can measure durations between events, and you can get the day of the week for arbitrary dates.

The following example prints the current day of the month. See the `Random` (p. 427) class for another example of how `Date` is used.

```
Date dt = new Date(); // Get current date and time.
System.out.println("Day of the month is " + dt.getDate());
```

Constructors

```
public Date();
```

Default constructor. Returns date object representing now (the moment the object was created).

```
public Date(int year, int month, int date);
public Date(int year, int month, int date, int hrs,
    int min);
public Date(int year, int month, int date, int hrs,
    int min, int sec);
```

These constructors take input in the following format: year = year minus 1900, month = number between 0 and 11, date = number between 1 and 31, hrs = number between 0 and 23, and minutes and seconds = number between 0 and 59.

```
public Date(long date);
```

This constructor uses an argument that represents the number of milliseconds since January 1, 1970, Greenwich Mean Time (GMT).

```
public Date(String s);
```

This constructor takes a string argument in the same format as the parse() method.

Class Methods

```
public static long parse(String s);
```

Returns a time value (number of milliseconds since January 1, 1970) after parsing a string; most standard syntaxes are accepted. The following format is always accepted: "Wed, 17 July 1995 13:30:00 GMT." American time zone abbreviations (such as PDT) are accepted, but time zone specification as "GMT+0900" (9 hours west of Greenwich) are recommended.

```
public static long UTC(int year, int month, int date, int hrs,
    int min, int sec);
```

Returns a time value (number of milliseconds since January 1, 1970) from the inputs. See Date constructors for interpretation of the numbers.

Instance Methods

```
public boolean after(Date when);
public boolean before(Date when);
```

These methods return true or false after comparing the current object to another Date object. For example, after() returns true if the current object is after the Date argument specified.

```
public int getDate();
public int getDay();
public int getHours();
public int getMinutes();
```

```
public int getMonth();
public int getSeconds();
```

All these methods return the specified component of the date, where month ranges between 0 and 11, date ranges between 1 and 31, hours range between 0 and 23, and minutes and seconds range between 0 and 59. getDay() returns a number between 0 and 6 representing the day of the week; 0 is Sunday.

```
public long getTime();
```

Returns the number of milliseconds since January 1, 1970, GMT.

```
public int getTimezoneOffset();
```

Returns the time zone offset, in minutes, that must be added to GMT to get the local time. The offset includes correction for daylight savings time.

```
public int getYear();
```

Returns the current year minus 1900.

```
public void setDate(int date);
public void setHours(int hours);
public void setMinutes(int minutes);
public void setMonth(int month);
public void setSeconds(int seconds);
public void setTime(long time);
public void setYear(int year);
```

These seven "set" methods all set a component of the date/time value. See the corresponding "get" method for the format.

```
public String toGMTString();
```

Returns a string representation of the date/time value using Internet GMT conventions. Sample output: "17 July 13:30:00 GMT."

```
public String toLocaleString();
```

Returns a string representation of the date/time value using local conventions. Exact format of this string is implementation-dependent.

Overridden Instance Methods

```
public boolean equals(Object obj);
public int hashCode();
public String toString();
```

These methods override method definitions in the Object class. The toString() method returns a string representation in the following standard format: "Sat Aug 12 04:30:00 PDT 1995."

Java 2 API Reference

Dialog Class

Full Name	`java.awt.Dialog`
Extends	`Window->Container->Component->Object`
Description	Public class. Creates a dialog box that may be modal. When a modal dialog box is displayed, the user cannot interact with any other parts of the application until the dialog box is closed. However, the modality of a dialog box does not affect the flow of control; a `Dialog` constructor, for example, returns immediately rather than wait for the dialog box to close. A dialog box may optionally have a title and be resizable. Dialog boxes generate all standard keyboard and mouse events as well as window events. Call `setVisible()` to display the dialog box. This method is inherited from the `Component` class (p. 210).

Constructors

```
public Dialog(Frame parent, boolean modal);
public Dialog(Frame parent, String title, boolean modal);
```

The dialog box must have a parent frame. The modal argument, if true, specifies that the dialog box is modal.

Instance Methods

```
public String getTitle();
public boolean isModal();
public boolean isResizable
public void setResizable(boolean resizable);
public void setTitle(String title);
```

These five methods get and set the dialog box attributes: title bar string, modality (true means that the dialog box is modal), and resizable condition (true means that the user can resize the dialog).

Dictionary Class

Full Name	`java.util.Dictionary`
Extends	`Object`
Description	Abstract public class; only subclasses can be instantiated. The role of this class in the API is that it defines some of the methods in the `Hashtable` class, although you can also inherit from it to create your own hashtable-like classes. See `Hashtable` for a description of methods.

Constructors

```
public Dictionary();
```

Default constructor. You cannot call this constructor, because `Dictionary` is an abstract class.

Instance Methods

```
abstract Enumeration elements();
public abstract Object get(Object key);
public abstract boolean isEmpty();
public abstract Enumeration keys();
public abstract Object put(Object key, Object value)
  throws NullPointerException;
public abstract Object remove(Object key);
public abstract int size();
```

For descriptions of these methods, see `Hashtable` class, page 274.

Dimension Class

Full Name	`java.awt.Dimension`
Extends	`Object`
Description	Public class. Creates a simple object containing height and width measurements.

A dimension object is used to store simple height and weight measurements. For example:

```
Dimension d;
d.width = 200;
d.height = 200;
```

Constructors

```
public Dimension();
public Dimension(Dimension d);
public Dimension(int width, int height);
```

The object can optionally be initialized in the constructor.

Instance Variables

```
public int height;
public int width;
```

Public instance variables. See earlier example for use.

Overridden Instance Methods

```
protected String toString();
```

Overrides method definition in the `Object` class.

DirectColorModel Class

Full Name   java.awt.image.DirectColorModel

Extends   ColorModel->Object

Description   Public class. Specifies a color model by specifying which bits in the pixel correspond to red, green, and blue values. This is useful for translating from color models that use RGB values but map them to different bit positions than the standard model. In general, there is never any need to use this class unless you're processing image data that does not use the default RGB model.

Constructors

```
public DirectColorModel(int bits, int rmask, int gmask,
   int bmask);
public DirectColorModel(int bits, int rmask, int gmask,
   int bmask, int amask);
```

The arguments specify number of bits per pixel; a bit mask for each of the colors red, green, and blue; and an optional mask for the alpha value. (See ColorModel, page 209, for information on the alpha value.) Each bit mask indicates which bits in each pixel value correspond to the given color.

Instance Methods

```
public final int getAlphaMask();
public final int getBlueMask();
public final int getGreenMask();
public final int getRedMask();
```

These methods return the bit masks assigned for the alpha and for each color.

Overridden Instance Methods

```
public final int getAlpha(int pixel);
public final int getBlue(int pixel);
public final int getGreen(int pixel);
public final int getRed(int pixel);
public final int getRGB(int pixel);
```

These methods override method definitions in the ColorModel class.

Double Class

Full Name   java.lang.Double

Extends   Number->Object

Description   Public final class. Serves as the wrapper class for the double primitive type. This class provides methods for converting between string, object, and numeric data. It also is useful for passing a double value by reference.

The following example converts a digit string to type double:

```
double d = (new Double(digitString)).doubleValue();
```

Constructors

```
public Double(double value);
public Double(String s) throws NumberFormatException;
```

The last constructor initializes from a digit string.

Class Variables

```
public final static double MAX_VALUE;
public final static double MIN_VALUE;
public final static double NaN;
public final static double NEGATIVE_INFINITY;
public final static double POSITIVE_INFINITY;
```

Constants. See the Glossary of Java Terminology and Concepts for meaning of the last three terms.

Class Methods

```
public static long doubleToLongBits(double value);
public static boolean isInfinite(double v);
public static boolean isNaN(double v);
public static double longBitsToDouble(long bits);
public static String toString(double d);
public static Double valueOf(String s);
```

The doubleToLongBits() and longBitsToDouble() class methods convert between a long and a double without changing the actual bit values. See below for a description of isNaN().

Instance Methods

```
public boolean isInfinite();
public boolean isNaN();
```

These methods return true if the current value is, respectively, positive or negative infinity, or "not a number." This is the only reliable way to test for an NaN (Not a Number) value, because NaN will always return false when compared to itself.

Overridden Instance Methods

```
public double doubleValue();
public float floatValue();
```

```
public int intValue();
public long longValue();
```

These methods return the double, float, int, or long equivalent of the value stored in the current object. The methods round as necessary, for there may be loss of precision.

```
public boolean equals(Object obj);
public int hashCode();
public String toString();
```

These methods override method definitions in the Object class.

EmptyBorder Class

Full Name   javax.swing.border.EmptyBorder

Extends   AbstractBorder->Object

Description   Public class. This class implements an empty border that takes up space but isn't visible. The purpose of this class is to create empty space around a component. Setting an empty border with margins (insets) provides a cushion of space around the component, no matter how it is handled by the container's layout manager. A border can be added to a component by calling the setBorder() method of the JComponent class (p. 300).

The following example sets a raised etched border for a label component named label:

```
label.setBorder(new EmptyBorder(10, 10, 10, 10));
```

Constructors

```
public EmptyBorder(int top, int left, int bottom,
    int right);
public EmptyBorder(Insets borderInsets);
```

These constructors create an EmptyBorder object by specifying the insets. (The first version specifies the same arguments you would pass to an Insets constructor.)

Instance Variables

```
protected int bottom;
protected int left;
protected int right;
protected int top;
```

These variables store the insets (margins) for each direction (in pixels).

Instance Methods

```
public Insets getBorderInsets();
```

Returns the four margins as an `Insets` object.

Overridden Instance Methods

```
public Insets getBorderInsets(Component c);
public Insets getBorderInsets(Component c, Insets insets);
```

These methods return the insets for the border; the second version first modifies the current insets by assigning the `insets` argument.

```
public boolean isBorderOpaque();
```

This method checks whether the border is opaque or transparent; opaque borders paint their own backgrounds, whereas transparent borders do not.

```
public void paintBorder(Component c, Graphics g,
   int x, int y, int width, int height);
```

Because the border is empty in this case, the `paintBorder()` method does nothing.

Enumeration Interface

Full Name	`java.util.Enumeration`
Description	Public interface. An object whose class implements this interface can be used to loop through a simple list of elements. This usually involves a `while` or `for` loop. A number of classes, such as `Vector` and `Hashtable`, return an enumeration as one way of providing access to child elements. Note that you can go through an enumeration only once; you cannot reset. (You can store the results of the enumeration in a vector or other structure as you go through it.)

The following example assumes you've been passed a string enumeration, strEnum. The example prints all the strings in the enumeration.

```
while (strEnum.hasMoreElements()) {
    String s = (String) strEnum.nextElement();
    System.out.println(s);
}
```

Interface Methods

```
public abstract boolean hasMoreElements();
```

Returns true if there are more elements left in the enumeration.

```
public abstract Object nextElement()
   throws NoSuchElementException;
```

Gets the next element and advances one position in the list. The object returned usually needs to be cast to a particular type — such as String in the example.

EtchedBorder Class

Full Name	javax.swing.border.EtchedBorder
Extends	AbstractBorder->Object
Description	Public class. This class implements an etched border. If you don't specify highlight/shadow colors when creating the border, it will derive the colors from the background color of the component that it borders. A border can be added to a component by calling the setBorder() method of the JComponent class (p. 300).

The following example sets a raised etched border for a label component named label:

```
label.setBorder(new EtchedBorder(EtchedBorder.RAISED));
```

Constructors

```
public EtchedBorder();
public EtchedBorder(int etchType);
public EtchedBorder(Color highlight, Color shadow)
public EtchedBorder(int etchType, Color highlight,
   Color shadow);
```

These constructors create bevel borders with varying degrees of detail in terms of the type of etched border and the colors used to shade the borders.

Class Variables

```
public static final int LOWERED;
public static final int RAISED;
```

Class constants. These constants specify the two different styles of etched border.

Instance Variables

```
protected int etchType;
protected Color highlight;
protected Color shadow;
```

These variables store the various pieces of information associated with an etched border, including the type of the border as well as the highlight and shadow colors.

Instance Methods

```
public int getEtchType();
public Color getHighlightColor(Component c);
public Color getHighlightColor();
public Color getShadowColor(Component c);
public Color getShadowColor();
```

These methods retrieve various pieces of information that describe the etched border.

Overridden Instance Methods

```
public Insets getBorderInsets(Component c);
public Insets getBorderInsets(Component c, Insets insets);
```

These methods return the insets for the border; the second version first modifies the current insets by assigning the insets argument.

```
public boolean isBorderOpaque();
```

This method checks whether the border is opaque or transparent; opaque borders paint their own backgrounds, whereas transparent borders do not.

```
public void paintBorder(Component c, Graphics g,
    int x, int y, int width, int height);
```

This method paints the border for a component using the specified border x, y position and size.

Event Class

Full Name java.awt.Event

Extends   Object

Description   Public class. An Event object contains detailed information on an event occurring at runtime, usually in response to a user action. When an event is generated, the Event object is passed from one component to the next until an event handler handles the event and returns true. The Event class also defines a number of useful constants that represent event types and key codes.

Note that the methods that use this class for handling events are deprecated beginning with Java 1.1, which means that such code is now considered non-standard. You should handle events by using the new event-handling model described in Chapter 4 of Part II.

Constructors

```
public Event(Object target, long when, int id,
  int x, int y, int key, int modifiers, Object arg);
public Event(Object target, long when, int id,
  int x, int y, int key, int modifers);
public Event(Object target, int id, Object arg);
```

All the arguments correspond to instance variables, described next.

Instance Variables

```
public Object arg;
```

An argument that contains additional information relevant to the event. This corresponds to the second argument passed to an action() event handler.

```
public int clickCount;
```

Number of consecutive mouse clicks (0 if event is not a mouse event).

```
public Event evt;
```

A reference to the next event in a linked list of events.

```
public int id;
```

id indicates type of event. Possible values are listed in the event-type constants. (See "Class Variables" in this topic.)

```
public int key;
```

The key that was pressed, if applicable. Special keys are represented as keycode constants. Alphanumeric keys are represented as their standard Unicode character values.

```
public int modifiers;
```

State of the modifier keys: these are the keys with "MASK" in their keycode name. The modifier states are combined, using bitwise OR (|), to produce a single integer field.

```
public Object target;
```

A reference to the object that generated the event (that is, where the event originated).

```
public long when;
```

Time stamp giving the time of the event.

```
public int x;
public int y;
```

These two fields give x,y coordinates of current position. For mouse events, this is the most recent mouse position.

Class Variables

```
public final static int ACTION_EVENT;
public final static int GOT_FOCUS, LOST_FOCUS;
public final static int KEY_ACTION;
public final static int KEY_ACTION_RELEASE;
public final static int KEY_PRESS, KEY_RELEASE;
public final static int LIST_DESELECT, LIST_SELECT;
public final static int LOAD_FILE;
public final static int MOUSE_DOWN, MOUSE_DRAG;
public final static int MOUSE_ENTER, MOUSE_EXIT;
public final static int MOUSE_MOVE, MOUSE_UP;
public final static int SAVE_FILE;
public final static int SCROLL_ABSOLUTE;
public final static int SCROLL_LINE_DOWN, SCROLL_LINE_UP;
public final static int SCROLL_PAGE_DOWN;
public final static int SCROLL_PAGE_UP;
public final static int WINDOW_DESTROY;
public final static int WINDOW_EXPOSE;
public final static int WINDOW_ICONIFY;
public final static int WINDOW_DEICONIFY;
public final static int WINDOW_MOVED;
```

These constants specify event IDs. Note that LOAD_FILE and SAVE_FILE are not generated in the current version of Java.

```
public final static int F1, F2, F3, F4, F5, F6, F7, F8, F9, F10,
    F11, F12;
```

Constants for function keys.

```
public final static int HOME, END;
public final static int LEFT, RIGHT;
public final static int PGDN, PGUP;
public final static int UP, DOWN;
```

Constants for other special keys.

```
public final static int ALT_MASK, CTRL_MASK;
public final static int SHIFT_MASK, META_MASK;
```

Modifier key codes. These are combined, using bitwise OR (|), to produce the modifier state. Use binary AND (&) to extract them. For mouse events, ALT_MASK indicates middle mouse button down, and META_MASK indicates right mouse button down.

Java 2 API Reference

Instance Methods

```
public boolean controlDown();
public boolean metaDown();
public boolean shiftDown();
```

These methods return the states of some of the modifier keys as simple Boolean conditions.

```
public void translate(int dx, int dy);
```

Translates the current coordinates of the event by adding dx and dy to x and y, respectively.

Overridden Instance Methods

```
public String toString();
```

Overrides the method definition in the Object class.

File Class

Full Name	java.io.File
Extends	Object
Description	Public class. A File object represents a node in the file system, either a file or a directory. You can use it to get attributes or children or to perform directory-service operations. To get file contents, create a stream object such as FileInput Stream. See Part II, Chapter 8, "Common Programming Tasks," for examples.
	Note that all Java file methods assume the use of the UNIX file separator ("/") in pathnames, regardless of platform. This convention may be irksome to non-UNIX programmers, but it is necessary for platform independence.

The following example gets the path of the current directory:

```
File f = new File(".");
String thePath = f.getAbsolutePath();
```

Constructors

```
public File(File dir, String name);
public File(String path);
public File(String path, String name);
```

A file or directory must be specified. In the first constructor, dir is another File object that happens to be a directory, and name specifies a file name within that directory. The second constructor takes a complete path/filename.

Class Methods

```
public final static String pathSeparator;
public final static char pathSeparatorChar;
public final static String separator;
public final static char separatorChar;
```

These methods return the separator used within pathnames and the drive-letter separator, respectively, used on the local system. In DOS and Windows, these separators are "\" and ":".

Instance Methods

```
public boolean canRead();
public boolean canWrite();
```

These methods return read/write permissions as true or false.

```
public boolean delete();
```

Attempts to delete the file and returns true if successful. If the File object refers to a directory, this method never succeeds.

```
public boolean exists();
```

Returns true if the file or directory specified by this object exists. A File object can be valid even if the filename referred to does not yet correspond to a disk file or directory. To create a new file, write to it; to create a new directory, use mkdir().

```
public String getAbsolutePath();
public String getName();
public String getParent();
public String getPath();
```

These methods return information about the file name. get-AbsolutePath() returns an absolute path name, even if the file object was constructed from a relative pathname. getName() returns a name without a path. getParent() returns null if the file object is the root directory.

```
public boolean isAbsolute();
public boolean isDirectory();
public boolean isFile();
```

Returns true if the specified condition is met. isAbsolute() returns false if the file object was constructed from a relative path. The File object may represent either a file or a directory.

```
public long lastModified();
```

Returns time of modification. See Date class (p. 231) for interpreting a long as a date.

```
public long length();
```

Returns length in number of bytes.

```
public String[] list();
public String[] list(FilenameFilter filter);
```

Returns an array of file names in the directory (assuming that the file object represents a directory). If filter is specified, only names not rejected by the filter are returned.

```
public boolean mkdir();
```

Uses the name contained in this file object to create a new directory. Thus, if the current File object contains the name "MyDir," then /MyDir is created as a new directory (under the parent directory specified in the object's path). Returns true if directory creation was successful.

```
public boolean mkdirs();
```

Does the same thing as mkdir() except that all intermediate directories that are new are also created. For example, if the full pathname is "/my/brandnew/folder," then potentially three new directories may be created. If /my already exists, then as many as two directories may be created.

```
public boolean renameTo(File dest);
```

Renames the file represented by this object. The new name is the name specified in dest. Returns true if successful.

Overridden Instance Methods

```
public boolean equals(Object obj);
public int hashCode();
public String toString();
```

These methods override method definitions in the Object class.

FileDescriptor Class

Full Name   java.io.FileDescriptor

Extends   Object

Description   Public final class. Represents an internally used handle for an open file or socket. Java applications and applet code should generally avoid using this class. Instead, use the File class to get general file and directory information, and use input and output streams for reading and writing to files. You can get an object of this type by calling getFD() through a FileInputStream or FileOutputStream object.

Constructors

```
public FileDescriptor();
```

Default constructor. Used internally. Java applications and applets should never call this constructor.

Class Variables

```
public final static FileDescriptor err;
public final static FileDescriptor in;
public final static FileDescriptor out;
```

Class variables (constants). These constants provide file descriptors for standard error, input, and output devices. As file descriptors, they can be used to create FileInputStream and FileOutputStream objects. However, it is generally easier to use System.err, System.in, and System.out.

Instance Methods

```
public boolean valid();
```

Returns true if the file descriptor is valid.

FileDialog Class

Full Name	java.awt.FileDialog
Extends	Dialog->Window->Container->Component->Object
Description	Public class. This class, a subclass of the Dialog class, adds the built-in functionality of a file-select dialog box. Generally, a FileDialog object does not need any additional components because its built-in capabilities are sufficient. As always, you display the dialog box by calling its setVisible() method. This method is inherited from the Component class (p. 210).

Constructors

```
public FileDialog(Frame parent, String title);
public FileDialog(Frame parent, String title, int mode);
```

A parent frame must be specified. The constructor always creates a modal dialog box: the mode in this case is either LOAD or SAVE, indicating either "Open File" or "Save As" dialog box. The default is LOAD.

Class Variables

```
public final static int LOAD;
public final static int SAVE;
```

These constants are the two possible values for the mode argument.

Instance Methods

```
public String getDirectory();
public String getFile();
public FilenameFilter getFilenameFilter();
public int getMode();
```

These methods get the current file directory path, filename, filename filter, and mode, respectively. Filename filter is described under setFilename Filter(), below. The mode is LOAD or SAVE.

```
public void setDirectory(String dir);
public void setFile(String file);
```

These methods set the file directory path and file name, respectively.

```
public void setFilenameFilter(FilenameFilter filter);
```

Sets the filename filter by specifying an object whose class implements the FilenameFilter interface. No such classes are provided in the API, but you can write your own. The filter determines which file names are displayed. (By default, all files in the directory path are displayed.) See FilenameFilter interface, page 249.

FileInputStream Class

Full Name   java.io.FileInputStream

Extends   InputStream->Object

Description   Public class. Creates a low-level input stream from a file. For easy file reading, construct a DataInputStream object from the FileInputStream object and then use DataInput Stream methods. See following example. Creating a FileInputStream object, if successful, automatically opens the file for reading.

This example gets a DataInputStream object for file STUFF.DAT. Note that the FileInputStream() constructor may throw an exception, if, for example, the file cannot be found. For this reason, the code must have a try-catch block.

```
try {
  FileInputStream fis = new FileInputStream("STUFF.DAT");
  DataInputStream dis = new DataInputStream(fis);
} catch(IOException e) {System.out.println(e);}
```

Constructors

```
public FileInputStream(File file)
  throws FileNotFoundException, IOException;
public FileInputStream(FileDescriptor fdObj);
```

```
public FileInputStream(String name)
   throws FileNotFoundException, IOException;
```

The third constructor is probably the most commonly used of these constructors. When specifying a path, remember to use the UNIX file separator ("/").

Instance Methods

```
public final FileDescriptor getFD() throws IOException;
```

Returns the FileDescriptor for this file.

Overridden Instance Methods

```
public int available() throws IOException;
public void close() throws IOException;
public int read() throws IOException;
public int read(byte b[]) throws IOException;
public int read(byte b[], int off, int len)
   throws IOException;
public long skip(long n) throws IOException;
```

These methods override method definitions in the InputStream class. See
InputStream (p. 286) for details.

```
protected void finalize() throws IOException;
```

Overrides method definition in the Object class. Calls the close() method.

FilenameFilter Interface

Full Name	java.io.FilenameFilter
Description	Public interface. Any object can implement this interface to serve as a filename filter; the filter determines which files to include in a display or a list. An example of a possible response is to include only those files with a .doc suffix.
	The API does not currently provide any filename filters, but you can write them yourself. The FileDialog class and the File.list() method use this interface.

Interface Methods

```
public abstract boolean accept(File dir, String name);
```

Returns true if the named file should be accepted (that is, displayed or listed).
This method is called once for each file or subdirectory. You can use the File
class to get the attributes of the file before deciding whether to accept it.
Remember to use UNIX filename conventions.

FileOutputStream Class

Full Name   java.io.FileOutputStream

Extends   OutputStream->Object

Description   Public class. Creates a low-level output stream to a file. For
               easy writing to a file, construct a DataOutputStream object
               from the FileOutputStream object and then use Data
               OutputStream methods. See the following example. Creating
               a FileOutputStream object, if successful, automatically
               opens the file for writing.

This example gets a DataOutputStream object for a file STUFF.DAT:

```
FileOutputStream fos = new FileOutputStream("STUFF.DAT");
DataOutputStream dos = new DataOutputStream(fos);
```

Alternatively, you can convert a FileOutputStream object into a PrintStream
object:

```
PrintStream ps = new PrintStream(new
    FileOutputStream("MY.TXT"));
```

Note that the FileOutputStream() constructor can throw an exception, so
you must add exception handling. See FileInputStream class, page 248.

Constructors

```
public FileOutputStream(File file) throws IOException;
public FileOutputStream(FileDescriptor fdObj);
public FileOutputStream(String name) throws IOException;
```

When specifying a path, remember to use the UNIX file separator ("/"). You
can use the third constructor, which takes a String argument, to specify a
path name directly. You can also build a stream around an existing File
object or a file descriptor.

Instance Methods

```
public final FileDescriptor getFD() throws IOException;
```

Returns the FileDescriptor for this file.

Overridden Instance Methods

```
public void close() throws IOException;
public void write(byte b[]) throws IOException;
public void write(byte b[], int off, int len)
    throws IOException;
public void write(int b) throws IOException;
```

These methods override method definitions in the OutputStream class.

```
protected void finalize() throws IOException;
```

Overrides the method definition in the Object class. Calls the close() method.

FilteredImageSource Class

Full Name	java.awt.image.FilteredImageSource
Extends	Object
Implements	ImageProducer
Description	Public class. Creates a new image source from an existing source by passing it through a filter. You can use the result- ing image source (or image producer) to create a new Image object. A FilteredImageSource constructor takes two inputs: an existing source and a filter. The result is a new image source that can used to create images. The Filtered ImageSource is a connector that takes in pixel data at one end (through the filter, an image consumer) and outputs pixel data at the other end. See the example for clarification.

The following figure illustrates the FilteredImageSource mechanism; the completed filter is both an image consumer and an image producer (or source).

The following code shows how this example is implemented. The first step is to create the filter itself to specify how much to crop:

```
CropImageFilter cropper = new CropImageFilter(20, 20,
    60, 60);
```

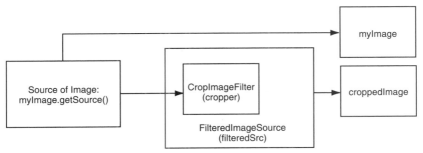

Using FilteredImageSource to crop an image

Next, the `FilteredImageSource` class is used to create a new image producer. This object uses the same source that the image `myImage` does, but it passes the data through the filter:

```
FilteredImageSource filteredSrc = new FilteredImagesource(
    myImage.getSource(),  // Use myImage's producer
    cropper );            // Crop by 20,20,60,60
```

The new variable, `filteredSrc`, is a bona fide image producer. This means that it can supply data to an image. The last line of code specifies `filteredSrc` as the new source of data for an image. The result is that `croppedImage` displays the same picture that `myImage` does, except that it is cropped.

```
Image croppedImage = createImage(filteredSrc);
```

Constructors

```
public FilteredImageSource(ImageProducer orig,
    ImageFilter imgf);
```

Creates an image producer from another image producer and a filter.

Overridden Instance Methods

```
public void addConsumer(ImageConsumer ic);
public boolean isConsumer(ImageConsumer ic);
public void removeConsumer(ImageConsumer ic);
public void requestTopDownLeftRightResend(ImageConsumer ic);
public void startProduction(ImageConsumer ic);
```

These methods implement the `ImageProducer` methods. See `ImageProducer` interface, page 283.

FilterInputStream Class

Full Name	java.io.FilterInputStream
Extends	InputStream->Object
Description	Public class. This class cannot be instantiated directly but is important as the superclass to all filtered-input classes: `BufferedInputStream`, `DataInputStream`, `LineNumberInputStream`, and `PushbackInputStream`. All these classes maintain an underlying input stream as an instance field and perform a filtering operation on the input. You can also write a filter class by subclassing `FilterInputStream` and overriding one or more methods.

Protected Instance Variables

```
protected InputStream in;
```

Instance variable referring to the underlying input stream. Because it is protected, it cannot be used outside the package, but it can be referred to in subclasses of `FilterInputStream`.

Overridden Instance Methods

```
public int available() throws IOException;
public void close() throws IOException;
public void mark(int readlimit);
public boolean markSupported();
public int read() throws IOException;
public int read(byte b[]) throws IOException;
public int read(byte b[], int off, int len)
   throws IOException;
public void reset() throws IOException;
public long skip(long n) throws IOException;
```

These methods override method definitions in the `InputStream` class.

FilterOutputStream Class

Full Name	`java.io.FilterOutputStream`
Extends	`OutputStream->Object`
Description	Public class. This class should not be instantiated directly but is important as the superclass to filtered-output classes: `BufferedOutputStream`, `DataOutputStream`, and `Print Stream`. All these classes maintain an underlying output stream as an instance field and perform a filtering operation before writing the output. You can also write a filter class by subclassing `FilterOutputStream` and overriding one or more methods.

Constructor

```
public FilterOutputStream(OutputStream out);
```

Instead of creating an instance of `FilterOutputStream` directly, you should use a subclass.

Protected Instance Variables

```
protected OutputStream out;
```

Instance variable referring to the underlying output stream. Because it is protected, it cannot be used outside the package, but it can be referred to in subclasses of `FilterOutputStream`.

Instance Methods

```
public void close() throws IOException;
public void flush() throws IOException;
public void write(byte b[]) throws IOException;
public void write(byte b[], int off, int len)
   throws IOException;
public void write(int b) throws IOException;
```

These methods override method definitions in the OutputStream class.

Float Class

Full Name	java.lang.Float
Extends	Number->Object
Description	Public final class. Serves as the wrapper class for the float primitive type. This class provides methods for converting between string, object, and numeric data. It also is useful for passing a float value by reference.

The following example converts a digit string to type float:

```
float flt = (new Float(digitString)).floatValue();
```

Constructors

```
public Float(float value);
public Float(double value);
public Float(String s);
```

The last constructor initializes from a string containing a floating-point expression.

Class Variables

```
public final static double MAX_VALUE;
public final static double MIN_VALUE;
public final static double NaN;
public final static double NEGATIVE_INFINITY;
public final static double POSITIVE_INFINITY;
```

See the "Glossary of Java Terminology and Concepts," for meaning of the last three terms.

Class Methods

```
public static long floatToIntBits(float value);
public static double intBitsToFloat(int bits);
public static boolean isInfinite(float v);
public static boolean isNaN(float v);
```

```
public static String toString(float d);
public static Double valueOf(String s);
```

The floatToIntBits() and intBitsToFloat() methods convert between an int and a float without changing the actual bit values. See the following description for isNaN().

Instance Methods

```
public boolean isInfinite();
public boolean isNaN();
```

These methods return true if the current value is, respectively, positive or negative infinity and "not a number." This is the only reliable way to test for a NaN value, because NaN will always return false when compared to itself.

Overridden Instance Methods

```
public double doubleValue();
public float floatValue();
public int intValue();
public long longValue();
```

These methods return the double, float, int, or long equivalent of the value stored in the current object. The methods round as necessary, for there may be loss of precision.

```
public boolean equals(Object obj);
public int hashCode();
public String toString();
```

These methods override method definitions in the Object class.

FlowLayout Class

Full Name	java.awt.FlowLayout
Extends	Object
Implements	LayoutManager
Description	Public class. Creates layout manager objects that lay out components from left to right, starting a new row when the right edge is reached. The behavior of these layout managers is described in Part II, Chapter 5, page 592.

The following example sets the current container to use an instance of FlowLayout with center alignment:

```
setLayout(new FlowLayout(FlowLayout.CENTER));
```

Constructors

```
public FlowLayout();
public FlowLayout(int align);
public FlowLayout(int align, int hgap, int vgap);
```

Optional arguments specify alignment and margins around components.

Class Variables

```
public final static int CENTER;
public final static int LEFT;
public final static int RIGHT;
```

These three constants are the possible values for alignment, which affects placement of components within each row.

Instance Methods

```
public void addLayoutComponent(String name, Component comp);
public void layoutContainer(Container target);
public Dimension minimumLayoutSize(Container target);
public Dimension preferredLayoutSize(Container target);
public void removeLayoutComponent(Component comp);
```

These five methods implement the LayoutManager interface; none of these methods is normally called by applications.

Overridden Instance Methods

```
public String toString();
```

This method overrides the method definition in the Object class.

FocusAdapter Class

Full Name	java.awt.event.FocusAdapter
Extends	Object
Implements	FocusListener
Description	Public class. A helper class that provides empty implementations of the methods defined in the FocusListener interface. This class serves as a convenience by allowing you to extend it and override only the listener response methods that you need to, as opposed to implementing all of the methods defined in the interface. To install an event handler for focus events, call the addFocusListener() method of the Component class (p. 210).

The following code defines an event handler for focus events. This handler only responds to the focusGained() method, although it could respond to focusLost() as well.

```
class MyFocusAdapter extends FocusAdapter {
    public void focusGained(FocusEvent e) {
        String msg = e.getSource().toString()
        + " about to get focus.";
        System.out.println(msg);
    }
}
```

Constructors

```
public FocusAdapter();
```

Instance Methods

```
public void focusGained(FocusEvent e);
public void focusLost(FocusEvent e);
```

These methods are called in response to a component gaining or losing the keyboard focus. The methods are called just before the focus changes.

FocusEvent Class

Full Name	java.awt.event.FocusEvent
Extends	ComponentEvent->AWTEvent->EventObject->Object
Description	Public class. This class encapsulates the information associated with a focus event, which is whether a component has gained or lost the keyboard focus. Focus events are generated by focus event sources and handled by objects that implement the FocusListener interface. An instance of the FocusEvent class is delivered to the focus listener event response methods to aid in handling focus events.

Constructors

```
public FocusEvent(Component source, int id,
    boolean temporary);
public FocusEvent(Component source, int id);
```

The source argument is the object with which the focus event is associated, id is an identifier that identifies the event, and temporary indicates whether the event is temporary or permanent.

Class Variables

```
public static final int FOCUS_FIRST;
public static final int FOCUS_GAINED;
public static final int FOCUS_LAST;
public static final int FOCUS_LOST;
```

Class constants. These constants are flags used to describe the focus event.

Java 2 API Reference

Instance Methods

```
public Object getSource();
```

Returns the object that generated the event. (This method is actually inherited from the EventObject class.)

```
public boolean isTemporary();
```

Returns true if the focus event is temporary.

FocusListener Interface

Full Name   java.awt.event.FocusListener

Description   Public interface. This interface defines methods that respond to focus events. Focus events are generated when a component gains or loses the keyboard focus. To handle focus events, you can implement the FocusListener interface, provide implementations of focus event response methods, and then register the listener class with an event source. Alternatively, you can extend the FocusAdaptor class and override only the focus event response method in which you are interested. To install an event handler for focus events, call the addFocusListener() method of the Component class (p. 210).

Interface Methods

```
public void focusGained(FocusEvent e);
public void focusLost(FocusEvent e);
```

These methods are called on a registered focus listener in response to a component gaining or losing the keyboard focus.

Font Class

Full Name java.awt.Font

Extends   Object

DescriptionPublic class. A Font object contains a complete specification for a text font. To get detailed information on height and width, you need to get a FontMetrics object by calling the getFontMetrics() method of a component or graphics object.

The following example specifies bold Courier font, 12-point size, and then sets it as the default font for the current frame or applet:

```
Font myFont = new Font("Courier", Font.BOLD, 12);
setFont(myFont);
```

Constructors

```
public Font(String name, int style, int size);
```

The second argument specifies one of the three constants listed next (BOLD, ITALIC, PLAIN); the third is a point size.

Class Variables

```
public final static int BOLD;
public final static int ITALIC;
public final static int PLAIN;
```

Constants specifying a font style. Bold and italic can be combined in the expression BOLD + ITALIC.

Class Methods

```
public static Font getFont(String nm);
public static Font getFont(String nm, Font font);
```

Returns a font object looked up in the system properties list database. The format is one of the following: name-style-pointsize, name-style, name-pointsize, and name. The defaults are plain and 12-point size. The second argument, if specified, is a default font.

Instance Methods

```
public String getFamily();
```

Returns the platform-specific family name of the font.

```
public String getName();
public int getSize();
public int getStyle();
public boolean isBold();
public boolean isItalic();
public boolean isPlain();
```

These six methods return basic information about a Font object.

Overridden Class Methods

```
public boolean equals(Object obj);
public int hashCode();
public String toString();
```

These methods override method definitions in the Object class.

FontMetrics Class

Full Name	java.awt.FontMetrics
Extends	Object

Java 2 API Reference

Description   Public class. A FontMetrics object provides detailed mea-
                     surements of font characteristics in terms of device units
                     (pixels). Although this class is public, you cannot instantiate
                     it directly; it has no public constructor. You can, however, get
                     a FontMetrics object by calling the getFontMetrics()
                     method of a Component or Graphics object.

The following example can be used from within an applet (or component
subclass) to get the height of the default font; this is the complete height of a
line of type, including leading. See Figure 3-3, page 548, for a diagram of font
metrics.

```
fm = getFontMetrics(getFont());
int height = fm.getHeight();
```

Instance Methods

```
public int bytesWidth(byte data[], int off, int len);
public int charsWidth(char data[], int off, int len);
```

These methods return the width of a string in this font; the string is
specified as an array of bytes or an array of characters. See also string
Width() below.

```
public int charWidth(char ch);
public int charWidth(int ch);
```

Returns the width of a single character in this font.

```
public int getAscent();
public int getDescent();
public Font getFont();
public int getHeight();
public int getLeading();
public int getMaxAdvance();
public int getMaxAscent();
public int getMaxDescent();
```

These eight methods return basic information about the font metrics. For a
chart showing the significance of each term, see Figure 3-3, page 548. The
getMax methods return the maximum metric of any character; other methods
return an average.

```
public int[] getWidths();
```

Returns an integer array containing the widths of the first 256 characters in
this font.

```
public int stringWidth(String str);
```

Returns the width of a string in this font. This tells you how much horizontal
space the string takes up when displayed in the font.

Overridden Instance Methods

```
public String toString();
```

Overrides method definition in the Object class.

Frame Class

Full Name	java.awt.Frame
Extends	Window->Container->Component->Object
Description	Public class. Creates a window that has borders and a menu bar. (This class is closer to the commonly accepted idea of "window" than the Java Window class is.) The use of frames is introduced in Chapter 5 on page 589. Frames generate all the standard keyboard and mouse events, as well as window events. Unlike other components, a frame is not displayed until setVisible() is called.

The following example displays a frame after setting title, cursor type, and size. setSize() and setVisible() are inherited from the Component class (p. 210).

```
Frame theFrame = new Frame("You're in the picture.");
theFrame.setCursor(Frame.HAND_CURSOR);
theFrame.setSize(150, 250);
theFrame.setVisible(true);
```

Constructors

```
public Frame();
public Frame(String title);
```

Frames have a number of attributes that are not specified in a constructor but can be set by specific methods.

Class Variables

```
public final static int CROSSHAIR_CURSOR;
public final static int DEFAULT_CURSOR;
public final static int E_RESIZE_CURSOR;
public final static int HAND_CURSOR;
public final static int MOVE_CURSOR;
public final static int N_RESIZE_CURSOR;
public final static int NE_RESIZE_CURSOR;
public final static int NW_RESIZE_CURSOR;
public final static int S_RESIZE_CURSOR;
public final static int SE_RESIZE_CURSOR;
public final static int SW_RESIZE_CURSOR;
public final static int TEXT_CURSOR;
```

Java 2 API Reference

```
public final static int W_RESIZE_CURSOR;
public final static int WAIT_CURSOR;
```

Constants specifying a cursor type. These constants can be given as input to the setCursor() method. For a description of these cursor types, see Table B-3 in Appendix B, "Useful Tables."

Instance Methods

```
public int getCursorType();
public Image getIconImage();
public MenuBar getMenuBar();
public String getTitle();
public boolean isResizable();
```

These five methods get information about basic frame attributes. Each of these attributes can also be set by a corresponding method.

```
public void remove(MenuComponent m);
```

Removes a menu component, generally a menu bar.

```
public void setCursor(int cursorType);
public void setIconImage(Image image);
public void setMenuBar(MenuBar mb);
public void setResizable(boolean resizable);
public void setTitle(String title);
```

These five methods set basic attributes of the frame. The setIconImage() and setMenuBar() methods assume that you have created an Image or MenuBar object that you can then pass as an argument. The setCursor() method takes one of the constants listed earlier.

Overridden Instance Methods

```
public void addNotify();
public void dispose();
```

These methods override method definitions in the Component class. addNotify() is used internally; dispose() closes the frame window and releases all system resources.

Graphics Class

Full Name	java.awt.Graphics
Extends	Object

Description   Abstract public class. Provides access to all of Java's drawing capabilities. You cannot directly instantiate this class by calling a constructor. However, the Component and Image classes support a getGraphics() method, and certain Component methods, such as paint(), pass an instance of a Graphics subclass.

Instance`Methods

```
public abstract void clearRect(int x, int y, int width,
   int height);
```

Clears the specified region, filling it with background color.

```
public abstract void clipRect(int x, int y, int width,
   int height);
```

Sets a clipping region for this graphics context, which results in the intersection of this rectangle with the current clipping rectangle, if any. This method is typically called just before the graphics object is passed to paint() or update().

```
public abstract void copyArea(int x, int y, int width,
   int height, int dx, int dy);
```

Copies the region at (x, y) to the region whose top left corner is (x + dx, y + dy).

```
public abstract Graphics create();
public Graphics create(int x, int y, int width, int height);
```

Creates a clone of the current graphics object, optionally specifying a subsection.

```
public abstract void dispose();
```

Immediately releases all system resources associated with the graphics object. This method is useful in programs that grab the display context directly to do quick drawing to the screen. Call dispose() at the end of a method such as paint() or at the end of a cycle of graphics operations. Remember that once dispose() is called, the graphics object becomes invalid.

```
public void draw3DRect(int x, int y, int width int height,
   boolean raised);
```

Draws a raised rectangle. If raised is true, then the rectangle is in the "up" position.

```
public abstract void drawArc(int x, int y, int width, int height,
   int startAngle, int arcAngle);
```

Draws an arc along the oval inscribed in a rectangle determined by the first four arguments. startAngle sets starting point in degrees, in which 0 is the three o'clock position. Positive numbers move counterclockwise; negative numbers move clockwise. arcAngle sets number of degrees to draw, again with negative meaning clockwise. Thus, setting startAngle and arcAngle to 0 and –180 draws a half-circle in the shape of a smile.

```
public void drawBytes(byte data[], int offset, int length,
    int x, int y);
public void drawChars(char data[], int offset, int length,
    int x, int y);
```

Similar to drawString except that arrays of bytes or char is used for string data.

```
public abstract boolean drawImage(Image img, int x, int y,
    Color bgcolor, ImageObserver observer);
public abstract boolean drawImage(Image img, int x, int y,
    ImageObserver observer);
public abstract boolean drawImage(Image img, int x, int y,
    int width, int height, Color bgcolor,
    ImageObserver observer);
public abstract boolean drawImage(Image img, int x, int y,
    int width, int height, ImageObserver observer);
```

Draws an image at x,y position, optionally specifying background color and size of region to fit the image into. (This is called scaling.) Usually, it is adequate to use the this keyword for the observer argument. If pixel data referred to by the image is not already loaded, drawImage() initiates loading. See also MediaTracker, page 394. Part II, Chapter 3 introduces use of drawImage() (p. 554).

```
public abstract void drawLine(int x1, int y1, int x2,
    int y2);
public abstract void drawOval(int x, int y, int width,
    int height);
public abstract void drawPolygon(int xPoints[],
    int yPoints[], int nPoints);
public void drawPolygon(Polygon p);
public void drawRect(int x, int y, int width, int height);
public abstract void drawRoundRect(int x, int y, int width,
    int height, int arcWidth, int arcHeight);
```

These methods draw the specified line or graphical shape. draw-RoundRect() uses degrees to specify the relative size of the rounded corner.

```
public abstract void drawString(String str, int x, int y);
```

Draws specified string, placing the baseline of the string y units from the top.

```
public void fill3DRect(int x, int y, int width, int height,
    boolean raised);
public abstract void fillArc(int x, int y, int width,
    int height, int startAngle, int arcAngle);
public abstract void fillOval(int x, int y, int width,
    int height);
public abstract void fillPolygon(int xPoints[],
    int yPoints[], int nPoints);
public void fillPolygon(Polygon p);
public abstract void fillRect(int x, int y, int width,
    int height);
public abstract void fillRoundRect(int x, int y, int width,
    int height, int arcWidth, int arcHeight);
```

These methods draw a shape and then fill it in with the foreground color. Similar to corresponding draw methods. fillArc() and fillRoundRect() use degree measurements; see drawArc() for other details on fillArc() arguments. The effect of fillArc () is to draw a pie section.

```
public abstract Rectangle getClipRect();
public abstract Color getColor();
public abstract Font getFont();
```

These methods return the current clipping region, foreground color, and current font, respectively.

```
public FontMetrics getFontMetrics();
public abstract FontMetrics getFontMetrics(Font f);
```

Returns a FontMetrics object, using the current font if one is not specified.

```
public abstract void setColor(Color c);
public abstract void setFont(Font font);
```

These methods set the foreground color and current font, respectively.

```
public abstract void setPaintMode();
public abstract void setXORMode(Color c);
```

These methods set the drawing mode to either normal drawing (setPaint Mode) or XOR mode. With XOR mode, drawing over the same region twice restores it to its original state. The color, c, is used in an XOR bit operation on existing pixels. Results can be unpredictable if more than two colors are in use.

```
public abstract void translate(int x, int y);
```

Alters the graphics context so that the point currently referred to as (x, y) becomes the new origin, (0, 0).

Overridden Instance Methods

```
public void finalize();
public String toString();
```

These methods override method definitions in the Object class. The finalize() method calls dispose, so that when a graphics object goes out of scope, it releases its system resources.

GregorianCalendar Class

Full Name	java.util.GregorianCalendar
Extends	Calendar->Object
Description	Public class. This class implements a standard Gregorian calendar that is a subclass of the Calendar class. A Gregorian calendar consists of two eras, BC and AD.

The GregorianCalendar class is a concrete sub-class of Calendar, and can therefore be created directly using the new operator and one of the Gregorian Calendar constructors. Following is an example of creating a Gregorian Calendar object for the current date and time in the Central Time Zone:

```
GregorianCalendar now =
    new GregorianCalendar(TimeZone.getTimeZone("CST"));
```

In this example, the static TimeZone.getTimeZone() method is called to obtain a TimeZone object representing the Central Time Zone.

Constructors

```
public GregorianCalendar();
public GregorianCalendar(TimeZone zone);
public GregorianCalendar(Locale aLocale);
public GregorianCalendar(TimeZone zone, Locale aLocale);
public GregorianCalendar(int year, int month, int date);
public GregorianCalendar(int year, int month, int date, int hour,
    int minute);
public GregorianCalendar(int year, int month, int date, int hour,
    int minute, int second);
```

Creates a Gregorian calendar based upon the specified time zone, locale, combination of time zone and locale, or the specific time fields year, month, date, hour, minute, and second.

Class Variables

```
public static final int AD;
public static final int BC;
```

Class constants. These constants represent the two eras associated with a Gregorian calendar.

Instance Methods

```
public boolean isLeapYear(int year);
```

Determines if the specified year is a leap year.

```
public final Date getGregorianChange();
public void setGregorianChange(Date date);
```

Gets and sets the point at which the calendar shifts from a Julian calendar to a Gregorian calendar; by default this is set to October 15, 1582.

Overridden Instance Methods

```
public void add(int field, int amount);
```

Adds the specified amount of time to the specified time field.

```
public int getActualMaximum(int field);
public int getActualMinimum(int field);
```

Retrieves the maximum and minimum values the specified field can have given the current date.

```
public int getGreatestMinimum(int field);
public int getLeastMaximum(int field);
```

Retrieves the greatest minimum value for the specified field, or the least maximum value for the field. For Gregorian calendar dates (as opposed to Julian dates), these methods return the same results as getMaximum() and getMinimum().

```
public int getMaximum(int field);
public int getMinimum(int field);
```

Retrieves the maximum and minimum values allowed for the specified field.

```
public void roll(int field, boolean up);
public void roll(int field, int amount);
```

Rolls the specified time field by the specified amount.

GridBagConstraints Class

Full Name	java.awt.GridBagConstraints
Extends	Object
Implements	Cloneable

Description   Public class. Specifies a set of layout constraints for one
               component. This class is used in conjunction with the Grid
               BagLayout class. The general procedure is as follows:
               create a set of constraints by using this class (GridBag
               Constraints) and then pass the sets of constraints along with
               the corresponding component by calling GridBagLayout.
               setConstraints(). Each component must be added to the
               container in addition to having its constraints specified to
               the layout manager.

The following example adds a component textA (a TextArea component) to a
layout managed by myGridBag, a layout manager of the GridBagLayout class.

```
GridBagConstraints textAConstr = new
    GridBagConstraints();
textAConstr.gridx = 0;     // Place in top left corner.
textAConstr.gridy = 0;
textAConstr.gridwidth = 3;     // Take up 3 x 2 cells.
textAConstr.gridheight = 2;
textAConstr.fill = GridBagConstraints.BOTH; // Fill cell.
// Assign weight 1.0, enabling component to grow.
textAConstr.weightx = textConstr.weighty = 1.0;
// Add the component.
myGridBag.setConstraints(textA, textAConstraints);
myContainer.add(textA);
```

Constructors

```
public GridBagConstraints();
```

Default constructor. The actual constraint values are set by manipulating
the instance variables.

Instance Variables

```
public int anchor;
```

Value specifying the zone (anchor) to place the component inside its cell.
Possible values are listed later in the topic and include CENTER, EAST, NORTH,
and so on. See "Class Variables."

```
public int fill;
```

One of four values — NONE, BOTH, HORIZONTAL, or VERTICAL — that indicates
which direction, if any, the component should grow in when the cell's space
is larger than the component's minimum size. See "Class Variables."

```
public int gridheight;
public int gridwidth;
```

Size of the component's cell, in terms of rows and columns. For example, a cell can take up a 2 × 2 section of the grid. A value of REMAINDER (see "Class Variables") in either dimension indicates that the cell should get all the space that is left in that dimension.

```
public int gridx;
public int gridy;
```

Position of the component. Using the special value RELATIVE (see "Class Variables"), in either coordinate, means positioning directly to the right (gridx) or just below (gridy) the previous component added.

```
public Insets insets;
```

An Insets object specifies margins around the component.

```
public int ipadx;
public int ipady;
```

Internal horizontal and vertical padding of the component. These fields create additional margins around the component, increasing the component's minimum size requirement.

```
public double weightx;
public double weighty;
```

Weights controlling how component grows in each direction as the container grows. A weight of 0.0 (the default) means that the component does not get extra space beyond its minimum size. A weight of 1.0 allows the component to grow as the available space does.

Class Variables

```
public final static int CENTER;
public final static int EAST;
public final static int NORTH;
public final static int NORTHEAST;
public final static int NORTHWEST;
public final static int SOUTH;
public final static int SOUTHEAST;
public final static int SOUTHWEST;
public final static int WEST;
```

These constants are possible values for the anchor field.

```
public final static int BOTH;
public final static int HORIZONTAL;
public final static int NONE;
public final static int VERTICAL;
```

These constants are possible values for the fill field.

```
public final static int REMAINDER;
```

This constant can be used in the gridWidth and gridHeight fields.

```
public final static int RELATIVE;
```

This constant can be used in the gridx and gridy fields.

Overridden Instance Methods

```
public Object clone();
```

Overrides the method definition in the Object class. This class produces cloneable objects.

GridBagLayout Class

Full Name	java.awt.GridBagLayout
Extends	Object
Implements	LayoutManager
Description	Public class. Creates layout managers providing the maximum flexibility in sizing and positioning components. When a container uses a GridBagLayout manager, each of its components must be assigned constraints. Use the GridBag Constraints class to create a set of constraints for each component. Then add the constraints by using the set Constraints() method.

See GridBagConstraints class (p. 267) for an example.

Constructors

```
public GridBagLayout();
```

Default constructor. All characteristics are set by calling setConstraints().

Instance Methods

```
public GridBagConstraints getConstraints(Component comp);
public void setConstraints(Component comp,
    GridBagConstraints constraints);
```

These methods get and set a GridBagConstraints object for the specified component. The setConstraints() method should be called once for each component to specify a set of constraints.

Instance Methods (Interface Methods)

```
public void addLayoutComponent(String name, Component comp);
public void layoutContainer(Container target);
public Dimension minimumLayoutSize(Container target);
```

```
public Dimension preferredLayoutSize(Container target);
public void removeLayoutComponent(Component comp);
```

These five methods implement the LayoutManager interface; none of these methods is normally called by applications.

Overridden Instance Methods

```
public String toString();
```

This method overrides the method definition in the Object class.

GridLayout Class

Full Name	java.awt.GridLayout
Extends	Object
Implements	LayoutManager
Description	Public class. Creates layout manager objects that align components into rows and columns not delineated by visible lines, as described in Chapter 5 on page 593.

The following example sets the current container to use an instance of GridLayout with five rows and three columns:

```
setLayout(new GridLayout(5, 3));
```

Constructors

```
public GridLayout(int rows, int cols);
public GridLayout(int rows, int cols, int hgap, int vgap)
    throws IllegalArgumentException;
```

You must specify number of rows and columns. Each grid cell is a region into which the layout manager attempts to fit a component. The optional hgap and vgap specify horizontal and vertical gap between grid cells.

Instance Methods

```
public void addLayoutComponent(String name, Component comp);
public void layoutContainer(Container target);
public Dimension minimumLayoutSize(Container target);
public Dimension preferredLayoutSize(Container target);
public void removeLayoutComponent(Component comp);
```

These five methods implement the LayoutManager interface; none of these methods is normally called by applications.

Overridden Instance Methods

```
public String toString();
```

This method overrides the method definition in the Object class.

HashMap Class

Full Name	java.util.HashMap
Extends	AbstractMap->Object
Description	Public class. This class implements a hash table that is based upon the Map interface. A hash map is similar to a hash table except that it is unsynchronized and permits null elements.

It is very straightforward to create hash maps using the constructors provided. Following is an example of creating a hash map with an initial capacity of 20 elements:

```
HashMap map = new HashMap(20);
```

Keep in mind that hash maps can be used to store virtually any kind of object along with a key that is used to access the object. As an example, you could store Dimension objects the sizes of rooms in your house in a hash map and access them via string keys. Following is an example of how you might go about adding such elements to the hash map:

```
map.put("Living room", new Dimension(14, 16));
map.put("Dining room", new Dimension(12, 14));
map.put("Play room", new Dimension(18, 20));
```

With the elements successfully added to the map, you can then search for them using their string keys:

```
Dimension room = null;
if (map.containsKey("Dining room"))
    room = (Dimension) map.get("Dining room");
```

You can also remove elements from the hash map by calling the remove() method and specifying the key:

```
map.remove("Play room");
```

To remove all elements from a hash map, simply call the clear() method:

```
map.clear();
```

Constructors

```
public HashMap();
```

Default constructor.

```
public HashMap(Map t);
```

Creates a hash map that is initialized with the specified map.

```
public HashMap(int initialCapacity);
public HashMap(int initialCapacity, float loadFactor);
```
Creates a hash map with the specified initial capacity and load factor.

Overridden Instance Methods
```
public void clear();
```
Clears the hash map.
```
public boolean containsKey(Object key);
```
Checks to see if the map contains a mapping for the specified key.
```
public boolean containsValue(Object value);
```
Checks to see if the map contains one or keys mapped to the specified value.
```
public Set entrySet();
```
Retrieves a set containing the entry mappings for the hash map.
```
public Object get(Object key);
```
Retrieves the value associated with the specified key.
```
public boolean isEmpty();
```
Checks to see if the hash map is empty.
```
public Set keySet();
```
Retrieves a set containing the key mappings for the hash map.
```
public Object put(Object key, Object value);
```
Adds a key/value mapping to the hash map.
```
public void putAll(Map t);
```
Adds all of the mappings in the specified map to the hash map.
```
public Object remove(Object key);
```
Removes the specified key and its associated value from the hash map.
```
public int size();
```
Retrieves the number of key/value mappings in the hash map.
```
public Collection values();
```
Retrieves a collection of values contained within the hash map.

Hashtable Class

Full Name	`java.util.Hashtable`
Extends	`Dictionary->Object`
Implements	`Cloneable`
Description	Public class. A `Hashtable` object is a collection that stores any number of objects of any type using a key to identify and retrieve each object. The stored objects are called elements. Keys may also be of any type, but all keys used in a given table should use the same type. The most useful methods are `put()`, which adds an element to the table, and `get()`, which retrieves it.

The following example stores two Social Security numbers using strings as keys to the table:

```
Hashtable ssnTable = new Hashtable();
ssnTable.put("Joe Bloe", new Long(123004444));
ssnTable.put("Jane Doe", new Long(456227777));
Long ssn = (Long)ssnTable.get("Joe Bloe");
System.out.println("Joe's SSN = " + ssn);
```

Constructors

```
public Hashtable();
public Hashtable(int initialCapacity);
public Hashtable(int initialCapacity, float loadFactor);
```

You can optionally specify initial capacity and load factor (a number between 0.0 and 1.0), although this is never required. The product of current capacity and load factor determines a temporary limit. As soon as this limit is exceeded, the table is automatically rehashed, gaining greater capacity. If you know in advance that a certain minimum capacity is needed, you can prevent some rehashing by specifying it in the constructor. A larger load factor more efficiently uses memory, but each lookup may require more time.

Instance Methods

```
public void clear();
```

Removes the entire contents of the table.

```
public boolean contains(Object value);
public boolean containsKey(Object key);
```

These methods return true if the specified element or key is found.

```
public Enumeration elements();
```

Returns an enumeration of all the elements. See also `keys()`, page 275.

```
public Object get(Object key);
```

Returns an element, looking it up by the specified key. Returns null if the element is not found. Note that the result must usually be cast to a particular type. (See example.)

```
public boolean isEmpty();
```

Returns true if there are no elements in the table.

```
public Enumeration keys();
```

Returns an enumeration of all the keys. See also elements(), page 274.

```
public Object put(Object key, Object value);
```

Adds an element to the table, assigning it the specified key. Returns the previous element assigned to this same key, or null if there was no previous element assigned.

```
public Object remove(Object key);
```

Remove a key and its corresponding element. This element is returned, and null is returned if the key was not mapped to any value.

```
public int size();
```

Returns number of elements.

Overridden Instance Methods

```
public Object clone();
public String toString();
```

These methods override method definitions in the Object class. For this class, the clone() method performs a relatively shallow copy; it clones the table but not the keys or the elements.

HyperlinkEvent Class

Full Name   javax.swing.event.HyperlinkEvent

Extends   EventObject->Object

Description   Public class. This class represents a hyperlink event that is delivered in response to a hyperlink being updated.

Constructors

```
public HyperlinkEvent(Object source,
   HyperlinkEvent.EventType type, URL u);
public HyperlinkEvent(Object source,
   HyperlinkEvent.EventType type, URL u, String desc);
```

Creates a hyperlink event based upon the specified event source, event type, URL, and description.

Instance Methods

```
public HyperlinkEvent.EventType getEventType();
```

Retrieves the type of the event.

```
public String getDescription();
```

Retrieves the description of the event.

```
public Object getSource();
```

Retrieves the object upon which the event originally occurred. (This method is actually inherited from the EventObject ancestor class.)

```
public URL getURL();
```

Retrieves the URL associated with the hyperlink event.

HyperlinkListener Interface

Full Name	javax.swing.event.HyperlinkListener
Extends	EventListener
Description	Public interface. This interface describes a hyperlink event listener that is used to handle hyperlink events.

Interface Methods

```
public void hyperlinkUpdate(HyperlinkEvent e);
```

This method is an event response method that is called when a hyperlink is updated.

Icon Interface

Full Name	javax.swing.Icon
Description	Public interface. This interface describes a small rectangular image that is used to provide graphical cues throughout an application's GUI. The ImageIcon class (p. 281) implements this interface and provides the most common way to create an icon using Swing.

Interface Methods

```
public int getIconHeight();
public int getIconWidth();
```

These methods get the height and width of the icon.

```
public void paintIcon(Component c, Graphics g,
    int x, int y);
```

This method paints the icon at the specified *x,y* position. The c argument is the component onto which the icon is painted.

Image Class

Full Name	`java.awt.Image`
Extends	`Object`
Description	Public class. An `Image` object represents a graphics image — an image from a file or an offscreen buffer. Different procedures apply for file images and buffer images. To get an image from a file, call the `getImage()` method of the `Applet` or `Toolkit` class. In this case, the `Image` object returned is not really the same as the data itself. The data must still be loaded, even though you have a valid object. Calling `Graphics.drawImage()` initiates actual loading. See also `MediaTracker`, page 394.
	To create an offscreen buffer, call the `createImage()` method of the `Component` class. (As a `Component` method, this method is inherited by many other classes, such as `Applet`.) This call returns a blank image, but, as suggested in the following example, you can draw to this image. When the image is ready, call `Graphics.drawImage()` to display it. See Part II, Chapters 3 and 6, for examples of both kinds of `Image` objects.

Java 2 API Reference

The following example creates an offscreen buffer the size of the applet's display area. Then it gets a `Graphics` object for drawing to this image. Note that `createImage()` and `size()` are applet methods inherited from the `Component` class.

```
int w = size().width;   // Get applet's width.
int h = size().height;  // Get applet's height.
Image buffer = createImage(w, h);  // Image is applet size.
Graphics g = buffer.getGraphics(); // Prepare to draw.
```

Several of the methods take an `ImageObserver` object as an argument. When one of these methods attempts to get data, the method returns immediately even if the requested data is not yet loaded. This circumstance is likely when the image is loading from a file. The `ImageObserver` object is called later, as new data is loaded. All classes derived from the `Component` class serve as image observers, so you can use a reference to a component (the `this` keyword often suffices).

Class Variables

```
public static Object UndefinedProperty;
```

This object is a special return value used by the `getProperty()` method of this class. Appropriate tests for equality (= =) will succeed, because there is only one instance of this object. Note that the object's name is an exception to the Java convention that only class names have initial caps.

Instance Methods

```
public abstract void flush();
```

Releases system resources being used to render the image. You usually do not need to call this method. It's provided to force correct redrawing of an image that may have changed.

```
public abstract Graphics getGraphics();
```

Returns a `Graphics` object that can be used to draw into the in-memory image.

```
public abstract int getHeight(ImageObserver observer);
```

Returns the height of the image in pixels. If sufficient data is not yet read to determine this, the value –1 is returned, and the `ImageObserver` object is called later.

```
public abstract Object getProperty(String name,
    ImageObserver observer);
```

Returns the value of the image property specified by the name argument. (Each image format defines its own set of properties. By convention, the "comment" property is often used to provide general information such as author and description.) If the image is not yet loaded, this method returns null, and the `ImageObserver` object is called later. If the specified property is not defined for this image, the method returns the special value `Image.UndefinedProperty`.

```
public abstract ImageProducer getSource();
```

Returns the image producer, an object that produces the actual pixel data. See `FilteredImageSource`, page 251, for an example.

```
public abstract int getWidth(ImageObserver observer);
```

Returns the width of the image in pixels. If sufficient data is not yet read to determine this, the value –1 is returned, and the `ImageObserver` object is called later.

ImageConsumer Interface

Full Name   `java.awt.image.ImageConsumer`

Description Public interface. This is an interface that you never need to implement or directly interact with in any way unless you are doing very low level manipulation of image data. This interface is visible to applications in the following way: image filters, such as `CropImageFilter`, are implicitly image consumers. The `PixelGrabber` class, which collects raw data, is also an image consumer.

An image consumer is an object that has requested data from an image producer. When the image producer is ready to send image data, it calls the appropriate methods of the image consumer. (Image consumers should not be confused with image observers, which monitor loading from disk.)

Interface Constants

```
public final static int IMAGEABORTED;
public final static int IMAGEERROR;
public final static int SINGLEFRAMEDONE;
public final static int STATICIMAGEDONE;
```

These constants are used by the imageComplete() method to indicate status. Values are mutually exclusive.

```
public final static int COMPLETESCANLINES;
public final static int RANDOMPIXELORDER;
public final static int SINGLEFRAME;
public final static int SINGLEPASS;
public final static int TOPDOWNLEFTRIGHT;
```

These constants are used by the setHints() method. They are flags that are OR'ed together.

Interface Methods

```
public abstract void imageComplete(int status);
```

When the image is complete, the image producer calls this method and passes a status indicator.

```
public abstract void setColorModel(ColorModel model);
```

Image producer calls this method to set a color model for the image.

```
public abstract void setDimensions(int width, int height);
```

Image producer calls this method to specify the image dimensions.

```
public abstract void setHints(int hintflags);
```

Image producer calls this method to set hints as to how it delivers pixel data. See "Interface Constants."

```
public abstract void setPixels(int x, int y, int w, int h,
   ColorModel model, byte pixels[], int off, int scansize);
public abstract void setPixels(int x, int y, int w, int h,
   ColorModel model, int pixels[], int off, int scansize);
```

The image producer calls this method to copy the actual pixel data. These two versions of the method are the same except for the pixel size (byte or int).

```
public abstract void setProperties(Hashtable props);
```

The image producer calls this method to set properties of the image.

ImageFilter Class

Full Name	java.awt.image.ImageFilter
Extends	Object
Implements	ImageConsumer, Cloneable
Description	Public class. This class is never used directly but is useful as the superclass to the CropImageFilter and RGBImage Filter classes. Image filters take data from an image-producing source (an image producer) and translate it some way. Use the FilterImageSource class to create a new image producer from a filter.

All the ImageFilter methods are used internally. There is rarely any need for application code to call these methods. However, it is possible to subclass ImageFilter to create your own filter.

Constructors

```
public ImageFilter();
```

Default constructor. This method performs no initialization.

Instance Variables

```
protected ImageConsumer consumer;
```

This is the field that contains the consumer, an object that receives the pixel data. Because this field is protected, you can refer to it only if you're sub-classing the ImageFilter class.

Instance Methods

```
public ImageFilter getFilterInstance(ImageConsumer ic);
```

Clones the image filter, setting the consumer field to the specified argument.

```
public void resendTopDownLeftRight(ImageProducer ip);
```

Requests that the image producer re-send the pixel data.

Instance Methods (from Interface)

```
public void imageComplete(int status);
public void setColorModel(ColorModel model);
public void setDimensions(int width, int height);
public void setHints(int hints);
public void setPixels(int x, int y, int w, int h,
   ColorModel model, byte pixels[], int off, int scansize);
public void setPixels(int x, int y, int w, int h,
   ColorModel model, int pixels[], int off, int scansize);
public void setProperties(Hashtable props);
```

These methods implement method declarations in the ImageConsumer interface.

Overridden Instance Methods

```
public Object.clone();
```

Overrides method definition in Object class.

Imagelcon Class

Full Name	javax.swing.ImageIcon
Extends	Object
Implements	Icon
Description	Public class. This class implements an image icon that is based on the Icon interface. Use of this class is the most common way to create an icon using the Swing architecture. See also Icon interface (p. 276).

Here is an example of creating a simple image icon from a filename:

```
ImageIcon icon = new ImageIcon("Rat.gif");
```

Here is another example that shows how to provide a text description of the icon:

```
ImageIcon icon = new ImageIcon("Rat.gif", "Dirty rat");
```

Constructors

```
public ImageIcon();
public ImageIcon(String filename);
public ImageIcon(String filename, String description);
public ImageIcon(URL location);
public ImageIcon(URL location, String description);
public ImageIcon(Image image);
public ImageIcon(Image image, String description);
```

Java 2 API Reference

```
public ImageIcon(byte[] imageData);
public ImageIcon(byte[] imageData, String description);
```

These constructors create image icons using various types of information such as a string filename, a URL, an Image object, or an array of raw image data. Each of the base constructors has an alternate constructor that accepts a string description to go with the image icon.

Instance Methods

```
public String getDescription();
public int getIconHeight();
public int getIconWidth();
public Image getImage();
public int getImageLoadStatus();
public ImageObserver getImageObserver();
```

These methods gets various property values. The getIconHeight() and getIconWidth() methods implement Icon interface methods.

```
protected void loadImage(Image image);
public void paintIcon(Component c, Graphics g, int x, int y);
```

These methods carry out basic operations necessary to render an icon. The paintIcon() method implements an Icon interface method.

```
public void setDescription(String description);
public void setImage(Image image);
public void setImageObserver(ImageObserver observer);
```

These methods set various properties of the icon.

Overridden Instance Methods

```
public String toString()
```

This method returns a string representation of the image icon, which is the description of the image icon if one has been specified.

ImageObserver Interface

Full Name	java.awt.image.ImageObserver
Description	Public interface. An object implements this interface to act as an observer during loading of an image; an image observer is notified as new data becomes available. All subclasses of the Java Component class implement this interface. Therefore, there usually is little need to implement this interface yourself.

Interface Constants

```
public final static int ABORT;
public final static int ALLBITS;
public final static int ERROR;
public final static int FRAMEBITS;
public final static int HEIGHT;
public final static int PROPERTIES;
public final static int SOMEBITS;
public final static int WIDTH;
```

These are status flags that indicate how much information of the image is now available; they are passed in the infoflags argument of imageUpdate(). For example, if the WIDTH flag is on, width data is now available. These flags are combined through bitwise OR (||).

Interface Methods

```
public abstract boolean imageUpdate(Image img,
    int infoflags, int x, int y, int width, int height);
```

This method is called when new data is available during loading. Java API components respond by causing a repaint.

ImageProducer Interface

Full Name   java.awt.image.ImageProducer

Description   Public interface. An image producer, or image source, produces the actual bits to construct an image. You can ignore the existence of image producers except when creating a new image source from data in memory (MemoryImageSource) or from a filter (FilteredImageSource). Once an image producer is available, you can use it to create a new image by calling the createImage() method of the Component class. See FilteredImageSource, page 251, for a complete example.

Interface Methods

```
public void addConsumer(ImageConsumer ic);
```

Adds the argument to the list of image consumers serviced by this image producer.

```
public boolean isConsumer(ImageConsumer ic);
```

Returns true if the image consumer is one of the consumers serviced by this image producer.

```
public void removeConsumer(ImageConsumer ic);
```

Informs the image producer that this image consumer no longer needs to be sent data.

```
public void requestTopDownLeftRightResend(ImageConsumer ic);
```

Requests resending the image data to this image consumer, in top-down, left-right order.

```
public void startProduction(ImageConsumer ic);
```

Requests that the image producer send the image data. Data is sent to this image consumer as well as all others on the list of consumers serviced by this image producer.

IndexColorModel Class

Full Name	java.awt.image.IndexColorModel
Extends	ColorModel->Object
Description	Public class. Specifies a color model that uses a finite number of colors, in which each number maps to a particular color. A color is translated by using the color number as an index into arrays that give intensity for red, green, and blue. This technique optionally supports one color that represents complete transparency. (Drawing in the transparent color lets the background show through.) In general, there is never any need to use this class unless you're processing image data that does not use the default RGB model.

Instance Methods

```
public IndexColorModel(int bits, int size, byte r[],
    byte g[], byte b[]);
public IndexColorModel(int bits, int size, byte r[],
    byte g[], byte b[], byte a[]);
public IndexColorModel(int bits, int size, byte r[],
    byte g[], byte b[], int trans);
```

The arguments include the number of bits per pixel in this model, the size of the color component arrays, the arrays themselves (including an optional alpha array), and an optional index indicating the number of the transparency color. If this index is used, all other color values are completely solid, or opaque. See ColorModel, page ___, for explanation of the alpha value.

```
public IndexColorModel(int bits, int size, byte cmap[],
    int start, boolean hasalpha);
public IndexColorModel(int bits, int size, byte cmap[],
    int start, boolean hasalpha, int trans);
```

These constructors work in a way similar to the constructors listed previously, except that a single array is used whose elements have packed RGB values. If hasalpha is true, it indicates that an alpha value is included in the packed RGB value. The trans argument is an optional index indicating the number of the transparency color. If this index is used, all other color values are completely solid, or opaque.

```
public final void getAlphas(byte a[]);
public final void getBlues(byte b[]);
public final void getGreens(byte g[]);
public final void getReds(byte r[]);
```

Returns the specified array.

```
public final int getMapSize();
```

Returns the number of elements in the color index.

Overridden Instance Methods

```
public final int getAlpha(int pixel);
public final int getBlue(int pixel);
public final int getGreen(int pixel);
public final int getRed(int pixel);
public final int getRGB(int pixel);
public final int getTransparentPixel();
```

These methods override method definitions in the ColorModel class.

InetAddress Class

Full Name	java.net.InetAddress
Extends	Object
Description	Public final class. Creates an Internet address from a specified machine name or IP address. An InetAddress object, in turn, is used by the DatagramPacket and Socket classes. Although this is a public, nonabstract class, it has no public constructors, so you cannot instantiate it directly. However, several class methods return InetAddress objects.

The following example gets an InetAddress object for the named computer:

```
InetAddress iaddr =
    InetAddress.getByName("java.sun.com");
```

Class Methods

```
public static InetAddress[] getAllByName(String host)
  throws UnknownHostException;
```

```
public static InetAddress getByName(String host)
    throws UnknownHostException;
```

The string argument is a machine name, such as java.sun.com, or a string representation of an IP address, such as 206.26.48.100. getAllByName() returns all the Internet addresses for the specified host.

```
public static InetAddress getLocalHost()
    throws UnknownHostException;
```

Gets the InetAddress object for the local machine.

Instance Methods

```
public byte[] getAddress();
public String getHostName();
```

These methods return the raw IP address and host name, respectively. Currently, IP addresses are 32 bits (4 bytes) but may eventually be 128 bits.

Overridden Instance Methods

```
public boolean equals(Object obj);
public int hashCode();
public String toString();
```

These methods override method definitions in the Object class.

InputStream Class

Full Name   java.io.InputStream

Extends   Object

Description Abstract public class. This class is the superclass for all input streams. Some of the subclasses have more efficient or specialized implementations than the default implementations provided in this class. Of the subclasses, DataInputStream is the most generally useful. See also FileInputStream, page 248.

Instance Methods

```
public int available() throws IOException;
```

Returns the number of bytes that can be read without waiting.

```
public void close() throws IOException;
```

Closes the stream and releases all system resources (such as file handles) associated with it.

```
public void mark(int readlimit);
```

If supported, this method sets a marker at the current file position in the stream. The next call to reset() moves back to the marked position. The readlimit is the maximum distance that such a reset can move. Not all subclasses necessarily support this method.

```
public boolean markSupported();
```

Returns true if the mark() method is supported.

```
public abstract int read() throws IOException;
```

Returns the next byte in the stream. Returns –1 if at end of the stream.

```
public int read(byte b[]) throws IOException;
public int read(byte b[], int off, int len)
    throws IOException;
```

Reads up to b.length or len bytes, whichever is smaller. Returns the number of bytes read, or –1 if at the end of the stream. The off argument gives a starting offset into the array.

```
public void reset() throws IOException;
```

Resets reading of input to the beginning of the stream, or to the marked position if the mark() method is supported.

```
public long skip(long n) throws IOException;
```

Skips n bytes in the stream before the next read.

InputVerifier Class

Full Name	javax.swing.InputVerifier
Extends	Object
Description	Public class. This class provides a means of verifying text that has been entered into a text field. If an input verifier is associated with a text component, the verifier will be used before focus leaves the component. Each verifier must be created custom by subclassing the InputVerifier class and then attaching an instance of it to a component by calling the setInputVerifier() method. This is a method of the Component class (p. 210).

Constructors

```
public InputVerifier();
```

Instance Methods

```
public boolean shouldYieldFocus(JComponent input);
```

Java 2 API Reference

This method is called when an attempt is made to move the focus from the specified component; this method calls the `verify()` method to determine if focus can move from the component.

```
public abstract boolean verify(JComponent input);
```

This method is called to verify the text contents of the specified component. You should override this method and provide your own implementation.

Insets Class

Full Name	`java.awt.Insets`
Extends	`Object`
Implements	`Cloneable`
Description	Public class. An `Insets` object contains four values specifying margins, in pixels. See the `insets()` method (p. 221) of the `Container` class and the `insets` field (p. 268) of the `Grid BagConstraints` class.

Constructors

```
public Insets(int top, int left, int bottom, int right);
```

Sets all four instance variables.

Instance Variables

```
public int bottom;
public int left;
public int right;
public int top;
```

Instance variables, directly accessible to other classes. Each specifies a margin.

Overridden Instance Methods

```
public Object clone();
public String toString();
```

These methods override method definitions in the `Object` class.

Integer Class

Full Name	`java.lang.Integer`
Extends	`Number->Object`
Description	Public final class. Serves as the wrapper class for the `int` primitive type. This class provides methods for converting between string, object, and numeric data. It also is useful for passing an `int` value by reference.

The following example converts a digit string to type int:

```
int i = Integer.parseInt(digitString);
```

Constructors

```
public Integer(int value);
public Integer(String s);
```

The second constructor initializes from a digit string.

Class Variables

```
public final static int MAX_VALUE;
public final static int MIN_VALUE;
```

Constants. Maximum and minimum values in the int range.

Class Methods

```
public static Integer getInteger(String nprop);
public static Integer getInteger(String nprop, int val);
public static Integer getInteger(String nprop, Integer val);
```

Returns the value of the named system property. The second argument, if specified, is returned if the property name is not found in the system properties table.

```
public static int parseInt(String s);
public static int parseInt(String s, int radix);
```

Returns the face value of a string of digits as an int.

```
public static String toBinaryString(int i);
public static String toHexString(int i);
public static String toOctalString(int i);
public static String toString(int i);
public static String toString(int i, int radix);
```

These methods return a string representation of the specified int value.

```
public static Integer valueOf(String s);
public static Integer valueOf(String s, int radix);
```

Returns an Integer object, initializing it from the digits in the string argument.

Instance Methods (from Number Class)

```
public double doubleValue();
public float floatValue();
public int intValue();
public long longValue();
```

These methods return the double, float, int, or long equivalent of the value stored in the current object.

Instance Methods (from Object Class)

```
public boolean equals(Object obj);
public int hashCode();
public String toString();
```

These methods override method definitions in the Object class.

ItemEvent Class

Full Name   java.awt.event.ItemEvent

Extends   AWTEvent->EventObject->Object

Description   Public class. This class encapsulates the information associated with an item event. Item events are generated by item event sources and handled by objects that implement the ItemListener interface. Item events are delivered to list components when an item is selected or deselected. An instance of the ItemEvent class is delivered to the item listener event response method to aid in handling item events.

Constructors

```
public ItemEvent(ItemSelectable source, int id, Object item,
    int stateChange);
```

The source argument is the object with which the item event is associated; id is an identifier that identifies the event; item is the item that has been selected or deselected; and stateChange is the new state of the item.

Class Variables

```
public static final int DESELECTED;
public static final int ITEM_FIRST;
public static final int ITEM_LAST;
public static final int ITEM_STATE_CHANGED;
public static final int SELECTED;
```

Class constants. These constants are flags used to describe the selection state change of the item associated with the event.

Instance Methods

```
public Object getItem();
public ItemSelectable getItemSelectable();
public int getStateChange();
```

These methods retrieve the originator of the item event, the item whose selection state has changed, and the new selection state of the item.

Overridden Instance Methods

```
public String paramString();
```

This method generates a parameter string that identifies the item event.

ItemListener Interface

Full Name   `java.awt.event.ItemListener`

Description   Public interface. This interface defines methods that respond
               to item events. Item events are semantic events that are gener-
               ated when an item in a list is selected or deselected. To handle
               item events, you must implement the `ItemListener` interface,
               provide an implementation of the `itemState`
               `Changed()` event response method, and then register an
               instance of the listener class with an event source. You
               can install an item event listener by calling the `addItem`
               `Listener()` method supported by the `AbstractButton` class
               (p. 165) and the `JComboBox` class (p. 297).

Interface Methods

```
public void itemStateChanged(ItemEvent e);
```

This method is called on a registered item listener in response to an item
event occurring.

ItemSelectable Interface

Full Name   `java.awt.ItemSelectable`

Description   Public interface. This interface describes a set of items for
               which zero or more can be selected. Objects that support
               the selection of such items are certain to implement the
               `ItemSelectable` interface.

Interface Methods

```
public void addItemListener(ItemListener l);
```

This method registers an item selectable listener for receiving item selection
events generated by the object that implements the ItemSelectable interface.

```
public Object[] getSelectedObjects();
```

Gets the currently selected items as an array.

```
public void removeItemListener(ItemListener l);
```

This method unregisters an item selectable listener that is registered to
receive item selection events generated by the object that implements the
ItemSelectable interface.

JApplet Class

Full Name	`javax.swing.JApplet`
Extends	`Applet->Panel->Container->Component->Object`
Implements	`RootPaneContainer`
Description	Public class. This GUI class extends the standard Abstract Windowing ToolKit (AWT) `Applet` class to support advanced features of the Swing architecture. This class is similar to `Applet` in many ways. The principal difference is that it supports specific panes that occupy different areas of the applet's onscreen area (or pane). In most applet code, the two most useful panes are the menu bar, and the content pane. Notably, you should almost always add components to an applet's content pane and not to the applet itself.
	Most of the useful methods of `JApplet` are inherited from the AWT `Applet` class (p. 173). These methods include `init()` and `paint()`, which are the two methods most commonly overridden by applet code.

The following code provides a simple skeleton for applet code using Swing classes. Note that the `init()` method gets a reference to the content pane, which is the container that you should add components to (other than menus), rather than the applet itself.

```
import.java.awt.*;
import.java.swing.*;

public class MyApplet extends JApplet {

    init() {
        Container pane = getContentPane();
        // Perform other initializations.
    }
    // Put other applet code here.
}
```

Constructors

```
public JApplet();
```

Instance Methods

```
public Container getContentPane();
public Component getGlassPane();
public JMenuBar getJMenuBar();
public JLayeredPane getLayeredPane();
public JRootPane getRootPane();
```

These methods return the panes of the applet, which control specific parts of the display area. Most of the time, you should work only with the content pane and the menu bar. You should not add components directly to the applet itself.

```
protected boolean isRootPaneCheckingEnabled();
```

This method returns true by default, which prevents components from being directly added to the applet (as opposed to the content pane). To enable adding components to the applet, first override this method and return false.

```
public void setContentPane(Container contentPane);
public void setGlassPane(Component glassPane);
public void setJMenuBar(JMenuBar menuBar)
```

These methods enable you to set new content pane, glass pane, and menu bar. Normally, the only one of these methods you need to call is setMenuBar().

Overridden Instance Methods

```
public void update(Graphics g);
```

This method forces a repaint of the applet, which results in the paint() method being called.

JButton Class

Full Name	javax.swing.JButton
Extends	AbstractButton->JComponent->Container-> Component->Object
Description	Public class. This GUI class implements a push button (or "command button") that supports advanced features of the Swing architecture. Most of the important methods of this class are inherited from the AbstractButton class (p. 165), such as addActionListener(), which installs an event handler for button selection.

Here is example code that creates a JButton object that uses both a string label and an icon. The button is then added to the content pane of the current applet or frame, and an event handler is installed. (Note: the applet implements the ActionListener interface and must be declared with an implements clause.)

```
ImageIcon icon = new ImageIcon("Plus.gif");
JButton button = new JButton("Add", icon);
button.addActionListener(this);
Container pane = getContentPane();
pane.add(button);
```

```
public void actionPerformed(ActionEvent e) {
    if (e.getSource == button) {
        JOptionPane.displayMessageDialog(this,
            "You clicked the button!");
    }
}
```

Constructors

```
public JButton();
public JButton(String text);
public JButton(Icon icon);
public JButton(Action a);
public JButton(String text, Icon icon);
```

These constructors support the creation of buttons using various pieces of initialization information such as text, an icon, an action, or a combination of text and an icon.

Instance Methods

```
public boolean isDefaultButton();
```

This method checks to see if the button is the default button in the container in which it resides.

```
public boolean isDefaultCapable();
```

This method checks to see if the button is capable of being the default button in the container in which it resides.

```
public void setDefaultCapable(boolean defaultCapable);
```

This method sets the button as the default button in the container in which it resides.

Overridden Instance Methods

```
protected void configurePropertiesFromAction(Action a);
```

This method sets the properties of the button based on the action argument.

```
protected String paramString();
```

This method generates a parameter string that identifies the button.

JCheckBox Class

Full Name   `javax.swing.JCheckBox`

Extends   `JToggleButton->AbstractButton->JComponent->Container->Component->Object`

Description   Public class. This class implements a checkbox that supports advanced GUI features of the Swing architecture. A checkbox is an independent component that shows either a check mark or an empty box, along with a label. Clicking the box toggles the component back and forth between the selected ("checked") and unselected states. The Swing architecture supports display of an icon in addition to, or in place of, an ordinary label. Note that many of the most useful methods of this class are defined in the `AbstractButton` class (p. 165), including the `AddItem Listener()` method, which installs event handlers for responding to changes in the state of the checkbox.

The following example adds a checkbox to the current applet or frame.

```
JCheckBox cb = new JCheckBox("Check this box for fun!");
Container pane = getContentPane();
pane.add(cb);
```

Constructors

```
public JCheckBox();
public JCheckBox(String text);
public JCheckBox(Icon icon);
public JCheckBox(Icon icon, boolean selected);
public JCheckBox(Action a);
public JCheckBox(String text, boolean selected);
public JCheckBox(String text, Icon icon);
public JCheckBox(String text, Icon icon, boolean selected);
```

These constructors support the creation of checkboxes using various pieces of initialization information such as text, an icon, an action, or a combination of text and an icon. You can also specify initial state of the checkbox by using the selected argument.

Instance Methods

```
public boolean isBorderPaintedFlat();
```

This method determines if the border of the checkbox should be painted flat.

```
public void setBorderPaintedFlat(boolean b);
```

This method sets whether the border of the checkbox should be painted flat.

Overridden Instance Methods

```
protected void configurePropertiesFromAction(Action a);
```

This method sets the properties of the checkbox based on the action argument.

```
protected String paramString();
```

This method generates a parameter string that identifies the checkbox.

JCheckBoxMenuItem Class

Full Name	javax.swing.JCheckBoxMenuItem
Extends	JMenuItem->AbstractButton->JComponent->Container->Component->Object
Description	Public class. This class implements a checkbox menu item that supports advanced GUI features of the Swing architecture, including optional picture (icon), check box, and text.

Constructors

```
public JCheckBoxMenuItem();
public JCheckBoxMenuItem(String text);
public JCheckBoxMenuItem(String text, boolean b);
public JCheckBoxMenuItem(Icon icon);
public JCheckBoxMenuItem(Action a);
public JCheckBoxMenuItem(String text, Icon icon);
public JCheckBoxMenuItem(String text, Icon icon, boolean b);
```

These constructors support the creation of checkbox menu items using various pieces of initialization information such as text, an icon, an action, or a combination of text and an icon. Also, two constructors that support setting the initial state of the checkbox via the b argument.

Instance Methods

```
public boolean getState();
public void setState(boolean b);
```

These methods get and set the selection state of the checkbox menu item.

Overridden Instance Methods

```
public Object[] getSelectedObjects();
```

This method returns an array containing a single item that is the label of the checkbox menu item, or null if the checkbox isn't selected.

```
protected String paramString();
```

This method generates a parameter string that identifies the checkbox menu item.

JColorChooser Class

Full Name	javax.swing.JColorChooser
Extends	JComponent->Container->Component->Object

Description   Public class. This class provides a standard GUI dialog box for selecting colors. By using this graphical component, the end user selects a choice from a palette of many colors. This color, in turn, is returned to the program as a Color value.

Here is an example of using the JColorChooser class to query the user for a color (the initial color is set to green):

```
Color color = JColorChooser.showDialog(this, "Select color",
   Color.green);
```

Constructors

```
public JColorChooser();
public JColorChooser(Color initialColor);
public JColorChooser(ColorSelectionModel model);
```

These constructors create a color-chooser dialog box with an optional initial color selected.

Class Methods

```
public static JDialog createDialog(Component c,
   String title, boolean modal, JColorChooser chooserPane,
   ActionListener okListener, ActionListener cancelListener);
```

Displays the color chooser as a non-modal dialog box. In calling the function, you must install event handlers that respond to the Ok and Cancel buttons.

```
public static Color showDialog(Component component,
   String title, Color initialColor);
```

Displays the color chooser as a modal dialog box. The method returns a Color value reflecting the user's choice.

Instance Methods

```
public Color getColor();
public void setColor(Color color);
public void setColor(int r, int g, int b);
public void setColor(int c);
```

These methods get and set the color selected in the color chooser.

JComboBox Class

Full Name   javax.swing.JComboBox

Extends   JComponent->Container->Component->Object

Description   Public class. This class supports a GUI combo box for selecting items from a list or entering text. The end user can click an arrow to display a popup list from which to select items. Many of the methods refer to one or more indexes; these are all zero-based, starting with index 0 referring to the first item.

The following example adds a combo box to the current applet or frame.

```
JCheckBox candidates = new JComboBox({"Bush", "Gore",
    "Buchanan", "Nader"});
Container pane = getContentPane();
pane.add(candidates);
```

This topic describes the most commonly used methods and fields.

Constructors

```
public JComboBox();
public JComboBox(Vector items);
public JComboBox(Object[] items);
```

These constructors support the creation of combo boxes by providing different approaches for initializing the list of items.

Instance Variables

```
protected String actionCommand;
protected boolean isEditable;
protected int maximumRowCount;
```

These instance variables store various properties of the combo box such as whether the combo box is editable.

Instance Methods

```
public void addActionListener(ActionListener l);
```

Adds an event handler for Action events generated when the end user makes a selection.

```
public void addItem(Object anObject);
```

Adds an item to the combo box.

```
public void addItemListener(ItemListener aListener);
```

Adds an event handler for events generated when the end user makes a selection. Supported for backward compatibility with AWT 1.1.

```
public Action getAction();
public String getActionCommand();
public Object getItemAt(int index);
public int getItemCount();
public int getMaximumRowCount();
```

Gets the state of various combo box properties. The `maximumRowCount` property specifies the number of visible rows that can be displayed; if the number of items exceeds this, the combo box uses a scrollbar.

```
public int getSelectedIndex();
public Object getSelectedItem();
public Object[] getSelectedObjects();
```

Gets the selected item by index number or zero-based index. If none are selected, the method returns –1 (first method) or null (second method). The `getSelectedObjects()` method is provided for backward compatibility with the AWT Choice class.

```
public void hidePopup();
```

Hides the popup containing the combo box list. See also `showPopup()`.

```
public void insertItemAt(Object anObject, int index);
```

Inserts item at specified zero-based index.

```
public boolean isEditable();
public boolean isLightWeightPopupEnabled();
public boolean isPopupVisible();
```

These methods return the state of one of the Boolean properties.

```
public void removeActionListener(ActionListener l);
```

Removes event handler installed with `addActionListener()`.

```
public void removeAllItems();
public void removeItem(Object anObject);
public void removeItemAt(int anIndex);
```

Removes specified item or items.

```
public void removeItemListener(ItemListener aListener);
```

Removes event handler installed with `addItemListener()`.

```
public boolean selectWithKeyChar(char keyChar);
```

Attempts to select an item corresponding to the specified key. Returns true if successful.

```
public void setAction(Action a);
public void setActionCommand(String aCommand);
public void setEditable(boolean aFlag);
public void setEditor(ComboBoxEditor anEditor);
public void setLightWeightPopupEnabled(boolean aFlag);
public void setMaximumRowCount(int count);
```

Java 2 API Reference

```
public void setModel(ComboBoxModel aModel);
public void setPopupVisible(boolean v);
```

These methods set various properties of the combo box.

```
public void setSelectedIndex(int anIndex);
public void setSelectedItem(Object anObject);
```

These methods select a list item, by index or by specifying the item itself.

```
public void showPopup();
```

Displays the combo box list.

Overridden Instance Methods

```
public boolean isFocusTraversable();
```

This method determines whether the combo box can receive the focus.

```
protected String paramString();
```

This method generates a parameter string that identifies the combo box.

```
public void setEnabled(boolean b);
```

This method enables or disables the combo box.

Java 2 API Reference

JComponent Class

Full Name   `javax.swing.JComponent`

Extends   `Container->Component->Object`

Description   Public class. This GUI class extends the standard Abstract Windowing ToolKit (AWT) Component class to support advanced features of the Swing architecture. The JComponent class serves as the base class for the majority of Swing components. Note that many of the most important methods of this class are inherited from the Component class (p. 210), including `paint()`, `repaint()`, and a number of the methods that install event handlers. See the Component class for a list of all of these event handler installers. Because this class extends the Component and Container classes, the JComponent inherits and works with the AWT framework as well as supporting the extended Swing features.

This topic describes most of the JComponent methods supported, except those that are for internal use only.

Constructors

```
public JComponent();
```

Class Variables

```
public static final String TOOL_TIP_TEXT_KEY;
public static final int UNDEFINED_CONDITION;
public static final int WHEN_ANCESTOR_OF_FOCUSED_COMPONENT;
public static final int WHEN_FOCUSED;
public static final int WHEN_IN_FOCUSED_WINDOW;
```

These constants describe the focus states of the component, along with the key that stores tooltip text for the component.

Class Methods

```
public static boolean isLightweightComponent(Component c);
```

This method returns true if the specified component is lightweight. A lightweight component does not correspond to a window on the native system, but is simply drawn as a graphic.

Instance Methods

```
public void addAncestorListener(AncestorListener listener);
```

Installs an event handler notified when any of the component's ancestor objects are moved or made visible or invisible.

```
public void addPropertyChangeListener(String propertyName,
    PropertyChangeListener listener);
```

Installs an event handler notified when any of the component's properties change.

```
public void addVetoableChangeListener(
    VetoableChangeListener listener);
```

Installs an event handler enabling the handler to veto any property changes in the component.

```
public void computeVisibleRect(Rectangle visibleRect);
```

Calculates a rectangle that is the intersection of the component and all its ancestors — in other words, the portion of the component that is visible on screen. This rectangle is placed in the visibleRect property, which you can get by calling getVisibleRect().

```
public JToolTip createToolTip();
```

In response to getToolTip(), this method is called to create a default tooltip object. You can override this class to provide your own tooltip. The tooltip is the popup Help window that appears when the mouse rests over a component.

```
public ActionListener getActionForKeyStroke(
    KeyStroke aKeyStroke);
```

This method returns the action listener, if any, for the corresponding keystroke.

```
public float getAlignmentX();
public float getAlignmentY();
```

These methods get the value of x and y alignments, which determine how the component is positioned. See corresponding "set" methods.

```
public boolean getAutoscrolls();
public Border getBorder();
public final Object getClientProperty(Object key);
protected Graphics getComponentGraphics(Graphics g);
public int getDebugGraphicsOptions();
public InputVerifier getInputVerifier();
public Insets getInsets(Insets insets);
public Component getNextFocusableComponent();
public KeyStroke[] getRegisteredKeyStrokes();
public JRootPane getRootPane();
public Point getToolTipLocation(MouseEvent event);
public String getToolTipText(MouseEvent event);
public String getToolTipText();
public Container getTopLevelAncestor();
public boolean getVerifyInputWhenFocusTarget();
public Rectangle getVisibleRect();
```

These methods get various properties of the component. The getClient Property() gets the value of a customized property added on by application code (see putClientProperty()). Several methods relate to a tooltip, which is the popup Help window that appears when the mouse rests over the component.

```
public void grabFocus();
```

This method is called by focus managers to shift focus to this component. To ask for focus from within the component's code, use requestFocus instead.

```
public boolean isFocusCycleRoot();
public boolean isManagingFocus();
public boolean isMaximumSizeSet();
public boolean isMinimumSizeSet();
public boolean isOptimizedDrawingEnabled();
public boolean isPaintingTile();
public boolean isPreferredSizeSet();
public boolean isRequestFocusEnabled();
public boolean isValidateRoot();
```

These methods return the state of various Boolean properties. See also "set" methods. A related method is the inherited isDoubleBuffered() method, also supported, which returns true if the double-buffering method is in use to reduce flickering during redrawing.

```
protected void paintBorder(Graphics g);
```

Repaints the component's border specified by the component's border property.

```
protected void paintChildren(Graphics g);
```

Causes a repaint of each child component in the child list. For information on how to add child components, see the Container class (p. 221), which contributes methods to this class.

```
protected void paintComponent(Graphics g);
```

Draws the component into the specified graphics context. Unless overridden, this method simply calls the component's paint method.

```
protected void processComponentKeyEvent(KeyEvent e);
```

This method is called if there are no matching actions for the keystroke. The default implementation does nothing. You can override to provide your own behavior.

```
public final void putClientProperty(Object key,
    Object value);
```

This method enables you to add your own properties. The method assigns the specified value to the property named by key. If the value argument is null, then the specified property (named by key) is cleared from the component's property list.

```
public void registerKeyboardAction(ActionListener anAction,
    KeyStroke aKeyStroke, int aCondition);
public void registerKeyboardAction(ActionListener anAction,
    String aCommand, KeyStroke aKeyStroke, int aCondition);
```

These methods register an Action object for a specified keystroke. When the user presses this key, the Action object's actionPerform() method is called.

```
public void removeAncestorListener(
    AncestorListener listener);
public void removePropertyListener(
    PropertyListener listener);
public void removeVetoableChangeListener(
    VetoableChangeListener listener);
```

These methods remove the specified event handler. See corresponding "add" methods.

```
public void repaint(Rectangle r);
```

These methods create a request to repaint the specified rectangle. Also see the version of repaint() inherited from the Component class (p. 210), which has the signature repaint(long tm, int x, int y, int width, int height); the first argument in that version is unused. The actual repainting is done by the paint() method inherited from the Component class. You can override paint() but should not call it directly.

```
public boolean requestDefaultFocus();
```

This is the method you should call to request that the component get the focus.

```
public void resetKeyboardActions();
```

Clears all keyboard action settings.

```
public void revalidate();
```

Requests that the system validate the component again.

```
public void setAlignmentX(float alignmentX);
public void setAlignmentY(float alignmentY);
```

These methods set alignment properties to a number between 0.0 and 1.0. A value of 0 indicates that the component should be placed closer to the left or top; a value of 1 indicates that the control should be placed closer to the right or bottom. 0.5 specifies placement at the halfway point.

```
public void setAutoscrolls(boolean autoscrolls);
public void setBorder(Border border);
public void setDebugGraphicsOptions(int debugOptions);
public void setDoubleBuffered(boolean aFlag);
public void setInputVerifier(InputVerifier inputVerifier);
public void setMaximumSize(Dimension maximumSize);
public void setMinimumSize(Dimension minimumSize);
public void setNextFocusableComponent(Component aComponent);
public void setOpaque(boolean isOpaque);
public void setPreferredSize(Dimension preferredSize);
public void setRequestFocusEnabled(boolean aFlag);
public void setToolTipText(String text);
public void setVerifyInputWhenFocusTarget(boolean flag);
```

These methods set various properties for the combo box. Note that the visibleRect property is set by calling computeVisibleRect() rather than a "set" method. See also "get" and "is" methods.

```
public void unregisterKeyboardAction(KeyStroke aKeyStroke);
```

Clears a keyboard action setting previously set with registerKeyboardAction().

Overridden Instance Methods

```
public boolean contains(int x, int y);
public void disable();
```

```
public void enable();
public Rectangle getBounds(Rectangle rv);
public Graphics getGraphics();
public int getHeight();
public EventListener[] getListeners(Class listenerType);
public Point getLocation(Point rv);
public Dimension getMaximumSize();
public Dimension getMinimumSize();
public Dimension getPreferredSize();
public Dimension getSize(Dimension rv);
public int getWidth();
public int getX();
public int getY();
public boolean hasFocus();
public boolean isDoubleBuffered();
public boolean isFocusTraversable();
public boolean isOpaque();
public void paint(Graphics g);
protected String paramString();
public void print(Graphics g);
public void printAll(Graphics g);
public void reshape(int x, int y, int w, int h);
public void setBackground(Color bg);
public void setEnabled(boolean enabled);
public void setFont(Font font);
public void setForeground(Color fg);
public void setVisible(boolean aFlag);
public void update(Graphics g);
```

These methods are overridden versions of methods defined in the parent
AWT Container and Component classes (pp. 221 and 210).

JDialog Class

Full Name	javax.swing.JDialog
Extends	Dialog->Window->Container->Component->Object
Implements	RootPaneContainer
Description	Public class. This class extends the standard Abstract Windowing ToolKit (AWT) Dialog class to support advanced GUI features of the Swing architecture. To customize a dialog box, you need to get its content pane by calling getContent Pane(), and then adding components to it.

Alternatively, you can save work in many cases by calling class methods of JOptionPane (p. 327) rather than creating a dialog box yourself.

Constructors

```
public JDialog();
public JDialog(Frame owner);
public JDialog(Frame owner, String title);
public JDialog(Frame owner, boolean modal);
public JDialog(Frame owner, String title, boolean modal);
```

These constructors create a dialog box with different pieces of initialization information; owner is the owner of the dialog box, title is the title of the dialog box, and modal determines whether the dialog box is modal. If no owner is specified, an invisible owner frame is created for the dialog.

Instance Methods

```
public Container getContentPane();
```

Gets the dialog's content pane. You can add elements to this pane and then call its add() method, defined in the Component class (p. 210).

```
public int getDefaultCloseOperation();
public Component getGlassPane();
public JMenuBar getJMenuBar();
public JLayeredPane getLayeredPane();
public JRootPane getRootPane();
```

These methods get various properties associated with the dialog, including the various panes that construct the internal spaces in the dialog's UI. Note that modal dialog's are not allowed to have heavyweight popup components. The default close operation, if not set, is HIDE_ON_CLOSE.

```
protected boolean rootPaneCheckingEnabled();
```

Returns true if an error is thrown whenever attempts are made to add components directly to the dialog rather than its content pane. This behavior can be turned off if needed; see "set" method.

```
public void setContentPane(Container contentPane);
public void setDefaultCloseOperation(int operation);
public void setGlassPane(Component glassPane);
public void setJMenuBar(JMenuBar menu);
public void setLayeredPane(JLayeredPane layeredPane);
```

These methods set various properties. If you choose, you can replace the default panes with customized versions. See also "get" methods.

```
public void setLocationRelativeTo(Component c);
```

Sets the location of the dialog relative to the specified component. The dialog is centered inside the component; if the component is not visible, the dialog is centered in the screen.

```
protected void setRootPane(JRootPane root);
protected void setRootPaneCheckingEnabled(boolean enabled);
```

These methods set various properties. See "get" methods.

Overridden Instance Methods

```
protected String paramString();
public void remove(Component comp);
public void setLayout(LayoutManager manager);
public void update(Graphics g);
```

These methods are overridden versions of methods defined in the parent AWT Dialog class.

JEditorPane Class

Full Name	javax.swing.JEditorPane
Extends	JTextComponent->JComponent->Container->Component->Object
Description	Public class. This class extends the JTextComponent (text-editing) class to provide a simple viewer for several types of content, including HTML, RTF, and plain text. An editor pane works as a simple browser. Each type of content is associated with a different "editor kit," which JEditorPane constructors automatically create for you. Note that to be used, the editor pane must be associated with a frame.

The following code creates a simple Web viewer by creating an editor pane, building a scrollbar pane around it, and then associating with a frame, which is then displayed.

```
public class Browser {
    public static void main(String[] args) {
        JEditorPane pane;
        try {
            pane = new JEditorPane(args[0]);
        }
        catch (IOException e) {
            e.printStackTrace(System.err);
            System.exit(1);
        }
```

Java 2 API Reference

```
    JFrame frame = new JFrame();
    frame.addWindowListener(new BasicWindowMonitor());
    frame.setContentPane(new JScrollPane(pane));
    frame.setSize(400, 400);
    frame.setVisible(true);
}
```

To make this code fully functional as a browser, you would need to add code for a HyperLinkListener object.

Constructors

```
public JEditorPane();
public JEditorPane(URL initialPage) throws IOException;
public JEditorPane(String url) throws IOException;
public JEditorPane(String type, String text);
```

These constructors create an editor pane with several different approaches to referencing the content to be edited. The arguments typically give the URL of a file to be edited. The constructors, except for the first, create the appropriate kind of editor kit.

Class Methods

```
public static EditorKit createEditorKitForContentType(
    String type);
public static String getEditorKitClassNameForContentType(
    String type);
```

These methods create an editor kit (or editor kit class name) for the appropriate content type. Content types supported by default include "application/rtf," "text/plain," "text/html," and "text/rtf."

```
public static void registerEditorKitForContentType(
    String type, String classname);
public static void registerEditorKitForContentType(
    String type, String classname, ClassLoader loader);
```

These methods are called to associate a content type with an editor kit class name. These are mostly for internal use only.

Instance Methods

```
public void addHyperlinkListener(HyperlinkListener l);
```

Sets a hyperlink listener, which can repond to hyperlink events. See HyperLink Listener.

```
public void fireHyperlinkUpdate(HyperlinkEvent e);
```

Fires a hyperlink event. This is mainly for internal use only.

```
public final String getContentType();
public EditorKit getEditorKit();
public EditorKit getEditorKitForContentType(String type);
public URL getPage();
```

These methods get various properties. The page contains the current content stream as a URL.

```
public void removeHyperlinkListener(HyperlinkListener l);
```

Removes an event handler previously added with addHyperLinkListener().

```
public final void setContentType(String type);
public void setEditorKit(EditorKit kit);
public void setEditorKitForContentType(String type,
    EditorKit k);
public void setPage(URL page) throws IOException;
public void setPage(String url) throws IOException;
```

These methods set various properties. The setPage() methods enable you to read a new page.

Overridden Instance Methods

```
public Dimension getPreferredSize();
public boolean getScrollableTracksViewportHeight();
public boolean getScrollableTracksViewportWidth();
public String getText();
public boolean isFocusCycleRoot();
public boolean isManagingFocus();
protected String paramString();
protected void processComponentKeyEvent(KeyEvent e);
protected void processKeyEvent(KeyEvent e);
public void replaceSelection(String content);
public void setText(String t);
```

These methods are overridden versions of methods defined in the parent JTextComponent class (p. 353).

JFileChooser Class

Full Name	javax.swing.JFileChooser
Extends	JComponent->Container->Component->Object
Description	Public class. This class provides a standard, scrollable GUI dialog box for selecting and viewing files. The user can use the mouse or keystrokes to find and select a file.

Normal use of this class involves calling one of the "show dialog" methods listed near the end of this topic; the methods return JFileChooser.CANCEL_OPTION if the user canceled the action. The filename selected can then be determined by calling the getSelectedFile() method. Note that all a file-chooser dialog box does is return a filename. You have to implement the appropriate response programmatically.

Here is an example of using the JFileChooser class to query the user for a filename:

```
JFileChooser chooser = new JFileChooser();
int retVal = chooser.showOpenDialog(this);
if (retVal == JFileChooser.APPROVE_OPTION)
    String fname = chooser.getSelectedFile().getName();
```

The this argument passed into showOpenDialog() is the parent component of the file chooser, which is typically the main application or applet window.

This topic describes the most commonly used methods of the class.

Constructors

```
public JFileChooser();
public JFileChooser(String currentDirectoryPath);
public JFileChooser(File currentDirectory);
```

These constructors create a file chooser, enabling you to optionally specify an initial directory to view.

Class Variables

```
public static final int CUSTOM_DIALOG;
public static final int OPEN_DIALOG;
public static final int SAVE_DIALOG;
```

The constants above provide a range of values for the dialogType property.

```
public static final int FILES_ONLY;
public static final int FILES_AND_DIRECTORIES;
public static final int DIRECTORIES_ONLY;
```

The constants above provide a range of values for the fileSelectionMode property.

```
public static final int APPROVE_OPTION;
public static final int CANCEL_OPTION;
public static final int ERROR_OPTION;
```

The constants above are possible return values of showDialog() and related methods..

These constants represent various settings and properties unique to the file chooser.

Instance Methods

```
public boolean accept(File f);
```

Returns true if the specified file should be displayed. You can filter files in the display by overriding this method.

```
public void addActionListener(ActionListener l);
```

Adds an event-handler that responds to user's pressing the Approve or Cancel button.

```
public void approveSelection();
public void cancelSelection();
```

These methods press the Approve or Cancel button programmatically, firing the appropriate events.

```
public void changeToParentDirectory();
```

Changes directory. See also setCurrentDirectory().

```
public void ensureFileIsVisible(File f);
```

Makes sure that specified file, if it is in the list, gets displayed. Causes scrolling if needed.

```
public int getApproveButtonMnemonic();
public String getApproveButtonText();
public String getApproveButtonToolTipText();
public File getCurrentDirectory();
public String getDescription(File f);
public String getDialogTitle();
public int getDialogType();
public int getFileSelectionMode();
```

Most of these methods get a property setting of the file chooser. The getDescription() method gets a brief description of the specified file, which might be used by a detailed directory view. The default for file SelectionMode() is JFileChooser.FILES_ONLY, but you can change this to JFileChooser.FILES_AND_DIRECTORIES or JFileChooser.DIRECTORIES_ONLY.

```
public Icon getIcon(File f);
public String getName(File f);
```

These methods return information on a specified file.

```
public File getSelectedFile();
public File[] getSelectedFiles();
```

These methods return the currently selected file or files. If no files are selected, getSelectedFile() returns null. If more than one file is selected, getSelectedFile() returns the first file in the list. The multiSelection Enabled property affects the behavior of these methods.

```
public String getTypeDescription(File f);
```

Gets a string describing the type of the specified file; can be used to help display file details.

```
public boolean isDirectorySelectionEnabled();
public boolean isFileSelectionEnabled();
public boolean isMultiSelectionEnabled();
public boolean isTraversable(File f);
```

These methods return the states of various Boolean properties. The isTraversable() property returns true if f is a directory and can be opened.

```
public void removeActionListener(ActionListener l);
```

Removes an event handler previously installed with addActionListener().

```
public void rescanCurrentDirectory();
```

Refreshes the list of files in the current directory; this is useful if you have reason to believe the directory contents have changed.

```
public void setApproveButtonMnemonic(char mnemonic);
public void setApproveButtonMnemonic(int mnemonic);
public void setApproveButtonText(String approveButtonText);
public void setApproveButtonToolTipText(String toolTipText);
public void setCurrentDirectory(File dir);
public void setDialogTitle(String dialogTitle);
public void setDialogType(int dialogType);
public void setFileSelectionMode(int mode);
public void setMultiSelectionEnabled(boolean b);
```

These methods set various properties of the file chooser. See "get" methods.

```
public void setSelectedFile(File file);
public void setSelectedFiles(File[] selectedFiles);
```

These methods select one or more files. Note that to effectively set multiple files, you may first need to call setMutliSelectionEnabled().

```
public int showDialog(Component parent,
  String approveButtonText);
public int showOpenDialog(Component parent);
public int showSaveDialog(Component parent);
```

These methods display the dialog and return a value indicating –1 if the user accepts a file and 0 if the user cancels the action. (You can get the file itself by calling the getSelectedFile() method.) The first method above displays an OK button with the specified text. The other two have an Open or Save button, as appropriate.

JFrame Class

Full Name	javax.swing.JFrame
Extends	Frame->Window->Container->Component->Object
Implements	RootPaneContainer
Description	Public class. This class extends the standard Abstract Windowing ToolKit (AWT) Frame class (p. 261) to support advanced GUI features of the Swing architecture. You use this component in roughly the same way as the AWT Frame class; however, instead of calling the add() method directly, you should first get a reference to the JFrame object's content pane and then add components to that pane. (See example below.) JFrame uses the Swing UI scheme that divides a frame into specific panels including layered pane, menu bar, content pane, and glass pane. To display a frame, call the setVisible() method of the Component class (p. 210).

Java 2 API Reference

The following code creates a JFrame object and adds a command button:

```
JFrame frm = new JFrame();
JButton btnOk = new JButton("OK");
frm.getContentPane().add(btnOk);
frm.setVisible(true);
```

Constructors

```
public JFrame();
public JFrame(String title);
public JFrame(GraphicsConfiguration gc);
public JFrame(String title, GraphicsConfiguration gc);
```

These constructors create a frame; the last three constructors use a string title, a graphics configuration, and a combination of the two to initialize the frame.

Class Variables

```
public static final int EXIT_ON_CLOSE;
```

Constant. This constant represents the exit-on-close feature of the frame, which exits an application automatically when the frame is closed.

Instance Methods

```
public Container getContentPane();
public int getDefaultCloseOperation();
public Component getGlassPane();
public JMenuBar getJMenuBar();
public JLayeredPane getLayeredPane();
public JRootPane getRootPane();
```

These methods get various properties of the class, including the specific panes that constitute the physical frame. (Of these, the content pane occupies the internal space of the frame.) The defaultCloseOperation property is set by default to WindowConstants.HIDE_ON_CLOSE. This setting causes the window to call setVisible(false) upon closing.

```
protected boolean isRootPaneCheckingEnabled();
```

If this method returns true, then attempts to add a component directly to the frame (rather than its content pane) throw an error.

```
public void setContentPane(Container contentPane);
public void setDefaultCloseOperation(int operation);
public void setGlassPane(Component glassPane);
public void setJMenuBar(JMenuBar menubar);
public void setLayeredPane(JLayeredPane layeredPane);
protected void setRootPane(JRootPane root);
protected void setRootPaneCheckingEnabled(boolean enabled);
```

These methods set various properties of the class. See corresponding "get" and "is" methods.

Overridden Instance Methods

```
protected String paramString();
protected void processKeyEvent(KeyEvent e);
protected void processWindowEvent(WindowEvent e);
public void remove(Component comp);
public void setLayout(LayoutManager manager);
public void update(Graphics g);
```

These methods are overridden versions of methods defined in the parent AWT Frame class.

JLabel Class

Full Name	javax.swing.JLabel
Extends	JComponent->Container->Component->Object
Implements	SwingConstants

Description   Public class. This class implements a label that is used to
display a string of text, an icon, or a combination of the two.
Labels are output-only components, which means they can't
receive input focus. This is a simple class that is similar to the
AWT Label class, except that it has extended features such as
the use of an icon.

Here is an example of creating a JLabel object and setting the horizontal and
vertical text position:

```
ImageIcon icon = new ImageIcon("Dog.gif");
JLabel label = new JLabel("Animals", icon, JLabel.CENTER);
label.setHorizontalTextPosition(JLabel.CENTER);
label.setVerticalTextPosition(JLabel.BOTTOM);
```

Constructors

```
public JLabel();
public JLabel(String text);
public JLabel(String text, int horizontalAlignment);
public JLabel(Icon image);
public JLabel(Icon image, int horizontalAlignment);
public JLabel(String text, Icon image,
    int horizontalAlignment);
```

These constructors create a label that includes text, an icon image, or both.
Some of the constructors also allow you to specify the horizontal alignment
of the text/image.

Instance Methods

```
public Icon getDisabledIcon();
public int getDisplayedMnemonic();
public int getHorizontalAlignment();
public int getHorizontalTextPosition();
public Icon getIcon();
public int getTextIconTextGap();
public Component getLabelFor();
public String getText();
public int getVerticalAlignment();
public int getVerticalTextPosition();
```

These methods get various property settings for the class. The vertical and horizontal alignment properties take the values TOP, BOTTOM, and CENTER; or LEFT,
RIGHT, and CENTER, depending on the orientation. All of these constants are
defined in SwingConstants, which is implemented by JLabel. (Therefore, the
name JLabel.CENTER, for example, is accepted.) getIconTextGap() returns the
space, in pixels, between the text label and icon, if any. The getLabelFor()

method returns the component, if any, that the label is specifically attached to; you can set this component with setLabelFor(), below.

```
public void setDisabledIcon(Icon disabledIcon);
public void setDisplayedMnemonic(char aChar);
public void setDisplayedMnemonic(int key);
public void setHorizontalAlignment(int alignment);
public void setHorizontalTextPosition(int textPosition);
public void setIcon(Icon icon);
public void setTextIconTextGap(int iconTextGap);
public void setLabelFor(Component c);
public void setText(String text);
public void setVerticalAlignment(int alignment);
public void setVerticalTextPosition(int textPosition);
```

These methods set various properties of the class. Set "get" methods.

Java 2 API Reference

JLayeredPane Class

Full Name	javax.swing.JLayeredPane
Extends	JComponent->Container->Component->Object
Description	Public class. This class supports a pane that allows components to be layered so that they overlap each other. Each component added to a layered pane receives a numeric depth, which determines where it resides (stacks) with respect to other components. This class takes advantage of the Container.add() method (p. 221), which enables you to specify an object as the second argument; with a layered panel, this argument may be an Integer object specifying the depth. Higher depth levels appear "on top" of lower ones. (See example that follows.)
	To get an instance of JLayeredPane, you can call the getLayeredPane() method of the JApplet or JFrame class (pp. 292 and 313).

The following example get a layered pane for the current applet (or frame) and adds buttons at two different levels of depth.

```
JLayeredPane layeredPan = getLayeredPane();
setContentPane(layeredPane);

JButton btnBotton = new JButton();
JButton btnTop = new JButton();
btnBottom.setBounds(10, 10, 60, 60);
btnTop.setBounds(30, 30, 60, 60);
```

```
// Add buttons at different depth levels; btnTop on top.

layeredPan.add(btnBottom, new Integer(1));
layeredPan.add(btnTop, new Integer(2));
```

Constructors

```
public JLayeredPane();
```

Class Variables

```
public static final String LAYER_PROPERTY;
public static final Integer DEFAULT_LAYER;
public static final Integer DRAG_LAYER;
public static final Integer FRAME_CONTENT_LAYER;
public static final Integer MODAL_LAYER;
public static final Integer PALETTE_LAYER;
public static final Integer POPUP_LAYER;
```

These constants identify special layers supported by the system. Except for
DEFAULT_LAYER, these numbers have high or low values; if your own layers
stay in the range 0 to 99, you avoid conflicts. (For example, FRAME_CONTENT_
LAYER is used only for the content pane background and menu bar. Its integer
setting is –30,000, virtually guaranteeing them to be below every other layer.)
Components are normally placed at the DEFAULT_LAYER, which is 0.

Class Methods

```
public static int getLayer(JComponent c);
public static JLayeredPane getLayeredPaneAbove(Component c);
public static void putLayer(JComponent c, int layer);
```

These methods search through the component hierarchy to find the layer of
the specified component. The getLayeredPaneAbove() method returns null if
the specified component is not found. The putLayer() method is similar to
the setLayer() method, described below, but it does not cause a repaint.

Instance Methods

```
public int getComponentCountInLayer(int layer);
```

Returns the current number of layers.

```
public Component[] getComponentsInLayer(int layer);
```

Returns an array containing all the components at the specified layer.

```
public int getIndexOf(Component c);
public int getLayer(Component c);
public int getPosition(Component c);
```

These methods get information about the specified component. getPosition() returns the component's position within its layer.

```
public int highestLayer();
public int lowestLayer();
```

Returns the depth number of highest or lowest layer.

```
public void moveToBack(Component c);
public void moveToFront(Component c);
```

Moves the component to the front or back of its layer.

```
public void setLayer(Component c, int layer);
public void setLayer(Component c, int layer, int position);
public void setPosition(Component c, int position);
```

These methods set the layer of a child component, its position within that layer, or both.

Overridden Instance Methods

```
public boolean isOptimizedDrawingEnabled();
public void paint(Graphics g);
protected String paramString();
public void remove(int index);
```

These methods are overridden versions of methods defined in the parent JComponent class. Of these, remove() is particularly useful as a way of getting rid of a component; this index is its absolute index within the pane, not within its layer. (You can get this index by calling the getIndexOf() method).

JList Class

Full Name   javax.swing.JList

Extends   JComponent->Container->Component->Object

Implements   Scrollable

Description   Public class. This class implements a list component that allows the user to select from a list of items. This class is similar to the AWT List class but supports some expanded features, such as the ability to set background and foreground colors for list items. The class also supports several selection modes, which you get and set with getSelectionMode() and setSelectionMode(). Many of the methods refer to one or more indexes; as elsewhere, these are zero-based.

Because this class implements the `Scrollable` interface, a `JList` object can be placed inside a `JScollPane` object, which is the principal way of providing scrollbars (since unlike its AWT equivalent, `JList` does not provide them itself).

Here is an example of creating a `JList` object that is initialized with an array of strings:

```
String[] colors = { "red", "green", "blue", "orange",
    "yellow", "purple", "black", "white" };
JList list = new JList(colors);
list.setSelectedIndex(4);        // Select fifth item.

// Add list to current content pane, with scrollbars.

JScrollPane scrollpane = new JScrollPane(list);
Container content = getContentPane();
content.add(scrollpane);
```

Constructors

```
public JList();
public JList(Vector listData);
public JList(Object[] listData);
```

These constructors create a list; the latter two constructors initialize the list with an array or vector.

Instance Methods

```
public void addListSelectionListener(
    ListSelectionListener listener);
```

Installs an event handler that responds to changes in list selection.

```
public void addSelectionInterval(int index0, int index1);
```

Adds the specified range to the set of selected items. This range contains the items from zero-based indexes index0 to index1, inclusive. See also setSelectionInterval().

```
public void clearSelection();
```

De-selects all items currently selected.

```
public void ensureIndexIsVisible(int index);
```

Causes scrolling, if necessary, to ensure that the specified item is visible.

```
public int getAnchorSelectionIndex();
public Rectangle getCellBounds(int index0, int index1);
public int getFirstVisibleIndex();
```

Java 2 API Reference

```
public int getFixedCellHeight();
public int getFixedCellWidth();
public int getLastVisibleIndex();
public int getLeadSelectionIndex();
public int getMaxSelectionIndex();
public int getMinSelectionIndex();
public Dimension getPreferredScrollableViewportSize();
```

These methods get various property settings. The getFixedCellHeight() and getFixedCellWidth() methods get the size, in pixels, of items in the list. You can explicitly set these with corresponding "get" methods. With other methods, the anchor and lead are the first and last positions, inclusive, of the most recent selection action. The min and max are the lowest and highest positions, inclusive, of all selected items.

```
public int getSelectedIndex();
public int[] getSelectedIndices();
public Object getSelectedValue();
public Object[] getSelectedValues();
```

These methods get the selected item or items, getting either the items themselves or zero-based indexes. If multiple selection is enabled, getSelected Index() and getSelectedValue() return the first item selected, if any. If no item is selected, these methods return –1 or null, as appropriate.

```
public Color getSelectionBackground();
public Color getSelectionForeground();
```

These methods return customized colors for items in the list.

```
public int getSelectionMode();
```

Returns the selection mode as one of the following constants of the List SelectionModel class: SINGLE_SELECTION, SINGLE_INTERVAL_SELECTION, and MULTIPLE_INTERVAL_SELECTION. The last two modes both permit multiple selection, but the second requires that any selection be part of a single continuous interval.

```
public int getVisibleRowCount();
```

Returns the number of rows currently visible on screen.

```
public Point indexToLocation(int index);
```

Returns the top left point (in pixels) of specified element, if visible, or null if not visible.

```
public boolean isSelectedIndex(int index);
public boolean isSelectionEmpty();
```

Returns true if item specified by zero-based index is selected. The second method returns true if no items are selected.

```
public int locationToIndex(Point location);
```

Returns the zero-based index of the item containing the specified point, in pixels.

```
public void removeListSelectionListener(
    ListSelectionListener listener);
```

Removes an event-handler installed by addListSelectionListener().

```
public void removeSelectionInterval(int index0, int index1);
```

Removes selection from interval specified by zero-based index0 to index1, inclusive.

```
public void setFixedCellHeight(int height);
public void setFixedCellWidth(int width);
public void setListData(Object[] listData);
public void setListData(Vector listData);
public void setSelectedIndex(int index);
public void setSelectedIndices(int[] indices);
public void setSelectedValue(Object anObject,
    boolean shouldScroll);
public void setSelectionBackground(Color clr);
public void setSelectionForeground(Color clr);
public void setSelectionInterval(int index0, int index1);
public void setSelectionMode(int selectionMode);
public void setVisibleRowCount(int visibleRowCount);
```

Most of these methods set various properties of the JList object; see corresponding "get" method.

JMenu Class

Full Name	javax.swing.JMenu
Extends	JMenuItem->AbstractButton->JComponent-> Container->Component->Object
Implements	MenuElement
Description	Public class. This class implements a menu that is capable of containing multiple menu items and separators. Within the menu, menu items are represented by the JMenuItem class (p. 325), while separators are represented by the JSeparator class. A number of methods use an index number (also called "position"); these indexes are zero-based.

The following example creates a menu and then adds several items to it. Although you cannot add icons directly, you can add a menu item with an icon by first creating a JMenuItem object and then specifying this object. This technique is used in the third statement below.

```
JMenu editMenu = new JMenu("Edit");
menuBar.add(editMenu);
editMenu.add(
    new JMenuItem( "Undo", new ImageIcon("Undo.gif") )
);
editMenu.addSeparator();
editMenu.add(new JMenuItem("Cut"));
editMenu.add(new JMenuItem("Copy"));
editMenu.add(new JMenuItem("Paste"));
```

Constructors

```
public JMenu();
public JMenu(String s);
public JMenu(Action a);
```

These constructors create a menu that is either empty or initialized with a string or action.

Instance Methods

```
public JMenuItem add(String s);
public JMenuItem add(Action a);
public JMenuItem add(JMenuItem menuItem);
```

These methods add a menu item from a string, action, or JMenuItem object. The method returns the resulting JMenuItem object in each case. See also insert().

```
public void addSeparator();
```

Adds a separator, which is a horizontal line. See also insertSeparator().

```
public int getDelay();
public JMenuItem getItem(int pos);
public int getItemCount();
public Component getMenuComponent(int n);
public int getMenuComponentCount();
public Component[] getMenuComponents();
public JPopupMenu getPopupMenu();
protected Point getPopupMenuOrigin();
```

These methods get various property settings for the JMenu object. The getMenuComponent() method returns the menu item at the specified position. The delay property specifies the number of milliseconds that menu items wait before appearing or disappearing; default setting is 0.

Java 2 API Reference

```
public void insert(String s, int pos);
public JMenuItem insert(JMenuItem mi, int pos);
public JMenuItem insert(Action a, int pos);
public void insertSeparator(int index);
```

Inserts an item at the specified position, which must be non-negative. All menu items at the position or later and shifted up by one. The insert Separator() method does the same thing, except that it places a horizontal line (separator) at the specified position.

```
public boolean isMenuComponent(Component c);
public boolean isPopupMenuVisible();
public boolean isTopLevelMenu();
```

Returns the state of a Boolean property. The isMenuComponent() returns true if the specified component is present in the menu.

```
public void remove(JMenuItem item);
public void removeMenuListener(MenuListener l);
```

Removes specified menu item or event handler.

```
public void setDelay(int d);
public void setMenuLocation(int x, int y);
public void setPopupMenuVisible(boolean b);
```

Sets one of the menu's properties. See "get" methods.

Overridden Instance Methods

```
public Component add(Component c);
public Component add(Component c, int index);
public void doClick(int pressTime);
public Component getComponent();
public MenuElement[] getSubElements();
public boolean isSelected();
public void menuSelectionChanged(boolean isIncluded);
protected String paramString();
protected void processKeyEvent(KeyEvent e);
public void remove(Component c);
public void remove(int pos);
public void removeAll();
public void setAccelerator(KeyStroke keyStroke);
public void setModel(ButtonModel newModel);
public void setSelected(boolean b);
```

These methods are overridden versions of methods defined in the parent JMenuItem class.

JMenuBar Class

Full Name	`javax.swing.JMenuBar`
Extends	`JComponent->Container->Component->Object`
Implements	`MenuElement`
Description	Public class. This class implements a menu bar that houses the menu for an applet or application. Menus within the menu bar are represented by the `JMenu` class.

Here is an example of code that creates a menu bar and then adds a menu and several menu items to it:

```
JMenuBar menuBar = new JMenuBar();
setJMenuBar(menuBar);
JMenu editMenu = new JMenu("Edit");
menuBar.add(editMenu);
editMenu.add(new JMenuItem("Undo",
  new ImageIcon("Undo.gif")));
editMenu.addSeparator();
editMenu.add(new JMenuItem("Cut"));
editMenu.add(new JMenuItem("Copy"));
editMenu.add(new JMenuItem("Paste"));
```

The menu bar can then be added to a frame by calling the `setMenuBar()` method of the `JFrame` class (p. 313).

```
myFrame.setMenuBar(menuBar);
```

Constructors

```
public JMenuBar();
```

Instance Methods

```
public JMenu add(JMenu c);
```

Adds a menu to the menu bar and returns a reference to that menu.

```
public int getComponentIndex(Component c);
```

Returns the zero-based index of the specified child component (which you can assume is a `JMenu` item) or -1 if the component is not found.

```
public Component getComponentAtIndex(int index);
public JMenu getHelpMenu();
public Insets getMargin();
public JMenu getMenu(int index);
public int getMenuCount();
```

These methods get various property settings for the menu bar. Some of these are read-only.

```
public boolean isBorderPainted();
public boolean isSelected();
```

These properties get boolean settings for the menu bar.

```
public void setHelpMenu(JMenu menu);
public void setBorderPainted(boolean b);
public void setMargin(Insets m);
```

These methods set various properties of the menu bar.

```
public void setSelected(Component c);
```

Makes the selected component the active menu bar. This is called when a mnemonic key for a menu is pressed.

JMenuItem Class

Full Name	`javax.swing.JMenuItem`
Extends	`AbstractButton->JComponent->Container->` `Component->Object`
Implements	`MenuElement`
Description	Public class. This class implements a menu item, which is typically a command that is capable of being invoked from a menu. A menu item functions much like a button appearing in a list (menu) with other buttons (menu items). A distinctive feature of Swing menu items is that they can contain both menu text (strings) and icons. This class works with the `JMenu` and `JMenuBar` classes (pp. 321 and 324). To respond to a menu item command, either initialize the menu item from an `Action` object or install an `ActionEvent` handler (p. 168). You can do the latter by calling the `addActionListener()` method inherited from `AbstractButton` class (p. 165).

Here is an example of code that creates several menu items, both with and without image icons:

```
JMenuItem undoItem = new JMenuItem("Undo",
    new ImageIcon("Undo.gif"));
JMenuItem cutItem = new JMenuItem("Cut");
JMenuItem copyItem = new JMenuItem("Copy");
```

Here is another example that shows how to set a mnemonic and accelerator for a menu item:

```
pasteItem = new JMenuItem("Paste");
pasteItem.setMnemonic(KeyEvent.VK_P);
pasteItem.setAccelerator(KeyStroke.getKeyStroke(
    KeyEvent.VK_V, ActionEvent.CTRL_MASK));
```

Once you create menu items, you can add them to a menu bar by calling the JMenuBar.add() method (p. 324). For example:

```
editMenu.add(pasteItem);
```

This topic describes the most commonly used methods. In addition to the methods listed here, the class provides methods to implement the MenuElement interface.

Constructors

```
public JMenuItem();
public JMenuItem(String text);
public JMenuItem(Icon icon);
public JMenuItem(Action a);
public JMenuItem(String text, Icon icon);
public JMenuItem(String text, int mnemonic);
```

These constructors create a menu item using a string, icon, action, or combination of a string and icon to initialize the item; the last constructor also specifies a keyboard mnemonic for the item. The mnemonic is a key identified by one of the integer constants in the KeyEvent class (p. 365).

Instance Methods

```
public KeyStroke getAccelerator();
public boolean isArmed();
```

These methods return property settings for the menu item.

```
public void setAccelerator(KeyStroke keyStroke);
public void setArmed(boolean b);
```

These methods set menu item properties. Setting the armed property to true is the equivalent of selecting the menu item.

```
public void updateUI();
```

Forces a refresh of the item's user interface.

Overridden Instance Methods

```
protected void configurePropertiesFromAction(Action a);
```

This method sets the properties of the menu item based on the action argument.

```
protected void init(String text, Icon icon);
```

This method initializes the menu item with the specified string and icon. If you only wish to set one of these arguments, pass null for the other argument.

```
protected String paramString();
```

This method generates a parameter string that identifies the menu item.

```
public void setEnabled(boolean b);
```

This method enables or disables the menu item.

JOptionPane Class

Full Name	javax.swing.JOptionPane
Extends	JComponent->Container->Component->Object
Description	Public class. This class provides a simplified mechanism for displaying a dialog box and, optionally, getting feedback from the user. The class is large because it provides an extremely wide set of options. The use of the class to show a modal dialog box requires only a single call to a class method. Alternatively, you can create a non-modal dialog by creating a JOptionPane instance and then closing it later. But use of a class method such as showMessageDialog() is by far the easiest way to use this class, as shown in the examples that follow.

The following example calls a JOptionPane class method to create a modal message dialog box.

```
JOptionPane.showMessageDialog(this,
    "You are running low on memory.", "Memory warning",
    JOptionPane.WARNING_MESSAGE);
```

The next example also creates a modal dialog box, but this method returns an integer indicating which button the user clicked.

```
int btn = JOptionPane.showConfirmDialog(this,
    "Are you sure you want to exit the application?",
    "Exit application", JOptionPane.YES_NO_OPTION);

if (btn == JOptionPane.YES_OPTION)
    // YES clicked, take appropriate action...
```

You check the return value of the showConfirmDialog() method to determine what button the user pressed to exit the dialog: YES_OPTION, NO_OPTION, OK_OPTION, CANCEL_OPTION, or CLOSED_OPTION.

Constructors

```
public JOptionPane();
public JOptionPane(Object message);
public JOptionPane(Object message, int messageType);
public JOptionPane(Object message, int messageType,
    int optionType);
public JOptionPane(Object message, int messageType,
    int optionType, Icon icon);
public JOptionPane(Object message, int messageType,
    int optionType, Icon icon, Object[] options);
public JOptionPane(Object message, int messageType,
    int optionType, Icon icon, Object[] options,
    Object initialValue);
```

These constructors create an option pane using various kinds of information. You should use a constructor only if you want to create a persistent, rather than a modal, dialog box. To do the latter, it is much easier to simply call one of the class methods.

Class Variables

```
public static final Object UNINITIALIZED_VALUE;
```

This is a constant used to indicate that no value has been selected for the pane.

```
public static final int ERROR_MESSAGE;
public static final int INFORMATION_MESSAGE;
public static final int PLAIN_MESSAGE;
public static final int QUESTION_MESSAGE;
public static final int WARNING_MESSAGE;
```

The constants above specify values for the messageType argument in class methods and constructors.

```
public static final int OK_CANCEL_OPTION;
public static final int YES_NO_CANCEL_OPTION;
public static final int YES_NO_OPTION;
```

The constants above specify values for the optionType argument in class methods and constructors. This determines what buttons are displayed.

```
public static final int CANCEL_OPTION;
public static final int CLOSED_OPTION;
public static final int DEFAULT_OPTION;
public static final int NO_OPTION;
public static final int OK_OPTION;
public static final int YES_OPTION;
```

The constants above are return values for class methods as well as getValue( ). For example, if the user clicks the OK button, the method returns JOptionPane.OK_OPTION.

Instance Variables

```
protected transient Icon icon;
protected transient Object initialSelectionValue;
protected transient Object initialValue;
protected transient Object inputValue;
protected transient Object message;
protected int messageType;
protected int optionType;
protected transient Object[] options;
protected transient Object[] selectionValues;
protected transient Object value;
protected boolean wantsInput;
```

These variables store information pertaining to the internal state of the option pane.

Class Methods

```
public static int showConfirmDialog(Component parentComponent, Object message);
public static int showConfirmDialog(Component parentComponent, Object message,
   String title, int optionType);
public static int showConfirmDialog(Component parentComponent, Object message,
   String title, int optionType, int messageType);
public static int showConfirmDialog(Component parentComponent, Object message,
   String title, int optionType, int messageType, Icon icon);
```

These methods display a dialog box that asks the user for confirmation, which may be Yes/No, Yes/No/Cancel, or OK/Cancel, depending on the optionType argument. (See "Class Variables.") The method returns a value indicating which button the user clicked.

```
public static String showInputDialog(Object message);
public static String showInputDialog(Component parentComponent, Object message);
public static String showInputDialog(Component parentComponent, Object message,
   String title, int messageType);
public static Object showInputDialog(Component parentComponent, Object message,
   String title, int messageType, Icon icon, Object[] selectionValues,
   Object initialSelectionValue);
```

These methods display a dialog box asking for string input from the user. The method returns the string the user typed. The message argument is typically a string, but some look-and-feels can meaningfully interpret other kinds of message forms, such as an icon. The selectionValues argument, used with the last version, is an array containing strings or icons; the dialog displays these as a list from which the user chooses. The icon argument can be null.

```
public static int showInternalConfirmDialog(Component parentComponent,
    Object message);
public static int showInternalConfirmDialog(Component parentComponent,
    Object message, String title, int optionType);
public static int showInternalConfirmDialog(Component parentComponent,
    Object message, String title, int optionType, int messageType);
public static int showInternalConfirmDialog(Component parentComponent,
    Object message, String title, int optionType, int messageType, Icon icon);
```

Similar to showConfirmDialog(), except that these methods use an internal dialog frame.

```
public static String showInternalInputDialog(Component parentComponent,
    Object message);
public static String showInternalInputDialog(Component parentComponent,
    Object message, String title, int messageType);
public static Object showInternalInputDialog(Component parentComponent,
    Object message, String title, int messageType, Icon icon,
    Object[] selectionValues, Object initialSelectionValue);
```

Similar to showInputDialog(), except that these methods use an internal dialog frame.

```
public static void showInternalMessageDialog(Component parentComponent,
    Object message);
public static void showInternalMessageDialog(Component parentComponent,
    Object message, String title, int messageType);
public static void showInternalMessageDialog(Component parentComponent,
    Object message, String title, int messageType, Icon icon);
```

Similar to showMessageDialog(), described later, except that these methods use an internal dialog frame.

```
public static int showInternalOptionDialog(Component parentComponent,
    Object message, String title, int optionType, int messageType, Icon icon,
    Object[] options, Object initialValue);
```

Similar to showOptionDialog(),except that this method uses an internal dialog frame.

```
public static void showMessageDialog(Component parentComponent, Object message);
public static void showMessageDialog(Component parentComponent, Object message,
    String title, int messageType);
public static void showMessageDialog(Component parentComponent, Object message,
    String title, int messageType, Icon icon);
```

These methods display a simple message box not requiring any choice on the part of the user. They do not return a value. The message object is typically a string, but some look-and-feels meaningfully interpret other object forms, such as an icon.

```
public static int showOptionDialog(Component parentComponent, Object message,
```

```
String title, int optionType, int messageType, Icon icon, Object[] options,
Object initialValue);
```

This method shows a dialog box for which you specify an array of options in an array; each element is a string or icon. The dialog represents each of these options as a separate button. The method returns the array index of the option selected by the user. The icon argument can be set to null.

Instance Methods

```
public JInternalFrame createInternalFrame(
    Component parentComponent, String title);
public Icon getIcon();
public Object getInitialSelectionValue();
public Object getInitialValue();
public Object getInputValue();
public int getMaxCharactersPerLineCount();
public Object getMessage();
public int getMessageType();
public int getOptionType();
public Object[] getOptions();
public Object[] getSelectionValues();
public Object getValue();
public boolean getWantsInput();
public void selectInitialValue();
public void setIcon(Icon newIcon);
public void setInitialSelectionValue(Object newValue);
public void setInitialValue(Object newInitialValue);
public void setInputValue(Object newValue);
public void setMessage(Object newMessage);
public void setMessageType(int newType);
public void setOptions(Object[] newOptions);
public void setValue(Object newValue);
public void setWantsInput(boolean newValue);
```

These methods get and set various properties for a persistent dialog box. Typically, you would only access such properties if you had first used a JOptionPane constructor to create a non-modal dialog and then manipulated it from within code. See "Class Methods," described earlier, for information on these properties.

JPanel Class

Full Name	javax.swing.JPanel
Extends	JComponent->Container->Component->Object

Description   Public class. This class provides support for a generic container that supports advanced features of the Swing architecture. Unlike its counterpart in the Abstract Windowing ToolKit (AWT), the JPanel class is a lightweight container.

Constructors

```
public JPanel();
public JPanel(LayoutManager layout);
public JPanel(boolean isDoubleBuffered);
public JPanel(LayoutManager layout, boolean
   isDoubleBuffered);
```

With the JPanel constructors, you can optionally specify a layout manager. You can also set the isDoubleBuffered property; if true, this turns on the double-buffering technique for graphics, which results in smoother movement at the cost of more memory usage.

JPasswordField Class

Full Name   javax.swing.JPasswordField

Extends   JTextField->JTextComponent->JComponent->
              Container->Component->Object

Description   Public class. This class implements a text-editing component that masks the text for entering passwords. The component shows that text is being entered, but the specific characters are masked so that the user can't tell what is being typed. The component generates an **ActionEvent** when the user pressed ENTER. (See JTextField for more information on event handling.)

The following code creates a JPasswordField component of 50-character width and adds it to the current content pane of the frame or applet.

```
JPasswordField passwrd = new JPasswordField(50);
Container content = getContentPane();
content.add(passwrd);
```

Constructors

```
public JPasswordField();
public JPasswordField(String text);
public JPasswordField(int columns);
public JPasswordField(String text, int columns);
```

These constructors create a password field that can be initialized with a string of text, a number of columns, or a combination of the two.

Instance Methods

```
public boolean echoCharIsSet();
public char getEchoChar();
public char[] getPassword();
public void setEchoChar(char c);
```

These methods get and set various pieces of information associated with the password field. As the user enters a character, the echo character (typically an asterisk) is displayed rather than the character actually typed. The get Password() method returns an array of char, but you can easily construct a string from this array by using a String constructor. Note that the getText() method, inherited from JTextComponent, does essentially the same thing but returns a string directly.

Overridden Instance Methods

```
public void copy();
public void cut();
```

These methods copy and cut text for the password field, preserving password-protection behavior for the component.

JPopupMenu Class

Full Name	javax.swing.JPopupMenu
Extends	JComponent->Container->Component->Object
Implements	MenuElement
Description	Public class. This class provides support for a popup menu that appears when the user clicks on a menu, or, in some cases, when the user right-clicks on a component. Note that the display of the popup is not automatic; you need to call the popup's show() method in response to an action. The popup menu disappears when a menu item is selected. See also MenuItem class (p. 401).
	Typically, you'll want to respond to rightmouse clicks. To add a mouse-action event handler that displays the popup at the right time, use the addMouseListener() method inherited from Component.

The following code is sufficient to create a simple popup menu:

```
JPopupMenu popup = new JPopupMenu("Edit Cmds");
popup.add(new JMenuItem("Cut"));
popup.add(new JMenuItem("Copy"));
```

The popup then needs to be displayed in response to an event. The following code displays a label and then displays the popup in response to a right mouse click.

```
Container content = getContentPane();
JLabel lab = new JLabel("Click right mouse button.");
lab.addMouseListener(new MyMouseAdapter());
//...

class MyMouseAdapter extends MouseAdapter {
    public void mousePressed(MouseEvent e) {
        if (
            (e.getModifiers() & InputEvent.BUTTON3_MASK) ==
            InputEvent.BUTTON3_MASK
        )
                popup.show(label, e.getX(), e.getY());
    }
}
```

Constructors

```
public JPopupMenu();
public JPopupMenu(String label);
```

These constructors create an empty popup menu, optionally with a title.

Class Methods

```
public static boolean getDefaultLightWeightPopupEnabled();
public static void setDefaultLightWeightPopupEnabled(
    boolean aFlag);
```

These class methods get and set the default behavior for popup menus generally. If a menu is lightweight, it uses up fewer system resources and acts more as a graphic than as a true window on the native environment.

Instance Methods

```
public Component add(Component c);
public JMenuItem add(JMenuItem menuItem);
public JMenuItem add(Action a);
public void addSeparator();
```

These methods add a menu item or a separator. If you add an argument of type Component rather than JMenuItem or Action, the component should implement the MenuElement interface. If you add an action, the resulting menu item displays an icon and text to its right; the method then returns the resulting JMenuItem object. A separator takes up a whole menu position. Note that with popup menus, the separator is a member of an internal class and is not an instance of JSeparator. See also "insert" methods.

```
public int getComponentIndex(Component c);
public Component getInvoker();
public String getLabel();
public Insets getMargin();
```

These methods get various property settings. The getComponentIndex() returns the zero-based index of the specified menu-item component, or –1 if the component is not an item of the menu. The invoker property is the component that hosts the popup menu.

```
public MenuElement[] getSubElements();
```

This method implements part of the MenuElement interface (p. 400).

```
public JMenuItem insert(Action a, int index);
public Component insert(Component component, int index);
```

These methods insert a menu item at specified zero-based index, using rules similar to corresponding "add" methods.

```
public boolean isBorderPainted();
public boolean isLightWeightPopupEnabled();
public boolean isPopupTrigger(MouseEvent e);
```

These methods return the state of various Boolean properties.

```
public void menuSelectionChanged(boolean isIncluded);
```

This method implements part of the MenuElement interface.

```
public void pack();
```

Causes menu items to be compressed to smallest possible size.

```
public void processKeyEvent(KeyEvent e, MenuElement[] path,
   MenuSelectionManager manager);
public void processMouseEvent(MouseEvent event,
   MenuElement[] path, MenuSelectionManager manager);
```

These methods help implement the MenuElement interface.

```
public void setBorderPainted(boolean b);
public void setInvoker(Component invoker);
public void setLabel(String label);
public void setLightWeightPopupEnabled(boolean aFlag);
public void setPopupSize(int width, int height);
public void setPopupSize(Dimension d);
public void setSelected(Component sel);
```

These methods set various properties of the popup menu. See "get" methods.

```
public void show(Component invoker, int x, int y);
```

Displays the popup menu at the specified coordinates of `invoker`, which is the host component of the popup menu. (Note that this method was never deprecated, even though the `show()` method of the `Component` class was replaced by `setVisible()`.)

Overridden Instance Methods

```
public boolean isVisible();
protected void paintBorder(Graphics g);
protected String paramString();
public void remove(int pos);
public void setLocation(int x, int y);
public void setVisible(boolean b);
```

These methods are overridden versions of methods defined in the parent `JComponent` class (p. 300).

JProgressBar Class

Full Name	`javax.swing.JProgressBar`
Extends	`JComponent->Container->Component->Object`
Implements	`SwingConstants`
Description	Public class. This class implements a GUI progress meter that is used to provide a visual indicator of the status of a lengthy operation. The visual indicator consists of a bar that fills to completion as an operation proceeds from start to finish; a numeric percentage can also be displayed on the progress bar.

The following example creates a progress bar and adds it to the current content pane of the applet. The progress bar displays a percentage figure. To set the foreground color, the code calls the `setForeground()` method inherited from the `Component` class (p. 210).

```
progress = new ProgressBar(JProgress.HORIZONTAL, 0, 500);
progress.setValue(250);
progress.setStringPainted(true);    // Display percentage.
progress.setForeground(Color.blue);

Container content = getContentPane();
content.add(progressbar);
```

Constructors

```
public JProgressBar();
public JProgressBar(int orient);
public JProgressBar(int min, int max);
public JProgressBar(int orient, int min, int max);
```

These constructors create a progress bar initialized with orientation, minimum, or maximum values, or a combination of all three. The orient argument specifies orientation. It can be set to JProgressBar.VERTICAL or JProgress. HORIZONTAL; the latter is the default. The min and max arguments determine the range over which the value property ranges; the default values are 0 and 100. (For example, if value is halfway between minimum and maximum, the progress bar shows 50 percent progress.) The value property must be set later with the setValue() method, unless you accept the default value of 50.

Instance Variables

```
protected transient ChangeEvent changeEvent;
protected ChangeListener changeListener;
protected BoundedRangeModel model;
protected int orientation;
protected boolean paintBorder;
protected boolean paintString;
protected String progressString;
```

These variables store information pertinent to the state of the progress bar.

Instance Methods

```
public void addChangeListener(ChangeListener l);
```

Installs an event handler for changes in value of the progress bar.

```
public int getMaximum();
public int getMinimum();
public int getOrientation();
```

These methods return the settings of various properties of the progress bar. For the meaning of these properties, see the constructors.

```
public double getPercentComplete();
public String getString();
```

These methods return the percent complete and the display string, respectively. The latter is displayed only if the stringPainted property is set to true. If the string property is left set to null (the default) and string Painted is true, a percentage figure (such as "50%") is displayed.

```
public int getValue();
```

Returns the value corresponding to the amount of progress; for example, if value is halfway between minimum and maximum, this represents 50 percent progress. A value setting three-quarters of the way between minimum and maximum represents 75 percent progress.

```
public boolean isBorderPainted();
public boolean isStringPainted();
```

Returns the setting of a Boolean property. If `stringPainted` is true, the progress bar displays the `string` property, or if `string` is left set to `null`, it displays a percentage figure.

```
public void removeChangeListener(ChangeListener l);
```

Removes an event handler previously installed with `addChangeListener()`.

```
public void setBorderPainted(boolean b);
public void setMaximum(int n);
public void setMinimum(int n);
public void setOrientation(int newOrientation);
public void setString(String s);
public void setStringPainted(boolean b);
public void setValue(int n);
```

These methods set various properties. See "get" methods and the constructors.

JRadioButton Class

Full Name	javax.swing.JRadioButton
Extends	JToggleButton->AbstractButton->JComponent->Container->Component->Object
Description	Public class. This class implements a radio button used to present one of a set of mutually exclusive choices. To use this class, first create an object of type `ButtonGroup` (p. ___). Then, after creating a radio button, use the `Button Group.add()` method to add each button to the group. Once this is done, selection of one button automatically causes de-selection of all other buttons in the group. To respond to button selection, install an event handler by calling the `addItem Listener()` methods inherited from the `AbstractButton` class (p. ___). Change in selection restuls in an `ItemEvent`.

The following code creates four radio buttons, groups them together, and adds them to the content pane of the current applet or frame. Because the choices are realized with radio buttons, it is impossible for the user to select more than one!

```
JRadioButton rbRep, rbDem, rbRef, rbGreen;
ButtonGroup group;

Container content = getContentPane();
Label lab = new JLabel("Vote for one ONLY!!!!");
content.add(lab);
```

```
group = new ButtonGroup();        // Create group.
rbRep = new JRadioButton("Bush");  // Create buttons.
rbDem = new JRadioButton("Gore");
rbRef = new JRadioButton("Buchanan");
rbGreen = new JRadioButton("Nader");

group.add(rbRep);                 // Put buttons in same group.
group.add(rbDem);
group.add(rbRef);
group.add(rbGreen);

content.add(rbRep);               // Add buttons to content pane.
content.add(rbDem);
content.add(rbRef);
content.add(rbGreen);
```

Constructors

```
public JRadioButton();
public JRadioButton(String text);
public JRadioButton(String text, boolean selected);
public JRadioButton(Action a);
public JRadioButton(Icon icon);
public JRadioButton(Icon icon, boolean selected);
public JRadioButton(String text, Icon icon);
public JRadioButton(String text, Icon icon, boolean selected);
```

These constructors create a radio button using various pieces of initialization information such as a string, action, icon, or a combination of them. Some of the constructors enable the radio button's selection state to be set via the selected argument.

JRadioButtonMenuItem Class

Full Name	`javax.swing.JRadioButtonMenuItem`
Extends	`JMenuItem->AbstractButton->JComponent->` `Container->Component->Object`
Description	Public class. A radio button menu item is a menu item like any other, but with an added feature: within any group of such menu items, exactly one of them appears in the selected state when the menu is displayed. Selecting any one of the menu items automatically de-selects the other items in the group. To use this class, first create an object of type `ButtonGroup` (p. 191).

Then, after creating a radio button, use the `ButtonGroup`.
`add( )` method to add each button to the group. JRadio
ButtonMenuItem inherits all the methods from the `JMenuItem`
class (p. 325). See also `JCheckBoxMenuItem`
(p. 296).

The following code creates four radio-button menu items, groups them
together, and adds them to a menu bar for the current applet or frame.
Because the choices are realized with radio button menu items, it is impossible for the user to select more than one!

```
JRadioButtonMenuItem miRep, miDem, miRef, miGreen;
ButtonGroup group;

Container content = getContentPane();
JLabel lab = new JLabel("Vote for one ONLY!!!!");
content.add(lab);

JMenuBar menubar = new JMenuBar();   // Create menubar and
setJMenuBar(menubar);                //  menu.
JMenu menu = new JMenu("Vote");
menubar.add(menu);

group = new ButtonGroup();                   // Create group.
miRep = new JRadioButtonMenuItem("Bush");  // Create items.
miDem = new JRadioButtonMenuItem("Gore");
miRef = new JRadioButtonMenuItem("Buchanan");
miGreen = new JRadioButtonMenuItem("Nader");

group.add(miRep);             // Put items in same group.
group.add(miDem);
group.add(miRef);
group.add(miGreen);

menu.add(miRep);              // Add items to menu.
menu.add(miDem);
menu.add(miRef);
menu.add(miGreen);
```

Constructors
```
public JRadioButtonMenuItem();
public JRadioButtonMenuItem(String text);
public JRadioButtonMenuItem(String text, boolean selected);
public JRadioButtonMenuItem(Action a);
public JRadioButtonMenuItem(Icon icon);
```

```
public JRadioButtonMenuItem(Icon icon, boolean selected);
public JRadioButtonMenuItem(String text, Icon icon);
public JRadioButtonMenuItem(String text, Icon icon,
   boolean selected);
```

These constructors create a radio button menu item using various pieces of initialization information such as a string, action, icon, or a combination of them. Some of the constructors enable the radio button menu item's selection state to be set via the selected argument.

JRootPane Class

Full Name	javax.swing.JRootPane
Extends	JComponent->Container->Component->Object
Description	Public class. This class provides support for a pane that orchestrates the window pane architecture of Swing windows. The JRootPane class is a lightweight container and forms the architectural basis for the JApplet, JFrame, JDialog, and JWindow classes. A root pane contains more specialized panes within it, including the content pane, layered pane, glass pane, and menu bar. With most applications, you typically work directly with the content pane (which includes most of the interior space of a typical component) and menu bar. For this reason, it usually isn't necessary to refer to the JRootPane class in most application and applet code.

Java 2 API Reference

Constructors

```
public JRootPane();
```

Instance Variables

```
protected Container contentPane;
protected JButton defaultButton;
protected Component glassPane;
protected JLayeredPane layeredPane;
protected JMenuBar menuBar;
```

These variables store various pieces of information related to the internal state of the root pane.

Instance Methods

```
public Container getContentPane();
public JButton getDefaultButton();
public Component getGlassPane();
public JMenuBar getJMenuBar();
public JLayeredPane getLayeredPane();
```

These methods get various property settings of the class.

```
public void setContentPane(Container content);
public void setDefaultButton(JButton defaultButton);
public void setGlassPane(Component glass);
public void setJMenuBar(JMenuBar menu);
public void setLayeredPane(JLayeredPane layered);
```

These methods set various properties of the class.

JScrollBar Class

Full Name	`javax.swing.JScrollBar`
Extends	`JComponent->Container->Component->Object`
Implements	`SwingConstants`
Description	Public class. This class provides a powerful and flexible implementation of a scrollbar component, which can function either an independent indicator (much like a slider or progress bar) or as a working scrollbar for a pane or other component. For example, by installing an event handler for an `Adjustment Event` (p. 170), you can link changes in the scroll bar directly to a pane. But note that you can often achieve the results more simply by using the `JScrollPane` class (p. 344).

The following code creates a vertical scrollbar, initializes it, and adds it to the right edge of the pane. The code also adds an event handler that can respond to changes to the scrollbar state. (Note that this class implements the `AdjustmentListener` interface and must be declared with an `implements` clause.)

```
Container content = getContentPane();
JScrollBar scrollbar = new JScrollBar(JScrollBar.VERTICAL,
    250, 25, 0, 500);
content.setLayout(new BorderLayout());
content.add(scrollbar, BorderLayout.EAST);
scrollbar.addAdjustmentListener(this);

public void adjustmentValueChanged(AdjustmentEvent e) {
    // Respond to changes here.
}
```

Constructors

```
public JScrollBar();
public JScrollBar(int orientation);
```

```
public JScrollBar(int orientation, int value, int extent,
    int min, int max);
```

These constructors create a scroll bar. The possible values for orientation are JScrollBar.HORIZONTAL and JScrollBar.VERTICAL, which is the default. The settings of min and max determine the limits over which the value property ranges; for example, a value setting halfway between min and max corresponds to the scrollbar indicator to sit at the halfway point. The extent argument corresponds to the width of the indictor (or "thumb") itself. The default values for extent, min, and max are 10, 0, and 100, respectively.

Instance Variables

```
protected int blockIncrement;
protected BoundedRangeModel model;
protected int orientation;
protected int unitIncrement;
```

These variables store the internal state of the scroll bar.

Instance Methods

```
public void addAdjustmentListener(AdjustmentListener l);
```

Installs an event handler for changes to the scrollbar value. See Adjustment Listener interface (p. 172).

```
public int getBlockIncrement();
public int getBlockIncrement(int direction);
public int getMaximum();
public int getMinimum();
public int getOrientation();
public int getUnitIncrement();
public int getUnitIncrement(int direction);
public int getValue();
```

These methods get various properties of the scroll bar. See constructors for description of max, min, value, and orientation properties. The block Increment and unitIncrement properties indicate the amount of movement in value given the user clicking the bar above or below the indicator (blockIncrement) and clicking one of the end arrows (unitIncrement).

```
public boolean getValueIsAdjusting();
```

Returns true if the scrollbar indicator is currently being dragged.

```
public int getVisibleAmount();
```

Returns the value of the extent property, which corresponds to the thickness of the indicator (or "thumb").

```
public void removeAdjustmentListener(AdjustmentListener l);
```

Removes an event handler installed with addAdjustmentListener().

```
public void setBlockIncrement(int blockIncrement);
public void setMaximum(int maximum);
public void setMinimum(int minimum);
public void setOrientation(int orientation);
public void setUnitIncrement(int unitIncrement);
public void setValue(int value);
public void setValueIsAdjusting(boolean b);
public void setValues(int newValue, int newExtent,
    int newMin, int newMax);
```

These methods set various properties. See "get" methods and the constructors. Note that calling setValue() moves the scrollbar indicator.

```
public void setVisibleAmount(int extent);
```

Sets the value of the extent property.

Overridden Instance Methods

```
public Dimension getMinimumSize();
public Dimension getMaximumSize();
```

These methods get the minimum and maximum sizes of the scroll bar.

```
public void setEnabled(boolean x);
```

This method enables or disables the scroll bar.

```
protected String paramString();
```

This method generates a parameter string that identifies the scroll bar.

JScrollPane Class

Full Name	javax.swing.JScrollPane
Extends	JComponent->Container->Component->Object
Implements	ScrollPaneConstants, Adjustable
Description	Public class. This Swing class provides a pane that gives you great flexibility in specifying and controlling the behavior of scrollbars. You can provide vertical scrollbars, horizontal scrollbars, or both; and each can be displayed on either at all times or only as needed. This class also provides access to the scrollbars themselves as functioning JScrollBar objects, if you wish, for more complete control over scrollbar behavior. (See JScrollBar class, p. 342.)

The typical use of this class is to build a `JScrollBar` object around another component, such as a list or text area. This other component is specified as the "view" object during initialization.

The following example creates a `JScrollPane` that adds scrolling support to a list:

```
String[] colors = { "red", "green", "blue", "orange",
    "yellow", "purple", "black", "white" };
JList list = new JList(colors);
list.setSelectedIndex(4);
JScrollPane scrollPane = new JScrollPane(list,
    JScrollPane.VERTICAL_SCROLLBAR_ALWAYS,
    JScrollPane.HORIZONTAL_SCROLLBAR_NEVER
);
```

This topic describes the most common methods and fields of the class.

Constructors

```
public JScrollPane();
public JScrollPane(Component view);
public JScrollPane(int vsbPolicy, int hsbPolicy);
public JScrollPane(Component view, int vsbPolicy,
    int hsbPolicy);
```

These constructors create a scroll pane with different types of initialization information; the view argument specifies the component for which the pane is to provide scrolling, while the vsbPolicy and hsbPolicy arguments specify vertical and horiztonal scroll bar policies for the scroll pane. These can be set to one of the following values, defined in ScrollPaneConstants and inherited by this class: VERTICAL_SCROLLBAR_ALWAYS, VERTICAL_SCROLLBAR_AS_NEEDED, and VERTICAL_SCROLLBAR_NEVER, as well as corresponding HORIZONTAL_ constants. The defaults are VERTICAL_AS_NEEDED and HORIZONTAL_AS_NEEDED.

Instance Variables

```
protected JScrollBar horizontalScrollBar;
protected int horizontalScrollBarPolicy;
protected Component lowerLeft;
protected Component lowerRight;
protected Component upperLeft;
protected Component upperRight;
protected JScrollBar verticalScrollBar;
protected int verticalScrollBarPolicy;
protected JViewport viewport;
```

Java 2 API Reference

These variables store the internal state of the pane. The Component fields contain the component currently visible at the indicated corner. See JScrollPane constructors for discussion of the scrollBarPolicy fields.

Instance Methods

```
public JScrollBar createHorizontalScrollBar();
public JScrollBar createVerticalScrollBar();
```

These methods force creation of a scrollbar.

```
public JScrollBar getHorizontalScrollBar();
public int getHorizontalScrollBarPolicy();
public JScrollBar getVerticalScrollBar();
public int getVerticalScrollBarPolicy();
```

These methods return settings of the common properties. Two of these methods return a reference to one of the actual scrollbars, if it exists, so that it can be manipulated directly as a JScrollbar object. (This isn't necessary for standard operation of the scrollbar pane, but it does give you added control if you want it.) These methods return null if the requested scrollbar does not currently exist.

```
public JViewport getViewport();
```

Returns the view onto the component featured in the pane. See JViewPort class (p. 361).

```
public void setHorizontalScrollBar(JScrollBar
horizontalScrollBar);
public void setHorizontalScrollBarPolicy(int policy);
public void setVerticalScrollBar(JScrollBar verticalScrollBar);
public void setVerticalScrollBarPolicy(int policy);
public void setViewport(JViewport viewport);
public void setViewportView(Component view);
```

Thes methods set various properties. See "get" methods and the JScrollPane constructors.

JSeparator Class

Full Name	javax.swing.JSeparator
Extends	JComponent->Container->Component->Object
Implements	SwingConstants
Description	Public class. When you call the addSeparator() method of the JMenu class, the Swing API creates an instance of JSeparator. You can create instances of this class directly, if you choose.

One use of this class is to create a vertical or horizontal line so that you can then add it to the layout of a container. This has the effect of separating other components.

Constructors

```
public JSeparator();
public JSeparator(int orientation);
```

These constructors create a separator; the latter constructor allows you to specify the orientation of the separator: this argument can be either JSeparator. HORIZONTAL (the default) or JSeparator.VERTICAL. These constants are defined in the interface.

Instance Methods

```
public int getOrientation();
public void setOrientation(int orientation);
```

These methods get and set the orientation of the separator.

JSlider Class

Full Name	javax.swing.JSlider
Extends	JComponent->Container->Component->Object
Extends	SwingConstants
Description	Public class. This class implements a GUI slider component that allows the user to slide an indicator (or "knob") back and forth within an interval. For example, you could use a JSlider object to represent a volume control. This class provides a functionality much like a scrollbar, but whereas a scrollbar is typically attached to the edge of a pane, sliders are intended to work independently. Sliders have unique visual features of their own, such as optional printing of a slider track, periodic notches ("ticks'), and periodic numbers, as on a radio tuner.

The following code creates a slider, adds it to the content pane, and installs an event handler for changes to the slider value. The slider displays major and minor ticks below the slider track.

```
Container content = getContentPane();
JScrollBar slider = new JSlider(JSlider.HORIZONTAL,
    0, 100, 50);
slider.setMajorTicks(10);
slider.setMinorTicks(5);
slider.setPaintTicks(true);
slider.setPaintLabels(true);
```

Java 2 API Reference

```
content.add(slider);
slider.addChangeListener(this);

public void stateChange(ChangeEvent e) {
    // Respond to changes here.
}
```

This topic describes the most common methods and variables of the class.

Constructors

```
public JSlider();
public JSlider(int orientation);
public JSlider(int min, int max);
public JSlider(int min, int max, int value);
public JSlider(int orientation, int min, int max,
    int value);
```

These constructors create a slider with varying degrees of initialization information. The orientation may be JSlider.VERTICAL or JSlider.HORIZONTAL (the default). The value determines the initial position of the slider indicator, relative to the min and max settings. The default settings for min, max, and value are 0, 100, and 50.

Instance Variables

```
protected ChangeListener changeListener;
protected int majorTickSpacing;
protected int minorTickSpacing;
protected int orientation;
protected boolean snapToTicks;
```

These variables store property values of the class.

Instance Methods

```
public void addChangeListener(ChangeListener l);
```

Installs an event handler that responds to changes in the slider's indicator knob (value property).

```
public int getExtent();
```

Returns the extent. This integer corresponds to the amount of movement caused by the PAGE UP and PAGE DOWN keys.

```
public boolean getInverted();
```

If true, the slider calibrates increasing values right-to-left (or bottom-to-top) rather than left-to-right or top-to-bottom.

```
public int getMajorTickSpacing();
```

Java 2 API Reference

Returns the spacing between major notches, or "ticks," displayed along the slider track. (Note that these are displayed only if `paintTicks` is `true` and `majorTickSpacing` is greater than 0.) The default value is 10.

```
public int getMaximum();
public int getMinimum();
```

These methods get the numeric limits of the slider track. The setting of `value`, relative to these two limits, determines position of the indicator knob. For example, if `value` is halfway between `minimum` and `maximum`, the indicator is halfway down the track.

```
public int getMinorTickSpacing();
```

Returns the spacing between minor notches, or "ticks," displayed along the slider track. (Note that these are displayed only if `paintTicks` is `true` and `minorTickSpacing` is greater than 0.) The default value is 2.

```
public int getOrientation();
```

Returns `JSliderBar.VERTICAL` or `JSliderBar.HORIZONTAL` (the default).

```
public boolean getPaintLabels();
public boolean getPaintTicks();
public boolean getPaintTrack();
public boolean getSnapToTicks();
```

These methods return various Boolean properties. If `paintLabels` is `true`, periodic numbers are displayed along the track, below each major tick. If `paintTicks` is `true`, major and minor ticks are displayed just below the slider track. If `paintTrack` is `true`, the slider bar (or "track") is displayed. If `snapToTicks` is `true`, the indicator adjusts to the nearest tick after each movement. The default for each of these if `false`, except for `paintTrack`. To set these properties, see "set" methods.

```
public int getValue();
```

Returns the setting of the `value` property, which corresponds to the location of the slider indicator, relative to the `minimum` and `maximum` settings.

```
public void removeChangeListener(ChangeListener l);
```

Removes an event handler installed by the `addChangeListener()` method.

```
public void setExtent(int extent);
public void setInverted(boolean b);
public void setMajorTickSpacing(int n);
public void setMaximum(int maximum);
public void setMinimum(int minimum);
public void setMinorTickSpacing(int n);
public void setOrientation(int orientation);
```

```
public void setPaintLabels(boolean b);
public void setPaintTicks(boolean b);
public void setPaintTrack(boolean b);
public void setSnapToTicks(boolean b);
public void setValue(int n);
```

These methods set common properties of the slider bar. See "get" methods. Note that changing the setting of the value property moves the slider indicator along the track.

JSplitPane Class

Full Name	javax.swing.JSplitPane
Extends	JComponent->Container->Component->Object
Description	Public class. This class provides support for a pane that is used to house two separate panes. The two panes within a split pane can be resized by the user to alter the amount of space given to each.

This class has a complex set of properties and methods. For information on this class, see documentation in the Javasoft web site.

JTabbedPane Class

Full Name	javax.swing.JTabbedPane
Extends	JComponent->Container->Component->Object
Description	Public class. This class provides support for a pane that establishes a tabbed user interface where the user can select different tabs to reveal different groups of components.

This class has a complex set of properties and methods. For information on this class, see documentation in the Javasoft web site.

JTable Class

Full Name	javax.swing.JTable
Extends	JComponent->Container->Component->Object
Description	Public class. This class implements a two-dimensional table component that presents information in rows and columns, much like a spreadsheet. The class has a large set of methods for customizing, initializing, editing, and selecting rows, columns, and cells within the table.

This class has a complex set of properties and methods, as well as a large set of helper classes, which are too complex to describe here. For information on this class, see documentation in the Javasoft web site.

JTextArea Class

Full Name	javax.swing.JTextArea
Extends	JTextComponent->JComponent->Container->Component->Object
Implements	Scrollable
Description	Public class. This class supports a text component that displays and supports editing of multiple lines of text. This class is similar in many ways to the AWT TextArea class. However, it does not support scrollbars by itself; to add scrollbars, place a JTextArea component in an instance of JScroll Pane (p. 344). Many of the most useful methods of this class are inherited from the JTextComponent class (p. 353); these methods include getText(), setText(), cut(), copy(), and paste().

The following code creates a text area with five rows and 60-character width, which it then initializes with several lines of text and adds to the content pane.

```
Container pane = getContentPane();
JTextArea area = new JTextArea(5, 60);
area.append("Here is a sample line of text.\n");
area.append("Here is a second line, and\n");
area.append("here is another.");
pane.add(area);
```

Constructors

```
public JTextArea();
public JTextArea(String text);
public JTextArea(int rows, int columns);
public JTextArea(String text, int rows, int columns);
```

These constructors create a text area that is initialized with an optional string, number of rows and columns, or a combination thereof.

Instance Methods

```
public void append(String str);
```

Appends a string to the end of the text.

```
protected int getColumnWidth();
public int getColumns();
public int getLineCount();
```

These methods get various property settings. `columnWidth` is the width in pixels of one column in the current font. `columns` is the number of visible columns that can be displayed in the current size, given the current font. (If the font is not monospace, column width is based on the letter "m.") `lineCount` is the number of lines currently displayed.

```
public int getLineEndOffset(int line)
   throws BadLocationException;
```

Returns the offset of the end-of-line delimiter (represented as "\n") for the specified line. The number returned is the offset from the beginning of the entire text.

```
public int getLineOfOffset(int offset)
   throws BadLocationException;
```

Returns the number of the line containing a character specified by an offset into the text.

```
public int getLineStartOffset(int line)
   throws BadLocationException;
```

Returns the offset of the character at the beginning of specified line.

```
public boolean getLineWrap();
```

Returns the value of `lineWrap`; if `true`, lines of text that exceed the visible column width wrap to the next line. If `lineWrap` is `false`, it's desirable to add scrollbars if the amount of text is going to exceed the display area. This property is `false` by default.

```
protected int getRowHeight();
public int getRows();
public int getTabSize();
```

These methods get various property settings. `rowHeight` is the height of one row in the current font. `rows` is the number of visible rows that can be displayed in the current size, given the current font. `tabSize` is the number of characters indented when the user presses the TAB key.

```
public boolean getWrapStyleWord();
```

Returns the setting of `wrapStyleWord`. If `true`, text wraps on word boundaries rather than character boundaries (the default).

```
public void insert(String str, int pos);
```

Inserts a string at the specified offset into the text.

```
public void replaceRange(String str, int start, int end);
```

Replaces characters in the indicated range with `str`.

```
public void setColumns(int columns);
public void setLineWrap(boolean wrap);
public void setRows(int rows);
public void setTabSize(int size);
public void setWrapStyleWord(boolean word);
```

These methods set various properties. See "get" methods.

Overridden Instance Methods

```
public Dimension getPreferredScrollableViewportSize();
public Dimension getPreferredSize();
public boolean getScrollableTracksViewportWidth();
public int getScrollableUnitIncrement(Rectangle visibleRect,
   int orientation, int direction);
public boolean isManagingFocus();
protected String paramString();
protected void processKeyEvent(KeyEvent e);
public void setFont(Font f);
```

These methods are overridden versions of methods defined in the parent JTextComponent class. The isManagingFocus() method returns true by default; this prevents the TAB key from moving focus to another control. To change this behavior, you can override this method and return false. The class also overrides the setFont() method, because a change to the text area's font requires several other properties (such as rowHeight) to be recalculated.

JTextComponent Class

Full Name	javax.swing.JTextComponent
Extends	JComponent->Container->Component->Object
Implements	Scrollable
Description	Public abstract class. This class implements common functionality for Swing components JTextField, JTextArea, JEditorPane, and JTextPane. Important methods include getText() and setText(), which enable you to read and edit the text displayed. The Swing text components are similar to their AWT counterparts TextComponent, TextField, and TextArea, but provide more flexibility.

This topic describes the most commonly used methods of the class. For example code, see JTextArea and JTextComponent.

Instance Methods

```
public void copy();
public void cut();
```

These methods perform editing functions Cut and Copy, respectively, on the currently selected text. The text is copied to the system clipboard.

```
public Color getCaretColor();
public int getCaretPosition();
public Insets getMargin();
```

These methods get various property settings. The margin property contains the insets between the component's border and the actual text.

```
public String getSelectedText();
```

Returns the selected (highlighted) text, if any. Although the end user normally selects text by using the mouse or the SHIFT key, text can also be selected programmatically. See "set" methods.

```
public Color getSelectedTextColor();
```

Returns the color used for rendering selected text.

```
public int getSelectionEnd();
public int getSelectionStart();
```

These methods return the starting and ending positions of the selected text, by offset. The selectionEnd property stores the offset of the first character past the end of the selection, so that the number of characters selected at any time is selectionEnd − selectionStart. If no text is currently selected, these methods return the same number.

```
public String getText();
public String getText(int offset, int len);
```

These methods return the text contents of the component. The first method returns all the text as a single string. The second method returns len characters beginning with the starting offset.

```
public boolean isEditable();
```

Returns the value of the boolean editable property, which is true by default.

```
public void paste();
public void replaceSelection(String content);
```

Replaces the currently selected text with the contents of the system clipboard, in the case of paste(), or with the specified string.

```
public void select(int selectionStart, int selectionEnd);
public void selectAll();
```

These methods cause text to be selected — the specified interval, in the case of the select(); or all the text, in the case of selectAll(). selectionStart is the offset of the first character selected, and the number of characters selected is selectionEnd − selectionStart.

```
public void setCaretColor(Color c);
public void setCaretPosition(int position);
public void setEditable(boolean b);
public void setMargin(Insets m);
public void setSelectedTextColor(Color c);
public void setSelectionEnd(int position);
public void setSelectionStart(int position);
public void setText(String t);
```

These methods set various properties of the class. See "get" methods.

JTextField Class

Full Name	`javax.swing.JTextField`
Extends	`JTextComponent->JComponent->Container->Component->Object`
Implements	`SwingConstants`
Description	Public class. This class implements a text field component that supports the editing of a single line of text. The class is similar to the AWT `TextField` component and also serves as base class to the `JPasswordField` class (p. 332). Note that many of the most useful methods of the class are inherited from `JTextComponent` (p. 353); these methods include `getText()` and `setText()`. An object of this class generates an `ActionEvent` when the user presses the ENTER key.

The following code creates a text field of 60-column width and adds it to the content pane of the applet or frame. When the user presses ENTER, the applet responds by displaying the text-field contents in a dialog box. (The class that contains this code implements the `ActionListener` interface and must be declared with an `implements` clause.)

```
Container pane = getContentPane();
JTextField tf = new JTextArea("Initial string", 60);
pane.add(tf);
tf.addActionListener(this);

public void actionPerformed(ActionEvent e) {
    if (e.getSource() == tf) {
        String msg = "String entered is: " + tf.getText();
        JOptionPane.displayMessageDialog(this, msg);
    }
}
```

Constructors

```
public JTextField();
public JTextField(String text);
public JTextField(int columns);
public JTextField(String text, int columns);
```

These constructors create a text field that is initialized with an optional string, number of columns, or both.

Instance Methods

```
public void addActionListener(ActionListener l);
```

Installs a handler for an action event. The user can activate the action associated with the text field by pressing the ENTER key.

```
public Action getAction();
protected int getColumnWidth();
public int getColumns();
```

These methods get various property settings. columnWidth is the width in pixels of one column in the current font. columns is the number of visible columns that can be displayed in the font. (If the font is not monospace, column width is based on the letter "m.")

```
public int getHorizontalAlignment();
```

Returns the setting of the alignment property; the default value, JTextField. LEFT specifies alignment against the left edge of the field (left justifying). Other possible values are JTextField.RIGHT and JTextField.CENTER.

```
public void removeActionListener(ActionListener l);
```

Removes an event handler previously installed with addActionListener().

```
public void setAction(Action a);
public void setColumns(int columns);
public void setHorizontalAlignment(int alignment);
```

These methods set various properties. See "get" methods.

Overridden Instance Methods

```
public Action[] getActions();
public Dimension getPreferredSize();
public boolean isValidateRoot();
protected String paramString();
public void setFont(Font f);
public void scrollRectToVisible(Rectangle r);
```

These methods are overridden versions of methods defined in the parent JTextComponent class (p. 353).; The class also overrides the setFont()

method, because a change to the text area's font requires several other properties (such as rowHeight) to be recalculated.

JTextPane Class

Full Name	javax.swing.JTextPane
Extends	JEditorPane->JTextComponent->JComponent->Container->Component->Object
Description	Public class. This class provides support for a pane that enables editing of different types of styled textual content. Unlike JEditorPane, JTextPane displays styled content such as HTML and RTF graphically, as opposed to showing it as simple text. Note that to fully use these features, you may need to take advantage of the Style, Attributes, and Document interfaces, which due to space considerations, are not described here. However, you can use all the methods inherited from JEditorPane (p. 307), JTextComponent (p. 353), and other ancestor classes.

Constructors

```
public JTextPane();
```

The default constructor creates a generic text pane.

Instance Methods

```
public void insertComponent(Component c);
public void insertIcon(Icon g);
```

JToggleButton Class

Full Name	javax.swing.JToggleButton
Extends	AbstractButton->JComponent->Container->Component->Object
Description	Public class. This class implements a toggle button, which is a button that is always set to one of two possible states (on/off). This class inherits useful methods from the AbstractButton class (p. ___), including setEnabled(), setIcon(), setSelected(), setText().
	A toggle button fires a ChangeEvent whenever there is a change in its state and a SelectionEvent when it is selected. To handle these events, use the addChange Listener() and addSelectionListener() methods, inherited from the AbstractButton class.

Java 2 API Reference

The following code creates a toggle button and adds it to the content pane of the current applet or frame.

```
Icon icon = new Icon("toggleb.gif");
Container content = getContentPane();
JToggleButton togglebtn = new JToggleButton(icon);
content.add(togglebtn);
addChangeListener(new MyChangeListener());
togglebtn.setSelected(true);
//...

class MyChangeListener implements ChangeListener {
    public void itemStateChanged(ItemEvent e) {
        System.out.println("Toggle button selected.");
    }
}
```

Constructors

```
public JToggleButton();
public JToggleButton(Icon icon);
public JToggleButton(Icon icon, boolean selected);
public JToggleButton(String text);
public JToggleButton(String text, boolean selected);
public JToggleButton(Action a);
public JToggleButton(String text, Icon icon);
public JToggleButton(String text, Icon icon,
    boolean selected);
```

These constructors create a toggle button that is capable of having an icon, text, or a combination of both. The initial selection state of the toggle button can also be specified via the `selected` argument in some of the constructors.

JToolBar Class

Full Name	javax.swing.JToolBar
Extends	JComponent->Container->Component->Object
Extends	SwingConstants
Description	Public class. This class implements a toolbar containing commonly used actions of an applet or application. You can attach any kind of components to the toolbar, but the most common practice is to add buttons, to which actions may be attached. (Or even more simply, add Action objects, which are automatically realized as buttons.)

The class provides an addAction( ) method; you can also use the add( ) method inherited from the Container class. When you add a toolbar to a pane, the pane should preferably use a BorderLayout manager (p. ___), so that you can attach the toolbar to an edge.

The following example creates a tool bar, adds a few buttons to it, and then adds the toolbar to the top part of a content pane named contentPane:

```
JToolBar toolbar = new JToolBar();
JButton button1 = new JButton(new ImageIcon("Cut.gif"));
toolbar.add(button1);
JButton button2 = new JButton(new ImageIcon("Copy.gif"));
toolbar.add(button2);
JButton button3 = new JButton(new ImageIcon("Paste.gif"));
toolbar.add(button3);
contentPane.add(toolbar, BorderLayout.NORTH);
```

Constructors

```
public JToolBar();
public JToolBar(int orientation);
public JToolBar(String name);
public JToolBar(String name, int orientation);
```

These constructors create a tool bar with an optional name and orientation (horizontal or vertical).

Instance Methods

```
public JButton addAction(Action a);
```

Adds an Action object as a toolbar button and returns it as a JButton reference, so that you can manipulate it as a button.

```
public void addSeparator();
public void addSeparator(Dimension size);
```

Adds blank space, separating the previously added items to the ones added after this method call. You can optionally specify the size of this space. Note that on a toolbar, this separator is unrelated to the JSeparator class.

```
public Component getComponentAtIndex(int i);
public int getComponentIndex(Component c);
```

These methods return the toolbar item at a particular index number or find the index of an item, if present. If the item cannot be found, get ComponentIndex( ) returns –1.

```
public Insets getMargin();
public int getOrientation();
```

```
public boolean isBorderPaint();
public boolean isFloatable();
```

These methods get various property settings. The orientation property is
JToolBar.HORIZONTAL by default. If the borderPainted property is true, the
toolbar automatically redraws its own border. If isFloatable is true, the
user can move the toolbar around its container by dragging the mouse on
a blank part of the toolbar. Both are true by default.

```
public void setBorderPainted(boolean b);
public void setFloatable(boolean b);
public void setMargin(Insets m);
public void setOrientation(int o);
```

These methods set various properties of the class. See "get" methods.

Overridden Instance Methods

```
protected void paintBorder(Graphics g);
```

This method paints the border around the tool bar.

```
protected String paramString();
```

This method generates a parameter string that identifies the tool bar.

JToolTip Class

Full Name	javax.swing.JToolTip
Extends	JComponent->Container->Component->Object
Description	Public class. This class implements a visual tip that appears over a component and provides brief description of that component to the user. This *tooltip*, as soon as it is attached to a component, appears as a small popup Help window whenever the mouse pointer rests over that component for a length of time. To attach a tooltip, you can override the createTool Tip() method of the JComponent class (p. ___). Alternatively, you can create the tool tip first and then call the tool tip's setComponent() method.

The following code creates a tooltip and attaches it to a button named
saveButton.

```
JToolTip mytooltip = new JToolTip();
mytooltip.setText("Saves to the current file.");
mytooltip.setComponent(saveButton);
```

Constructors

```
public JToolTip();
```

Creates an empty tool tip object. Text must be provided by calling the
`setTipText()` method.

Instance Methods

```
public JComponent getComponent();
public String getTipText();
public void setComponent(JComponent c);
public void setTipText(String tipText);
```

These methods get and set various pieces of information associated with the
tool tip. The `component` property (which is `null` by default), specifies the
component to which the tool tip is attached. The `tipText` contains the text
to display.

JTree Class

Full Name	`javax.swing.JTree`
Extends	`JComponent->Container->Component->Object`
Description	Public class. This class implements a tree component, which is used to display information in a hierarchical tree consisting of nodes and leaves. This class has a vast set of capabilities for constructing and editing a tree structure complete with many kinds of nodes, complete with functions for selecting, expanding, and collapsing nodes. The complex nature of the class, however, does not make it easy to use.

This class has a complex set of properties and methods, as well as a large set
of helper classes, which are too complex to describe here. For information on
this class, see documentation in the Javasoft Web site.

JViewport Class

Full Name	`javax.swing.JViewport`
Extends	`JComponent->Container->Component->Object`
Description	Public class. This class implements a viewport that provides a logical window (or *view*) through which you can see underlying data. A viewport usually contains a larger amount of text or graphics than can be displayed within a frame. What's displayed on screen, then, is a view into the underlying component. As the view position moves, you see different parts of the component. One of the key methods is the `getView Position()` method, which determines what part of the component to view.

A natural use for this class is to implement scrolling of a pane to which scrollbars are attached. Scrollbar event handlers need only call `setViewPosition()` and `getViewPostion()` of the viewport to cause the appropriate movement through the viewed component. However, the `JScrollPane` class (p. 344) implements scrolling automatically for you. The `JViewport` class is available for situations in which you need more customized forms of scrolling.

The following code adds a viewport to the current applet or frame. The viewport shows points from point (50, 50) to (250, 250) of the picture:

```
Container content = getContentPane();
Icon icon = new Icon("bigpict.gif");
JViewport vp = new JViewPort();
vp.setView(icon);
vp.setViewPosition(Point(50, 50));   // Top left = 50, 50
vp.setViewSize(200, 200);            // View 200 by 200 pixels.
content.add(vp);
```

Constructors

```
public JViewport();
```

Creates an empty viewport. You attach a component for viewing by calling the setView() method.

Instance Variables

```
protected transient Image backingStoreImage;
protected boolean backingStore;
protected boolean isViewSizeSet;
protected Point lastPaintPosition;
protected boolean scrollUnderway;
```

These variables store important pieces of information regarding the state of the viewport. If the backingStoreEnabled property is true (see "Instance Methods"), the viewport uses the backingStoreImage field for double buffering.

Instance Methods

```
public void addChangeListener(ChangeListener l);
```

Installs an event handler that responds to changes in the view position, size, or extent.

```
public Dimension getExtentSize();
```

Gets the size of the component being viewed.

```
public Component getView();
```

Gets the component being viewed. (This is set by calling the setView( ) method).

```
public Point getViewPosition();
```

Gets the point within the underlying component that is displayed in the viewport's top-left corner. (This is set by calling the setView() method.) For example, a view position of (10, 10) means that the viewport starts viewing at position (10, 10) within the component. Thus, point (5, 5) would not be visible.

```
public Rectangle getViewRect();
public Dimension getViewSize();
```

These methods return information about the area being viewed: viewSize is the size of the viewport (unless the component is smaller, in which case it is the size of the component); viewRect combines the top-left corner (vewPosition) with the viewSize dimension.

```
public boolean isBackingStoreEnabled();
```

Returns true if double-buffering is enabled for smoother scrolling.

```
public void removeChangeListener(ChangeListener l);
```

Removes an event handler previously installed with addChangeListener( ).

```
public void setBackingStoreEnabled(boolean b);
public void setExtentSize(Dimension newExtent);
public void setView(Component view);
public void setViewPosition(Point p);
public void setViewSize(Dimension newSize);
```

These methods set various properties of the viewport. See "get" methods.

```
public Point toViewCoordinates(Point p);
public Dimension toViewCoordinates(Dimension size);
```

These methods translate point or dimension data into data used within the view. The default behavior is to simply return the argument that was passed. You would override these methods if supporting logical coordinates that differed from physical ones.

JWindow Class

Full Name	javax.swing.JWindow
Extends	Window->Container->Component->Object
Implements	RootPaneContainer

Description   Public class. This class corresponds closely to the AWT Window
                class, adding nothing but a JRootPane component (although
                others can be added programmatically). In most application and
                applet code, you should use JFrame (p. ___) in preference,
                because frames have useful features such as
                a menu bar and close button. The JWindow class provides
                nothing but a plain border. With AWT, you might use a Window
                class for a popu menu; but with Swing, the JMenuPopup class
                is provided for you. The only situation in which you'd need to
                use the JWindow class would be if you wanted a completely
                plain window with no adornments (which you might use, for
                example, to display temporary graphics as in a "splash"
                screen).

Constructors

```
public JWindow( );
public JWindow(Frame owner);
public JWindow(Window owner);
```

These constructors enable you to optionally specify an owner window or
frame.

Instance Methods

```
public Container getContentPane( );
public Component getGlassPane( );
public JLayeredPane getLayeredPane( );
public JRootPane getRootPane( );
public void setContentPane(Container contentPane);
public void setGlassPane(Component glassPane);
public void setLayeredPane(JLayeredPane layeredPane);
protected void setRootPane(JRootPane root);
```

These methods get and set the specific panes of the window. The content
pane contains the interior space of the window.

Overridden Instance Methods

```
protected String paramString( );
```

This method generates a parameter string that identifies the window.

```
public void remove(Component comp);
```

This method removes a component that has been added to the window.

```
public void setLayout(LayoutManager manager);
```

This method sets the layout manager for the window.

KeyAdapter Class

Full Name	java.awt.event.KeyAdapter
Extends	Object
Implements	KeyListener
Description	Public class. A helper class that provides empty implementations of the methods defined in the KeyListener interface (p. ___). This class serves as a convenience by allowing you to extend it and override only the listener response methods that you need, as opposed to implementing all of the methods defined in the interface. After deriving an event-handling class from this one, you need to register it as an event listener.

Here is an example of a class that extends KeyAdapter to process key presses:

```
class MyKeyAdapter extends KeyAdapter {
  public void keyPressed(KeyEvent e) {
    int code = e.getKeyCode();
  }
}
```

The following code installs this handler for a component named text1.

```
text1.addKeyListener(new MyKeyAdapter());
```

Constructors

```
public KeyAdapter();
```

Instance Methods

```
public void keyPressed(KeyEvent e);
public void keyReleased(KeyEvent e);
public void keyTyped(KeyEvent e);
```

These methods are called in response to a key on the keyboard being typed, pressed, or released.

KeyEvent Class

Full Name	java.awt.event.KeyEvent
Extends	InputEvent->ComponentEvent->AWTEvent-> EventObject->Object

Description   Public class. This class encapsulates the information
associated with a key event. Key events are generated by
key event sources and handled by objects that implement
the KeyListener interface (p. 370). An instance of the
KeyEvent class is delivered to the key listener event response
methods to aid in handling key events.

Here is an example of using the KeyEvent class to check whether the HOME
key was typed:

```
class MyKeyAdapter extends KeyAdapter {
  public void keyTyped(KeyEvent e) {
    if (e.getKeyText() == "HOME")
      System.out.println("You pressed the HOME key!");
  }
}
```

The following code installs this handler for a component named text1.

```
text1.addKeyListener(new MyKeyAdapter());
```

Constructors

```
public KeyEvent(Component source, int id, long when,
  int modifiers, int keyCode, char keyChar);
public KeyEvent(Component source, int id, long when,
  int modifiers, int keyCode);
```

The source argument is the object with which the key event is associated; id
is an identifier that identifies the event; when contains the time that the event
occurred; modifiers contains a set of flags that indicate the keyboard modifiers that were used with the key; keycode contains the virtual key code for
the key; and keyChar is the Unicode character generated by the key event.

Class Variables

```
public static final int KEY_FIRST, KEY_LAST;
public static final int KEY_TYPED, KEY_PRESSED;
public static final int KEY_RELEASED;
public static final int VK_ENTER;
public static final int VK_BACK_SPACE;
public static final int VK_TAB;
public static final int VK_CANCEL;
public static final int VK_CLEAR;
public static final int VK_SHIFT, VK_CONTROL, VK_ALT;
public static final int VK_PAUSE;
public static final int VK_CAPS_LOCK;
public static final int VK_ESCAPE;
public static final int VK_SPACE;
```

```
public static final int VK_PAGE_UP, VK_PAGE_DOWN;
public static final int VK_END;
public static final int VK_HOME;
public static final int VK_LEFT, VK_RIGHT;
public static final int VK_UP, VK_DOWN;
public static final int VK_COMMA;
public static final int VK_MINUS;
public static final int VK_PERIOD;
public static final int VK_SLASH;
public static final int VK_0, VK_1, VK_2, VK_3, VK_4, VK_5,
    VK_6, VK_7, VK_8, VK_9;
public static final int VK_SEMICOLON;
public static final int VK_EQUALS;
public static final int VK_A, VK_B, VK_C, VK_D, VK_E, VK_F,
    VK_G, VK_H, VK_I, VK_J, VK_K, VK_L, VK_M, VK_N, VK_O,
    VK_P, VK_Q, VK_R, VK_S, VK_T, VK_U, VK_V, VK_W, VK_X,
    VK_Y, VK_Z;
public static final int VK_OPEN_BRACKET;
public static final int VK_BACK_SLASH;
public static final int VK_CLOSE_BRACKET;
public static final int VK_NUMPAD0, VK_NUMPAD1, VK_NUMPAD2,
    VK_NUMPAD3, VK_NUMPAD4, VK_NUMPAD5, VK_NUMPAD6,
    VK_NUMPAD7, VK_NUMPAD8, VK_NUMPAD9;
public static final int VK_MULTIPLY;
public static final int VK_ADD;
public static final int VK_SEPARATER;
public static final int VK_SUBTRACT;
public static final int VK_DECIMAL;
public static final int VK_DIVIDE;
public static final int VK_DELETE;
public static final int VK_NUM_LOCK, VK_SCROLL_LOCK;
public static final int VK_F1, VK_F2, VK_F3, VK_F4, VK_F5,
    VK_F6, VK_F7, VK_F8, VK_F9, VK_F10, VK_F11, VK_F12,
    VK_F13, VK_F14, VK_F15, VK_F16, VK_F17, VK_F18, VK_F19,
    VK_F20, VK_F21, VK_F22, VK_F23, VK_F24;
public static final int VK_PRINTSCREEN;
public static final int VK_INSERT;
public static final int VK_HELP;
public static final int VK_META;
public static final int VK_BACK_QUOTE, VK_QUOTE;
public static final int VK_KP_UP, VK_KP_DOWN;
public static final int VK_KP_LEFT, VK_KP_RIGHT;
public static final int VK_DEAD_GRAVE;
```

Java 2 API Reference

```
public static final int VK_DEAD_ACUTE;
public static final int VK_DEAD_CIRCUMFLEX;
public static final int VK_DEAD_TILDE;
public static final int VK_DEAD_MACRON;
public static final int VK_DEAD_BREVE;
public static final int VK_DEAD_ABOVEDOT;
public static final int VK_DEAD_DIAERESIS;
public static final int VK_DEAD_ABOVERING;
public static final int VK_DEAD_DOUBLEACUTE;
public static final int VK_DEAD_CARON;
public static final int VK_DEAD_CEDILLA;
public static final int VK_DEAD_OGONEK;
public static final int VK_DEAD_IOTA;
public static final int VK_DEAD_VOICED_SOUND;
public static final int VK_DEAD_SEMIVOICED_SOUND;
public static final int VK_AMPERSAND;
public static final int VK_ASTERISK;
public static final int VK_QUOTEDBL;
public static final int VK_LESS;
public static final int VK_GREATER;
public static final int VK_BRACELEFT;
public static final int VK_BRACERIGHT;
public static final int VK_AT;
public static final int VK_COLON;
public static final int VK_CIRCUMFLEX;
public static final int VK_DOLLAR;
public static final int VK_EURO_SIGN;
public static final int VK_EXCLAMATION_MARK;
public static final int VK_INVERTED_EXCLAMATION_MARK;
public static final int VK_LEFT_PARENTHESIS;
public static final int VK_NUMBER_SIGN;
public static final int VK_PLUS;
public static final int VK_RIGHT_PARENTHESIS;
public static final int VK_UNDERSCORE;
public static final int VK_FINAL;
public static final int VK_CONVERT;
public static final int VK_NONCONVERT;
public static final int VK_ACCEPT;
public static final int VK_MODECHANGE;
public static final int VK_KANA;
public static final int VK_KANJI;
public static final int VK_ALPHANUMERIC;
public static final int VK_KATAKANA;
```

```
public static final int VK_HIRAGANA;
public static final int VK_FULL_WIDTH;
public static final int VK_HALF_WIDTH;
public static final int VK_ROMAN_CHARACTERS;
public static final int VK_ALL_CANDIDATES;
public static final int VK_PREVIOUS_CANDIDATE;
public static final int VK_CODE_INPUT;
public static final int VK_JAPANESE_KATAKANA;
public static final int VK_JAPANESE_HIRAGANA;
public static final int VK_JAPANESE_ROMAN;
public static final int VK_KANA_LOCK;
public static final int VK_INPUT_METHOD_ON_OFF;
public static final int VK_CUT;
public static final int VK_COPY;
public static final int VK_PASTE;
public static final int VK_UNDO;
public static final int VK_AGAIN;
public static final int VK_FIND;
public static final int VK_PROPS;
public static final int VK_STOP;
public static final int VK_COMPOSE;
public static final int VK_ALT_GRAPH;
public static final int VK_UNDEFINED;

public static final char CHAR_UNDEFINED;
```

Class constants. These constants are virtual key codes used to describe keys that are capable of being pressed on the keyboard.

Instance Methods

```
public char getKeyChar();
public int getKeyCode();
public static String getKeyModifiersText(int modifiers);
public static String getKeyText(int keyCode);
public int getModifiers();
public Object getSource();
public boolean isActionKey();
public void setKeyChar(char keyChar);
public void setKeyCode(int keyCode);
public void setModifiers(int modifiers);
public void setSource(Object newSource);
```

These methods get and set properties associated with the key event. The getSource() method returns the object that generated the event. (This method is actually inherited from EventObject.) The getModifiers() method returns a bit mask that can be AND'ed with these fields from the InputEvent class: ALT_GRAPH_MASK, ALT_MASK, CTRL_MASK, and SHIFT_MASK. By using the modifiers field, you can determine the state of various shift keys.

KeyListener Interface

Full Name   java.awt.event.KeyListener

Description   Public interface. This interface defines methods that respond
               to key events. Key events are generated when a key on the key-
               board is typed, pressed, or released; typing a key consists of
               pressing and releasing it. To handle key events, you can imple-
               ment the KeyListener interface, provide implementations of
               key event response methods, and then register the listener
               class with an event source. Alternatively, you can extend the
               KeyAdaptor class and override only the key
               event response methods in which you are interested.

See KeyAdapter and KeyEvent topics (pp. 365 and 365) for example code.

Interface Methods

```
public void keyPressed(KeyEvent e);
public void keyReleased(KeyEvent e);
public void keyTyped(KeyEvent e);
```

These methods are called on a registered key listener in response to a key on the keyboard being typed, pressed, or released.

KeyStroke Class

Full Name   javax.swing.KeyStroke

Extends   Object

Description   Public class. This class represents a key that has been typed
               on the keyboard, including the character code of the key along
               with any modifiers (Shift, Alt, Ctrl, and so on) that apply to the
               stroke.

Class Methods

```
public static KeyStroke getKeyStroke(char keyChar);
public static KeyStroke getKeyStroke(Character keyChar,
   int modifiers);
public static KeyStroke getKeyStroke(int keyCode,
   int modifiers, boolean onKeyRelease);
public static KeyStroke getKeyStroke(int keyCode,
   int modifiers);
```

```
public static KeyStroke getKeyStroke(String s);
public static KeyStroke getKeyStrokeForEvent(
   KeyEvent anEvent);
```

These methods return a KeyStroke object using different types of information to describe the key stroke. See KeyEvent class (p. 365) for interpretation of values.

Instance Methods

```
public char getKeyChar();
public int getKeyCode();
public int getModifiers();
public boolean isOnKeyRelease();
```

These methods retrieve various pieces of information associated with the keystroke. See KeyEvent class (p. 365) for interpretation of keycode and modifier values.

Overridden Instance Methods

```
public boolean equals(Object anObject);
public int hashCode();
public String toString();
```

These three methods override method definitions in the Object class (p. 407).

Label Class

Full Name	java.awt.Label
Extends	Component->Object
Description	Public class. Creates a simple component that displays a single line of read-only text. Label objects generate no events and cannot get focus. They are useful for labeling other components that do not have their own built-in label or caption.

The following example adds a label to the current frame or applet:

```
Label lab1 = new Label("OK");
add(lab1);
```

Constructors

```
public Label();
public Label(String label);
public Label(String label, int alignment);
```

Specifying label text and alignment is optional.

Class Variables

```
public final static int CENTER;
public final static int LEFT;
public final static int RIGHT;
```

These three constants are the possible values for text alignment.

Instance Methods

```
public int getAlignment();
public String getText();
public void setAlignment(int alignment);
public void setText(String label);
```

These methods get and set basic attributes of the label. The alignment argument can take any of the class variables as a setting: CENTER, LEFT, RIGHT.

Overridden Instance Methods

```
public synchronized void addNotify();
```

Overrides method definition in the Component class.

LayoutManager Interface

Full Name   java.awt.LayoutManager

Description   Public interface. This interface defines a set of services that a class must implement to be a layout manager. Note that only code within container classes calls these methods. Java applets and applications do not call these methods directly.

Interface Methods

```
public abstract void addLayoutComponent(String name,
    Component comp);
```

This method is called when a component is added to a container using the add(String, Component) method. The layout manager interprets the string; therefore, the meaning is dependent on the particular layout manager.

```
public abstract void layoutContainer(Container target);
```

This is the method where most of the work is done. It is called when the container needs to be laid out. The layout manager should respond by resizing and moving each component in the container as appropriate.

```
public abstract Dimension minimumLayoutSize(
    Container target);
```

This method returns the minimum layout size for the container after calculating the size required by all its components.

```
public abstract Dimension preferredLayoutSize(
   Container target);
```

This method returns the preferred layout size for the container after calculating the size that would best fit the preferred size for all the components.

```
public abstract void removeLayoutComponent(Component comp);
```

This method is called to inform the layout manager that the specified component is being removed from its container.

LineBorder Class

Full Name	javax.swing.border.LineBorder
Extends	AbstractBorder->Object
Description	Public class. This class implements a line border with an arbitrary thickness and a solid color.

Here is an example of setting a line border for a label component named label:

```
label.setBorder(new LineBorder(Color.red, 2));
```

Constructors

```
public LineBorder(Color color);
public LineBorder(Color color, int thickness);
public LineBorder(Color color, int thickness,
   boolean roundedCorners);
```

These constructors create line borders with varying degrees of detail in terms of the color and thickness, as well as whether or not they have rounded corners.

Instance Variables

```
protected Color lineColor;
protected boolean roundedCorners;
protected int thickness;
```

These variables store the various pieces of information associated with a line border, including the thickness and color of the border, as well as whether or not it has rounded corners.

Class Methods

```
public static Border createBlackLineBorder();
public static Border createGrayLineBorder();
```

These methods create default line borders with black or gray lines.

Instance Methods

```
public Color getLineColor();
public boolean getRoundedCorners();
public int getThickness();
```

These methods retrieve various pieces of information that describe the line border.

Overridden Instance Methods

```
public void paintBorder(Component c, Graphics g, int x,
    int y, int width, int height);
```

This method paints the border for a component using the specified border x,y position and size.

```
public Insets getBorderInsets(Component c);
public Insets getBorderInsets(Component c, Insets insets);
```

These methods retrieve the insets for the border; the latter version acts upon the Insets object that is passed as an argument.

```
public boolean isBorderOpaque();
```

This method checks whether the border is opaque or transparent; opaque borders paint their own backgrounds, whereas transparent borders do not.

Java 2 API Reference

LineNumberInputStream Class

Full Name	`java.io.LineNumberInputStream`
Extends	`FilterInputStream->InputStream->Object`
Description	Public class. Creates an input stream that tracks the number of lines read. The current line count advances when any of the following is read: a newline, a carriage return, or a newline/carriage-return pair. The class does not embed line numbers into the stream; they are only used within the class.

Constructors

```
public LineNumberInputStream(InputStream in);
```

Creates a line-numbered stream from another input stream.

Instance Methods

```
public int getLineNumber();
```

Returns the number of the current line being read.

```
public void setLineNumber(int lineNumber);
```

Resets the current line number. For example, if you set the current number to 10, the next line read would be numbered 11, the one after that 12, and so on.

Overridden Instance Methods

```
public int available() throws IOException;
public void mark(int readlimit);
public int read() throws IOException;
public int read(byte b[], int off, int len)
    throws IOException;
public void reset() throws IOException;
public long skip(long n) throws IOException;
```

These methods override method definitions in the InputStream class.

LinkedList Class

Full Name	java.util.LinkedList
Extends	AbstractSequentialList->AbstractList->AbstractCollection->Object
Description	Public class. This class implements a linked list based upon the List interface.

To create an empty linked list, you simply use the default LinkedList constructor:

```
LinkedList list = new LinkedList();
```

If you wanted to store a palette of colors in a linked list, you would add each Color object using the add() method:

```
list.add(Color.black);
list.add(Color.white);
list.add(Color.blue);
list.add(Color.green);
list.add(Color.orange);
list.add(Color.red);
list.add(Color.yellow);
```

In this example, the standard Color constants are used, but you could also create custom colors using the new operator and one of the Color constructors (page ___). This version of the add method adds each element to the end of the list. You can also specify an index to the add() method to insert an element at a specific point within the list. To get an object from the list, you can specify the index of the element to the get() method:

```
Color c = (Color) list.get(3);
```

Since linked lists are zero-based, this will retrieve the fourth element in the list. It is more common to access a linked list with an iterator, as opposed to accessing elements by index. To obtain an iterator for a linked list, call the `listIterator()` method and pass it the index of the first element you'd like included in the iterator:

```
ListIterator iterator = list.listIterator(0);
```

In this example, 0 is passed into the `listIterator()` method so that the entire list is included in the iterator. Once you obtain a `ListIterator`, you can access the list using familiar traversal methods such as `previous()` and `next()`.

To remove all elements from a linked list, call the `clear()` method:

```
list.clear();
```

Constructors

```
public LinkedList();
```

Default constructor.

```
public LinkedList(Collection c);
```

Creates a linked list initialized with the specified collection.

Instance Methods

```
public void addFirst(Object o);
public void addLast(Object o);
```

Adds the specified element to the beginning or end of the linked list.

```
public Object getFirst();
public Object getLast();
```

Retrieves the first or last element in the linked list.

```
public Object removeFirst();
public Object removeLast();
```

Removes the first or last element in the linked list.

Overridden Instance Methods

```
public boolean add(Object o);
public void add(int index, Object element);
```

Adds the specified object to either the end of the linked list or at the specified index in the list.

```
public boolean addAll(Collection c);
public boolean addAll(int index, Collection c);
```

Adds the specified collection to either the end of the linked list or at the specified index in the list.

```
public void clear();
```

Clears the linked list of all elements.

```
public boolean contains(Object o);
```

Checks to see if the linked list contains the specified object.

```
public Object get(int index);
```

Retrieves the object at the specified index in the linked list.

```
public int indexOf(Object o);
public int lastIndexOf(Object o);
```

Retrieves the first or last occurrence of the specified object as a list index.

```
public ListIterator listIterator(int index);
```

Retrieves a list iterator for the linked list starting at the specified index.

```
public Object remove(int index);
public boolean remove(Object o);
```

Removes the object at the specified list index or the specified object from the linked list.

```
public Object set(int index, Object element);
```

Sets the element at the specified list index with the specified object.

```
public int size();
```

Determines the number of elements in the linked list.

```
public Object[] toArray();
public Object[] toArray(Object[] a);
```

Retrieves an array containing all of the elements in the linked list. The a parameter allows you to specify an array that determines the runtime type of the array returned by toArray().

List Interface

Full Name	java.util.List
Extends	Collection
Description	Public interface. This interface describes an ordered collection, also known as a sequence. Elements within the list can be accessed by an integer index.

Interface Methods

```
public boolean add(Object o);
public void add(int index, Object element);
```

Adds the specified object to the end of the list or at the specified index in the list.

```
public boolean addAll(Collection c);
public boolean addAll(int index, Collection c);
```

Adds the specified collection to either the end of the list or at the specified index in the list.

```
public void clear();
```

Clears the list of all elements.

```
public boolean contains(Object o);
public boolean containsAll(Collection c);
```

Checks to see if the list contains the specified object or collection.

```
public Object get(int index);
```

Retrieves the object at the specified index in the list.

```
public int indexOf(Object o);
```

Retrieves the first occurrence of the specified object as a list index.

```
public boolean isEmpty();
```

Checks to see if the list is empty.

```
public Iterator iterator();
```

Retrieves an iterator for the list that can be used to iterate through the elements.

```
public int lastIndexOf(Object o);
```

Retrieves the last occurrence of the specified object as a list index.

```
public ListIterator listIterator();
public ListIterator listIterator(int index);
```

Retrieves a list iterator for the entire list or a partial list starting at the specified index.

```
public boolean remove(Object o);
public Object remove(int index);
```

Removes the object at the specified list index or the specified object from the list.

```
public boolean removeAll(Collection c);
```

Removes the elements from the list that are contained in the specified collection.

```
public boolean retainAll(Collection c);
```

Removes the elements from the list except those that are contained in the specified collection.

```
public Object set(int index, Object element);
```

Sets the element at the specified list index with the specified object.

```
public int size();
```

Determines the number of elements in the list.

```
public List subList(int fromIndex, int toIndex);
```

Retrieves a sub-list containing the elements within specified start and end indices.

```
public Object[] toArray();
public Object[] toArray(Object[] a);
```

Retrieves an array containing all of the elements in the list. The parameter allows you to specify an array that determines the runtime type of the array returned by toArray().

List Class

Full Name	java.awt.List
Extends	Component->Object
Description	Public class. A List object is a component featuring a scrollable list of items from which the user can select one or more items by clicking on them. Objects of this type generate standard keyboard and mouse events. Mouse clicks generate ActionEvent and ItemEvent, respectively, for the user making a definite choice (for example, by double clicking) and for item selection. Use the addActionListener() and addItemListener() methods to install event handlers as appropriate.

The following example creates and initializes a List component and adds it to the current frame or applet. The list has three visible rows and permits multiple selection.

```
List countryList = new List(3, true);
countryList.addItem("Oh Canada!");
```

Java 2 API Reference

```
countryList.addItem("La Belle France");
countryList.addItem("USA");
add(Countrylist);
```

Several methods use an index into the list to specify a position. This index is zero-based; the first item in a list is in position zero, the second is in position 1, and so on.

Constructors

```
public List();
public List(int rows, boolean multipleSelections);
```

The rows argument specifies the number of visible rows. Specifying 0 lets the layout manager determine the row size. (This produces good results with BorderLayout but poor results with FlowLayout.) The multipleSelections argument, if true, specifies that the user can select any number of items at the same time.

Instance Methods

```
public void addActionListener(ActionListener l);
```

Adds an event handler for action events; these are events that indicate choosing a command on the part of the user.

```
public void addItem(String item);
public void addItem(String item, int index);
```

Adds an item, optionally specifying position with a zero-based index. All list items are simple strings.

```
public void addItemListener(ItemListener l);
```

Adds an event handler for changes in item selection.

```
public boolean allowsMultipleSelections();
```

Returns true if multiple selections are allowed.

```
public void clear();
```

Clears the list of all items.

```
public int countItems();
```

Returns the number of items in the list.

```
public void delItem(int position);
public void delItems(int start, int end);
```

These methods delete one or more items. In the case of delItems(), all items from start to end positions, inclusive, are deleted. All arguments are zero-based indexes.

```
public void deselect(int index);
```

Removes selection from the specified item if currently selected. The argument is a zero-based index.

```
public String getItem(int index);
```

Returns the item specified by a zero-based index.

```
public int getRows();
```

Returns the number of visible rows. This is not necessarily the same as the number of items.

```
public int getSelectedIndex();
public int[] getSelectedIndexes();
```

Returns the zero-based index of the currently selected item or items. get SelectedIndex() returns –1 if no item is selected or if there are multiple selections.

```
public String getSelectedItem();
public String[] getSelectedItems();
```

Returns the selected item or items. getSelectedItem() returns null if there is no selection or if there are multiple selections.

```
public int getVisibleIndex();
```

Returns the zero-based index of the last item made visible by a call to makeVisible().

```
public boolean isSelected(int index);
```

Returns true if the specified item is selected. Index is zero-based.

```
public void makeVisible(int index);
```

Scrolls the list, if necessary, so that the specified item is visible to the user. The index is zero-based.

```
public Dimension minimumSize(int rows);
public Dimension preferredSize(int rows);
```

These methods return the minimum and preferred size, respectively, assuming that the list had the specified number of visible rows.

```
public void removeActionListener(ActionListener l);
public void removeItemListener(ItemListener l);
```

Removes a previously installed event handler.

```
public void replaceItem(String newValue, int index);
```

Assigns a new string value to the specified item. Index is zero-based.

```
public void select(int index);
```

Causes the specified item to be selected. Index is zero-based. The value −1 deselects all items.

```
public void setMultipleSelections(boolean v);
```

Turns the multiple-selection capability on or off, depending on the argument v.

Overridden Instance Methods

```
public void addNotify();
public Dimension minimumSize();
public Dimension preferredSize();
public void removeNotify();
```

These methods override method definitions in the Component class.

ListResourceBundle Class

Full Name	java.util.ListResourceBundle
Extends	ResourceBundle->Object
Description	Public class. This class is used to package resources in a list for a specific locale and acts as an important means of organizing information for internationalization.

To bundle strings into a list resource bundle, you must create a class that derives from ListResourceBundle. Following is an example of how you might organize common U.S. English phrases into a list resource bundle:

```
public class PhraseBundle extends ListResourceBundle {
  static final Object[][] contents = {
    // Localized U.S. English phrases
    { "Enter", "Hello" },
    { "Exit", "Goodbye" },
    { "Apology", "I'm sorry" },
    { "Grateful", "Thank you" }
  };

  public Object[][] getContents() {
    return contents;
  }
}
```

As you can see, the label strings are stored in a static array that is accessible through the getContents() method. This is the standard protocol for bundling string lists in a ListResourceBundle object. The bundle actually contains pairs of strings; the first string in each pair is the key, while the second string is the locale-sensitive information. The string keys are what an internationalized program uses to obtain locale-sensitive information from the resource bundle. Consequently, the key part of the string list is the same across all locales.

The PhraseBundle class only identifies data for one locale, which just so happens to be the United States. To bundle data for another locale, you must create a new class whose name consists of the resource bundle name with the locale code appended to the end. For example, the PhraseBundle class for the French language would be named PhraseBundle_fr. Following is the code for this class:

```
public class PhraseBundle_fr extends ListResourceBundle {
    static final Object[][] contents = {
    // Localized French phrases
    { "Enter", "Allo" },
    { "Exit", "Adieu" },
    { "Apology", "Je navre" },
    { "Grateful", "Grace" }
    };

    public Object[][] getContents() {
        return contents;
    }
}
```

To extract strings from a list resource bundle, you must obtain the bundle using the static getBundle() method, and then use the getString() method to retrieve a localized string from the bundle:

```
ResourceBundle phrases = ResourceBundle.getBundle("PhraseBundle",
    Locale.US);

String enterStr = phrases.getString("Enter");
String exitStr = phrases.getString("Exit");
String apologyStr = phrases.getString("Apology");
String gratefulStr = phrases.getString("Grateful");
```

The interesting thing about this code is that you could easily switch to the French locale by simply changing the second parameter to the getBundle() method:

```
ResourceBundle phrases = ResourceBundle.getBundle("PhraseBundle",
    Locale.FRANCE);
```

By specifying the French locale when obtaining the resource bundle, the `PhraseBundle_fr` class is automatically returned from the `getBundle()` method.

Constructors

```
public ListResourceBundle();
```

Overridden Instance Methods

```
public Enumeration getKeys();
```

Retrieve an enumeration containing all of the keys in the list resource bundle.

```
public final Object handleGetObject(String key);
```

Retrieve an object from the list resource bundle using the specified key.

ListSelectionEvent Class

Full Name	`javax.swing.event.ListSelectionEvent`
Extends	`EventObject->Object`
Description	Public class. This class represents a list selection event that is delivered in response to an item or items in a list being selected or deselected.

Constructors

```
public ListSelectionEvent(Object source, int firstIndex,
    int lastIndex, boolean isAdjusting);
```

Creates a list selection event based upon the specified event source, starting list index, ending list index, and adjustment flag. The adjustment flag specifies whether or not this is one of a series of rapidly generated events.

Instance Methods

```
public int getFirstIndex();
```

Obtains the index of the first item selected.

```
public int getLastIndex();
```

Obtains the index of the last item selected.

```
public Object getSource();
```

Retrieves the object upon which the event originally occurred. (This method is actually inherited from the `EventObject` ancestor class.)

```
public boolean getValueIsAdjusting();
```

Checks to see if this event is part of a list adjustment.

```
public String toString();
```
Obtains a string representation of the event.

ListSelectionListener Interface

Full Name   `javax.swing.event.ListSelectionListener`

Extends   `EventListener`

Description   Public interface. This interface describes a list selection event listener that is used to handle list selection events.

Interface Methods
```
public void valueChanged(ListSelectionEvent e);
```
This method is an event response method that is called when the selection of a list changes.

Locale Class

Full Name   `java.util.Locale`

Extends   `Object`

Description   Public class. This class represents a specific geographical, political, or cultural region for purposes of localizing an applet or application. This is important in internationalized code so that it displays information according to the user's native language and culture.

Creating locales is pretty simple; you simply provide the appropriate language and country code strings to the `Locale` constructor. For example, the following code creates a locale for Austria:
```
Locale l = new Locale("de", "AT");
```
This locale can then be used to perform locale-specific operations in an application. If an attempt is made to use an unsupported locale, Java tries a more general version of the locale by dropping the country. So, for this example the more general German language locale would be tried if the Austrian locale failed. If both locales fail, Java resorts to the default locale, which is hopefully supported by the application. If not, a `MissingResourceException` exception is thrown.

Constructors
```
public Locale(String language, String country);
public Locale(String language, String country, String variant);
```

Creates a locale based upon the specified language and country. The `variant` argument allows you to specify additional information regarding the locale.

Class Variables

```
public static final Locale CANADA;
public static final Locale CANADA_FRENCH;
public static final Locale CHINA;
public static final Locale CHINESE;
public static final Locale ENGLISH;
public static final Locale FRANCE;
public static final Locale FRENCH;
public static final Locale GERMAN;
public static final Locale GERMANY;
public static final Locale ITALIAN;
public static final Locale ITALY;
public static final Locale JAPAN;
public static final Locale JAPANESE;
public static final Locale KOREA;
public static final Locale KOREAN;
public static final Locale PRC;
public static final Locale SIMPLIFIED_CHINESE;
public static final Locale TAIWAN;
public static final Locale TRADITIONAL_CHINESE;
public static final Locale UK;
public static final Locale US;
```

Class constants. These constants represent built-in languages and countries supported by the `Locale` class.

Class Methods

```
public static Locale[] getAvailableLocales();
```

Retrieves a list of all the currently installed locales.

```
public static Locale getDefault();
```

Retrieves the default locale for the current environment.

```
public static String[] getISOCountries();
```

Retrieves a list of all the ISO two-character country codes.

```
public static String[] getISOLanguages();
```

Retrieves a list of all the ISO two-character language codes.

```
public static void setDefault(Locale newLocale);
```

Sets the default locale for the current environment.

Instance Methods

```
public String getCountry();
public final String getDisplayCountry();
```

Retrieves the two-character country code and full country string for the current locale.

```
public String getDisplayCountry(Locale inLocale);
```

Retrieves the full country string for the specified locale.

```
public final String getDisplayLanguage();
```

Retrieves the full language string for the current locale.

```
public String getDisplayLanguage(Locale inLocale);
```

Retrieves the full language string for the specified locale.

```
public final String getDisplayName();
```

Retrieves the full locale name string for the current locale.

```
public String getDisplayName(Locale inLocale);
```

Retrieves the full locale name string for the specified locale.

```
public final String getDisplayVariant();
```

Retrieves the full variant string for the current locale.

```
public String getDisplayVariant(Locale inLocale);
```

Retrieves the full variant string for the specified locale.

```
public String getISO3Language() throws MissingResourceException;
```

Retrieves a three-character abbreviation of the current locale's language.

```
public String getISO3Country() throws MissingResourceException;
```

Retrieves a three-character abbreviation of the current locale's country.

```
public String getLanguage();
```

Retrieves the two-character language code for the current locale.

Long Class

Full Name	java.lang.Long
Extends	Number->Object
Description	Public final class. Serves as the wrapper class for the long primitive type. This class provides methods for converting between string, object, and numeric data. It also is useful for passing a long value by reference.

The following example converts a digit string to type long:

```
long lng = Long.parseLong(digitString);
```

Constructors

```
public Long(long value);
public Long(String s);
```

The second constructor initializes from a digit string.

Class Variables

```
public final static long MAX_VALUE;
public final static long MIN_VALUE;
```

Constants. Maximum and minimum values in the long range.

Class Methods

```
public static Long getLong(String nm);
public static Long getLong(String nm, long val);
public static Long getLong(String nm, Long val);
```

Returns the value of the system property named. The second argument, if specified, is returned if the property name is not found in the system properties table.

```
public static long parseLong(String s);
public static long parseLong(String s, long radix);
```

Returns the face value of a string of digits as a long.

```
public static String toString(long i);
public static String toString(long i, long radix);
```

Returns a string representation of the long value.

```
public static Long valueOf(String s);
public static Long valueOf(String s, long radix);
```

Returns a Long object, initializing it from the digits in the string argument.

Instance Methods (from Number Class)

```
public double doubleValue();
public float floatValue();
public int intValue();
public long longValue();
```

These methods return the double, float, int, or long equivalent of the value stored in the current object.

Instance Methods (from Object Class)

```
public boolean equals(Object obj);
public long hashCode();
public String toString();
```

These methods override method definitions in the Object class.

LookAndFeel Class

Full Name   `javax.swing.LookAndFeel`

Extends   `Object`

Description   Public class. "Look and Feel" is the scientific name the Java architects came up with to designate a whole set of visual details for the Java platform. There are at least three main types of look-and-feel settings: Windows, Motif, and Metal. For example, with the Windows look-and-feel, all the components — such as sliders, progress bars, and menus, to name just a few — are rendered so as to closely approximate the look of controls on the Windows platform. Small details of component behavior may also be influenced by a look-and-feel.

The purpose of this class is to make the look of a Swing application largely independent of the platform on which it actually runs.

Although it is possible to create an entirely new look-and-feel, doing so involves writing a large amount of graphics code for extremely low level Swing classes that are outside the scope of this book. It's nice to know that the capability is there, though.

Here is an example that sets an application to conform to the Windows look and feel:

```
try {
    UIManager.setLookAndFeel(
        "com.sun.java.swing.plaf.windows.WindowsLookAndFeel");
}
catch (Exception e) {
}
```

Although the LookAndFeel class isn't used directly in this code, it is certainly at work behind the scenes. Here is another example that sets an application to the native look and feel:

```
try {
    String laf = UIManager.getSystemLookAndFeelClassName();
    UIManager.setLookAndFeel(laf);
```

Java 2 API Reference

```
}
catch (Exception e) {
}
```

The details of this class are outside the scope of this book. See information on the Javasoft Web site at http://java.sun.com.

Map Interface

Full Name	`java.util.Map`
Description	Public interface. This interface describes a map collection that is used to map keys to values. Values within a map are referenced using a unique key.

Interface Methods

```
public void clear();
```
Clears the map.

```
public boolean containsKey(Object key);
```
Checks to see if the map contains a mapping for the specified key.

```
public boolean containsValue(Object value);
```
Checks to see if the map contains one or keys mapped to the specified value.

```
public Set entrySet();
```
Retrieves a set containing the entry mappings for the map.

```
public Object get(Object key);
```
Retrieves the value associated with the specified key.

```
public boolean isEmpty();
```
Checks to see if the map is empty.

```
public Set keySet();
```
Retrieves a set containing the key mappings for the map.

```
public Object put(Object key, Object value);
```
Adds a key/value mapping to the map.

```
public void putAll(Map t);
```
Adds all of the mappings in the specified map to the map.

```
public Object remove(Object key);
```
Removes the specified key and its associated value from the map.

```
public int size();
```
Retrieves the number of key/value mappings in the map.

```
public Collection values();
```
Retrieves a collection of values contained within the map.

Math Class

Full Name	`java.lang.Math`
Extends	`Object`
Description	Public final class. All fields of this class are class fields — they have no connection to individual data objects of type `Math`. Instead, the `Math` class provides a collection of static methods and two useful constants: `E` and `PI`. The `Math` class is like a mini-library made up of mathematical functions. This class has no constructor, and there is no reason to instantiate it.

The following example produces a random number from 1 to n. The first step is to execute `random()`, which produces a number in the range 0.0 to 1.0. Note that the `floor()` method could be applied to get a number in the range 0 to n-1.

```
int r = Math.ceil(Math.random() * n);
```

Class Variables

```
public final static double E = 2.7182818284590452354;
public final static double PI = 3.14159265358979323846;
```

Constants. Given the limits of double precision, these amounts are the closest approximations of the irrational numbers e and pi.

Class Methods

```
public static double abs(double a);
public static float abs(float a);
public static int abs(int a);
public static long abs(long a);
```

Returns the absolute value of the amount specified.

```
public static double acos(double a);
public static double asin(double a);
public static double atan(double a);
```

Returns the result of an inverse trig function.

```
public static double atan2(double a, double b);
```

Returns the angle component of the polar coordinates for point (a, b), where a and b use the Cartesian coordinate system.

```
public static double ceil(double a);
```

Returns the lowest integer amount that is equal to or greater than the argument.

```
public static double cos(double a);
```

Returns the cosine of the argument.

```
public static double exp(double a);
```

Returns e to the power of a (in which e is the natural logarithm base).

```
public static double floor(double a);
```

Returns the highest integer amount that is equal to or less than the argument.

```
public static double IEEEremainder(double f1, double f2);
```

Returns the remainder as defined by IEEE, when f1 is divided by f2. The remainder is the amount left over after an integer quotient is found.

```
public static double log(double a);
```

Returns the natural logarithm of a.

```
public static double max(double a, double b);
public static float max(float a, float b);
public static int max(int a, int b);
public static long max(long a, long b);
```

Returns the maximum of two numbers, where both have the same type.

```
public static double min(double a, double b);
public static float min(float a, float b);
public static int min(int a, int b);
public static long min(long a, long b);
```

Returns the minimum of two numbers, where both have the same type.

```
public static double pow(double a, double b);
```

Returns a to the power of b.

```
public static double random();
```

Returns a psuedo-random number between 0.0 and 1.0. For more sophisticated random-number generation (such as Gaussian distribution), use the Random class. However, Math.random() is adequate for most code that uses a random number.

```
public static double rint(double a);
public static long round(double a);
public static int round(float a);
```

All these methods return the nearest integer value. The difference is that
rint() returns a double rather than an integer type and favors even numbers
in rounding: 2.5 rounds to 2.0, although 2.51 rounds up to 3.0.

```
public static double sin(double a);
public static double sqrt(double a);
public static double tan(double a);
```

These methods return a sine, square root, and tangent, respectively.

MatteBorder Class

Full Name   javax.swing.border.MatteBorder

Extends   EmptyBorder->AbstractBorder->Object

Description   Public class. This class implements a matte border that is
                painted in a solid color or with a tiled icon image. The purpose
                of this class is to create a border between a component and its
                surroundings rendered with a particular color or pattern of your
                choice. A MatteBorder object that uses a pattern sets a
                tileIcon property.

Constructors

```
public MatteBorder(int top, int left, int bottom, int right,
   Color matteColor);
public MatteBorder(Insets borderInsets, Color matteColor);
public MatteBorder(int top, int left, int bottom, int right,
   Icon tileIcon);
public MatteBorder(Insets borderInsets, Icon tileIcon);
public MatteBorder(Icon tileIcon);
```

These constructors create matte borders by specifying the size in different
ways and also by using a solid color or tiled icon image as the border
appearance.

Instance Variables

```
protected Color color;
protected Icon tileIcon;
```

These variables store the various pieces of information associated with a
matte border, including the color and tile icon of the border.

Instance Methods

```
public Insets getBorderInsets();
```

This method retrieves the insets of the border.

```
public Color getMatteColor();
public Icon getTileIcon();
```

These methods retrieve the matte color and tile icon of the matte border.

Overridden Instance Methods

```
public Insets getBorderInsets(Component c);
public Insets getBorderInsets(Component c, Insets insets);
```

These methods retrieve the insets for the border; the latter version acts on the Insets object that is passed as an argument.

```
public boolean isBorderOpaque();
```

This method checks whether the border is opaque or transparent; opaque borders paint their own backgrounds, whereas transparent borders do not.

```
public void paintBorder(Component c, Graphics g, int x,
    int y, int width, int height);
```

This method paints the border for a component using the specified border *x,y* position and size.

MediaTracker Class

Full Name   java.awt.MediaTracker

Extends   Object

Description   Public class. A MediaTracker object monitors the progress of loading an image from disk or a remote site. After creating the tracker, you assign an image to it by calling addImage(). A single tracker can monitor any number of images as long as they are being loaded for the same component. The most important methods are checkID() and waitForID(), which check progress and wait for completion, respectively.

The following example creates a MediaTracker object that monitors loading for an Image object, imgFromFile. checkID() returns true if the image is completely loaded. For MediaTracker used in context, see the example in Part II, Chapter 3 on page 555.

```
MediaTracker tracker = new MediaTracker(this);
tracker.addImage(imgFromFile, 1);
// ...
boolean b = tracker.checkID(1);  // Image loaded?
```

Constructors

```
public MediaTracker(Component comp);
```

A media tracker always monitors a component, which must be specified.

Class Variables

```
public final static int ABORTED;
public final static int COMPLETE;
public final static int ERRORED;
public final static int LOADING;
```

These constants are status codes returned by the statusAll() and statusID() methods.

Instance Methods

```
public void addImage(Image image, int id);
public void addImage(Image image, int id, int w, int h);
```

Registers an image to be tracked, assigning that image an ID number of your choice. The purpose of the ID is to identify the image so that it can be referred to in other MediaTracker methods. The w and h arguments should be specified when you're doing scaling.

```
public boolean checkAll();
public boolean checkAll(boolean load);
public boolean checkID(int id);
public boolean checkID(int id, boolean load);
```

These four methods check loading status, returning true if the specified image has finished loading (checkID) or if all images tracked have finished loading (checkAll). If the load argument is included and is true, then the method initiates loading if not already started.

```
public Object[] getErrorsAny();
public Object[] getErrorsID(int id);
public boolean isErrorAny();
public boolean isErrorID(int id);
```

These four methods return information about errors encountered during loading. You can check on all images being tracked or on a single image identified by its ID.

```
public int statusAll(boolean load);
public int statusID(int id, boolean load);
```

Returns status using one of the four status codes defined in the class.

```
public void waitForAll();
public boolean waitForAll(long ms)
   throws InterruptedException;
public void waitForID(int id);
public boolean waitForID(int id, long ms)
   throws InterruptedException;
```

Java 2 API Reference

These methods wait for the specified image or images and do not return until the image has finished loading, an error is encountered, or ms milliseconds (if specified) have elapsed. Note that calling one of these methods from within the main thread may be a risk, especially if you're loading data from a remote site. The UI is inoperable while the main thread is in a waiting state.

MemoryImageSource Class

Full Name	`java.awt.image.MemoryImageSource`
Extends	`Object`
Implements	`ImageProducer`
Description	Public class. Creates an image source that produces an image from raw pixel data in memory. The resulting image producer can be used to create a new image by calling the `createImage()` method of the `Component` class. This class is the converse of the `PixelGrabber` class, which gets raw pixel data from the image.

The following example loads a 300×200 image from buffer, an integer array containing pixel data:

```
MemoryImageSource mem = new MemoryImageSource(300, 200,
    buffer, 0, 300);
Image myImage = createImage(mem);
```

Constructors

```
public MemoryImageSource(int w, int h, ColorModel cm,
    byte pix[], int off, int scan);
public MemoryImageSource(int w, int h, ColorModel cm,
    byte pix[], int off, int scan, Hashtable props);
public MemoryImageSource(int w, int h, ColorModel cm,
    int pix[], int off, int scan);
public MemoryImageSource(int w, int h, ColorModel cm,
    int pix[], int off, int scan, Hashtable props);
public MemoryImageSource(int w, int h, int pix[], int off,
    int scan);
public MemoryImageSource(int w, int h, int pix[], int off,
    int scan, Hashtable props);
```

The arguments specify size, integer or byte pixel array source, offset into the array, and scan size (typically the same as width). You can optionally specify a color model and a properties table. If a color model is not specified, the default RGB model is used.

Instance Methods

```
public void addConsumer(ImageConsumer ic);
public boolean isConsumer(ImageConsumer ic);
public void removeConsumer(ImageConsumer ic);
public void requestTopDownLeftRightResend(ImageConsumer ic);
public void startProduction(ImageConsumer ic);
```

These methods implement method declarations in the ImageProducer interface (p. 283).

Menu Class

Full Name	java.awt.Menu
Extends	MenuItem->MenuComponent->Object
Implements	MenuContainer
Description	Public class. Creates a pull-down menu that can be added to a menu bar by calling MenuBar.add( ). A menu bar, in turn, can be added to a frame by calling Frame.setMenuBar( ). Menus may optionally be tear-off menus if it is supported by the platform. The default is a standard menu. See also MenuItem, page 401.

Assume that MyFrameClass is a subclass of Frame. The following MyFrame Class( ) constructor sets a menu bar with one menu (Commands), under which are two items (Do and Exit). See MenuItem class (p. 401) for event-handling code.

```
MyFrameClass() {
    // Assume miDo, miExit declared as instance vars.
    miDo = new MenuItem("Do");
    miExit = new MenuItem("Exit");

    Menu m = new Menu("Commands");    // Create menu.
    m.add(miDo);                      // -> Add items.
    m.add(miExit);

    MenuBar mb = new MenuBar();       // Create menu bar.
    mb.add(m);                        // -> Add menu.
    setMenuBar(mb);                   // Call Frame.setMenuBar().
}
```

Constructors

```
public Menu(String label);
public Menu(String label, boolean tearOff);
```

You can optionally specify a `tearOff` argument, which, if true, causes the menu to be created as a tear-off menu.

Instance Methods

```
public MenuItem add(MenuItem mi);
public void add(String label);
```

Adds the specified item as a string or `MenuItem` object. In either case, the resulting item is stored as a `MenuItem` object. Nested menus are possible, because the `Menu` class is a subclass of `MenuItem` and therefore a `Menu` object can be given as an argument to `add()`.

```
public void addSeparator();
```

Adds a separator bar in the next menu position.

```
public int countItems();
public MenuItem getItem(int index);
public boolean isTearOff();
```

These methods return information about the menu. `getItem()` returns the specified menu as a `MenuItem` object. Index is zero-based.

```
public void remove(int index);
public void remove(MenuComponent item);
```

Removes the menu item specified by zero-based index or by reference to the object.

Overridden Instance Methods

```
public void addNotify();
public void removeNotify();
```

These methods override method definitions in the `MenuComponent` and `MenuItem` classes. These methods are both used internally.

MenuBar Class

Full Name	`java.awt.MenuBar`
Extends	`MenuComponent->Object`
Implements	`MenuContainer`
Description	Public class. Creates a menu bar that may be added to a frame by calling `Frame.setMenuBar()`. A menu bar must be added to a frame to be displayed. A menu bar is a series of menu names; clicking one pulls down the selected menu.

See `Menu` class (p. 397) for an example.

Constructors

```
public MenuBar();
```

Instance Methods

```
public synchronized Menu add(Menu m);
```

Adds a menu to the bar.

```
public int countMenus();
```

Returns the current number of menus on the bar.

```
public Menu getHelpMenu();
public Menu getMenu(int i);
```

These methods return the requested Menu object. Index is zero-based.

```
public synchronized void remove(int index);
public synchronized void remove(MenuComponent m);
```

Removes the specified menu from the bar. Index is zero-based.

```
public synchronized void setHelpMenu(MenuComponent item);
```

Causes the menu to be specified as a help menu, which is placed in a reserved location on the menu bar.

Overridden Instance Methods

```
public synchronized void addNotify();
public synchronized void removeNotify();
```

These methods override method definitions in the MenuComponent and MenuItem classes. These methods are both used internally.

MenuComponent Class

Full Name   java.awt.MenuComponent

Extends   Object

Description   Abstract public class. Because this class is abstract, you can-
               not use it to directly create an object. However, this class is the
               superclass of three menu-related classes — MenuBar, Menu,
               and MenuItem — and it includes methods useful in
               all these subclasses.

Constructors

```
public MenuComponent();
```

Instance Methods

```
public Font getFont();
public MenuContainer getParent();
```

These methods return font and container much as Component methods do.

```
public MenuComponentPeer getPeer();
public boolean postEvent(Event evt);
public void removeNotify();
```

These three methods are mainly used internally.

```
public void setFont(Font f);
```

Sets a font used to display menu or menu bar text.

Overridden Instance Methods

```
public String toString();
```

Overrides the method definition in the Object class.

MenuContainer Interface

Full Name   java.awt.MenuContainer

Description   Public interface. This interface defines a set of methods
that a class must implement to be a container of other menu
structures. Menu-container classes include Frame, Menu,
and MenuBar. It is unlikely you'll ever need to implement this
interface yourself.

Interface Methods

```
public abstract Font getFont();
```

Returns the current font.

```
public abstract boolean postEvent(Event evt);
```

Used internally, to pass along events not handled to a container.

```
public abstract void remove(MenuComponent m);
```

Removes the specified object, which belongs to a class derived from
MenuComponent; these classes include Menu and MenuItem.

MenuElement Interface

Full Name   javax.swing.MenuElement

Description   Public interface. This interface is implemented by any element
that appears within a Swing menu. Implementing the methods
in this interface ensures that a class is able to respond to the
basic commands that the Swing architecture requres for consistent menu behavior.

MenuElement is implemented by the JMenu, JMenuBar, JMenuItem, and JPopupMenu classes (pp. 321, 324, 325, and 333).

Interface Methods

```
public Component getComponent();
```

This method retrieves the component responsible for painting the menu in which the menu element appears.

```
public MenuElement[] getSubElements();
```

This method retrieves the subelements associated with a menu element; of course, this method only applies to menu elements that contain subelements.

```
public void menuSelectionChanged(boolean isIncluded);
```

This method adds or removes the menu element from the current menu selection; this method is called automatically by a MenuSelection object.

```
public void processKeyEvent(KeyEvent event, MenuElement[] path,
    MenuSelectionManager manager);
public void processMouseEvent(MouseEvent event, MenuElement[] path,
    MenuSelectionManager manager);
```

These methods process mouse and key events that impact the menu element.

MenuItem Class

Full Name	java.awt.MenuItem
Extends	MenuComponent->Object
Description	Public class. Creates an item on a pull-down menu, which can be added to a Menu object by calling Menu.add(). When a MenuItem object is selected, it generates an ActionEvent. Call the addActionListener() method to install the appropriate event handler.

The following example subclasses Frame and responds to selection of miDo or miExit, two menu items.

```
class MyFrame extends Frame implements ActionListener {
    MenuItem miDo, miExit;

    // Insert MyFrameClass() constructor.
    // from "Menu Class" topic.
     miDo.addActionListener(this);
     miExit.addActionListener(this);
```

Java 2 API Reference

```
public void actionPerformed(ActionEvent e) {
   if (e.getSource() == miDo)
      System.out.println("Do activated!");
   else if (e.getSource() == miExit) {
      System.out.println("Exit activated!");
      System.exit(1);
   }
}


}
```

Constructors

```
public MenuItem(String label);
```

Menu item must be identified by a label.

Instance Methods

```
public synchronized void addNotify();
```

Used internally.

```
public void disable();
public void enable();
public void enable(boolean cond);
```

These methods disable or enable the menu item. A disabled item is grayed out and cannot be selected. enable() with an argument can be used to enable (true) or disable (false).

```
public String getLabel();
public boolean isEnabled();
```

These methods return the label and enabled state of the menu item.

```
public void setLabel(String label);
```

Specifies a new label.

MouseAdapter Class

Full Name	`java.awt.event.MouseAdapter`
Extends	`Object`
Implements	`MouseListener`

Description   Public class. A helper class that provides empty implementations of the methods defined in the `MouseListener` interface.
This class serves as a convenience by allowing you to extend it
and override only the listener response methods that you need,
as opposed to implementing all of the methods defined in the
interface. After deriving an event-handling class from this one,
you need to register it as an event listener.

Here is an example of a class that extends `MouseAdapter` to process mouse
clicks:

```
class MyMouseAdapter extends MouseAdapter {
  public void mouseClicked(MouseEvent e) {
    System.out.println("You clicked the mouse button!");
  }
}
```

An object `button1` that uses this class can install the event handler as follows:

```
button1.addMouseListener(new MyMouseAdapter());
```

Constructors

```
public MouseAdapter();
```

Instance Methods

```
public void mouseClicked(MouseEvent e);
public void mouseEntered(MouseEvent e);
public void mouseExited(MouseEvent e);
public void mousePressed(MouseEvent e);
public void mouseReleased(MouseEvent e);
```

These methods are called in response to a mouse button being clicked,
pressed, or released, or the mouse entering or exiting a component.

MouseEvent Class

Full Name   `java.awt.event.MouseEvent`

Extends   `InputEvent->ComponentEvent->AWTEvent->`
`EventObject->Object`

Description   Public class. This class encapsulates the information associated with a mouse event, which includes mouse button clicks
and mouse motion. Mouse events are generated by mouse
event sources and handled by objects that implement the
`MouseListener` interface. An instance of the `MouseEvent`
class is delivered to the mouse listener event response methods to aid in handling mouse events.

Java 2 API Reference

Here is an example of using the MouseEvent class to determine the location of the mouse pointer upon releasing the mouse button:

```
class MyMouseAdapter extends MouseAdapter {
  public void mouseReleased(MouseEvent e) {
    System.out.println("Mouse X position = " + e.getX());
    System.out.println("Mouse Y position = " + e.getY());
  }
}
```

An object button1 that uses this class can install the event handler as follows:

```
button1.addMouseListener(new MyMouseAdapter());
```

Constructors

```
public MouseEvent(Component source, int id, long when, int
modifiers,
    int x, int y, int clickCount, boolean popupTrigger)
```

The source argument is the object with which the mouse event is associated; id is an identifier that identifies the event; when contains the time that the event occurred; modifiers contains a set of flags that indicate the modifiers that were used when the event occurred; x and y are the location of the mouse pointer; clickCount is the number of mouse clicks associated with the event; and popupTrigger specifies whether the event is a trigger for a popup menu.

Class Variables

```
public static final int MOUSE_CLICKED;
public static final int MOUSE_DRAGGED;
public static final int MOUSE_ENTERED;
public static final int MOUSE_EXITED;
public static final int MOUSE_FIRST;
public static final int MOUSE_LAST;
public static final int MOUSE_MOVED;
public static final int MOUSE_PRESSED;
public static final int MOUSE_RELEASED;
```

Class constants. These constants are flags used to describe the type of the mouse event.

Instance Methods

```
public int getClickCount();
```

Returns the number of successive clicks. (For example, 2 indicates a double-click.)

```
public Point getPoint();
Returns mouse position as a Point object.public int getX();
public int getY();
```

Returns mouse position as x and y coordinates.

```
public boolean isPopupTrigger();
```

Returns true if the mouse event is a trigger for a popup menu.

```
public void translatePoint(int x, int y);
```

Translates the mouse pointer coordinates by adding the value of the x and y arguments.

MouseListener Interface

Full Name	`java.awt.event.MouseListener`
Description	Public interface. This interface defines methods that respond to mouse events. Mouse events are generated when a mouse button is clicked, pressed, or released, or when the mouse pointer enters or exits a component; a mouse button click is a mouse button press followed by a release. To handle mouse events, you can implement the `MouseListener` interface, provide implementations of mouse event response methods, and then register the listener class with an event source. Alternatively, you can extend the `MouseAdaptor` class and override only the mouse event response methods in which you are interested. Events associated with the movement of the mouse are handled by the `MouseMotionListener` interface.

Interface Methods

```
public void mouseClicked(MouseEvent e);
public void mouseEntered(MouseEvent e);
public void mouseExited(MouseEvent e);
public void mousePressed(MouseEvent e);
public void mouseReleased(MouseEvent e);
```

These methods are called on a registered mouse listener in response to a mouse button being clicked, pressed, or released, or the mouse entering or exiting a component.

MouseMotionAdapter Class

Full Name	`java.awt.event.MouseMotionAdapter`
Extends	`Object`
Implements	`MouseMotionListener`

Description   Public class. A helper class that provides empty implementations of the methods defined in the MouseMotionListener interface. This class serves as a convenience by allowing you to extend it and override only the listener response methods that you need, as opposed to implementing all of the methods defined in the interface. After deriving an event-handling class from this one, you need to register it as an event listener.

Here is an example of a class that extends MouseMotionAdapter to process mouse movements:

```
class MyMouseMotionAdapter extends MouseMotionAdapter {
  public void mouseMoved(MouseEvent e) {
    System.out.println("You moved the mouse!");
  }
}
```

An object button1 that uses this class can install the event handler as follows:

```
button1.addMouseMotoinListener(new MyMouseMotionAdapter());
```

Constructors

```
public MouseMotionAdapter();
```

Instance Methods

```
public void mouseDragged(MouseEvent e);
public void mouseMoved(MouseEvent e);
```

These methods are called in response to the mouse being dragged or moved.

MouseMotionListener Interface

Full Name   java.awt.event.MouseMotionListener

Description   Public interface. This interface defines methods that respond to mouse motion events. Mouse motion events are generated when the mouse is dragged or moved over a component. To handle mouse motion events, you can implement the Mouse MotionListener interface, provide implementations of mouse motion event response methods, and then register the listener class with an event source. Alternatively, you can extend the MouseMotionAdaptor class and override only the mouse motion event response method in which you are interested. Events associated with mouse buttons are handled by the MouseListener interface.

Interface Methods

```
public void mouseDragged(MouseEvent e);
public void mouseMoved(MouseEvent e);
```

These methods are called on a registered mouse motion listener in response to the mouse being dragged or moved.

Object Class

Full Name	java.lang.Object
Extends	This class is the only Java class that has no superclass.
Description	Public class. As the ancestor class to all other classes in Java (whether API or not), the Object class defines universal methods inherited by all classes. Several of these methods— clone(), equals(), finalize(), and toString()—generally need to be overridden by a subclass to be useful. Note that notify() and wait() are intended mainly for internal use.

Constructors

```
public Object();
```

Instance Methods

```
public boolean equals(Object obj);
```

Compares contents of the specified object, obj, to those of the current object. Subclasses of Object may override this method to perform meaningful comparisons; for example, in the String class, this method returns true if string contents are equal. The test-for-equality operator (= =) returns true only if two object variables refer to the same object in memory. This condition is much more restrictive than testing contents for equality.

```
public final Class getClass();
```

Returns a Class object, which provides information on the current object's class.

```
public int hashCode();
```

Used internally. Some classes override this method to make it easier to work with hash tables. (See Hashtable class, page ___.) Classes that override this method tend to be those often used as hash-table keys.

```
public final void notify();
public final void notifyAll();
```

Used internally. The Thread class calls these methods to wake up a thread that has been waiting for ownership of the current object. This approach is related to use of the synchronize keyword.

```
public String toString();
```

Returns a string representation of the current object. Many API classes override toString() to provide meaningful string representations for the particular data they contain.

```
public final void wait();
public final void wait(long timeout);
public final void wait(long timeout, int nanos);
```

Used internally. The Thread class calls these methods to request ownership of the current object. This is related to use of the synchronize keyword.

```
protected Object clone() throws CloneNotSupportedException,
    OutOfMemoryError;
```

Returns a complete copy of the object's contents. A subclass may override clone() and make it public. In the API, only classes that implement Cloneable provide usable implementations of clone(). API classes that do not implement Cloneable throw an exception if this method is called. Note that with objects, cloning is not the same as assignment (=), which merely causes one object variable to refer to the same memory location as another variable.

```
protected void finalize() throws Throwable;
```

This method is called just before the object is destroyed by the garbage collector. This is the closest thing to a destructor in Java. In contrast to a destructor, there is no guarantee as to when this method is called.

Observable Class

Full Name	java.util.Observable
Extends	Object
Description	Public class. An Observable object has the ability to maintain a list of observers, which can include any object whose class implements the Observer interface. When a method of an Observable object knows of a change to its state, it should call the notifyObservers() method, which in turn notifies all the observers in the list. Although the Observable class by itself is not useful, it is useful as a superclass to other classes.

Constructors

```
public Observable();
```

Instance Methods

```
public void addObserver(Observer o);
```

Adds an observer to the list.

```
public int countObservers();
```

Returns the number of observers.

```
public void deleteObserver(Observer o);
public void deleteObservers();
```

Removes observers: either a specified observer or all observers in the list.

```
public boolean hasChanged();
```

Returns true if the current object has changed since the last notification. Instead of notifying observers of every minute change, an observable object can instead choose to call the clearChanged() and setChanged() methods to adjust an internal flag. Observers can call hasChanged() to get the state of this flag. clearChanged() and setChanged() are described at the end of this topic.

```
public void notifyObservers();
public void notifyObservers(Object arg);
```

Notifies observers of a change. The method can optionally specify an argument. Interpreting this argument is application-defined.

Protected Instance Methods

```
protected void clearChanged();
protected void setChanged();
```

These are protected methods, meaning that they can only be called from within the package or a class derived from Observable. These two methods turn the internal "has changed" flag on and off, respectively. See hasChanged(), above, for more information.

Observer Interface

Full Name	java.util.Observer
Description	Public interface. Declares a method—update()—which is required for an object to act as an observer. The object that is watched is an instance of an Observable subclass. You register an observer by calling the Observable object's addObserver() method. When the Observable object changes, it notifies all its observers.

Java 2 API Reference

The terminology may be confusing, because the two names are so close. But remember that an `Observable` object is watched, and it sends out notification. An object that implements `Observer` is a watcher, and it receives the notification, responding in any way appropriate.

Interface Methods

```
public abstract void update(Observable o, Object arg);
```

This method is called when the target object (the one whose class is derived from `Observable`) broadcasts a notification by calling its `notifyObservers()` method. The first argument specifies the exact source of the notification. The second argument is a supplemental argument whose use is application-defined; its use is up to you.

OutputStream Class

Full Name	`java.io.OutputStream`
Extends	`Object`
Description	Abstract public class. This class is the superclass for all output streams. Some of the subclasses have more efficient or more specialized implementations than the default implementations provided in this class.

Of the subclasses, `DataOutputStream` and `PrintStream` (text output) are the most widely used. See also `FileOutputStream`, page ___.

Instance Methods

```
public void close() throws IOException;
```

Closes the stream and releases all system resources associated with it (such as file handles).

```
public void flush() throws IOException;
```

Forces the internal buffer, if any, to be immediately written to the stream. The buffer is then emptied.

```
public void write(byte b[]) throws IOException;
public void write(byte b[], int off, int len)
    throws IOException;
```

Writes a series of bytes to the stream. The number of bytes is `len`, if specified, or all the bytes in the array `b`, if `len` is not specified. The `off` argument gives a starting offset in the array.

```
public abstract void write(int b) throws IOException;
```

Writes one byte to the stream using the eight low-order bits of b.

Pageable Interface

Full Name	`java.awt.print.Pageable`
Description	Public interface. This interface encapsulates the information necessary to represent a series of pages to be printed.

Interface Constants

```
public static final int UNKNOWN_NUMBER_OF_PAGES;
```

This constant represents an unknown number of pages, and is returned by the `getNumberOfPages()` method if the number of pages to be printed is unknown.

Interface Methods

```
public int getNumberOfPages();
public PageFormat getPageFormat(int pageIndex)
   throws IndexOutOfBoundsException;
public Printable getPrintable(int pageIndex)
   throws IndexOutOfBoundsException;
```

These methods retrieve the number of pages to be printed, the format of a specific page, and the `Printable` object associated with the pages.

PageFormat Class

Full Name	`java.awt.print.PageFormat`
Extends	`Object`
Description	Public class. This class describes the formatting of a printed page, which consists of the size and orientation of the page.

Constructors

```
public PageFormat();
```

Default constructor. This creates a page with a default size (8.5" x 11") and orientation (portrait).

Class Variables

```
public static final int LANDSCAPE;
public static final int PORTRAIT;
public static final int REVERSE_LANDSCAPE;
```

Class constants. These constants identify different orientation types for a page.

Instance Methods

```
public double getHeight();
public double getImageableHeight();
```

Java 2 API Reference

```
public double getImageableWidth();
public double getImageableX();
public double getImageableY();
public double[] getMatrix();
public int getOrientation();
public Paper getPaper();
public double getWidth();
public void setOrientation(int orientation)
    throws IllegalArgumentException;
public void setPaper(Paper paper);
```

Overridden Instance Methods

```
public Object clone();
```

This method returns a copy of this PageFormat object.

Panel Class

Full Name	java.awt.Panel
Extends	Container->Component->Object
Description	Public class. A panel is a container that has no window of its own. There are no visible borders around a panel. This class is useful for grouping components or for subdividing a window. Panels are used to group components in Part II, Chapter 4.

Constructors

```
public Panel();
```

Instance Methods

```
public synchronized void addNotify();
```

Overrides method definition in Component. Used internally.

Paper Class

Full Name	java.awt.print.Paper
Extends	Object
Description	Public class. This class represents the physical character-istics of a piece of paper and is used in conjunction with printing.

Constructors

```
public Paper();
```

Default constructor. This creates a default paper size that is 8.5″ × 11″ with 1″ margins.

Instance Methods

```
public double getHeight();
```

These methods retrieve the width and height of the page, in 1/72nd of an inch.

```
public double getImageableWidth();
public double getImageableHeight();
public double getImageableX();
public double getImageableY();
```

These methods retrieve the imageable (printable) x and y coordinates of the upper-left corner of the page, as well as the imageable width and height of the page, in 1/72nd of an inch.

```
public double getWidth();
public void setImageableArea(double x, double y,
    double width, double height);
```

This method sets the imageable (printable) x and y coordinates of the upper-left corner of the page, as well as the imageable width and height of the page, in 1/72nd of an inch.

```
public void setSize(double width, double height);
```

This method sets the size of the page, in 1/72nd of an inch.

Overridden Instance Methods

```
public Object clone();
```

This method returns a copy of this Paper object.

PasswordAuthentication Class

Full Name	java.net.PasswordAuthentication
Extends	Object
Description	Public class. This class stores the user name and password associated with a network authentication and is used by the Authenticator class.

Constructors

```
public PasswordAuthentication(String userName, char[] password);
```

Creates a PasswordAuthentication object using the specified user name and password.

Instance Methods

```
public char[] getPassword();
public String getUserName();
```

These methods retrieve the password and user name associated with the authentication.

PipedInputStream Class

Full Name   java.io.PipedInputStream

Extends   InputStream->Object

Description Public class. Creates a stream that reads from a data pipe. A data pipe is a channel of information between two threads. One thread (the source) sends data through the pipe while the other thread (the sink) reads the data put there. If the sink attempts a read after having read all the data in the pipe, it is blocked until more data is sent.

You create a data pipe by setting up a pair of threads, one using a PipedInputStream object and the other using a PipedOutputStream object. Each stream must connect to the other stream. You can use the constructors or the connect() method of each object to set up these connections.

Constructors

```
public PipedInputStream();
public PipedInputStream(PipedOutputStream src)
    throws IOException;
```

If src is not specified here, you must specify it with connect(). The output stream must also connect to this input stream.

Instance Methods

```
public void connect(PipedOutputStream src)
    throws IOException;
```

Connects to an output stream (src). The output stream must also connect to this input stream.

Overridden Instance Methods

```
public void close() throws IOException;
public int read(byte b[], int off, int len)
    throws IOException;
public int read() throws IOException;
```

These methods override method definitions in the InputStream class.

PipedOutputStream Class

Full Name	`java.io.PipedOutputStream`
Extends	`OutputStream->Object`
Description	Public class. Creates a stream that writes to a data pipe. A data pipe is a channel of information between two threads. One thread (the source) sends data through the pipe while the other thread (the sink) reads the data put there. When the source writes data to the pipe, it remains there until both streams are closed.
	You create a data pipe by setting up a pair of threads, one using a `PipedInputStream` object and the other using a `PipedOutputStream` object. Each stream must connect to the other stream. You can use the constructors or the `connect()` method of each object to set up these connections.

Constructors

```
public PipedOutputStream();
public PipedOutputStream(PipedInputStream snk)
   throws IOException;
```

If sink is not specified here, you must specify it with connect(). The input stream must also connect to this output stream.

Instance Methods

```
public void connect(PipedInputStream snk)
   throws IOException;
```

Connects to an input stream (snk). The input stream must also connect to this output stream.

Overridden Instance Methods

```
public void close() throws IOException;
public void write(byte b[], int off, int len)
   throws IOException;
public void write(int b) throws IOException;
```

These methods override method definitions in the InputStream class.

PixelGrabber Class

Full Name	`java.awt.image.PixelGrabber`
Extends	`Object`
Implements	`ImageConsumer`

Java 2 API Reference

Description   Public class. Gets raw pixel data from an image, which you can store in memory and analyze. Pixels are returned using the default RGB model. This class is of use to programs that need to store pixel data in memory for some reason. Note that the `MemoryImageSource` class performs a converse operation.

The following example uses the `PixelGrabber` class to extract raw pixel data from an existing image, `myImage`:

```
int w = myImage.getWidth(this);
int h = myImage.getHeight(this);
int buffer[] = new int[w * h];
PixelGrabber grabber = new PixelGrabber(myImage, 0, 0,
   w, h, buffer, 0, w);
grabber.grabPixels();
```

Constructors

```
public PixelGrabber(Image img, int x, int y, int w, int h,
   int pix[], int off, int scansize);
public PixelGrabber(ImageProducer ip, int x, int y, int w,
   int h, int pix[], int off, int scansize);
```

Arguments specify the image source, the shape and size of the region, a destination array, an offset to the position in the array to receive the first pixel, and the scan size of each row (which is typically the same as the width argument, w).

Instance Methods

```
public boolean grabPixels();
public boolean grabPixels(long ms);
```

Starts copying pixels from the image. The method does not return until it's finished getting pixels or until the specified number of milliseconds (ms) has elapsed, whichever comes first.

```
public int status();
```

Returns the same status codes as used in the `ImageObserver` interface.

Instance Methods (from Interface)

```
public void imageComplete(int status);
public void setColorModel(ColorModel model);
public void setDimensions(int width, int height);
public void setHints(int hints);
public void setPixels(int srcX, int srcY, int srcW,
   int srcH, ColorModel model, byte pixels[], int srcOff,
   int srcScan);
public void setPixels(int srcX, int srcY, int srcW,
```

```
    int srcH, ColorModel model, int pixels[], int srcOff,
    int srcScan);
public void setProperties(Hashtable props);
```

These methods implement methods declared in the ImageConsumer interface.

Point Class

Full Name	java.awt.Point
Extends	Object
Description	Public class. Creates a two-dimensional point containing an x and a y integer value.

Constructors
```
public Point(int x, int y);
```

Instance Variables
```
public int x;
public int y;
```
These instance variables contain the x and y values stored in the object.

Instance Methods
```
public void move(int x, int y);
```
Sets x and y to the values specified.

```
public void translate(int x, int y);
```
Adds the specified values to the current values of x and y.

Overridden Instance Methods
```
public synchronized void equals();
public int hashCode();
public String toString();
```
These methods override methods in the Object class.

Polygon Class

Full Name	java.awt.Polygon
Extends	Object

Description   Public class. Creates an *n*-sided figure that can be passed to the drawPolygon() and fillPolygon() methods of the Graphics class. Java creates the polygon by "connecting the dots," using a series of points. With drawPolygon(), the last point of the polygon should usually be the same as the first point so that the figure connects back to where it started.

The following example creates a triangle connecting the points (10, 10), (10, 100), and (200, 100):

```
Polygon poly = new Polygon();
poly.addPoint(10, 10);
poly.addPoint(10, 100);
poly.addPoint(200, 100);
poly.addPoint(10, 10);
```

Constructors

```
public Polygon();
public Polygon(int[] xpoints, int[] ypoints, int npoints);
```

The second version initializes the first *n* points, although they can always be added.

Instance Variables

```
public int npoints;
public int[] xpoints;
public int[] ypoints;
```

These instance variables store the number of vertices (points), the set of *x* coordinates, and the set of *y* coordinates. Points are stored as *x* and *y* coordinates in matching positions. For example, the first point is (xpoints[0], ypoints[0]).

Instance Methods

```
public void addPoint(int x, int y);
```

Adds a vertex (a point) to the polygon.

```
public Rectangle getBoundingBox();
```

Returns the smallest rectangular area that includes the entire polygon.

```
public boolean Inside(int x, int y);
```

Returns true if the specified point is located in the interior of the polygon.

Printable Interface

Full Name   java.awt.print.Printable

Description   Public interface. This interface defines a method used to print a page. A printed page consists of an object that implements this interface, as well as a `PageFormat` object.

Interface Constants

```
public static final int NO_SUCH_PAGE;
public static final int PAGE_EXISTS;
```

These constants indicate that a page exists and that there is no such page.

Interface Methods

```
public int print(Graphics graphics, PageFormat pageFormat,
    int pageIndex) throws PrinterException;
```

This method is used to print a page into a graphics context. The graphics argument is the graphics context, `pageFormat` is the format of the page, and `pageIndex` is the index of the page to be printed.

PrinterGraphics Interface

Full Name   java.awt.print.PrinterGraphics

Description   Public interface. This interface is used by `Graphics` objects to enable the printing of graphical information. To print a page of graphics, a `Graphics` object must implement the `Printer Graphics` interface and then be passed to a `Printable` object. The main function of the `PrinterGraphics` interface is to provide a means for an application to obtain the printer job that controls the rendering request for printing.

Interface Methods

```
public PrinterJob getPrinterJob();
```

This method retrieves the printer job that controls the rendering request for printing.

PrinterJob Class

Full Name   java.awt.print.PrinterJob

Extends   Object

Description   Public class. This class serves as the print engine for controlling the printing of pages. Applications use this class to control printing parameters such as the number of copies, as well as to display a GUI for altering detailed print settings.

Constructors

```
public PrinterJob();
```

Class Methods

```
public static PrinterJob getPrinterJob();
```

This method creates a new printer job and returns a `PrinterJob` object through which printing can be controlled.

Instance Methods

```
public abstract void cancel();
public PageFormat defaultPage();
public abstract PageFormat defaultPage(PageFormat page);
public abstract int getCopies();
public abstract String getJobName();
public abstract String getUserName();
public abstract boolean isCancelled();
public abstract PageFormat pageDialog(PageFormat page);
public abstract void print() throws PrinterException;
public abstract boolean printDialog();
public abstract void setCopies(int copies);
public abstract void setJobName(String jobName);
public abstract void setPageable(Pageable document) throws
NullPointerException;
public abstract void setPrintable(Printable painter, PageFormat
format);
public abstract void setPrintable(Printable painter);
public abstract PageFormat validatePage(PageFormat page);
```

PrintStream Class

Full Name	`java.io.PrintStream`
Extends	`FilterOutputStream->OutputStream->Object`
Description	Public class. Prints text representations of Java data. Common uses of this class include console output (System.out), output to a text file, and output to a socket stream. (See `FileOutputStream`, page 250, and `Socket`, page 450.) There is no exact converse to `PrintStream` on the input side, but you can use `DataInputStream` to read lines of text, which you then parse. All the print methods discard the high-order eight bits of Unicode characters.

The following example uses the `System.out` object, an instance of `PrintStream`, to print a prompt string. The `flush()` method — unnecessary with `println()` — forces immediate printing of the string. See Chapter 8, page 665, for a code in the context of an example.

```
System.out.print("Enter a number: ");
System.out.flush();
```

Constructors

```
public PrintStream(OutputStream out);
public PrintStream(OutputStream out, boolean autoflush);
```

The out argument is another output stream. This argument is often a
FileInputStream object that can be constructed from a filename. If autoflush
is specified and is true, output is automatically flushed at the end of each
line of text (the default behavior).

Instance Methods

```
public boolean checkError();
```

Flushes the output stream and returns true if an error has been encountered.

```
public void print(boolean b);
public void print(char c);
public void print(char s[]);
public void print(double d);
public void print(float f);
public void print(int i);
public void print(long l);
public void print(Object obj);
public void print(String s);
```

All the print() methods output a text representation of the argument by calling the object's toString() method. The stream must be flushed if you want
to force immediate printing.

```
public void println();
public void println(boolean b);
public void println(char c);
public void println(char s[]);
public void println(double d);
public void println(float f);
public void println(int i);
public void println(long l);
public void println(Object obj);
public void println(String s);
```

All the println() methods perform the same action as their print() counterparts except that they add a newline character at the end and flush the stream.

Overridden Instance Methods

```
public void close();
public void flush();
```

Java 2 API Reference

```
public void write(byte b[], int off, int len) throws IOException;
public void write(int b) throws IOException;
```

These methods override method definitions in the OutputStream class.

Process Class

Full Name	java.lang.Process
Extends	Object
Description	Abstract public class. The Runtime.exec() method returns an instance of this class when you execute a file. (Actually, it returns an instance of a subclass, but the effect is the same.) Processes are vaguely similar to threads, but a process originates in a separate executable file and not in the current program. Processes have their own I/O streams. Applets that are run from browsers can start threads but not processes.

Instance Methods

```
public abstract void destroy();
```

Kills the process.

```
public abstract int exitValue() throws
    IllegalThreadStateException;
```

Returns the exit value; call this only after the process is killed or else an exception will be thrown.

```
public abstract InputStream getErrorStream();
public abstract InputStream getInputStream();
public abstract OutputStream getOutputStream();
```

Gets the requested error, input, or output stream associated with the process.

```
public abstract int waitFor();
```

The current thread waits for the process to complete, returning immediately if the process has already terminated.

ProgressMonitor Class

Full Name	javax.swing.ProgressMonitor
Extends	Object

Description   Public class. This class provides support for a progress monitor that is used to keep track of the progress of a lengthy operation. The ProgressMonitor class automatically assesses the length of an operation and displays a window indicating the progress status if the operation still has a way to go.

Constructors

```
public ProgressMonitor(Component parentComponent,
    Object message, String note, int min, int max)
```

Creates a progress monitor using the specified minimum and maximum values for the progress operation.

Instance Methods

```
public void close();
public int getMaximum();
public int getMillisToDecideToPopup();
public int getMillisToPopup();
public int getMinimum();
public String getNote();
public boolean isCanceled();
public void setMaximum(int m);
public void setMillisToDecideToPopup(
    int millisToDecideToPopup);
public void setMillisToPopup(int millisToPopup);
public void setMinimum(int m);
public void setNote(String note);
public void setProgress(int nv);
```

ProgressMonitorInputStream Class

Full Name   javax.swing.ProgressMonitorInputStream

Extends   FilterInputStream->InputStream->Object

Description   Public class. This class provides a progress monitor that is specially designed to monitor the progress of reading from an input stream.

Constructors

```
public ProgressMonitorInputStream(Component parentComponent,
    Object message, InputStream in);
```

Creates a progress monitor input stream based on the specified input stream.

Instance Methods

```
public ProgressMonitor getProgressMonitor();
```

This method retrieves the underlying progress monitor associated with the progress monitor input stream.

Overridden Instance Methods

```
public void close() throws IOException;
public int read() throws IOException;
public int read(byte[] b) throws IOException;
public int read(byte[] b, int off, int len)
  throws IOException;
public void reset() throws IOException;
public long skip(long n) throws IOException;
```

These methods are overridden versions of methods defined in the parent FilterInputStream class (p. ___).

Properties Class

Full Name	java.util.Properties
Extends	Hashtable->Dictionary->Object
Description	Public class. Creates a properties table; this is a special kind of hash table (see Hashtable class, page ___) in which keys and elements are always strings. Property tables have built-in support for reading and writing to streams. They also have a built-in mechanism for providing default property values. Properties tables are used by a number of other classes in Java, such as the System class. To set property values, use the put() method inherited from Hashtable.

The following example gets the value of the os.name property in the system properties table. For a list of all these properties, see Table B-6 in Appendix B, "Useful Tables."

```
Properties sysProp = System.getProperties();
String sysName = sysProp.getProperty("os.name");
```

Constructors

```
public Properties();
public Properties(Properties defaults);
```

You can optionally specify a table that contains default values for the new table.

Instance Variables

```
protected Properties defaults;
```

Protected instance variable. (Because it is protected, it cannot be accessed except by subclasses.) This variable contains a reference to another Properties table that contains default values. When a property name is looked up and the name is not found, its value is then looked up in the default table. The defaults field is null if there is no default property table.

Instance Methods

```
public String getProperty(String key);
public String getProperty(String key, String defaultValue);
```

Returns the property value for the specified name (key). If the search for the name fails, the default property table, if any, is searched.

```
public void list(PrintStream out);
```

Outputs the table to a print stream. This is useful for debugging purposes.

```
public void load(InputStream in);
```

Loads the property table from the specified input stream.

```
public Enumeration propertyNames();
```

Returns an enumeration of all the property names along with names in the default table, if any. See Enumeration interface, page ___.

```
public void save(OutputStream out, String header);
```

Saves the property table to the specified output stream.

PropertyResourceBundle Class

Full Name	java.util.PropertyResourceBundle
Extends	ResourceBundle->Object
Description	Public class. This class is used to package a set of properties for a specific locale, and acts as an important means of organizing information for internationalization.

Constructors

```
public PropertyResourceBundle(InputStream stream)
  throws IOException;
```

Creates a PropertyResourceBundle object from the specified input stream; the input stream is usually associated with a text file containing a list of properties.

Overridden Instance Methods

```
public Enumeration getKeys();
```

Retrieve an enumeration containing all of the keys in the property resource bundle.

```
public Object handleGetObject(String key);
```

Retrieve an object from the property resource bundle using the specified key.

PushbackInputStream Class

Full Name	java.io.PushbackInputStream
Extends	FilterInputStream->InputStream->Object
Description	Public class. This class contains an extra one-character buffer that can be used to "unread" the last character read. This is often useful for syntax parsers.

Constructors

```
public PushbackInputStream(InputStream in);
```

The constructor creates a PushbackInputStream around the specified input stream.

Instance Variables

```
protected int pushBack;
```

Protected instance variable that stores a pushed-back character after a call to unread(). Because this variable is protected, it cannot be accessed from outside the package, except by a derived class. A value of –1 indicates that there is currently no pushed-back character.

Instance Methods

```
public void unread(int ch) throws IOException;
```

Pushes back a character. The next time read() is called, this character is read first. Calling unread() twice before a read() operation throws an exception.

Overridden Instance Methods

```
public int available() throws IOException;
public boolean markSupported();
public int read() throws IOException;
public int read(byte bytes[], int offset, int length)
   throws IOException;
```

These methods override method definitions in the InputStream class. The available() method adds 1 to the total of available data if there is a pushed-back character stored. The markSupported() method always returns false for this class. Also note that read() empties the one-character buffer.

Random Class

Full Name	`java.util.Random`
Extends	`Object`
Description	Public class. Creates objects that can be used to generate a series of psuedo-random numbers. The `Math.random()` method is often simpler to use.

Constructors

```
public Random();
public Random(long seed);
```

Using the time as a seed is recommended, as in `Random((new Date()).getTime())`. See also `setSeed()`, below.

Instance Methods

```
public double nextDouble();
public float nextFloat();
```

These methods return the next random number as a floating-point value between 0.0 and 1.0.

```
public double nextGaussian();
```

Returns the next random number from a Gaussian (normal) distribution, with mean value of 0.0 and standard deviation of 1.0.

```
public int nextInt();
public long nextLong();
```

These methods return the next random number as an integer ranging over the data type's range.

```
public void setSeed(long seed);
```

Resets the pseudo-random series. Using the current time is recommended.

RandomAccessFile Class

Full Name	`java.io.RandomAccessFile`
Extends	`Object`
Implements	`DataInput, DataOutput`
Description	Public class. Creates an object that can be used for random access. The unique features of such a stream are that it can be used to read or write at the same time, and you can call the `seek()` method to move directly to any file position.

Java 2 API Reference

Otherwise, almost all the methods here are found in Data
InputStream or DataOutputStream. Typical random-access
algorithms assume equal-length records, which may, in turn,
require the use of equal-length string data. One solution is
to equalize string lengths with calls to StringBuffer.
setLength().

The following example opens the file RAN.DAT with read/write permission,
moves to record position 30, and writes an integer *n*. Assume that recsize
and n are declared and initialized elsewhere.

```
try {
   RandomAccessFile rf = new
      RandomAccessFile("RAN.DAT", "rw");
   rf.seek(recsize * 30);
   rf.writeInt(n);
} catch (IOException e) {System.out.prinln(e);}
```

Constructors

```
public RandomAccessFile(File file, String mode)
   throws IOException;
public RandomAccessFile(String name, String mode)
   throws IOException;
```

The mode is either r (read) or rw (read/write). Successfully creating the
object automatically opens the file for random-access I/O.

Instance Methods

```
public void close() throws IOException;
```

Closes the stream and releases all system resources associated with it (such
as file handles).

```
public final FileDescriptor getFD() throws IOException;
```

Returns the FileDescriptor for this file.

```
public long getFilePointer() throws IOException;
```

Returns the current value of the file pointer. This is an offset from the beginning of the file.

```
public long length() throws IOException;
```

Returns the current length of the file.

```
public abstract int read() throws IOException;
```

Returns the next byte in the stream. Returns –1 if at end of the stream.

```
public int read(byte b[]) throws IOException;
public int read(byte b[], int off, int len)
    throws IOException;
```

Reads up to b.length or len bytes, whichever is smaller. Returns the number of bytes read, or –1 if at the end of the stream. The off argument gives a starting offset into the array.

```
public final boolean readBoolean() throws IOException;
public final byte readByte() throws IOException;
public final char readChar() throws IOException;
public final double readDouble() throws IOException;
public final float readFloat() throws IOException;
```

Each of these methods reads an instance of a primitive data type.

```
public final void readFully(byte b[]) throws IOException,
    EOFException;
public final void readFully(byte b[], int off, int len)
    throws IOException, EOFException;
```

Reads enough bytes to fill the array or reads len bytes if specified. In either case, this method causes the current thread to wait until all the data requested is read.

```
public final int readInt() throws IOException;
```

Reads an instance of an int.

```
public final String readLine() throws IOException;
```

Reads a character string up to the first newline, carriage return, newline/carriage-return pair, or end of input stream.

```
public final long readLong() throws IOException;
public final short readShort() throws IOException;
public final int readUnsignedByte() throws IOException;
public final int readUnsignedShort() throws IOException;
```

Each of these methods reads an instance of a primitive data type. Although unsigned byte and unsigned short are not Java data types, Java can read them correctly and return them in an int field that has sufficient range to store the number read.

```
public final String readUTF() throws IOException;
```

Reads a string in the Unicode transformation format (UTF). This format reads the first two bytes as an unsigned short integer indicating the length of the string. The rest of the data consists of UTF-8 character encoding. The UTF-8 format, which is compatible with ASCII, is described in Table B-5 in Appendix B, "Useful Tables." See also writeUTF(), page ___.

```
public void seek(long pos) throws IOException;
```

Sets the file pointer to a new position.

```
public int skipBytes(int n) throws IOException;
```

Advances the file pointer n bytes before the next file I/O operation.

```
public void write(byte b[]) throws IOException;
public void write(byte b[], int off, int len)
   throws IOException;
```

Writes a series of bytes to the stream. The number of bytes is len, if specified, or all the bytes in the array b if len is not specified. The off argument gives a starting offset in the array.

```
public abstract void write(int b) throws IOException;
```

Writes one byte to the stream using the eight low-order bits of b.

```
public final void writeBoolean(boolean v)
   throws IOException;
public final void writeByte(int v) throws IOException;
```

Writes an instance of a primitive data type, boolean or int.

```
public final void writeBytes(String s) throws IOException;
```

Writes a string to the output stream, converting each character to a byte by discarding the eight high bits. Note that readLine() will not read such a string correctly unless you terminate it with a newline or carriage return. See also writeUTF(), below which is more reliable.

```
public final void writeChar(int v) throws IOException;
public final void writeChars(String s) throws IOException;
public final void writeDouble(double v) throws IOException;
public final void writeFloat(float v) throws IOException;
public final void writeInt(int v) throws IOException;
public final void writeLong(long v) throws IOException;
public final void writeShort(int v) throws IOException;
```

Each of these methods writes the appropriate primitive data type.

```
public final void writeUTF(String str) throws IOException;
```

Writes a string in the Unicode transformation format (UTF). This format writes the first two bytes as an unsigned short integer indicating the length of the string. The rest of the data consists of UTF-8 character encoding. The UTF-8 format, which is compatible with ASCII, is described in Table B-5 in Appendix B, "Useful Tables." See also readUTF().

Rectangle Class

Full Name	java.awt.Rectangle
Extends	Object
Description	Public class. Creates a rectangle represented as a point (top-left corner), width, and height. The Rectangle class is frequently useful in specifying clipping regions for repainting. Note that to draw rectangles, you need to use the Graphics class. As with polygons, rectangles are not automatically displayed.

The following example creates a rectangle from the union of two other rectangles. The new rectangle has x and y coordinates of (10, 10), width 290, and height 290.

```
Rectangle rect1 = new Rectangle(10, 10, 150, 200);
Rectangle rect2 = new Rectangle(50, 50, 250, 250);
Rectangle rectNew = rect1.union(rect2);
```

Constructors

```
public Rectangle();
public Rectangle(Dimension d);
public Rectangle(int width, int height);
public Rectangle(int x, int y, int width, int height);
public Rectangle(Point p);
public Rectangle(Point p, Dimension d);
```

If a value is not specified, a default value of 0 is assumed.

Instance Variables

```
public int height;
public int width;
public int x;
public int y;
```

Public instance variables. You can manipulate these directly.

Instance Methods

```
public void add(int newx, int newy);
public void add(Point pt);
public void add(Rectangle r);
```

All these methods expand the rectangle object so that it contains the specified point or rectangle.

```
public void grow(int h, int v);
```

Increments the width (h, for horizontal) and height (v, for vertical).

```
public boolean inside(int x, int y);
```

Returns true if the given point is contained in the rectangle.

```
public Rectangle intersection(Rectangle r);
```

Returns the rectangle that results from the intersection of the current object and Rectangle r.

```
public boolean intersects(Rectangle r);
public boolean isEmpty();
```

These methods return true or false for the specified condition.

```
public void move(int x, int y);
public void reshape(int x, int y, int width, int height);
public void resize(int width, int height);
```

These methods directly specify new values for the rectangle's instance variables.

```
public void translate(int dx, int dy);
```

Increments the rectangle's *x* and *y* values.

```
public Rectangle union(Rectangle r);
```

Returns the rectangle that results from the union of the current object and Rectangle r.

Overridden Instance Methods

```
public boolean equals(Object obj);
public int hashCode();
public String toString();
```

All these methods override method definitions in the Object class.

ResourceBundle Class

Full Name	java.util.ResourceBundle
Extends	Object
Description	Public class. This class represents a bundle of information that is specific to a given locale. The ResourceBundle class is used to create objects that contain localized information for internationalized programs. Specific resource bundles that contain information must be derived from ResourceBundle.

Resource bundles are typically obtained via the static getBundle() method. Following is an example of obtaining a resource bundle named SpeechBundle using the Italian locale:

```
ResourceBundle speech = ResourceBundle.getBundle("SpeechBundle",
    Locale.ITALIAN);
```

Keep in mind that the actual SpeechBundle class must be a class derived from ResourceBundle or one of its sub-classes such as ListResourceBundle or PropertyResourceBundle.

Constructors

```
public ResourceBundle();
```

Class Methods

```
public static final ResourceBundle getBundle(String baseName)
    throws MissingResourceException;
public static final ResourceBundle getBundle(String baseName,
    Locale locale);
public static ResourceBundle getBundle(String baseName,
    Locale locale, ClassLoader loader)
```

These methods obtain a resource bundle based upon the specified base name, locale, and loader. Resource bundles are always created using these methods, as opposed to using the ResourceBundle constructor.

Instance Methods

```
public Locale getLocale();
```

Retrieves the locale associated with the resource bundle.

```
public final Object getObject(String key)
    throws MissingResourceException;
```

Retrieves an object from the resource bundle using the specified key.

```
public final String getString(String key)
    throws MissingResourceException;
```

Retrieves a string from the resource bundle using the specified key.

```
public final String[] getStringArray(String key)
    throws MissingResourceException;
```

Retrieves an array of strings from the resource bundle using the specified key.

RGBImageFilter Class

Full Name	java.awt.image.RGBImageFilter
Extends	ImageFilter

Description   Abstract public class. Creates a color filter for images. The use of this class is somewhat similar to using the `CropImage Filter` class, but with this difference: instead of instantiating this class directly, you create a color filter by subclassing this class. In the majority of cases, the one method that you need to override is `filterRGB()`; you use this method to determine how to translate each pixel.

Protected Instance Methods

```
protected boolean canFilterIndexColorModel;
protected ColorModel newmodel;
protected ColorModel origmodel;
```

Protected instance variables. (Because they are protected, they cannot be accessed from outside, but subclass code can refer to them.) You can choose to set canFilterIndexColorModel to true and then use an IndexColorModel object rather than filter pixels individually.

Instance Methods

```
public IndexColorModel filterIndexColorModel(
   IndexColorModel icm);
```

If canFilterIndexColorModel is true, this method returns the IndexColor Model object to be used. Otherwise, the returned value is ignored.

```
public abstract int filterRGB(int x, int y, int rgb);
```

Converts a pixel by taking the position and current RGB value and outputting a new RGB value. When subclassing, you should override this method unless you are going to use an IndexColorModel object. This is usually the only method you should be interested in overriding.

```
public void filterRGBPixels(int x, int y, int w, int h,
   int pixels[], int off, int scansize);
```

Processes pixels in a buffer by sending them, one by one, through the filterRGB() method. You should never override this method.

```
public void substituteColorModel(ColorModel oldcm,
   ColorModel newcm);
```

Replaces use of the old color model with the new color model.

Overridden Instance Methods

```
public void setColorModel(ColorModel model);
public void setPixels(int x, int y, int w, int h,
   ColorModel model, byte pixels[], int off, int scansize);
public void setPixels(int x, int y, int w, int h,
   ColorModel model, int pixels[], int off, int scansize);
```

These methods override method definitions in the ImageFilter class.

Runnable Interface

Full Name   java.lang.Runnable

Description   Public interface. Any class that implements this interface can
                 define the behavior of a thread. After writing the class, you hook
                 it up to a thread in the following way: create an instance of your
                 class; specify this instance as an argument to a Thread con-
                 structor. This constructor, of course, creates a thread. When
                 this thread is started, it calls the run() method defined in your
                 class.

Interface Methods

```
public run();
```

This method is called in response to a thread's start() method. A thread is
hooked to a particular Runnable class.

Runtime Class

Full Name   java.lang.Runtime

Extends   Object

Description   Public class. This class provides a connection to the capabili-
                 ties of the local computer as well as interaction with the Java
                 interpreter (Sometimes called the Java Virtual Machine.) Some
                 of these capabilities — such as exec() — can be used by appli-
                 cations but (for security reasons) are not allowed in browser-run
                 applets. See also System class, page ___, which supports
                 related capabilities.

Class Methods

```
public static Runtime getRuntime();
```

Returns the system's Runtime object.

Instance Methods

```
public Process exec(String command);
public Process exec(String command, String envp[]);
public Process exec(String cmdarray[]);
public Process exec(String cmdarray[], String envp[]);
```

Executes a new process on the local machine; this process may be an executable that runs outside the Java interpreter. The cmdarray argument, if
specified, is an array of strings in which the first string is the command

name. The envp argument, if specified, is an array of strings; each envp string has the form "name = value."

```
public void exit(int status);
```

Causes the Java program to exit, passing the specified exit code to the system.

```
public long freeMemory();
```

Returns the amount of unused memory; this is always less than the amount returned by totalMemory(). Calling gc() may result in some objects being destroyed, thereby increasing free memory.

```
public void gc();
```

Requests that the garbage collector (which normally runs as a low-priority background process) be invoked right away to start destroying objects no longer used.

```
public InputStream getLocalizedInputStream(InputStream in);
public OutputStream getLocalizedOutputStream(
  OutputStream out);
```

These methods get localized input and output streams; such streams convert between the local character code and Unicode. This is not normally necessary for ASCII characters.

```
public void load(String filename)
  throws UnsatisfiedLinkError;
public void loadLibrary(String libname)
  throws UnsatisfiedLinkError;
```

Mainly used internally. These methods load native-code implementations. load() specifies a complete path name, whereas loadLibrary() relies on the system to search in the library directories.

```
public void runFinalization();
```

Requests that the Java interpreter call the finalize() method for all objects that have been destroyed. Normally, an object's finalize() method may not necessarily be run right away.

```
public long totalMemory();
```

Returns the total amount of memory available to the Java interpreter, including memory currently used by objects and variables. See freeMemory(), above.

```
public void traceInstructions(boolean on);
public void traceMethodCalls(boolean on);
```

Causes Java to print a statement or method trace if the interpreter supports this feature. Calling these methods with on set to false turns off the tracing.

Scrollable Interface

Full Name   javax.swing.Scrollable

Description   Public interface. This interface describes information necessary
                  to keep track of the state of scrolling data in a viewport.
                  Classes must implement this interface in order to support a
                  scrolling view. A class that implements this interface can be
                  given scrollbars by being placed inside a JScrollPane object.
                  See JScrollPane (p. 344) for details.

Interface Methods

```
public Dimension getPreferredScrollableViewportSize();
public int getScrollableBlockIncrement(
   Rectangle  visibleRect, int orientation, int direction);
public boolean getScrollableTracksViewportHeight();
public boolean getScrollableTracksViewportWidth();
public int getScrollableUnitIncrement(Rectangle visibleRect,
   int orientation, int direction);
```

Scrollbar Class

Full Name   java.awt.Scrollbar

Extends   Component->Object

Description   Public class. A Scrollbar object encapsulates the standard
                  scroll-bar control found in GUI environments. In Java, scroll bars
                  are best positioned in a container by using a Border
                  Layout manager and assigning the scroll bar to an edge of the
                  container. Scroll bars generate all standard keyboard and
                  mouse events except MOUSE_DOWN and MOUSE_UP.

The following example adds a horizontal scroll bar to the current frame or
applet. Values corresponding to scroll bar position run from 0 to 100, and the
initial position is halfway (50).

```
Scrollbar sb = new Scrollbar(Scrollbar.HORIZONTAL, 50,
   25, 0, 100);
add(sb);
```

Constructors

```
public Scrollbar();
public Scrollbar(int orientation);
public Scrollbar(int orientation, int value, int visible,
   int minimum, int maximum);
```

Optionally set scroll-bar attributes. The minimum and maximum attributes specify integers corresponding to the end points. The value attribute corresponds to the current position of the scroll-bar indicator, which changes in response to user actions. Thus, if minimum and maximum are 100 and 200, a value of 150 indicates the scroll-bar midpoint. A value of 190 is close to the right (or bottom) end point. The visible attribute means "size of a visible page," and its effect is to determine the page increment (the amount of movement when the user clicks the bar on either side of the indicator).

Class Variables

```
public final static int HORIZONTAL;
public final static int VERTICAL;
```

Possible values for the orientation attribute.

Instance Methods

```
public int getLineIncrement();
public int getMaximum();
public int getMinimum();
public int getOrientation();
public int getPageIncrement();
public int getValue();
public int getVisible();
```

All these "get" methods all set various attributes of the scroll bar. (See the Scrollbar constructor, page 437, for descriptions.) The visible and page increment attributes are closely related although not necessarily equal to each other. Calling getValue() reports the current position of the scroll-bar indicator.

```
public void setLineIncrement(int l);
public void setPageIncrement(int l);
public void setValue(int value);
public void setValues(int value, int visible, int minimum, int
  maximum);
```

These "set" methods set the various scroll-bar attributes. (See the Scrollbar constructor, page 437, for information.) Calling setValue() moves the scroll-bar indicator.

Overridden Instance Methods

```
public void addNotify();
```

Overrides the method definition in the Component class.

ScrollPane Class

Full Name   java.awt.ScrollPane

Extends   `Container->Component->Object`

Description   Public class. This class implements a container that supports
                  horizontal and vertical scrolling for one child component.

Constructors

```
public ScrollPane();
```

Default constructor.

```
public ScrollPane(int scrollbarDisplayPolicy);
```

Creates a ScrollPane object with the specified display policy, which is one
of the following values: SCROLLBARS_AS_NEEDED, SCROLLBARS_ALWAYS, or
SCROLLBARS_NEVER.

Class Variables

```
public static final int SCROLLBARS_AS_NEEDED;
public static final int SCROLLBARS_ALWAYS;
public static final int SCROLLBARS_NEVER;
```

Class constants. These constants describe the display policies supported by
the scroll pane, which determine when the scroll pane is to be shown.

Instance Methods

```
public Adjustable getHAdjustable();
```

Retrieves the state of the horizontal scrollbar as an Adjustable object.

```
public int getHScrollbarHeight();
```

Retrieves the height of a horizontal scrollbar.

```
public int getScrollbarDisplayPolicy();
```

Obtains the display policy for the scrollbars.

```
public Point getScrollPosition();
```

Retrieves the position of the child window being displayed in the upper-left
corner of the view port.

```
public Adjustable getVAdjustable();
```

Retrieves the state of the vertical scrollbar as an Adjustable object.

```
public Dimension getViewportSize();
```

Obtains the size of the view port.

```
public int getVScrollbarWidth();
```

Retrieves the width of a vertical scrollbar.

```
public void setScrollPosition(Point p);
public void setScrollPosition(int x, int y);
```

Sets the position of the child window; the specified position within the child window is placed in the upper left corner of the view port.

Overridden Instance Methods

```
public void addNotify();
public void doLayout();
public AccessibleContext getAccessibleContext();
public String paramString();
public void printComponents(Graphics g);
public final void setLayout(LayoutManager mgr);
```

These methods override method definitions in the Component and Container classes.

ScrollPaneConstants Interface

Full Name   javax.swing.ScrollPaneConstants

Description   Public interface. This interface serves as a convenient location to store constants used within a scroll pane. The constants in this interface are used by the JScrollPane class (p. 344).

Interface Constants

```
public static final String VIEWPORT
public static final String VERTICAL_SCROLLBAR
public static final String HORIZONTAL_SCROLLBAR
public static final String ROW_HEADER
public static final String COLUMN_HEADER
public static final String LOWER_LEFT_CORNER
public static final String LOWER_RIGHT_CORNER
public static final String UPPER_LEFT_CORNER
public static final String UPPER_RIGHT_CORNER
public static final String LOWER_LEADING_CORNER
public static final String LOWER_TRAILING_CORNER
public static final String UPPER_LEADING_CORNER
public static final String UPPER_TRAILING_CORNER
public static final String VERTICAL_SCROLLBAR_POLICY
public static final String HORIZONTAL_SCROLLBAR_POLICY
```

These string constants are keys that identify specific properties of JScrollPane objects.

```
public static final int VERTICAL_SCROLLBAR_AS_NEEDED
public static final int VERTICAL_SCROLLBAR_NEVER
public static final int VERTICAL_SCROLLBAR_ALWAYS
public static final int HORIZONTAL_SCROLLBAR_AS_NEEDED
public static final int HORIZONTAL_SCROLLBAR_NEVER
public static final int HORIZONTAL_SCROLLBAR_ALWAYS
```

These constants provide settings for the hsbPolicy and vbsPolicy properties
of JScrollPane objects.

SecurityManager Class

Full Name   java.lang.SecurityManager

Extends   Object

Description   Abstract public class. Applications that browse the net, view
               applets, or download classes across the network can install
               a security manager by subclassing this class and writing and
               overriding methods. The security manager is installed by calling
               System.setSecurityManager(). A new security manager
               cannot be installed if there is already one in place; applets,
               therefore, cannot install one.

               Before a potentially sensitive operation is performed, the
               appropriate "check" method of the security manager (if any) is
               called. The method responds by doing nothing or by throwing a
               SecurityException, thus preventing the operation. The
               default behavior for each method is to throw an exception. Note
               that applications do not have a security manager unless the
               program installs one. The Netscape browser and applet viewer
               install different security managers, which is why applet viewer
               is able to be more lenient.

Instance Methods

```
public void checkAccept(String host, int port)
    throws SecurityException;
```

Checks whether a port may be accessed.

```
public void checkAccess(Thread g) throws SecurityException;
```

Checks whether the thread may be modified.

```
public void checkAccess(ThreadGroup g)
    throws SecurityException;
```

Checks whether the thread group may be modified.

```
public void checkConnect(String host, int port)
  throws SecurityException;
public void checkConnect(String host, int port,
  Object context) throws SecurityException;
```

Checks whether the specified port may be connected to. See also getSecurityContext() (p. 443).

```
public void checkCreateClassLoader()
  throws SecurityException;
```

Checks whether the program may create a new class loader.

```
public void checkDelete(String file)
  throws SecurityException;
```

Checks whether the file may be deleted.

```
public void checkExec(String cmd) throws SecurityException;
```

Checks whether the file may be executed.

```
public void checkExit(int status) throws SecurityException;
```

Checks whether the program may call exit() with the specified status code.

```
public void checkLink(String lib) throws SecurityException;
```

Checks whether the program may dynamically load a library.

```
public void checkListen(int port) throws SecurityException;
```

Checks whether the program may wait for a connection request.

```
public void checkPackageAccess(String pkg)
  throws SecurityException;
public void checkPackageDefinition(String pkg)
  throws SecurityException;
```

Checks whether the program may load and define classes in the package, respectively.

```
public void checkPropertiesAccess()
  throws SecurityException;
public void checkPropertyAccess(String key)
  throws SecurityException;
```

Checks whether the program may use the systems properties table and access the specified property, respectively.

```
public void checkRead(FileDescriptor fd)
  throws SecurityException;
public void checkRead(String file)
```

```
    throws SecurityException;
  public void checkRead(String file, Object context)
    throws SecurityException;
```

Checks whether the program may read the file. See also getSecurityContext() below.

```
    public void checkSetFactory() throws SecurityException;
```

Checks whether the program may set a socket factory or stream handler factory.

```
    public boolean checkTopLevelWindow(Object window);
```

Returns true if the program is trusted to make the specified window visible.

```
    public void checkWrite(FileDescriptor fd)
      throws SecurityException;
    public void checkWrite(String file)
      throws SecurityException;
```

Checks whether the program may write to the file.

```
    public boolean getInCheck();
```

Returns true if a security check is in progress.

```
    public Object getSecurityContext();
```

Returns an object that encapsulates a security context. This object can be given as an argument to checkConnect() and checkRead(). If a trusted method is asked to open a socket or read a file on behalf of another method, then that other method's security context is passed: the security manager needs to know whether that other method would be allowed to read or connect on its own.

SequenceInputStream Class

Full Name	java.io.SequenceInputStream
Extends	InputStream->Object
Description	Public class. Creates a single input stream from two or more separate input streams. As soon as the end of one stream is read, the next byte is read from the next stream in the sequence. This happens seamlessly so that the sequence is read as a single, unbroken stream.

Constructors

```
    public SequenceInputStream(Enumeration e);
    public SequenceInputStream(InputStream s1, InputStream s2);
```

Java 2 API Reference

If an enumeration is specified, each object returned by the enumeration must be an `InputStream` object. (You can implement your own enumerations; see `Enumeration` interface, page ___.)

Overridden Instance Methods

```
public void close() throws IOException;
public int read() throws IOException;
public int read(byte buf[], int pos, int len)
    throws IOException;
```

These methods override method definitions in the `InputStream` class.

ServerSocket Class

Full Name	`java.net.ServerSocket`
Extends	`Object`
Description	Public final class. Creates an object that listens for a connection request from another machine. (The machine making the connection request is called a client.) To initiate listening, you call the `accept()` method. As soon as a connection is made, it returns a `Socket` object that you can use to communicate with the client.

The following example waits for a client computer to contact this computer (the server). Then the program establishes input and output streams to talk to the client. Port number 8189 is used, because it is not used by system services, for which ports 0-1023 are reserved.

```
try {
    ServerSocket server = new ServerSocket(8189);
    Socket client = server.accept();
    InputStream fromClient = client.getInputStream();
    OutputStream toClient = client.getOutputStream();
    // ...
    client.close();
} catch (IOException e) System.out.println(e);
```

In communicating with the client, usually it is easiest to use `DataInputStream` and `DataOutputStream` (or `PrintStream`) objects:

```
DataInputStream dis = new DataInputStream(fromClient);
PrintStream psToClient = new PrintStream(toClient);
psToClient.println("Greetings, client.");
```

Constructors

```
public ServerSocket(int port) throws IOException;
public ServerSocket(int port, int count) throws IOException;
```

Java 2 API Reference

These constructors create a server socket around the specified local port (specifying 0 asks for the first free port). The optional count argument specifies a maximum number of client connection requests to store in a queue.

Class Methods

```
public static void setSocketFactory(SocketImplFactory fac)
    throws IOException, SocketException;
```

Specifies a new SocketImplFactory to use. Application code typically never calls this method. It is used by code that needs to modify the socket implementation for a particular platform.

Instance Methods

```
public Socket accept() throws IOException;
```

Initiates listening for a client connection request. The method does not return until a request is received. Returns a Socket object that can be used to send or receive data to the client.

```
public void close() throws IOException;
```

Closes the socket and frees the port.

```
public InetAddress getInetAddress();
public int getLocalPort();
```

These methods return the Internet address and the server's local port number, respectively.

Overridden Instance Methods

```
public String toString();
```

Overrides method definition in the Object class.

Set Interface

| Full Name | java.util.Set |
| Description | Public interface. This interface describes a collection of elements where no two elements are alike. |

Interface Methods

```
public boolean add(Object o);
```

Adds the specified object to the set if it is not already in the set.

```
public boolean addAll(Collection c);
```

Adds the specified collection of objects to the set if they are not already in the set.

Java 2 API Reference

```
public void clear();
```

Clears the set of all elements.

```
public boolean contains(Object o);
```

Checks to see if the set contains the specified object.

```
public boolean containsAll(Collection c);
```

Checks to see if the set contains the specified collection of objects.

```
public boolean isEmpty();
```

Checks to see if the set contains any elements.

```
public Iterator iterator();
```

Retrieves an iterator for the set.

```
public boolean remove(Object o);
```

Removes the specified object from the set.

```
public boolean removeAll(Collection c);
```

Removes the specified collection of objects from the set.

```
public boolean retainAll(Collection c);
```

Removes the all elements from the set except for the specified collection of objects.

```
public int size();
```

Determines how many elements are in the set.

```
public Object[] toArray()
public Object[] toArray(Object[] a)
```

Retrieves an array containing all of the elements in the set. The a parameter allows you to specify an array that determines the runtime type of the array returned by toArray().

Short Class

Full Name	java.lang.Short
Extends	Number->Object
Description	Public class. This class serves as a standard wrapper for primitive short values.

Constructors

```
public Short(short value);
public Short(String s) throws NumberFormatException;
```

Creates a Short object using either a primitive short value or a string containing a base 10 number.

Class Variables

```
public static final short MIN_VALUE;
public static final short MAX_VALUE;
```

These constants represent the minimum and maximum values allowed for a short value.

```
public static final Class TYPE;
```

This constant is an object representing the primitive short type.

Class Methods

```
public static Short decode(String nm)
   throws NumberFormatException;
```

Decodes a Short object out of a string containing a number; the number in the string can be in decimal, hexadecimal, or octal format.

```
public static short parseShort(String s)
   throws NumberFormatException;
public static short parseShort(String s, int radix)
   throws NumberFormatException;
```

Parses a short out of a string containing a short number.

```
public static Short valueOf(String s)
   throws NumberFormatException;
public static Short valueOf(String s, int radix)
   throws NumberFormatException;
```

Parses a Short object out of a string containing a short number.

Instance Methods

```
public int compareTo(Short anotherShort);
public int compareTo(Object o);
```

Compares this short to the specified Short object or other object; the return value is 0 if the objects are numerically equal, less than 0 if this short is less than the argument, and greater than 0 if this short is greater than the argument.

Java 2 API Reference

Overridden Instance Methods

```
public byte byteValue();
public double doubleValue();
public float floatValue();
public int intValue();
public long longValue();
public short shortValue();
```

These methods return the value of this short as a byte, double, float, int, long, or short.

SimpleTimeZone Class

Java 2 API Reference

Full Name	java.util.SimpleTimeZone
Extends	TimeZone->Object
Description	Public class. This class extends the TimeZone class to implement a time zone compatible with a Gregorian calendar.

Constructors

```
public SimpleTimeZone(int rawOffset, String ID);
public SimpleTimeZone(int rawOffset, String ID, int startMonth,
   int startDay, int startDayOfWeek, int startTime, int endMonth,
   int endDay, int endDayOfWeek, int endTime);
public SimpleTimeZone(int rawOffset, String ID, int startMonth,
   int startDay, int startDayOfWeek, int startTime, int endMonth,
   int endDay, int endDayOfWeek, int endTime, int dstSavings);
```

Creates a SimpleTimeZone object based upon the specified arguments. The rawOffset argument is a base time offset relative to Greenwich Mean Time (GMT).

Instance Methods

```
public int getDSTSavings();
```

Retrieves the amount of time used to advance the clock for daylight savings time, in milliseconds.

```
public void setEndRule(int month, int dayOfMonth, int time);
public void setEndRule(int month, int dayOfWeekInMonth,
   int dayOfWeek, int time);
public void setEndRule(int month, int dayOfMonth,
   int dayOfWeek, int time, boolean after);
```

Sets the end rule for daylight savings time using the specified arguments.

```
public void setDSTSavings(int millisSavedDuringDST);
```

Sets the amount of time used to advance the clock for daylight savings time, in milliseconds.

```
public void setStartRule(int month, int dayOfMonth, int time);
public void setStartRule(int month, int dayOfWeekInMonth,
    int dayOfWeek, int time);
public void setStartRule(int month, int dayOfMonth,
    int dayOfWeek, int time, boolean after);
```

Sets the start rule for daylight savings time using the specified arguments.

```
public void setStartYear(int year);
```

Sets the start year for daylight savings time using the specified year.

SizeRequirements Class

Java 2 API Reference

Full Name	javax.swing.SizeRequirements
Extends	Object
Description	Public class. This is a special class used by layout managers to calculate the size and position of objects.

Constructors

```
public SizeRequirements();
public SizeRequirements(int min, int pref, int max,
    float a);
```

The first constructor is the default constructor; the second constructor creates a SizeRequirements object with the specified minimum, preferred, maximum, and alignment values.

Instance Variables

```
public float alignment;
public int maximum;
public int minimum;
public int preferred;
```

These variables store minimum, preferred, maximum, and alignment values, which constitute the size requirements of a component.

```
Class Methodspublic static int[] adjustSizes(int delta,
    SizeRequirements[] children);
```

This method adjusts the specified array of sizes by a specified amount (delta).

```
public static SizeRequirements
  getAlignedSizeRequirements(SizeRequirements[] children);
public static SizeRequirements
  getTiledSizeRequirements(SizeRequirements[] children);
```

These methods determine the amount of space required to tile or align a set of components.

```
public static void calculateAlignedPositions(int allocated,
   SizeRequirements total, SizeRequirements[] children,
   int[] offsets, int[] spans);
public static void calculateTiledPositions(int allocated,
   SizeRequirements total, SizeRequirements[] children,
   int[] offsets, int[] spans);
```

These methods calculate the positions and sizes of a set of components so that they are tiled or aligned.

Overridden Instance Methods

```
public String toString();
```

Overrides the method definition in the Object class.

Socket Class

Java 2 API Reference

Full Name	`java.net.Socket`
Extends	`Object`
Description	Public final class. Creates a socket, which is an object, built around a local port, that provides the capability to communicate with another machine. To perform I/O, you call `Socket` methods to get input and output streams. You read or write to these streams just as you would read or write to file streams.
	You can create a socket directly and use it as a client socket; this presumes that the other machine is a server that can listen to and respond to a request for a connection. You can also get a socket from the `ServerSocket` class; in this latter case, you use the socket to read and write data as a server.

The following example reads data from port 13 (the daytime system service) of the server named `java.sun.com`.

```
try {
   Socket sock = new Socket("java.sun.com", 13);
   printInstream(sock.getInputStream());
} catch (IOException e) {System.out.println(e);}
```

This example assumes that `printInstream()` is a method in your program that prints the contents of an input stream. Here is one way of writing such a method:

```
static void printInstream(InputStream in)
  throws IOException {
```

```
DataInputStream dis = new DataInputStream(in);
String s = "";
do {
  System.out.println(s);
  s = dis.readLine();
} while (s != null);
}
```

Constructors

```
public Socket(InetAddress address, int port)
  throws IOException;
public Socket(InetAddress address, int port, boolean stream)
  throws IOException;
public Socket(String host, int port) throws IOException;
public Socket(String host, int port, boolean stream)
  throws IOException;
```

You specify destination address and destination port (the local port is assigned for you). For specification of host, see InetAddress class (p. 285). If the optional stream argument is true, then a connection-based protocol (TCP) that supports stream I/O is used. This is the default. If the argument is false, then the connectionless User Datagram Protocol is used.

Class Methods

```
public static void setSocketImplFactory(SocketImplFactory
  fac) throws IOException, SocketException;
```

Specifies a new SocketImplFactory to use. Application code typically never calls this method. It is used by code that needs to modify the socket implementation for a particular platform.

Instance Methods

```
public void close() throws IOException;
```

Closes the socket and frees the port.

```
public InetAddress getInetAddress();
```

Gets the InetAddress object that encapsulates the other machine's address.

```
public InputStream getInputStream() throws IOException;
```

Returns an input stream. You can use this stream to read data as you would any other input stream. Incoming data is read from the port.

```
public int getLocalPort();
```

Returns the local port being used by this socket.

```
public OutputStream getOutputStream() throws IOException;
```

Returns an output stream. You can use this stream to write data as you would any other input stream. Data written is sent to the machine on the other end of the network connection.

```
public int getPort();
```

Returns the port number in use by the other machine.

Overridden Instance Methods

```
public String toString();
```

Overrides method definition in the Object class.

SoftBevelBorder Class

Java 2 API Reference

Full Name   `javax.swing.border.SoftBevelBorder`

Extends   `BevelBorder->AbstractBorder->Object`

Description   Public class. This class implements a soft bevel border, which is a bevel border with softened corners.

Constructors

```
public SoftBevelBorder(int bevelType);
public SoftBevelBorder(int bevelType, Color highlight,
; Color shadow);
public SoftBevelBorder(int bevelType,
   Color highlightOuterColor, Color highlightInnerColor,
   Color shadowOuterColor, Color shadowInnerColor);
```

These constructors create soft bevel borders with varying degrees of detail in terms of the colors used to shade the borders.

Overridden Instance Methods

```
public Insets getBorderInsets(Component c);
```

This method retrieves the insets for the border.

```
public boolean isBorderOpaque();
```

This method checks whether the border is opaque or transparent; opaque borders paint their own backgrounds, whereas transparent borders do not.

```
public void paintBorder(Component c, Graphics g, int x,
   int y, int width, int height);
```

This method paints the border for a component using the specified border *x,y* position and size.

SortedMap Interface

Full Name   java.util.SortedMap

Description   Public interface. This interface describes a map collection that is sorted in ascending order according to the keys contained within.

Interface Methods

```
public Comparator comparator();
```

Retrieves the comparator used to compare keys for sorting; this method returns null if the keys are to be compared according to their natural order.

```
public Object firstKey();
```

Retrieves the first key in the sorted map.

```
public SortedMap headMap(Object toKey);
```

Retrieves a sub-map of the map whose keys are less than the specified key.

```
public Object lastKey();
```

Retrieves the last key in the sorted map.

```
public SortedMap subMap(Object fromKey, Object toKey);
```

Retrieves a sub-map of the map containing the keys within the specified key range.

```
public SortedMap tailMap(Object fromKey);
```

Retrieves a sub-map of the map whose keys are greater than the specified key.

Java 2 API Reference

Stack Class

Full Name   java.util.Stack

Extends   Vector->Object

Description   Public class. Creates a stack mechanism onto which you can push and pop any type of objects. A stack is a collection in which the main access is a last-in-first-out (LIFO) mechanism. Popping the stack returns the last item pushed onto the stack.

The following example creates a stack, pushes two strings, and pops the last one off. Note that the pop() return value needs to be cast from Object to whatever type you're using (in this case, String).

```
Stack mystack = new Stack();
```

```
mystack.push("First item.");
mystack.push("Second item.");
String topOfStack = (String) mystack.pop();
```

Constructors

```
public Stack();
```

Instance Methods

```
public boolean empty();
```

Returns true if the stack contains no objects.

```
public Object peek();
public Object pop();
public Object push(Object item);
```

These methods perform the peek, pop, and push operations. peek() returns the top object without removing it, whereas pop() both returns this object and removes it from the stack. push() places a new item on the top of the stack and returns that item. Remember to cast the return value of push(), as shown in the example.

```
public int search(Object o);
```

Returns 0-based position of the object from top of the stack, or –1 if the object is not found.

StreamTokenizer Class

Full Name	`java.io.StreamTokenizer`
Extends	`Object`
Description	Public class. Creates an input stream with built-in support for tokenizing input. Tokenizing is the process of breaking text into words and symbols. This class is somewhat similar to `java.util.StringTokenizer` but is more sophisticated. Among other things, this class can interpret comments, quoted strings, and numbers.

Generally, this class is most useful to people writing compilers, interpreters, and other programs that analyze complex input.

Constructors

```
public StreamTokenizer(InputStream I);
```

Constructor. Builds a `StreamTokenizer` object around the specified input stream.

Class Variables

```
public final static int TT_EOF;
public final static int TT_EOL;
public final static int TT_NUMBER;
public final static int TT_WORD;
```

Constants indicating type of input just read. TT_EOF and TT_EOL indicate end of file and end of line, respectively. TT_NUMBER indicates a number was read, and TT_WORD indicates a word.

Instance Variables

```
public double nval;
public String sval;
public int ttype;
```

Instance variables that store temporary information used during tokenization. nval and sval store last number and string (word) just read, respectively. ttype is equal to one of the four TT_* constants or the value of an ordinary character (typically an operator or other non-word symbol).

Instance Methods

```
public void commentChar(int ch);
```

Recognizes specified character as end-of-line comment symbol in the stream. A forward slash (/) is a comment symbol by default.

```
public void eolIsSignificant(boolean flag);
```

If true, EOL is recognized as a token. If false, EOL is treated as a whitespace (the default).

```
public int lineno();
```

Returns number of current line read.

```
public void lowerCaseMode(boolean fl);
```

If true, tokens are converted to all lowercase.

```
public int nextToken();
```

Returns the type of the next token. After a call to nextToken(), this value is available in the type field. Depending on type, the token's contents may be stored in nval or sval.

```
public void ordinaryChar(int ch);
public void ordinaryChars(int low, int hi);
```

The specified character (or all characters in the range) loses any special meaning and is treated as an ordinary character. When the character is read, it is treated as a one-character token, and ttype is set to the value of this character. Operators, for example, are usually ordinary characters. See also wordChars(), below.

```
public void parseNumbers();
```

Specifies that numbers are to be handled separately from words. Numeric data is stored in nval, and token type is TT_NUMBER instead of TT_WORD. This is the default condition.

```
public void pushBack();
```

Causes the next call to nextToken() to return the current value of the ttype field.

```
public void quoteChar(int ch);
```

Specifies a quotation mark symbol. When any quotation mark is encountered, all input up to the next occurrence of the same symbol is read into a string; ttype is set to ch, and the string is stored in sval. (See "Class Variables.") By default, both single and double quotation marks are quote characters.

```
public void resetSyntax();
```

Resets the syntax table so that all characters are treated as ordinary characters. See ordinaryChar(), page 455.

```
public void slashSlashComments(boolean flag);
public void slashStarComments(boolean flag);
```

When flag is true, each of these methods enables recognition of C++ and C comment symbols, respectively. These symbols are not recognized by default.

```
public void whitespaceChars(int low, int hi);
```

Specifies that characters in the range low to hi, inclusive, are whitespace characters. By default, this includes standard whitespace characters such as space and tab.

```
public void wordChars(int low, int hi);
```

Specifies that the characters in the range low to hi, inclusive, are treated as word characters. A word consists of one of these characters followed by any combination of word characters and digits. By default, all letters are word characters.

Overridden Instance Methods

```
public String toString();
```

Overrides the method definition in the Object class.

String Class

Full Name	`java.lang.String`
Extends	`Object`
Description	Public final class. Represents a character string. Although there are other ways to represent a string, Java uses the `String` class as the standard format. String literals are translated into `String` objects by the Java compiler.
	Once created, a `String` object cannot change. This fact is usually not noticeable, for `String` operations constantly create new strings. But if you're going to do large amounts of string manipulation, consider using the `StringBuffer` class or an array of `char`. The final results can be translated back into `String` form.
	In addition to the many methods listed here, you can use the concatenation operator (+). The `String` class is unique in supporting its own operator.

The following example creates two strings — s1 and s2 — containing the values "the end" and "THE END." The equalsIgnoreCase() method returns the value true in this case.

```
String s1 = "the" + " " + "end";
String s2 = s1.toUpperCase();
System.out.println("Length of s1 is: " + s1.length());
if (s1.equalsIgnoreCase(s2))
    // ...
```

Constructors

```
public String();
public String(byte ascii[], int hibyte);
public String(byte ascii[], int hibyte, int offset,
    int count) throws StringIndexOutOfBoundsException;
public String(char value[]);
public String(char value[], int offset, int count)
    throws StringIndexOutOfBoundsException;
public String(String value);
public String(StringBuffer buffer);
```

The string can be initialized from another string, from an ASCII array, from an array of char (Unicode), or from a StringBuffer object.

Class Methods

```
public static String copyValueOf(char data[]);
public static String copyValueOf(char data[], int offset,
    int count);
```

Returns the value of the char data as an equivalent String object.

```
public static String valueOf(boolean b);
public static String valueOf(char c);
public static String valueOf(char data[]);
public static String valueOf(char data[], int offset,
    int count);
public static String valueOf(double d);
public static String valueOf(float f);
public static String valueOf(int i);
public static String valueOf(long l);
public static String valueOf(Object obj);
```

All these methods allocate new strings, initializing them from the argument data. Where the argument is numeric, valueOf() translates it into a string representation of the digits.

Instance Methods

```
public char charAt(int index) throws
    StringIndexOutOfBoundsException;
```

Returns the character at the zero-based index.

```
public int compareTo(String anotherString);
```

Returns 1, 0, or –1, depending on whether the current object is greater, equal to, or less than, respectively, the string argument. Less than means listed earlier in an alphabetical arrangement.

```
public String concat(String str);
```

Returns a new string that is the concatenation of the string argument onto the current string.

```
public boolean endsWith(String suffix);
```

Returns true if the last characters in the current string match the suffix.

```
public boolean equalsIgnoreCase(String anotherString);
```

Performs a comparison in which case is ignored: true equals TRUE.

```
public void getBytes(int srcBegin, int srcEnd, byte dst[],
    int dstBegin);
public void getChars(int srcBegin, int srcEnd, char dst[],
    int dstBegin);
```

Copies characters from the current string to the destination location.
getBytes() uses the eight low-order bits of the character.

```
public int indexOf(int ch);
public int indexOf(int ch, int fromIndex);
public int indexOf(String str);
public int indexOf(String str, int fromIndex);
```

Searches for first occurance of specified character or string. You can optionally specify where to begin the search. See also lastIndexOf() below and
substring() (p. 460). Returns –1 if search target is not found.

```
public String intern();
```

Returns an identical string that is from a set of unique strings. No strings are
repeated in this set. This means that if string1 and string2 have identical
contents, then string1.intern() and string2.intern() refer to the same
object in memory.

```
public int lastIndexOf(int ch);
public int lastIndexOf(int ch, int fromIndex);
public int lastIndexOf(String str);
public int lastIndexOf(String str, int fromIndex);
```

This method is the same as indexOf() except that the search starts at the
back of the string and moves toward the front.

```
public int length();
```

Returns the number of characters in the string.

```
public boolean regionMatches(boolean ignoreCase,
   int toffset, String other, int ooffset, int len);
public boolean regionMatches(int toffset, String other,
   int ooffset, int len);
```

Compares a subset of the current string to a subset of other, the string argument. toffset is a zero-based index into this string, and ooffset is an index
into other.

```
public String replace(char oldChar, char newChar);
```

Returns a new string created by replacing every occurrence of oldChar with
newChar.

```
public boolean startsWith(String prefix);
public boolean startsWith(String prefix, int toffset);
```

Returns true if the first characters in the current string match prefix. You can
optionally look for prefix starting at toffset, a zero-based index.

Java 2 API Reference

```
public String substring(int beginIndex);
public String substring(int beginIndex, int endIndex)
    throws StringIndexOutOfBoundsException;
```

Returns the substring at the specified zero-based index. If endIndex is not specified, substring() returns all the characters from beginIndex onward.

```
public char[] toCharArray();
```

Returns the char array equivalent to the current string.

```
public String toLowerCase();
public String toUpperCase();
```

Returns a new string made by converting the current string to all uppercase or all lowercase.

```
public String trim();
```

Returns a string created by removing all whitespace from the current string.

Overridden Instance Methods

```
public boolean equals(Object anObject);
public int hashCode();
public String toString();
```

These methods override method definitions in the Object class. equals() is especially useful for determining equality of contents. toString() returns a reference to the string; it does not clone a new string.

StringBuffer Class

Full Name	java.lang.String
Extends	Object
Description	Public final class. This class is similar to the String class. The main difference is that StringBuffer objects can be internally modified. For example, append() adds characters to the end of the buffer and returns a reference to the current object, unlike String.concat(), which creates a completely new object. As with Vector objects, StringBuffer objects automatically grow as needed. When you are finished manipulating string data, you can efficiently convert back to string form by calling StringBuffer.toString() or a String constructor.

The following example uses a StringBuffer object to insert a word. The results are then converted back to String format.

```
StringBuffer strBuf = new StringBuffer("the end");
strBuf.insert(4, "living ");
String s = new String(strBuf);
```

Constructors

```
public StringBuffer();
public StringBuffer(int length);
public StringBuffer(String str);
```

If a length argument is specified, it sets the initial capacity. (The buffer can grow beyond this capacity, but each capacity adjustment takes processor time.)

Instance Methods

```
public StringBuffer append(boolean b);
public StringBuffer append(char c);
public StringBuffer append(char str[]);
public StringBuffer append(double d);
public StringBuffer append(float f);
public StringBuffer append(int i);
public StringBuffer append(long l);
public StringBuffer append(Object obj);
public StringBuffer append(String str);
```

Appends a string, or string representation of the argument, onto the end of the current string. Returns a reference to the current object.

```
public int capacity();
```

Returns the current capacity of the string buffer.

```
public char charAt(int index);
```

Returns the character at the zero-based index. See also setCharAt(), page 462.

```
public void ensureCapacity(int minimumCapacity);
```

Ensures that the string buffer can store at least this many items.

```
public void getChars(int srcBegin, int srcEnd char dst[],
   int dstBegin);
```

Copies indicated characters from the string buffer (from srcBegin to srcEnd) into destination char array.

```
public StringBuffer insert(int offset, boolean b);
public StringBuffer insert(int offset, char c);
public StringBuffer insert(int offset, char str[]);
public StringBuffer insert(int offset, double d);
public StringBuffer insert(int offset, float f);
```

Java 2 API Reference

```
public StringBuffer insert(int offset, int i);
public StringBuffer insert(int offset, long l);
public StringBuffer insert(int offset, Object obj);
public StringBuffer insert(int offset, String str);
```

Inserts a substring into the middle of the string buffer using a string or a string representation of the specified argument. The offset is a zero-based index. Returns a reference to the current object.

```
public int length();
```

Returns the current length. This is not necessarily the same as capacity.

```
public StringBuffer reverse();
```

Reverses the order of all characters in the string. Returns a reference to the current object.

```
public void setCharAt(int index, char ch);
```

Changes the value of the character at the zero-based index.

```
public void setLength(int newLength);
```

Sets a new length. If this is greater than current length, the method pads the end of the string with nulls. If this is less than the current length, the method deletes characters at the end.

```
public String toString();
```

Overrides method definition in the Object class. This creates a String equivalent of the string buffer.

StringTokenizer Class

Full Name	java.util.StringTokenizer
Extends	Object
Implements	Enumeration
Description	Public class. Creates an object that breaks up contents of a string, returning one item at a time. Each item (called a token) is a series of characters surrounded by delimiters; in other words, a word, symbol, or number. For example, the string "Big Ugly Fish" contains three tokens. Delimiters include whitespace characters by default, but you can optionally specify a string that contains delimiter characters. See the constructors. Also, for a more powerful tokenizing class, see StreamTokenizer class (p. ___).

The following example gets the contents of a text field, Text1, and then prints all the items in that text field, each on a separate line:

```
StringTokenizer st = new StringTokenizer(Text1.getText());
while(st.hasMoreTokens())
    System.out.println(st.nextToken());
```

Constructors

```
public StringTokenizer(String str);
public StringTokenizer(String str, String delim);
public StringTokenizer(String str, String delim,
    boolean returnTokens);
```

The returnTokens argument, if true, causes the delimiters to be returned as tokens in addition to the items in between.

Instance Methods

```
public int countTokens();
```

Returns the number of tokens found.

```
public String nextToken() throws NoSuchElementException;
public String nextToken(String delim);
```

Gets the next token. You can optionally specify new delimiters, which affect tokenization of the remainder of the string.

```
public boolean hasMoreTokens();
```

Returns true if there are any remaining tokens in the string.

Overridden Instance Methods

```
public Object nextElement() throws NoSuchElementException;
public boolean hasMoreElements();
```

These methods implement methods in the Enumeration interface.

SwingConstants Interface

Full Name   javax.swing.SwingConstants

Description Public interface. This interface serves as a convenient location to store constants used throughout the Swing toolkit. By implementing this interface, a class inherits all these constants and can use them as if they were declared in the class itself.

Interface Constants

```
public static final int CENTER;
public static final int TOP;
public static final int LEFT;
public static final int BOTTOM;
public static final int RIGHT;
public static final int NORTH;
public static final int NORTH_EAST;
public static final int EAST;
public static final int SOUTH_EAST;
public static final int SOUTH;
public static final int SOUTH_WEST;
public static final int WEST;
public static final int NORTH_WEST;
public static final int HORIZONTAL;
public static final int VERTICAL
public static final int LEADING;
public static final int TRAILING;
```

These constants represent general positioning characteristics throughout the Swing toolkit.

SwingUtilities Class

Full Name   javax.swing.SwingUtilities

Extends   Object

Description   Public class. This class contains a suite of helper methods used throughout the Swing toolkit.

Class Methods

```
public static final boolean
isRectangleContainingRectangle(Rectangle a,
  Rectangle b)
public static Rectangle getLocalBounds(Component aComponent)
public static Window getWindowAncestor(Component c)
public static Point convertPoint(Component source, Point aPoint,
  Component destination)
public static Point convertPoint(Component source, int x, int y,
  Component destination)
public static Rectangle convertRectangle(Component source,
  Rectangle aRectangle, Component destination)
public static Container getAncestorOfClass(Class c, Component
comp)
```

```
public static Container getAncestorNamed(String name, Component
comp)
public static Component getDeepestComponentAt(Component parent,
int x,
  int y)
public static MouseEvent convertMouseEvent(Component source,
  MouseEvent sourceEvent, Component destination)
public static void convertPointToScreen(Point p, Component c)
public static void convertPointFromScreen(Point p, Component c)
public static Window windowForComponent(Component aComponent)
public static boolean isDescendingFrom(Component a, Component b)
public static Rectangle computeIntersection(int x, int y, int
width,
  int height, Rectangle dest)
public static Rectangle computeUnion(int x, int y, int width,
  int height, Rectangle dest)
public static Rectangle[] computeDifference(Rectangle rectA,
  Rectangle rectB)
public static boolean isLeftMouseButton(MouseEvent anEvent)
public static boolean isMiddleMouseButton(MouseEvent anEvent)
public static boolean isRightMouseButton(MouseEvent anEvent)
public static int computeStringWidth(FontMetrics fm, String str)
public static String layoutCompoundLabel(JComponent c,
FontMetrics fm,
  String text, Icon icon, int verticalAlignment,
  int horizontalAlignment, int verticalTextPosition,
  int horizontalTextPosition, Rectangle viewR, Rectangle iconR,
  Rectangle textR, int textIconGap)
public static String layoutCompoundLabel(FontMetrics fm, String
text,
  Icon icon, int verticalAlignment, int horizontalAlignment,
  int verticalTextPosition, int horizontalTextPosition,
  Rectangle viewR, Rectangle iconR, Rectangle textR, int
textIconGap)
public static void paintComponent(Graphics g, Component c,
Container p,
  int x, int y, int w, int h)
public static void paintComponent(Graphics g, Component c,
Container p,
  Rectangle r)
public static void updateComponentTreeUI(Component c)
public static void invokeLater(Runnable doRun)
public static void invokeAndWait(Runnable doRun)
```

Java 2 API Reference

```
      throws InterruptedException, InvocationTargetException
public static boolean isEventDispatchThread()
public static int getAccessibleIndexInParent(Component c)
public static Accessible getAccessibleAt(Component c, Point p)
public static AccessibleStateSet getAccessibleStateSet(Component c)
public static int getAccessibleChildrenCount(Component c)
public static Accessible getAccessibleChild(Component c, int i)
public static Component findFocusOwner(Component c)
public static JRootPane getRootPane(Component c)
public static Component getRoot(Component c)
public static boolean notifyAction(Action action, KeyStroke ks,
   KeyEvent event, Object sender, int modifiers)
public static void replaceUIInputMap(JComponent component, int type,
   InputMap uiInputMap)
public static void replaceUIActionMap(JComponent component,
   ActionMap uiActionMap)
public static InputMap getUIInputMap(JComponent component,
   int condition)
public static ActionMap getUIActionMap(JComponent component)
```

These methods are used throughout the Swing toolkit to carry out various utility functions.

System Class

Full Name	`java.lang.System`
Extends	`Object`
Description	Public final class. This class, along with `Runtime`, provides access to a number of useful system functions. Some methods appear in both classes; `exit()`, `gc()`, `load()`, and `loadLibrary()` respond by calling methods of the same name in `Runtime`. Especially useful are the class variables `err`, `in`, and `out`, which provide access to basic console I/O. The `System` class consists entirely of class fields that are accessed as `System.variable` and `System.method()`. This class cannot be instantiated.

Instance Variables

```
public static PrintStream err;
public static InputStream in;
public static PrintStream out;
```

Each of these is a unique object available to the entire program. These objects provide access to system input, output, and error output.

Class Methods

```
public static void arraycopy(Object src, int src_position,
    Object dst, int dst_position, int length);
```

This is a general-purpose fast-copy routine. The src and dst arguments must be arrays of primitive data. Data areas may be part of the same array and may overlap.

```
public static long currentTimeMillis();
```

Returns the number of milliseconds since January 1, 1970, Greenwich Mean Time. Equivalent to (new Date()).getTime().

```
public static void exit(int status);
```

Causes the Java program to exit, passing the specified status code to the system.

```
public static void gc();
```

Requests that the garbage collector (which normally runs as a low-priority background process) be invoked right away to start destroying objects no longer used.

```
public static Properties getProperties();
```

Returns the system properties table.

```
public static String getProperty(String key);
public static String getProperty(String key, String def);
```

Looks up a property in the system properties table. If the property name is not found and if the def argument is specified in getProperty(), then def is returned.

```
public static SecurityManager getSecurityManager()
    throws SecurityException;
```

Returns a reference to the currently assigned security manager.

```
public static void load(String filename);
public static void loadLibrary(String libname);
```

Mainly used internally. These methods load native-code implementations. load() specifies a complete pathname, whereas loadLibrary() relies on the system to search in the library directories.

```
public static void runFinalization();
```

Requests that the Java interpreter call the finalize() method for all objects that have been destroyed. Normally, an object's finalize() method may not necessarily be run right away.

```
public static void setProperties(Properties props);
```

Replaces the systems property table with the properties table specified in the argument. Note that this throws an exception if the security manager does not allow it.

```
public static void setSecurityManager(SecurityManager s);
```

Sets a security manager, throwing a `SecurityException` if a security manager is already assigned.

TextArea Class

Java 2 API Reference

Full Name	`java.awt.TextArea`
Extends	`TextComponent->Component->Object`
Description	Public class. Creates a multiline edit box. Remember that this class inherits all the methods of `TextComponent`, including the `setText()` and `getText()` methods. Consult Text Component class (p. ___) if you can't find a method here.
	TextArea objects generate all standard keyboard and mouse events except `mousePressed` and `mouseReleased`. A `TextArea` object may create an internal scroll bar, but it is not under the programmer's control.

The following example creates a text area with 10 rows, 50 columns, and initial text. Later, the contents are retrieved into the string variable `multiLine`.

```
TextArea myTextBox = new TextArea("Some text", 10, 50);
add(myTextBox);    // Add to current applet or frame.
// ...
String multiLine = myTextBox.getText();
```

Constructors

```
public TextArea();
public TextArea(int rows, int cols);
public TextArea(String text);
public TextArea(String text, int rows, int cols);
```

If rows and columns are not specified, the default is 0. This produces good results when the `TextArea` object is at the Center zone with a `BorderLayout` manager, because it results in the text area using all the space in the container. The default of 0 for rows and columns does not produce good results with `FlowLayout` manager.

Instance Methods

```
public void appendText(String str);
```

Appends the indicated string onto the end of the existing text.

```
public int getColumns();
public int getRows();
```

These methods get the number of visible columns and rows.

```
public void insertText(String str, int pos);
```

Inserts a text string into existing text at the zero-based position indicated. For example, a value of 0 for pos means to insert text at the beginning of the string.

```
public Dimension minimumSize(int rows, int cols);
public Dimension preferredSize(int rows, int cols);
```

These methods return minimum and preferred size, given the number of visible rows and columns specified.

```
public void replaceText(String str, int start, int end);
```

Replaces the text between the two positions with the indicated string. The positions are zero-based indexes; see the select() method of the Text Component class (p. 469).

Overridden Instance Methods

```
public Dimension minimumSize();
public Dimension preferredSize();
public void addNotify();
```

Overrides method definition in the Component class.

TextComponent Class

Full Name	java.awt.TextComponent
Extends	Component->Object
Description	Public class that has no constructors and cannot be instantiated directly. This class contains common methods for the TextField and TextArea classes.

Instance Methods

```
public String getSelectedText();
```

Returns selected text, if any. This is the text that the user has highlighted.

```
public int getSelectionEnd();
public int getSelectionStart();
```

These methods get the ending and starting positions of the selected (highlighted) text. getSelectionEnd() returns the position of the last character inside the selection, so the methods return the same value — equal to current position — when no text is highlighted. If text is highlighted, the difference

between the two values yields the number of characters selected. See
select() below.

```
public String getText();
```

Returns the entire text contents of the object as a single string.

```
public boolean isEditable();
```

Returns true if the object is in the editable state. See setEditable() below.

```
public void select(int selStart, int selEnd);
public void selectAll();
```

These methods set the selection highlight to the indicated positions and to
the entire contents, respectively. The first version uses indexes. If the cursor
sits in front (to the left) of the first character, the index of that position is
zero. The index of the position in front of the second character is 1, and so
on. Thus, select (0,1) selects the first character of the string; select (0,2)
selects the first two.

```
public void setEditable(boolean t);
```

Sets the object to the editable state (true) or noneditable state (false). If it is
editable (the default setting), the user can enter and delete text.

```
public void setText(String t);
```

Sets the entire text contents of the object to the specified string.

Overridden Instance Methods

```
public void removeNotify();
```

Overrides method definition in the Component class. Used internally.

TextField Class

Full Name	java.awt.TextField
Extends	TextComponent->Component->Object
Description	Public class. Creates a single-line text-entry component. This class supports an optional echo-character feature for password protection. Remember that this class inherits all the TextComponent methods, including setText() and getText(). Consult TextComponent class (p. 469) if you can't find a method here.
	TextField objects generate the standard keyboard and mouse events exceptmousePressed and mouseReleased. When the user presses Return, an Action event is generated.

The following example creates a text field with 50 columns and some initial text. Later, the contents are retrieved into the string variable theText.

```
TextField myTextField = new TextField("Some text", 50);
add(myTextField);    // Add to current applet or frame.
// ...
String theText = myTextField.getText();
```

Constructors

```
public TextField();
public TextField(int cols);
public TextField(String text);
public TextField(String text, int cols);
```

You can optionally specify starting text and width in columns. If you don't specify a width, the size is determined by the container's layout manager.

Instance Methods

```
public boolean echoCharIsSet();
```

Returns true if character echoing is in use. This condition is set by setEchoCharacter(), and it results in the same character being echoed no matter what is typed.

```
public int getColumns();
```

Returns the number of columns; this tells you how many characters can be visible at one time.

```
public char getEchoChar();
```

Returns the current echo character, if any. See setEchoCharacter(), below.

```
public Dimension minimumSize(int cols);
public Dimension preferredSize(int cols);
```

Returns minimum and preferred size of the text field object, given the specified number of columns.

```
public void setEchoCharacter(char c);
```

Sets an echo character, which causes the same character to be echoed as the user types. For example, if "*" is the echo character, then "*" appears in response to each keystroke rather than the character typed. The typical use of this feature is for password entry.

Overridden Instance Methods

```
public void addNotify();
public Dimension minimumSize();
public Dimension preferredSize();
```

These methods override method definitions in the Component class.
addNotify() is used internally.

Thread Class

Full Name	java.lang.Thread
Extends	Object
Implements	Runnable
Description	Public class. Creates independent threads of execution; these are tasks that run concurrently with the program's main thread. An important method is start(), which causes the thread to start executing the run() method of the target object. This object is specified in the Thread constructor. See Chapter 6 for an introduction to threads.

The following example starts a background thread (bkgrnd) and puts the current thread to sleep:

```
// When bkgrnd starts, it will use run() from THIS class.
Thread bkgrnd = new Thread(this);
//...
bkgrnd.start();
try {
  Thread.sleep(500);
} // Sleep for .5 secs.
catch (InterruptedException e) {
  ;
}
```

Constructors

```
public Thread();
public Thread(Runnable target);
public Thread(Runnable target, String name);
public Thread(String name);
public Thread(ThreadGroup group, Runnable target);
public Thread(ThreadGroup group, Runnable target,
  String name);
public Thread(ThreadGroup group, String name);
```

The target is an object whose class implements the Runnable interface. When
the thread starts, the run() method of target's class is called. If no target is
specified, then the run() method of the thread itself is used. Although
Thread.run() does nothing, you can subclass Thread and override the run()
method. You can optionally give a name to the thread.

Class Variables

```
public final static int MAX_PRIORITY = 10;
public final static int MIN_PRIORITY = 1;
public final static int NORM_PRIORITY = 5;
```

Constants. These constants indicate the maximum, minimum, and average priority level. You can set priority level for a thread by calling its setPriority() method.

Class Methods

```
public static int activeCount();
public static Thread currentThread();
public static void dumpStack();
public static int enumerate(Thread tarray[]);
```

All of these methods apply to the currently executing thread. activeCount() returns the number of active threads in the thread group; currentThread() returns a reference to the thread; dumpStack() prints a stack trace; and enumerate() gets all the threads in the thread group.

```
public static void sleep(long millis) throws
InterruptedException;
public static void sleep(long millis, int nanos) throws
InterruptedException;
```

Causes current thread to wait for the specified time.

```
public static void yield();
```

Temporarily pauses and lets other threads execute.

Instance Methods

```
public void checkAccess() throws SecurityException;
```

Throws an exception if the security manager does not allow access to this thread.

```
public final String getName();
public final int getPriority();
public final ThreadGroup getThreadGroup();
```

These methods return basic information about the attributes of the thread.

```
public final boolean isAlive();
```

Returns true if the thread is alive. A live thread is one that has been started and has not died.

```
public final boolean isDaemon();
```

Returns true if the thread is a daemon. Daemon threads exist only to support other threads. The Java interpreter stops executing when the only live threads are daemons. See also `setDaemon()`, below.

```
public final void join() throws InterruptedException;
public final void join(long millis) throws InterruptedException;
public final void join(long millis, int nanos)
   throws InterruptedException;
```

The thread that calls this method waits until this thread (the thread through which join was called) dies; for example, `thread1.join()` means pause until thread1 dies. A maximum waiting time may be specified.

```
public void run();
```

This method implements the `Runnable` interface. Does nothing, but subclasses may override it.

```
public final void setDaemon(boolean on)
   throws IllegalThread-StateException;
public final void setName(String name);
public final void setPriority(int newPriority)
   throws IllegalArgumentException;
```

These methods set the daemon condition, name, and thread priority. See also `isDaemon()`, page 473.

```
public void start() throws IllegalThreadStateException;
```

Starts thread execution. Response is to spin off the thread by executing the `run()` method implemented by the target object. (See `Thread` constructors.)

```
public String toString();
```

Overrides method definition in the `Object` class.

ThreadGroup Class

Full Name	`java.lang.ThreadGroup`
Extends	`Object`
Description	Public class. A `ThreadGroup` object is useful for operating on a set of related threads. Several of the `ThreadGroup` methods return a `SecurityException`; this exception is generated when the security manager does not permit the currently executing thread to make the requested change. Thread groups may be nested inside each other.

Constructors

```
public ThreadGroup(String name);
public ThreadGroup(ThreadGroup parent, String name)
  throws NullPointerException;
```

The thread group may be made the child of another thread group.

Instance Methods

```
public int activeCount();
public int activeGroupCount();
```

Returns the number of active threads in the group (plus all child groups) and the number of active child thread groups (plus all their descendants), respectively.

```
public final void checkAccess() throws SecurityException;
```

Throws an exception if the security manager does not allow access to this thread group.

```
public final void destroy() throws IllegalThreadStateException;
```

Destroys the contents of the thread group and all child groups (nested to any level). An exception is thrown if there is an active thread in the group.

```
public int enumerate(Thread list[]);
public int enumerate(Thread list[], boolean recurse);
public int enumerate(ThreadGroup list[]);
public int enumerate(ThreadGroup list[], boolean recurse);
```

Copies all active threads, or all active thread groups, into an array. Use activeCount() or activeGroupCount() to determine how big the array needs to be.

```
public final int getMaxPriority();
```

Gets the maximum priority permitted in this group. See also setMaxPriority(), page 476.

```
public final String getName();
public final ThreadGroup getParent();
public final boolean isDaemon();
```

These methods return basic information about the thread group. A daemon thread group is automatically destroyed when its last thread has stopped. See also setDaemon(), page 476.

```
public void list();
```

Prints information useful for debugging purposes.

```
public final boolean parentOf(ThreadGroup g);
```

Returns true if this thread group is the parent of the specified group g.

```
public final void setDaemon(boolean daemon)
    throws SecurityException;
```

Sets the daemon condition on or off. A daemon thread group is automatically destroyed when its last thread has stopped.

```
public final void setMaxPriority(int pri)
    throws SecurityException;
```

Sets the maximum priority for threads in the group. Does not affect threads that already have a higher priority.

```
public void uncaughtException(Thread t, Throwable e);
```

Responds to an uncaught exception that stops one of the threads in the group. The default response is to do nothing if the exception is `ThreadDeath` but otherwise to call `e.printStackTrace()`. You can override this method to specify different behavior.

Overridden Instance Methods

```
public String toString();
```

Overrides the method definition in the `Object` class.

ThreadLocal Class

Full Name	java.lang.ThreadLocal
Extends	Object
Description	Public class. This class supports thread-local variables, which are variables for which a copy is assigned to each thread that accesses one. In other words, if a thread accesses a thread-local variable, the thread receives its own copy of the variable.

Constructors

```
public ThreadLocal();
```

Instance Methods

```
public Object get();
```

Gets the value of the thread-local variable.

```
public void set(Object value);
```

Sets the value of the thread-local variable.

Throwable Class

Full Name   `java.lang.Throwable`

Extends   `Object`

Description   Public class. This is the ancestor class for all exception classes. The methods defined in this class (which are all inherited by every exception class) are useful for debugging purposes.

Constructors

```
public Throwable();
public Throwable(String message);
```

These constructors are rarely used, because `Throwable` is not often instantiated directly.

Instance Methods

```
public Throwable fillInStackTrace();
```

Fills in the stack trace and returns the exception, which is convenient if you rethrow it. "Fills in" means that if and when a stack trace is printed (see `printStackTrace()`), previous exceptions are not reported, and a new exception is reported at the line of code that calls `fillInStackTrace()`.

```
public String getMessage();
```

Gets the error-message text associated with the exception.

```
public void printStackTrace();
public void printStackTrace(PrintStream s);
```

Prints a stack trace, optionally sending the output to a specified print stream. A stack trace lists each program location that threw or passed along an exception.

```
public String toString();
```

Overrides the method definition in the `Object` class. The string representation generally identifies the particular exception class.

Timer Class

Full Name   `javax.swing.Timer`

Extends   `Object`

Description   Public class. This class provides support for a timing function that triggers an action event at a specified rate. The `Timer` class has many interesting uses that range from establishing the frame rate of an animation to creating a digital stopwatch. The `Timer` class indicates that a period of time has elapsed by sending an action event to registered listeners.

Constructors

```
public Timer(int delay, ActionListener listener);
```

This creates a `Timer` object with the specified delay and action listener.

Instance Variables

```
protected EventListenerList listenerList;
```

This variable stores the list of listeners that receive action event notifications from the timer.

Instance Methods

```
public void addActionListener(ActionListener listener);
public int getDelay();
public int getInitialDelay();
public EventListener[] getListeners(Class listenerType);
public static boolean getLogTimers();
public boolean isCoalesce();
public boolean isRepeats();
public boolean isRunning();
public void removeActionListener(ActionListener listener);
public void restart();
public void setCoalesce(boolean flag);
public void setDelay(int delay);
public void setInitialDelay(int initialDelay);
public static void setLogTimers(boolean flag);
public void setRepeats(boolean flag);
public void start();
public void stop();
```

TimeZone Class

Full Name   `java.util.TimeZone`

Extends   `Object`

Description   Public class. This class represents a time zone that supports daylight savings time.

Constructors

```
public TimeZone();
```

Class Variables

```
public static final int SHORT;
public static final int LONG;
```

Class constants. These constants represent the two types of time zone descriptions, short and long.

Class Methods

```
public static String[] getAvailableIDs();
public static String[] getAvailableIDs(int rawOffset);
```

Gets the available time zone IDs; the rawOffset argument allows you to limit the available IDs to time zones with the specified offset.

```
public static TimeZone getDefault();
```

Retrieves the default time zone for the current environment.

```
public static TimeZone getTimeZone(String ID);
```

Retrieves the time zone associated with the specified time zone ID.

```
public static void setDefault(TimeZone zone);
```

Sets the default time zone for the current environment.

Instance Methods

```
public final String getDisplayName();
```

Obtains the display name for the time zone.

```
public final String getDisplayName(Locale locale);
```

Obtains the display name for the time zone based upon the specified locale.

```
public final String getDisplayName(boolean daylight, int style);
public String getDisplayName(boolean daylight, int style,
    Locale locale);
```

Obtains the display name for the time zone based upon the specified arguments, including the daylight savings time, style, and locale of the time zone.

```
public String getID();
```

Retrieves the ID of the time zone.

```
public boolean hasSameRules(TimeZone other);
```

Checks to see if the time zone has the same rules and offset as the specified time zone.

```
public void setID(String ID);
```

Sets the ID of the time zone.

TitledBorder Class

Full Name	javax.swing.border.TitledBorder
Extends	AbstractBorder->Object
Description	Public class. This class implements a titled border, which is a border with the addition of a string title.

Constructors

```
public TitledBorder(String title);
public TitledBorder(Border border);
public TitledBorder(Border border, String title);
public TitledBorder(Border border, String title,
   int titleJustification, int titlePosition);
public TitledBorder(Border border, String title,
   int titleJustification, int titlePosition, Font titleFont);
public TitledBorder(Border border, String title,
   int titleJustification, int titlePosition, Font titleFont,
   Color titleColor);
```

These constructors create titled borders with varying degrees of detail in terms of the title justification, position, font, and color.

Class Variables

```
public static final int DEFAULT_POSITION
public static final int ABOVE_TOP
public static final int TOP
public static final int BELOW_TOP
public static final int ABOVE_BOTTOM
public static final int BOTTOM
public static final int BELOW_BOTTOM
public static final int DEFAULT_JUSTIFICATION
public static final int LEFT
public static final int CENTER
public static final int RIGHT
public static final int LEADING
public static final int TRAILING
protected static final int EDGE_SPACING
protected static final int TEXT_SPACING
protected static final int TEXT_INSET_H
```

Class constants. These constants represent the different styles associated with the text positioning in a titled border.

Instance Variables

```
protected Border border;
protected String title;
protected Color titleColor;
protected Font titleFont;
protected int titleJustification;
protected int titlePosition;
```

These variables store the various pieces of information associated with a titled border, including the border, string title, position, justification, font, and color. The values for justification and position take one of the constants listed earlier.

Instance Methods

```
public Border getBorder();
protected Font getFont(Component c);
public Dimension getMinimumSize(Component c);
public String getTitle();
public Color getTitleColor();
public Font getTitleFont();
public int getTitleJustification();
public int getTitlePosition();
public void setBorder(Border border);
public void setTitle(String title);
public void setTitleColor(Color titleColor);
public void setTitleFont(Font titleFont);
public void setTitleJustification(int titleJustification);
public void setTitlePosition(int titlePosition);
```

These methods get and set various property values. The values for justification and position take one of the constants listed earlier.

Overridden Instance Methods

```
public void paintBorder(Component c, Graphics g,
    int x, int y, int width, int height);
```

This method paints the border for a component using the specified border *x,y* position and size.

```
public Insets getBorderInsets(Component c);
public Insets getBorderInsets(Component c, Insets insets);
```

These methods retrieve the insets for the border; the latter version acts on the Insets object that is passed as an argument.

```
public boolean isBorderOpaque();
```

This method checks whether the border is opaque or transparent; opaque borders paint their own backgrounds, whereas transparent borders do not.

Toolkit Class

Full Name	`java.awt.Toolkit`
Extends	`Object`
Description	Abstract public class. A Toolkit object provides a link to platform-dependent graphics. The `getImage()` method, like its counterpart in the `Applet` class, is useful for loading image files. The `Toolkit` class also has methods that return information on fonts and screen-display characteristics. Because this class is abstract, you cannot instantiate it directly; however, you can call `Component.getToolkit()`.

The following example uses the `Toolkit` class to supply a `getImage()` method for applications. It is similar to the `Applet.getImage()` method that loads image files.

```
Toolkit tk = Toolkit.getDefaultToolkit();
// ...
Image getImage(String filename) {
  return tk.getImage(filename)
}
Image getImage(URL url) {
  return tk.getImage(url)
}
```

Class Methods

```
public static Toolkit getDefaultToolkit();
```

Because this method is a class method, you can always call it directly (but remember to include the class prefix). Returns a reference to the current toolkit in use.

Instance Methods

```
public abstract int checkImage(Image image,
    int width, int height,  ImageObserver observer);
```

Returns the status of image loading using the same return flags that the ImageObserver class uses. This method is mostly for internal use. Applications and applets should usually use a MediaTracker object instead.

```
public abstract Image createImage(ImageProducer producer);
```

Used internally. To get an `Image` object, you should use `getImage()` or `Component.createImage()` instead. The latter is used for offscreen buffering.

```
public abstract ColorModel getColorModel();
public abstract String[] getFontList();
```

These methods return the color model and list of fonts supported on the current platform. The color model is mainly for internal use. It is used to translate RGB colors into the system's own color scheme if necessary.

```
public abstract FontMetrics getFontMetrics(Font font);
```

Returns a `FontMetrics` object for the specified font.

```
public abstract Image getImage(String filename);
public abstract Image getImage(URL url);
```

Returns an `Image` object that contains instructions for loading an image file from disk or a network site. Actual loading is initiated by calling `Graphics.drawImage()`.

```
public abstract int getScreenResolution();
public abstract Dimension getScreenSize();
```

These methods return information about the current platform. The screen resolution is returned in number of dots per inch.

```
public abstract boolean prepareImage(Image image,
    int width, int height, ImageObserver observer);
```

Used internally, by `Component.prepareImage()`. You probably never need to call this method yourself.

```
public abstract void sync();
```

Ensures that the screen image is completely up-to-date. This is sometimes useful because some graphics methods may use buffering of screen data.

TreeMap Class

Full Name	java.util.TreeMap
Extends	AbstractMap->Object
Description	Public class. This class implements a tree map based upon the SortedMap interface.

Constructors

```
public TreeMap();
```

Default constructor.

```
public TreeMap(Comparator c);
```

Creates a tree map that utilizes the specified comparator for sorting its keys.

```
public TreeMap(Map m);
public TreeMap(SortedMap m);
```

Creates a tree map that is initialized with the specified map or sorted map.

Instance Methods

```
public Comparator comparator();
```

Retrieves the comparator used to compare keys for sorting; this method returns null if the keys are to be compared according to their natural order.

```
public Object firstKey();
```

Retrieves the first key in the tree map.

```
public SortedMap headMap(Object toKey);
```

Retrieves a sub-map of the tree map whose keys are less than the specified key.

```
public Object lastKey();
```

Retrieves the last key in the tree map.

```
public SortedMap subMap(Object fromKey, Object toKey);
```

Retrieves a sub-map of the tree map containing the keys within the specified key range.

```
public SortedMap tailMap(Object fromKey);
```

Retrieves a sub-map of the tree map whose keys are greater than the specified key.

Overridden Instance Methods

```
public void clear();
```

Clears the tree map.

```
public boolean containsKey(Object key);
```

Checks to see if the tree map contains a mapping for the specified key.

```
public boolean containsValue(Object value);
```

Checks to see if the tree map contains one or keys mapped to the specified value.

```
public Set entrySet();
```

Retrieves a set containing the entry mappings for the tree map.

```
public Object get(Object key);
```

Retrieves the value associated with the specified key.

```
    public Set keySet();
```
Retrieves a set containing the key mappings for the tree map.

```
    public Object put(Object key, Object value);
```
Adds a key/value mapping to the tree map.

```
    public void putAll(Map map);
```
Adds all of the mappings in the specified map to the tree map.

```
    public Object remove(Object key);
```
Removes the specified key and its associated value from the tree map.

```
    public int size();
```
Retrieves the number of key/value mappings in the tree map.

```
    public Collection values();
```
Retrieves a collection of values contained within the tree map.

TreeSet Class

Full Name	java.util.TreeSet
Extends	AbstractSet->AbstractCollection->Object
Description	Public class. This class implements a tree set based upon the Set interface.

Constructors
```
    public TreeSet();
    public TreeSet(Comparator c);
```
Creates a tree set that utilizes the specified comparator for sorting its keys.

```
    public TreeSet(Collection c);
    public TreeSet(SortedSet s);
```
Creates a tree set that is initialized with the specified collection or sorted set.

Instance Methods
```
    public Comparator comparator();
```
Retrieves the comparator used to compare keys for sorting; this method returns null if the keys are to be compared according to their natural order.

```
    public Object first();
```
Retrieves the first element in the tree set.

```
    public SortedSet headSet(Object toElement);
```

Retrieves a subset of the tree set whose elements are less than the specified element.

```
public Object last();
```

Retrieves the last element in the tree set.

```
public SortedSet subSet(Object fromElement, Object toElement);
```

Retrieves a subset of the tree set containing the elements within the specified element range.

```
public SortedSet tailSet(Object fromElement);
```

Retrieves a subset of the tree set whose elements are greater than the specified element.

Overridden Instance Methods

```
public boolean add(Object o);
```

Adds the specified object to the tree set.

```
public boolean addAll(Collection c);
```

Adds the specified collection of objects to the tree set.

```
public void clear();
```

Clears the tree set.

```
public boolean contains(Object o);
```

Checks to see if the tree set contains the specified object.

```
public boolean isEmpty();
```

Checks to see if the tree set is empty.

```
public Iterator iterator();
```

Retrieves an iterator for the tree set.

```
public boolean remove(Object o);
```

Removes the specified object from the tree set.

```
public int size();
```

Retrieves the number elements in the tree set.

URL Class

Full Name	java.net.URL
Extends	Object

Description   Public final class. A URL object represents a uniform resource
                  locator (URL) and can be used to download data from the Web
                  page that the URL identifies. The URL class is a relatively sim-
                  ple mechanism for downloading information. For more complete
                  control over the communication channel, you can use
                  a URLConnection object, which you can get by calling
                  openConnection(). Some of the most common URL
                  methods are getContent() and openStream(), which
                  perform downloading.

The easiest way to specify a URL is to use a single string. For example:

```
URL u = new URL(
  "http://java.sun.com/products/apiOverview.html");
```

This string combines these substrings: protocol ("http"), host ("java.sun.
com"), and file ("products/apiOverview.html"). These elements could have
been specified separately. The protocol "http" means Hypertext Transport
Protocol.

Constructors

```
public URL(String spec) throws MalformedURLException;
```

Constructor specifying the URL location as a single string.

```
public URL(String protocol, String host, int port,
  String file) throws MalformedURLException;
public URL(String protocol, String host, String file)
  throws MalformedURLException;
```

Constructors specifying the protocol, host, and file separately; these make up
parts of the URL specification string, as explained earlier. If no destination
port is specified, then the http default (80) is assumed.

```
public URL(URL context, String spec)
  throws MalformedURLException;
```

Constructor specifying a relative spec. The missing information is supplied
by the context argument. For example, spec might specify only the file portion of the URL.

Class Methods

```
public static void setURLStreamHandlerFactory(
  URLStreamHandlerFactory fac) throws Error;
```

Sets the stream handler factory. Normal program code rarely calls this
method.

Instance Methods

```
public final Object getContent() throws IOException;
```

Downloads the URL contents as a Java object.

```
public String getFile();
public String getHost();
public int getPort();
public String getProtocol();
```

These methods get information specified in the constructor.

```
public String getRef();
```

Returns the reference (or anchor) of this URL. This suffix is used in some URL specifications and is preceded by a pound sign (#). The reference acts as a tag that identifies a particular part of the file.

```
public URLConnection openConnection() throws IOException;
```

Returns a URLConnection object for this URL.

```
public final InputStream openStream() throws IOException;
```

Returns an input stream that can be used to read the location. This presumes the location is a file.

```
public boolean sameFile(URL other);
```

Returns true if the URL argument refers to the same host, port, and file as this URL.

```
public String toExternalForm();
```

Returns a string representation of this URL.

Overridden Instance Methods

```
public boolean equals(Object obj);
public int hashCode();
public String toString();
```

These methods override method definitions in the Object class (p. ___).

URLConnection Class

Full Name	java.net.URLConnection
Extends	Object
Description	Abstract public class. You cannot directly instantiate this class, but you can get an instance by calling the openConnection() method of the URL class. This class can be used to download information from an Internet location, and it supports a much larger set of methods than URL.

Some of these methods are of interest to only a few programmers, although getInputStream() and getOutputStream() are often useful, as are the date/time methods getLast Modified() and setIfModifiedSince().

Class Methods

```
public static boolean getDefaultAllowUserInteraction();
public static void setDefaultAllowUserInteraction(Boolean
    defaultallowuserinteraction);
```

These methods get and set the default value of the AllowUserInteraction setting. See getAllowUserInteraction(), below.

```
public static String getDefaultRequestProperty(String key);
public static void setDefaultRequestProperty(String key,
    String value);
```

These methods get and set default values for properties downloaded from the URL.

```
public static void setContentHandlerFactory(
    ContentHandlerFactory fac) throws Error;
```

Sets the content handler factory. Normal program code rarely calls this method.

Instance Methods

```
public abstract void connect();
```

Opens a communications link for the URL. No effect if connection has already been made.

```
public boolean getAllowUserInteraction();
```

If true, the context allows user interaction such as responding to a dialog box.

```
public Object getContent() throws IOException,
    UnknownServiceException;
```

Downloads the URL contents as a Java object.

```
public String getContentEncoding();
```

Returns the content-encoding string for the URL, or null if it is not known.

```
public int getContentLength();
```

Returns the length of the URL resource, or –1 if it is not known.

```
public String getContentType();
```

Returns a string describing the content type, or null if it is not known.

```
public long getDate();
```

Returns the sending date of the URL resource as the number of milliseconds since January 1, 1970, GMT.

```
public boolean getDefaultUseCaches();
```

If true, the protocol uses caches as often as possible.

```
public boolean getDoInput();
public boolean getDoOutput();
```

These methods return true if the respective I/O operation is allowed. The default is to enable input but not output.

```
public long getExpiration();
```

Returns the expiration date as the number of milliseconds since January 1, 1970, GMT.

```
public String getHeaderField(int n);
public String getHeaderField(String name);
```

Returns the value of the specified header field.

```
public long getHeaderFieldDate(String name, long Default);
public int getHeaderFieldInt(String name, int Default);
```

Returns the numeric value of the specified header field, returning Default if the field is missing.

```
public String getHeaderFieldKey(int n);
```

Returns the key for the *n*th header field.

```
public long getIfModifiedSince();
```

Returns the value of the ifModifiedSince field. If this is nonzero, it indicates a time stamp; data is fetched only if it has a time stamp later than this date. Time is measured in milliseconds since January 1, 1970, GMT.

```
public InputStream getInputStream() throws IOException,
    UnknownServiceException;
```

Returns an input stream for reading data from the URL location. Data is read as if from a file.

```
public long getLastModified();
```

Returns a time stamp giving the time of last modification of the URL resource.

```
public OutputStream getOutputStream() throws IOException,
    UnknownServiceException;
```

Returns an output stream for writing data to the URL location. Data is written as if to a file.

```
public String getRequestProperty(String key);
```

Gets the value of the requested property.

```
public URL getURL();
```

Returns the associated URL object for this connection.

```
public boolean getUseCaches();
```

If true, Java is enabled to use caches for reading and writing to the URL connection. If false, Java is required to reload after each read or write. You set this condition with setUseCaches().

```
public void setAllowUserInteraction(
  boolean allowuserinteraction);
public void setDefaultUseCaches(boolean defaultusecaches);
public void setDoInput(boolean doinput);
public void setDoOutput(boolean dooutput);
public void setIfModifiedSince(long ifmodifiedsince);
public void setRequestProperty(String key, String value);
public void setUseCaches(boolean usecaches);
```

These methods set the value of various properties. See the corresponding "get" methods.

```
public String toString();
```

Overrides method definition in the Object class.

URLDecoder Class

Full Name	java.net.URLDecoder
Extends	Object
Description	Public class. This class is a utility class that contains a single static method, decode(), used to convert a MIME-formatted string into a normal string.

Constructors

```
public URLDecoder();
```

Class Methods

```
public static String decode(String s);
```

Converts the specified MIME-formatted string into a normal string.

URLEncoder Class

Full Name	`java.net.URLEncoder`
Extends	`Object`
Description	Public class. A URLEncoder object supports a method that translates URL strings into a standard, internationally accepted form. Note that you cannot instantiate this class, but you don't need to, because its one method is a class method.

Class Methods

```
public static String encode(String s);
```

Returns a string that has the same content as the argument but is translated into URL canonical form. This form restricts characters to an internationally accepted (and hence portable) subset of ASCII. The method converts each space to a plus sign (+) and converts each non-alphanumeric character (other than the underscore) into the form %*XX*, where *XX* is two hexadecimal digits.

Vector Class

Full Name	`java.util.Vector`
Extends	`Object`
Implements	Cloneable
Description	Public class. A vector object is similar to an array but is more flexible; a vector automatically grows as new members are needed. You can also call `trimToSize()` to trim a vector when desired, so that it gets rid of excess capacity. Vectors have a wealth of other useful functions for adding, removing, and deleting elements. Vectors have one major limitation in comparison to arrays: elements must be objects and not primitive data. Consequently, types such as `int` must first be converted to a wrapper-class equivalent (in this case, `Integer`). Strings, however, are objects and can be added directly.

The following example creates a vector, adds three elements, and then returns the first element. Note that the return value of `elementAt()` needs to be cast from `Object` to whatever type you're using (in this case, `String`).

```
Vector vec = new Vector();
vec.addElement("Here is a string.");
vec.addElement("'Nuther string.");
vec.addElement("Third string.");
String firstElem = (String) vec.elementAt(0);
```

Constructors

```
public Vector();
public Vector(int initialCapacity);
public Vector(int initialCapacity, int capacityIncrement);
```

You can optionally specify the initial capacity and the amount by which capacity grows each time it is exceeded.

Instance Methods

```
public final void addElement(Object obj);
```

Adds the specified element to the vector.

```
public final int capacity();
```

Returns the current capacity. Remember, this is increased whenever the number of elements exceeds it.

```
public final boolean contains(Object elem);
```

Returns true if the specified object is currently an element of the vector.

```
public final void copyInto(Object anArray[]);
```

Copies the contents of the vector into an array.

```
public final Object elementAt(int index)
    throws ArrayIndexOutOfBoundsException;
```

Returns the element at the specified zero-based index. The return value must usually be cast to a particular type.

```
public final Enumeration elements();
```

Returns the contents of the vector into an enumeration. See Enumeration interface.

```
public final void ensureCapacity(int minCapacity);
```

Ensures that the vector can store at least this number of items.

```
public final Object firstElement()
    throws NoSuchElementException;
```

Returns the first element in the vector. See also elementAt() above and lastElement() (p. 494).

```
public final int indexOf(Object elem);
public final int indexOf(Object elem, int index);
```

Searches the vector for the specified element and returns its zero-based index, optionally starting at a specified index. Returns –1 if the item is not found.

```
public final void insertElementAt(Object obj, int index)
    throws ArrayIndexOutOfBoundsException;
```

Inserts a new element at the specified position (a zero-based index), bumping the elements that follow it up by one index. See also setElementAt() below.

```
public final boolean isEmpty();
```

Returns true if the vector contains no elements.

```
public final Object lastElement()
    throws NoSuchElementException;
```

Returns the last element. See also firstElement() (p. 493) and elementAt() (p. 493).

```
public final int lastIndexOf(Object elem);
public final int lastIndexOf(Object elem, int index);
```

Similar to indexOf() except that the search starts at the back and moves toward the front.

```
public final void removeAllElements();
public final boolean removeElement(Object obj);
public final void removeElementAt(int index)
    throws ArrayIndexOutOfBoundsException;
```

These methods remove the specified element or elements. If an individual element is removed, indexes of elements that follow it are shifted down by one.

```
public final void setElementAt(Object obj, int index)
    throws ArrayIndexOutOfBoundsException;
```

Replaces the specified item with a new value. Indexes are zero-based.

```
public final void setSize(int newSize);
```

Sets a new size. If this is greater than the current size, the method pads the end of the vector with null items. If this is less than the current size, the method deletes items at the end.

```
public final int size();
```

Returns the number of elements.

```
public final void trimToSize();
```

Reduces the capacity of the vector to that of the number of elements. This maximizes storage efficiency.

Overridden Instance Methods

```
public Object clone();
public final String toString();
```

These methods override method definitions in the Object class (p. ___).

ViewportLayout Class

Full Name	javax.swing.ViewportLayout
Extends	Object
Implements	LayoutManager
Description	Public class. This class implements a layout manager that is designed specifically for use with viewports. See JViewport (p. 361) for more information.

Constructors

```
public ViewportLayout();
Instance Methodspublic void addLayoutComponent(String name,
Component c);
public void layoutContainer(Container parent);
```

This method is called automatically to lay out the components in the specified container.

```
public Dimension minimumLayoutSize(Container parent);
public Dimension preferredLayoutSize(Container parent);
```

These methods determine the minimum and preferred layout size of the specified container.

```
public void removeLayoutComponent(Component c);
```

Void Class

Full Name	java.lang.Void
Extends	Object
Description	Public class. This class serves as a standard wrapper for the primitive void type.

Class Variables

```
public static final Class TYPE;
```

This constant is an object representing the primitive void type.

WeakHashMap Class

Full Name	java.util.WeakHashMap
Extends	AbstractMap->Object

Java 2 API Reference

Description   Public class. This class implements a weak hash map, which is
                  a hash map whose entries are automatically removed when
                  their keys are no longer in use.

Constructors

```
public WeakHashMap();
```

Default constructor.

```
public WeakHashMap(Map t);
```

Creates a weak hash map that is initialized with the specified map.

```
public WeakHashMap(int initialCapacity);
public WeakHashMap(int initialCapacity, float loadFactor);
```

Creates a weak hash map with the specified initial capacity and load factor.

Overridden Instance Methods

```
public void clear();
```

Clears the weak hash map.

```
public boolean containsKey(Object key);
```

Checks to see if the map contains a mapping for the specified key.

```
public Set entrySet();
```

Retrieves a set containing the entry mappings for the weak hash map.

```
public Object get(Object key);
```

Retrieves the value associated with the specified key.

```
public boolean isEmpty();
```

Checks to see if the weak hash map is empty.

```
public Object put(Object key, Object value);
```

Adds a key/value mapping to the weak hash map.

```
public Object remove(Object key);
```

Removes the specified key and its associated value from the weak hash map.

```
public int size();
```

Retrieves the number of key/value mappings in the weak hash map.

Window Class

Full Name   java.awt.Window

Extends   `Container->Component->Object`

Description Public class. Although the class can be used directly, its child classes — `Frame` and `Dialog` — are much more commonly used. The `Frame` class adds visible borders and a menu bar and is actually closer to the common notion of window.

Constructors

```
public Window(Frame parent);
```

Creates a window that has a default `BorderLayout` manager.

Instance Methods

```
public synchronized void dispose();
```

Closes the window and releases all its resources. Unlike most Java resources, windows are not automatically destroyed by the garbage collector; this is because windows are maintained by the native window manager. You must explicitly call `dispose()` to remove a window.

```
public final String getWarningString();
```

Returns the warning string that is displayed when there is a `SecurityManager` object and it determines that the current window is insecure.

```
public synchronized void pack();
```

Lays out child components in their preferred size.

```
public void toBack();
public void toFront();
```

These methods move the window to the front or back of the layers of visible windows.

Overridden Instance Methods

```
public synchronized void addNotify();
public Toolkit getToolkit();
public synchronized void setVisible(boolean b);
```

These methods override method definitions in Component. The `setVisible()` method is particularly useful for windows: if passed `true`, it displays the window and moves it to the front of other windows.

WindowAdapter Class

Full Name	`java.awt.event.WindowAdapter`
Extends	`Object`
Implements	`WindowListener`

Description   Public class. A helper class that provides empty implementations of the methods defined in the `WindowListener` interface. This class serves as a convenience by enabling you to extend it and override only the listener response methods that you need, as opposed to implementing all of the methods defined in the interface. After deriving an event-handling class from this one, you need to register it as an event listener.

Here is code that uses the `WindowAdapter` class to shut down an application in response to the frame window closing.

```
class WindowHandler extends WindowAdapter {
  public void windowClosing(WindowEvent e) {
    System.exit(0);
  }
}
```

Constructors

```
public WindowAdapter();
```

Instance Methods

```
public void windowActivated(WindowEvent e);
public void windowClosed(WindowEvent e);
public void windowClosing(WindowEvent e);
public void windowDeactivated(WindowEvent e);
public void windowDeiconified(WindowEvent e);
public void windowIconified(WindowEvent e);
public void windowOpened(WindowEvent e);
```

These methods are called in response to a window being activated, closed, closing (window is about to close), deactivated, de-iconified (restored from icon), iconified (minimized), or opened. These methods implement the `WindowListener` interface.

WindowConstants Interface

Full Name   `javax.swing.WindowConstants`

Description   Public interface. This interface serves as a convenient location to store constants used to control the closing of windows. These constants are used by the `getDefaultClose Operation()` and `setDefaultCloseOperation()` methods of the `JFrame` and `JDialog` classes.

Interface Constants

```
public static final int DISPOSE_ON_CLOSE;
public static final int DO_NOTHING_ON_CLOSE;
public static final int HIDE_ON_CLOSE;
```

These constants are used by the JFrame and JDialog classes to control the closing of windows.

WindowEvent Class

Full Name	java.awt.event.WindowEvent
Extends	ComponentEvent->AWTEvent->EventObject->Object
Description	Public class. This class encapsulates the information associated with a window event. Window events are generated by window event sources and handled by objects that implement the WindowListener interface. An instance of the Window Event class is delivered to the window listener event response methods to aid in handling window events.

Java 2 API Reference

Constructors

```
public WindowEvent(Window source, int id);
```

The source argument is the object with which the window event is associated, and id is an identifier that identifies the event.

Class Variables

```
public static final int WINDOW_ACTIVATED;
public static final int WINDOW_CLOSED;
public static final int WINDOW_CLOSING;
public static final int WINDOW_DEACTIVATED;
public static final int WINDOW_DEICONIFIED;
public static final int WINDOW_ICONIFIED;
public static final int WINDOW_FIRST;
public static final int WINDOW_LAST;
public static final int WINDOW_OPENED;
```

Class constants. These constants are flags used to describe the specific type of window event.

Instance Methods

```
public Window getWindow();
```

This method retrieves the window associated with the event.

Overridden Instance Methods

```
public String paramString();
```

This method generates a parameter string that identifies the window event.

WindowListener Interface

Full Name   java.awt.event.WindowListener

Description   Public interface. This interface defines methods that respond to window events. Window events are generated when a window is opened, closing, closed, iconified (minimized), de-iconified (restored), activated, or deactivated. To handle window events, you can implement the WindowListener interface, provide implementations of window event response methods, and then register the listener class with an event source. Alternatively, you can extend the WindowAdaptor class and override only the component event response methods in which you are interested.

Interface Methods

```
public void windowActivated(WindowEvent e);
public void windowClosed(WindowEvent e);
public void windowClosing(WindowEvent e);
public void windowDeactivated(WindowEvent e);
public void windowDeiconified(WindowEvent e);
public void windowIconified(WindowEvent e);
public void windowOpened(WindowEvent e);
```

These methods are called in response to a window being activated, closed, closing (window is about to close), deactivated, de-iconified (restored from icon), iconified (minimized), or opened.

A Java Programming Tutorial

This part provides an introduction to programming using the Java language. It begins by introducing you to Java applets and applications, the two major types of Java programs. From there, you learn about the major building blocks of the Java programming language, along with some of the many features built into the Java 2 API. Some highlights of this part of the book include a close look at the new Swing graphical user interface toolkit that was added in Java 2 (Chapter 5), as well as an introduction to the popular JavaBeans technology (Chapter 7). This part of the book also includes coverage of Java 2 event handling, animation, and many other facets of Java development.

IN THIS PART

Chapter 1 Applets and Oranges

Chapter 2 Java Building Blocks

Chapter 3 Fun with Graphics

Chapter 4 Components and Events

Chapter 5 Moving to Swing

Chapter 6 Animation and Threads

Chapter 7 Working with JavaBeans

Chapter 8 Common Programming Tasks

Applets and Oranges

Before you can develop programs with Java, you need to understand some basic procedures. This chapter shows you how to produce the two major kinds of Java programs: applets and applications.

A Java *applet* is a program embedded inside a Web page. When the Web page is viewed, the applet is automatically and transparently downloaded across the Internet along with other contents of a page, including text and graphics. The applet is then executed by the browser within the context of the Web page. The applet serves as the interactive, intelligent part of the page, and requires a Java-compliant Web browser in order to function. (While a Java-compliant browser supports the execution of applets, it is possible for the user to disable Java support for security purposes.) Java's most popular use to date is to create applets.

A Java *application* is more or less the same kind of beast with which you are familiar if you've programmed in other languages. It runs directly on a local machine, be it a client or server. Unlike applets, which typically execute within a Web page, Java applications have relatively few restrictions and can perform all the basic functions that are performable in most other languages. Java is a good, general-purpose programming language. And Java's built-in application programming interface (API) makes it easy to write applications that can establish network connections, write to the disk, or display information.

● **CROSS-REFERENCE**

In spite of the chapter title, you can't really use Java to create oranges, although you can color things orange if you like. More about that in Chapter 3, "Fun with Graphics," page 539.

Ultimately, you may find applets more interesting due to their relationship with Web pages, but we begin by examining applications, because they are closer to the traditional model of software development.

Preparing to Run Java

If you haven't done so already, then you should install the Java Software Development Kit (Java SDK). The Java SDK contains all the executables you need to create applications and applets as well as all the Java standard classes and helpful utilities such as appletviewer, which enables you to view applets quickly and easily. You can download the Java SDK from Sun Microsystems' Java Web site: `ftp://java.sun.com/`

● **CROSS-REFERENCE**

To learn more about classes, see the section "What Are Classes and Methods?" (p. 511) later in this chapter. For now, however, you may prefer to just enter and run some programs.

Downloading from the Sun Microsystems site provides a current version. You can use the Java SDK free of charge. As of this writing, the latest release of the Java SDK is 1.3, even though the platform is still known as Java 2.

● **NOTE**

You can download the Java SDK for free from the JavaSoft Web site at `http://java.sun.com`. The download can be carried out as one large file that is approximately 30MB in size, or as a series of smaller files.

Any text editor can be used to write Java programs. Java does not require the use of an integrated development environment, although some are available (such as Microsoft's Visual J++).

Applications: Remember the main

A simple Java application uses main( ) as a point of entry, just as with C and C++ applications. The following application prints the text "Hello Java!" followed by a blank line. As with all applications, you run it directly on your local computer.

```
class HelloJava {
  public static void main(String args[]) {
    System.out.println("Hello Java!");
  }
}
```

If you enter this program into a file yourself, be sure that you name it using the .java extension. In building Java programs, it is usually easiest to give the source file the same base name as the class containing main( ), for example, HelloJava.java.

Compiling and running the application

After entering the source code in the file HelloJava.java, compile the application using this command:

```
javac HelloJava.java
```

If this command is successful, the Java compiler (javac.exe) produces a class file, HelloJava.class. If the compile was unsuccessful, go back and make sure you entered the program correctly.

HelloJava.class represents the program in an intermediate binary form. You can now run the program, but only with the aid of the Java interpreter (java.exe):

```
java HelloJava
```

Anytime that you want to run the program, enter the preceding code. Of course, if you change the program you must recompile it.

Figure 1-1 summarizes the Java development process for applications.

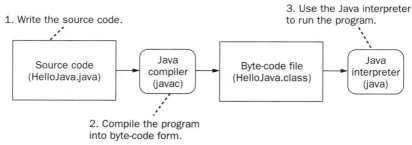

Figure 1-1   *Developing and running Java applications*

Understanding the code

The first thing you should notice about the application is that all the
code is contained inside a class declaration. Almost all statements in all
Java programs must appear inside classes. The first line starts the declaration of the class HelloJava, which gives its name to the program:

```
class HelloJava {
   ...
}
```

The class contains a declaration of a single method, main(). A
method is the same as a function except that it's defined inside a class
and often operates on an object. For now (until we discuss objects),
think of a method as another kind of function. The three middle
lines define the method, main():

```
public static void main(String args[]) {
   System.out.println("Hello Java!");
}
```

As in C and C++, the main keyword has a special meaning: it's
the program entry point. When you execute the application, the Java
interpreter looks for a method with the signature public static
void main(). The attributes may seem arbitrary (static and void are
actually quite meaningful), but for now, you should just remember
to use them.

The statement inside the method does all the work of the application. This statement calls the println() method of the System.out
object. This method call looks similar to a function call, but println()
cannot be called directly. Figure 1-2 shows a syntactical analysis of
this statement.

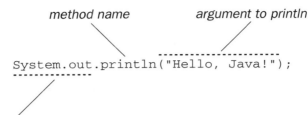

Figure 1-2 *Analysis of a call to println*

There are several differences between the Java and the C++ ways of coding within the example. For example:

- Unlike C++, Java considers main() a method and not a function, so main () must be given exactly the attributes shown. As with all methods, main() must be defined entirely inside the class. Java does not use prototypes.

- In Java, the arguments to main() have type String and not C++'s char*. As you might expect, arguments to main() are command-line arguments. String is a special class defined in the Java language. String, rather than arrays of char, is used for most string handling.

- The call to println() uses both a class and an object reference. The context operator (::)is not used in Java. Instead, Java uses dot syntax (.) for class references as well as object references. In C++, the call is written as System::out.println().

- Unlike C++, Java doesn't terminate the class declaration with a semicolon (;). Java's syntax is simpler in this respect. Semicolons are used only to terminate individual statements. You never use them after a closing brace (}).

Summary: Application syntax

In general, the simplest applications have the following syntax:

```
class program_name {
  public static void main(String args[]) {
    statements
  }
}
```

In the preceding code, substitute the name of your own program for *program_name*. You can use any name you want for *args*, although args works fine.

●—**CROSS-REFERENCE**————————————————

For the use of this argument, see "main() Method," in Part I, "Java 2 Language Reference," page 67.

Any number of other methods can be defined as long as they are placed inside the class declaration. (Remember that methods are the Java version of functions.) A more complete syntax is as follows:

```
class program_name {
  variable_declarations

  public static void main(String args[]) {
    statements
  }

  static return_type method_name(argument_list) {
    statements
  }

  ...
}
```

In Chapter 2 (see p. 523), I discuss how and why to use Java to create more than one class. Similar to a structure type in C/C++, classes can define data fields. They can also declare functions, which are called *methods*.

In the meantime, you can experiment by adding more statements to this simple application. For example, here is a variation on the sample application that uses several statements:

```
class HelloJava {
  public static void main(String args[]) {
    System.out.println("This is an example of");
    System.out.println("a program that prints");
    System.out.println("several lines.");
  }
}
```

What are Classes and Methods?

1

This book talks a lot about classes. If you have a background in C++ or any other object-oriented programming language, you may be comfortable with this concept. Even if you have programmed in C++, you'll notice that in Java, classes take on an expanded role.

In Java, classes are the basic unit of program organization. With few exceptions, you can say that *a Java program is a collection of classes*. The simplest programs contain a class with the same name as the program and a method called main() within that class. (More about methods in a moment.) In this case, a single class holds all the program code.

Why write more than one class? Because classes in Java can perform many roles. For example, a class can:

- Create a new data type, complete with its own methods and data fields. Each instance of the type is an object. This is generally how classes are used in C++, and you'll learn how to do this in Chapter 2.

- Create a collection of static functions, which can be called without reference to an object. For example, the Java library puts useful math functions into a class.

- Create a collection of useful constants.

In short, then, a class is the fundamental unit of program organization. For convenience, classes can be grouped into larger units called *packages*, which can span multiple source files. (A class, in contrast, must be declared entirely inside a single source file.) Don't worry about packages yet; the next chapter explains them in detail.

This book also talks a lot about *methods*. A function defined inside a class is a method. In C++, these are called member functions. In Java, *all* functions must be methods; that is, each must be defined inside some class.

Applets: Getting into a Web Page

Applets are not necessarily harder to write than applications, but they require a different structure. Remember that applets are programs that run inside a Web page rather than directly on a local computer. Here is a simple applet:

```
public class HelloApplet extends java.applet.Applet {
    public void paint(java.awt.Graphics g) {
```

```
        g.drawString("Hello Java!", 5, 20);
    }
}
```

If you enter this program and save it as a file, name it HelloApplet.java. The base name of the file *must* match the name of the class (HelloApplet). If you use a filename other than HelloApplet.java, make sure that the filename changes as well. The reason the names must match is that HelloApplet is a public class, which means the class is available for use by other classes.

Compiling and running the applet

After entering the applet source code, run the Java compiler on the source file just as you would for an application:

```
javac HelloApplet.java
```

If this command is successful, the Java compiler (javac.exe) produces the applet's class file, HelloApplet.class. If the compile was unsuccessful, go back and make sure you entered the program exactly.

The file HelloApplet.class represents the applet in intermediate binary form. The next step is to place the applet in a Web page, which may be a very simple page. The <applet> tag in the HTML file creates the link to the applet and sets the size of the applet's display area.

To create a Web page for the applet, enter the following code in a text file and name the file HelloApplet.html.

```
<html>
<head>
</title>Hello Applet</title>
</head>

<body>
Here is an applet.
<p>
<applet code="HelloApplet.class" width="400" height="400">
</applet>
</body>
</html>
```

Most of the commands in this file are fairly standard. In fact, you can reuse the same HTML code for other applets. The critical line, the only one that must change, is the <applet> tag. In the following code, you can substitute the name of another applet for HelloApplet.

```
<applet code="HelloApplet.class" width="400" height="400">
```

To view the applet, open the HTML file in a Web browser. The Web browser reads the HTML and responds by loading and running the applet. When the browser reads the <applet> tag, it displays the applet within a region of the browser window whose size is determined by the <applet> tag.

When developing applets, it's convenient to use the applet viewer utility provided by the Java SDK. This utility cannot be used to browse the Web, but it can read HTML files and display applets available on the local computer. The appletviewer serves as a handy alternative to using a Web browser when testing applets. The appletviewer takes a single argument — the HTML file:

```
Appletviewer HelloApplet.html
```

●—NOTE———————————————————————————————————————

When you first attempt to use the appletviewer utility, it displays a copyright message and requires your acceptance. You must click OK to proceed, and unless you have a large monitor, it may be difficult to see the OK button. Scroll the appletviewer window, if necessary, until you can see the button.

Figure 1-3 summarizes the applet development process.

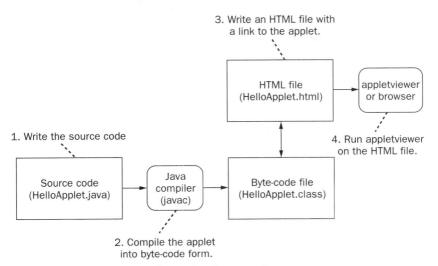

Figure 1-3 *Developing and running Java applets*

Understanding the code

As with applications, all the code in an applet is contained inside a class declaration. This class declaration is a little more complex for applets:

```
public class HelloApplet extends java.applet.Applet {
   ...
}
```

The applet class declaration uses the extends keyword to indicate that the applet class HelloApplet inherits from java.applet.Applet, which is a class defined in the Java API. This class provides a series of built-in capabilities. When a class inherits from another class, it gains all of the parent class's members, including variables and methods. Therefore, HelloApplet takes on attributes of the generic java.applet.Applet class but can add its own code, to create a specific applet.

●—CROSS-REFERENCE————————————————————

To find out more about inheritance, see the section "Background: Inheritance" on page 563 of Chapter 4.

The java.applet.Applet class provides a special method, paint(), that tells Java how to repaint the screen. It doesn't repaint the whole screen, but only that portion assigned to the applet. The class HelloApplet overrides the paint() method and provides its own, custom version of this method:

```
public void paint(java.awt.Graphics g) {
   g.drawString("Hello Java!", 5, 20);
}
```

When the Java interpreter needs to repaint the applet for any reason, it calls the applet's paint() method and passes a graphics object (g). This object provides access to the display area. Although it's similar to a display context in Windows programming, it is easier to use. You can use the graphics object to call graphics methods such as drawString(). The arguments to drawString() are the string to be printed ("Hello, Java!") followed by the x and y coordinates at which to place the top-left corner of the string. These coordinates are in pixels.

You must override the paint() method in order to draw graphics that are specific to your applet. If you do not override the paint() method, the applet uses the default implementation of paint(), which does nothing. You can override a number of useful methods for the applet, including `init()`, which performs initialization, and `start()`, which is called to start the applet running. (You might override the latter if the applet makes use of threads, which allow you to have several subprograms running at once.) You can override as many or as few of these predefined applet methods as you need.

Unlike applications, applets don't have a `main()` method. An applet is loaded and executed by a program already running — the Web browser. The browser starts the applet by loading a class that inherits from `java.applet.Applet`, as explained earlier, and then calling its `init()` method. In this case, that class is `HelloApplet`.

One last difference between applets and applications is security; applets are required by default to conform to a very stringent security model that limits them in a variety of ways, whereas applications have no security limitations. Until Java 1.1, this distinction between applets and applications was significant because applets had no way to dodge the security limitations. However, Java 1.1 ushered in digital security signatures, which allow applets to be digitally signed and therefore deemed safe. Digitally signed applets are also referred to as *trusted applets*. The stringent applet security model is not applied to digitally signed applets, meaning that these applets have the capability to do things applets of the past could not do, such as writing files.

There are several differences between the Java and the C++ ways of coding within the example. For example:

- The expressions `java.applet.Applet` and `java.awt.Graphics` are examples of classes referred to through their packages — `java.applet` and `java.awt`. There is nothing exactly like packages in C or C++, but their use here is somewhat like namespaces in ANSI C++. The next chapter provides much more information about packages, including how to get rid of the package qualifiers in class names.

- The classes themselves are `Applet` and `Graphics`. By convention, only class names have initial capital letters. This makes it easier to determine parts of the language at a glance. Any name preceding a class name must be a package name, which typically aren't capitalized. Packages are used to organize groups of classes.

●—CROSS-REFERENCE

To find out more about packages, see "package Statement" in Part I, "Java 2 Language Reference," page 79.

- Both the class `HelloApplet` and the `paint()` method must be declared public. Java supports `public`, `private`, and `protected` for methods and variables, but only `public` for classes. (Other modifiers are supported: see "Classes" (p. 34), "Methods" (p. 69), and "Variables" (p. 99) in Part I, "Java 2 Language Reference.")

- Unlike C++, Java has no terminating semicolon (`;`) at the end of the class declaration.

Summary: Applet syntax

Applets can be much more elaborate than the following examples, but the syntax summary provides an idea of what to expect in every applet, including the simplest ones:

```
public class applet_name extends java.applet.Applet {
  public void paint(java.awt.Graphics g) {
    statements
  }

  [ public void init( ) {
    statements
  } ]

  [other_methods]
}
```

Here, the brackets indicate optional items. In addition to `paint()` and `init()`, you can define a number of methods that have special meaning inside an applet. For example, some methods are called in response to an event such as a mouse click.

How Java Works on Multiple Platforms

It may seem inconvenient that Java requires both a compiler and an interpreter. However, this is one of the things that make Java platform-independent. The compiled form of a program is a bytecode file; bytecodes consists of binary instructions for a hypothetical processor. Each platform (Windows, Mac, UNIX, etc.) has its own Java interpreters (such as java.exe, Web browsers, and appletviewer) that decode the instructions for the local system. An interpreter works by reading a bytecode instruction, carrying out an action immediately, and then reading the next instruction.

The same bytecode files can be executed on all Java-compatible platforms because each platform has its own interpreter (see Figure 1-4). Each interpreter carries out instructions as appropriate for its platform. At the same time, the intent of Java's designers was to make behavior across all platforms as consistent as possible. This is one reason that many of Java's features are implemented at a fairly high level of abstraction.

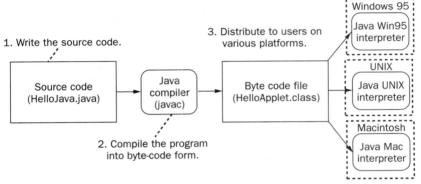

Figure 1-4 *Java program running on multiple platforms.*

in plain english in p
sh in plain english i
glish in plain englis
in plain english in p
sh in plain english i
glish in plain englis
in plain english in p
glish in plain englis
in plain english in p
sh in plain english i
glish in plain englis
in plain english in p
sh in plain english i
glish in plain englis
in plain english in p
lish in plain englis
in plain english in p
sh in plain english i
glish in plain englis
in plain english in p
sh in plain english i
lish in plain englis
in plain english in p
lish in plain englis

Java Building Blocks

Java's program structure is not exactly like that of any other programming language. Java has a unique architecture that organizes programs into packages, classes, and objects. These terms have specific technical meanings in Java. Java also has a special feature called interfaces, which is discussed in Chapter 5.

Because the general concept of a Java class is close to the C++ concept of class, if you have a background in C++, you're ahead of the game. However, classes are even more important in Java because all method definitions and variables must be placed inside classes. Nothing is global!

Doing More with Classes

Chapter 1 (page 511) introduced a simple class used in an application. Interestingly, the entire program consisted of just this class declaration:

```
class HelloJava {
  public static void main(String args[]) {
    System.out.println("Hello Java!");
  }
}
```

Here, the class declaration consists of a single method, called main(). However, classes can consist of any number of two basic kinds of class members, which are called *fields*:

- Variables
- Methods

Remember that methods are the Java equivalent of functions. The following program demonstrates the use of a variable and several methods. Note that double is the Java double-precision floating-point type.

```
class PrintTemps {
  static double fahr;

  public static void main(String args[]) {
    System.out.println("Here is a Fahr/Cent table.");
    printValues();
  }

  static void printValues() {
    for (fahr = 0.0; fahr <= 100.0; fahr += 10.0) {
      System.out.print(fahr);
      System.out.print('\t');
      System.out.println(convert(fahr));
    }
  }

  static double convert(double f) {
    return (f - 32.0) / 1.8;
  }
}
```

The fahr variable and all of the methods defined in this program are declared static. In Java, static variables and methods are the simplest kinds of items to declare. When a variable is static, there is only one copy of it in the program. In the next section, you'll learn about non-static variables, which are data fields of an object. A non-static variable does not just appear once; each object of the class has its own copy of the variable. (Non-static methods are similar; they act on individual objects.) For now, just remember that until you start creating objects, every variable and method you declare must be static — starting with main( ), the entry point of an application.

There's another consequence of static: static methods can refer only to fields of the class that are also static. This is why the variable, fahr, and the other two methods — printValues( ) and convert( ) — must be declared with the static keyword. The sequence of the program is as follows:

1. The program entry point, main( ), gets called first.
2. main( ) calls the functions printValue( ) and convert( ). Because main( ) is static, the other methods must also be static, or main( ) cannot call them.

Given this catch-22, how do nonstatic methods ever get called? Simple: the restriction against using nonstatic fields is lifted when main( ) uses fields of other classes. For example, the print( ) and println( ) methods (discussed in the next section) are nonstatic and belong to an object.

●—NOTE

For the most part, the use of static in Java is identical to its use in C++. However, static can't be used with global functions, because Java does not support global functions.

The print statements in this example point out some useful features of Java. First, the System.out object supports both print( ) and println( ); the difference between these two methods is that after println( ), Java prints a new line. Pascal programmers should feel right at home seeing these two old friends. The System.out object, incidentally, is an instance of the standard Java PrintStream class, which is where you'll find these methods declared.

In C++ terms, print( ) and println( ) are overloaded methods. This means that they can take a variety of arguments. You can give print( ) or println( ) an argument having any of Java's primitive types such as int and float:

```
System.out.print(fahr);
System.out.print('\t');
System.out.println(convert(fahr));
```

The expression '\t' is a special character representing a tab.

The rest of the example is straightforward if you know C or C++. If not, the `for` statement probably looks new to you. Look up the topic "for Statement" in Part I, p. 53, for more information. The addition-increment operator is also used here (`fahr += 10.0`). This is shorthand for the following:

```
fahr = fahr + 10.0
```

A Class that Creates Objects

In all but the most trivial programs, you'll probably have a number of different classes. A Java program is essentially a collection of classes.

So far, classes have been used as the basis for Java programs. In Java, it is the name of the class, and not the name of the source file, that determines the program name. To use the program in the preceding section as an example, you could put the code in a file named `myfile.java` and then compile the code by using this filename as follows:

```
javac myfile.java
```

But you do not necessarily run the program by entering the file name. To run the program, you feed the name of the class containing `main()` to the Java interpreter. If you glance back at the example, you'll see that this class name is `PrintTemps`. In fact, the executable file created by the previous compile command is `PrintTemps.class`, not `myfile.class`. Therefore, the following command runs the program, no matter what the name of the source file is:

```
java PrintTemps
```

As was suggested in Chapter 1 (see p. 511), it simplifies things to give the file and the class the same name. Applets require giving the file and the class the same name because the applet class is public. In fact, the file name and class name must match for all public classes.

Therefore, one use for classes is to represent a main program (applet or application). Another use for classes, and probably the use most familiar to C++ programmers, is to create a new data type. Classes are very much like structures in C, records in Pascal, and user-defined types in Visual Basic. The big difference — and what makes Java object-oriented — is that you can give classes built-in functions, which are more appropriately referred to as methods.

Creating data types

The following example uses classes two ways. One class represents the main program (TestFractions), and the other class creates a composite data type (Fraction).

```java
class TestFractions {
  public static void main(String args[]) {
    Fraction fract1 = new Fraction();
    Fraction fract2 = new Fraction();
    fract1.setValues(5, 8);
    fract2.setValues(7, 11);
    if (fract1.compare(fract2) > 0)
      System.out.println("5/8 is > 7/11");
    else
      System.out.println("5/8 is not > 7/11");
  }
}

class Fraction {
  int numerator, denominator;

  void setValues(int n, int d) {
    numerator = n;
    denominator = d;
  }

  int compare(Fraction otherFract) {
    int us = numerator * otherFract.denominator;
    int them = denominator * otherFract.numerator;

    if (us > them)
      return 1;
    else if (us == them)
      return 0;
    return -1;
  }
}
```

This is the first example that deals explicitly with objects. Objects provide a lot to digest, so I've kept it simple. The central feature of this example is that it introduces a new type of your own creation, Fraction. The purpose of most classes is just that: to define a new type. The type can be composed of any combination of other types, including boolean; char; byte; short; int; long; float; and double. In this case, Fraction is a type made up of two integers named numerator and denominator (see Figure 2-1). There are also two methods — setValues and compare — that help you manipulate the objects.

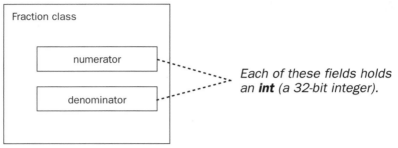

Figure 2-1 *Structure of the Fraction class*

The first thing that main() does is to create two objects of the Fraction type:

```
Fraction fract1 = new Fraction();
Fraction fract2 = new Fraction();
```

In Java, creating an object is generally a two-step process. You define an object variable (in this case, fract1) and then use the new operator to allocate an object in memory. Note that this step is not required when you create a variable of a primitive (built-in) type, such as int or double. The creation of fract1 and the Fraction object could have been done in two separate lines:

```
Fraction fract1;
fract1 = new Fraction();
```

However, Java is very liberal about initialization of variables. You can combine these two statements into one, creating both the variable (fract1) and the object to which it refers:

```
Fraction fract1 = new Fraction();
```

The rest of the example calls methods through the two objects fract1 and fract2. If you're not familiar with objects and methods, keep on reading. Otherwise, you can skip the section titled "Background: Object Orientation."

Allocating objects

If you're a C++ programmer, you may have noticed that there is no use of a delete operator, free() function, or other memory cleanup mechanism in the source code. This is not a careless omission: Java does not have a delete operator or similar such functionality.

Instead, all unused objects in memory are intelligently cleaned up by the Java garbage collector, which runs as a background thread. You can forget about freeing memory, knowing that the Java interpreter will take care of this programming issue for you. Life is easy!

●─NOTE

In C++, you never need to allocate object variables and objects separately. In other words, C++ lets you create objects the obvious way:

```
Fraction fract1, fract2;
```

In Java, an object variable such as `fract1` or `fract2` is only a reference; this means that before `fract1` or `fract2` can be used, it must first be associated with actual objects. The new operator creates the objects. Another difference illustrated in this example is that the `main()` function can freely refer to fields of the `Fraction` class. Unlike C++, fields of Java classes are not private by default.

Background: Object Orientation

The preceding section introduced objects and object-oriented programming. The basic idea of object orientation is simple: programs designed around data structures. The individual instances of user-defined data types (classes) are called objects.

●─NOTE

Java, unlike C++, does not consider instances of primitive data—such as `int` or `double`—to be objects. The distinction is important, because only objects, but not primitive data, require the use of the new operator in order for creation to occur.

The first hurdle in understanding object orientation is to be clear on the difference between classes and objects. The relationship is roughly the same as that of a data type to specific values. For example, the `Fraction` class defines a type with two integer fields: numerator and denominator. `Fraction` is the class, while the variables `fract1` and `fract2` in the `TestFractions` application class refer to individual objects of the `Fraction` class. `Fraction` defines the data fields, but `fract1` and `fract2` hold specific values for those fields (see Figure 2-2).

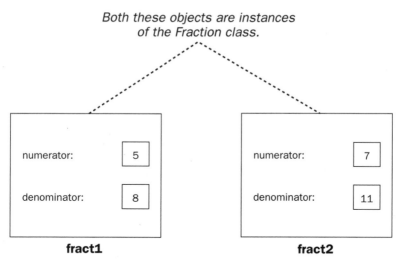

Both these objects are instances
of the Fraction class.

| numerator: | 5 | | numerator: | 7 |
| denominator: | 8 | | denominator: | 11 |

fract1   **fract2**

Figure 2-2   *Objects of the Fraction class*

Manipulating objects with methods

In Java, even function code is organized around classes and objects. The function code, of course, is made up of methods. Generally, a method provides a way of communicating with, or manipulating objects of, a particular class. The Fraction methods, for example, let you manipulate Fraction objects.

Here's the definition for setValues(), a simple method of the Fraction class:

```
void setValues(int n, int d) {
   numerator = n;
   denominator = d;
}
```

As a Fraction method, this method can be applied to instances (objects) of the Fraction class, such as fract1. The method can be called by using the following syntax:

```
fract1.setValues(5, 8);
```

Because setValues() is called through the object fract1, this statement has the effect of setting values in fract1. When the method adjusts the values of numerator and denominator, it is fract1's fields, and not those of another object, that get set. In contrast, the next statement sets the values of fract2's fields:

```
fract2.setValues(7, 11);
```

When you make the call `fract1.setValues()`, Java assumes that the variable names in the `setValues()` definition — `numerator` and `denominator` — are fields of `fract1`. When you call the method through `fract2`, it's assumed they're fields of `fract2`.

This should be clear, but one point is easy to miss: although the methods operate on objects, they are declared in the class. The objects `fract1` and `fract2` respond in similar ways to `setValues()`, because they belong to the same class. Another class might implement `setValues()` in a different way.

The bottom line is that individual objects have their own data values, but they share the same code. Figure 2-3 illustrates this idea; `fract1` and `fract2` have their own data but share the methods defined for the `Fraction` class.

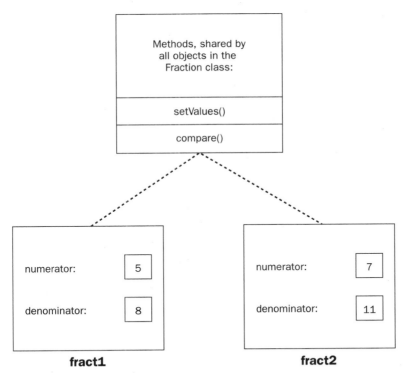

Figure 2-3 *Code and data in the Fraction class*

Thus, a class is essentially a structure definition that, optionally, can have methods. The methods provide built-in functionality for objects of the class. You can use the methods to manipulate and communicate with the objects.

But how is a method different from a C function? The most significant differences are:

- Method definition code can make unqualified references to variables in the same class. For example, you can use numerator rather than *object*.numerator:

```
myFract.numerator     // Qualified (valid anywhere)
numerator             // Unqualified (valid in Fraction
class)
```

●─NOTE─────────────────────────────────────

This last example uses the line-comment symbol (//), which indicates that the rest of the line is a comment. This is the same comment symbol used in C++.

- When you call a method, references to unqualified variables are considered fields of the current object (the object through which the call was made). This is significant, because the method can refer to any field of the current object, even fields declared private.
- Method definition code can make unqualified references to other methods of the same class, even those declared private.

●─NOTE─────────────────────────────────────

The previous discussion does not apply to static variables and methods. Static methods are limited to referring only to static variables of the class.

Using constructors

The purpose of the setValues() method is to set initial values for the two variables numerator and denominator. It's more efficient to do this with a *constructor*, which is a method that is automatically called when a new object is created. Java constructors follow almost exactly the same rules that C++ constructors follow. A Java constructor has the same name as the class itself, but it has no return type (not even void). You can write any number of constructors as long as they have different argument lists. For example:

```
class Fraction {
    int numerator, denominator;

    // Constructors
    Fraction() {
```

```
    numerator = denominator = 0;
  }

  Fraction(int n, int d) {
    numerator = n;
    denominator = d;
  }
```

2

...

With the `Fraction(int, int)` constructor defined, the `main()`
method in the `TestFractions` class can declare, allocate, and initialize
the two `Fraction` objects all at once:

```
class TestFractions {
  public static void main(String args[]) {
    Fraction fract1 = new Fraction(5, 8);
    Fraction fract2 = new Fraction(7, 11);
```

...

The arguments to the expression new `Fraction()` determine
which constructor gets called. In this case, the constructor called is
the one that takes two integer arguments.

Program Organization and Packages

A Java program is basically a collection of classes. Each class that is
compiled gets placed in its own class file. But how do you organize
these classes?

Any class that has a properly declared `main()` method can serve as
a program entry point. That class can then refer to any other class in
the current directory (or in a directory searched by Java). This gives
Java a freewheeling, open-ended structure as compared to C and C++,
which do not have such a structure. Some of the differences between
Java and C/C++ are:

- Java doesn't require anything special to make classes in one file
  available to another file. The only consideration is that if one
  file is dependent on class declarations in another file, then the
  other file must exist in either compiled or source-code form at
  compile time, and the class must be declared as `public`. (Thus,
  if you do things in the right order, even mutual cross-references
  between source files are not a problem.)

- Within any given source file, Java classes can be declared in any order. Methods can also be defined in any order, regardless of how they cross-reference each other.

- Consequently, Java has no concept of prototypes, external declarations, or header files. Forward references to classes and methods are not a problem.

- All the fields of a Java class are accessible to other classes except for fields that are specifically declared private. (This is automatically true only if the classes are in the same package, a fact to which I'll return after introducing the concept of packages in the next section.)

The only problem with this rule of classes having automatic access to each other is that you can accumulate many classes. This arrangement is fine until you have so many classes that you run out of names. The obvious solution is to create a different directory for each software project, so that you can reuse the same names in different projects without conflict.

But sometimes you may develop classes that you want to make available to all your projects. In fact, as an object-oriented language, Java encourages this kind of reuse. To help facilitate the development of class libraries, Java provides a feature called the *package*. Class names in a package do not conflict with those in another package, because each package creates its own namespace.

How packages work

Classes are always stored in individual files, regardless of packages, but all the members of a package are stored in the same subdirectory. The use of packages also changes the rules by which classes can refer to each other. In effect, packages provide an extra layer of encapsulation, because not all classes in a package are visible to code outside the package.

To place a source file in a package, you place a `package` statement at the beginning of the file. This statement, if included, must be the first statement in the file.

```
package package_name;
```

The `package_name` must be the same as the name of the subdirectory in which the class file is to be placed. The name can contain embedded dots (`.`), as explained in the next section, to show that it is in a nested subdirectory.

Being placed in a package has these effects on a class:

- Other classes in the same package can refer to the class, even if they're declared in another file. This is standard behavior.

- However, a class can be referenced from outside the package only if the class is declared `public`. Public classes have special restrictions: there can be no more than one public class in any given source file, and it must have the same name as the base name of the source file.

Most classes in the Java API are public; otherwise, you could not use them in your own code. Everything in the API is organized into packages.

Figure 2-4 illustrates the effect of the package statement on three source files. Note that the package name, `cars`, is the same as the name of the subdirectory containing the package. This is required. Figure 2-4 uses arrows to show how classes in this example are able to access other classes.

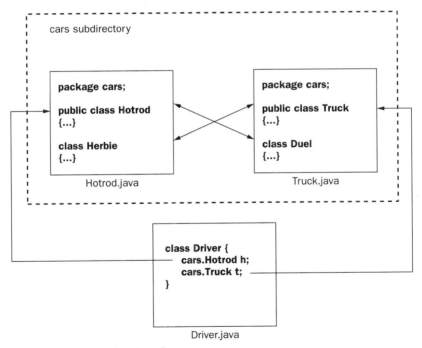

Figure 2-4 *Example of package use*

Two files — Hotrod.java and Truck.java — are placed in the cars package. Because they are in the same package, all the classes in these files (Hotrod, Herbie, Truck, Duel) can refer to one another. The class Driver is defined in Driver.java and is not part of the cars package. Therefore, Driver can refer only to the package's public classes: Hotrod and Truck. These class names must match the names of their respective source files, because they are public classes.

There is another consideration to remember when writing your own packages: Because a class is public does not mean that its fields are accessible outside the package. The default access level for all fields (both variables and methods) is to be accessible within the current package but not from outside. If a class is public, then declaring a field public makes the field accessible outside the package as well. If the class is not public, declaring the field public has no effect. See the topic "public Keyword" in Part I, p. 83, for more information.

The four vital points to remember are:

- The package name must be the same as the name of subdirectory containing the class.
- Only public classes are available to code outside the package.
- The name of a public class must be the same as the base name of the source file.
- A field is not visible outside its package unless both the class and that field are declared public.

Packages and directory structure

In Java, some package names have embedded dots (.) to separate parts of the name. Such a name indicates that the classes in the package are to be found several levels down in the package hierarchy. For example, consider this package name:

```
package briano.util.tools;
```

Because this name has three parts (briano, util, and tools), the package is to be found three levels down in the package system. Figure 2-5 illustrates the relationship of the name to the package structure, and how it parallels the directory structure of a file system. The first subdirectory (in this case, briano) must be located under a directory that the Java interpreter would normally search; by default, it will search the current directory, although you can use the CLASSPATH variable to have the interpreter search other directories, as explained in the next section. The rest of the package name traces a path through the directories.

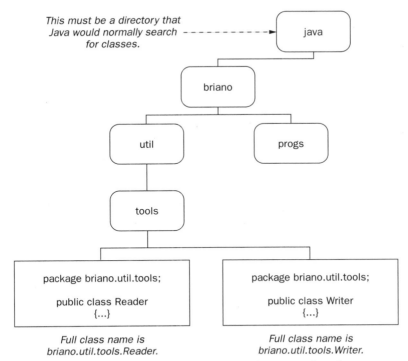

This must be a directory that Java would normally search for classes. ----------▶ java

briano

util   progs

tools

package briano.util.tools;

public class Reader
{...}

package briano.util.tools;

public class Writer
{...}

Full class name is briano.util.tools.Reader.

Full class name is briano.util.tools.Writer.

Figure 2-5 *Directory structure for package briano.util.tools*

Inside the source files for the classes themselves, the package statement must spell out the entire package name — in this case, briano.util.tools.

When using the Java API, the standard packages have names such as java.awt.image and java.awt.peer, even though there is probably no java\awt\image or java\awt\peer subdirectory on your computer. However, when the Java SDK interpreter runs a program, it looks in the \java\lib directory (actually the \lib directory under the Java home directory) to find the file classes.zip. When unzipped, this file contains the complete directory structure for the API as well as all the API classes. You should not attempt to unzip this file yourself since the Java interpreter is designed to access the files from within the classes.zip ZIP file.

How Java searches for classes and packages

There are a number of Java utilities that search for class files, including the Java compiler and the Java interpreters. In every case, Java searches for class files as follows:

1. If the CLASSPATH environment variable is set, Java searches all directories listed in this environment variable, in the order listed, as well as ZIP and JAR files in the directories.

2. Otherwise, Java searches the current directory.

If the class is part of a package, Java uses the package name to look for a subdirectory under one of the directories it would normally search for classes. For example, assume that on a Windows 2000 system the CLASSPATH environment variable is set to this:

    CLASSPATH=C:\mystuff;C:\java\packages

Java could resolve a reference to class mathpack.Trig by finding the file in either of these locations:

    C:\mystuff\mathpack\Trig.class
    C:\java\packages\mathpack\Trig.class

In setting CLASSPATH, it is a good idea to use the current-directory symbol (.) so that Java always searches the current directory first. Doing so preserves Java's default search behavior.

    CLASSPATH=.;C:\mystuff;C:\java\packages

Regardless of how the CLASSPATH environment variable is set, Java also looks for API classes in the classes.zip file in the lib directory of the Java home directory. This file typically has the file path \java\lib\classes.zip.

●—NOTE

File names in this section assume the Windows/MS-DOS convention, which uses a backslash (\) for directory paths. UNIX uses a forward slash (/) instead. UNIX also uses a colon (:) rather than a semicolon (;) to separate directories in CLASSPATH. When path and filenames are specified as arguments to Java API methods, Java uses the UNIX conventions, unless otherwise specified, regardless of development and target platforms.

The import statement

Most of the packages you'll want to use are in the Java API. Some of the API classes have long package names, such as java.awt.image. ImageObserver. You can also create your own custom packages that contain custom classes.

The import statement lets you refer directly to classes in a package, effectively giving the classes within the package a local scope for coding purposes. The import statement neither changes the way that Java searches for classes nor affects any of the rules that apply to accessing classes and fields in a package. When you first start using Java, the import statement looks a lot like the C #include statement, but its purpose is quite different: The only effect of the Java import statement is to let you refer to a class by a shorter (unqualified) name. Look at the introductory applet example from the previous chapter:

```java
public class HelloApplet extends java.applet.Applet {
  public void paint(java.awt.Graphics g) {
    g.drawString("Hello Java!", 5, 20);
  }
}
```

References to java.applet.Applet and java.awt.Graphics can be replaced by Applet and Graphics, respectively, as long as you first use import statements:

```java
import java.applet.Applet;
import java.awt.Graphics;
public class HelloApplet extends Applet {
  public void paint(Graphics g) {
    g.drawString("Hello Java!", 5, 20);
  }
}
```

In this case, the use of import statements does not impact the size of the executable, although it does make the code somewhat easier to read. However, in complex applications, some class names may appear many times. In this case, use of the import statement reduces the amount of typing that you must do.

Another way to use an import statement is with the following syntax:

```java
import package.*;
```

This statement has the effect of importing the names of all classes and interfaces in the indicated package. For instance, the previous example could be rewritten as follows:

```
import java.applet.*;
import java.awt.*;
public class HelloApplet extends Applet {
    public void paint(Graphics g) {
        g.drawString("Hello Java!", 5, 20);
    }
}
```

The only exception to the usage of the import statement is that classes and interfaces in the java.lang package can always be referred to directly without importing. In other words, all of the classes and interfaces in the java.lang package are imported automatically.

Fun with Graphics

3

If you've programmed for typical hardcore GUI systems such as Windows, a pleasant surprise awaits you: Java provides you with the same basic functionality, but in a simpler, cleaner programming model. At its heart is the `Graphics` object, which is easy to use once you understand the `object.method` syntax.

If you haven't programmed for a GUI system before, don't worry; there isn't any weird GUI programming stuff to unlearn.

So, let's plunge into the colorful world of graphics. The examples in this chapter don't do anything terribly fancy — they basically just display information — but upcoming chapters will add the capability to get information and to animate the graphics.

Applets, Applications, and Graphics

First, a word about the role of graphics in Java programming generally. As Chapter 1 pointed out, there are two main kinds of Java programs: applications and applets. Yet, in many books on Java, graphics seem to be the exclusive province of applets. Applications often seem to be relegated to simple utilities and console applications. This might well lead you to ask whether Java graphics are reserved for applet use only. The answer is a resounding no. However, it turns out that applets are a little easier to get started with by learning Java graphics.

The trick to drawing graphics in any Java program is to get a valid `Graphics` object, which is required for performing graphics operations. However, you can't just call the `Graphics` class constructor. You must get a `Graphics` object passed to you by something called a *component*, which is an onscreen graphical object that can be displayed, moved, sized, and treated as the source of events. (An example would be a command button.)

Getting a `Graphics` object is easy to do in an applet, because every applet has at least one built-in component: the applet itself. A component can respond to events, and it is notified when it is time to update the screen. Getting a `Graphics` object in an application requires a little more work, because you have to establish the framework yourself. For simplicity's sake, this chapter focuses on applets, but the last section in Chapter 4 (p. 583) explains how to introduce components and graphics into an application.

In an application, you can create components by using certain features of the Abstract Windowing ToolKit (AWT), which is explained in the next chapter. The first step is to create and show a `Frame` object. Until you learn how to create components, however, it's easiest to create graphics effects by programming simple applets. So, this chapter focuses on applets.

The Graphics Object

In Java, you perform most graphics operations by manipulating the `Graphics` object directly. After you get the object, you call its methods to do everything: write text, draw figures, and specify fonts and colors. The most common way to get the `Graphics` object is to write a `paint()` method, in which you are passed a `Graphics` object automatically:

```
public class HelloApplet extends java.applet.Applet {
    public void paint(java.awt.Graphics g) {
```

```
        // Paint the applet here.
    }
}
```

The applet itself is also an object. There can be many instances of an applet, because the user can use the appletviewer to clone multiple versions of an applet.

The Graphics object, g, provides a reference to the applet's display area (see Figure 3-1). Keep in mind that g is an argument, and you can use any argument name you wish. If passed in through paint(), g provides a reference to the part of the display area that needs to be repainted, an area known as the *clipping rectangle*. The clipping rectangle contains just the area in need of updating; use of this rectangle optimizes painting, because it reduces the actual screen real estate to be refreshed. You can draw all over the applet's display area, but only the region in the clipping rectangle is updated.

Often, the applet's entire display area needs to be redrawn. This is the case, for example, when the applet is first displayed. In some cases, however, only a corner needs to be redrawn, such as when a window overlaps the applet but then is moved away. The clipping rectangle contains just this area that needs to be redrawn.

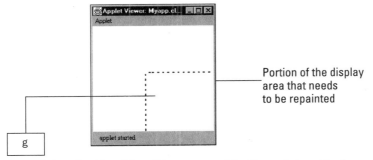

Figure 3-1   *The Graphics object, g, used in the paint method*

None of this has any effect on the way you write the paint() method except that the purpose of paint() is to restore an existing image. If the image needs to change, you must make sure that the entire area affected is repainted, either by calling repaint() to refresh the screen or by grabbing the Graphics object directly. At the end of this chapter in the section titled "Grabbing a Graphics Context (Scribble)" is an example of the latter technique.

In any case, after you have the Graphics object, you can call its methods to perform any graphics action that you want to execute. As elsewhere, these statements use the object.method syntax. On page 526 in Chapter 2, we stated that methods are often used to manipulate objects of a particular class. In this case, calling a method through the Graphics object results in graphics of some sort being drawn on the display area; the specific graphics are dependent upon the specific method called.

```
import java.awt.*;

public class Myapplet extends java.applet.Applet {
  public void paint(Graphics g) {
    g.SetColor(Color.blue);
    g.SetFont(new Font("Arial", Font.BOLD, 12));
    g.drawString("Hello there Java!", 20, 20);
  }
}
```

Displaying Text

The drawString() method is Java's principal method for displaying text on the screen. The other two methods — drawChar() and drawBytes() — do exactly the same thing except that they accept string data in a different format.

The following example displays the string "How do you take your Java?", placing the baseline of the string 10 pixels from the left edge and 30 pixels from the top edge.

```
g.drawString("How do you take your Java?", 10, 30);
```

The drawString() method and the other two drawing methods use the current settings for background color, foreground color, and font properties. The next section explains how to change color settings.

Setting background and foreground colors

Background color is a property of the applet and should be set in the applet's init() method using the setBackground() method. Because both of these methods are fields of the applet class, you can refer to setBackground() directly from within init(). You don't need to qualify the reference as object.method.

```
import java.awt.*;
import java.applet.*;
```

```
public class Myapplet extends Applet {
  public void init() {
    setBackground(Color.blue);
  }

  public void paint(Graphics g) {
    g.drawString("The field is blue.", 20, 20);
  }
}
```

The background color should be set in the init() method because the background color is used to fill the display area before paint() is ever called.

The expression Color.blue is a constant defined in the Color class. This constant is declared static, meaning it's a class variable. Consequently, you can refer to this constant directly through the class using the syntax *class.field*. You don't have to first create a Color object.

The Color class is a good example of a class with a dual purpose: it defines a set of useful constants, and it defines Color as an object type. Many classes in the API work this way. They define useful constants, but they can also be used to create objects. When a field is a class field, there is exactly one copy of it, and it does not depend on object creation. (Class variables are stored as if they were global variables.) In the API, you can see which fields are class fields, because they are declared with the static keyword.

●—CROSS-REFERENCE

To learn more about the static keyword, see "static Keyword" in Part I, "Java 2 Language Reference," page 87.

All this means that the Color class provides a set of useful constants (red, blue, cyan, white, black, gray, and so on), but the class can also be used to create new objects of type Color. In Java, a class can be used in multiple ways.

●—NOTE

In C++, you would refer to the expression Color.blue as Color::blue. C++ also supports static class variables, but uses the scope-resolution operator (::) to qualify references through a class.

Aside from background color, common attributes of the display area are set through the Graphics object. To set foreground color, call the setColor() method from within paint(). The following example applet sets both foreground and background colors:

```java
import java.awt.*;
import java.applet.*;
public class Myapplet extends Applet {
  public void init() {
    setBackground(Color.blue);
  }

  public void paint(Graphics g) {
    g.setColor(Color.red);
    g.drawString("Red on blue.", 20, 20);
  }
}
```

Again, setColor() and drawString() are qualified references, because they are methods of class Graphics, whereas setBackground() is a method of the applet and does not need to be qualified.

● **CROSS-REFERENCE**

For a complete list of Color constants, see "Color Class" in Part I (p. 207).

Setting the font

To specify a font, create a Font object and then pass that object to the setFont() method. Java lets you do this in a single statement:

```java
g.setFont(new Font("Helvetica", Font.PLAIN, 12));
```

The arguments to the Font constructor are the font name, a number indicating font style, and the point size. The statement is interesting because it uses the Font object in two ways. Font.PLAIN is a class field that can be used before a font object is created. Then the method call new Font() calls a Font class constructor to create the object.

The following example specifies a font that is both bold and italic:

```java
g.setFont(new Font("Arial", Font.BOLD + Font.ITALIC, 14));
```

You can also set the font in the applet's init() method. The init() method is called just once — when the applet is loaded. Sometimes it's useful to set the font as a graphics method; for example, if you need to change fonts during a repaint. But if you're going to stick to one font, it's more efficient to set it once in init() by calling the applet's own setFont() method. Remember that when applied to the applet, setFont() does not need to be qualified if it is called from within another applet method. In other words, you don't have to use the object.method syntax if a method is being called from within the object that it is defined, as the following code demonstrates:

```
public void init() {
  setFont(new Font("Arial", Font.BOLD + Font.ITALIC, 14));
}
```

●—CROSS-REFERENCE———————————————————————
For a list of supported fonts, see Appendix B (p. 679).

Using font metrics

A number of text operations require measurement of font properties. In the most obvious and common case, you want to display more than one line of text in an applet. To print the second line, you would need to know how far to move down. This distance depends on the height of the current font.

The following example prints two lines of red text in 14-point Arial font against a white background:

```
import java.awt.*;
import java.applet.*;
public class Print2 extends Applet {
  FontMetrics fm;
  int y;

  public void init() {
    setBackground(Color.white);
    Font myFont = new Font("Arial", Font.PLAIN, 14);
    setFont(myFont);
    fm = getFontMetrics(myFont);
    y = fm.getHeight();
  }

  public void paint(Graphics g) {
    g.setColor(Color.red);
    g.drawString("First line of text.", 5, 20);
    g.drawString("Second line of text.", 5, 20 + y);
  }
}
```

This example introduces the use of the `FontMetrics` class. This class is declared in the `java.awt` package, so the `import` statements already cover it. All the classes could have been imported individually, although that would have made the applet source code a couple of lines longer:

●─**CROSS-REFERENCE**───────────────────────

For more information about the `FontMetrics` class, see "FontMetrics Class" in Part I, "Java 2 API Reference," page 259.

```
import java.awt.Graphics;
import java.awt.Font;
import java.awt.FontMetrics
import java.applet.Applet;
```

This applet must do a number of operations just once. For efficiency's sake, these operations are performed in the `init()` method, which the appletviewer or browser calls once when the applet is loaded. After the font is created and the distance between lines is calculated, there is no need to do these operations again. As in a previous example, the background color must also be set in `init()`.

```
public void init() {
            setBackground(Color.white);
    Font myFont = new Font("Arial", Font.PLAIN, 14);
            setFont(myFont);
            fm = getFontMetrics(myFont);
            y = fm.getHeight();
}
```

In this applet, information must be communicated between the `init()` method and the `paint()` method. Specifically, the height y is calculated in `init()` and is later used in `paint()`. This communication requires the use of instance variables rather than temporary or local variables. Remember that instance variables are variables declared at the class level but which are not declared `static`:

```
FontMetrics fm;
int y;
```

When run, the applet `Print2` produces the display shown in Figure 3-2.

Figure 3-2   *The Print2 applet displaying two lines of text*

This applet specifies a particular font, but you can always use the default font if you want. Once a font has been set, you can get font metrics for the current font by calling the applet's getFont() method:

```
fm = getFontMetrics(getFont());
```

● **NOTE** ─────────────────────────────────

You might think that you can create a FontMetrics object by using a constructor, but FontMetrics is an abstract class and cannot be directly instantiated. You must call the applet's getFontMetrics() method to get a FontMetrics object. The applet actually hands you an instance of a FontMetrics subclass. In Java, a subclass can be used anywhere its superclass (parent class) can be used. This means that the object you get back from getFontMetrics() is fully usable.

● **CROSS-REFERENCE** ─────────────────────────

To find out more about superclasses, see "super Keyword" in Part I, "Java 2 Language Reference," page 92.

Using other font metrics: A summary

The FontMetrics class supports a series of measurements for each font. Each of these measurements can be accessed through the appropriate get method of FontMetrics. For example, in the previous example, fm. getHeight() returns the height of the font. See Part I, p. 259, for a complete list of methods.

Figure 3-3 shows the available font measurements in a graphical context. The characters shown are representative of all other characters in the font.

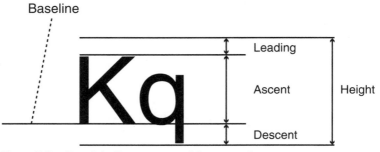

Figure 3-3 *Graphical summary of font metrics*

Drawing Figures

The Graphics class supports a large set of methods for operations such as drawing lines, drawing circles and squares, and filling in regions. All of them can be called through the Graphics object g.

```
public void paint(Graphics g) {
   // Draw a line from (0, 0) to (150, 100)
   g.drawLine(0, 0, 150, 100);
   // Draw square at (170, 20), size 100 x 100
   g.drawRect(170, 20, 100, 100);
   // Draw circle at (120, 100), in area size 80 x 80
   g.drawOval(120, 100, 80, 80);
}
```

This example, when put into an applet and executed, gives the output shown in Figure 3-4. To see all the output, you may need to resize the appletviewer window after starting the applet. An alternative is to change the width and height attributes of the <APPLET> tag in the HTML file so that the size of the window is at least 300 by 200 units.

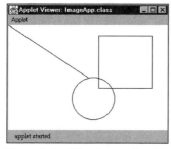

Figure 3-4 *Viewing a simple graphical applet in the appletviewer window*

In the case of the `drawLine()` method, the arguments specify two endpoints using *x,y* coordinates. The call to `drawLine()` in this example draws a line from the point (0, 0) to the point (150, 100).

In the case of `drawRect()` and `drawOval()` — and many other graphics methods as well — the first two arguments specify a corner, and the last two specify width and height. Thus, the call to `drawRect()` specifies an upper-left corner of (170, 20), a width of 100, and a height of 100. Calls to `drawOval()` interpret arguments the same way, except that they draw an oval inscribed within the indicated rectangle. Figure 3-5 shows an example of another oval.

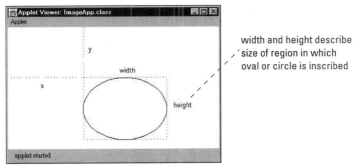

width and height describe size of region in which oval or circle is inscribed

Figure 3-5 *Arguments to the drawOval() method*

One of the more versatile Java graphics methods is `drawPolygon()`, which takes as its argument a set of any number of points. At runtime, Java connects the dots to produce a polygon as elaborate as you want. (Its cousin, `fillPolygon()`, uses similar mechanics.) This method is relatively simple to use. Most of the work lies in determining which points to connect.

To use `drawPolygon()`, you may first need to draw a diagram of the figure that you want to create, and then determine the coordinates. Figure 3-6 shows the figure to be drawn and the coordinates of each of its six points.

The next step is to write out the point values, placing the x and y coordinates in two columns (see Table 3-1).

Although there are only six points, this table has seven rows. This is because the `drawPolygon()` function does not connect the dots back to the first point unless that point is listed at the end.

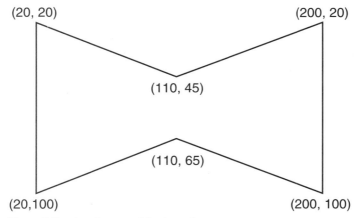

Figure 3-6   *A polygon with six points*

Table 3-1   *Coordinates for a polygon with six points*

x Value	y Value
20	20
110	45
200	20
200	100
110	65
20	100
20	20

Using the information in Table 3-1, we can create two integer arrays: an x array and a y array. These arrays, along with the number of points (seven), are given as arguments to the drawPolygon() method. Java enables you to create arrays either by using the new operator or by initializing with an aggregate, as done in the example that follows.

●─CROSS-REFERENCE────────────

For more information on initializing arrays, see the topics "Aggregates" (p. 21) and "Arrays" (p. 23) in Part I.

```
public void paint(Graphics g) {
    int xArray[] = {20, 110, 200, 200, 110, 20, 20};
```

```
    int yArray[] = {20, 45, 20, 100, 65, 100, 20};
    g.drawPolygon(xArray, yArray, 7);
}
```

The use of the drawPolygon() method may not seem novel because you can create the same effect by repeatedly calling the drawLine() method. The real power of polygons comes when you use the fillPolygon() method to color in the region that you construct. For example:

```
public void paint(Graphics g) {
    int xArray[] = {20, 110, 200, 200, 110, 20, 20};
    int yArray[] = {20, 45, 20, 100, 65, 100, 20};
    g.fillPolygon(xArray, yArray, 7);
}
```

Another way to create this same applet is to use the API Polygon class, which defines a data type that is essentially an ordered collection of points. After creating a Polygon object, you can use the addPoint() method repeatedly to add all the points you want.

The following example creates the same polygon in the context of a complete applet. The polygon is allocated and initialized in the init() method. As mentioned before, it's always more efficient to do things in the init() method if they need to be done only once. Similarly, in the previous examples, it would have been more efficient to initialize the arrays in the init() method.

Remember that any information communicated between different methods must be represented by class or instance variables and not by local variables. That is the case with the variable poly in this example. As an instance variable, it is declared outside of methods but must be allocated, as well as initialized, in init().

The Polygon class is part of the java.awt package, so it is automatically imported by the first import statement.

```
import java.awt.*;
import java.applet.*;
public class PolyApp extends Applet {
    // Object variable referring to poly is declared
    // at class level.
    Polygon poly;

    // init() method.
    // All the actions here need to be performed just once.
    public void init() {
        poly = new Polygon();
        poly.addPoint(20, 20);
        poly.addPoint(110, 45);
```

```
            poly.addPoint(200, 20);
            poly.addPoint(200, 100);
            poly.addPoint(110, 65);
            poly.addPoint(20, 100);
            poly.addPoint(20, 20);
        }

        // paint() method.
        // The polygon already exists, just needs to be redrawn.
        public void paint(Graphics g) {
            g.fillPolygon(poly);
        }
    }
```

When the applet is loaded by the appropriate command of an HTML file, the applet runs and produces the output shown in Figure 3-7.

Figure 3-7   *Effe0ct of the fillPolygon() method*

Blasting Pictures to the Screen

An important technique in graphics programming is to display a stored image from a file or Web site. In Java, displaying images centers on use of the Image class. This class defines a data type that represents any kind of stored graphical image. Whereas a Graphics object is a temporary handle for a drawing area, an object of type Image is persistent, which means that its contents don't go away when a program ends. As you'll see here and in later chapters, the Graphics and Image classes are often used together, but they have distinctly different uses.

The following application loads an image file and displays the image on screen. This application assumes that you have a file named joe.surf.yellow.small.gif (this is all one file name) on your disk and that it's located in the directory \java\demo\Image-Test\graphics. If you installed the JDK with \java as your home directory, the file should be in that location.

```
import java.awt.*;
import java.applet.*;
public class ImageApp extends Applet {
  Image joe;

  public void init() {
    String file = "/java/demo/ImageTest/graphics/"
      + "joe.surf.yellow.small.gif";

    joe = getImage(getDocumentBase(), file);
    if (joe == null) {
      System.out.println("joe not found.");
      System.exit(0);
    }
  }

  public void paint(Graphics g) {
    g.drawImage(joe, 0, 0, this);
  }
}
```

The first field in the class is an object variable named joe, of type Image. As with all object variables, joe is only a reference; you must assign joe an actual object before it can be useful.

```
Image joe;
```

The statements in the init() method create an image and assign it to joe. First, the code creates a string that specifies the file location and name. In the following code, the String class's concatenation operator (+) helps split the statement into two physical lines for convenience.

●—NOTE——————————————————————

Following the UNIX convention, Java API methods always use the forward slash (/), rather than the backward slash (\), to separate directory names. The Java interpreter running on the target computer translates file pathnames as appropriate for the local system.

```
String file = "/java/demo/ImageTest/graphics/"
  + "joe.surf.yellow.small.gif";
```

The next statement calls the applet's getImage() method to load the image file into memory. It also constructs an Image object for — and assigns the object to — the variable joe. The first argument must have type URL, a class in the java.net package. A URL is a uniform resource locator, and it can specify any available Web page.

Thus, the getImage() method can easily load image files from remote locations. In this case, all we want is a URL for the local machine. It turns out the applet's getDocumentBase() method returns this URL. The second argument to getImage() specifies the filename.

```
joe = getImage(getDocumentBase(), file);
```

The getImage() method does not need to be called more than once, no matter how many times the image is drawn. Therefore, the call to getImage(), along with the string assignment, is placed in the init() method.

The paint() method is the logical place to do the drawing of the image. The drawImage() method puts up the image in the display area. The first three arguments specify the Image object and the x,y coordinates at which to place the image. The coordinates specify the top-left corner of the image relative to the applet's display area.

```
public void paint(Graphics g) {
   g.drawImage(joe, 0, 0, this);
}
```

The fourth argument uses the this keyword, which refers to the current object — that is, the object for which the code is being executed. In applet code, this simply refers to the applet itself. (Remember that an applet is an object.)

●—NOTE

In C++, the this keyword is a *pointer* to the current object. Java has no pointers, and it treats this as a reference. The C++ equivalent to Java's use of this is *this.

In any case, the drawImage() method expects an object of type ImageObserver as its fourth argument. An image observer is an object that plays a role in the loading of the image. If not all of the image data is available when needed, the image observer says, in effect, "Inform me when more data becomes available." The image observer then updates the image using the new data as it becomes available.

It might be time-consuming to write your own image observer. Fortunately, all applets — as well as all classes derived from Component — function as image observers. The easy solution is therefore to provide this (a reference to the applet) as the fourth argument.

When the applet is first loaded, you'll probably notice that painting joe takes a little time. This is because the file is being loaded into memory while painting happens. However, subsequent painting of joe (try iconizing and then restoring the applet) is very fast.

If you want, you can cause the application to display the image in one fell swoop. This involves using a media tracker to monitor the loading of the image. To use this approach, make the following changes:

1. Add an implements Runnable clause to the applet declaration and declare a MediaTracker object as an instance variable:

```
public class ImageApp implements Runnable {
MediaTracker tracker;
// Rest of class...
```

2. Insert the following lines of code at the very end of the init() method. These statements initialize the media tracker and start a new thread:

```
tracker = new MediaTracker(this);
tracker.addImage(joe, 0);
Thread runner = new Thread(this);
runner.start();
```

3. Add the following run() method to your applet class. You must use the name "run." This code causes a repaint as soon as loading is complete:

```
// run() method. Defines thread behavior.
public void run() {
   try {tracker.waitForID(0);}
   catch(InterruptedException e){;}
   repaint();
}
```

4. Rewrite the paint() method so that it doesn't draw the image unless it is completely loaded:

```
public void paint(Graphics g) {
   if (tracker.checkID(0, true))
      g.drawImage(joe, 0, 0, this);
}
```

Many of the concepts used in this code may be new. For now, just go ahead and use the code. The concept of threads, as well as the try and catch keywords, is introduced in Chapter 6. You might also look at "MediaTracker Class" (p. 394) in Part I.

The new code uses a two-prong strategy. First, it spins off a separate process, or *thread*, which waits for loading to finish. This waiting happens by calling the waitForID() method. As soon as loading is complete, the thread causes an immediate repaint and dies — this is all it does.

Second, the code for `paint()` is altered so that image drawing is prevented during loading. This is necessary because it's possible for repaints to occur at any time. The call to `checkID` returns a Boolean: before loading is complete, this method returns `false`. After that, it always returns `true`.

Grabbing a Graphics Context (Scribble)

This section features the Java version of the now-famous Scribble app (harking back to one of the author's Visual Basic days).

In most applets and applications, you use a `Graphics` object within `paint()` and then forget it. For certain kinds of applications, however, you need to grab the `Graphics` object and do a quick operation directly to the display. The `Scribble` applet does just that: every time the mouse is dragged, `Scribble` grabs the `Graphics` object and draws a line. The Scribble applet has several key features:

- It calls `addMouseListener(this)` and `addMouseMotion Listener(this)` to say "Use this class as its own mouse and mouse-motion event handler." Beginning with Java 1.1, you must explicitly register event-handling classes. In this case, the `Scribble` class registers itself as the handler for both kinds of events. Events could have been handled in a separate class, but for convenience, everything here is done in the `Scribble` class.

- The `Scribble` class implements the `MouseListener` and `MouseMotionListener` interfaces. In Java 1.1 and later, a class must implement the appropriate interface (or interfaces) to be a valid event handler.

- `Scribble` methods `mousePressed()` and `mouseDragged()` have the code that actually responds to the mouse actions of interest. (`Scribble` implements other interface methods, such as `mouseReleased()`, with empty definitions.) The next chapter discusses event handlers and the flow of events in greater detail.

- The applet grabs the `Graphics` object directly by calling its `getGraphics()` method. Scribble would be too slow if you had to wait for a repaint after each mouse move.

- The applet releases the graphics object quickly by calling the `Graphics` object's `dispose()` method, which forces the release of the graphics context associated with the object.

The use of `dispose()` is key to the smooth working of the applet. If you attempt to write Scribble without calling this method, you may find (as I did) that after a large number of mouse moves, the applet locks up. The `dispose()` method ensures that the graphics context is immediately released back to the system, which means it is no longer in memory. Be advised, however, that once `dispose()` is called, the `Graphics` object cannot be used again until the next call to `getGraphics()`.

Here is the complete code for Scribble:

```java
import java.awt.*;
import java.awt.event.*;
import java.applet.*;

public class Scribble extends Applet implements MouseListener,
  MouseMotionListener {
  int oldX, oldY;

  public void init() {
    // Register the event handlers
    addMouseListener(this);
    addMouseMotionListener(this);
  }

  public void mouseMoved(MouseEvent evt) {
  }

  public void mouseDragged(MouseEvent evt) {
    Graphics g = getGraphics();
    g.drawLine(oldX, oldY, evt.getX(), evt.getY());
    g.dispose();
    oldX = evt.getX();
    oldY = evt.getY();
  }

  public void mouseEntered(MouseEvent evt) {
  }

  public void mouseExited(MouseEvent evt) {
  }

  public void mousePressed(MouseEvent evt) {
    oldX = evt.getX();
    oldY = evt.getY();
  }
```

```
public void mouseReleased(MouseEvent evt) {
}

public void mouseClicked(MouseEvent evt) {
}
}
```

Figure 3-8 shows a sample Scribble display.

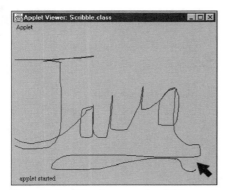

Figure 3-8   *The famous Scribble applet*

After you read Chapter 6, you should be able to figure out how to restore the display by replenishing from an offscreen buffer. This technique involves drawing simultaneously to the screen and the buffer after each mouse move and then overriding paint() so that it copies the buffer to the screen. This approach enables Java to correctly restore the display after resizing or iconizing, something it cannot do now.

Components and Events

4

Drawing everything from scratch is usually the hard way to do things. For most programs, you'll want to take advantage of Java's built-in graphical objects. These objects are provided in Java's Abstract Windowing ToolKit (AWT), a set of classes provided in the java.awt package. In fact, you've already used the AWT, because graphics are also a part of this package.

The AWT provides easy ways to create dialog boxes, text boxes, buttons, scroll bars, and many other kinds of graphical objects, which are called components. As in other GUI systems, these objects interact with the user and respond to events.

The Java AWT Hierarchy

Before we dive into the world of components and events, it's useful to understand how components relate to the elements presented in the last few chapters. Figure 4-1 shows the part of the Java API class hierarchy that includes components and applets.

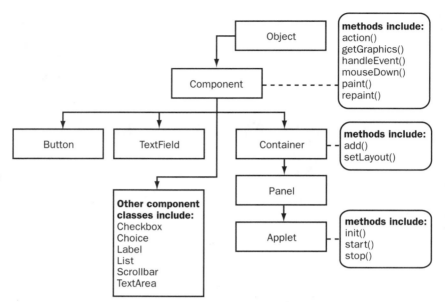

Figure 4-1   *Components and applets in the class hierarchy*

The relationships in Figure 4-1 are not physical ones; this hierarchy relates to inheritance. (See the next section for an explanation of inheritance.) The Applet class has the characteristics of all the classes it inherits from.

The Applet class inherits many of its most important methods, including paint(), from the Component class. If you look up the Applet class in Part I, "Java 2 API Reference," you'll notice that many of the methods aren't listed. This is due to the fact that they are defined in the Component class, which means you may need to also consult Component to find a method.

The Applet class also inherits from the Container class. The Container class provides the capability to physically contain other components. Any class that inherits from Container can create objects that function as containers — a container can hold other objects within its borders. Thus, an applet can contain other components.

Finally, the Applet class inherits from Panel. A panel is a window subsection not marked by a physical border. If you look at an applet closely, you'll see that it does not completely occupy all the space inside the browser or applet viewer. An applet has characteristics of a component, a container, and a panel.

Java does not support multiple inheritance, so each class has only one direct superclass. However, a class may have many indirect superclasses (ancestors), as is the case with the `Applet` class.

Figure 4-1 suggests how important the `Component` class is. In theory, you can write a `paint()` method for any component and perform graphics operations. Of course, many components have built-in displays, such as a label on a button, so you won't want to override `paint()` in those cases. You might, however, want to override `paint()` for a panel, which is blank by default.

Background: Inheritance

If you've programmed in C++ or another object-oriented language, feel free to skip this section. If you are a C person, or a BASIC person, or just want a quick review, read on.

Inheritance is a popular feature of object orientation. It is a simple idea, although much has been written about it. Inheritance applies to classes; objects are involved only as far as their classes are affected. The rest is easy.

●—**CROSS-REFERENCE**———————————————————

To learn more about object orientation, see "Background: Object Orientation" in Chapter 2, page 525.

Essentially, if class B inherits from class A, B automatically gets all of A's fields. B gets all of A's built-in behavior, because B inherits all of A's methods. The only exception is constructors — B must define its own. The Java interpreter will, by default, call A's default constructor to help create an object of type B. But generally, you should write the appropriate constructors for each individual class.

In Java, the `extends` keyword creates inheritance relationships. Consider three simple classes: A, B, and C. Each class is the subclass (or child class) of the one before it, and each successive subclass adds additional fields. A subclass need not add new fields, but most of them do. Any declarations in a class either add to or override the fields of its superclass (or parent class).

```
class A {
   int a, b;

   void setFields(int newA, int newB) {
     a = newA; b = newB;
   }
}
```

```
class B extends A {
  double x, y;
}

class C extends B {
  int c;

  int getC() {
    return c;
  }

  setFields (int newA, int newB) {
    a = newA;
    c = b = newB;
  }
}
```

Figure 4-2 shows how these inheritance relationships work. Each successive generation adds new fields. Note that by inheriting from B, C gets all of A's fields as well.

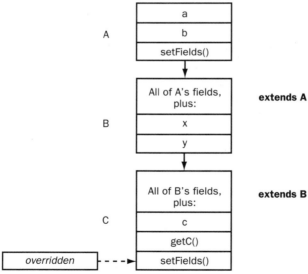

Figure 4-2 *A sample inheritance hierarchy*

There is one other twist in this example. Class C defines the setFields() method, even though it was already defined in Class A. (If the argument list differed in type information, they would be separate, overloaded methods, but here they have the same signature.) So, in this case, C overrides the definition of setFields(). This is an important phenomenon in Java. Often, you will customize the behavior of an API class by subclassing that class and then overriding one or more methods. In fact, this is exactly what happens when you write an applet — you subclass the `Applet` class and then override applet methods such as `paint()` and `init()`.

Furthermore, this sort of subclassing works because Java observes an important rule (as does C++): anywhere an instance of a class is expected, an instance of a subclass is accepted as well. Thus, the browser or applet viewer expects to create an instance of `Applet`, but you cause it to create an instance of your applet instead — even though your applet is actually just a subclass of `Applet`.

For now, the most important thing to remember is that some of the most important fields of a class are often inherited from ancestor classes. In the case of `Applet`, both `Component` and `Container` contribute important methods. Admittedly, this argument sometimes makes it more difficult to look up a method in the API because not all the methods are in one place. However, if you clearly understand the purpose and scope of each class in the hierarchy, it is usually clear where to look for a method.

Overview of Java UIs

Java uses a different model for generating user interfaces (UIs) than is used in other programming languages. Instead of positioning components on a container by specifying exact size and position, Java uses a layout manager. A layout manager sizes and positions all the components according to a general scheme.

"But wait!" you say. "How can Java presume to position my components for me? I know best where they should go!"

If you were creating a user interface for a specific platform, this might be true. Java, however, is designed to create programs for multiple platforms. When you're developing a program on a Macintosh, you can lay out a user interface so that it looks good on . . . well, a Macintosh. But other platforms may have different sizes and resolutions. What's more, when you write an applet you may not have any control of the size of the applet window.

Java's solution is to assign a layout manager to each container. (The applet is a container, but Java also supports other kinds of containers, such as windows, panels, and dialog boxes.) The layout manager is an object that determines the size and position of the immediate children. If the size of the container changes, the layout manager will reposition everything in the container according to a general scheme.

The basic procedure for creating and displaying a component is simple:

1. Define a variable to refer to the component. (Actually, this step is required only if you need a way to refer to the component later.)

2. Create the component by using the new operator.

3. Add the component to a container by calling the container's add() method.

For example, the following statements create a button and add it to a container. "Click me!" is displayed on the button. The Button constructor sets this text.

```
Button theButton;
// ...
theButton = new Button("Click me!");
theContainer.add(theButton);
```

The order in which you add components affects how the layout manager positions the components. For example, if the layout manager is an instance of the FlowLayout class, it positions the components from left to right in the order they were created.

Although every container has a default layout manager, you can assign a new layout manager by calling the container's setLayout() method. For example:

```
theContainer.setLayout(new BorderLayout());
```

The Java API provides a series of standard layout-manager classes — FlowLayout, BorderLayout, GridLayout, and GridBagLayout — but it is possible to write your own. You learn much more about layout managers, including the box layout that is new to Java 2, in Chapter 5.

An Applet with Components

Applets aren't the only kind of graphical programs that Java can produce. However, let's first look at how an applet with components works. Later, we'll examine an application with the same components.

The following applet, simple as it is, demonstrates issues that are common to more complex applets. This applet features two text boxes, labels for the text boxes, and a command button.

```
import java.awt.*;
import java.applet.*;
public class ConvApplet extends Applet {
  // Instance variables for components.
  // These must be declared here; if local, then other methods
```

```
//  (to be added later) wouldn't be able to use them.
Label      labF, labC;
TextField textF, textC;
Button     convButton;

public void init() {
  labF = new Label("Fahr:");
  add(labF);
  textF = new TextField(15);
  add(textF);

  labC = new Label("Cent:");
  add(labC);
  textC = new TextField(15);
  add(textC);
  convButton = new Button("Convert");
  add(convButton);
  }
}
```

The only method overridden here is init(). It's not necessary to write anything for paint(), because once the five components are added to the applet, they are automatically redrawn as needed.

The code that creates and adds the components is straightforward. Here, I've spaced the statements so that it is easy to see pairs of related statements: the first statement creates a component; the second statement adds it to the applet. The add() method does not need to be qualified here, because it is being applied to the applet itself. Here is the first pair of statements:

```
labF = new Label("Fahr:");
add(labF);
```

The argument to the Label constructor specifies the label text. In the next pair of statements, the argument to the TextField constructor specifies the size in characters.

```
textF = new TextField(15);
add(textF);
```

As elsewhere in Java, the new operator must be used to allocate an object in memory, unless the type is primitive data. (In addition to new, you can allocate strings and arrays by using string literals and set aggregates.) There is no delete operator, because Java cleans up unused memory itself.

I used an HTML file with the following <APPLET> tag to test this applet:

```
<APPLET code="ConvApplet.class" width=300 height=200>
```

After compiling the applet and loading the HTML file, I got the results shown in Figure 4-3. The results on your computer may differ.

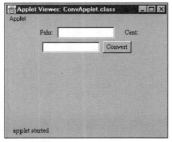

Figure 4-3   *The ConvApplet program, first cut*

This arrangement is clearly unsatisfactory. In fact, it's awful! One problem is that Java used the `FlowLayout` manager (the default) because no layout manager was specified. The `FlowLayout` manager style works fine for some applets, but not for this applet.

Another problem is that the labels don't stay with their associated text boxes. This is easy to fix by introducing panels. The applet itself is a panel, and you can create any number of other panels. Essentially, a panel is a container that is part of another container. There are no visible borders around a panel, but a panel acts as a grouping mechanism.

The revised strategy for this application creates a panel around the first two components and a panel around the second. Figure 4-4 shows the resulting container/component relationships.

The following revised applet code uses panels and the `Border-Layout` class. Because an object of this class is in use, components are added to the applet in specific zones, or anchors. The zones determine what part of the applet a component is attached to: "North," "South," "East," "West," or "Center."

The labels and the text boxes are not added directly to the applet; instead, they are added to panels. Remember that panels are containers as well as components of the applet. Each panel retains its own layout manager, so within the panels, the zones are not used. When a component is added to a panel, the `add()` method must be qualified, as in `panF.add(textF)`.

```
import java.awt.*;
import java.applet.*;

public class ConvApplet extends Applet {
    Panel       panF, panC;
```

```
Label     labF, labC;
TextField textF, textC;
Button    convButton;

public void init() {
  setLayout(new BorderLayout());
  panF = new Panel();
  panC = new Panel();
  labF = new Label("Fahr:");
  panF.add(labF);              // Add to panel.
  textF = new TextField(15);
  panF.add(textF);             // Add to panel.
  add("North", panF);          // Add panel to applet.
  labC = new Label("Cent:");
  panC.add(labC);              // Add to panel.
  textC = new TextField(15);
  panC.add(textC);             // Add to panel.
  add("Center", panC);         // Add panel to applet.
  convButton = new Button("Convert");p
  add("South", convButton);
  }
}
```

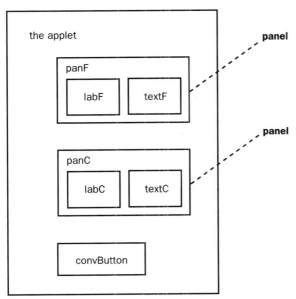

Figure 4-4 *Container relationships involving panels*

Figure 4-5 shows the final look of the applet.

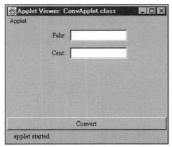

Figure 4-5 *Applet using panels and BorderLayout.*

Responding to Events

Interactive Web pages and applications can react to user actions. This is what events are all about. An event is an occurrence — typically a user action of some kind — that a component can respond to in one of its methods. In Java, events flow from one component to another until a component handles the event and returns true. Mouse clicks and keystrokes are among the more interesting events.

Java has seen various approaches to handling events since its inception a few short years ago. The event-handling approach that finally stuck was introduced in Java 1.1 and is called the *delegation event model*. The main premise behind the delegation event model is to separate event-handling code and core application code. It became apparent in the Java 1.0 event model that event handling was too closely linked with core application code, resulting in an often-complex blend of user interface code and back-end application code. For large applications, it is better to isolate user interface code as much as possible from back-end application code.

The delegation event model establishes the concept of *event types*, in which each type of event is given a unique class type that is derived from a common event class. Event objects of a given event type, also called *event state objects*, are passed between event sources and listeners to constitute an event notification. *Event sources* are capable of generating events, whereas *event listeners* are designed to respond to events. An event is propagated from an event source to an event listener when the event source invokes a method on the listener and passes an object of the given event type.

Event listeners are connected to event sources through a registration mechanism that requires a listener to call a registration method on a source. When the registration method is called, the source is informed to send event notifications to the listener. Registered listeners can also be unregistered, or removed as listeners from a source. Event sources are required to support the addition and removal of listeners through a pair of public event registration methods.

When an event occurs in an event source, the source sends an event notification to any registered listener. The event notification is sent via a method call on each registered listener. Listeners are required to implement an event listener interface that contains a list of methods that can be called by an event source in response to an event. These methods are known as *event response methods* because listeners implement them in order to provide code that responds to an event.

The Java 2 API supports a variety of event types and associated event listener interfaces. These event types are conceptually divided into two different types: low-level events and semantic events. *Low-level events* are events used to convey information about a low-level input or graphical user interface interaction such as a mouse move, key press, or focus change. *Semantic events*, on the other hand, are events used to convey information about a high-level graphical user interface interaction that has meaning within the context of a certain component. For example, an item event is fired whenever a menu item changes. Several low-level events, such as key presses, are fired to arrive at the menu change, which results in a single semantic event.

Low-level events

Low-level events are fired in response to a low-level input or graphical user interface interaction such as a key press or component focus change. The Java 2 API defines a set of event classes that represents the different types of low-level events. These classes are used to generate event state objects that are passed between a source and listener when an event occurs. The low-level event classes supported by the Java 2 API are:

- ComponentEvent
- ContainerEvent
- FocusEvent
- KeyEvent
- MouseEvent
- WindowEvent

●—**NOTE**

All event classes (low-level and semantic) are derived from the AWTEvent class, which encapsulates general characteristics shared by all events. The AWTEvent class is so generic that you typically never interact with it directly. This is evident by the fact that there is no event listener interface defined for AWTEvent. A semantic event is an event that is fired in response to an action that is based on the semantics of a particular object, such as an item change in a list. Semantic events differ from low-level events in that semantic events are related to the specific function of an object.

Figure 4-6 shows the inheritance tree for the low-level event classes. The next several sections describe these event classes in more detail and indicate when they are fired. They also provide a glimpse at the event listener interface associated with each event type. Forgive me if the next several sections look like a reference; I just want to give you a quick idea as to how events are managed by the Java API. A more complete reference for these events be found in Part I, "Java 2 API Reference."

Figure 4-6 shows the inheritance tree for the low-level event classes.

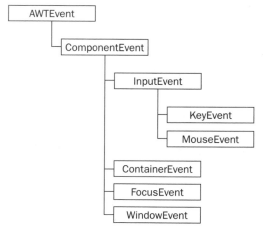

Figure 4-6 *The inheritance tree for the low-level event classes*

ComponentEvent

The ComponentEvent class encapsulates component-level events such as resizes, moves, and visibility changes. For example, when a component is resized, a `ComponentEvent` event is fired. The listener interface for `ComponentEvent` is `ComponentListener`, which supports the following event response methods:

- `componentMoved()` — called when a component is moved
- `componentResized()` — called when a component is resized
- `componentHidden()` — called when a component is hidden
- `componentShown()` — called when a component is shown

ContainerEvent

The `ContainerEvent` class encapsulates container-level events including the addition and removal of components. When a component is added to or removed from a container, a `ContainerEvent` event is fired. The listener interface for `ContainerEvent` is `ContainerListener`, which supports the following event response methods:

- `componentAdded()` — called when a component is added to a container
- `componentRemoved()` — called when a component is removed from a container

FocusEvent

The `FocusEvent` class is used to convey focus changes within components. There are two types of focus changes supported by the `FocusEvent` class: permanent and temporary. A permanent focus change occurs when the focus directly changes from one component to another. An example of a permanent focus change is the user moving from one component to another using the Tab key. A temporary focus change occurs when a component loses or gains focus indirectly based on some other operation such as a dialog box being displayed. The difference between the two types of focus changes is that temporary focus changes are eventually restored. Both types of focus changes are represented by the `FocusEvent` class; to distinguish between the two, you can call the `isTemporary()` method.

The listener interface for `FocusEvent` is `FocusListener`, which supports the following event response methods:

- `focusGained()` — called when a component gains focus
- `focusLost()` — called when a component loses focus

KeyEvent

The KeyEvent class encapsulates component-level keyboard events such as key presses and releases. For example, when a component has focus and a key is pressed or released, a KeyEvent event is fired. As you saw in Figure 4-6, the KeyEvent class is derived from InputEvent, which is an organizational class used to group input event types. Input events are delivered to listeners before being processed by their source, which gives listeners an opportunity to consume the events. The listener interface for KeyEvent is KeyListener, which supports the following event response methods:

- keyPressed() — called when a key is pressed
- keyReleased() — called when a key is released
- keyTyped() — called when a key is typed, which consists of a key press/release combination

MouseEvent

The MouseEvent class represents component-level mouse events such as mouse moves and button clicks. For example, a MouseEvent event is fired whenever the mouse is moved or clicked over a component. Additionally, there are events corresponding to the mouse entering and leaving a component's surface area. Like KeyEvent, the MouseEvent class is derived from InputEvent because it represents mouse input events.

There are two listener interfaces used with the MouseEvent class: MouseListener and MouseMotionListener. The event response methods defined in the MouseListener interface are:

- mousePressed() — called when the mouse button is pressed
- mouseReleased() — called when the mouse button is released
- mouseClicked() — called when the mouse button is clicked, which consists of a button press/release combination
- mouseEntered() — called when the mouse pointer enters a component's surface area
- mouseExited() — called when the mouse pointer exits a component's surface area

The MouseMotionListener interface is designed specifically to handle mouse movement events; it supports the following event response methods:

- mouseMoved() — called when the mouse pointer is moved over a component

- `mouseDragged()` — called when the mouse pointer is moved over a component with the mouse button held down

WindowEvent

The `WindowEvent` class encapsulates window-level events such as a window being activated or closed. The listener interface for `WindowEvent` is `WindowListener`, which supports the following event response methods:

- `windowActivated()` — called when a window is activated
- `windowDeactivated()` — called when a window is deactivated
- `windowOpened()` — called when a window is opened
- `windowClosed()` — called when a window is closed
- `windowClosing()` — called when a window is in the process of being closed, but hasn't yet closed
- `windowIconified()` — called when a window is minimized to iconic form
- `windowDeiconified()` — called when a window is restored from iconic form

Semantic events

Semantic events are fired in response to high-level graphical user interface interactions that have meaning within the context of a certain component. For example, an item selection in a list results in an `ItemEvent` event being generated, which, in this case, is specific to the list's functionality. The Java API defines a set of event classes that represent the different types of semantic events. The semantic event classes supported by the Java 2 API are:

- `ActionEvent`
- `AdjustmentEvent`
- `ItemEvent`
- `TextEvent`

Figure 4-7 shows the inheritance tree for the semantic event classes. The next several sections describe these event classes in more detail and indicate when and why they are fired.

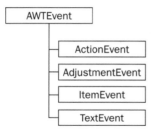

Figure 4-7   *The inheritance tree for the semantic event classes*

ActionEvent

The ActionEvent class encapsulates component-specific actions such as clicking a button component or a menu item. Following are the AWT objects capable of firing ActionEvent events, along with why they fire them:

- Button — fires an action event when clicked
- List — fires an action event when an item is double-clicked
- MenuItem — fires an action event when an item is clicked
- TextField — fires an action event when the Enter key is pressed

The event listener interface for ActionEvent is ActionListener, which only defines one event response method — actionPerformed() — which is called when a component-specific action occurs.

AdjustmentEvent

The AdjustmentEvent class encapsulates component-specific value changes such as the value of a scrollbar being changed. Scrollbars are actually the only AWT components that fire AdjustmentEvent events. The event listener interface for AdjustmentEvent is AdjustmentListener, which only defines one event response method — adjustmentValueChanged() — which is called when a component-specific value adjustment occurs.

ItemEvent

The ItemEvent class encapsulates component-specific item changes such as selecting an item from a list. The AWT objects capable of firing ItemEvent events, along with why they fire them, are:

- Choice — fires an item event when a choice item is selected
- List — fires an item event when a list item is selected

- `Checkbox` — fires an item event when a checkbox is checked or unchecked
- `CheckboxMenuItem` — fires an item event when a checkbox menu item is checked or unchecked

The event listener interface for `ItemEvent` is `ItemListener`, which only defines one event response method — `itemStateChanged()` — which is called when a component-specific item change occurs.

TextEvent

The `TextEvent` class models events are fired in response to a change in the text of a text component. The text components capable of firing `TextEvent` events, along with why they fire them, are:

- `TextArea` — fires a text event when the text changes
- `TextField` — fires a text event when the text changes

The event listener interface for `TextEvent` is `TextListener`, which only defines one event response method — `textValueChanged()` — which is called when the text changes in a text component.

Event delivery

To effectively process and manage events, you must thoroughly understand the event delivery process. The event delivery process involves three objects: an event source, an event listener, and an event state object. The process begins when an event listener notifies a source that it wants to listen to a particular type of event. It does this by calling an event listener registration method provided by the source. Once the listener is registered, the source is ready to deliver events to it. Whenever a change occurs in the source that generates an event, the source creates an event state object describing the event and sends it out to the listener. The source does this by calling one of the event response methods defined in the listener's event listener interface, and passes along the event state object.

Event delivery is completely synchronous, which means that an event is guaranteed complete delivery without interruption. However, there are no rules regarding the order in which an event is delivered to a group of listeners. There are two primary types of event delivery: unicast and multicast.

Unicast and multicast delivery

The standard AWT components support multiple event listeners, which means that multiple event listeners can be registered with and receive events from a single event source. This type of event delivery is known as *multicast event delivery* because an event is broadcast to multiple event listeners simultaneously. With multicast event delivery, event listeners can be added and removed at will via event listener registration methods, and the event source is responsible for keeping track of the listeners and dispatching events to each. Figure 4-8 illustrates multicast event delivery.

Figure 4-8   *Multicast delivery of an event to multiple listeners*

Although multicast event delivery is the most popular and versatile type of event delivery, the delegation event model also supports *unicast event delivery*, in which only one listener is permitted to listen to a source at a time. Unicast event sources can have only one registered listener at any given time. Event listener registration methods for unicast sources are designed to throw an exception if an attempt is made to register more than one listener. Figure 4-9 illustrates unicast event delivery.

Figure 4-9   *Unicast delivery of an event to a single listener*

It's important to understand that unicast event delivery is a more limited form of delivery and should only be used when necessary. That all of the standard AWT components are multicast event sources indicates the Java architect's perception of unicast event delivery. Nevertheless, there may be circumstances in which you need to limit the delivery of an event to a single listener. In such circumstances, unicast event delivery is a lifesaver.

Unicast event sources are distinguished from multicast sources by their event listener registration methods being capable of throwing the TooManyListeners exception. This is often the only clue as to the type of event delivery supported by a component. As an example, the following event listener registration method supports multicast delivery:

```
public void addCrunchListener(CrunchEvent e);
```

In this example, the CrunchEvent event can be fired to multiple listeners that have been registered with the addCrunchListener() registration method. If a CrunchEvent event source is unicast, it would supply the following addCrunchListener() method:

```
public void addCrunchListener(CrunchEvent e) throws
TooManyListeners;
```

The only difference between the two addCrunchListener() methods is the addition of the throws clause to the latter. If more than one event listener is registered with this method, a TooManyListeners exception is thrown.

Delivery concerns

Although event delivery under the delegation event model is typically a very smooth process, there are a few concerns worth mentioning. One potential problem arises when an event listener throws exceptions back to an event source. The problem relates to how an event source should react to such an exception. Unfortunately, there are no rules governing what should happen in a situation such as this. Java 2 stipulates that the manner in which an event source deals with listener-generated exceptions is entirely implementation dependent, which means that you must consult the documentation for a particular source to learn how it handles listener-generated exceptions.

Another problem associated with event delivery occurs when the group of event listeners registered with a multicast source is updated during the delivery of an event. In this situation, it is technically possible for a listener to be removed from the source before its event has been delivered. When this happens, it is possible for an event to be delivered to a listener that is no longer registered, which certainly seems as if it is a problem. There are no strict rules governing how event sources are to deal with this problem, so you should consult the documentation of an event source if you are worried about this problem. Fortunately, this problem isn't likely to cause trouble in most Java programs because event listeners are typically thrown away once they are unregistered.

Event adapters

Event listeners are provided in the Java 2 API as interfaces, instead
of as classes, because event listeners are used as a means for Java
programs to provide application-specific code that responds to event
notifications. This means that there is no default behavior ever associated with event response methods. Because event listener interfaces
are comprised entirely of event response methods, there is no reason
to provide a specific implementation. Classes that want to respond to
events must implement an event listener interface and provide implementations for all the event response methods defined in the interface.

One problem with this event listener approach is that it requires a
class to implement all the event response methods defined in a listener
interface. Without implementing all the methods, the class would
remain abstract, and could not be instantiated and used. This isn't an
issue in situations where most or all of the event response methods
defined in an interface are going to be used by a class. However, what
about the situation in which you want to implement only a single
event response method and the interface provides a variety of methods? Because you are required to provide implementations for all the
methods in the interface, you would have to add empty do-nothing
methods for all the methods that you aren't interested in. This situation is annoying because you have to add unnecessary code.

Fortunately, there is a simple solution to this problem. The Java
API provides a set of *event adapters*, which are "convenience classes"
used to make the process of implementing event listener interfaces
cleaner. Event adapters enable you to implement only the event
response methods that you need, freeing you from the hassle of writing a bunch of useless empty methods. Event adapters are classes,
not interfaces, so you must derive from them rather than implement
them. That they are classes is what enables you to selectively provide
event response methods.

There is an event adapter class associated with each low-level
event listener interface. Each event adapter implements all the
methods defined in its corresponding event listener interface. Why
are there no event adapters for semantic event listener interfaces?
Because each semantic event listener interface defines only one
event response method, and because there is only one method to
be implemented, there is no "convenience" to be gained by using
an adapter class.

Event adapters are painfully simple classes. Just so you believe
me, let's take a quick look at the KeyAdapter event adapter class.

Following is the code for the KeyAdapter class, taken straight from the Java 2 API source:

```
public abstract class KeyAdapter implements KeyListener {
  public void keyTyped(KeyEvent e) {}
  public void keyPressed(KeyEvent e) {}
  public void keyReleased(KeyEvent e) {}
}
```

It doesn't get much simpler than that! As you can see, the KeyAdapter class just implements the KeyListener interface and provides do-nothing methods for all the event response methods defined in the interface.

As you just learned, event adapters are used to help clean up the process of responding to events. However, using an event adapter class isn't always as simple as just deriving from the appropriate class and implementing some methods. A common problem is the situation in which you want to use an event adapter class directly with an applet or application class. The problem is that applets and applications already have a parent class and therefore can't be derived from an adapter class. This is an annoying problem because there is no way to circumvent Java's single inheritance design.

One possible solution is to create a separate event-handler class that derives from the adapter class, but the event handler is likely to need access to private and protected members of the application class. Because Java has no facility similar to C++'s friend classes, it's not really possible to give the event-handler class access to the members of the application class. What to do?

The answer is a Java feature called inner classes, which provides just the mechanism necessary to solve this problem; you can implement an adapter class that is a member of an application class. The adapter class definition is completely contained within the application class, and is derived from a suitable AWT event adapter class. This allows you to only implement the specific methods you need, in addition to being able to access private and protected members of the application.

Following is source code for an applet called ClickMe, which demonstrates the difference between using an event adapter inner class and implementing an event listener interface directly:

```
import java.awt.*;
import java.applet.*;
```

```
import java.awt.event.*;

public class ClickMe extends Applet implements ActionListener
{
  private Button    button;
  private AudioClip clickClip, thanksClip;

  public void init() {
    // Load the audio clips
    clickClip = getAudioClip(getCodeBase(), "ClickMe.au");
    thanksClip = getAudioClip(getCodeBase(), "ThankYou.au");

    // Create and add the button
    button = new Button("Click me!");
    add(button);

    // Register the applet with the button as a listener
    button.addActionListener(this);
    button.addMouseListener(new ClickMeAdapter());
  }

  public void actionPerformed(ActionEvent e) {
    // Play thanks clip in response to button action events
    thanksClip.play();
  }

  class ClickMeAdapter extends MouseAdapter {
    // Play click clip in response to button mouse entry
events
    public void mouseEntered(MouseEvent e) {
      clickClip.play();
    }
  }
}
```

The ClickMe applet contains a button that plays an audio clip upon being clicked (Figure 4-10). A button click results in an ActionEvent event being fired, which is responded to directly by the ClickMe applet class. This is apparent by the fact that the applet class implements the ActionListener interface, in addition to the registration of the applet as an action event listener. The action event response method actionPerformed() is directly implemented in the ClickMe applet class, and is responsible for playing a "thank you" audio clip.

Figure 4-10   *The ClickMe applet*

Up to now the ClickMe applet seems no different than any other delegation event-handling applet that directly implements an event listener interface. However, the ClickMe applet also uses an adapter inner class to respond to mouse movement events. The adapter inner class is named ClickMeAdapter, and is defined within the scope of the ClickMe applet class. The ClickMeAdapter class is purely a helper class used within the context of the ClickMe applet class; it overrides the mouseEntered() method to play a "click me" audio clip whenever the mouse pointer enters the button's surface area. An instance of the ClickMeAdapter class is created and used as the argument to the addMouseListener() registration method in the init() method. That's all it takes to create and register an adapter inner class.

The result of the event response methods in the ClickMe applet is that when the mouse pointer enters the button's surface area a "click me" audio clip is played that encourages the user to click the button. When the user clicks the button, a "thank you" audio clip is played.

An Application with Components

It's easy to write an application that does everything that an applet can do, including graphics operations and adding components. One way to write the application is as follows:

1. Instead of subclassing Applet, write your applet code as a subclass of Frame.

2. Add a windowClosing() event response method that exits the application in response to the frame window closing.

3. Write a class containing main(). In the definition for main(), create an object of your Frame subclass and then call the setTitle(), setSize(), and show() methods for that object.

Note that you could also add an init() method and call it from main() if you wanted to give the application a similar feel as an applet. If you're adapting code from an applet, you probably already have an init() method definition. However, if you write an application from scratch, it's more efficient to place this same code in a constructor.

The following code is a version of ConvApplet, called ConvPrg, which is written as an application:

```
import java.awt.*;
import java.awt.event.*;

class ConvPrg {
  public static void main(String args[]) {
    ConvFrame frm = new ConvFrame();
    frm.setTitle("ConvFrame program");
    frm.setSize(300, 200);
    frm.show();
  }
}

class ConvFrame extends Frame {
  public ConvFrame() {
    // Register the event handlers
    addWindowListener(new WindowHandler());
  }

  class WindowHandler extends WindowAdapter {
    public void windowClosing(WindowEvent e) {
      System.exit(0);
    }
  }

  // Place the rest of the class declarations here.
  // Include all the methods and variables you'd normally
  // put in an applet...
}
```

The Frame class inherits from the Component, Container, and Window classes. You can use Frame, as is done here, to generate a new window. A major difference between user interfaces of applets and those of applications is that in applications, you must generate the initial window yourself. In addition, the application has responsibility for responding to user requests to close the window.

In the windowClosing() method in the WindowHandler event adaptor, it's important to call the System.exit() method in order to exit the application properly. Otherwise, you couldn't shut down the application by closing the frame window.

When writing applications, you cannot call API methods that are defined only in the Applet class. For example, you cannot call

`Applet.getImage()`. Usually, however, you can use an alternative mechanism in applications. For example, to load an image, first get the frame's toolkit object and then call `getImage()` through this object. The following method illustrates this technique:

```
// You can add this method to your frame classes to enable
// frame code to load images.
Image getImage(String filename) {
  Toolkit tk = getToolkit();
  return tk.getImage(filename);
}
```

For more information on the `Toolkit` class, see Part I, "Java 2 API Reference," page 482.

4

in plain english in p
sh in plain english in
glish in plain english
in plain english in p
sh in plain english in
glish in plain english
in plain english in p
glish in plain english
in plain english in p
sh in plain english in
glish in plain english
in plain english in p
sh in plain english in
glish in plain english
in plain english in p
lish in plain english
in plain english in p
sh in plain english in
glish in plain english
in plain english in pl
sh in plain english in
lish in plain english
in plain english in pl
glish in plain english

Moving to Swing

5

The most dramatic improvement to the Java 2 platform from previous versions is the addition of the Swing toolkit, which is a suite of GUI classes and interfaces that supercedes many of the standard Abstract Windowing ToolKit (AWT) classes and interfaces. The Swing toolkit represents a major restructuring of Java's GUI feature set, not to mention many new and more powerful GUI components. A significant feature in Swing is the capability for Java applets and applications to alter their look and feel for a given environment. This enables the same program to blend into both Macintosh and Windows environments, for example.

Although the Swing application framework replaces many components of the traditional Java AWT, it does work in concert with core parts of the AWT. In other words, Swing works hand-in-hand with the AWT to provide a more enhanced GUI for applets and applications. You'll find that the Swing architecture is more flexible than the older AWT architecture, which ultimately results in more options for constructing GUIs in Java.

Swing and the AWT

Before Java 2, Java's support for GUI construction was based entirely on the AWT. This changed in Java 2 with the introduction of the Swing toolkit, which supplements, and in some ways replaces, the old AWT. Many of the new Swing classes are actually derived from AWT classes, which means that you can think of Swing as an extension to the AWT. As an example, the AWT Component class has a Swing counterpart named JComponent. In general, the names of Swing classes that derive from and/or replace existing AWT classes begin with the letter J.

Because Swing overlaps the AWT in many ways, it's logical to ask why Swing is necessary. The main reason for the addition of Swing has to do with a limitation in the AWT. Components in the AWT are known as *heavyweight components* because they are associated with native components, or *peers*, on a given operating system. For example, an AWT button uses an underlying Windows peer when running on the Windows platform. Although this approach sounds logical, it results in platform dependencies that make it difficult to build truly cross-platform GUIs.

Swing is built around the concept of *lightweight components*, which are peerless components; lightweight components have no underlying native component. This means that most Swing components are 100 percent Java and therefore don't have any variance across different platforms. To accommodate users' desire to have Java GUIs resemble native GUIs, Swing employs a "pluggable" look-and-feel architecture that enables you to set the look and feel of a GUI dynamically. Figure 5-1 shows the relationship between heavyweight AWT components and lightweight Swing components.

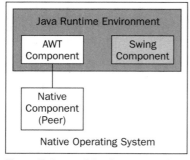

Figure 5-1 *Unlike heavyweight AWT components, lightweight Swing components don't rely on underlying native components.*

Inside Swing

Swing is a full-featured GUI framework that injects many interesting new features into Java in addition to those offered by the AWT. The major features supported by the Swing toolkit are:

- Lightweight component framework
- Pluggable look-and-feel architecture
- Enhanced layout managers
- Powerful set of reusable GUI components
- Standard dialog boxes
- Tool tips
- Keyboard mnemonics

The AWT includes a set of *layout managers* that are used to determine how components are physically arranged within a container. Swing builds on this support for layout managers by introducing four new layout managers, including one that significantly simplifies the layout of components in complex user interfaces. Swing also adds a huge set of components to help make user interfaces richer and more powerful. Swing's standard dialog boxes also provide a means of performing common GUI tasks such as allowing the user to browse and select a file or a color.

Other interesting Swing GUI improvements are tool tips and keyboard mnemonics. *Tool tips* are small pop-up windows that provide help information within the context of a GUI element. *Keyboard mnemonics* provide a means of assigning hot-keys to common tasks.

Getting started with Swing frames

Frames form the basis of all Swing user interfaces. More specifically, a *frame* is a container that serves as the main window for an application. Because they serve as main application windows, frames support familiar GUI window features such as a title, border, and buttons for sizing and closing the frame. Frames are represented by the `JFrame` class, which replaces the AWT's `Frame` class. `JFrame` is one of the few heavyweight Swing components because it represents a physically distinct window.

NOTE

Although the `JFrame` class is a heavyweight component, most Swing components are lightweight components. A few Swing components, such as `JFrame`, are exceptions to the lightweight rule because they physically require a native window in order to function properly.

The `JFrame` class is actually very similar to the AWT's `Frame` class. In fact, you can convert an AWT application to Swing by simply changing the application's frame class from `Frame` to `JFrame`. However, the `JFrame` class introduces the concept of a content pane, which is a special component that takes on the job of managing the frame's interior. Any GUI modifications made to a Swing frame, such as adding components, must actually be made to the frame's content pane. This is accomplished by first retrieving the content pane with a call to the `getContentPane()` method:

```
JFrame frame = new JFrame();
Container contentPane = frame.getContentPane();
contentPane.add(new Button("OK"));
```

In this example, a button is indirectly added to the Swing frame by adding it to the frame's content pane.

Understanding panes

A *content pane* is responsible for managing the interior of a frame, which makes it an important part of all Swing GUIs. A *pane* is simply a generic Swing container. Multiple panes are used in Swing to create an architecture that can support rich GUI features. There are five fundamental types of Swing panes:

- Root pane
- Layered pane
- Content pane
- Menu bar
- Glass pane

Pane architecture's purpose is to provide a means of supporting both lightweight and heavyweight components within a single GUI. The root pane is a virtual pane that serves as a container for the other four pane types. Because lightweight components don't have peers, the layered pane takes on the chore of determining how they overlap each other. The content pane is the central pane to which you add components to construct a user interface. The menu bar is on the same layer as the content pane and provides a place for an application's menu. Finally, the glass pane resides on a layer above all others and allows you to draw graphics on top of components; the glass pane is invisible by default.

The layered pane is interesting because it determines how components overlap each other. It does this by establishing a Z-order for each layer, which you can think of as a number indicating the depth of a layer with respect to the screen. In other words, the screen is the highest layer with a theoretical Z-order of infinity, while other layers have decreasing Z-orders behind the screen. The JLayeredPane class defines a set of constant layer identifiers that specify the Z-order of common layers. These constants, in order of increasing Z-order, are:

- FRAME_CONTENT_LAYER — the content pane and menu bar reside in this layer
- DEFAULT_LAYER — most components reside in this layer
- PALETTE_LAYER — palettes and floating toolbars reside in this layer
- MODAL_LAYER — dialog boxes reside in this layer
- POPUP_LAYER — pop--up menus and tool tips reside in this layer
- DRAG_LAYER — components that are being dragged temporarily reside in this layer

By default, components are added to the default layer identified by the DEFAULT_LAYER constant. You can also specify an explicit integer layer when adding components to a container, which gives you finer control over the layering of components.

Mixing Swing with the AWT

Even though Swing peacefully coexists with the Java AWT, Swing represents a departure from the way in which GUIs were constructed using the AWT in prior versions of Java. However, Java 2 is still backward compatible with earlier Java versions, which means that you have the freedom to use the traditional AWT approach to building GUIs or the new Swing approach.

Java 2's support for both the old and new Java GUI approaches isn't without complication. Consider the issue of mixing lightweight and heavyweight components, which is inevitable with the two GUI architectures. For example, if you create two buttons, a Button and a JButton, the first button is a heavyweight component with a peer while the second is a peerless lightweight component. Java has to be capable of allowing these two components to peacefully coexist within a common GUI framework, which is why it employs the root pane architecture.

Although Java is equipped to handle a mixing of component types, it isn't a good idea to mix older AWT components with new Swing components if you are building an application with a Swing user interface. The Swing components are designed specifically to fit into the Swing architecture and therefore are the components of choice for constructing Swing GUIs.

Laying Out GUIs with Swing

The Swing architecture has lots to offer in terms of creating powerful GUIs, which are of utmost importance in developing intuitive applets and applications. Although specific GUI features are often encapsulated within the confines of a given Swing component, an application's GUI typically involves the orchestration of multiple components. Components must be carefully arranged in a Swing GUI to achieve maximum impact and ease of use. Swing includes special layout managers that make it possible to carefully control the positioning of components in a GUI.

Actually, the Java AWT fully supports layout managers and has for some time, but Swing builds on this support with a notable new layout manager that is quite simple to use, yet very powerful. I'm referring to the box layout, which is very useful above and beyond the standard AWT layouts: flow, grid, border, card, and grid bag.

Getting to know layout managers

Components in a Swing GUI are always housed by a container, to which the components are added. This container is often the content pane of an application's frame window. Every container in Java has an associated layout manager that determines how components are physically arranged within the container. Layout managers are typically associated with a special type of container known as a panel. A panel is a windowless container; panels don't have windows because they typically utilize the window of the parent content pane. Because every panel has a layout manager associated with it, you can create nested panels within other panels to facilitate an elaborate organization of components.

Layout managers greatly simplify the physical arrangement of components, making them a very important part of a GUI's design. The basic layout managers supported by the Java AWT are:

- Flow
- Grid
- Border
- Card
- Grid bag

In addition to these layout managers, the Swing toolkit introduces a box layout manager that can be used to construct complex GUIs. The box layout manager serves as a good alternative to the grid bag layout manager, which is difficult to use in most situations. The Swing toolkit actually introduces four new layout managers, including the box layout manager. However, the remaining three Swing layout managers are used internally by Swing and are rarely useful by themselves for constructing GUIs.

Layout managers provide a means of arranging components in a container using relative positioning, which means that the components are positioned relative to each other. Relative positioning is important because it helps to alleviate problems associated with variations across different computing platforms. For example, resolutions and window sizes can vary greatly from platform to platform, in which case components that are positioned at absolute locations may not look like you would expect.

You can still position components at absolute locations in Java, but it's a good idea to avoid doing so if at all possible. Fortunately, layout managers go a long way toward alleviating the need to use absolute positioning. For example, the box layout manager has some slick features that enable you to fine-tune the relative positioning of components.

Using layout managers

Layout managers are implemented in Java as classes that you can instantiate. However, layout managers themselves are not GUI components; layout managers are invisible objects used to control how GUI components are arranged within a container. Layout manager classes are all required to implement the `LayoutManager` interface. Creating a layout manager is much like creating any other Java object:

```
FlowLayout flow = new FlowLayout();
```

This example creates a `FlowLayout` object, about which you will learn more shortly. Most layout managers also enable you to specify the spacing between components. For example, the following code shows how to create a flow layout manager with centered components that have 4 pixels between them in the X direction and 8 pixels in the Y direction:

```
FlowLayout flow = new FlowLayout(FlowLayout.CENTER, 4, 8);
```

Perhaps even more important than creating a layout manager is assigning it to a container. The `Container` class defines a method named setLayout() that sets the layout for a container:

```
getContentPane().setLayout(flow);
```

In this example, the layout manager for the content pane of a frame window is set to a flow layout manager by calling the setLayout() method. You can also set the layout manager for a new container in the container's constructor when you first create it:

```
JPanel panel = new JPanel(new FlowLayout());
```

Notice that the container in this example is actually created as a panel using the `JPanel` class. After the layout manager is set for a container, the layout manager will physically arrange any components added to the container.

The flow layout manager

The *flow layout manager* is the default layout manager for panels and is represented by the `FlowLayout` class. The flow layout manager arranges components across a container in rows from left to right. When a row fills with components, the components wrap around and a new row is started. You can arrange the rows in a flow layout manager to be aligned left, right, or centered. By default, components are aligned centered in a flow layout manager. Figure 5-2 shows how components are arranged when added to a panel using the flow layout manager.

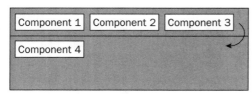

Figure 5-2 *The flow layout manager arranges components across a container in rows from left to right.*

Because the flow layout manager is the default layout manager for panels, you don't have to explicitly set it in a panel if you want to use it. However, content panes don't use the flow layout manager as the default layout manager, so you must explicitly set the flow layout manager if you're working with a content pane. The following code sets a content pane to the flow layout manager and adds a few buttons:

```
Container contentPane = getContentPane();
contentPane.setLayout(new FlowLayout());
contentPane.add(new JButton("One"));
contentPane.add(new JButton("Two"));
contentPane.add(new JButton("Three"));
contentPane.add(new JButton("Four"));
contentPane.add(new JButton("Five"));
```

5

The grid layout manager

The *grid layout manager*, which is represented by the GridLayout class, arranges components in a grid of rows and columns. Similar to the flow layout manager, the grid layout manager arranges components from left to right, but they conform to a fixed arrangement of rows and columns. For example, you may create a grid layout as a 3×2 grid that is capable of holding six components. The first two components added will be placed in the first row, the second two in the second row, and so forth. Figure 5-3 shows how components are arranged when using the grid layout manager.

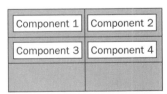

Figure 5-3 *The grid layout manager arranges components from left to right in a fixed arrangement of rows and columns.*

A major difference between the grid layout manager and the flow layout manager is that components in a grid layout are sized the same to fit into each grid cell. You set the number of cells by passing the number of rows and columns into the GridLayout constructor:

```
GridLayout grid = new GridLayout(3, 2);
```

The following code sets a content pane to a 2×4 grid layout manager and adds a few buttons:

```
Container contentPane = getContentPane();
contentPane.setLayout(new GridLayout(2, 4));
contentPane.add(new JButton("One"));
contentPane.add(new JButton("Two"));
contentPane.add(new JButton("Three"));
contentPane.add(new JButton("Four"));
contentPane.add(new JButton("Five"));
```

The border layout manager

The *border layout manager* is the default layout manager for the content pane of frames and is represented by the BorderLayout class. The border layout manager is very different from the flow and grid layout managers in that it arranges components in the geographic directions north, south, east, and west, along with another component in the center.

You specify the direction location of a component when you add it to a container by calling the add() method and passing one of the following BorderLayout constants as the second parameter: NORTH, SOUTH, EAST, WEST, or CENTER. For example:

```
add(new JButton("OK"), BorderLayout.NORTH);
```

If you don't add a component to a certain position, no physical space is set aside for the position. Figure 5-4 shows how components are arranged within a border layout manager.

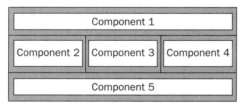

Figure 5-4 *The border layout manager arranges components in the geographic directions north, south, east, and west, along with another component in the center.*

The following code sets a content pane to a border layout manager and adds a few buttons:

```
Container contentPane = getContentPane();
contentPane.setLayout(new BorderLayout());
```

```
contentPane.add(new JButton("One"), BorderLayout.NORTH);
contentPane.add(new JButton("Two"), BorderLayout.WEST);
contentPane.add(new JButton("Three"), BorderLayout.CENTER);
contentPane.add(new JButton("Four"), BorderLayout.EAST);
contentPane.add(new JButton("Five"), BorderLayout.SOUTH);
```

The card layout manager

The *card layout manager*, which is represented by the CardLayout class, is a layout manager that arranges multiple panels so that they act like a stack of cards. A card layout manager consists of a group of panels with only one of the panels visible at any given time. You display different cards by calling the first(), last(), next(), and previous() methods on a CardLayout object and passing in the parent container. Each panel card can use its own layout manager to arrange the components it contains. Figure 5-5 shows how a card layout manager can be used to organize panels that themselves use other types of layouts. In this figure, the card layout is responsible for managing which panel is displayed at a given time.

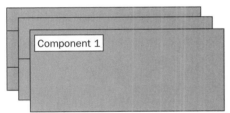

Figure 5-5   *The card layout manager arranges components on panels that act similar to a stack of cards, with only one visible at a given time.*

The card layout is handy for creating wizard-style interfaces in which the user is presented with a sequence of GUIs implemented as card panels. The following code sets a content pane to a card layout, adds a few panels, and sets the card layout to display the last panel added:

```
Container contentPane = getContentPane();
CardLayout card = new CardLayout();
contentPane.setLayout(card);
contentPane.add(new JPanel());
contentPane.add(new JPanel());
contentPane.add(new JPanel());
card.last(contentPane);
```

The box layout manager

The *box layout manager* is by far the most versatile of the layout managers. It is represented by the BoxLayout class and provides a means of arranging components horizontally or vertically next to each other. What makes the box layout so powerful is its support for nesting and its capability to fine-tune the spacing between components; you can create very intricate GUIs using nested box layouts. Part of the box layout's power comes from the fact that it respects a component's minimum, maximum, and preferred size, if specified. Unlike other layout managers, the box layout has a special container class named Box that is used in conjunction with the BoxLayout class. Figure 5-6 shows how interesting arrangements of components can be created by using the box layout.

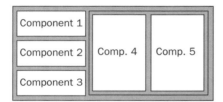

Figure 5-6 *The box layout manager arranges components horizontally or vertically next to each other.*

Remember that boxes in a box layout manager are invisible — their role is simply to determine the layout of visible components. In Figure 5-6, the first three components are added to a vertical box. The remaining two components are added to a nested horizontal box that sits alongside the vertical box.

The box layout manager takes an interesting approach to aligning components: you provide a floating point number between 0.0 and 1.0 that determines how a component is aligned with other components in the box. Figure 5-7 shows how different alignment values affect a vertical box.

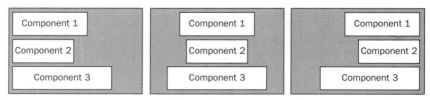

Figure 5-7 *Alignment values determine how components are aligned within the box layout manager.*

As Figure 5-7 shows, alignment values of 0.0, 0.5, and 1.0 are used to set the alignment of components in a box layout, respectively. In addition to tweaking the alignment, you can use invisible fillers to create space between components using the box layout. The Box class provides these types of invisible fillers:

- Rigid areas
- Glue
- Filler

Rigid areas are used to create fixed-size spaces between components in a single direction; *glue* is used to maximize the space between components in a single direction; and *filler* is used to create an invisible component with a minimum, maximum, and preferred size. Figure 5-8 shows how rigid areas, glue, and filler are used to control the space between components in the box layout manager.

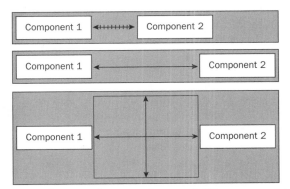

Figure 5-8   *Rigid areas, glue, and filler are used to control space between components in the box layout manager.*

To create a rigid area, you use the createRigidArea() method on a Box object. The createHorizontalGlue() and createVerticalGlue() methods are used to create glue between components. Finally, you must create an instance of the Box.Filler inner class to use filler.

The grid bag layout manager

Although the box layout manager is extremely versatile, the AWT provides a layout manager called grid bag that provides the most flexibility of all the layouts. Of course, increased flexibility often comes at a price. In the case of the grid bag layout manager, the price is the complexity of coding required to create an intricate GUI.

The *grid bag layout manager* is similar to the grid layout manager except that it provides greater control over the size and position of the cells in the grid. For example, grid bag layout manager lets you specify that some cells span multiple columns. You can also control the physical arrangement of components within specific cells in the grid.

In most cases, you can use nested box layouts instead of the grid bag layout manager. I encourage this approach because the box layout manager is much easier to understand and use than the grid bag layout manager. If you're just dying to find out how the grid bag layout manager works, please refer to the `GridBagLayout` and `GridBagConstraints` classes in the Java 2 API documentation.

5 Using Swing Components

Perhaps the most exciting aspect of the Swing toolkit is the suite of new components it introduces for building Java GUIs. Swing components include icons, labels, buttons, borders, lists, and combo boxes, to name a few. The remainder of this section explores some of these components and how they are used to build GUIs.

Icons

Icons are used in Swing GUIs to provide visual cues associated with GUI features. The `Icon` interface defines the general characteristics of a Swing icon, including methods used to work with the icon. Java provides a class named `ImageIcon` that implements the `Icon` interface and provides a simple way to create icons based on GIF or JPEG images. To create an icon based on an image, simply provide the name of the image file as the parameter to the `ImageIcon` constructor:

```
ImageIcon icon = new ImageIcon("Fish.gif");
```

Optionally, you can also provide a second parameter that identifies a text description of the icon:

```
ImageIcon icon = new ImageIcon("Fish.gif", "Big fishy");
```

The text description for an icon is not displayed, but it is available for informational purposes via a call to the `getDescription()` method.

The `ImageIcon` class isn't actually a Java component, which means that you can't use it by itself within a GUI. The `ImageIcon` class must always be used in conjunction with components such as the `JLabel`

component, which you will learn about shortly. The following code is
an example of using an image icon with a label component:

```
Container contentPane = getContentPane();
ImageIcon icon = new ImageIcon("Fish.gif");
contentPane.add(new JLabel(icon));
```

The results of this code are shown in Figure 5-9. As you can see,
the image icon of a fish is drawn within the confines of an applet.
More specifically, the image icon is drawn within a label component
in the applet.

Figure 5-9   *The image icon example code results in an image of a fish
being displayed within a label component.*

You are probably familiar with images used on toolbar buttons in
many popular applications such as Web browsers. You may notice
that when these buttons become disabled, the images on them take
on a gray, colorless appearance. A grayed image provides a visual cue
to let you know that a particular button is disabled. In Java, image
icons are used to represent images in most components, including
buttons, and are therefore responsible for offering a grayed look in
response to a component becoming disabled.

Swing uses a gray filter to carry out a default graying feature for
the ImageIcon class. This means that Swing automatically generates a
grayed version of any images that you use with the ImageIcon class,
which keeps you from having to provide an additional grayed image.
If you want to create a custom icon class of your own you must provide a suitable graying feature.

Labels

Labels are output-only components that are used to present both text
and graphical information to the user. You often see labels used in

conjunction with input components such as text edit fields. Labels are represented in Swing by the JLabel class. The following code is an example of creating a simple text label:

```
Container contentPane = getContentPane();
JLabel label = new JLabel("Surprise!");
contentPane.add(label);
```

The results of this code are shown in Figure 5-10.

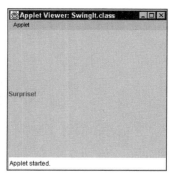

Figure 5-10   *The text label example code results in a string of text being displayed within a label component.*

You already learned how to create an icon label by passing an icon as the only parameter to the JLabel constructor. You can also combine text and an icon to create a more compelling and informative label:

```
Container contentPane = getContentPane();
ImageIcon icon = new ImageIcon("Cake.gif");
JLabel label = new JLabel("Surprise!", icon,
  JLabel.CENTER);
contentPane.add(label);
```

The results of this code are shown in Figure 5-11.

The JLabel class supports a set of alignment constants that are used to specify the horizontal and vertical alignment of the label's contents. For example, the TOP, LEFT, BOTTOM, RIGHT, and CENTER constants are used to determine the horizontal and vertical alignment of text within a text label. The JLabel class also supports geographic alignment constants such as NORTH and NORTH_EAST.

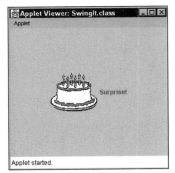

Figure 5-11 *The text/icon label example code results in a string of text and an image being displayed within a label component.*

You set the horizontal and vertical alignment of a label using the setHorizontalAlignment() and setVerticalAlignment() methods. You can also use the same constants to set a label's text position with respect to its icon by calling setHorizontalTextPosition() and setVerticalTextPosition(). The following code is an example of setting the horizontal and vertical text position of a label:

```
label.setHorizontalTextPosition(JLabel.CENTER);
label.setVerticalTextPosition(JLabel.BOTTOM);
```

The previous code demonstrates how alignment constants are used to establish the positioning of label contents. These alignment constants are all defined in the SwingConstants interface, which is implemented by all Swing components that require alignment. The alignment constants defined in the SwingConstants interface are:

LEFT	WEST
RIGHT	NORTH_WEST
TOP	NORTH
BOTTOM	NORTH_EAST
CENTER	HORIZONTAL
EAST	VERTICAL
SOUTH_EAST	LEADING
SOUTH	TRAILING
SOUTH_WEST	

Buttons

A commonly used GUI component is the button. Swing supports buttons via the JButton class, which provides support for a basic push button with text and/or an icon. Following are examples of creating JButton components:

```
JButton b1 = new JButton("OK");
JButton b2 = new JButton(icon);
JButton b3 = new JButton("OK", icon);
```

In addition to the JButton class, Swing also includes the JToggleButton, JCheckBox, and JRadioButton classes, which are types of buttons. A toggle button is a two-state button that remains pushed-in after you click it; when you click it again, it returns to the unpushed-in state. A checkbox is a type of toggle button that displays a check mark next to a line of text. Finally, radio buttons are used in groups to provide a mutually exclusive series of choices; only one radio button in a group can be selected at any given time.

When a button is pushed, it generates an action event. You register an event listener to handle button action events by calling the addActionListener() method on a button. You must then implement the ActionListener interface in the event listener class by providing a suitable actionPerformed() method. You can determine which button was pushed by calling the getSource() method on the ActionEvent object passed into the actionPerformed() method, and then casting it to a JButton.

Borders

Although Swing components such as labels and buttons are visually appealing by themselves, it is possible to dress them up a little to improve the overall look of a GUI. You do so with *borders*, which are special classes that determine the appearance of the outer edge of components. Like icons, borders aren't actually components. Java's border classes are located in the javax.swing.border package, and include support for these types of borders:

- Empty border
- Line border
- Etched border
- Bevel border
- Soft bevel border
- Matte border

These borders provide a variety of different looks around the outer edge of components. You set the border for a component by calling the setBorder() method and passing in a border object. For example, the following code sets the border for a label to a line border that is magenta in color and 2 pixels wide:

```
label.setBorder(new LineBorder(Color.magenta, 2));
```

The EtchedBorder, BevelBorder, and SoftBevelBorder classes all accept a parameter indicating whether the border is to be raised or lowered in appearance. Examples of setting each type of appearance are:

```
label1.setBorder(new EtchedBorder(EtchedBorder.RAISED));
label2.setBorder(new BevelBorder(BevelBorder.LOWERED));
```

Finally, the MatteBorder class accepts a tiled icon that is used to draw the border around a component:

```
label.setBorder(new MatteBorder(new ImageIcon("Daisy.gif")));
```

Java supports two types of borders that are built around the types you just learned about: compound borders and titled borders. Compound borders are represented by the CompoundBorder class and enable you to nest a border within the insets of another border. Titled borders are represented by the TitledBorder class and enable you to place title text along the edge of a border.

Borders might not seem like that big of a deal at this point because they only determine how the outer edge of a component is drawn. However, you have to consider the ramifications of using borders throughout an entire user interface. By carefully using bevel and etched borders, for example, you can create intuitive and visually appealing user interfaces with a three-dimensional look. More specifically, you could set the bevel border for some components to have a raised look, while setting others for a lowered look. This visual effect can significantly help the organization of a user interface. Besides, users have come to expect slick user interfaces in modern graphical applications, so you should aspire to give them what they want. Borders help make this job a little easier.

Lists and combo boxes

Lists and *combo boxes* are GUI components that manage lists of items. The user selects items from a list or combo box by clicking on them with the mouse or navigating through the list with the arrow keys on the keyboard. Swing supports lists and combo boxes with the JList and JComboBox classes. Lists are used to list a series of text and/or icon items from which the user can select one or more items. You can create a list from an array by passing the array into the constructor for the JList object:

```
Container contentPane = getContentPane();
String[] days = { "Sunday", "Monday", "Tuesday",
  "Wednesday", "Thursday", "Friday", "Saturday" };
JList list = new JList(days);
contentPane.add(list);
```

Figure 5-12 shows how this list looks in the context of an applet.

Figure 5-12   *The list example code results in a list component containing the days of the week.*

You might have noticed that the list in the figure doesn't have scroll bars, which means that it doesn't support scrolling. Many components require support for scrolling when their contents become larger than their physical view space. Swing makes it very easy to support scrolling in a component by using the JScrollPane class. The JScrollPane class implements a scrolling pane that serves as a container for components that require scrolling functionality. The JScrollPane class assesses the scrolling needs of a component and determines whether it should display scroll bars for altering the component's view space. In most cases, you can rely on the default behavior of the JScrollPane class and avoid writing custom scrolling code.

If you simply create a list and add it to a pane, the list won't support scrolling. To support scrolling, you must create a JScrollPane object and pass the list into its constructor:

```
JScrollPane scrollPane = new JScrollPane(list);
contentPane.add(scrollPane);
```

To select an item in a list, call the `setSelectedIndex()` method and pass in the zero-based index of the list item:

```
list.setSelectedIndex(3);
```

You can also select multiple items in a list by passing the starting and ending indices of the items to the `setSelectionInterval()` method:

```
list.setSelectionInterval(2, 4);
```

Lists generate list selection events when you select an item in a list. To handle a list event, you implement the `ListSelectionListener` interface, which defines a single method — `valueChanged()`. The following code is an example of printing the list item that was selected using the `getSelectedValue()` method in the `JList` class:

```
public void valueChanged(ListSelectionEvent e) {
   System.out.println(list.getSelectedValue());
}
```

Combo boxes are similar to lists in that they provide a GUI for selecting items from a list of choices. Unlike lists, combo boxes only display a single item; multiple items are revealed in a drop-down window when you activate the combo box. Combo boxes are limited in that they only allow one item to be selected at a time. On the other hand, combo boxes are flexible in that they can enable users to manually enter new items. Combo boxes also save on screen space because they only open to reveal choices when you click them. The `JComboBox` class is similar in many ways to `JList`, which means that working with combo boxes in Java code is similar to using lists.

More Swing components

In addition to the Swing components that you learned about in this chapter, Swing also supports other components that are useful in certain situations. These other components and the Swing classes that carry out their functionality are:

- Table — `JTable`
- Text components — `JTextField`, `JPasswordField`, `JTextArea`, `JTextPane`
- Scroller — `JScrollBar`, `JScrollPane`
- Slider — `JSlider`
- Progress bar — `JProgressBar`, `JProgressMonitor`
- Tree — `JTree`

Although these components are all very powerful and serve an important role in certain GUI scenarios, the details of using them are beyond the scope of this chapter. Using them isn't much different from using the other Swing components that you've already worked with in this chapter.

Using Menus and Toolbars

As you well know, menus are a common part of applications in practically every GUI environment. Swing provides a suite of classes for creating just about any menu that you could possibly need. The JMenuBar class forms the basis for Swing menus by serving as the main menu bar for an application. The JMenu class represents individual drop-down menus in menu bars. Menu items within a drop-down menu can be one of the following types:

- Normal menu item
- Checkbox menu item
- Radio button menu item

As powerful as menus can be, they are surprisingly easy to work with. To create a menu you first create a JMenuBar object and then set it as the menu bar for the application frame by calling the setJMenuBar() method:

```
JMenuBar menuBar = new JMenuBar();
setJMenuBar(menuBar);
```

With the menu bar in place, you can start creating and adding drop-down menus:

```
JMenu editMenu = new JMenu("Edit");
menuBar.add(editMenu);
```

The final step is to create and add menu items to the drop-down menus:

```
editMenu.add(new JMenuItem("Cut"));
editMenu.add(new JMenuItem("Copy"));
editMenu.add(new JMenuItem("Paste"));
```

The previous code assumes that you want to create basic text-only menu items. You can also create menu items with icons:

```
editMenu.add(new JMenuItem("Undo",
  new ImageIcon("Undo.gif")));
```

The JCheckBoxMenuItem and JRadioButtonMenuItem classes work very much like JMenuItem in that they can be created as text-only or as text with an icon.

Although the vast majority of users are comfortable navigating menus via the mouse, it is nonetheless very important to provide a keyboard interface for interacting with menus. This is accomplished through keyboard mnemonics and accelerators. A *mnemonic* enables you to navigate through the hierarchy of a menu to select a menu item or invoke a menu command, usually in conjunction with the Alt key. An *accelerator* provides a means of directly accessing a specific menu item without navigating through the menu hierarchy.

An underlined character in the name of a menu item identifies a mnemonic. Accelerator keys are also visible in menu items; an accelerator key combination is identified to the right of a menu item. To set the mnemonic and accelerator for a given menu item, you simply call the setMnemonic() and setAccelerator() methods on the item:

```
copyItem = new JMenuItem("Copy");
copyItem.setMnemonic(KeyEvent.VK_C);
copyItem.setAccelerator(KeyStroke.getKeyStroke(KeyEvent.VK_C,
  ActionEvent.CTRL_MASK));
```

This code sets the mnemonic character for the Copy menu item to C and then sets the accelerator to the key combination Ctrl+C. Other key masks, such as SHIFT_MASK and ALT_MASK, can also be used when setting an accelerator.

Although not as critical, toolbars have become about as standard as menus in modern graphical applications. *Toolbars* provide a means of accessing commonly used application features from an array of buttons or other components positioned along a bar at the top of an application's main window frame. Actually, toolbars can be positioned anywhere in an application's frame but the top is the most popular location.

The JToolBar class represents a Swing toolbar that acts as a container. Creating a toolbar using the JToolBar class is as simple as constructing an object and adding components to it:

```
JToolBar toolbar = new JToolBar();
JButton button = new JButton(new ImageIcon("Cut.gif"));
toolbar.add(button);
button = new JButton(new ImageIcon("Copy.gif"));
toolbar.add(button);
button = new JButton(new ImageIcon("Paste.gif"));
toolbar.add(button);
contentPane.add(toolbar, BorderLayout.NORTH);
```

In this example, a toolbar is created and three icon buttons are added to it. Notice that unlike menus, which require the calling of a special method to set them, toolbars are added to the content pane of a frame window.

Because toolbar buttons typically don't contain text, they don't have an action command associated with them by default. You must explicitly set the action command for icon toolbar buttons so that they have the appropriate command string when they generate action events. This is accomplished by calling the setActionCommand() method:

```
button.setActionCommand("Edit");
```

A common problem in GUI applications is coordinating GUI actions that are common to multiple components. For example, you may have a menu item for the Paste command as well as a toolbar button. It's important for these two GUI elements to generate the same events and share the same state information (enabled, disabled, etc.). Swing provides a special interface called Action that solves this problem by enabling you to create general action commands and then add them to a toolbar or menu. The appropriate GUI element is automatically created and a common event listener is registered. For example:

```
PasteAction paste = new PasteAction("Paste", pasteIcon);
editMenu.add(paste);
toolbar.add(paste);
paste.setEnabled(false);
```

This code demonstrates how to create a single paste action and add it to a menu and a toolbar. The call to setEnabled() results in both the Paste menu item and the Paste toolbar button being disabled. The PasteAction class is a class that you must create to implement the Action interface.

If you don't care about the state of GUI elements matching, there is a simpler approach to coordinating actions among multiple components. All you have to do is set the action command strings to match. This results in a single actionPerformed() method responding to both menu item and toolbar button events.

Actions come into play when more than one GUI element invokes the same command within an application. A good example is the File Save command that is found in most applications. You would typically have a menu item and a toolbar button for this command. You already know that you can set the two GUI elements to the same action command for them to generate the same action event. However, what if you want to disable them if no changes have been made to necessitate saving. This is where the real power of actions is revealed.

By using actions, the two GUI elements are effectively handled as one. You can enable or disable the action itself instead of the GUI elements. These settings are then automatically reflected in all of the GUI elements that were created from the action. The primary limitation of actions is that they can only be used to create JMenuItem and JButton objects. In other words, you can't use them with radio buttons or checkboxes. Even so, actions provide a clean way to synchronize the appearance and functionality of menu items and toolbar buttons.

There is one last topic to touch on that relates to toolbars: *tool tips*, which are small text windows that appear when the user pauses with the mouse cursor over a component. Because tool tip windows are designed to be unobtrusive, the text associated with a tool tip should be very concise. Fortunately, it is very simple to set tool tips for a component. A call to the setToolTipText() method is all that is required:

```
button.setToolTipText("Copy");
```

This code sets the tool tip text for a button to the string "Copy", which is displayed whenever the user pauses with the mouse cursor over the button. Although tool tips are primarily used with icon buttons, you can assign tool tips to any Swing component to help make its usage clearer.

Dialog Boxes, Option Panes, and Choosers

Although you can display and retrieve information by placing components directly in the content pane of an applet or application window, there are situations in which it is helpful to place these components in a separate window that is displayed temporarily. This type of window is known as a *dialog box* and provides a means of displaying a "temporary" user interface that displays or retrieves information, and then goes away. *Option panes* are standard dialog boxes that make it easier to accomplish certain tasks, alleviating the need to construct a custom dialog box GUI. *Choosers* are specialized dialog boxes designed to retrieve commonly sought information from the user such as a filename or a color.

Swing supports dialog boxes through the JDialog class, which contains a content pane to which you add dialog box components.

Constructing a custom dialog box GUI is very similar to constructing an application GUI through the content pane of a frame window. Swing supports option panes through the JOptionPane class, which provides a variety of different static methods that can be used to create standard dialog boxes such as message dialog boxes, confirmation dialog boxes, and input dialog boxes, among others. Swing also supports choosers, which are standard dialog boxes tailored to very specific tasks such as browsing for a file or selecting a color.

The alternative to standard dialog boxes is custom dialog boxes, which are dialog boxes whose GUI is entirely determined by you. The JDialog class serves as the container for creating custom dialog boxes. To create a custom dialog box, you derive a class from the JDialog class and create an instance of it. You then create and add components to the dialog object just as if you were constructing a GUI within the content pane of a frame window. In fact, dialogs actually have content panes that you use identically to content panes in frame windows. The border layout is the default layout used for dialog content panes, which is also similar to content panes in frame windows.

Using option panes

Because option panes are standard dialog boxes, they are very easy to display and use. The most straightforward way to use option panes is to call one of the static methods defined in the JOptionPane class:

- showMessageDialog()
- showConfirmDialog()
- showInputDialog()
- showOptionDialog()

These methods take similar parameters that are used to customize the appearance and functionality of the dialog boxes. For example, each method accepts a "message type" parameter that determines the look and feel of the dialog, along with the default icon that is displayed. This parameter can be one of these constants: ERROR_MESSAGE, INFORMATION_MESSAGE, WARNING_MESSAGE, QUESTION_MESSAGE, or PLAIN_MESSAGE. The following code is an example of creating a message dialog box:

```
JOptionPane.showMessageDialog(this,
   "You are running low on memory.", "Memory warning",
   JOptionPane.WARNING_MESSAGE);
```

Confirmation dialog boxes are different from message dialog boxes in that they present multiple buttons. These constants are used to identify the buttons in a confirmation dialog: YES_NO_OPTION, YES_NO_CANCEL_OPTION, OK_CANCEL_OPTION. The following code is an example of creating a confirmation dialog box:

```
JOptionPane.showConfirmDialog(this,
  "Are you sure you want to exit the application?",
  "Exit application", JOptionPane.YES_NO_OPTION);
```

The return value of the showConfirmDialog() method identifies the button that was pressed by the user to exit the dialog box: YES_OPTION, NO_OPTION, OK_OPTION, CANCEL_OPTION, or CLOSED_OPTION.

Creating input and option dialog boxes is similar to creating message and confirmation dialog boxes, the main difference being that you provide additional parameters to the latter two dialogs to specify a set of options from which the user can select.

Using choosers

Choosers are specialized dialog boxes designed to retrieve information from the user within the context of a commonly performed task. For example, browsing a disk drive or network for a file is a common task that users perform. Swing includes a file chooser that provides a powerful GUI for performing this task. There is also a color chooser, which is a very intuitive GUI used to select colors. The JFileChooser and JColorChooser classes implement file and color choosers in Java.

The easiest way to use the Swing color chooser is to call the static showDialog() method in the JColorChooser class:

```
Color color = JColorChooser.showDialog(this, "Select color",
  Color.green);
```

The first parameter is the parent container. The second parameter is the caption to be displayed in the chooser dialog box. The third parameter is the color to be initially selected. The showDialog() method returns the color that the user selected.

To create a file chooser, you must first create an instance of the JFileChooser class and then call the showOpenDialog() or showSaveDialog() method:

```
JFileChooser chooser = new JFileChooser();
int retVal = chooser.showOpenDialog(this);
```

The parameter to showOpenDialog() is the parent container for the dialog box. The return value of this method indicates the button that was pressed by the user to exit the dialog: APPROVE_OPTION or

CANCEL_OPTION. You can then determine the name of the file selected by calling the getName() method.

Pluggable Look and Feel

One problem with a cross-platform GUI such as Swing is that it typically uses the least-common denominator of generic GUI features because it has to be capable of working on a variety of different platforms. A second problem is that applications designed with a "generic" GUI all tend to have a generic look that doesn't mesh well with the underlying native GUI. Java 2 addresses both of these problems in Swing with a "pluggable look and feel" feature.

By using a pluggable look and feel, a Swing GUI is capable of querying the underlying native GUI and taking on its look and feel. This means that a single Java application will look and feel like a native Windows application when run on Windows and will look and feel like a native Macintosh application when run on a Mac. Currently, Swing supports four different look and feels:

- Java (Metal)
- Windows
- Macintosh
- Motif

If you don't explicitly set the look and feel of an applet or application, Swing automatically uses the Java look and feel, which is also known as Metal. So, all of the Swing code you've developed thus far uses the Java look and feel. Although it doesn't make too much sense, you could set the look and feel of an application to Windows or Motif even if it is run on a different platform. However, the Macintosh look and feel is only available on the Macintosh platform.

Setting the look and feel of an applet or application is surprisingly simple given the sweeping GUI changes that result from it. The Java API provides a class named UIManager that includes static methods for setting the look and feel with relative ease. The following code is an example of using the setLookAndFeel() method to set the look and feel of an application to the Windows look and feel.

```
try {
  UIManager.setLookAndFeel(
    "com.sun.java.swing.plaf.windows.WindowsLookAndFeel");
}
catch (Exception e) {
}
```

In this example, the class name of the Windows look-and-feel class is passed into the setLookAndFeel() method. The following look-and-feel classes are supported in the Java 2 API and correspond to the looks and feels that were discussed previously:

- javax.swing.plaf.metal.MetalLookAndFeel
- com.sun.java.swing.plaf.windows.WindowsLookAndFeel
- com.sun.java.swing.plaf.mac.MacLookAndFeel
- com.sun.java.swing.plaf.motif.MotifLookAndFeel

If you want your applet or application to assume the native look and feel of the platform on which it is running, you can call the getSystemLookAndFeelClassName() method to determine the native look and feel. This is the preferred approach to ensure that an applet or application takes on the look and feel of the native platform on which it is running. The following code is an example of setting an application to the native look and feel:

```
try {
   String laf = UIManager.getSystemLookAndFeelClassName();
   UIManager.setLookAndFeel(laf);
}
catch (Exception e) {
}
```

Although the look and feel of an application can be set dynamically at any time, you should initially set it in the main() method for the application before doing anything else. This is important because the look and feel should be set prior to creating any components.

6

Animation and Threads

Animation is a word that shares a root with *animal* and *animate*. It's easy to see why: animated objects, like animals, have the power to move of their own accord. When you use Java's animation capabilities, you can create objects that move around the screen without prompting by the user. Although this chapter doesn't go into the fine points of advanced animation, it does introduce basic animation techniques that enable applets to move objects around the screen.

In Java, animation requires the use of *threads*, a concept that is explained in this chapter. The thread capability is a feature of the Java API that harnesses the power of modern computers. Although threads are called *processes* in some programming languages, the basic idea is the same: a thread is a background task that runs independently of the main program. Like a second-unit director in a movie company, a thread goes off and works on its own schedule.

The Java Thread/Animation Model

In Java, a second thread handles animation (see Figure 6-1); the first thread is the main program itself. (If you are new to the concept of threads, you may want to skip ahead to the next section, "Background: Threads," p. 619.) You create the second thread by using the Thread class. You can have as many extra threads as you have thread objects. First, create an object of the Thread class and then call its start() method. In response to start(), the Java interpreter calls your run() method, which you can define in the same class that starts the thread. The run() method is the starting point for all threads other than the program's main thread.

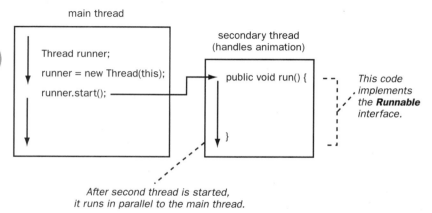

Figure 6-1   *The Java thread programming model*

Creating a thread

Figure 6-1 includes what may at first look like a strange line of code:

```
runner = new Thread(this);
```

In plain English, what this statement means is this:

When runner starts, use the run() method defined in this class.

The argument to the Thread constructor is significant because of the object's class. Java looks at the object's class to find a run() method there. The run() method becomes associated with this particular thread.

The this keyword refers to the applet itself. (In general, this refers to the current object.) Therefore, in this example, Java uses the run() method defined in the applet class.

Suppose you specified a different object in the constructor:

```
runner2 = new Thread(threadDirector);
```

In this case, Java would look at threadDirector and determine its class. Then, when runner2 was started, it would call the run() method defined in threadDirector's class.

Java is flexible when it comes to creating multiple threads with different behavior. For each thread, you can specify a different object and therefore a different run() method (unless, of course, the objects are of the same class).

Implementing the runnable interface

There's another piece to the puzzle of creating multithreaded Java programs. The preceding section described how a class defines thread behavior by defining a run() method:

```
public void run() {
  Put_your_thread_behavior_here
}
```

6

The placeholder Put_your_thread_behavior_here refers to code that implements the actual thread activity. Later sections of this chapter develop this code and show how it works in the context of a complete application.

Only one other thing is required: The class that includes this method must declare that it implements the Runnable interface. This is easily done with the implements keyword.

Java uses the term *interface* in a special way. (Actually, it is nearly identical to the concept as used in Microsoft's Component Object Model.) An interface is a set of services that a class agrees to implement. These "services" are actually abstract methods. A class implements these methods by providing definitions for them.

In the case of the Runnable interface, a class must implement just one method: run(). In effect, implementing Runnable is a way of saying, "I agree to provide a definition for run()." Requiring that a class implement Runnable is Java's way of making sure that a run() method can be called when a thread is started.

Background: Threads

Java threads are no different from multithread programming concepts in other programming languages. If you're familiar with the concept, you can safely skip this section.

What is a thread?

Modern computer systems have multitasking capability that enables several programs to run at once. In actuality, the programs aren't running at the same time (unless the computer has parallel processors), but the processor switches so quickly between programs that they appear to run simultaneously. What's more, each program can proceed, usually at acceptable speed, without waiting for the other programs to terminate.

Threads are a special form of multitasking. They introduce the following twist: when a program is multithreaded, two or more tasks can be running that originate in the same program. The upshot of this is that a single program can cause multiple activities to occur simultaneously. This capability is useful if a program needs to print a document or do intense computation in the background, for example, while still managing to interact with the user in a timely manner.

All programs automatically have at least one thread. This thread, which we might call the main thread, is the one that starts when the program is loaded into memory. To add a second, third, or fourth thread, a program uses the Thread class and the Runnable interface.

Why are threads needed for animation?

In the old world of DOS programming — if you ever programmed in DOS — you could act as if you were the only game in town. If you wanted to show an animation demo, for example, you probably just went ahead and did it. Graphical user interface (GUI) systems, however, require everyone to be a good citizen, and Java is no exception.

Even after your applet starts an animation effect, it should continue being fully responsive to the user. Maybe the user will want to pull down the Applet menu, for example, or perform an action to close the applet window. But if your applet or application were single-threaded and went into an infinite loop to do animation, it would no longer be able to respond to methods such as paint(), not to mention event response methods such as mouseClicked() and mouseMoved(). From the user's point of view, the user interface (UI) would suddenly become inoperable.

Multithreading is the solution. After the animator thread is started, it can go off and do its own thing. The main thread continues, running in parallel, all the time responding to user actions. The secondary thread goes off and does the fun stuff, while the main thread sticks around to interact with the user. If the user resizes the applet window, for example, the main thread is the one that calls paint() in response to that event. The animator thread doesn't know anything about it.

The Basic Animation Applet

Once you understand the use of threads in Java, it's easy to start writing applets that use animation techniques because most animated applets use the same boilerplate thread code to carry out animation. In other words, the thread-specific code will likely be very similar across all of your animated applets.

● NOTE

You can write animated applications as well as animated applets. You can adapt the following applet code to work in an application, as described in on page 583 of Chapter 4, "Components and Events." However, most applications are single-thread and do not have start() methods.

The following applet contains the basic code for animation. In a real example, you could substitute a different value for time_delay, which specifies a delay in milliseconds. In this case, a value of 100 causes a periodic delay of 1/10th of a second. You can either set the variable time_delay to a different constant or simply insert the constant directly where time_delay appears in the code.

```
import java.awt.*;
import java.applet.*;

public class Animator extends Applet implements Runnable {
  Thread runner;
  int time_delay = 100;  // Substitute your own value for
                         //  time_delay.

  public void start() {
    runner = new Thread(this);
    runner.start();
  }

  public void run() {
    while(true) {
      // Advance animation and cause repaint.
      try {
        Thread.sleep(time_delay);
      } catch (InterruptedException e) {
        ;
      }
    }
  }

  public void paint(Graphics g) {
```

```
    // Paint current animation
  }
}
```

Much of what you see here is standard code for creating, start-ing, and pausing the animation thread. You can use this standard code in one applet after another. Here, I've named this thread runner, although you can give it any name you like.

This code creates a thread that is used to establish a timing loop for controlling animation in the applet. You will likely use code very similar to this in all of your animated applets. Table 6-1 summarizes applet methods that are called and describes how an animated applet should respond.

Table 6-1   *Applet methods that the animation thread should respond to*

Applet Method	Situation and recommended response
init()	The applet has just been loaded into memory. This is the logical place to allocate objects owned by the applet.
start()	Either the applet has just started or else the user is resuming operation after making the applet pause. Although you can check the thread's state and choose to suspend the thread when it is paused, it is usually sufficient (and simpler) to create a new thread.

The real animation work takes place in the run() and paint() methods. The run() method includes some interesting code that you may not have seen before:

```
while(true) {
  // Advance animation and cause repaint.
  try {
    Thread.sleep(time_delay);
  } catch (InterruptedException e) {
    ;
  }
}
```

This method employs the try and catch keywords, which are part of the Java exception-handling syntax. If this seems complex or alien right now, don't worry. Just include the try and catch state-ments as they appear here, substituting a time_delay value of your choice. This value is in milliseconds (thousandths of a second). For example, if you wanted the applet to pause half a second between each drawing, you would use the value 500.

CROSS-REFERENCE

To learn more about classes, see "Exception Handling" in Part I, "Java 2 Language Reference," page 46.

In case you're curious, here's what's going on: the sleep() method causes the current thread to go to sleep for the specified number of milliseconds. When the interval elapses, the system wakes up the thread. In the meantime, however, it's possible that something might interrupt the thread before it is scheduled to wake. Such a situation generates an exception of type InterruptedException. The code must respond to this exception, which it does by using the catch keyword. In this case, the exception handler doesn't do anything, although it could (such as displaying an error message).

Java does not require all exceptions to be handled. Exception handling is optional for exceptions derived from the RuntimeException class. However, because the InterruptedException type is not derived from RuntimeException, it must be handled or the Java compiler complains.

NOTE

Java's rules for exception handling are nearly the same as those for ANSI C++. The principal difference is that Java requires that exception classes be derived, directly or indirectly, from the Throwable class.

Creating a Simple Animation

The following example creates a simple animation: a big black dot that moves down and across the screen. Most of this example is the same as the code template in the previous section. The additions are the definition of two coordinate variables, x and y; statements in the run() method that increment these values and force a repaint; and a call to the fillOval() method to draw the dot.

Be forewarned that you will almost certainly see a noticeable flickering when you run the applet. Don't worry. We'll take care of that problem in the next section, "Smoothing Out the Animation."

```
import java.awt.*;
import java.applet.*;

public class Animator extends Applet implements Runnable {
    Thread runner;
    int x, y;    // Current coordinates of the dot
```

```java
public void init() {
  x = y = 0;  // Start in top left corner.
}

public void start() {
  runner = new Thread(this);
  runner.start();
}

public void run() {
  while(true) {
    x += 4;     // Move x to new location.
    y += 4;     // Move y to new location.
    repaint(); // Force a repaint now.
              try {
      Thread.sleep(250);  // Pause .25 secs.
    } catch (InterruptedException e) {
      ;
    }
  }
}

public void paint(Graphics g) {
  g.fillOval(x, y, 50, 50);  // Paint the dot.
}
}
```

In this example, I have commented all statements that involve some change or addition to the basic animation thread code that you've already seen; uncommented lines are part of the boilerplate animation thread code.

Smoothing Out the Animation

You may feel that the annoying flickering of the dot in the sample animation code in the prior section spoiled the fun. This flickering is caused by inefficient drawing and redrawing of the dot and its surrounding background. The techniques for smooth animation presented in this section have the effect of updating the screen much more efficiently.

Not all animation presents the complex challenges of a moving image. For example, if a figure stays in place but displays changing pictures, you need only to clip the picture's area before redrawing (this will be the same rectangle every time) and then override update() so that all it does is call paint().

NOTE

The techniques presented in the next two sections—clipping and double buffering—are not dependent on each other. Sometimes using just one or the other is enough. Double buffering is the more powerful technique, and you can often get good results using it alone. On my system, I found that the animation ran 10 percent faster using both techniques rather than using double buffering only. A slightly more optimal performance, therefore, was achieved by using both techniques.

Technique 1: Clipping

The technique of *clipping* restricts repainting to as small an area as possible. In the example presented earlier, the applet redraws the entire display just to repaint the dot. A better approach is to determine exactly what needs to be redrawn and then call the `clipRect()` graphics method to limit the repainting.

This technique is straightforward. Obviously, the old dot needs to be erased and a new one drawn at the new location. If you merge the two affected areas, you get the total area that requires repainting. Figure 6-2 shows how this clipping area is determined. The resulting area must be in the shape of a rectangle, so that the corners are filled out.

1. Current picture
of the dot.

2. Dot must be erased
at the old location.

3. Dot is drawn in at
the new location.

4. Clipping region is the union
of the old and new locations.

Figure 6-2   *Determining the clipping rectangle*

Technique 2: Double buffering

The default behavior (that is, without double buffering) for updating the screen does the following:

1. Fill the display area with the background color.
2. Call the paint() method to draw foreground lines, text, figures, and so on.

This approach is fine for static displays, where the graphics are repainted only occasionally. However, for animation programs that may replenish images several times a second, it involves too much redrawing.

Animation should be as smooth as possible. Ideally, the image and its surrounding background should be painted together in a single drawing operation. The solution is *double buffering*, a technique that uses an offscreen image stored in memory.

With double buffering, the program paints into this offscreen image, drawing and redrawing as necessary. Then, when the image is complete, the code blasts it to the screen in a single smooth operation. Figure 6-3 summarizes double buffering as a two-step process.

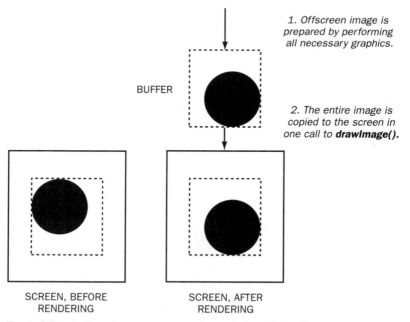

1. Offscreen image is prepared by performing all necessary graphics.

BUFFER

2. The entire image is copied to the screen in one call to **drawImage()**.

SCREEN, BEFORE RENDERING

SCREEN, AFTER RENDERING

Figure 6-3   *Animating movement through double buffering*

Remember that screen operations are costly, both in time and in the effect on the eye. Buffering is a way of achieving screen-access economy.

The revised animation code

The following code shows the clipping and double-buffering techniques in use together. Combining these techniques makes for the fastest, smoothest animation possible with Java.

First, some new instance variables are added to the applet:

```
Image buffer;
int curw, curh;
```

The Image object, named buffer, is the offscreen drawing area. Its dimensions are made to match the applet's width and height, which are stored in curw and curh, respectively. If these dimensions change for any reason (the user might resize the applet, for example), buffer must be resized immediately.

Aside from the variable definitions, all the new code is in the run() method, shown next. This code introduces a couple of important techniques. After determining the clipping region, it writes to the buffer by getting the buffer's graphics object and calling update(), passing the object as an argument. This approach tricks the applet into updating the buffer instead of the screen. Then the code blasts the image to the screen by getting the applet's graphics object and calling drawImage(). It does not wait for a repaint, which would be too slow.

Both operations use the getGraphics() method. As I mentioned in the section "Applets, Applications, and Graphics" in Chapter 3 (page 540), you cannot get a valid graphics object by calling the Graphics constructor directly. But any component or image will gladly pass you its Graphics object if you call getGraphics(). The following is the new version of the run() method:

```
public void run() {
  while(true) {
    // Create new buffer if none exists OR
    // if applet is resized.
    if ( (buffer == null) ||
      (curw != getWidth()) ||
      (curh != getHeight()) ) {
      buffer = createImage(getWidth(), getHeight());
      curw = getWidth();
      curh = getHeight();
    }
```

```
       // Determine clipping region.
       Rectangle oldRect = new Rectangle(x, y, 51, 51);
       x += 4;
       y += 4;
                           Rectangle newRect = new Rectangle(x, y,
   51, 51);
       Rectangle r = newRect.union(oldRect);

       // Update offscreen buffer instead of the screen.
       Graphics g = buffer.getGraphics();
       g.clipRect(r.x, r.y, r.width, r.height);
       update(g);

       // Copy buffer directly to display in a single drawing
       // operation.
       g = getGraphics();
       g.clipRect(r.x, r.y, r.width, r.height);
       g.drawImage(buffer, 0, 0, this);
                           try {
         Thread.sleep(250);
       }   // Pause .25 secs.
       catch (InterruptedException e) {
         ;
       }
     }
   }
```

Final Touches: Follow the Bouncing Ball

If you take the Animator example code from earlier in this chapter
(p. 621) and add the variables and the new version of run() as shown
in the preceding section, you should get smooth movement. (It actually is slightly jerky because it is moving four pixels at a time, but
you can experiment with that.) In any event, the flicker should
be gone.

   This last section adds a finishing touch to make the applet more
interesting to watch. Right now, the dot moves down and to the right
until it vanishes off the screen, never to return unless the user selects
the Reload command from the Applet menu. (Boring.) It's much more
fun to bounce the ball off the walls of the application. And it's easy to
code — here's how:

- If the left edge of the dot is at coordinate zero or less, start
  moving right.

- If the right edge of the dot is equal to or greater than the right edge of the applet (indicated by the applet's width), start moving left.
- Otherwise, continue in the current direction.
- Make similar adjustments along the y axis.

To make these adjustments, horizontal and vertical movements are controlled by the instance variables deltaX and deltaY, respectively. The values are adjusted, if needed, after each movement.

Here's the completed applet, in its entirety, using deltaX and deltaY to control movement:

```java
import java.awt.*;
import java.applet.*;

public class Animator extends Applet implements Runnable {
  Thread runner;
  int x, y;   // Current coordinates of the dot
  Image buffer;
  int curw, curh;
  int deltaX, deltaY;   // Current direction of move

  public void init() {
    x = y = 0;   // Start in top left corner.
    deltaX = deltaY = 4; // Move down and right to start.
  }

  public void start() {
    runner = new Thread(this);
    runner.start();
  }

  public void run() {
    while(true) {
      // Create new buffer if none exists OR
      // if applet is resized.
      if ( (buffer == null) || (curw != getWidth()) ||
        (curh != getHeight()) ) {
        buffer = createImage(getWidth(), getHeight());
        curw = getWidth();
        curh = getHeight();
      }

      // Determine clipping region.
      Rectangle oldRect = new Rectangle(x, y, 51, 51);
      x += deltaX;
```

6

```
        y += deltaY;
        Rectangle newRect = new Rectangle(x, y, 51, 51);
        Rectangle r = newRect.union(oldRect);

        // Update offscreen buffer instead of the screen.
        Graphics g = buffer.getGraphics();
        g.clipRect(r.x, r.y, r.width, r.height);
        update(g);

        // Copy buffer directly to display in a single drawing
        // operation.
        g = getGraphics();
        g.clipRect(r.x, r.y, r.width, r.height);
        g.drawImage(buffer, 0, 0, this);

        // Make directional adjustments if we hit a wall.
        if (x <= 0)
          deltaX = 4;
        else if (x + 50 >= getWidth())
          deltaX = -4;
        if (y <= 0)
          deltaY = 4;
        else if (y + 50 >= getHeight())
          deltaY = -4;
        try {
          Thread.sleep(250);
        } // Pause .25 secs.
        catch (InterruptedException e) {
          ;
        }
      }
    }

    public void paint(Graphics g) {
      g.fillOval(x, y, 50, 50);  // Paint the dot.
    }
  }
```

When you run this applet, you'll notice that the dot now bounces off the edges of the applet window like a bouncing ball. This is a good example of how it isn't too difficult to control animation once the core code is in place.

Working with JavaBeans

J ust as manufactured components helped speed the revolution, software components have great promise for increasing efficiency in software development. A software component is an independent structure that can industrial be tested, perfected, and then used in endless applications. Developers don't have to write the same code over and over. A component contains capabilities in a fully reusable form.

The JavaBeans architecture is a software component model integrated into the Java 1.1 platform and beyond. JavaBeans build upon the reusability of Java by defining an infrastructure for extensible, reusable objects. JavaBeans components go a step beyond traditional Java objects in that they can be queried to assess their capabilities. These components also work with special graphical user interface (GUI) editors that can view, customize, and manipulate components at design time. In short, JavaBeans have "design-time behavior" that aids graphical programming in which you draw the user interface.

What are JavaBeans?

As a software component model, the JavaBeans architecture was designed to support certain standard features or services. Although not all component models tout these features, the JavaBeans architects felt it necessary that JavaBeans support them all to be a viable technology.

The JavaBeans component model

The following component model services are directly supported by JavaBeans:

- Introspection
- Event handling
- Persistence
- Visual layout
- Application builder support
- Distributed computing support

Introspection is the mechanism that exposes the functionality of components to the outside world. Introspection is a critical aspect of a component model because it is responsible for dictating how applications and other components access the functionality of a component. This mechanism enables JavaBeans components to be installed and used seamlessly within a visual development tool. Such a tool can query the components and learn about the functionality that the components offer.

Event handling is what enables a component to generate notifications whenever the state of the component changes. Components generate event notifications to all interested parties such as applications or other components. A simple example of a component event is a mouse click; events can also be more abstract. JavaBeans components adhere to the same delegation event model that forms the foundation of Java 2 event handling.

Persistence is the means by which a component is stored to, and retrieved from, a nonvolatile location such as a hard disk. Persistence enables components to be safely stored away and re-created later. Persistence is important because it enables developers to customize and store Beans within the context of an application under development. When the application is deployed for use, files containing the customized Beans are also shipped; persistence makes this possible.

● **NOTE**

JavaBeans components are often referred to as *Beans* for short.

The *visual layout* of a component is the physical position of a component within its own space, and the position of a component with respect to other components sharing space in the same container. Beans aren't required to have a visual appearance, but many of them are visual. An example of a visual Bean is a button; an example of a nonvisual Bean is a spell checker.

Application builder support enables components to be manipulated graphically to build applications. The specific support required by JavaBeans is the capability of exposing component properties and behaviors to application builder tools through special user interfaces. JavaBeans application builder support works hand-in-hand with introspection to provide a means for JavaBeans to integrate well within visual development tools.

Distributed computing support is necessary to enable the execution of components in applications built on a distributed network such as the Internet. Distributed networks are very complex systems and incur a significant amount of overhead on behalf of a component. For this reason, JavaBeans is designed to leverage solutions from existing distributed computing technologies.

JavaBeans versus ordinary Java objects

A potential source of confusion surrounding JavaBeans is its relationship to the rest of Java. With Java generally being regarded as the end-all technology for the future of software, it almost seems like JavaBeans is unnecessary. Yet even though earlier versions of Java were powerful, they lacked widespread reusability and interoperability. JavaBeans is the technology that filled this gap in the Java platform.

A critical difference between JavaBeans and ordinary Java objects is the capability of multiple Beans to interact with each other dynamically. What this means is that a Bean can be compiled and distributed in executable form with no API documentation, and then reused with other Beans with no programming effort. The interaction is dynamic because the connection between the Beans occurs while the Beans are executing. Contrast this with the static interaction common to normal Java objects, which involves programmatically connecting objects together at the source-code level.

As an illustration of what dynamic object interaction means in practical terms, imagine being able to purchase a couple of objects that perform different functions, for example, statistical analysis and

graphing. Now consider how nice it would be to "wire" these two
objects together using a visual tool and have the graphing object graph
data processed by the statistical analysis object; all of this with no programming, mind you. This scenario is impossible without JavaBeans!

Perhaps the clearest distinction between JavaBeans and the rest
of Java is that Java is a programming language and runtime system,
whereas JavaBeans is an API based on Java. JavaBeans is part of the
core Java 2 API, although it was initially developed as an independent Java-based technology.

Inside a Bean

A Bean, like any Java object, is composed of two kinds of things: data
and methods that act on data. The data part of a Bean completely
describes its state, while the methods provide a means for the Bean's
state to be modified and for actions to be taken accordingly. Also, as
with any Java class, a Bean class can have private, protected, and
public methods — the latter enabling the outside world to communicate with the Bean.

●—NOTE————————————————————————

Beans also communicate with the outside world through events generated when the internal state of a Bean or its properties change. This is
discussed in the next section.

Public Bean methods are often grouped according to their function, in which case they form interfaces. Beans expose their functionality to the outside world through interfaces. Interfaces are important
because they specify the protocol by which a particular Bean is inter-
acted with externally; a programmer need only know a Bean's interfaces to be able to successfully manipulate and interact with the Bean.

Bean properties

A JavaBean property is a piece of data accessed externally through a
formal interface. The data itself is not declared public, but stored in a
private member, which is then accessed indirectly as shown in this
section.

Bean properties have special features that go beyond ordinary
data. To begin with, properties are modifiable at design time through
visual property editors or through straight coding. By altering property values, an application developer can customize both the appearance and behavior of Beans. This customization is carried out either

visually or programmatically, depending on the development tools being used.

Although properties often have built-in Java data types such as int and long, they can also have class and interface types. In this way, a property can really have any data type you choose, including your own custom type. You can even create a property that does not correspond to a stored piece of data but is computed dynamically, as needed.

Properties often cause changes in the appearance of a Bean upon being modified. As an example, consider a graphical user interface Bean that has its background color represented by a property. If this color property is changed, the Bean must be immediately repainted to reflect the new color on screen. Otherwise, the property would no longer correspond to what the user sees.

You declare a property in the same way you declare an ordinary member variable. But in addition, each property has at least one accessor method. Here is the declaration of an integer property named **speed**, along with its accessor methods:

```
private int speed;

public int getSpeed() {
  return speed;
}

public void setSpeed(int s) {
  speed = s;
}
```

The following common scenarios all involve access of properties. In each case, the appropriate accessor methods are called:

- Within the Java language, properties are accessed programmatically via explicit calls to public accessor methods. (In the previous example, this would mean calling getSpeed() and setSpeed() explicitly.)

- Properties are accessed visually via property sheets in application builder tools.

- Properties appear as object fields in scripting environments such as JavaScript or VBScript. Thus in JavaScript, unlike Java itself, you could set speed this way:
  ```
  myobject.speed = 10
  ```

- Properties are used to persistently store and retrieve the state of a Bean.

Accessor methods

An *accessor method* is a public method defined in a Bean that enables access to the value of a particular property. Accessor methods typically come in pairs: one to read the data and one to write it.

Accessor methods responsible for reading a Bean's properties are known as *getter methods*, while those responsible for writing a Bean's properties are known as *setter methods*. Getter and setter methods form the sole interface between a Bean's properties and the outside world, because properties can't be publicly accessed directly.

Getter and setter methods are straightforward in their definitions. The following getter and setter methods provide access to an integer Bean property named `speed`:

```
public int getSpeed();
public void setSpeed(int s);
```

The first method is the getter method, which is evident by the fact that it is returning (getting) an integer value.

The second method is the setter method, and returns a void value but accepts an integer value as its only argument. Notice that the methods are named `getSpeed()` and `setSpeed()`, to clearly signify their purpose. These method names aren't coincidental, as you learn a little later in the chapter in the section titled "Property design patterns."

Properties aren't required to always have pairs of accessor methods. It is perfectly acceptable for a property to have only a getter method, for example, in which case the property would be read-only. Likewise, it is possible, although less likely, to make a property write-only by providing only a setter method.

Advanced Bean properties

In addition to the basic Bean properties that you've already learned about, JavaBeans supports three additional property types:

- Indexed properties
- Bound properties
- Constrained properties

The next few sections explore each of these property types and their relevance to JavaBeans programming.

Indexed properties

Although most properties represent a single piece of information, it is possible to associate multiple values with a property by using *indexed properties*. Indexed properties contain any number of elements of the same type, accessed through a single integer index; hence, the name "indexed property." In this way, indexed properties work very much like ordinary Java arrays.

Like all Bean properties, indexed properties are accessed through accessor methods. However, indexed properties often support an additional pair of accessor methods because it is useful to be able to access either an individual element or the entire array of elements. So, indexed properties have two pairs of accessor methods; one pair gets and sets individual properties in the property array via an index, while the other pair gets and sets the entire array of properties as a single entity. The accessor methods for an indexed property of type Color named palette are:

```
public Color getPalette(int index);
public void setPalette(int index, Color color);
public Color[] getPalette();
public void setPalette(Color[] colors);
```

The first two accessor methods for the palette indexed property get and set an individual element from the property array, which is evident by the integer index required by each method. The last two methods get and set the palette property array as a whole, which is evident by the array brackets ([ ]) used when defining the property type. These last two methods are powerful because they enable you to get and set the entire property array at once.

As with single-valued (non-indexed) properties, you are free to implement any accessor method that you choose. For example, you may not want to allow direct access to the entire array of properties, in which case you wouldn't implement the second pair of accessor methods. Optionally, you could make an indexed property read-only by eliminating both setter methods.

Bound properties

Indexed properties aren't the only type of advanced property supported in JavaBeans. It is sometimes useful for an application to know when a Bean property changes. JavaBeans supports this capability through *bound properties*, which are properties that provide a notification service upon being changed. Bound properties are registered with an outside party (an application, applet, or Bean) that is interested in knowing about changes in the property. Whenever the value of a bound property changes, the interested party is notified. These properties are called bound properties because they are effectively bound to an outside party via changes in their value.

The mechanism by which a bound property is connected with an interested party begins with two event-listener registration methods: `addPropertyChangeListener()` and `removePropertyChange Listener()`. These methods enable an application, applet, or other Bean (listener) to bind to a property, thereby making the property bound. The definitions for these methods are:

```
public void addPropertyChangeListener(
  PropertyChangeListener l);
public void removePropertyChangeListener(
  PropertyChangeListener l);
```

When an interested party wants to bind itself to a property, it must call `addPropertyChangeListener()` and pass in an object implementing the `PropertyChangeListener` interface. The `PropertyChangeListener` interface supports the `property Change()` method, which is called whenever the bound property is changed. In other words, whenever the bound property changes, the `propertyChange()` method is called on the listener object that is passed into `addPropertyChangeListener()`. The `removePropertyChangeListener()` method can be called to break a property binding.

Figure 7-1 shows how a property change event is delivered to a property change listener when the value of a bound property changes.

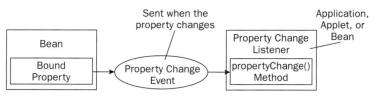

Figure 7-1 *A property change event is delivered from a Bean to a property change listener whenever a bound property changes.*

Constrained properties

JavaBeans also supports *constrained properties*, which are properties that enable an outside party to validate or reject a change. When the user of a Bean attempts to change the value of a constrained property, the value is first checked with an outside validation source. Property change rejections come in the form of `PropertyVeto Exception` exceptions, which are handled by the Bean containing the property. When such an exception occurs, the Bean is responsible for reverting the property back to its prior value and issuing a new property change notification for the reversion.

A practical example of an instance in which a constrained property is handy is a property that represents a date. An application might want to validate a change in the date property to make sure it stays within a particular range, such as the current year. If an attempt is made to set the property to a date outside of the current year, the application can reject the change.

The mechanism by which a constrained property is connected with a validation source is similar to the listener registration mechanism for bound properties. A Bean supporting constrained properties must implement two event-listener registration methods: `addVetoable ChangeListener()` and `removeVetoableChangeListener()`. These methods are used to register listeners with the Bean containing the properties that they want to validate or constrain. The definitions for these methods are:

```
public void addVetoableChangeListener(
   VetoableChangeListener l);
public void removeVetoableChangeListener(
   VetoableChangeListener l);
```

As with the registration of listeners for bound properties, when an interested party wants to register itself as validating a constrained property, it must call `addVetoableChangeListener()` and pass in an object implementing the `VetoableChangeListener` interface. The `VetoableChangeListener` interface supports the `vetoable Change()` method, which is used to validate the constrained property. Constrained property listeners can be removed by calling the `remove VetoableChangeListener()` method.

Figure 7-2 shows how a property veto exception is thrown whenever a vetoable change listener rejects a constrained property change.

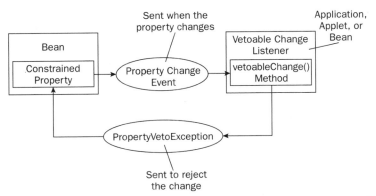

Figure 7-2 *A property veto exception is thrown whenever a vetoable change listener rejects a constrained property change.*

Understanding Bean Introspection

A fundamental feature of JavaBeans is the capability to expose information about themselves. Application builder tools and developers need to be able to take a prepackaged Bean and have a consistent, automated way to find out how it works. The mechanism that exposes the structure and functionality of a Bean to the outside world is called *introspection*. Introspection is a fundamental part of JavaBeans because it is the means by which Beans are integrated into different environments.

What type of information must a Bean expose for introspection purposes? Typically, the built-in JavaBeans introspection mechanism analyzes a Bean for its public properties, methods, and events, which is usually enough information for an application builder tool or developer to be able to use a Bean. How exactly does a Bean support introspection? Beans provide introspection information about themselves in two ways:

1. By conforming to JavaBeans design patterns
2. By explicitly providing information about themselves

A design pattern is a naming convention recognized by application building tools and scripting languages. For example, the principal convention supported for accessing JavaBeans properties is the get*Propname* and set*Propname* convention described earlier. Use of such a design pattern provides an automatic form of introspection.

●—NOTE

The Java language itself does not recognize any particular design patterns. Java, therefore, does not know when you have defined a property. To set or get a property within Java code, you must explicitly call the accessor methods.

Alternatively, Bean developers can explicitly provide information about a Bean that is made available to the JavaBeans introspection facility. This approach to supporting introspection gives developers a fine degree of control over how a Bean will appear externally. Because design patterns provide a default, automatic form of introspection support, this explicit approach is completely optional.

Introspection that uses design patterns is automatic because JavaBeans analyzes the naming and type signatures for public methods in a Bean to determine what properties, methods, and events the Bean makes available for public use. In this way, all Bean developers must do is adhere to design patterns for their Beans to support introspection.

The use of these patterns alleviates the need for developers to provide information explicitly.

There are a variety of different design patterns for specifying everything from simple properties to event sources. All design patterns rely on some type of consistent naming convention for methods and their related arguments and data types. Remember that the automatic approach to introspection provided by design patterns is not only convenient from the perspective of JavaBeans, but it also has the intended side effect of encouraging Bean developers to write more structured code. The two major types of design patterns are:

- Property design patterns
- Event design patterns

Property design patterns

Property design patterns are used to identify the properties of a Bean. These were introduced earlier in the section "Bean properties," page 636. These include accessor methods, which are the means by which the JavaBeans automatic introspection facility determines the properties of a Bean. Basically, anytime the JavaBeans introspector encounters a public getter or setter method, it assumes the member variable being get or set is a property and then exposes the property to the outside world.

The design patterns for properties vary a little based on the type of property. The different property design patterns are:

- Simple property design patterns
- Boolean property design patterns
- Indexed property design patterns

To understand how these design patterns affect the accessor methods for properties, consider these properties:

```
private int numLegs;
private boolean insect;
```

Suitable accessor methods that adhere to both the simple property and Boolean design patterns are:

```
public int getNumLegs() {
  return numLegs;
}

public void setNumLegs(int nl) {
  numLegs = nl;
}
```

```
public boolean isInsect() {
  return insect;
}

public void setInsect(boolean i) {
  insect = i;
}
```

The simple property design patterns basically boil down to prepending the word *get* or *set* onto the front of the property name to arrive at the names of the getter and setter methods. It's also important to use appropriate data type of the property in the methods. The Boolean design patterns differ only in the getter method, which requires you to prepend the word *is* instead of *get*. This helps point out that the return value of the method is a true/false value.

Event design patterns

Event design patterns are used to identify the events that a Bean is capable of broadcasting. Events are important because they allow a Bean to inform an interested party of internal state changes. Events come in a variety of different forms, but some common ones are mouse clicks and drags. For example, when the user drags the mouse over a button Bean, the Bean might broadcast an event that can be handled and responded to by an interested party.

Beans send event notifications to event listeners that have registered themselves with a Bean. Beans provide special event registration methods to facilitate the registration process. The event registration methods come in pairs, with one method allowing interested parties to be added as listeners, and the other allowing listeners to be removed. The automatic JavaBeans introspection facility uses this pair of methods to determine the events a Bean is capable of broadcasting. The design patterns governing the event registration methods are:

```
public void addEventTypeListener (EventTypeListener x);
public void removeEventTypeListener (EventTypeListener x);
```

In these design patterns, *EventType*Listener refers to the object type of the event listener being registered; this object is required to implement the *EventType*Listener interface. The placeholder *EventType* should be replaced by a particular kind of event (such as Mouse in the following example), but Listener is typed in literally. Applying the event design patterns to an event listener of type MouseListener yields these method definitions:

```
public void addMouseListener(MouseListener x);
public void removeMouseListener(MouseListener x);
```

The event design patterns described thus far apply to multicast event sources, which are Beans that support multiple event listeners. JavaBeans also supports unicast event sources, which are Beans that only support one event listener at any given time. If an attempt is made to register more than one listener with a unicast Bean, the `add()` registration method throws a `TooManyListenersException` exception. The design pattern for this method is:

```
public void addEventListenerType(EventListenerType x)
    throws TooManyListeners;
```

The only difference between this design pattern and the one for multicast Beans is the specification of the `TooManyListeners` exception.

Explicit Bean information

Although the automatic approach to introspection afforded by applying design patterns is useful and powerful, there may be situations in which you want or need to explicitly provide information about a Bean for introspection purposes. JavaBeans supports the explicit inclusion of Bean information through Bean information classes. A *Bean information class* is a special class that can contain the following information about a Bean:

- Description of a Bean
- Icons for visually representing the Bean in design tools, toolbars, and so on
- Properties of a Bean
- Events broadcast by a Bean
- Methods supported by a Bean

Bean information classes must implement the `BeanInfo` interface, which defines methods used to determine information about a Bean. A Bean's information class must be named the same as the Bean class, with the word *BeanInfo* appended. So, if you have a Bean named `Widget`, then the Bean information class must be named `WidgetBeanInfo`.

When explicitly providing Bean information using a Bean information class, you have the freedom of providing as much or as little information as you want. For example, it is possible to explicitly provide information about a Bean's properties, yet allow the automatic introspection facility to determine the Bean's supported methods and events.

Bean Persistence

A fundamental requirement of the JavaBeans technology is that Beans must be capable of being saved and restored in a consistent manner. *Persistence* is the mechanism by which Beans are stored to, and retrieved from, a nonvolatile location such as a hard disk. To understand why persistence is important, consider the life cycle of a Bean:

1. Creation
2. Customization
3. Usage
4. Destruction

The life cycle of a Bean takes place within the context of a single application; when the application ends, all the Beans it contains are destroyed and forgotten. However, a Bean may form part of a user interface or otherwise provide a semi-permanent building block of an application. The Bean, for example, may have been customized by an application building tool at design time. The Bean is therefore part of the application's initial settings. In such a case, it's important that every time the application runs, it reloads the Bean object with its settings intact.

Persistence alters the life cycle of a Bean by allowing Beans to be stored and later resurrected in precisely the same state they were in when originally stored:

1. Creation or persistent retrieval
2. Customization
3. Usage and/or persistent storage
4. Destruction

Now that you understand the basics surrounding persistence and why it's important, let's consider two other related issues:

- What information gets persistently stored in a Bean?
- Where is this information stored?

You already know that Beans consist of data and methods that act on the data. The persistent portion of a Bean is usually some subset of the Bean's data. Remember that the whole point of persistence is to enable Beans to be restored in the exact same state they were in when saved. Your first impulse might be to say that all of a Bean's data should be persistently stored. However, this approach doesn't always work because:

- Bean data sometimes includes temporary information that has no meaning beyond a specific Bean instance

- Bean data often includes references to other Beans; such references can't be stored using persistence alone

The first problem has to do with the fact that some Bean data simply isn't necessary to store persistently. For example, consider a Bean member variable that keeps track of the state of the mouse button. Clearly, this is information that shouldn't be stored because the state of the mouse button is likely to change before the Bean is restored. To indicate that a member variable shouldn't be persistently stored, you use the `transient` keyword in its declaration. By default, all of a Bean's non-transient member variables are automatically stored persistently.

The second persistence problem occurs because persistence doesn't attempt to restore relationships between Beans; it is only concerned with saving individual Beans. Because connections between Beans are typically established within an application builder tool, JavaBeans leaves it up to these tools to implement their own mechanism for maintaining connections between Beans.

Although the primary storage location for persistent Beans is files, they are by no means the only option. Beans can also be stored in databases, which could be useful in certain situations. Admittedly, this route is less common than storing Beans in files, but it's worth mentioning because it shows the extensibility of JavaBeans persistence. By default, the JavaBeans persistence facility automatically stores Beans in files.

7

Serialization

Persistence in JavaBeans is tightly linked to *serialization*, which is the process of reading or writing an object as a stream of bytes. Serialization is extremely useful for storing and retrieving Java objects to and from nonvolatile locations such as files. JavaBeans uses serialization in its automatic approach to persistence, which involves the storing and retrieving of Beans based upon their properties.

The key to serialization is the representation of an object's state in a serialized form that is capable of being restored. When serialized, an object is converted to a series of bytes that sufficiently represents the state of the object. From the perspective of JavaBeans, it isn't important exactly how a Bean is resolved into bytes, as long as the Bean can be completely restored from the bytes.

It is important to note that serialization provides one specific approach to persistence. Serialization comes into play automatically in JavaBeans persistence when a Bean provides no direct serialization support of its own. In this way, you can think of serialization as the default approach to persistence taken by JavaBeans. To take advantage of this automatic form of persistence, Beans must simply implement the `Serializable` interface, which is mainly a formality because the interface defines no methods. Beans that don't use automatic serialization must support persistence by providing an externalization mechanism, which is a means of storing and retrieving an object through some type of custom, externally defined format.

Versioning

An important issue related to persistence and serialization is *versioning*, which is the inevitable tendency of an object to evolve over time and gain new functionality. Versioning is significant in terms of persistence because an object can be saved under one version and then restored later under a newer version. This creates a tricky problem because different versions of an object often have different state information. Versioning raises some interesting questions about object identity, including what constitutes a backwardly compatible change to an object.

The Java serialization facility deals with versioning by enforcing a set of rules that ensure compatibility across different object versions. These rules dictate the evolution of objects by restricting the kinds of changes that can be made in newer versions. More specifically, you can only add new properties and interfaces to an object, as opposed to being able to modify existing properties and interfaces. This might seem to be an annoyance, but it guarantees that the new version of an object will work with code based on the old version.

The serialization facility in Java addresses versioning in these ways:

- It supports reading an object from a stream that was written by an older version

- It supports writing an object to a stream that is to be read by an older version

- It identifies and loads objects that match the version used to write the stream

- It supports communication between different versions of an object executing in different virtual machines

● NOTE

Because most Beans rely on serialization as their default form of persistence, Bean versioning is seldom a problem as long as Bean developers observe the versioning rules imposed by Java's automatic serialization facility.

Customizing Beans

Customization, which is the editing of Beans in a design-time environment, is critical to JavaBeans because it provides the means by which Beans are manipulated in application builder tools. The idea behind customization is that it makes application development easier and smoother because of the visual manipulation and reuse of objects. The JavaBeans approach to customization is much simpler and more automatic than similar attempts by other component models. The result is that Bean developers have to put forth very little effort in order for their Beans to be customizable in application builder tools.

Although much of a Bean's support for customization is provided automatically by JavaBeans, there certainly are situations in which developers have to provide Bean-specific customization support. Because the additional overhead incurred by this customization support is only required by a Bean at design time, the overhead is kept physically separate from the runtime portion of a Bean. A Bean intended for a runtime setting is not shipped with the customization support, which allows the Bean to remain very compact. This is particularly important for Beans used in a distributed network environment where the size of an applet or application is critical due to bandwidth considerations.

The specific support for Bean customization comes in a variety of forms:

- Property editors
- Property sheets
- Customizers

Property editors

Property editors, which are visual user interfaces for editing a particular property type, form the first line of support for JavaBeans customization. Property editors are at the root of JavaBeans customization because they are implemented at the property level. By providing property editors for every conceivable property type, it becomes possible to visually edit an entire Bean purely through a series of property editors.

It's impossible to predict and provide property editors for every conceivable property type a Bean might use. However, JavaBeans provides property editors for built-in Java data types such as integers, Booleans, strings, fonts, and colors. Figure 7-3 shows the font property editor provided by JavaBeans.

Figure 7-3 *The standard JavaBeans font property editor provides a GUI for editing font properties.*

Notice how the font property editor uses drop-down lists to enable you to change the various aspects of a font property. The JavaBeans color property editor provides a similar user interface, as Figure 7-4 shows.

Figure 7-4 *The standard JavaBeans color property editor provides a GUI for editing color properties.*

The color property editor allows you to specify a color either by using red, green, and blue (RGB) values, or by selecting a common color from a drop-down list. This property editor also provides a very useful visual feature by displaying the color you are editing.

Although the standard JavaBeans property editors are quite handy, Beans sometimes use custom property types, in which case there is no standard editor. In this case, it is up to the Bean developer to provide a custom property in order for the Bean to be visually customizable. This may seem like a big requirement for Bean developers, but it guarantees that all Beans support customization. JavaBeans provides enough standard property editors that you typically don't have to worry about implementing your own. Even if you do, they aren't too difficult to develop.

Property sheets

Although property editors serve a very important purpose at the property level, the editing of properties always takes place within the context of a complete Bean. In other words, customizing a Bean usually involves interacting with a group of property editors because most Beans have more than one editable property. JavaBeans organizes the customizable properties of a Bean into a special GUI called a *property sheet*. Property sheets are usually implemented as windows that either contain or launch individual property editors such as the standard font and color property editors.

A good example of a property sheet can be found in the BeanBox, which is a Bean testing tool that is part of the JavaBeans Development Kit (BDK). You learn more about the BDK later in the chapter in the section titled "Testing Beans in the BeanBox." For now, look at Figure 7-5, which shows the Properties window in the BeanBox. The BeanBox Properties window is a property sheet.

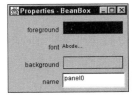

Figure 7-5   *The BeanBox Properties window is a good example of a property sheet.*

Notice that the property sheet includes property editors for the various properties in the Bean, which, in this case, is a button. The property editor for the `label` property is simple enough to use directly in the property sheet. Others, including the ones for the `foreground`, `background`, and `font` properties, are contained in dialog boxes that are displayed whenever you click on the property in the property sheet. It's important to understand that the property sheet isn't responsible for managing the details of each individual property editor; property editors are completely self-contained user interfaces. All a property sheet must do is give each property editor a place to reside.

Customizers

Although property sheets are functional and intuitive in their approach to providing a means of visually editing Beans, JavaBeans offers a more powerful approach to Bean customization: this approach uses *customizers*, which are GUI objects that provide a highly intuitive means of visually editing Bean properties. By intuitive, I mean that customizers don't simply display a group of property editors; instead, they provide a user interface custom-tailored to a specific Bean that is more intuitive from the user's perspective. Customizers are similar to property sheets in that they enable you to edit a complete Bean; but customizers typically take a very different approach when it comes to the user interface.

Customizers often employ a wizard interface, which is a user interface that presents a series of steps that are traversed by the user sequentially. Customizers sometimes use a wizard interface in the context of a series of questions, which is certainly a more intuitive approach than editing Bean properties directly using a property sheet. Customizers are designed to be used primarily with complex Beans whose customization could really benefit from a more intuitive user interface; it is sufficient to use property sheets to edit most simple Beans.

JavaBeans supports customizers through the `Customizer` interface, which is an interface that defines the basic overhead required of a customizer. Although this interface serves as a good jumpstart, developing a customizer can require a significant coding effort.

Creating a Simple Bean

You've now learned enough about JavaBeans to take a look at a fully functional Bean. The `MyLabel` Bean is a simple Bean that displays a string of text as a label. Although this is a very basic Bean, it demonstrates the use of properties, accessor methods, and persistence, as well as automatic support for introspection. The code for the `MyLabel` Bean is:

```java
import java.awt.*;
import java.io.Serializable;

public class MyLabel extends Canvas implements Serializable {
  private String label;

  // Constructors
  public MyLabel() {
    this("I'm a label!");
  }

  public MyLabel(String l) {
    // Allow the superclass constructor to do its thing
    super();

    // Set the label property
    label = l;

    // Set a default size
    setSize(75, 50);
  }

  // Accessor methods
```

```
public String getLabel() {
  return label;
}

public void setLabel(String l) {
  label = l;
}

// Other public methods
public synchronized void paint(Graphics g) {
  int width = getSize().width;
  int height = getSize().height;

  // Paint the background
  g.setColor(getBackground());
  g.fillRect(0, 0, width, height);

  // Paint the label (foreground) text
  g.setColor(getForeground());
  g.setFont(getFont());
  FontMetrics fm = g.getFontMetrics();
  g.drawString(label, (width - fm.stringWidth(label)) / 2,
    (height + fm.getMaxAscent() - fm.getMaxDescent()) / 2);
}
}
```

The MyLabel Bean has a single string property named label, along with getter and setter methods for the property. The default constructor for the Bean calls the detailed constructor with a default value for the label property. The detailed constructor does the actual work of initializing the Bean by assigning the label property value and setting the initial size of the Bean. The paint() method is responsible for painting the label text.

The Bean supports automatic persistence by implementing the Serializable interface. Remember that this interface defines no methods, so it isn't necessary to use a method to implement the interface; simply using the implements keyword in the class declaration is sufficient. Automatic persistence works fine in this Bean because the only property is of a standard Java data type, which is easily serialized.

Similar to persistence, introspection in MyLabel is supported automatically. This is because the getter and setter methods for the label property adhere to the property design patterns that you learned about earlier in the chapter in the section titled "Property design patterns." Because the Bean has no events, event design patterns don't enter the picture.

Beans are compiled using a Java compiler just like any other Java classes. The development of Beans differs from normal Java classes when it comes time to use them. The next section tackles how Beans are packaged using Java archives.

Packaging Beans in JAR Files

Java supports an interesting feature known as *Java archives* that provide a means of bundling multiple files into a single, compressed archive file. Java archive files, also called *JAR files*, are very similar to the ZIP and TAR files that are popular on Windows and Unix platforms, respectively. The rationale behind the creation of the JAR technology was to allow Java class files and resources to be bundled together for easier and more efficient distribution. Not surprisingly, JAR files provide the perfect distribution mechanism for JavaBeans.

The Java 2 SDK ships with a JAR utility that enables you to create and manipulate JAR files. Like all other Java SDK tools, the JAR utility is a command-line tool; its syntax is:

```
jar Options [Files]
```

The optional `Files` argument specifies the files to be used when working with a JAR file and varies according to the `Options`. The `Options` argument specifies options that determine how the JAR utility manipulates a JAR file. Table 7-1 presents a list of the more commonly used options.

Table 7-1   *JAR utility options*

f	Identify the name of the archive as the first file in the Files argument
c	Create a new archive
m	Create a manifest file for an archive based on an external manifest file (the external manifest file is provided as the second file in the `Files` argument)
t	List the contents of an archive
x	Extract all the files in an archive, or just the files provided in the `Files` parameter

●─TIP───────────────────────────

Unlike most command-line tools, the JAR utility doesn't require the use of a / or – when specifying options.

To find out what files are contained in a JAR file, you simply use the f and t options with the JAR utility like this:

```
jar ft SomeArchive.jar
```

The f option is necessary to inform the JAR utility of the JAR file whose contents you want to list. The results of this command will include all the files contained within the SomeArchive.jar JAR file.

Creating a JAR file is a little more involved than simply listing the contents, but not much. For example, the following command packages Java classes into a JAR file:

```
jar fc MyArchive.jar *.class
```

In this example, the f option is used to specify the name of the new JAR file to be created, MyArchive.jar. The c option indicates that a new JAR file is to be created containing all files matching the *.class wildcard (all Java classes in the current directory).

●─TIP───────────────────────────

You can use more than one wildcard in the JAR utility command line. For example, to include all the classes, GIF images, and AU sounds in the current directory, you would include these wildcards: *.class *.gif *.au.

Packaging a Bean in a JAR file involves an extra piece of information not required when packaging normal Java classes: the manifest file that contains information about the Beans in a JAR file. You must provide a manifest file for the JAR file and specify it when creating the JAR file. Following is an example of how the MyLabel Bean is packaged using the JAR utility:

```
jar fcm MyLabel.jar MyLabel.mf *.class
```

In this example, the f option is used to specify the name of the new JAR file to be created, MyLabel.jar. The c option indicates that a new JAR file is to be created containing all files matching the *.class wildcard (all Java classes in the current directory, including the JavaBeans component class). Finally, the m option specifies that an external manifest file, MyLabel.mf, is to be included as the manifest file for the JAR file. A *manifest file* is a text file with information about what Beans are included in a JAR file; JAR files are capable of containing multiple Beans.

The last part of the JAR file creation is critical because JAR files containing Beans must have a manifest file identifying the Beans. This is necessary so that application builder tools can quickly analyze the manifest file and determine what Beans are in the JAR file. Following is the listing for the `MyLabel.mf` manifest file:

```
Manifest-Version: 1.0

Name: MyLabel.class
Java-Bean: True
```

The first line of the manifest file simply states the version of JAR used to create the archive, which is 1.0 in Java 2. The third line lists the name of the Bean class, `MyLabel.class`. Finally, the last line indicates that the class is in fact a Bean class. This is necessary because JAR files can also be used to package normal Java classes.

> **● NOTE**
>
> If a JAR file contains more than one Bean, the third and fourth lines of the manifest file are repeated for each different Bean.

Testing Beans in the BeanBox

You learned earlier in the chapter in the section titled "Property sheets" that the BeanBox is a tool used to test Beans. More specifically, the BeanBox serves as a test container that allows Beans to execute in an environment that simulates how Beans will be used in the real world. For example, the BeanBox supports both runtime and design-time modes that enable you to test a Bean as it would execute both in a completed application and in a visual development tool. The BeanBox is part of the JavaBeans Development Kit that ships separately from the standard Java 2 SDK. Along with the BeanBox, the BDK includes valuable example Beans with complete source code.

Although the BeanBox is a standalone Java application, you don't execute it using the standard Java interpreter. Instead, the BDK ships with a batch file called run that is used to run the BeanBox. The reason for using a batch file to execute the BeanBox instead of using the Java interpreter directly is that the BeanBox requires certain settings be in the environment path, which the batch file handles. To run the BeanBox, just execute the run batch file, which is located in the beanbox directory beneath the main BDK installation directory.

●─TIP───────────────────────────────────

The run batch file is actually named run.bat on the Windows platform and run.sh on the Unix platform. This batch is executed at the command line and requires the Java SDK's bin directory to be part of the PATH.

The BeanBox takes a few moments to initialize and start up, but once it starts it displays four different windows: a ToolBox window, a BeanBox window, a Properties window, and a Method Tracer window. These windows form the primary parts of the BeanBox interface and are shown in Figures 7-6 through 7-9.

Figure 7-6 *The ToolBox window displays all of the Beans installed in the BeanBox.*

The ToolBox window displays all of the Beans installed in the BeanBox. These are the Beans available to be tested in the BeanBox and consist of the example Beans provided with the BDK, along with any that you add. Notice that some of the Beans have graphical icons associated with them to make their usage a little more obvious. The ToolBox window is where you select Beans to be inserted in the BeanBox window (Figure 7-7) for testing.

The BeanBox window is where Beans are actually inserted and tested. This window is akin to a form design window in an application builder tool; you lay out Beans in the BeanBox window and visually manipulate them as desired. The BeanBox window also serves as the main application window for the BeanBox application because it contains the menu of available BeanBox commands.

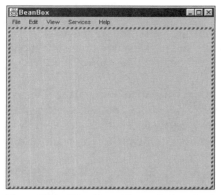

Figure 7-7 *The BeanBox window is the actual container used to test Beans.*

The Properties window (Figure 7-8) provides an interface for editing the properties of a Bean. You learned about it earlier in the chapter in the section titled "Property sheets" when you examined the role of property sheets in Bean customization.

Figure 7-8 *The Properties window allows you to customize the properties of a Bean.*

The Method Tracer window (Figure 7-9) only applies to Beans that have been designed to have information displayed about their called methods. This useful debugging tool tracks the internal workings of a Bean.

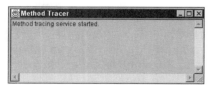

Figure 7-9 *The Method Tracer window is a debugging window that tracks the internal workings of a Bean.*

The four windows in the BeanBox user interface combine to make an interesting tool that is indispensable for testing your own Beans. To use the tool, you simply load the Bean that you want to test by following these steps:

1. Select Loadjar from the File menu in the BeanBox window.

2. When prompted for a file, browse and select the JAR file containing your Bean.

3. Your Bean will then be added to the bottom of the ToolBox window; you might need to scroll down to see it. Click on the Bean in this window.

4. Move the mouse over the BeanBox window and notice that the mouse cursor has changed to a crosshair; this indicates that you are inserting a Bean object into the BeanBox. Click in the BeanBox window wherever you want the Bean to be inserted.

With the Bean successfully loaded and inserted into the BeanBox, it is ready to be customized. The following steps describe how to customize the `MyLabel` Bean:

1. Click on the Bean in the BeanBox window to make sure it is selected; the Properties window will change to reflect the Bean's properties. In addition to the `label` property that you created in the Bean, properties that are inherited from the `Component` class and are standard in most Beans are also shown in the BeanBox window.

2. To change the color of the Bean's background click on the gray box in the Property Sheet window to display a property editor for the background color property.

3. The property editor includes a drop-down list of colors. Select a color and notice how the Bean changes.

4. Click the Done button to accept the new background color.

5. Now try changing the label of the Bean by clicking in the box to the right of the word *label* in the Property Sheet window.

6. Type a new label such as `Hello!` and watch how it affects the Bean.

After you are finished customizing a Bean, it's useful to be able to see how it will operate in a runtime setting. You can easily test a Bean in its runtime mode using the BeanBox. So far, you've been working with the Bean in a design-time setting. To test the Bean in a runtime setting, simply select View from the BeanBox menu and then select Disable Design Mode. All of the windows will then disappear except the BeanBox window, and the Bean will execute as if it were in a completed application. You can return to design-time mode by selecting Enable Design Mode from the View menu.

Advanced JavaBeans

The core JavaBeans technology hasn't changed much since Java 1.1. However, two advanced enhancements to the technology have occurred as of Java 2. The two improvements to the JavaBeans technology that were ushered in by Java 2 are:

- Extensible Runtime Containment and Services Protocol
- Drag and Drop Subsystem

The Extensible Runtime Containment and Services Protocol is a technology that enables a Bean to discover information about the container in which it resides. You can think of this protocol as somewhat of a reverse introspection facility because introspection usually involves the container learning about the Bean. A primary benefit to using the Extensible Runtime Containment and Services Protocol is that it enables you to nest Beans within other Beans, yet it still allows every Bean to have complete access to services offered by the Bean container.

The Drag and Drop Subsystem in Java 2 isn't necessarily directly targeted at JavaBeans, but it does impact JavaBeans considerably. Although Java is designed to be entirely cross-platform with no native coding, it is readily apparent that Java applications need to be able to communicate effectively with native applications. The Drag and Drop Subsystem supports native drag-and-drop in Java, which allows Java applications to interact via drag-and-drop with native applications and retain the native feel of the action. This is important for JavaBeans because drag-and-drop is a feature commonly used with Beans.

Both the Extensible Runtime Containment and Services Protocol and the Drag and Drop Subsystem are beyond the scope of this chapter.

EJB: JavaBeans and the Enterprise

One last issue worth addressing before closing the topic of JavaBeans is Enterprise JavaBeans, also known as *EJB*. Enterprise JavaBeans is a technology built on JavaBeans that is designed to address the needs of enterprise application middleware. If you aren't too familiar with middleware, it is the piece of an enterprise application that sits between the client and server and typically handles the processing of business rules. Because there are architectural advantages to breaking down business processing logic into discrete functional units, it made sense for the Java architects to utilize JavaBeans.

Enterprise JavaBeans is not part of the standard Java 2 platform; instead, it is part of the broader Java 2 Enterprise Edition, which is also known as J2EE. J2EE is beyond the scope of this book.

7

in plain english in p
sh in plain english in
glish in plain englis
in plain english in p
sh in plain english in
glish in plain englis
in plain english in p
glish in plain englis
in plain english in p
sh in plain english in
glish in plain englis
in plain english in p
sh in plain english in
glish in plain englis
in plain english in p
lish in plain englis
in plain english in p
sh in plain english in
glish in plain englis
in plain english in p
sh in plain english in
lish in plain englis
in plain english in p
glish in plain englis

Common Programming Tasks

J ava does things a little differently than does C, C++, or
Basic. Although many aspects of Java programming are
simpler than C++ and other approaches to GUI application
development, Java's approach to some common tasks is not
always obvious. This chapter helps you to learn to use Java
quickly by summarizing how to accomplish tasks in the following areas:

- Converting between numbers and strings
- Console input and output
- Graphical interface input and output
- Basic file operations

Converting between Numbers and Strings

Typically, data is displayed as a string but crunched as a number.
Converting between these formats is therefore a common part of
most Java programs. The next three sections survey this topic,
which was introduced in Chapter 4, "Components and Events."

String to integer

Converting a digit string to an integer is easy, because the Java API provides the Integer.parseInt() method to do it in one step. The following example reads the digits in aString and stores the value in i:

```
int i = Integer.parseInt(aString);
```

The Long.parseLong() method does the same thing except that the result is stored in a long integer:

```
long lng = Long.parseLong(aString);
```

These two methods — parseInt() and parseLong() — are *class* methods and can be used almost like global functions. No object creation is required of these methods.

String to floating point

Reading a floating-point string requires two steps:

1. Create a Double object initialized from the string.

2. Use the doubleValue() method to convert from object to primitive data.

Figure 8-1 illustrates this process.

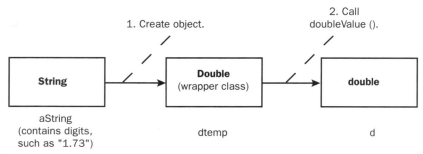

Figure 8-1 *Converting string to type double*

The following example illustrates the two steps, reading from the digits in a string variable named aString:

```
Double dtemp = Double(aString); // 1. Create object
double d = dtemp.doubleValue();  // 2. Call doubleValue()
```

If you want more-compact code, you can combine the two steps, creating a temporary object on the fly and then calling the method. For example:

```
double d = (new Double(aString)).doubleValue();
```

The process is approximately the same for storing results as a float (single-precision) value. The main difference is that you call floatValue() rather than doubleValue():

```
float f = (new Float(aString)).floatValue();
```

Numeric to string

Converting numeric values to strings is easy. One approach is to use String.valueOf(). Although this is a class method, it returns a string object — namely, the string representation of a number:

```
int i = 101;
String aString = String.valueOf(i);
System.out.println("The value of i is " +
   String.valueOf(i));
```

String.valueOf() is overloaded so that you can give it any type of numeric input.

Another approach is to combine a numeric value with another string by using the string concatenation operator (+). In such an expression, Java automatically converts the number to a string representation.

```
System.out.println("The value of i is " + i);
```

Java performs this conversion even if the string is empty. For example, the following code initializes a string as a representation of the integer i:

```
String aString = "" + i;
```

Console Input and Output

You've already seen many examples of console output. The System.out object provides two overloaded methods — print() and println() — that can be used to print to the screen in a Java application:

```
System.out.print("Print text, continue line... ");
System.out.println("Print text, then add a newline.");
```

●─**NOTE**───────────────────────────────────────

The only quirk with using print() is that to force an immediate printing without a newline, you must call the flush() method to flush the
buffer. This is not necessary with println(), because the built-in
newline automatically flushes the buffer.

The technique for getting input from the console is more complicated. The System.in object is an instance of the InputStream class,
which does not provide an easy way to read a whole line of input.
The solution is to convert System.in to an instance of another class —
BufferedReader — which provides the readLine() method:

```java
import java.io.*;
// ...
String s = "";
BufferedReader ds =
    new BufferedReader(new InputStreamReader(System.in));
try {
    s = ds.readLine();
} catch(IOException e) {
    ;   // Do nothing
}
```

The BufferedReader object is actually created from an Input
StreamReader object. This layering of object creation is necessary to
properly set up a stream for reading from the console. Because the
readLine() method has the possibility of throwing an IOException
exception, the code must place each call to readLine() inside a try-
catch block. (This requirement is annoying here, because it's
unlikely that standard input would throw an exception.)

The following example shows repeated use of console input
and output in a small program. To make the programming easier,
almost all the input/output handling is moved to a utility function,
promptForInt(), which takes care of prompting, exception handling,
and integer conversion.

```java
import java.io.*;

// main program - reads three integers and prints total
class ConsoleTest {
    public static void main(String args[]) {
        int a, b, c, total;
        a = promptForInt("Enter 1st integer: ");
        b = promptForInt("Enter 2nd integer: ");
        c = promptForInt("Enter 3rd integer: ");
        total = a + b + c;
```

```
          System.out.println("The total is: " + total);
       }

       // promptForInt() - reads a string from the console and
       // returns first integer read.
       static int promptForInt(String prompt) {
         System.out.print(prompt);
         System.out.flush();
         String s = "";
         BufferedReader ds =
           new BufferedReader(new InputStreamReader(System.in));
         try {
           s = ds.readLine();
         } catch (IOException e) {
           System.out.println(e);
         }
         return Integer.parseInt(s);
       }
     }
```

A limitation of this program is that it permits entry of only one integer per line. If you want, you can enter and read multiple items in a line by building a StringTokenizer object around the line read and then using StringTokenizer methods:

```
import java.util.*;
//...
StringTokenizer st = new StringTokenizer(s);
i = Integer.parseInt(st.nextToken()); // read a number
```

For more information, see StringTokenizer class (p. 462) in the "Java 2 API Reference" in Part I.

Basic File Operations

Only applications can read or write to disk files or even read a directory. As a rule, net browsers prevent file operations, because permitting file operations would enable an applet to destroy everything on your disk, or otherwise breach security.

This section gives a brief introduction to file operations. For more complete information, see the summary of the java.io package (p. 138) in Part I, "Java 2 API By Category"

Reading the directory

The File class provides access to the directory system. This class is part of the java.io package, as are all Java API classes that support file operations. A File object represents one node in the file/directory system — either a single file or a single directory:

- If the File object represents a file, you can use the object to get file attributes but not contents. (See the next section for information about getting file contents.)
- If the File object represents a directory, you can use the object to get a list of directory items as well as other directory attributes. You can also use this object to create new subdirectories.

The following program prints the contents of the current directory:

```
import java.io.*;

class Dir {
  public static void main(String args[]) {
    File myDir = new File(".");
    String theList[] = myDir.list();
    int n = theList.length;
    for (int i = 0; i < n; i++)
      System.out.println(theList[i]);
  }
}
```

The first statement in the program creates a File object that represents the current directory, specified by a single dot (".") in DOS/UNIX notation:

```
File myDir = new File(".");
```

The program calls File.list() to get a list of children for this node (that is, the current directory). This list is returned as an array of strings, which we assign to the array variable theList. Although Java arrays are similar to C/C++ arrays, each Java array contains its own length attribute. The program uses this attribute to determine how many items to print:

```
String theList[] = myDir.list();
int n = theList.length;
for (int i = 0; i < n; i++)
  System.out.println(theList[i]);
```

For more information on the File class, refer to Part I, "Java 2 API Reference," page 244.

Reading file contents

If you come from the C, C++, or Basic world, you probably use a three-step process to read a file: open, read, and close the file. Java automates some of this process and uses exception handling to report conditions such as "File not found."

To open a file for reading, create a FileInputStream object, initializing with a string or other object. Java implicitly opens the file for reading. For example, you can use a File object to initialize a FileInputStream object:

```
File f = new File("STUFF.TXT");
FileInputStream fis = new FileInputStream(f);
```

You can also initialize a FileInputStream object directly from a string name:

```
FileInputStream fis = new FileInputStream("STUFF.TXT");
```

The example in this section reads a file by creating both types of objects — File and FileInputStream — and reading the name of a file from the command line. Figure 8-2 illustrates the general strategy.

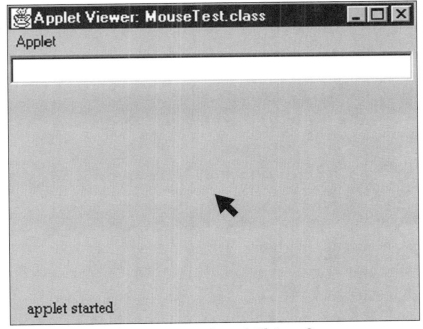

Figure 8-2 *Use of command line, File, and FileInputStream*

The program first reads the file name. Then it creates a `File` object and uses this object to determine length. Finally, it creates a `FileInput Stream` object to read contents. The length is stored in the variable n, so the program reads n bytes. Here is the complete application:

```java
import java.io.*;

class FileRead {
  public static void main(String args[]) {
    if (args.length < 1) {
      System.out.println("Specify file.");
      System.exit(0);
    }
    File f = new File(args[0]);
    int len = (int) f.length();
    byte ascii[] = new byte[len];
    try {
      FileInputStream fis = new FileInputStream(f);
      fis.read(ascii, 0, len);
      String theText = new String(ascii);
      System.out.println(theText);
    } catch(IOException e) {
      System.out.println(e);
    }
  }
}
```

This program first checks the command line and exits immediately if there is no argument:

```java
if (args.length < 1) {
  System.out.println("Specify file.");
  System.exit(0);
}
```

Next, the program creates a `File` object and determines file length. An array named `ascii` is created to hold ASCII data from a text file. The program takes advantage of Java's dynamic sizing of arrays to allocate an array just big enough to hold the data.

```java
File f = new File(args[0]);
int len = (int) f.length();
byte ascii[] = new byte[len];
```

Finally, the program creates a `FileInputStream` object and reads data into the array. There are two statements that can raise an exception here: the `FileInputStream` constructor may report that the file cannot be found, and the `read()` method may report that data is not available to be read. Both statements are placed inside a `try` block to catch I/O exceptions.

```
try {
  FileInputStream fis = new FileInputStream(f);
  fis.read(ascii, 0, len);
  String theText = new String(ascii);
  System.out.println(theText);
} catch(IOException e) {
  System.out.println(e);
}
```

A subtlety of this program is that text-file data is assumed to be stored in ASCII format, whereas Java strings use Unicode. These formats are compatible except that Unicode characters are 16 bits wide rather than 8 bits wide. Fortunately, the `String` class provides a constructor that converts an array of ASCII bytes to a bona fide Java string, and it is used to initialize `theText`.

Other file-handling techniques

The Java API provides a `FileOutputStream` class, which does for output what `FileInputStream` does for input. You may also want to take advantage of the many specialized file I/O streams in the Java API (all part of the `java.io` package). In almost all cases, the procedure for using a specialized I/O stream is as follows:

1. Create a `FileInputStream` or `FileOutputStream` object. Remember to catch exceptions, which can be raised by constructors for these classes.

2. Use this object to initialize another stream object.

For example, `DataInputStream` provides methods for reading many kinds of data in a structured way rather than reading raw bytes; for this reason, it is frequently easier to use than `FileInput Stream`, especially when you are working with data files created by Java applications. The following code creates a `DataInputStream` object from a `FileInputStream` object:

```
FileInputStream fis = new FileInputStream("STUFF.TXT");
DataInputStream dataFile = new DataInputStream(fis);
```

The exception to this general procedure is the `RandomAccessFile` class, which constructs an object directly from a file name. See Part I, "Java 2 API Reference" (page 427), for more information on the `Random AccessFile` class.

Java Exceptions and Errors

A

J ava exceptions and unrecoverable errors are implemented as classes, all of them derived from the
Throwable class. These classes fall into three broad categories:

- Optional exceptions, derived from RuntimeException
- Mandatory exceptions
- Unrecoverable errors

Exception Classes Generally

Nearly all exception classes have two constructors: a default
constructor and a constructor that takes a String argument.
Other methods are inherited from the Throwable class; these
methods include methods for getting an exception message text
and for printing a stack trace. See "Throwable Class" in Part I,
"Java 2 Reference," page 477. The general pattern for exception-
class constructors is that of the Exception class itself:

```
Exception();
Exception(String msg);
```

Optional Exceptions (RuntimeException)

All the exceptions in this group are derived, directly or indirectly, from the RuntimeException class, which itself is a subclass of Exception (see Table A-1). Handling these exceptions is always optional.

Table A-1 *Optional Exceptions (derived from RuntimeException)*

Exception class	Package (if not java.lang)	Superclass (if not RuntimeException)
ArithmeticException		
ArrayIndexOutOf BoundsException		IndexOutOfBounds Exception
ArrayStoreException		
ClassCastException		
Concurrent Modification Exception	java.util	
EmptyStackException	java.util	
IllegalArgument Exception		
IllegalComponent	java.awt	IllegalState ExceptionState Exception
IllegalMonitorState Exception		
IllegalStateException		
IllegalThreadState Exception		IllegalArgument Exception
ImagingOpException	java.awt.image	
IndexOutOfBounds Exception		
MissingResource Exception	java.util	
NegativeArraySize Exception		
NoSuchElement Exception	java.util	

Exception class	Package (if not java.lang)	Superclass (if not RuntimeException)
NullPointerException		
NumberFormat Exception		IllegalArgument Exception
RasterFormatException	java.awt.image	
SecurityException		
StringIndexOutOfBounds Exception		IndexOutOfBounds Exception
UnsupportedOperation Exception		

Remember that catching a superclass exception (such as Illegal-ArgumentException) implicitly catches all its subclasses as well.

Mandatory Exceptions

The exceptions in this group are not derived from the Runtime Exception class. Whenever you call a method that throws one of these exceptions, you must respond by catching the exception or by placing a throws clause in the caller's method declaration (see Table A-2).

Table A-2 *Mandatory Exceptions*

Exception class	Package (if not java.lang)	Superclass (if not exception)
AWTException	java.awt	
BindException	java.net	SocketException
CharConversion Exception	java.io	IOException
ClassNotFoundException		
CloneNotSupported Exception		
ConnectException	java.net	SocketException
EOFException	java.io	IOException

Continued

A

Table A-2 *Continued*

Exception class	Package (if not java.lang)	Superclass (if not exception)
FileNotFoundException	java.io	IOException
FontFormatException	java.awt	
IllegalAccessException		
InstantiationException		
InterruptedException		
InterruptedIOException	java.io	IOException
InvalidClassException	java.io	ObjectStream Exception
InvalidObjectException	java.io	ObjectStream Exception
IOException	java.io	
MalformedURL Exception	java.net	IOException
NoRouteToHost Exception	java.net	SocketException
NoSuchFieldException		
NoSuchMethodException		
NotActiveException	java.io	ObjectStream Exception
NotSerializable	java.io	ObjectStream Exception Exception
ObjectStreamException	java.io	IOException
OptionalDataException	java.io	ObjectStream Exception
PrinterAbortException	java.awt.print	PrinterException
PrinterException	java.awt.print	
PrinterIOException	java.awt.print	PrinterException
ProtocolException	java.net	IOException
SocketException	java.net	IOException
StreamCorrupted Exception	java.io	ObjectStream Exception
SyncFailedException	java.io	IOException

Exception class	Package (if not java.lang)	Superclass (if not exception)
TooManyListeners Exception	java.util	
UnknownHostException	java.net	IOException
UnknownService Exception	java.net	IOException
UnsupportedEncoding Exception	java.io	IOException
UnsupportedLookAnd FeelException	javax.swing	
UTFDataFormat Exception	java.io	IOException
WriteAbortedException	java.io	ObjectStream Exception

Remember that catching a superclass exception (such as IO-Exception) also catches all its subclasses.

Errors

The Error class is another class that extends the Throwable class. Classes derived from Error represent unrecoverable errors such as running out of memory. These errors should not be caught. When they occur, the interpreter prints an error message and terminates. The only class derived from Error that is not fatal is ThreadDeath, which does not affect other threads and does not cause the program to terminate.

Useful Tables

This Appendix is divided into three sections: graphics tables, text-handling tables, and miscellaneous tables.

Graphics Tables

This section summarizes the meaning of several types of constants that are useful in graphics and text operations: fonts, colors, and cursor types. Table B-1 lists Java fonts and their Windows equivalents. Java font names can be passed to constructors in the Font class.

Table B-1 *Java Fonts*

Font in Java	Font on a Windows system
Java default font (no font specified)	Arial
Courier	Courier New
Dialog	MS Sans Serif
DialogInput	MS Sans Serif
Helvetica	Arial
TimesRoman	Times New Roman
ZapfDingbats	Wingdings

Table B-2 lists the color constants provided in the Color class. These same constants are listed in Part I, Section 7, "Java 2 API Reference," page 208.

Table B-2 *Color Class Constants*

Color.black	Color.magenta
Color.blue	Color.orange
Color.cyan	Color.pink
Color.darkGray	Color.red
Color.gray	Color.white
Color.green	Color.yellow
Color.lightGray	

Table B-3 summarizes cursor types, which can be set in the setCursor() method of the Frame class.

Table B-3 *Java Cursor Settings*

Cursor	Description
Frame.CROSSHAIR_CURSOR	Cursor using a simple crosshair.
Frame.DEFAULT_CURSOR	Default cursor used if you don't specify a cursor. Appears as an arrow.
Frame.E_RESIZE_CURSOR	Resizing cursor for right edge.
Frame.HAND_CURSOR	Hand pointing at the current position.
Frame.MOVE_CURSOR	Move-window cursor.

Cursor	Description
Frame.NE_RESIZE_CURSOR	Resizing cursor for the top-right corner.
Frame.NW_RESIZE_CURSOR	Resizing cursor for the top-left corner.
Frame.N_RESIZE_CURSOR	Resizing cursor for the top edge.
Frame.SE_RESIZE_CURSOR	Resizing cursor for the bottom-right corner.
Frame.SW_RESIZE_CURSOR	Resizing cursor for the bottom-left corner.
Frame.S_RESIZE_CURSOR	Resizing cursor for the bottom edge.
Frame.TEXT_CURSOR	Cursor used in editable text fields. Usually appears as a large I-shaped divider.
Frame.WAIT_CURSOR	Usually an hourglass or watch picture of some kind, indicating that the user should wait while an operation is being carried out.
Frame.W_RESIZE_CUSOR	Resizing cursor for the left edge.

Text-Handling Tables

Most text handling in Java is straightforward. There are several situations, however, in which you need to handle text characters in a special way: when you want to embed special characters into strings, and when you read and write to text files. As mentioned throughout this book, the Unicode character set can represent many characters beyond those in the English alphabet. However, a complete guide to Unicode is beyond the scope of this book.

Table B-4 summarizes escape sequences recognized in Java strings. You can use these sequences to embed some of the more standard special characters. Remember that each character is actually stored in two bytes.

Table B-4   *Java Escape Sequences*

Escape sequence	Description
\b	Backspace
\t	Tab
\n	Newline

Continued

Table B-4 *Continued*

Escape sequence	Description
\f	Form feed
\"	Double quotation mark
\'	Single quotation mark
\\	Backslash
\r	Carriage return
\\xxx	Character with octal value *xxx* in the Unicode system, in which *xxx* is between \000 and \377. This corresponds to the decimal range 0 to 255; you can use octal only to represent values that require no more than 1 byte.
\uxxxx	Character with hexadecimal value *xxxx* in the Unicode system. This encoding enables you to represent the entire possible Unicode range; you can represent any unsigned 2-byte integer value.

The next table is relevant to file input and output operations. When you read and write text strings to data files, you can use the UTF-8 encoding scheme. In fact, this is recommended for best results, although you must use it consistently. For more information, see `DataInputStream` and `DataOutputStream` in Section 7 (p. 227 and p. 230).

Table B-5 shows how the UTF-8 encoding scheme handles various characters in the Unicode range. Methods such as `DataOutputStream. writeUTF()` perform the encoding for you. Notably, all ASCII characters are translated into strings of exactly one character per byte, a compact arrangement that makes them easy to read if you scan the file. This works because the lowest 128 Unicode characters correspond to ASCII characters with the same value.

Table B-5 *UTF-8 encodings*

Start of Range	End of Range	Required Bits	Binary Sequence (x = 1 or 0)
\u0000	\u007F	7	0xxxxxxx
\u0080	\u07FF	11	110xxxxx 10xxxxxx
\u0800	\uFFFF	16	1110xxxx 10xxxxxx 10xxxxxx

Miscellaneous Tables

This final section includes two tables of importance, especially for applications: the default system properties table and a summary of class and field modifiers.

Table B-6 lists the default system properties. These properties are contained in the table that you get by calling `System.get-Properties()`. You can also look up individual properties in this table by calling `System.getProperty()`. Browsers do not grant applets the right to read all these properties — any information that would reveal private information about the user is denied to applets.

Table B-6   *Default System Properties*

Property Name	Description	Can applet read?
java.version	Version number of Java interpreter running on system.	yes
java.vendor	String identifying vendor of Java interpreter.	yes
java.vendor.url	Java vendor's URL.	yes
java.home	Home directory on local machine where Java is installed.	no
java.class.version	Version number of the Java API in use.	yes
os.name	Name of the operating system running.	yes
os.version	Version number of the operating system.	yes
file.separator	File separator used in path names (Windows, UNIX, and Mac use \, /, and :, respectively).	yes
path.separator	Directory-name separator used in paths (: or ;).	yes
line.separator	Line separator used in text files and elsewhere (\n or \r\n). As with other separators, this is platform-specific.	yes
user.name	The username recognized in the local environment.	no
user.home	The home directory of the current user.	no
user.dir	The current working directory.	no

B

In addition, the API uses several other properties whose value you can change to customize behavior. These properties include awt.toolkit (specifies the name of the class that implements the Toolkit class), awt.appletWarning (specifies the warning string that appears in applet windows), and awt.font.fontname, which specifies the font corresponding to fontname. You could, for example, specify a different font for awt.font.fontname, thus creating an alias or altering the interpreter's standard set of fonts.

Table B-7 summarizes the relationship of Java modifiers to classes and fields. Unlike those in C++, Java classes have a smaller set of modifiers available than does methods or variables.

Table B-7   *Class and Field Modifiers in Java*

Modifier	Classes?	Variables?	Methods?	Description
abstract	yes	no	yes	Classes: cannot be instantiated. Methods: the method definition is not provided in this class. Class must also be abstract.
(default access)	yes	yes	yes	Class or field is visible everywhere within the package but not outside the package.
final	yes	yes	yes	Classes: cannot be subclassed. Variables: cannot be modified. Methods: cannot be overridden.
native	no	no	yes	Code is provided by a dynamic link library rather than Java code. The method is implemented in another language, such as C or C++.
private	no	yes	yes	Field is not visible outside the class.
private	no	yes	yes	Field is not visible outside the class except in subclasses.

B

Modifier	Classes?	Variables?	Methods?	Description
`protected`	no	yes	yes	Field is not visible outside the package except in subclasses.
`public`	yes	yes	yes	Classes: class is visible outside package. Fields: field is visible outside the package, but only if class is also public (otherwise, field has default access).
`static`	no	yes	yes	Field is a class field (can be accessed as *class.field* as well as *obj.field*).
`synchronized`	no	no	yes	Only one thread may execute the method at a time.
`volatile`	no	yes	no	Value is subject to change without warning; Java is instructed to never store in a register or temporary location. This attribute cannot be used with `final`.

Interfaces follow the same rules that classes follow except as follows:

- Interfaces are automatically abstract whether declared so or not.
- Interface methods are automatically abstract and do not need to be explicitly declared so (doing so is always optional).
- Interface methods can take only `abstract` and `public` as modifiers.
- Interfaces can have variables, but the variables must be declared `final static`.
- Interfaces cannot be declared `final`.

B

Glossary

abstract class

A class with one or more abstract methods. An abstract class cannot be used directly to create objects. However, an abstract class can be a useful place to declare a set of methods common to a number of subclasses. A good example in the Java API is the Number class in the java.lang package. The subclasses of Number include Integer, Long, Float, and Double. Abstract classes are similar to interfaces, because both of these constructs include abstract methods. However, Java recognizes abstract classes and interfaces as two separate parts of the language, and imposes different rules on them. See the topic "abstract Keyword" (p. 20) for more information.

abstract method

A method that has no implementation—that is, no function-definition code. The implementation must be filled in by a subclass. Abstract methods appear only in abstract classes and interfaces. When you declare a class that inherits from an abstract class, you must provide implementations for all the methods (unless you're declaring another abstract class). Similarly, when a class implements an interface, it must provide implementations for all the abstract methods. An abstract method is therefore like a stand-in or prototype for an actual method definition to be provided elsewhere. The concept of pure virtual functions in C++ is the same as abstract methods in Java. See the topic "abstract Keyword" (p. 20) for more information.

abstraction
The process of making something simpler by hiding the details. There are many reasons that hiding the details can be desirable, especially in a multiplatform language such as Java. For example, the Java Socket class is an abstraction of the idea of a network connection. Different platforms can have widely varying ways of connecting to a network, complete with their own procedures and protocols. Even if you master all the protocols for all the possible platforms, having to deal with them all means maintaining many different versions of the code. However, when you work with Socket, which is the Java network abstraction, you don't have to concern yourself with the details of any particular platforms. Similarly, many classes may be thought of as being abstractions for something potentially complex or nonstandardized (the Thread class, for example). One virtue of object-oriented programming is that it encourages data abstraction in the form of classes. Be aware, however, that abstraction is more a philosophy or a general quality than something measurable or precise.

Abstract Windowing ToolKit (AWT)
The AWT is a set of classes and interfaces in the Java API that is devoted to building graphical user interfaces (GUIs) in Java applets and applications. The java.awt package serves as the root package for AWT classes and interfaces. The AWT forms the basis of the Swing toolkit, which provides advanced GUI features.

The AWT is also an important part of the Java API (see "API"). It provides windows, buttons, checkboxes, scroll bars, events, and other components of interest to GUI programmers. These features can be used in both applets and applications. The AWT consists of classes and interfaces provided in the java.awt package. For an in-depth introduction to AWT, see Part II, Chapter 4, "Components and Events."

The AWT also contains layout managers, each of which uses a general strategy for sizing and positioning components inside a container. If the user resizes a window, for example, the container's layout manager repositions the components.

accelerator
An accelerator is an alternative approach to entering a command in an application that is quicker than navigating through a menu hierarchy. Accelerators actually associate menu commands with special key

combinations. An accelerator key combination is identified visually to the right of a menu item. Examples of accelerators include Ctrl+X, Ctrl+C, and Ctrl+V, which correspond to the Cut, Copy, and Paste commands in most applications. Accelerators are also sometimes referred to as keyboard shortcuts.

access level
The visibility of a field relative to other classes. Java supports five access levels, not just three as in C++. In addition to public, private, and protected, Java provides the default access level. Unlike access levels in C++, Java's default access level is not the same as private. The default visibility of a field is to be accessible to all classes in the same package. You must specifically declare a field private to restrict its access by other classes.

API
Application programming interface. In general, an API is a set of any combination of classes, functions, variables, and methods that provides a general model for creating applications. In simple terms, this means working with certain standard functions and classes rather than programming close to the hardware. The Java API is particularly helpful to programmers, because it generalizes universal features of modern computers, such as displays, threads, network connections, and mouse and keyboard input, and is guaranteed to work consistently on all Java-compatible platforms. In addition, the Java API uses a programming model that is conceptually simpler than most other widely used GUI systems. All items in the Java API are contained in packages, interfaces, and classes, as required by the structure of the Java language. Also, the Java API supports the creation of different types of programs such as applications, applets, and servlets.

applet
A program that runs inside a Web page. This is currently the most popular use for Java programming, although Java can be used in other ways. (See "application.") Java programs that are structured as applets must be derived from the general class `java.applet.Applet`, which means that the `java.applet.Applet` class provides functionality used by all applets.

applet viewer
A utility for viewing applets that is provided in the Java Development Kit (JDK). End users typically run a Java applet by using a Java-compatible Web browser and accessing the appropriate Web page on the Internet. However, the applet viewer utility is convenient for developers who want

to run an applet on their local computer. When you run applet viewer, you specify an HTML file that has a link to the appropriate applet. See Chapter 1, "Applets and Oranges," for more information.

application

A stand-alone Java program that can be run directly on a local computer without the need to access it across the Web. Although Java's most glamorous use is the creation of applets, Java applications are also potentially very useful. A Java application can do anything that most other high-level languages can do. Moreover, the Java API provides an easy-to-use mechanism for writing applications that communicate across the network. Another advantage is that Java applications can run without change on any Java-compatible platform, just as applets can.

array

An organized collection of data in which each element has the same base type. As with most other programming languages, an element of a Java array can be accessed through a numeric index. As in C and C++, indexes are always zero-based. If the name of an array is A, the first element is A[0], the second is A[1], and so on. Java arrays are objects allocated with the new operator. Multidimensional arrays are treated as true arrays of arrays. As a consequence, you can, if you choose, allocate each row of a multidimensional array separately and give each row a different size. For more information, see the topic "Arrays," page 23.

ASCII

American Standard Code for Information Interchange: the standard format for mapping printable characters to bytes of data. ASCII is used in virtually all personal computers in the United States and other English-speaking countries. The ASCII character set is not large enough to represent the character sets of all human languages, so Java uses the Unicode system, which maps each character to 2 bytes of data rather than to 1 byte of data. The first 128 Unicode characters correspond to ASCII characters.

AWT

See Abstract Windowing ToolKit (AWT).

bitmap (.bmp file)

A binary representation of a rectangular screen image using pixel data. Each dot, or pixel, in the image maps to an element of data in the bitmap. The pixel in the top-left corner maps to the first element, the adjacent pixel on the right maps to the second element, and so on. Bitmaps can have any rectangular area: a subsection of the screen, the entire screen, or even a larger area. In GUI systems, a principal way to display an image is to copy a bitmap to the screen. Although there are other ways to display graphics (such as drawing lines), a bitmap has the advantage of containing the complete snapshot of an area. Note that .bmp is Microsoft's bitmap format; there are others, such as .xbm (Xbitmap format).

Boolean expression
An expression that has one of only two possible values: true or false. Control structures such as if and while require the use of Boolean expressions. In C, C++, Microsoft Visual Basic, and some other programming languages, Boolean values are treated as just another way to use integers. For example, a numeric expression that evaluates to 0 is considered false, and all other values are considered true. Java, by using an approach similar to Pascal, treats Boolean values as distinct from integers and provides a separate data type, boolean. Java's approach is straightfoward, because the results of all comparisons (such as Sum > 0) are Boolean, as you would expect. However, some programming tricks picked up from C and C++ — such as using while(n) instead of while(n!=0) — do not work. See the topics "Boolean expression" (p. 27), "true Keyword" (p. 97), and "false Keyword" (p. 51) for more information. See also Glossary entry "short-circuit logic" (p. 720).

border
A border is a special GUI component that is used to establish the appearance of the outside edge of another component. For example, you would use a border to provide a 3D beveled edge to a button.

border layout
The border layout is a layout manager that arranges components in the geographic directions north, south, east, and west, along with another component in the center. The border layout is the default layout manager for the content pane of frames. There is no direct relationship between the border layout and border components.

box layout
The box layout is a layout manager that provides a means of arranging components horizontally or vertically next to each other. The box layout is unique among layout managers because of the flexibility it offers when you nest box layouts within each other. Additionally, you can fine-tune the spacing between components within a box layout to create very intricate GUIs.

button
A button is a GUI component that invokes a command or sets a value when clicked by the user. Regular buttons are used to invoke commands, whereas radio buttons, toggle buttons, and checkboxes provide

a means of setting values. In actuality, buttons themselves don't invoke commands or set values, but instead trigger special handlers that carry out the tasks.

byte codes

Binary data representing a Java program. Byte codes are the intermediate language between Java and ordinary machine language. When you run the Java compiler, it translates your program into a series of `.class` files, each containing byte codes for a particular class. A Java interpreter reads these codes when you execute the program. Byte codes consist of binary, not human-readable data, containing instructions to a hypothetical Java computer (the Java Virtual Machine). The interpreter simulates this machine.

The use of byte codes is one of the things that make Java platform-independent. No matter which computer compiles a Java program, any other Java-enabled computer can run it. As explained in Chapter 1, "Applets and Oranges," each platform has its own Java interpreter. This arrangement differs from most software development, in which a compiler produces machine instructions aimed at a particular processor and operating system.

C

A popular computer language created by Brian Kernighan. Originally created as a tool for writing the UNIX operating system, C has eclipsed nearly all other traditional programming languages in popularity, with the exception of Basic. Much of C's success lies in its combining high-level control and data structures with useful and powerful operators, such as shift and bit operations. Java inherits much of C's syntax, although Java has some major differences and is more nearly akin to C++.

C++

The standard object-oriented version of C, created by Bjarne Stroustrup. At least superficially, C++ is the language closest to Java. As a rule, however, C++ and Java are too different from each other to make it particularly easy to port code from one to the other. An important difference is that C and C++ rely heavily on the use of pointers, whereas Java eliminates pointers. Because they were creating a language for Internet applications, Java's designers omitted pointers because of the memory problems they present. Moreover, Java is a leaner, smaller language and does not support some of the more obscure features of C++. On the other hand, C++ programmers will find that Java's use of such concepts as classes, references, and the `new` operator make Java familiar and easy to learn.

card layout
The card layout is a layout manager that arranges multiple panels so that they act like a stack of cards; only one of the panels is visible at any given time. The card layout is useful for creating wizard style interfaces, where the user is presented with a sequence of GUIs implemented as card panels.

cast
An operator that changes the type of an expression. The result is a new, temporary value that has the same value as its operand but a different type. Sometimes the compiler casts data for you. For example, in the declaration double d = 1; the integer 1 is implicitly cast to double and then assigned to d. Explicit casts are needed when an assignment results in loss of precision, for example, when you assign a floating-point constant (stored by default as type double) to a variable of type float. You also need a cast when you assign an expression to a variable of subclass type. For example, the vector.elementAt() method returns an Object type. Any variable you assign the result to belongs to a subclass of Object (because every class is, directly or indirectly, a subclass of Object). Therefore, the result needs to be cast. You can go in the other direction — assigning to a variable of superclass type — without an explicit cast. See the topic "casts," page 30, for example code.

character string
See "string," page 721.

character, Unicode
A 16-bit value used to represent a printable character on the display. Although an 8-bit (ASCII) value is sufficient to represent all characters in the English alphabet, it is too small to represent all characters from certain other natural languages. See "Unicode," page 725.

chooser
A chooser is a specialized dialog box used to retrieve standard information from the user within the context of a commonly performed task. For example, Swing includes a file chooser that provides a powerful GUI for browsing for files, along with a color chooser for selecting colors.

combo box
A combo box is a GUI component that allows the user to select an item from a list. Unlike lists, however, combo boxes only display a single item; multiple items are revealed in a drop-down window when you activate the combo box. Combo boxes also can serve as edit fields and allow users to manually enter new items that are added to the list.

component

A component is a graphical object that performs a function within a graphical user interface (GUI). Components are the building blocks of Java application GUIs. Examples of Java components include buttons, combo boxes, menus, and toolbars.

container

A container is a component that serves as a context for grouping together other components. Containers play a vital role in Java's GUI architecture in that they are the only components capable of housing other components. Examples of Java containers include panes, toolbars, and dialog boxes.

class

The most basic unit, or division, in a Java program. A class is a collection of variable declarations or function code (called *methods*) or both. Once a class is declared, you can use it to create any number of objects. The class's variable declarations determine each object's data fields, and methods determine object behavior. Another way to think of a class is to consider it a user-defined type and to consider objects as instances of such a type. The concept of a Java class is similar to a C++ class, C structure, Pascal record, or Visual Basic module. Java does not support the C++ `structure` and `union` keywords; instead, the `class` keyword must be used to declare all user-defined types.

Classes have other uses. Sometimes they are simply convenient program divisions. A class can include static fields, which are like global variables and functions except in their scope. In Java, a class might be the starting point of a program or a general pattern for other classes (an *abstract class*). However, the most common use of a class is as a type used to generate objects.

class method

A method that applies to an entire class and not to individual objects. Class methods are declared static. The principal feature of class methods is that you can call such a method through its class (as *class.method( )*) rather than having to create an object and then call the method through the object (as *object.method( )*).

For example, one of the class methods of the `Integer` class is `parseInt( )`. The following is a valid method call even if no `Integer` objects have been created:

```
int n = Integer.parseInt(inputstring);
```

Class methods have an important restriction: they can refer to other fields only if they are class fields (static). Another restriction is that class methods cannot use the `this` keyword. See also "instance method," page 704.

class variable

A variable that is shared by an entire class rather than stored in individual objects. Class variables are declared static. The principal feature of a class variable is that you can refer to it through its class (as `class.variable`) rather than having to create an object and then refer to the variable through the object (as `object.variable`).

For example, you can refer to the BOLD and ITALIC variables of the Font class even if no Font objects have been created:

```
Font.BOLD
Font.ITALIC
```

In the API, many class variables are constants, so they are not variables in the traditional sense. However, the syntax is the same. See also "instance variable," page 704.

CLASSPATH

An environment variable, or setting, maintained by the local operating system. If CLASSPATH is defined, the Java interpreter searches the CLASSPATH directories when it looks for a class; otherwise, it searches only the current directory. When you set CLASSPATH, you should include the current-directory symbol ("." in DOS and UNIX) to preserve the default behavior.

client

The user of a service provided by another computer, database, or object. In network operations, a client computer initiates a network connection with another computer, called a server, and then makes requests through function calls. A client may request the server to send information, store data, or execute some other task. The terms client and server are used most often in network operations, but sometimes used in database operations and in some object-oriented programming. See also "server," page 720.

compiler, Java

A program, called `javac.exe` on Windows platforms and javac on UNIX/Linux platforms, that translates Java source code into byte codes. The byte codes, in turn, can be run on any Java-compatible platform by using a Java interpreter. Traditionally, compilers translate source code into machine instructions so that it can be executed directly on a computer.

The Java compiler does roughly the same thing but translates the program into byte-code format, which consists of instructions to a virtual (imaginary) machine. See also "interpreter, Java," page 706.

component (Component class)

An independent graphical object capable of receiving and responding to events. Components are often called controls in other programming systems. In the Java API, all standard components are defined in the `java.awt` package. Examples include applets, windows, buttons, frames, choice boxes, and labels. In the Java API, the `java.awt.Component` class is a high-level abstract class that includes attributes and methods common to all components. Specific classes that inherit from the Component class are `Applet`, `Button`, `Frame`, `Choice`, `Label`, as well as many others.

constant

A value that does not change throughout the course of a program. Java variables declared `final` are constants; the compiler does not permit changes to these variables. For more information, see "final Keyword," page 51. Constants also include literal values, such as quoted strings and digits.

constructor

A method that is automatically called when an object is created. Constructors, though optional, are useful for performing initialization of objects. As in C++, a constructor has no return type and has the same name as the class for which it is written. See the topic "Constructors," page 39.

container (Container class)

A component that can physically contain other components. The standard containers defined in the Java API include windows, frames, and dialog boxes. These containers are defined in classes in the `java.awt` package, and all of them inherit from the `Container` class. The `Applet` class is also a container class, although it is located in the `java.applet` package.

copy constructor

A constructor that tells how to create an object from another object of the same class. The signature of a copy constructor is *class*(*class*). Copy constructors do not have quite the same importance in Java that they do in C++, because Java does not pass objects by value. However, they are still useful.

critical section

See "synchronized methods and threads," page 722.

delegation event model
The delegation event model is the event model employed by Java 2, which involves registering event listeners with event sources in order for events to be delivered from one object to another. This model is very efficient because the only events that are delivered are those for which a listener has specifically been registered. Java used several other event models in previous versions before finally arriving at the delegation event model, which is extremely flexible.

dialog box
A dialog box is a special window that provides a means of displaying a "temporary" user interface that displays or retrieves information, and then goes away. Constructing a custom dialog box GUI is very similar to constructing an application GUI through the content pane of a frame window.

Double-buffering
A technique for smoothing the effects of animation in graphics programs. In double-buffering, a program manipulates an internal graphics display that is not seen by the user but is stored in memory. When a series of graphics changes have been completed, the in-memory display is copied to the display through a single operation that copies pixel info to the screen. Double-buffering requires more memory but is often the only technique for achieving smooth animation effects that do not flicker.

encapsulation
Protecting part of an object from the outside world; it amounts to declaring a method or variable `private`. It is a good policy to make the contents of a class (and thus an object) private except for the parts that must interact with other classes. These points of interaction should, ideally, be as few as possible. The advantage of encapsulating some or most of the class is that the internals of the class can be freely rewritten without breaking the code that uses the class. Another advantage is that it's frequently useful to hide the details. These are fundamental principles of object-oriented design, although they are helpful in traditional programming as well.

Encapsulation is often used in a slightly more general sense, meaning roughly "an abstraction for." For example, the `String` class can be considered to encapsulate the contents and attributes of character strings. (See "string," page 721.) An object of type `String` in Java represents the capabilities that you associate with an array of characters. This object can do all the same things that a character string can do, but it hides most of the details of how the data is stored, ultimately making the `String` class easier to work with.

escape sequence

A two-character sequence that represents a single special character, such as a tab (\t) or newline (\n). As in C and C++, Java escape sequences begin with the backslash. See the topic "Strings" (p. 89) for a list of escape sequences.

event

An event is something that occurs within an object that an application or other object might want to know about and to which it might possibly react. Examples of events include mouse clicks and key presses. Each GUI component in the Java supports certain events that are applicable to the function of the component.

event adapter

An event adapter is a helper class that makes the code for handling events much cleaner. More specifically, an event adapter alleviates the need to implement all of the event response methods in an event listener interface, allowing you to implement only the methods you need.

event listener

An event listener is an object that is capable of responding to events that are typically generated by GUI components. You connect an event listener to an event source in order to receive and respond to events. An event listener is responsible for implementing event response methods that are called in response to specific types of events.

event response method

An event response method is a special method that is implemented by an event listener and that is called in response to an event.

event source

An event source is an object that is capable of generating events. Most GUI components are event sources because they typically generate events in response to user interactions. As an example, a button generates action events when you click it with the mouse.

exception

An unusual occurrence during program execution that requires immediate handling. Most exceptions are runtime errors of some kind, although some exceptions (such as reaching the end of a file) do not necessarily indicate catastrophe. Java's exception-handling syntax, which is close to that in ANSI C++, enables you to centralize exception-handling code so it is easier to maintain. When an exception is reported (or thrown), execution is automatically transferred to the closest exception handler no matter what method was executing when the exception was thrown. See the topic "Exception Handling" (p. 46) for more information.

event

An action, normally a user action such as a keystroke or a mouse event, that your program can respond to at runtime through specific methods. For example, the `mouseDown()` method is called when the user presses a mouse button at runtime. Only certain kinds of graphical objects, called components, receive events. You write event-handling code by subclassing the component's class (for example, `Button`) and overriding the event-handling methods by writing your own method definitions. See Chapter 4, "Components and Events."

field

An item in a class declaration. Fields determine the attributes of each object in the class (except for fields declared static). A field may be either a variable or a method. Fields are called members in C structures and C++ classes. Java's designers had a passion for borrowing from C++ but changing the terminology, perhaps to keep C++ programmers from becoming complacent. In Java terminology, a variable (data member in C++) may actually be a constant.

finalizer method

A method that all classes inherit from the `Object` class but don't necessarily implement. The `finalizer()` method is the closest thing in Java to a C++ destructor; it includes code executed when an object is about to be removed from memory. The purpose of this method is to clean up resources that were being used by the object. However, because almost all such cleanup is automatic in Java, writing a `finalizer()` method is usually unnecessary.

firewall

A security layer that protects parts of a network from outsiders. For example, it may be desirable to connect a proprietary network, such as a LAN, to the Internet, while making only parts of the network available to the outside world. Other parts are protected through a firewall. Creation and maintenance of a firewall are generally low-level systems issues.

fixed point

An alternative format for representing fractional values, used in the Java Database Connectivity (JDBC) `Numeric` class. A fixed-point variable is an integer with a built-in scale. For example, a scale of two means that instead of storing the number of dollars, you store the number of cents — a value stored as 179 would be displayed as 1.79. If the scale were three, the value would be displayed as 0.179. In contrast, the floating-point format cannot store 1.79 or 0.179 precisely. Although values are displayed in decimal radix, they are stored in binary. This conversion of fractional data from one radix to another involves loss of data, and the floating-point format accumulates errors in dollars-and-cents calculations. Understandably, the fixed-point format is more popular with accountants.

floating point

A data type that can represent fractions; floating point can also represent very large quantities. Floating-point number formats use scientific notation, which includes sign, mantissa, and exponent. (Don't worry if you don't recognize these terms, because there's almost never any practical reason for dissecting a floating-point number.) The important thing to know is that Java uses the same floating-point formats for all platforms — you can rely on the value of a float or double variable. Other programming languages do not always enforce a binary standard, so transfer of data between platforms is unreliable. The other thing to know about floating-point data is that there is a trade-off: integers can be processed faster, whereas floating-point numbers take longer to process but can hold much larger and smaller quantities. Yet the gap between integer and floating-point efficiency is narrowing as more and more hardware platforms contain powerful built-in floating-point coprocessors. Even so, you should avoid using floating point, when an integer variable would suffice.

flow layout

The flow layout arranges components across a container in rows from left to right and is the default layout manager for panels. When adding components to a flow layout, the components appear next to each other moving from left to right across the container, and then scroll down and continue the same pattern on another line.

frame

A frame is a container that serves as the main window for an application. Because frames serve as main application windows, they support familiar UI window features such as a title, border, and buttons for sizing and closing the frame.

FTP

File Transfer Protocol is the standard protocol used in network communications for downloading files. The World Wide Web supports this protocol in a transparent way; a Web user automatically logs into the target server by clicking the appropriate link. File-downloading locations on the Web are identified by the ftp: prefix.

garbage collector
A lazy programmer's dream come true: a background thread, run by the Java interpreter, that releases memory used by objects that are no longer around. Because of the garbage collector, you generally don't need to explicitly destroy objects or release memory even though you must explicitly create them using the new operator. Unused objects are simply cleaned up when you're not looking, so to speak. Typically, the garbage collection process takes over when all the variables referring to a particular object in memory have gone out of scope (although the Java interpreter could be optimized to start garbage collection even sooner). The garbage collector runs as a low-priority thread, minimizing its impact on program efficiency. It gets priority whenever memory is scarce.

GIF (.gif file)
Graphics Interchange Format: a popular format for storing graphics images that is used widely in Web pages and Java applications. If you examine the Java SDK, you'll find a number of examples of .gif files that you can readily load into a Java Image object. Unlike bitmap (.bmp) files, the GIF format uses space-compression techniques to store an image (See also "JPEG," page 708.)

glue
Glue is a special object used in the box layout to maximize the space between components in one direction (horizontal or vertical). Glue forms an important part of the box layout in that it helps to fine-tune the positioning of components.

grid bag layout
The grid bag layout is a layout manager that provides the most flexibility of all the layouts, but at the cost of considerable complexity. The grid bag layout is similar to a grid layout except that you have a lot more control over the size and position of the cells in the grid. For example, in a grid bag layout you can specify that some cells span multiple columns as well as control the physical arrangement of components within specific cells in the grid.

grid layout
The grid layout is a layout manager that arranges components in a grid (table) of rows and columns. Like the flow layout, the grid layout arranges components from left to right, but they conform to a fixed arrangement of rows and columns, as opposed to simply scrolling to form new lines of components.

GUI

Graphical user interface. GUI systems are famous for being easy to use and notoriously difficult to program. When you write applets, the Java API provides a strong offering of GUI features — windows, buttons, scroll bars, graphics, mouse events, and so on — in a form that is relatively easy to program. A particularly strong advantage of Java is that you can use it to create GUI programs that run, without change, on different kinds of computers.

heavyweight component

A heavyweight component is a component that has an underlying native component, or peer, associated with it. For example, an AWT button is a heavyweight component because it uses an underlying Windows peer when running on the Windows platform. Heavyweight components are heavily tied to the underlying operating system and therefore assume the look and feel of the underlying native components. Lightweight components don't rely on underlying native components, and are therefore more flexible in taking on a different look and feel.

host

A synonym for *server.* You can think of a client as "visiting" a server and being treated to guest services. Note that the client must be a good guest by behaving itself and using the correct procedures (protocol) to make requests.

HotJava

A Web browser developed by Sun Microsystems to support Java applets. Netscape and other vendors soon followed suit by adding Java support to their browsers. HotJava is itself an application written entirely in Java, thus demonstrating the power of the language.

HTML

Hypertext Markup Language is the standard markup language for encoding a Web page. An HTML file consists mainly of a series of tags: commands, enclosed in angle brackets (<>), that cause a browser to display text and graphics. In addition, a Java-compatible browser recognizes the <APPLET> tag, which specifies a subclass of the Java `Applet` class to load and run.

HTTP

Hypertext Transport Protocol is the protocol used by World Wide Web servers for providing hypertext documents, or Web pages. *Hypertext* enables a document to contain text, images, and sounds, as well as links (or jumps) to other pages or resources, even within the same document. The reason that Web URLs start with `http:` is that they use the HTTP protocol. See "FTP," page 700, for an example of another protocol.

icon
An icon is an image that provides visual cues associated with GUI features. Icons are regularly used with Swing menu items and buttons, as well as other components.

implement
In Java, this term has a specific technical meaning in addition to its more general meaning: to implement a method is to provide a method definition (the statements between the braces: {}); to implement an interface is to provide definitions for all the methods in the interface. In Java, as in other object-oriented systems, different classes may provide different definitions for the same method. Each definition is a different implementation.

In general usage, to implement means to fulfill or complete something. The Java usage is consistent with this general idea. A method declaration implies the idea of a certain task or activity; an implementation defines one way to perform that task. Similarly, an interface declares a list of services; an implementation for an interface defines a way to perform those services. Java also supports an `implements` keyword (see p. 58), and a version of Java on a particular platform is sometimes called an implementation of Java.

infinity
See "POSITIVE_INFINITY" (p. 716) and "NEGATIVE_INFINITY" (p. 712).

inheritance
Defining a new class or interface in terms of an existing class or interface. Inheritance, which conjures up visions of family trees and biological classification schemes, is a highly touted feature of object-oriented programming. But inheritance is probably best viewed as a convenient way of repeating all the fields of one class inside another class without having to retype the declarations. For example, when class A inherits from class B, A automatically has all the same fields that B does, including method declarations and definitions, if any. (However, the private fields of B are not visible in A.) B is then the superclass of A. Any explicit declarations in A create additional or overridden fields. A can reuse, adapt, and amend the code already created for B.

Java limits inheritance to single inheritance, meaning that any given class inherits directly from only one superclass. Yet, a class may inherit *indirectly* from other classes, because B may have its own superclass, and that superclass may have another superclass, and so on. This arrangement creates an inheritance hierarchy, at the root of which is the `Object` class defined in the Java API. Thus, all classes inherit from `Object`, although there may be intervening generations. For more information, see the topic "extends Keyword," page 49.

Although Java restricts inheritance to single inheritance, it lets a class implement any number of interfaces. Implementing an interface is a variation on inheritance; in C++, it is the same as inheriting from a purely abstract class. Nevertheless, interfaces have special restrictions that classes do not have. Limiting multiple inheritance to interfaces reduces the possible complexity that the Java compiler must deal with. For more information, see "interface."

inner class
An inner class is a class that is defined within the scope of another class. Inner classes are often used with event adapters to make event handling cleaner.

instance
Simply put, an object. The fact that object-oriented terminology uses both *object* and *instance* to mean the same thing may seem like a plot to confuse the novice. However, the term *instance* emphasizes an object's relationship to its class and is sometimes useful for this reason. For example, suppose there is a Car class used to create the objects herbie, hotrod, and chittybang. All of these objects have their fields defined in the Car declaration. It's convenient to speak of herbie, hotrod, and chittybang as "instances of Car."

instance method
A method that operates on individual objects (instances). All methods not declared static are instance methods. Unlike class methods, instance methods have unlimited access to all other fields (variables and methods) in the same class, even those that are nonstatic or private. Generally, an instance method's main purpose is to manipulate an object or communicate with it in some way. Unlike a class method, an instance method can be called only through an object. For example, you can call the setLabel() method of the Button class only after creating a Button object:

```
Button b = new Button();
b.setLabel("My button.");
```

If setLabel() were a class method rather than an instance method, the expression "Button.setLabel("My button")" would be legal — which it is not. See also "class method," page 694.

instance variable
A variable that represents a field of an object (that is, an instance). All variables are instance variables unless declared static. You must create an object before referring to an instance variable. You then refer to

the variable through the object and not through its class. For example, the variable `width` is an instance variable of the `Dimension` class. The variable `width` takes up storage inside the instance `d`:

```
Dimension d = new Dimension();
int w = d.width;
```

If `width` were a class variable rather than an instance variable, then `Dimension.width` would be a legal expression — which it is not. See also "class variable," page 695.

instantiation
Instantiation means creating an object of a particular class. A class that has at least one object is said to be instantiated. Some classes (abstract classes in particular) cannot be instantiated, meaning that you cannot use them to create objects directly. The term is almost unnecessary, but object-oriented devotees seem to like it.

integer
The common way that numbers are stored in computers: as simple whole-number quantities that do not have a fractional part. Although some kinds of calculations require fractions (see "floating point," page 700), a program typically has many calculations that do not involve fractions at all. For example, a common type of variable is a loop variable, which counts iterations through a loop. For such situations, it is more efficient to use an integer than a floating-point number. Java integer types include `byte`, `short`, `int`, and `long`. In Java, all integer types store negative as well as positive numbers. (See "two's complement," page 724, for more information on negative numbers.)

interface
Simply put, a list of services. An interface consists of abstract methods — and, optionally, constants — but you can think of it as a contract between the class that implements it and the class's users. By implementing an interface, you agree to provide definitions for each method declared in the interface (a method being a "service"). Implementing an interface is similar to subclassing an abstract class.

Beyond that, interfaces are sometimes used in the API almost as if they were classes. For example, certain API methods have the return type `Enumeration`. This means that you get back an object whose class implements the `Enumeration` interface. In this case, you don't know what the object's actual class is. However, you don't care; the only thing that matters is that you can call any `Enumeration` method through this object. In effect, you can treat `Enumeration` as if it were the object's class.

The Java concept of interface is close to that of abstract class. In C++, an abstract class is exactly what you would use in place of an interface. The main difference is that abstract classes are not bound to all the restrictions that interfaces are bound to. Java limits multiple inheritance to interfaces that, in turn, have greater restrictions. Consequently, the Java compiler is leaner, because some of the messier problems of multiple inheritance never arise.

On a final note: Don't confuse Java's use of *interface* with the rather general use of the term in *C++ In Plain English*. In Java, *interface* has a much narrower and more technical meaning.

interpreter, Java
A program that reads Java byte codes (stored in .class files) and responds by performing actions. The program java.exe is an interpreter, as is the applet viewer program and any Java-compatible Web browser. You can think of byte codes as instructions for a virtual, or imaginary, processor. A Java interpreter decodes these instructions by executing them on its platform. Because each platform has its own Java interpreter, a Java program and compiler can target just one virtual machine, in effect making Java a universal language. It is theoretically possible that a computer could be developed that would process Java byte codes directly; until then, interpreters suffice. See also "compiler, Java," page 695.

introspection
The ability of a JavaBean to expose information about itself to the external world. Important aspects of introspection include the ability to expose attributes as *properties* (p. 717) and to expose event-handling behavior. At design time, an application building tool uses introspection techniques to examine a Bean and enable graphical editing of its capabilities by the Bean user. Introspection is one of the abilities that most distinguishes a Bean from an ordinary Java object, because ordinarily you cannot understand the capabilities of an object without access to documentation or source code. See Chapter 7 for more information.

invisible filler
An invisible filler is used in the box layout to create space between components. Invisible fillers play an important role in establishing the box layout's capability of fine-tuning the position of components.

Java
A computer programming language that is highly object-oriented, smaller than C++, and targeted for new environments such as the Internet. Much more so than other languages, Java is a unified language: Java has a built-in API and a precise binary standard for all

its data types. Unlike C and C++, Java has tighter security features that make it safer for distribution across a network; for example, you cannot use Java to read and write random memory addresses. The ever-increasing adoption of the Java format and widespread availability of Java interpreters make it an ideal language for writing programs to be distributed throughout the microcomputer and minicomputer world as well as for use in specialized computerized devices of the future. (See "compiler, Java," page 695, and "interpeter, Java," page 706.)

JavaScript
A programming language based on Java and C that can be embedded directly into HTML files. JavaScript has some similarities to Java, but it is a separate language; it is neither a macro language for generating Java code nor a tool for creating Java applications. People with little programming experience may prefer to learn JavaScript, because it is a smaller language. However, it is much less flexible than Java and lacks many of Java's object-oriented features, such as inheritance. JavaScript was designed to integrate tightly into HTML browsers, with direct access to browser objects. This makes it better at interacting directly with elements of Web pages. Although generally slower than Java, JavaScript usually loads faster because it's embedded in the Web page.

JavaBeans
Java's answer to Microsoft's ActiveX controls, JavaBeans is a technology for creating custom Java components that can be dragged and dropped into a visual development environment. The predecessor to ActiveX and JavaBeans was Visual Basic custom controls, which established the success of a component-based model of developing software. JavaBeans and ActiveX are not necessarily mutually exclusive. An important difference is that JavaBeans is an extension to the Java API (in Java 1.1 and not covered here). JavaBeans is covered extensively in Part II, Chapter 7, "Working with JavaBeans."

Java compiler (javac)
See "compiler, Java," page 695.

Java interpreter (java)
See "interpreter, Java," page 706.

Java Virtual Machine
A term that means almost the same thing as Java interpreter. When the Java compiler translates a program, it produces machine instructions for a hypothetical system called the Java Virtual Machine. (The instructions are called *byte codes*.) On any given computer, the Java interpreter executes these instructions, thus simulating Virtual Machine behavior. However, the Java Virtual Machine is more than just a way to interpret

individual instructions; it is the entire runtime environment supporting Java programs. Thus, the Java Virtual Machine provides features such as background threads and garbage collection.

JDBC
Java database connectivity: the Java 1.1 extension for interacting with database systems. The `java.sql` package contains the set of classes and interfaces that support all the JDBC capabilities, using SQL statements to execute commands.

Java SDK
Java Software Development Kit (SDK). You can download the Java SDK free by using the Internet and going to the JavaSoft home page (`http://javasoft.com`). It is also available on CD-ROM. The Java SDK includes a Java compiler, an interpreter, demos, and applet viewer, as well as other useful utilities such as a debugger.

JPEG (.jpg file)
Joint Photographic Experts Group: a graphics-image format that, like GIF, uses compression techniques to store an image in a smaller space than required by a standard bitmap (`.bmp`) file. The JPEG format produces the best compression for a single photographic image by eliminating redundant picture information. (For example, a field of solid blue sky is reduced to a few bytes indicating the pattern.) Contrast this compression technique with MPEG (see p. 711).

keyword
A word that has a predefined meaning in a language. Common Java keywords include `if`, `else`, `while`, and `do`, which are all inherited from C/C++, as well as `extends`, `implements`, `package`, and `interface`, which are new in Java. The main thing to know about keywords is that you cannot choose them as names for your own variables. Yet, it probably isn't worth your time to memorize lists of keywords. Picking meaningful, highly specific names will usually avoid conflicts. Beyond that, the Java compiler will tell you when there is a problem. For a table of keywords, see the topic "Keywords," page 65.

label
A label is an output-only component that is used to present both text and graphical information to the user. You often see labels used in conjunction with input components such as text edit fields. Labels can also be used with icons to present graphics or a combination of graphics and text.

layout manager

A layout manager is an object associated with a container that determines how components are physically arranged within the container. Layout managers are often referred to simply as layouts. The Java 2 API includes several different layout managers for accomplishing different arrangements of components.

lightweight component

A lightweight component, also known as a peerless component, is a component with no underlying native component. The primary benefit to lightweight components is that they are 100% Java, which alleviates inconsistencies across different platforms. Most of the components in the Swing toolkit are lightweight components, as opposed to the heavyweight Abstract Windowing ToolKit (AWT) components.

list

A list is a GUI component that allows the user to select one or more text and/or icon items from a list of possibilities.

local variable

A variable declared inside a method, a compound statement, or (in Java only) a `for` statement. Memory occupied by a local variable is returned as soon as it goes out of scope. See the topic "for Statement" (p. 53) for information about Java's unique use of local variables inside a `for` loop.

Local variables have a purpose limited to a specific section of code, such as a loop or calculation. In contrast, variables declared at the class level (called *class variables* and *instance variables*) have longer life spans and can share information between methods. One principle of good programming is to always use local variables except when a larger scope is needed. Unlike C and C++, Java has no true global variables, although class variables have global life span and storage. See also "scope" (p. 719) and "stack" (p. 721).

lock

See "synchronized methods and threads," page 722.

low-level event

A low-level event is an event that is fired in response to a low-level input or graphical user interface interaction such as a key press or mouse click.

MAX_VALUE

A constant, defined in the number classes `Integer`, `Long`, `Float`, and `Double`, that is equal to the highest positive value the type in question can hold. Note that these wrapper classes give ranges and other information for the primitive data types `int`, `long`, `float`, and `double`, but wrapper classes are not identical to primitive data types.

members

See "field," page 699.

menu

A menu is a GUI component that provides a hierarchical user interface for selecting commands and altering settings within an applet or application. A Swing menu consists of a menu bar that is a container for individual drop-down menus; these menus contain individual menu items that represent commands or settings.

method

A function or subroutine declared inside a class. In Java, methods are the only functions or subroutines allowed. In other words, you must place all function code inside class declarations. As with C functions, a Java method may or may not return a value, depending on its return type. (A `void` method returns no value.) By default, methods in Java are late bound and polymorphic. For information on how to declare methods, see the topic "Methods," page 69.

All methods are either instance methods or class methods. A method declared static is a *class* method and works very much like a global function in the way that it is used. For example, the class method `Math.random()` has nothing to do with individual objects and, except for the `Math` prefix, is like a C function. A method not declared static is an instance method. Generally, the purpose of such a method is to program behavior into individual objects. For example, the method might manipulate the state of a particular object through which it is called.

MIDI

Musical Instrumental Digital Interface: a format for storing audio data. MIDI can store musical information in a compact format and is especially useful for communication of data between computers, synthesizers, and muscial instruments.

MIN_VALUE

A constant, defined in the number classes `Integer`, `Long`, `Float`, and `Double`, equal to the lowest value that the type in question can hold. This is the negative number of greatest magnitude (farthest from zero).

Note that these wrapper classes give ranges and other information for the primitive data types `int`, `long`, `float`, and `double`, but wrapper classes are not identical to primitive data types.

mnemonic
A mnemonic provides a keyboard user interface for navigating through the hierarchy of a menu to select a menu item or invoke a menu command, usually in conjunction with the Alt key. An underlined character in the name of a menu item visually identifies a mnemonic. Mnemonics differ from accelerators in that accelerators automatically invoke a command, while mnemonics provide a means of navigating menus. You can still invoke commands with mnemonics, but they are carried out through the menu.

MPEG
Motion Picture Experts Group: a format for storing video (and, optionally, audio) information. Unlike JPEG, which is a single-image format, MPEG reduces redundant picture information within groups of frames. Specifically, MPEG eliminates most individual frames in favor of data that summarizes changes between them. MPEG produces the highest compression for video, but JPEG is still preferred for some purposes. MPEG is designed only for distribution, and not for editing, because of its elimination of individual frames.

multicast event delivery
Multicast event delivery involves an event being broadcast to multiple event listeners simultaneously; multiple event listeners can be registered with a multicast event source. Multicast event delivery makes it possible for several objects to listen and respond to a single event.

multithreaded program
A program that uses more than one thread, or sequence of execution. In a sense, each thread operates as an independent program except that all threads share common program code and resources. All Java programs have at least one thread. (In addition, running in the background are threads you don't see such as the Java garbage collector.) By running more than one thread, a program gains the ability to do more than one activity at a time. See "thread," page 723.

NaN
Not a Number, a special floating-point value that indicates an undefined result. Certain mathematical operations produce this value—most notably, division by zero in a floating-point expression. Unlike integer division, floating-point division produces this result rather than throwing an exception. The constants `Float.NaN` and `Double.NaN` represent the

NaN value for the `float` and `double` types, respectively. When NaN is tested for equality to itself, it returns false, so use `Float.isNaN()` or `Double.isNaN()` to test for this value.

native code

The machine language of the local processor. In reality, a computer never executes any code except native code. All other types of programming code must somehow be translated. This translation is performed by other programs, called compilers and interpreters, which themselves are directly or indirectly running native code.

For the most part, the existence of native code and translators is not an issue in Java programming unless you want to step outside the Java language and plug in external code modules. These modules may be written in C, C++, or assembly language before being compiled into machine language. Java provides the `native` keyword for implementing a method with non-Java code. This technique is strictly prohibited in applets, because native code, once executed, circumvents all security checks.

NEGATIVE_INFINITY

A special floating-point value that indicates an overflow involving a negative number. Unlike integer arithmetic, floating-point operations produce this result rather than throwing an exception. The constants `Float.NEGATIVE_INFINITY` and `Double.NEGATIVE_INFINITY` represent this value for the `float` and `double` types, respectively. In any comparison, negative infinity is always lower than any other value represented by the type, although it is equal to itself.

null

A special value indicating "no object assigned." In Java, object variables are references, which means that they can be associated with different objects in memory at different times. A null value means that the variable is currently not associated with any object. In Java, the `null` keyword is a predefined value that can be assigned to an object variable or tested for equality with the variable.

object

A packet of data with both state and behavior. An object is an instance of a data structure that knows how to respond to a set of messages. In Java, messages are actually method calls, which are like function calls except that they involve a reference to a particular object. For example, a method call such as `myobject.clearAllFields()` might tell myobject to zero out all its data fields. A Java object is therefore like a C structure or Pascal record with the added feature of responsiveness, or intelligence. (Note, however, that it is also valid for an object to consist only of data fields.)

One of the major confusions in object-oriented programming, when people first approach the subject, is the distinction between objects and classes. An object responds to method calls at runtime, but all methods are declared and defined in an object's class, which provides complete type information. Objects of the same class therefore tend to have similar behavior, although differences in state (the particular values stored in the data fields) can affect what happens during execution of a method.

object orientation
An approach to program design and coding that is one of the essential features of Java. Although object orientation has many things in common with traditional, structured programming, there is one fundamental difference: the major division is not between code and data but between individual objects, which are self-contained units having both state (data) and behavior (code). The general model of object orientation is that of a network of objects, each able to respond intelligently to messages from other objects. Object orientation has proved to be increasingly appropriate for modern programming systems, because graphical, event-driven systems act very much like collections of independent objects. In Java, object structure and behavior are programmed by writing a class.

One of the major goals of object orientation is to facilitate and encourage reusable code. Object-oriented languages, including Java, support inheritance, which is a useful technique for reusing and adapting code.

one-based indexing
An indexing scheme in which the first position is 1, the second position is 2, the third position is 3, and so on. This approach may seem the obvious way to do things, but most of Java uses zero-based indexing instead. JDBC classes (`java.sql`) use one-based indexing to indicate column position.

option pane
An option pane is a standard dialog box that makes it easier to accomplish certain tasks, alleviating you from having to construct a custom dialog box GUI. As an example, you can use an option pane to ask the user a Yes/No question or to simply display a message.

overloading
Reusing a method name so that you define different versions for different argument types. For example, suppose you want to write a function, `square_it()`, that works with both `int` and `double`. The Java

solution is to write two versions of the function: `square_it(int)` and `square_it(double)`. Each has a different signature and method definition.

Overloading is resolved at compile time: the Java compiler knows how to evaluate a method call such as `square_it(5)`. Java knows that `int` is the type of the argument, 5, and so calls `square_it(int)`. Overloading is basically a convenience — it eliminates the need to generate different method names for each argument type, such as `square_it_int()` and `square_it_double()`. Contrast this with polymorphism (see "polymorphism," page 715), which is a runtime, not a compile-time, operation.

Another type of overloading is *operator overloading*, which Java does not currently let you extend to your own classes. In operator overloading, the meaning of an operator (such as + or *) is determined by the types of its operands. In Java, the only class that overloads an operator is `String`, which defines its own operation for the plus sign (+).

overriding
The process of inheriting a method from a superclass but substituting a new method definition. Because Java classes can override any method definition (except those declared final), there can be multiple definitions of the same method. Java methods are polymophic; this means that the appropriate method definition for an object is always called at runtime, regardless of how that object is accessed.

package
A collection of related classes placed in the same subdirectory. The most commonly used packages are in the API, which uses packages to help organize API classes into meaningful groups. Another use for packages is to set aside a group of classes as a separate subproject in a large software project. Packages create a layer of software insulation over and above classes. When you refer to a class inside another package, the class referred to must be declared public. Also, you must prefix the name of the class with the name of its package or else use the `import` keyword. (But note that the API class `java.lang` is an exception; access to that class is automatic.)

The intricacies of packages, directories, and searching for `.class` files may at first be counterintuitive to C and C++ programmers, because there is nothing exactly like them in these other languages. For more information, consult Chapter 2, "Java Building Blocks."

pane
A pane is a generic Swing container. Different types of panes are used in conjunction in the Swing architecture to provide support for rich GUI features.

pixel
Picture element: a single dot on the display screen. A pixel is the smallest unit of distance on the screen as well as being the smallest unit in an off-screen buffer. Many graphics formats use pixels as units, although some formats use compression techniques to save space. Pixel data includes all information needed to display a single dot, including color and intensity.

platform
A combination of processor, computer architecture, and operating system. The platform is simply the underlying type of system on which you are running. For example, an Intel processor running Windows 95 is one platform; a Macintosh is another platform, and UNIX is yet another. Until Java, there was no widely available technique for writing a program that could run, without change, on multiple platforms.

pluggable look and feel
Pluggable look and feel is a feature of Swing that allows you to set the look and feel of a GUI dynamically. By using a pluggable look and feel, a Swing GUI is capable of querying the underlying native GUI and taking on its look and feel. The look and feel of a GUI comprises such graphical parameters as color schemes, component styles, and 3D shading effects, to name a few.

pointer
A variable that stores an address in memory. Support for pointer operations makes C, C++, and Assembly language very powerful, but it also makes them dangerous. A C programmer can use pointer operations to overwrite large sections of memory (often unintentionally). Certain highly specialized kinds of software will always require pointers; for example, you generally need C, C++, or Assembly language to write a new operating system. Java, however, is a sophisticated application-writing language in which security issues are important. Despite its similarity to C++, therefore, Java eliminates pointers in favor of other techniques. See the topic "Pointers," page 80.

polymorphism
The capability of responding to the same message in infinitely many ways (from the Greek for "many forms"). Polymorphism may sound esoteric, but it is what enables you to define custom responses to standard API methods, such as `paint()` and `mouseDown()`. Polymorphism enables you to subclass an existing class C, override methods, and have other software treat an instance of your subclass as though it were an instance of C. Other software need have no foreknowledge of your subclasses. So, for example, the Abstract Windowing ToolKit (AWT)

thinks that it is calling `Button.action()`, when actually it is calling your implementation of the `action()` method. In effect, polymorphism lets you plug your own code into an existing structure.

The mechanism that makes this possible is late binding, which means that the address of the actual implementation to be called is not determined until runtime. The object's exact type is known at runtime, so calls are correctly resolved. Consequently, the knowledge of how to respond to method calls is built into an individual object. Program control is decentralized. Polymorphism is realized by using virtual functions in C++ and through callback functions in C. By default, all methods are polymorphic in Java unless declared final.

POSITIVE_INFINITY

A special floating-point value that indicates an overflow involving a positive number. Unlike integer arithmetic, floating-point operations produce this result rather than throw an exception. The constants `Float.POSITIVE_INFINITY` and `Double.POSITIVE_INFINITY` represent this value for the `float` and `double` types, respectively. In any comparison, positive infinity is always greater any other value represented by the type, although it is equal to itself.

primitive data type

One of the data types predefined in the Java language, most of which are numeric: `boolean`, `char`, `byte`, `short`, `int`, `long`, `float`, and `double`. Java variables having a primitive data type work very much as they do in other programming languages. Unlike objects, primitive data is allocated directly in memory by simply declaring variables. The `new` keyword is not used unless you are creating arrays. For a table describing primitive data sizes and ranges, see the topic "Data Types," page 41.

private access

An access level for fields: a method or variable declared private can be accessed only within the method definitions of its own class. This corresponds closely to the C++ use of `private`. The `private` keyword cannot be applied to class declarations. However, a class that is not public is accessible only within its own package, making it private as far as code outside the package is concerned. For more information, see "private Keyword," page 81, or Table B-7 in Appendix B, page 684.

progress bar

A progress bar is a GUI component that provides a visual representation of the status of an incomplete process. For example, you might display a progress bar while loading images in an applet or copying files in a disk utility application.

property

A string value stored in a simple table. To access a value, you use another string called a *key*. For example, in the Java system properties table, the key `file.separator` returns a string containing the file separator character. (This is "\" for Windows systems and "/" for UNIX systems.) Property tables are relatively simple structures that do not require JDBC. You can create property tables for your own purposes, and Java provides a system property table that contains information of general use. For more information, see the `Properties` (p. 424) and `System` (p. 466) classes, and Table B-6 in Appendix B, page 683.

A JavaBean can have one or more Bean properties, which is a different concept from the one just described. A Bean property is a piece of data accessed indirectly through accessor methods. An application builder tool can use the accessor methods to let a developer view and edit the Bean properties graphically at design time. In effect, a property is a higher-level piece of data than a simple data member. When you set a color property, for example, the Bean can respond by repainting itself to show the results of a new color. See Chapter 7 for more information.

protected access

An access level for fields: a method or variable can be declared protected. This is the intermediate access level between public and private. A field declared protected cannot be accessed outside its package, except in subclasses; and a field declared private protected cannot be accessed outside its class at all, except in subclasses. For more information, see "protected Keyword," page 82, or Table B-7 in Appendix B, page 684.

protocol

An agreed-on procedure, or set of rules, for communication, especially across a network. Without a common protocol, two computers could send each other random streams of data, and the result would be chaos. A protocol enables computers to talk to each other in a meaningful way: a computer follows a protocol to initiate a conversation; inform the other if data is to be sent and how much; and indicate what, if any, response is expected.

public access

An access level for fields as well as a modifier for class declarations. A class declared public is accessible everywhere, even outside its package. Only one class can be declared public in each source file, and it must have the same name as the source file. A field declared public has the same visibility as its class; this means that public has no effect on fields unless the class is also public. For more information, see "public Keyword," page 83, or Table B-7 in Appendix B, page 684.

raising an exception
See "throwing an exception," page 724.

reference
A variable, argument, or return value that refers to an object. In Java, all object variables are references. Java references look exactly like ordinary variables (there is no reference operator, as in C++), but there are a couple of critical differences. First, a reference variable cannot be used until associated with an actual object. The object is usually created with the new operator and is then associated with a variable through assignment (=). Second, assigning one reference to another does not create a copy of the object but rather causes both references to refer to the same thing. For example, if A and B are references, A = B causes A to be associated with the same object that B is. Nevertheless, there is still only one copy of the data.

Consequently, a reference is like a handle or a pointer, although it looks like an ordinary variable. The most important point is that there are only a few ways to create new objects in memory. Passing a reference, whether through assignment, return value, or argument value, simply passes a handle to an existing object. If you need to create a new copy—for example, so that you can modify the new copy while retaining the original data—use clone( ), if available, or use a copy constructor. If you've programmed extensively in C++, you've already seen references. But remember that in Java, all object variables and return types are automatically references, so there is no need for a reference operator (&). If you've programmed in C, you can think of references as pointers without the pointer syntax. For more information, see the topic "References," page 84.

reserved word
A word that cannot be used for variable names. Most reserved words are keywords. A few are reserved for possible use by future versions of Java. See "keyword," page 708.

result set
A result from a database query structured in tabular format. Although some simple queries return integers, most of them involve result sets. The JDBC package java.sql provides the ResultSet interface for reading the contents of a result set and ResultSetMetaData for inspecting the structure of a given result set.

rigid area
A rigid area is a special object used in box layouts to create fixed-size spaces between components in one direction (horizontal or vertical). Rigid areas form an important part of the box layout in that they help fine-tune the positioning of components.

scope

The visibility of a variable or method within a program. Despite its apparent similarity to C and C++, Java has different scope rules. The rules for declaring and using local variables are roughly the same as in C++. Java has no global variables, so all variables, except local variables, are declared at the class level. Here, the visibility of a variable is determined by its access level and the visibility of its class. For the complete rules applying to access levels, see the topics "public Keyword" (p. 83), "private Keyword" (p. 81), and "protected Keyword" (p. 82).

security features, Java

Features of Java intended to make for safe surf on the Internet. Java security is an issue with two sides: how to create applications that prevent invading code — viruses or Trojan horses — from being loaded, and how to place restrictions on applets so that they cannot invade other systems. Java places few restrictions, other than bounds checking, type checking, and elimination of pointer operations, on applications. Generally, you are writing applications for use on your own computer, so applications are assumed to be safe. Applications can optionally use the Java API to download information from the network. The `java.lang.SecurityManager` class can be used by applications to filter out certain types of code during downloading. It is up to you to subclass `Security Manager` to impose restrictions for downloading code.

Java-enabled browsers (for example, the applet viewer and the Netscape Navigator and Internet Explorer browsers) are designed to restrict anyone from writing applets that could violate the integrity of any user's system. The restrictions imposed by these interpreters prevent applets from doing any of the following: reading, writing, or trashing files on the local computer; opening a new network connection (a socket); executing a program on the local machine; or using native methods. (Native methods automatically evade all security checks.) The potential effects of these actions in the hands of an evil programmer could be catastrophic. For example, permitting an applet to execute local programs would give an applet writer the ability to execute an MS-DOS command such as `DEL *.*` or `FORMAT C:` on the local computer.

semantic event

A semantic event is an event that is fired in response to an action that is based on the semantics of a particular object, such as an item change in a list. Semantic events differ from low-level events in that semantic events are related to the specific function of an object.

server
The provider of a service. In network operations, a server is a computer that waits to be contacted by another computer (called a *client*) and then responds to requests. To be useful, a server must run continually or at least during a window of time known to the client. The term *server* also is used in other contexts, including database operations and object-oriented programming.

short-circuit logic
The technique that Java uses to evaluate Boolean conditions combined with logical AND (&&) and logical OR (||). This is a technique that Java has in common with other programming languages such as C++. Java evaluates only enough of a Boolean expression to determine a true or false result. For example, with logical AND, if the first operand is evaluated as false, this renders the overall outcome false and the remainder of the expression isn't evaluated. See also "Boolean expressions" (p. 27).

signature
A method declaration giving complete type information. For example:

```
int Class1.max(int, int)
```

A signature uniquely identifies a specific method as understood by the compiler; this does not include argument names, which are arbitrary and can differ each time a method is used. Because of method overloading (see "overloading," page 713), the compiler differentiates methods not by name but by signature.

signed data
Integer data that can represent both positive and negative numbers. In Java, all numeric types are signed. See "two's complement," page 724, for details of how negative numbers are represented.

slider
A slider is a GUI component that allows the user to graphically select a value by sliding a knob within a bounded range of values. An example of a good usage of a slider is a volume control in a multimedia application.

socket
A network connection in a Java program. You open a network connection by creating an object of the Socket class. When creating the object, you specify a string containing the host or an Internet address as well as a port number. The Java API throws an exception if it cannot successfully connect. Once the connection is made, you can then use the socket to get objects of the InputStream and OutputStream

classes; these are the same classes used for stream-based file input and output. For more information, see "Socket Class" (p. 450) and "ServerSocket Class" (p. 444) in the "Java 2 API Reference."

SQL
Structured Query Language: a widely recognized standard language for querying, sorting, and modifying a database. SQL is relatively independent of database architecture. For this reason, it is used by JDBC to interact with a variety of databases. JDBC methods enable you to build and execute SQL statements and execute them.

stack
A last-in-first-out (LIFO) storage mechanism. Stacks are highly useful in computer programming. The essence of a stack is that you can push as many items as you want on top of the stack. Then, when you start popping items off the stack, they are removed in reverse order, beginning with the last item to be pushed onto the stack. At any time, you can push new items on top of the stack.

Stacks have two uses. First, most modern processors use an internal stack to keep track of subroutine calls, arguments, and values of local variables. This stack usage is automatic, and you generally have no direct access to it unless you are writing assembly language. A stack can also be used as a storage mechanism in your own programs. The API provides the `Stack` class for handling groups of objects for which you want LIFO access.

static initializer
An initializer for an entire class, consisting of code in braces ({}) followed by the `static` keyword. Static initializers are useful for initializing static variables and other operations that should be performed once for the entire class. For more information, see "static Keyword," page 87.

string
A sequential group of characters, typically forming a word, phrase, or sentence in a natural language such as English. Technically, strings should be called character strings or text strings, although they are usually called strings for short. Strings are used often in computer programming, because there is often a need to display readable text.

In Java, a string is represented as an object of type `String`. A string literal is a quoted string, and it automatically has type `String`. String data is not null-terminated, and you should not treat strings as arrays of type `char`, although you can convert any `String` object to an array of `char` by calling the `toCharArray()` method of the `String` class. Doing so, in fact, might be useful if you needed to dissect a string by character. However, the Java String class has a large number of useful methods, generally making character-by-character operations (the kind you would write in C) unnecessary. See "String Class," page 457, in the "Java 2 API Reference" for more information. For some examples of simple string-handling code, see the topic "Strings," page 89.

Individual objects of type String cannot be modified. Nevertheless, string operations are easy to do with the String objects; for example, when you apply the concatenation operator (+) on two strings, Java creates a new String object so that neither of the operands is modified. However, for efficient, complex string operations, you should convert a string to an object of type StringBuffer. Such objects can be modified without causing additional objects to be created.

subclass

A class that inherits from another class. Subclasses are also called *child classes* or *derived classes*. A class may have any number of subclasses, though it may have only one direct superclass. See "Inheritance," page 703.

superclass

A class that provides the base declarations for another class. (See "inheritance," page 703.) Superclasses are also called *parent classes* or *base classes*. In Java, a class may only have one superclass, although a class may have many indirect superclasses. (For example, C inherits from B, which inherits from A. A is an indirect superclass of C.) If no superclass is specified, the superclass is automatically the Object class in the java.lang package of the API. For more information, see the topic "extends Keyword," page 49.

Swing toolkit

The Swing toolkit is a set of classes and interfaces that serve as an extension to the Java Abstract Windowing ToolKit (AWT). Swing provides replacements for many of the classes in the AWT. In general, Swing classes and interfaces are more extensible and powerful than their AWT counterparts. Although it is possible to mix AWT and Swing components, doing so can cause problems and is not recommended.

synchronized methods and threads

A technique for avoiding simultaneous execution of certain sections of code, often called *critical sections*, by more than one thread. Before a thread executes such code, it may need a way to temporarily lock out other threads, because if two threads operate on the same resource simultaneously, they may interfere with each other to disastrous effect. (Consider two threads attempting to write over the same file record or sort the same array at the same time.) The solution is for one thread to wait until another finishes and relinquishes its lock. Java provides an easy way to implement locks by using the synchronized keyword. Although you don't manipulate locks directly, locks are used as appropriate for the given platform. The synchronized keyword provides a high level of abstraction that works effectively on many different systems. For more information, see "synchronized Keyword," page 94.

system property
See "property," page 717. For a list of system properties, see Table B-6 in Appendix B, page 683.

table
A table is a GUI component that allows the user to view and manipulate data in a two-dimensional table format, similar to a spreadsheet. Tables are extremely powerful and provide a great deal of functionality if you have the need for a spreadsheet-style user interface in an application.

thread
An independent sequence of execution, much like a separate process. (But note that some operating systems make a distinction between threads and processes.) Every program has at least one thread; when a program starts a second or third thread, it gains the capability to do more than one thing at a time. For example, a program might have one thread that responds to user input, another thread to animate a bouncing ball, and a third thread that prints a document in the background. Although in actuality a single processor can do only one thing at a time, almost all CPUs made today have the capability to achieve the practical effect of simultaneous running of threads. Multithreaded code should easily be able to take advantage of parallel-processor platforms, with threads truly running concurrently, when they become available.

Java encapsulates the capabilities of threads on all platforms by providing the Thread class in the API. Starting a second, third, or other thread is as easy as declaring a Thread object and calling its start() method. When you create a thread, you specify an object that implements the Runnable interface. Implementing Runnable guarantees that the object's class has a run() method. When the thread is started, Java calls this method.

One way to use threads is to implement Runnable in the class that uses the thread. Another way is to use Thread subclasses for which you override run() with your own thread behavior. For examples, see Chapter 6, "Animation and Threads."

throwing an exception
The act of generating an exception, which has the effect of transferring control to the nearest exception handler of the appropriate type. As described in the glossary entry "exception" (p. 698), an exception is an unusual occurrence that requires immediate handling. In many, but not all, cases, an exception indicates an error of some kind. Another typical case that generates an exception is an attempt to read past the end of a file. The API raises exceptions as appropriate. In addition, you can raise exceptions yourself by using the `throw` keyword. For more information, see the topic "Exception Handling," page 46.

toolbar
A toolbar is a GUI component that serves as a container for buttons and other components and is typically positioned along a bar at the top of an application's main window frame. Toolbars can be positioned anywhere in an application's frame, but the top is the most popular location.

tooltip
A tooltip is a small text window that appears when the user pauses with the mouse cursor over a component. Tooltip windows are designed to be unobtrusive, so the text associated with a tooltip is typically very concise.

tree
A tree is a GUI component that enables the user to view and manipulate a set of hierarchical data as an outline. A good example of a tree is the hierarchical file view used in most file explorer applications. Trees are extremely useful for providing a user interface to view and manipulate any kind of hierarchical data.

two's complement
A popular format for representing signed integers (numbers that can be negative). A negative number is represented by taking the corresponding positive number, inverting all the digits through bitwise negation, and adding 1. For example, to get –1 for the `byte` integer type, we take 00000001, invert it to get 11111110, and finally add 1: 11111111. One of the consequences of two's complement arithmetic is that any number with a 1 in its leftmost digit is negative. The great majority of microprocessors being made today include efficient built-in support for two's complement arithmetic. For this reason, Java uses two's complement as its binary standard for integer data. Remember that two's complement arithmetic is performed under the covers and generally does not affect you unless you analyze bit patterns.

unicast event delivery
Unicast event delivery involves an event being broadcast to a single event listener; only one event listener can be registered with a unicast event source. Unlike multicast event delivery, unicast event delivery only allows one event listener to receive and respond to an event generated by an event source.

Unicode
A scheme for representing individual characters in terms of numeric values. Unicode is similar to the ASCII system, but a Unicode character occupies 16 bits (2 bytes) rather than 8 bits. All implementations of Java use Unicode characters, because Unicode's 16-bit character size enables it to represent character sets for natural languages other than English. However, the lowest 128 Unicode values are equal to their ASCII counterparts. Java is a language designed to produce applications that run without change in many environments. Unicode is therefore a logical choice for the character set, because it does not pose the same limitations that ASCII does. The importance of making software available for an international audience is a sign of our times — and of the international acceptance of computers.

unsigned data
An integer data type that does not represent any negative numbers. In a language such as C, unsigned types are occasionally useful, because, given a particular size, an unsigned integer can represent twice as many positive numbers as a signed integer can represent. Java does not support any unsigned data. In Java, the lack of unsigned types is made palatable by the fact that int and long have relatively large ranges, making unsigned types almost unnecessary.

URL
Uniform resource locator, which is a string of characters containing the address of an Internet location (although a URL can also refer to the local computer). URLs can be relative, but a complete URL contains at least three major parts in the form protocol://server/file. For example, in the URL http://stay.com/now/please, the protocol is http: (see "HTTP," page 702), the server name is stay.com, and the file on that server is /now/please. (A network server is also called a *host*.) The Java URL class supports the specification and use of URLs.

variable
A named location for holding data. Generally speaking, a variable is a value that may change during the course of the program; a variable has a name — such as i, n, count, amount, temperature, and so on — so that you can refer to it in the source code. In Java, variables come in

three major varieties: local variables, declared inside methods or even smaller code blocks; instance variables, declared at the class level; and class variables, declared at the class level but also declared static. Unlike most languages, Java has no facility for declaring global variables. For more information, see "class variable" (p. 695), "instance variable" (p. 704), and "local variable" (p. 709).

Variables work in roughly the same way in Java as they do in other languages. There is one peculiarity, though, in addition to the lack of global variables: variables of a user-defined type (a class) do not actually contain data because they are references. This means that they must be associated with an existing object before they can be used. Most often, the object itself is allocated by using new. Variables that have a primitive data type (such as int, long, or float) are not references and work just as they do in other languages.

variable, class
See "class variable," page 695.

variable, instance
See "instance variable," page 704.

variable, local
See "local variable," page 709.

Visual J++
Microsoft's integrated development environment for Java programs. Visual J++ provides an environment similar to Visual C++, which automates some of the tasks of designing and writing a program. The code generated by Visual J++ is Java code, and the standard rules apply.

WAV (.wav file)
A format for storing audio data, used on Windows systems. WAV files are sometimes embedded in Web pages and used in Java applications.

wrapper class
An API class that stores a simple numeric value. A primitive-data value such as an int is not part of the class hierarchy, does not inherit from Object, and therefore cannot be stored in a collection-class object such as Vector or Stack. However, an int can be converted to its wrapper class, Integer, and then stored in a Vector or Stack object. A wrapper class creates an object around a single bit of primitive data. Wrapper classes also provide useful methods for dealing with primitive data, such as Integer.parseInt(). The API's wrapper classes are Integer, Long, Float, Double, Character, and Boolean.

zero-based indexing
An indexing scheme in which the first position is 0, the second position is 1, the third position is 2, and so on. For consistency with C and C++, the Java language and core API use zero-based indexing in every situation involving an index. Thus, for example, `myArray[9]` refers to the tenth (and not the ninth) element of `myArray`. The exception is JDBC (`java.sql`), which uses one-based indexing to indicate column positions.

Z-order
Z-order applies to a layered pane and is a number that indicates the depth of the layer with respect to the screen. In other words, the screen is the highest layer with a theoretical Z-order of infinity, while other layers have decreasing Z-orders behind the screen. Z-order is what allows you to layer panes on top of one another. You can think of Z-order as a number that indicates the position of each card (layered pane) in a deck of cards relative to the top of the deck (the screen).

Index

Symbols & Numbers

#define directive, 43
#if directive, 58
#include directive, 60–61
% (modulus) operator, 73
?: (conditional operator), 38
3-D drawing, 106

A

absolute values, 106
abstract border, 106
abstract classes, 6
    defined, 687
abstract keyword, 20
abstract methods, 6
    creating, 20
    defined, 687–688
AbstractAction class, 164
AbstractBorder class, 164–165
AbstractButton class, 165–166
abstraction, 388
accelerators, 688–689
access level, 689
accessor methods, JavaBeans, 638
action events, 112
    responding to, 106, 123
Action interface, 166–168
ActionEvent class, 168–169, 576
ActionListener interface, 169–170
adapters, events, 580–583
Adjustable interface, 171–172
adjustment events, 106, 112
    responding to, 123
AdjustmentEvent class, 170–171, 576
AdjustmentListener interface, 172–173

aggregates, 6, 21–23
allocation of objects, 524–525
animation, 617
    clipping, 625
    code revision, 627–628
    creating, 623–624
    double buffering, 626–627, 697
    smoothing, 624–628
    threads and, 620
animation applet, 621–623
API (application programming interface)
    classes, 153–161
    defined, 689
    interfaces, 153–161
    reference, 105–129
applet class, 173–175
applet viewer, 689–690
AppletContext interface, 175–176
applets
    animation applet, 621–623
    code, 514–516
    compiling, 512–513
    components, 566–570
    defined, 689
    graphics and, 540
    initializing, 117
    overview, 511–516
    parameters, 106
    references, 114
    running, 512–513
    Scribble, 556–558
    starting, 106, 126
    Swing and, 127
    syntax, 516
    trusted applets, 515
appletviewer, 513

729

application builder support, components, 635
applications
　compiling, 507–508
　components, 583–585
　defined, 690
　entry point, 6, 529
　graphics and, 540
　running, 507–508
　syntax, 509–510
arcs, drawing, 106, 111
arguments
　command-line, 6
　methods, 9
　values, default, 42
ArrayList class, 176–178
arra@index H:ys, 23–25. *See also* vector objects
　aggregates, 6
　creating, 6
　defined, 690
　flexible, 106
　growing, 115
　length, 6, 118
　size, 126
　vectors, 124
arrow keys, 106
ASCII (American Standard Code for Information Interchange), 690
assignments, 9, 25–26
attributes, files, 106, 113, 114
　reading, 122
audio clips, 106
　playing, 121
AudioClip interface, 178–179
Authenticator class, 179
auto keyword, 26
AWT (Abstract Windowing Toolkit), 292–293
　defined, 388
　events, 180
　hierarchy, 561–563
　Swing and, 588, 591–592
AWTEvent class, 180, 572

B

background color, 106, 125, 542–544
Bean information class (JavaBeans), 645
BeanBox (JavaBeans), 656–660
bell-curve distribution, 106
bevel borders, 106, 126, 181–182
　soft, 452
BevelBorder class, 181–182
bit fields, 26
bitmap, 690–691
BitSet class, 182–183
bitwise operators, 6, 8, 26–27
bold, 107
　setting, 125
Book class, 183–184
Boolean class, 184–185
Boolean conditions, testing, 6
Boolean constants, false, 7
boolean data type, 41
Boolean expressions, 6, 27–28
　conditional operator, 38
　defined, 691
Boolean variables, 6
Border interface, 185–186
border layout, 691
border layout manager, 596–597
BorderLayout class, 186
borders
　bevel, 106, 126, 181–182
　　soft, 452
　components, 121
　compound, 108, 220–221
　defined, 691

empty, 112, 238–239
etched, 112, 240–241
line, 118, 373–374
matte, 119, 393–394
Swing toolkit, 604–605
titled, 128, 480–482
bound properties, JavaBeans, 639–640
Box class, 187
box layout, 107, 691
box layout manager, 598–599
BoxLayout class, 187–188
break statement, 6, 11, 28–29
brightening color, 107
BufferedInputStream class, 188–189
BufferedOutputStream class, 188–189
buffers
　animation, 626–627, 697
　double buffering, 697
　string, 460–462
bundles, 432–433
Button class, 190–191
ButtonGroup class, 191–192
buttons, 107, 204
　command button, 293–294
　defined, 691–692
　radio buttons, JRadioButton class, 338–339
　Swing and, 127
　Swing toolkit, 604
Byte class, 192–193
byte codes defined, 692
byte data type, 6, 29, 41
byte variables, creating, 6
ByteArrayInputStream class, 193–194
ByteArrayOutputStream class, 194–195
bytes
　reading from file, 107
　strings, conversion, 109

C

C programming language, 692
C + + programming language, 692
Calendar class, 195–198
Canvas class, 199
card layout, 693
card layout manager, 597
card stack layout, 107
CardLayout class, 199–200
case keyword, 10, 30
case, testing, 107
case-insensitive strings, 107
cast operator, 693
casting, 6, 30–32
　implicit, 32
catch keyword, 6, 7, 32
catching exceptions, 6
ChangeEvent class, 200
ChangeListener interface, 200–201
char data type, 6, 33–34, 41
Character class, 201–202
character strings, String class, 457–460
character type, testing, 128
character variables, 6
　size, 6
characters
　case, converting, 109
　dimensions, 107
　processing, 107
　reading from files, 107
　testing, 107
　Unicode, 682, 693, 725
　width, 129
　writing to files, 107
check marks, menus, 121, 204–205
Checkbox class, 202–203

checkboxes, 109
    Swing and, 127, 296
CheckboxGroup class, 203-204
CheckboxMenuItem class, 204-205
child components, printing, 121
Choice class, 205-206
choosers
    defined, 693
    Swing toolkit, 613-614
circles, drawing, 107
Class class, 206-207
class declarations, code, 508
class fields, 6
class information, 114
class keyword, 6, 34-36
class members, 6
class modifiers, 6
classes, 114
    abstract, 6, 687
    AbstractAction, 164
    AbstractBorder, 164-165
    AbstractButton, 165-166
    ActionEvent, 168-169, 576
    AdjustmentEvent, 170-171, 576
    API, 153-161
    applet, 173-175
    ArrayList, 176-178
    Authenticator, 179
    AWTEvent, 180, 572
    BevelBorder, 181-182
    BitSet, 182-183
    Book, 183-184
    Boolean, 184-185
    BorderLayout, 186
    Box, 187
    BoxLayout, 187-188
    BufferedInputStream, 188-189
    BufferedOutputStream, 188-189
    Button, 190-191
    ButtonGroup, 191-192
    Byte, 192-193
    ByteArrayInputStream, 193-194
    ByteArrayOutputStream, 194-195
    Calendar class, 195-198
    Canvas, 199
    CardLayout, 199-200
    ChangeEvent, 200
    Character, 201-202
    Checkbox, 202-203
    CheckboxGroup, 203-204
    CheckboxMenuItem, 204-205
    Choice, 205-206
    Class, 206-207
    Color, 207-209
    ColorModel, 209-210
    Component, 210-218, 562
    ComponentAdapter, 218
    ComponentEvent, 218-219, 572-573
    CompoundBorder, 220-221
    Container, 221-222
    ContainerEvent, 573
    CropImageFilter, 222-223
    Cursor, 223-224
    DatagramPackage, 224-225
    DatagramSocket, 225-226
    DataInputStream, 227-229
    DataOutputStream, 230-231
    Date, 231-233
    declaring, 6
        methods, 520-522
    defined, 694
    deriving, 7
    Dialog, 234
    Dictionary, 234-235
    Dimension, 235

DirectColorModel, 236
Double, 236-238
EmptyBorder, 238-239
Error, 677
EtchedBorder, 240-241
Event, 241-244
exceptions, 673
File, 244-246
FileDescriptor, 246-247
FileDialog, 247-248
FileInputStream, 248-249
FileOutputStream, 250-251
FilteredImageSource, 251-252
FilterInputStream, 252-253
FilterOutputStream, 253-254
Float, 254-255
FlowLayout, 255-256
FocusAdapter, 256-257
FocusEvent, 257-258, 573
Font, 258-259
FontMetrics, 259-261, 545-548
Frame, 261-262
Graphics, 262-266, 548-552
GregorianCalendar, 266-267
GridBagConstraints, 267-270
GridBagLayout, 270-271
GridLayout, 271
HashMap, 272-273
Hashtable, 274-275
HyperlinkEvent, 275-276
Image, 277-278, 552-556
ImageFilter, 280-281
ImageIcon, 281-282
importing, 8
IndexColorModel, 284-285
InetAddress, 285-286
information, 107
inner, 8, 61-62, 704
InputStream, 286-287
InputVerifier, 287-288
Insets, 288
Integer, 288-290
ItemEvent, 290-291, 576-577
JApplet, 292-293
java.awt package, 132-134
java.awt.event package, 135-137
java.awt.image package, 137-138
java.awt.print package, 138
java.io package, 138-140
java.lang package, 140-141
java.net packages, 141-142
java.util package, 142-144
javax.swing package, 142-144
javax.swing.border package, 149
javax.swing.event package, 149
javax.swing.text package, 150
JButton, 293-294
JCheckBox, 294-295
JCheckBoxMenuItem, 296
JColorChooser, 296-297
JComboBox, 297-300
JComponent, 300-305
JDialog, 305-307
JEditorPane, 307-309
JFileChooser, 309-313
JFrame, 313-314
JLabel, 314-316
JLayeredPane, 316-318
JList, 318-321
JMenu, 321-323
JMenuBar, 324-325
JMenuItem, 325-327
JOptionPane, 327-331
JPanel, 331-332

Continued

classes *(continued)*
  JPasswordField, 332-333
  JPopupMenu, 333-336
  JProgressBar, 336-338
  JRadioButton, 338-339
  JRadioButtonMenuItem, 339-341
  JRootPane, 341-342
  JScrollBar, 342-344
  JScrollPane, 344-346
  JSeparator, 346-347
  JSlider, 347-350
  JSplitPane, 350
  JTabbedPane, 350
  JTable, 350-351
  JTextArea, 351-353
  JTextComponent, 353-355
  JTextField, 355-357
  JTextPane, 357
  JToggleButton, 357-358
  JToolBar, 358-360
  JToolTip, 360-361
  JTree, 361
  JViewport, 361-363
  JWindow, 363-364
  KeyAdapter, 365
  KeyEvent, 365-370, 574
  KeyStroke, 370-371
  Label, 371-372
  LineBorder, 373-374
  LineNumberInputStream, 374-375
  LinkedList, 375-377
  List, 379-380
  ListResourceBundle, 382-384
  ListSelectionEvent, 384-385
  Locale, 385-387
  Long, 387-389
  LookAndFeel, 389-390
  Math, 391-393
  MatteBorder, 393-394
  MediaTracker, 394-396
  MemoryImageSource, 396-397
  Menu, 397-398
  MenuBar, 398-399
  MenuComponent, 399-400
  MenuItem, 401-402
  methods, 694-695
  modifiers, 684-685
  MouseAdapter, 402-403
  MouseEvent, 403-405, 574-575
  MouseMotionAdapter, 405-406
  Object, 407-408
  object creation, 522-525
  Observable, 408-409
  OutputStream, 410
  overview, 511
  packages, 9
  PageFormat, 411-412
  Panel, 412
  Paper, 412-413
  PasswordAuthentication, 413-414
  PipedInputStream, 414
  PipedOutputStream, 415
  PixelGrabber, 415-417
  Point, 417
  Polygon, 417-418
  PrinterJob, 419-420
  PrintStream, 420-422
  Process, 422
  ProgressMonitor, 422-423
  ProgressMonitorInputStream, 423-424
  Properties, 424-425
  PropertyResourceBundle, 425-426
  public, 10, 531-532
  PushbackInputStream, 426
  Random, 427

  RandomAccessFile, 427-430
  Rectangle, 431-432
  ResourceBundle, 432-433
  RGBImageFilter, 433-435
  Runtime, 435-436
  RuntimeException, 674-675
  Scrollbar, 437-438
  ScrollPane, 438-440
  searches, 534
  SecurityManager, 441-443
  SequenceInputStream, 443-444
  ServerSocket, 444-445
  Short, 446-448
  SimpleTimeZone, 448-449
  SizeRequirements, 449-450
  Socket, 450-452
  SoftBevelBorder, 452
  Stack, 453-454
  stack collection, 126
  StreamTokenizer, 454-456
  String, 457-460
  string, 89
  StringBuffer, 460-462
  StringTokenizer, 462-463
  subclasses, 10
    defined, 722
  superclasses
    defined, 722
    extends keyword, 49-50
  SwingUtilities, 464-466
  System, 466-468
  TextArea, 468-469
  TextComponent, 469-470
  TextEvent, 577
  TextField, 470-472
  Thread, 472-474
  ThreadGroup, 474-476
  ThreadLocal, 476
  Throwable, 477
  Timer, 477-478
  TimeZone, 478-480
  TitledBorder, 480-482
  Toolkit, 482-483
  TreeMap, 483-485
  TreeSet, 485-486
  URL, 486-488
  URLConnection, 488-491
  URLDecoder, 491
  URLEncoder, 492
  variables, 695
  Vector, 492-495
  ViewportLayout, 495
  Void, 495
  WeakHashMap, 495-496
  Window, 496-497
  WindowAdapter, 497-498
  WindowEvent, 499-500, 575
  wrapper, 726
CLASSPATH environment, 695
clauses, 7
client sockets, opening, 120
clients, 107
  creating, 108
  defined, 695
clipping
  animation, 625
  rectangles, 108, 125, 541
Cloneable interface, 207
code
  applets, 514-516
  class declarations and, 508
  critical sections, 7, 696
  revising, animation and, 627-628
collections
  maps, 390-391

sorting, 453
sequences, List interface, 377–379
color, 109
  background, 106, 542–544
  black, 107
  blue, 107
  brightening, 107
  constants, 108
  Cyan, 110
  darkening, 110
  filters, 108
  foreground, 114, 125, 542–544
  hue, 116
  images, filters, 433–435
  JColorChooser class, 296–297
  numbers, 108
color chooser, Swing and, 127
Color class, 207–209
color class constants, graphics and, 680
color model, 108, 284–285
ColorModel class, 209–210
combo boxes
  defined, 693
  JComboBox class, 297–300
  Swing and, 127
  Swing toolkit, 605–607
command button, 109, 293–294
command-line arguments, 6
commands, menu commands, 119
comments, 6, 8, 36–37
  multi-line, 9
Comparable interface, 210
compilers defined, 695–696
compiling
  applets, 512–513
  applications, 507–508
Component class, 210–218, 562
  components, 696
ComponentAdapter class, 218
ComponentEvent class, 218–219, 572–573
ComponentListener interface, 219–220
components, 106, 540
  adding, 108
  applets, 566–570
  application builder support, 635
  applications, 583–585
  borders, 121
  child, printing, 121
  Component class, 696
  containers, 114, 115
  contents, printing, 121
  defined, 694
  dimensions, 110
  distributed computing support, 635
  grouping, 115
  heavyweight, 588, 702
  height, 116
  hiding, 116
  JavaBeans and, 634–635
  layering, 316–318
  lightweight, 588, 709
  painting, 120
  position, 121
  removing, 108, 123
  showing, 126
  single-line text-entry, 470–472
  size, 114, 126
  Swing and, 127
  Swing toolkit
    borders, 604–605
    buttons, 604
    combo boxes, 605–607
    icons, 600–601
    labels, 601–603
    list boxes, 605–607

text, 128
text editing, 111
text-editing, 332–333
visual layout, 635
width, 129
compound borders, 108, 220–221
compound statements, 6, 37–38
CompoundBorder class, 220–221
condition expression, 54
conditional (?:) operator, 38
conditional expressions, 6
conditional operator, 7
conditions
  Boolean, testing, 6
  on/off, 120
connections, networks, 179
console
  input/output, 665–667
  reading from/writing to, 108
console metrics, 108
const keyword, 38
constants
  color, 108
  color class, graphics and, 680
  defined, 696
  events, 108, 112
  null, 8, 75–76
  scroll pane, 108, 440–441
  Swing, 463–464
  symbolic, 7
  values, 7
  windows, 108
constrained properties, JavaBeans, 640–641
constraints, layout, 267–270
constructing objects, 6
constructors, 39, 380–382, 528–529
  calling, 6
  copy constructor, 696
  creating, 7
  defined, 696
  superclass, 10
Container class, 221–222
  containers, 696
ContainerEvent class, 573
containers
  components, 115
  Container class, 696
  defined, 694
  events, 112
    responding to, 123
  panels, 412
  references, 108
  scrolling, 438–440
  Swing and, 331–332
content panes, 590
contents, files, 669–671
context operator, 39–40
continue statement, 6, 40–41
converting
  between data types, 7
  float data type, 113
  numbers to strings, 665
  numbers/strings, 663–665
  strings
    to floating points, 664–665
    to integers, 664
coordinates
  points, 417
  scroll bar, 125
  translating, 109, 128
copy constructor, 696
critical sections of code, 7, 696
CropImageFilter class, 222–223
Cursor class, 223–224
cursor settings, graphics and, 680–681

D

darkening color, 110
data members, 41
data pipes, PipedInputStream class and, 414
data types, 41–42, 110
    boolean, 41
    byte, 6, 29, 41
    casting, 6, 30–32
    char, 6, 33–34, 41
    character, 128
    converting between, 7
    creating, 523–524
    double, 7, 42, 44–45
    float, 7, 42, 52–53
    int, 41, 63–64
    long, 8, 41, 67
    primitive, 9, 716
    short, 10, 41, 87
    unsigned, 725
DatagramPacket class, 224–225
DatagramSocket class, 225–226
DataInput interface, 226–227
DataInputStream class, 227–229
DataOutput interface, 229
DataOutputStream class, 230–231
Date class, 231–233
date, current, 110
declarations
    classes, 6
        methods, 520–522
    exceptions, 7
    extern, 50–51
    struct, 92
    typedef, 98
default keyword, 42–43
defining methods, 8
    order, 530
delegation event model, 570, 697
delete operator, 8, 43
delivering events, 577–579
deriving classes, 7
destructors, 43–44
dialog boxes, 109
    creating, 110
    defined, 697
    JFileChooser class, 309–313
    JOptionPane class, 327–331
    modal, 234
    Swing and, 127
    Swing toolkit, 611–612
    titles, 125, 128
Dialog class, 234
Dictionary class, 234–235
Dimension class, 235
dimensions
    components, 110
    images, 114
DirectColorModel class, 236
directives
    #define, 43
    #if, 58
    #include, 60–61
directories
    access, 111
    contents, 111
    creating, 109, 118
    new, 111
    reading, 668
    searching, 124
    structure, packages and, 532–533
display
    refreshing, 123
    repainting, 123
displaying
    images, 552–556
    text, 542–548

dispose( ) method, 557
distributed computing support, components, 635
do keyword, 7, 8, 44
do loops, 7
do-nothing statement, 7
documentation, 7
documents, printing, 121
double buffering, animation, 626–627, 697
Double class, 236–238
double data type, 7, 42, 44–45
    converting, 111
    range, 121
    reading from/writing to, 111
double variables, 7
downloading Java SDK, 506–507
drawImage( ) method, 554–555
drawing
    arcs, 106, 111
    figures, 548–552
    Graphics class, 262–266
    in-memory image and, 111
    lines, 111
    methods, 111
    rectangles, 431–432
    shapes, 111
    squares, 126
drawLine( ) method, 549
drawPolygon( ) method, 549–552
drawRect( ) method, 549
drawString( ) method, 542–548

E

echo characters, 470
edit boxes, multiline, 468–469
editing text, 111
    multiple lines, 351–353
    panes, 357
    string manipulation, 111
editors, 307–309
EJB (Enterprise JavaBeans), 660–661
else clause, 7
else keyword, 7, 8, 45
empty statements, 7, 45–46
EmptyBorder class, 238–239
encapsulation, defined, 697
Enumeration interface, 239–240
enumerations, 112
    cycling through, 110
equality, objects, 112
Error class, 677
errors, 677
    standard, 112
        I/O, 126
escape sequences, 681–682
    defined, 698
    strings, 10
etched borders, 112
EtchedBorder class, 240–241
Event class, 241–244
event delivery, 577–579
event design patterns, JavaBeans, 644–645
event handling, JavaBeans, 634
event listeners, 570
event response methods, 571, 698
event sources, 570, 698
event state objects, 570
event types, 570
events
    action, 106, 112
    ActionEvent class, 168–169
    adapters, 580–583, 698
    adjustment, 106, 112
    AdjustmentEvent class, 170–171
    AWT, 180
    AWTEvent class, 180, 572

ChangeEvent class, 200
component, 219–220
ComponentEvent class, 218–219, 572–573
components, 112
constants, 108, 112
ContainerEvent class, 573
defined, 698, 699
delegation event model, 570, 697
Event class, 241–244
focus, 112, 258
FocusEvent class, 257–258, 573
HyperlinkEvent class, 275–276
item, 290–291
ItemEvent class, 290–291, 576–577
key events
    KeyEvent class, 365–370
    KeyListener interface, 370
KeyEvent class, 365–370
keystroke, 112
listeners, 698
ListSelectionEvent class, 384–385
low-level, 571–575, 709
mouse, 112
    methods, 405, 406–407
    MouseEvent class, 403–405
    responding to, 119
MouseEvent class, 403–405
multicast event deliver, 711
responding to, 123–124, 570–583
semantic, 571, 575–577, 719
TextEvent class, 577
Timer class, 477–478
unicast event delivery, 725
window, 499–500
WindowEvent class, 499–500
windows, 113
exception classes, 477
    overview, 673
exception handling, 7, 46–49
exceptions, 7
    catching, 6
    declaring, 7
    defined, 698
    mandatory, 675–677
    methods, 113
    optional, 674–675
    throwing, 724
executing statements, repeating, 10, 53–55
exponential functions, 113
expressions
    Boolean, 27–28
    defined, 691
    condition, 54
    conditional, 6
    increment, 54–55
    initializer, 54
    integer test, 8
extends keyword, 49–50
extern declarations, 50–51

F

false conditions, 7
false keyword, 8, 51
fields, 530
    bit fields, 26
    defined, 699
    modifiers, 684–685
    text fields, JTextField class, 355–357
figures, drawing, 548–552
file chooser, Swing and, 127
File class, 244–246
file descriptors, 114
File dialog box, 113
file operations, 667–671
file pointer, moving, 119

file separators, 115, 125
FileDescriptor class, 246–247
FileDialog class, 247–248
FileInputStream class, 248–249
FilenameFilter interface, 249
FileOutputStream class, 250–251
files
    access, 113
    attributes, 106, 113, 114
        reading, 122
    closing, 108
    contents
        reading, 669–671
        tokenizing, 128
    modifying, 110
    opening, 120
    reading from, 113, 122
    renaming, 123
    selecting, 124
    sequence, 122
    sequences, reading from, 125
    series, reading from, 125
    size, 126
    virtual, 129
    writing to, 113
filler, box layout managers, 599
fillOval( ) method, 623
FilteredImageSource class, 251–252
FilterInputStream class, 252–253
FilterOutputStream class, 253–254
filters
    color, 108
    image, 108
    images, 113, 116, 280–281
        color, 433–435
final keyword, 7, 9, 10, 51–52
finalize( ) method, 43–44
finalizer method, 699
firewalls, 699
fixed point, 699–700
flags, bit flags, 182–183
Float class, 254–255
float data type, 7, 42, 52–53
    converting, 113
    range, 121
float variables, 7
floating-points
    converting from strings, 664–665
    defined, 700
    rounding, 124
flow layout, 700
flow layout manager, 594–595
FlowLayout class, 255–256
flushing buffers, 107
focus
    events, 112, 258
    moving, 113
    requesting, 123
FocusAdapter class, 256–257
FocusEvent class, 257–258, 573
FocusListener interface, 258
Font class, 258–259
font metrics, 114, 115, 119, 545–547
FontMetrics class, 259–261, 545–548
fonts, 114
    current, 114
    graphics and, 679–680
    height, 116
    menu items, 125
    properties, 114, 115
    setting, 125, 544–545
    style, 125, 127
    for loops, 8
for statement, 8, 10, 53–55
foreground color, 114, 125, 542–544

forward references, 530
Frame class, 261-262
frame window, Swing and, 127
frames
    creating, 109
    defined, 700
    icon, 125
    JFrame class, 313-314
    resizing, 123
    Swing, 589-590
    titles, 125, 128
free( ) function, 524-525
friend keyword, 55
FTP (File Transfer Protocol), 700
function overloading, 72
functions, 55
    free( ), 524-525
    logarithmic, 118
    mathematical, 119
    system, 466-468
    trigonometric, 128

G

garbage collection, 8
    defined, 701
Gaussian distribution, 114
getGraphics( ) method, 556
getImage( ) method, 553-554
GIF files, 701
global variables, 50-51
glue, 701
goto statement, 56
graphics, 539
    applets and, 540
    applications and, 540
    color class contants, 680
    cursor settings, 680-681
    fonts, 679-680
    Sync and, 128
    synchronization, 115
    tables, 679-681
Graphics class, 262-266, 548
graphics context, 115
graphics object, 540-542, 548-552
graphics operations, 115
GregorianCalendar class, 266-267
grid bag layout manager, 599-600, 701
grid layout, 701
grid layout manager, 595-596
GridBagConstraints class, 267-270
GridBagLayout class, 270-271
GridLayout class, 271
growing arrays, 115
GUI (graphical user interface)
    defined, 702
    Swing and, 592-600
        checkbox, 295

H

hash maps, 495-496
HashMap class, 272-273
Hashtable class, 274-275
heavyweight components, 588
    defined, 702
hexadecimal notation, 8, 56
hierarchies
    AWT, 561-563
    tree, 116
    trees, 128
host, 702
HotJava, 702
HTML (Hypertext Markup Language), 702
HTTP (Hypertext Transport Protocol), 702
HyperlinkEvent class, 275-276

HyperlinkListener interface, 276

I

I/O streams, 129
Icon interface, 276-277
icons, 116
    defined, 703
    image icons, 281-282
    Swing toolkit, 600-601
identifiers, 8, 56-57
    names, 8
if statements, 7, 8, 57
Image class, 277-278, 552-556
image data, raw, 122
image filters, 108, 113, 116
image objects, 114
    creating, 110
image sources, 114
    memory and, 396-397
ImageConsumer interface, 278-280
ImageFilter class, 280-281
ImageIcon class, 281-282
ImageObserver interface, 282-283
ImageObserver object, 554-555
ImageProducer interface, 283-284
images
    color, filters, 433-435
    creating from source, 110
    cropping, 110
    dimensions, 111, 114
    displaying, 111, 552-556
    filters, 280-281
        color, 433-435
    height, 116
    loading, 109, 117, 118
        monitoring, 119
        tracking, 128, 394-396
    pixel data and, 121
    properties, 115, 121
    size, 126
    source, creating, 251-252
    width, 129
implementation
    defined, 703
    interfaces, 8
    keywords, 8
    runnable interfaces, 619
    thread behavior, 117
implements keyword, 58-59
implicit casting, 32
import statement, 8, 59-60, 535-536
in-memory image, drawing to, 111
increment expression, 54-55
IndexColorModel class, 284-285
indexed properties, JavaBeans, 638-639
indexing, one-baed, 713
indexing, zero-based, 727
InetAddress class, 285-286
ingeter variables, 8
inheritance, 8, 61, 563-565
    defined, 703-704
    parents and, 563
init( ) method, 515
    background color, 543
initializer expression, 54
inner classes, 8, 61-62
    defined, 704
input
    console, 665-667
    lines read, 374-375
    numbered lines, 120
input streams
    monitoring, 119
    SequenceInputStream class, 443-444

input/output errors, 126
InputStream class, 286–287
InputVerifier class, 287–288
Insets class, 288
instance method, 704
instance variable, 704
instanceof operator, 8, 10, 63
instances
    defined, 704
    objects, 9
instantiation, 705
int data type, 41, 63–64
    range, 121
Integer class, 288–290
integer test expressions, 8
integers
    converting from strings, 664
    defined, 705
    reading to/from files, 117
interface keyword, 8, 64–65
interfaces, 64–65
    Action, 166–168
    ActionListener, 169–170
    Adjustable, 171–172
    AdjustmentListener, 172–173
    API, 153–161
    AppletContext, 175–176
    AudioClip, 178–179
    Border, 185–186
    ChangeListener, 200–201
    Cloneable, 207
    Comparable, 210
    ComponentListener, 219–220
    DataInput, 226–227
    DataOutput, 229
    defined, 705–760
    Enumeration, 239–240
    FilenameFilter, 249
    FocusListener, 258
    HyperlinkListener, 276
    Icon, 276–277
    ImageConsumer, 278–280
    ImageObserver, 282–283
    ImageProducer, 283–284
    implementing, 8
    ItemListener, 291
    ItemSelectable, 291
    KeyListener, 370
    LayoutManager, 372–373
    List, 377–379
    ListSelectionListener, 385
    Map, 390–391
    MenuContainer, 400
    MenuElement, 400–401
    MouseListener, 405
    MouseMotionListener, 406–407
    Observer, 409–410
    Pageable, 411
    Printable, 418–419
    Runnable, 435
    runnable, implementing, 619
    Scrollable, 437
    ScrollPaneConstants, 440–441
    Set, 445–446
    SortedMap, 453
    SwingConstants, 463–464
    WindowConstants, 498–499
    WindowListener, 500
    wizard-style, 597
Internet addresses
    creating, 285–286
    specifying, 126
interpreters, Java, 706
introspection, JavaBeans, 634, 642–645
    defined, 706

invisible filters, 706
italic text, 117
    setting, 125
item events, 290–291, 291
ItemEvent class, 290–291, 576–577
ItemListener interface, 291
ItemSelectable interface, 291

J

JApplet class, 292–293
JAR files, JavaBeans, 654–656
Java
    defined, 706–707
    platforms, multiple, 516–517
    running, 506–507
Java SDK (Software Development Kit), 506, 708
    downloading, 506–507
Java Virtual Machine, 707–708
java.applet package, 132
java.awt package, 132–134
java.awt.event package, 135–137
java.awt.image package, 137–138
java.awt.print package, 138
java.io package, 138–140
java.lang package, 140–141
java.net package, 141–142
java.util.package, 142–144
JavaBeans, 633
    accessor methods, 638
    Bean information class, 645
    BeanBox, 656–660
    component model, 634–635
    creating, 652–654
    customizing, 649–652
    defined, 707
    EJB (Enterprise JavaBeans), 660–661
    event design patterns, 644–645
    event handling, 634
    introspection, 634, 642–645
    JAR files, 654–656
    objects and, 635–636
    overview, 634–636
    persistence, 634, 646–648
    properties, 636–637
        bound, 639–640
        constrained, 640–641
        indexed, 638–639
    property design patterns, 643–644
    property editors, 649–650
    property sheets, 650–651
    serialization, 647–648
    testing beans, 656–660
    versioning, 648
JavaScript, 707
javax.swing package, 142–144
javax.swing.border package, 149
javax.swing.event package, 149
javax.swing.text package, 150
JButton class, 293–294
JCheckBox class, 294–295
JCheckBoxMenuItem class, 296
JColorChooser class, 296–297
JComboBox class, 297–300
JComponent class, 300–305
JDBC (Java database connectivity), 708
JDialog class, 305–307
JEditorPane class, 307–309
JFileChooser class, 309–313
JFrame class, 313–314, 590
JLabel class, 314–315
JLayeredPane class, 316–318
JList class, 318–321
JMenu class, 321–323
JMenuBar class, 324–325

JMenuItem class, 325–327
JOptionPane class, 327–331
JPanel class, 331–332
JPasswordField class, 332–333
JPEG files, 708
JPopupMenu class, 333–336
JProgressBar class, 336–338
JRadioButton class, 338–339
JRadioButtonMenuItem class, 339–341
JRootPane class, 341–342
JScrollBar class, 342–344
JScrollPane class, 344–346
JSeparator class, 346–347
JSlider class, 347–350
JSplitPane class, 350
JTabbedPane class, 350
JTable class, 350–351
JTextArea class, 351–353
JTextComponent class, 353–355
JTextField class, 355–357
JTextPane class, 357
JToggleButton class, 357–358
JToolBar class, 358–360
JToolTip class, 360–361
JTree class, 361
JViewport class, 361–363
JWindow class, 363–364

K

key events
KeyEvent class, 365–370
KeyListener interface, 370
KeyAdapter class, 365
keyboard
    input, 117
        reading, 122
    KeyStroke class, 370–371
    reading from, 122
    strings, reading, 127
KeyEvent class, 365–370, 574
KeyListener interface, 370
KeyStroke class, 370–371
keystroke events, 112
    handling, 116
    responding to, 117, 124
keywords, 65–66. *See also* reserved words
    abstract, 20
    accessing, 8
    auto, 26
        case, 10, 30
    catch, 6, 7, 32
    class, 6, 34–36
    const, 38
    default, 42–43
    defined, 708
    do, 7, 8, 44
    else, 7, 8, 45
    extends, 49–50
    false, 7, 51
    final, 7, 9, 10, 51–52
    friend, 55
    implementing, 8
    implements, 58–59
    interface, 8, 64–65
    main, 508
    native, 9, 74
    private, 9, 81–82
    protected, 10, 82–83
    public, 10, 82–83
    register, 85
    return, 10, 85–86
    static, 6, 10, 87–89
    struct, 92–93
    super, 10

synchronized, 7, 11, 94–95
this, 6, 9, 96–97
throw, 7, 11, 97
throws, 97
true, 11, 97–98
try, 7, 98
virtual, 101
void, 10, 101–102
volatile, 11, 102

L

Label class, 371–372
labels, 8, 66
    creating, 109, 118
    defined, 708
    JLabel class, 314–316
    statements, 8
    Swing and, 127
    Swing toolkit, 601–603
layers, components, 316–319
layout
    constraints, 267–270
        @index H:custom, 110, 118
    flow, 700
    grid, 701
layout managers, 125, 592–594
    border, 596–597
    box, 598–599
    card, 597
    defined, 709
    flow, 594–595
    grid, 595–596
    grid bag, 599–600
    Swing and, 592–600
    ViewportLayout class, 495
LayoutManager interface, 372–373
lightweight components, 588, 709
line borders, 118, 373–374
line comments, 8
LineBorder class, 373–374
LineNumberInputStream class, 374–375
lines read, 374–375
lines, drawing, 111, 118, 549
linked lists, 375–376
LinkedList class, 375–377
list boxes, 115, 118, 125
    creating, 109
    item selection, 124
    Swing toolkit, 605–607
List class, 379–380
List interface, 377–379
ListResourceBundle class, 382–384
lists
    defined, 709
    JList class, 318–321
    linked, 375–376
    selections, 384–385
    Swing and, 127
ListSelectionEvent class, 384–385
ListSelectionListener interface, 385
literals, string, 10, 81
loading images
    tracking, 128, 394–396
local variables, 709
Locale class, 385–387
locks, 709
logarithmic functions, 118
Long class, 387–389
long data type, 8, 41, 67, 118, 387–389
    range, 121
long integers, 118
    reading from string, 122
long variables, 8
LookAndFeel class, 389–390

loops
    advancing, 6
    breaking out, 6
    conditions and, 8
    do, 7
    for, 8
low-level events, 571–575, 709
low-level network I/O, 118
lowercase, converting to, 118

M

main keyword, 508
main( ) method, 6, 67–69, 507–510
    creating, 8
mandatory exceptions, 675–677
Map interface, 390–391
maps
    collections, 390–391
        sorting, 453
        hash maps, 495–496
        tree maps, 483–485
margins, 288
masking passwords, 119
masks, 8
Math class, 391–393
mathematical functions, 119
matte borders, 119
MatteBorder class, 393–394
MAX_VALUE constant, 710
MediaTracker class, 394–396
memory, 119
    image sources and, 396–397
MemoryImageSource class, 396–397
menu bar, 106, 125
    creating, 109, 119
    frames, 119
    JMenuBar class, 324–325
    MenuBar class, 398–399
    Swing and, 127
Menu class, 397–398
menu commands, responding to, 119, 123
menu items, 106
    check marks, 204–205
    creating, 109
    disabling, 111
    enabling, 112
    fonts, 125
    JMenu class, 321–323
    JMenuItem class, 325–327
    radio buttons, 339–341
    removing, 123
    separating, 125
    Swing and, 127
menu separator, 106, 125
MenuBar class, 398–399
MenuComponent class, 399–400
MenuContainer interface, 400
MenuElement interface, 400–401
MenuItem class, 401–402
menus, 106, 710
    check marks, 121
    creating, 109
    JPopupMenu class, 333–336
    Menu class, 397–398
    Swing and, 127
    Swing toolkit, 608–611
methods, 69–72
    abstract, 6, 687–688
        creating, 20
    accessor, JavaBeans, 638
    argument list, 9
    class declarations, 520–522
    class methods, 6
    classes, 694–695

constructors, 39
defined, 710
defining, 8, 508, 510
    order, 530
dispose( ), 557
drawImage( ), 554–555
drawLine( ), 549
drawPolygon( ), 549–552
drawRect( ), 549
drawString( ), 542–548
event response methods, 571
fillOval( ), 623
finalize( ), 43–44
finalizer, 699
getGraphics( ), 556
getImage( ), 553–554
init( ), 515
instance, 704
main( ), 6, 67–69, 507–510
MenuContainer interface, 400
modifiers, 9, 70
mouse events, 405, 406–407
mouseDragged( ), 556
mousePressed( ), 556
multiple versions, 9
native code, 9, 712
objects and, 526–528
overloading, 9, 72
overriding, 9, 714
overview, 511
paint( ), 514
painting, 120
polygons, 121
print( ), 521
protected, 10
public, 10
setBackground( ), 542–544
setFont( ), 544–545
static, 521
string, 126
Swing toolkit, 464–466
synchronized, 722–723
text string, 128
values, returning, 10
metrics
    console, 108, 124
    font metrics, 545–547
MIDI (Musical Instrument Digital Interface), 710
MIN_VALUE constant, 710–711
mnemonics, 711
modal dialog boxes, 234
modal setting, 119
modifiers
    class, 6, 684–685
    fields, 684–685
    methods, 9, 70
modulus (%) operator, 73
modulus operator, 9, 10
mouse
    cursor, bitmap, 223–224
    events, 112
        handling, 116
        methods, 405, 406–407
        responding to, 119, 124
MouseAdapter class, 402–403
mouseDragged( ) method, 556
MouseEvent class, 403–405, 574–575
MouseListener interface, 405
MouseMotionAdapter class, 405–406
MouseMotionListener interface, 406–407
mousePressed( ) method, 556
MPEG files, 711
multicast event delivery, 578–579, 711
multiline comment, 9
multiline edit boxes, 468–469

multiple platforms, 516–517
multithreaded programs, 711
music, 119, 121

N

names
    identifiers, 8
    packages, 532
    variables, 8
namespace, 73
NaN, 711–712
native code, methods, 9, 712
native keyword, 9, 74
network client, creating, 109
network server, creating, 109
networks, 108
    connections, 179
    operations, performing, 120
    reading across, 122
new operator, 6, 9, 74–75
null
    constant, 9, 75–76
    defined, 712
    object variables, 9
numbered line input, 120
numbers
    converting to strings, 665
    random, 427
    strings, converting between, 663–665

O

Object class, 407–408
object orientation, 525–529, 713
objects, 76–77
    allocating, 524–525
    allocating space, 6
    arrays and, 23
    comparing, 210
    creating, 399–400
    creation, classes and, 522–525
    defined, 712–713
    equality, 112
    event state objects, 570
    Graphics, 548–552
    graphics, 540–542
    image objects, 114
    ImageObserver, 554–555
    instances, 9
    JavaBeans, 635–636
    methods and, 526–528
    notifying, 120
    references, 9
    testing, 128
Observable class, 408–409
Observer interface, 409–410
octal notation, 9, 76
on/off conditions, 120
one-based indexing, 713
operation@index H:s, 91–92
operator overloading, 11, 79
operators, 77–79
    accessing, 9
    assignment, 25–26
    bitwise, 6, 8, 26–27
    conditional (?:), 7, 38
    context, 39–40
    delete, 8, 43
    groups, 78
    instanceof, 8, 10, 63
    modulus (%), 9, 10, 73
    new, 6, 9, 74–75
    precedence, 9, 77–79
    shift, 86

shift operators, 10
ternary, 77–78
unary, 77
option buttons, 204
    creating, 110
option pane
    defined, 713
    Swing and, 127
    Swing toolkit, 612–613
optional exceptions, 674–675
orientation of objects, 525–529, 713
output, 120
    console, 665–667
    to file, 120
OutputStream class, 410
overloading
    defined, 713–714
    methods, 9, 72
    operators, 11, 79
overriding methods, 9
    defined, 714

P

package statement, 9, 79–80
packages, 9, 511, 529–536
    defined, 714
    directory structure and, 532–533
    importing, 8
    java.applet, 132
    java.awt, 132–134
    java.awt.event, 135–137
    java.awt.image, 137–138
    java.awt.print, 138
    java.io, 138–140
    java.lang, 140–141
    java.net, 141–142
    java.util, 142–144
    javax.swing, 142–144
    javax.swing.border, 149
    javax.swing.event, 149
    javax.swing.text, 150
    names, 532
    searches, 534
packets, datagrams, 224–225
Pageable interface, 411
PageFormat class, 411–412
pagination, 120
Paint mode, 102
    setting, 125
paint( ) method, 514, 540
painting
    components, 120
    methods, 120
    regions, 123
    shapes, 120
Pane, 120–121
Panel class, 412
panels
    containers, 412
    creating, 110
panes
    content, 590
    defined, 714
    option panes, 713
    splitting, 126, 350
    Swing, 590–591
    Swing class, 344–346
    tabbed, 350
    text editing, 357
Paper class, 412–413
parameters, applets, 106, 121
parents
    inheritance and, 563
    references, 121

PasswordAuthentication class, 413–414
passwords
    masking, 119
    PasswordAuthentication class, 413–414
    Swing and, 127
        pathnames, 121
        pausing, 121
        persistence, JavaBeans, 634, 646–648
        pi, 121
        PipedInputStream class, 414
PipedOutputStream class, 415
pipes, data, 121, 414–415
pixel data, 121
    PixelGrabber class, 415–417
    saving from image, 124
PixelGrabber class, 415–417
pixels, 714
platforms, 714
    multiple, 516–517
pluggable look and feel, Swing and, 614–615
    defined, 715
Point class, 417
pointers, 9, 80–81
    defined, 715
points (coordinates), 417
Polygon class, 417–418
polygons
    creating, 110
    drawing, 549
    methods, 121
    points, 106
    Polygon class, 417–418
polymorphism, 715–716
popup menus
    JPopupMenu class, 333–336
    Swing and, 127
ports, closing, 108
precedence, operators, 9, 77–79
primitive data types, 9, 716
    byte, 29
    short, 446–448
print( ) method, 521
Printable interface, 418–419
PrinterJob class, 419–420
printing, 109, 121
    components
        child, 121
        contents, 121
    Pageable interface, 411
    PageFormat class, 411–412
    paper, 412–413
    print engine, 419–420
    Printable interface, 418–419
    PrintStream class, 420–422
priorities, threads, 121, 125
private access, 716
private keyword, 9, 81–82
private variable, 9
Process class, 422
processes, 617. See also threads
    starting, 121
program entry point, 529
programming languages
    C, 692
    C++, 692
    Visual J++, 726
progress bar, 336–338, 716
    monitoring, 423–424
    Swing and, 127
progress monitor, creating, 122
ProgressMonitor class, 422–423
ProgressMonitorInputStream class, 423–424
properties
    defined, 717
    fonts, 114, 115

images, 115, 121
JavaBeans, 636–637
    bound, 639–640
    constrained, 640–641
    indexed, 638–639
organizing, 425–426
setting, 125
settings, 114
system, 121, 128, 683
tables, 129
Properties class, 424–425
property design patterns, JavaBeans, 643–644
property editors, JavaBeans, 649–650
property sheets, JavaBeans, 650–651
PropertyResourceBundle class, 425–426
protected access, 717
protected keyword, 10, 82–83
protocol, 717
prototypes, 530
public access, 717
public classes, 531–532
public keyword, 10, 82–83
pull-down menus
    Menu class, 397–398
    MenuItem class`, 401–402
Push button, 121
push buttons, creating, 110
PushbackInputStream class, 426

R

Radio button, 121
    Swing and, 127
radio buttons, 204
    creating, 110
    JRadioButton class, 338–339
    menu items, 339–341
random access, 121, 427–430
    records, writing, 129
Random class, 427
random numbers, 121, 427
random-access records, 122
RandomAccessFile class, 427–430
range, 121
raw image data, 122
read-only text, Label class, 371–372
reading
    directories, 668
    file contents, 669–671
Rectangle class, 431–432
rectangles
    clipping, 108, 125, 541
    creating, 110
    drawing, 549
    rounded, 124
    union, 128
references, 84–85
    applets, 114
    defined, 718
    forward references, 530
    new operator and, 74
    objects, 9
    parents, 121
regions, painting, 123
register keyword, 85
remainder, 123
renaming files, 123
repainting, forcing, 114, 123
representation, strings, 126
reserved words, 66, 718
resolution, screen, 123, 124
ResourceBundle class, 432–433
resources, ListResource class, 382–384
responding to events, 570–583
result sets, 718

return keyword, 10, 85–86
RGB values, 115
    creating color, 124
RGBImageFilter class, 433–435
rigid areas, box layout managers, 599, 718
rounded rectangles, 124
rounding floating-points, 124
RTT (runtime type information) operators, 63
Runnable interface, 435
runnable interfaces, implementing, 619
running
    applets, 512–513
    applications, 507–508
    Java, 506–507
Runtime class, 435–436
RuntimeException class, 674–675

S

scope, 719
screen height, 116
screen metrics, 124
screen resolution, 123, 124
screen width, 129
        Scribble applet, 556–558
scroll bar
    coordinates, 125
    creating, 110
    JScrollBar class, 342–344
    position, 121
    Swing and, 127
scroll pane constants, 108
Scrollable interface, 437
Scrollbar class, 437–438
ScrollPane class, 438–440
ScrollPaneConstants interface, 440–441
searches
    classes, 534
    directories, 124
    packages, 534
    strings, 124
    vectors, 124
security, 719
    checks, 121, 124
security manager, 441–443
SecurityManager class, 441–443
semantic events, 571, 575–577, 719
separator, Swing and, 127
sequence of files, 122
SequenceInputStream class, 443–444
sequences, List interface, 377–379
serialization, JavaBeans, 647–648
server sockets, opening, 120
servers
    acting as, 125
    creating, 125
    defined, 720
ServerSocket class, 444–445
Set interface, 445–446
setBackground( ) method, 542–544
setFont( ) method, 544–545
shapes, 126
    drawing, 111
    painting, 120
Shift keys, codes for, 126
shift operators, 10, 86
Short class, 446–448
short data type, 10, 41, 87
        Short class, 446–448
short variables, 10
short-circuit logic, 720
signatures, 720
signed data, 720
SimpleTimeZone class, 448–449

SizeRequirements class, 449–450
sleeping, 126, 129
sliders
    defined, 720
    JSlider class, 347–350
    Swing and, 127
smoothing animation, 624–628
Socket class, 450–452
sockets
    client, opening, 120
    creating, 450–452
    defined, 720–721
    server, opening, 120
SoftBevelBorder class, 452
SortedMap interface, 453
sound, producing, 126
space allocation, 6
special keys, codes, 126
splitter windows, 126, 129
splitting panes, 350
spreadsheets, 126
SQL (Structured Query Languge), 721
squares, drawing, 126
Stack class, 453–454
stack collection class, 126
stacks, 453–454, 721
statements
    break, 6, 11, 28–29
    compound, 6, 37–38
    continue, 6, 40–41
    do-nothing, 7
    empty, 7, 45–46
    executing, repeating, 10, 53–55
    for, 8, 10, 53–55
    goto, 56
    if, 7, 8, 57
    import, 8, 59–60, 535–536
    labels, 8
    package, 9, 79–80
    switch, 8, 11, 28–29, 93–94
    while, 11, 103
static initializers, 150, 721
static keyword, 6, 10, 87–89
static methods, 521
static text, 126
status bar, 126
stream I/O, 110
streaming
    input, 126
    output, 126
        OutputStream class, 410
        PrintStream class, 420–422
StreamTokenizer class, 454–456
String class, 89, 457–460
string literals, 10
string methods, 126
StringBuffer class, 460–462
strings, 10, 89–92, 462–463, 721–722
    buffers, 460–462
    bytes, conversion, 109
    contents, tokens, 128
    converting
        from numbers, 665
        to floating points, 664–665
        to integers, 664
    creating, 10
    escape sequences, 10
    length, 10
    literals, 81
    numbers, converting between, 663–665
    operations, 91–92
    reading
        from file, 126

from keyboard, 127
representation, 126
searches, 124
text
  appending, 106
  methods, 128
  replacing, 123
text editing, 111
variables, 89–90
writing to file, 127
StringTokenizer class, 462–463
struct declarations, 92
structure, directories, 532–533
styles, fonts, 127
subclasses, 10
  defined, 722
super keyword, 10, 92–93
superclass constructors, 10
superclasses, 127
  defined, 722
  extends keyword, 49–50
Swing architecture
  checkbox, 295, 296
  command button, 293–294
  components, JTextComponent class, 353–355
  containers, 331–332
  panes, 344–346
Swing toolkit, 587, 722
  AWT and, 588, 591–592
  choosers, 613–614
  components
    borders, 604–605
    buttons, 604
    combo boxes, 605–607
    icons, 600–601
    labels, 601–603
    list boxes, 605–607
  dialog boxes, 611–612
  frames, 589–590
  GUIs and, 592–600
  layout managers and, 592–600
  menus, 608–611
  methods, 464–466
  option pane, 612–613
  overview, 589
  panes, 590–591
  pluggable look and feel, 614–615
  tool bar, 608–611
SwingConstants interface, 463–464
SwingUtilities class, 464–466
switch branches
  case keyword, 30
  default, 7
switch statements, 8, 11, 93–94
  breaking, 28–29
  labels, 66
sychronized keyword, 10
symbolic constants, 7
Sync, graphics, 128
synchronization, graphics, 115
synchronized keyword, 7, 94–95
synchronized methods, 722–723
synchronized threads, 722–723
syntax
  aggregates, 21–23
  applets, 516
  applications, 509–510
System class, 466–468
system functions, 466–468
system properties, 121, 128
  default, 683

T
tables
  creating, 128
  defined, 723
  graphics, 679–681
  JTable class, 350–351
  properties, 129
  properties table, 424–425
  Swing and, 127
templates, 96
ternary operators, 77–78
testing JavaBeans, 656–660
text
  components, 128
  displaying, 111, 542–548
  editing panes, 357
  read-only, Label class, 371–372
  select/replace, 124
  setting, 125
  static, 126
  strings, replacing, 123
  Unicode, 682
  validating, 129
text area, Swing and, 128
text fields
  JTextField class, 355–357
  Swing and, 128
text strings, methods, 128
text verification, 287–288
text-editing components, 332–333
text-handling, 681–682
TextArea class, 468–469
TextComponent class, 469–470
TextEvent class, 577
TextField class, 470–472
this keyword, 6, 9, 96–97
Thread class, 472–474
thread-local variables, 476
ThreadGroup class, 474–476
ThreadLocal class, 476
threads, 128, 555, 617
  animation and, 620
  behavior, 117
  creating, 109, 618–619
  defined, 723
  multithreaded programs, 711
  overview, 619–620
  priorities, 121, 125
  Runnable interface, 435–436
  starting, 126
  suspending, 127
  synchronized, 722–723
throw keyword, 7, 11, 97
Throwable class, 477
throwing exceptions, defined, 724
throws keyword, 97
time zones, 448–449
time, current, 110, 128
Timer class, 477–478
timers
  creating, 128
  setting, 125
TimeZone class, 478–480
titled borders, 128, 480–482
TitledBorder class, 480–482
titles
  dialog boxes, 128
  frames, 128
toggle button
  JToggleButton class, 357–358
  Swing and, 128
tokenizing input, 454–456

tokens
  file contents, 128
  string contents, 128
tool bar
  defined, 72r
  JToolBar class, 358–360
  Swing and, 128
  Swing toolkit, 608–611
toolkit, 114, 128
Toolkit class, 482–483
tooltips, 360–361
  defined, 724
  Swing and, 128
tree maps, 483–485
TreeMap class, 483–485
trees
  defined, 724
  hierarchical, 128
  JTree class, 361
  Swing and, 128
TreeSet class, 485–486
trigonometric functions, 128
true keyword, 11, 97–98
trusted applets, 515
try keyword, 7, 98
two's complement, 724
typedef declarations, 98

U

UIs (user interfaces), 565–566
  layout, 118
unary operators, 77
unicast event delivery, 578, 725
Unicode, 682, 693, 725
union of rectangles, 128
unsigned types, 98–99, 725
uppercase converting to, 128
URL (Uniform Resource Locator), 129
  defined, 725
URL class, 486–488
URLConnection class, 488–491
URLDecoder class, 491
URLEncoder class, 492
user input, JOptionPane class, 327–331
UTF-encodings, 682
utilities
  appletviewer, 513
  JAR, 654–656
  Swing and, 128

V

validation, text, 129
values
  absolute, 106
  arguments, default, 42
  constants, 7
  variables, assigning, 6
variables, 99–101
  Boolean, 6
  byte, creating, 6
  character, 6
    size, 6
  classes, 695

defined, 725–726
double, 7
float, 7
global, 50–51
instance, 704
integer, 8
local, 709
long, 8
naming conventions, 8
private, 9
protected, 10
public, 10
short, 10
strings, 89–90
thread-local, 476
values, assigning, 6
Vector class, 492–495
vectors
  arrays, 124
  searches, 124
verification, text, 287–288
versioning, JavaBeans, 648
versions of Java, xii
ViewportLayout class, 495
viewports, JViewport class, 361–363
virtual files, 129
virtual keyword, 101
Visual J++ programming language, 726
visual layout, components, 635
Void class, 495
void keyword, 10, 101–102
volatile keyword, 11, 102

W

waiting, 129
WAV files, 726
WeakHashMap class, 495–496
while statement, 11, 103
Window class, 496–497
window events, 499–500
WindowAdapter class, 497–498
WindowConstants interface, 498–499
WindowEvent class, 499–500, 575
WindowListener interface, 500
windows
  constants, 108
  creating, 110
  displaying, 111, 129
  events, 113
    responding to, 124
  panes, 341–342
  resizing, 123
  showing, 126
  splitter, 126
  splitting, 129
  Swing and, 128
wizard-style interfaces, 597
wrapper classes, 726

X–Y–Z

XOR painting mode, 129
Z-order, 727
zero-based indexing, 727

Two Books in One!

CONCISE TUTORIALS
Each In Plain English guidebook delivers concise, targeted tutorials—no hand-holding, no coddling, just the skills you need to get up and running fast.

READY-REFERENCE HELP
Each book also features topic-sorted and A-to-Z reference sections that answer your questions quickly and help you get the job done, day after day.

In Plain English. All the tools you need to get up to speed—and get results.

For more information, visit our website at:
www.mandtbooks.com